Camera Austria International

Laboratory for Photography and Theory

Edited by · Museum der Moderne Salzburg

With texts by

Reinhard Braun
Christine Frisinghelli
Toshiharu Ito
Christiane Kuhlmann
Maren Lübbke-Tidow
Sandra Križić Roban
Roberta Valtorta

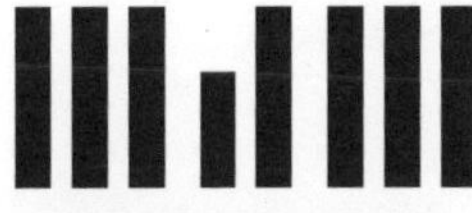

Museum der Moderne
Salzburg

Spector Books

Contents

Dialogs 1–8

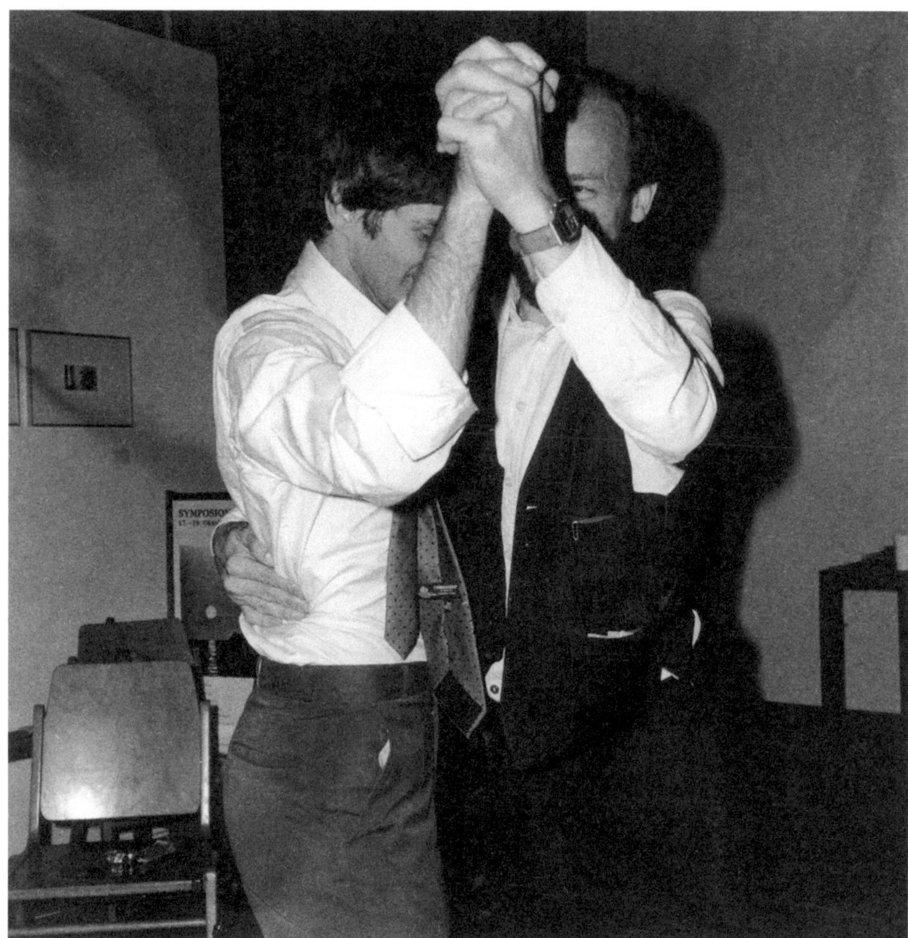

Mark Haworth-Booth and Manfred Willmann,
Symposion on Photography VI: "The Power (and the Glory) of Photography," 1984.
Photo: Harald Strobl

Preface

Since the late 1970s, Camera Austria has been an essential authority for critical debate on the medium of photography—not just in Austria, but worldwide. Indeed, it is impossible to overestimate the significance of the dedicated work performed by Christine Frisinghelli, Manfred Willmann and Seiichi Furuya, the founders of the association in Graz, who are still active to this day. Their development of the Symposia on Photography in Austria and publishing of the magazine *Camera Austria International* came at a time when photography was struggling to be recognized within the canon of fine art throughout Europe, and represents an important contribution to an international infrastructure of professional networking and exchange.

Camera Austria is part of the avant-garde movement in Graz that established itself in the late 1950s as an association of artists in the Forum Stadtpark. From its beginnings as a private gallery, run by Manfred Willmann and hosted in the café pavilion of the Graz city park, the photo gallery achieved widespread recognition in Austria, particularly after its separation from the Forum's film & photo department in 1976 and the establishment of the photo gallery within the context of the Forum Stadtpark association. From 1980 onwards, the departmental magazine *Camera Austria International* formed a visual counterpart to *manuskripte,* a literary magazine published by Forum Stadtpark. This created the foundation for an inquisitive, critical, and consistent examination of images and launched a theoretical investigation of the medium which has continued for more than 40 years.

Salzburg has its own tradition in the Fotohof, which developed as a collective from the initiatives of Salzburg College. Primarily in its role as a publishing house for Austria's photographers, it reflects the country's photographic history. But here in western Austria and especially here at the Museum der Moderne Salzburg, the developments that emanated from Camera Austria have not passed us by. Their influence has been felt via Otto Breicha, founding director of the Museum der Moderne, or, as it was called at the time, the Moderne Galerie und Graphische Sammlung–Rupertinum. Breicha was the person who exhibited contemporary photography alongside a donation by art collector Friedrich Welz, a collection of modern graphic prints that formed the basis of the museum's foundation. This meant that our museum was the first, and for many years the only one, in Austria consistently dedicated to this medium. Breicha developed his passion for photography during his activities in Graz, both as a member of the board of directors for the steirischer herbst festival and as editor of the magazine *Protokolle,* which from its first edition in 1966 also saw itself as a showcase for contemporary photography. Further, the reaction to discussions held in Graz is reflected in the photography collection of the Museum der Moderne, which is comprised of the museum's own collection and that of the Austrian Federation.

I am very happy that our successful completion of this exhibition project, with its intensive research into the history and development of Camera Austria, also represents a cooperative venture that can be regarded as an important contribution to the study of the history of art and photography in Austria. It serves as a medium in which to reflect, and reflect upon, the institution, its focuses and networks. Moreover, it is a successful endeavor to place photography in and from Austria in an international context.

This extraordinary project could not have been realized without the close cooperation between the Museum der Moderne Salzburg and the Camera Austria Association in Graz. My thanks go first and foremost to guest curator Christine Frisinghelli, co-founder of Camera Austria, and to Christiane Kuhlmann, curator for photography and media art at the Museum der Moderne, who developed the idea for this exhibition along with my predecessor Sabine Breitwieser. Thanks are equally due to those who have been so dedicated in advancing this ambitious project, above all Christina Penetsdorfer, assistant curator at the Museum der Moderne, who was diligently involved in editing this publication. Special thanks are also due to Reinhard Braun, artistic director of Camera Austria, and his entire team. They made the research material and loan collection available and attended to the development of the project as critical partners in dialogue. Maren Lübbke-Tidow, former editor of *Camera Austria International,* made a number of important and greatly appreciated conceptual contributions to the project. In addition, I would like to thank Susanne

Greimel for her very capable organization of the loan procedures and the whole team at the Museum der Moderne for their professional work. My thanks also go to the Arts and Culture Division of the Federal Chancellery of Austria, in particular to Gudrun Schreiber, director of the Department of Visual Arts, Architecture, Design, Fashion, Photography, Video, and Media Arts, for her valuable support.
I would especially like to thank all the artists represented in the exhibition, as well as all the other lenders who have made our project possible in the first place.

Thorsten Sadowsky
Director Museum der Moderne Salzburg

Showing and Reading What There Is to See

For more than 40 years, Camera Austria has been an institution for photography in Graz, a discussion platform, an exhibition center, a publishing house, an archive, a library, and an organizer of workshops and symposia. For almost thirty years, the institution has also presented its eponymous Camera Austria Award for Contemporary Photography.

An exhibition on this forum, which, in all its complexity, has been a byword internationally for artistic and theoretical engagement with photography since the mid-1970s, is a huge task. It can only showcase aspects of this process in a fragmentary fashion, selectively follow certain lines, and make a number of chosen themes and specific continuities visible. The current presentation constitutes a preliminary overview from outside of the institution itself, for which the term "laboratory," which forms part of the name of the Camera Austria Association, is particularly appropriate. The laboratory is a work space in which experiments, measurements, and analyses are conducted and where quality is controlled; in the world of analog photography, at least, it is also the actual location where pictures are developed. In addition, the laboratory aspect indicates that it is an experimental setup, and that the focus is on raising questions rather than providing formalized answers.

In this respect, the exhibition at the Museum der Moderne Salzburg reflects the experimental and illuminative nature of the wide range of photographic and theoretical approaches that the Graz-based institution has focused on since its inception. To quote from the preface to the sixth Symposion on Photography in 1984, "The Power (and the Glory) of Photography": "This corresponds with the fundamental question that was raised in each symposion, not only in the sixth, i.e. the question concerning the nature of photography. With other words, each of the precedent symposions was also dedicated to the attempt to discover, in the wide range of possible applications of photography as well as in today's theory of photography, the power of the medium, at the same time however, depending on the different, sometimes even opposed point of views of the participants, to leave its definition in suspense."[1] The various fields of the application, languages, and contradictions of photography were considered as a specific quality of the medium, which is

why Gottfried Bechtold, Bernhard Johannes Blume, Giovanni Chiaramonte, Bernard Faucon, John Gossage, Inge Morath, and Helmut Newton were all invited to this symposium—a potentially explosive mixture, and proof of the great diversity in the curators' intellectual approaches and their broad range of activities.

The Premise of the Exhibition

In his text "Work on Pictures," Reinhard Braun proposes the thesis, with regard to Camera Austria, that "there is no point in returning to the past."[2] That is correct as a strategy for the institution. One of the tasks of museums is the evaluation and contextualization of their own inventory.

Bearing this in mind, it is important for Museum der Moderne Salzburg to examine the activities that have developed from Camera Austria. Since 1981 the museum has been home not only to its own photographic collection, with its emphasis on post-1945 Austrian fine-art photography, but also to that of the Austrian Federation. The overall collection comprises more than 22,000 works; it includes large individual collections of works by Camera Austria artists[3] Seiichi Furuya, Branko Lenart, Helmut Tezak, and Manfred Willmann as well as by the contributors to the exhibitions and symposia such as Sabine Bitter and Helmut Weber, Friedl Kubelka, Tatiana Lecomte, Ulrike Lienbacher, Michaela Moscouw, Eva Maria Ocherbauer, Michael Schuster, Nicole Six & Paul Petritsch, Hartmut Skerbisch, and Christian Wachter, to name just a few. Both threads of the collection have developed in parallel to the discussions conducted in Graz.

In addition, there is also a direct connection with Graz via Otto Breicha, the founding director of Salzburg's Museum of Modern Art and Graphic Collection–Rupertinum, which is the original core of the Museum der Moderne Salzburg. Breicha was head of the Kulturhaus der Stadt Graz from 1972 to 1980 and can be considered one of the initiators of the discussion on contemporary photography in Austria.[4]

Set against this background, the exhibition displays a significant segment of Austrian artistic and photographic history, whose development has taken a different course than in Germany, the Netherlands, or the United States. In the 1970s, there was a lack of educational institutions, collections, funding opportunities, and even a publicly conducted discourse on photography. As a consequence, a number of disparate centers developed on the initiative of individual artists—centers which then became active in the further development and public perception of Austrian photography.[5] Like Salzburg's Fotohof, Vienna's Fotogalerie, or the FLUSS Society for the Promotion of Photo and Media Art, Camera Austria is one such initiative. Willmann's preface in the first edition of *Camera Austria International* has an almost defiant tone, a kind of knee-jerk reaction to the sluggishness of the institutions: "Camera Austria is the only magazine dealing with the diverse activities playing out in the field of photography in Austria: with the work of photographers, with the activity of photo clubs, and with the projects of exhibition-makers."[6]

Manfred Willmann first started to regularly exhibit national and international photography in 1974, when he founded Graz's Fotogalerie Schillerhof, followed a year later by the Fotogalerie in the Forum Stadtpark. Initially alone, he was subsequently joined by Christine Frisinghelli. These ventures then developed into a project that involved not only looking at pictures with a curious eye and a sense of rigor but also reflecting on the medium theoretically.[7] The Symposion on Photography—which took place annually from 1979 to 1997, and then once again in 2003 upon the opening of the new, enlarged exhibition and editing rooms in the Eisernes Haus building in Graz, directly adjacent to the Kunsthaus—formed a considerable part of their work and were a significant result of this project.

The international perception of Camera Austria, however, is primarily based on the regular publication of the symposia's artistic and theoretical contributions in the magazine, which has appeared since 1980 in both English and German editions. The illustrations, in particular, which were printed on thick, high-quality paper, made a positive impression on photographers, leading British photographer Paul Graham, for example, to nominate *Camera Austria International* as the 1988 photographic book of the year in *Creative Camera*. Another method of communicating via photography was the compilation of exhibitions with Austrian and European photographers in other locations, such as the *Photography in Austria* exhibition, which Christine Frisinghelli curated together with Ute Eskildsen for the Museum Folkwang in Essen in 1987, as well as *Another Continent* for the Metropolitan Museum of Photography in Tokyo in 1994.[8]

The aim of the Salzburg exhibition is not to map the history of Camera Austria's evolution in a linear way but rather to highlight thematic and discursive emphases that have had an influence on the development of photography in Austria. At the same time, the exhibition also explicitly references international positions.

The Graz Forum can be seen as a kind of window opening out onto a vista of different photographic trends and orientations while simultaneously rendering Austrian photographers visible. The fact that the institution is not a one-way street but, above all, a very active network conducting a lively exchange of information and ideas between Graz and the world at large can be seen in a letter by US photographer Robert Adams to Christine Frisinghelli, written in October 1995, after Adams had received the international Spectrum Award for Photography at the Sprengel Museum. He wrote, "Thank you again…for bringing *Listening to the River* to Graz. Without you and Thomas [Weski], my efforts would never have reached so wide a European audience. I don't know how to express my appreciation enough."[9]

The Principle of Contemporaneity

The ninth Photography Symposion took place in October 1987 on the subject of "Contemporaneity," a somewhat unmanageable term less focused on revealing the temporal parallels between fine-art photography positions than on presenting the artists as participants in the current events of the time. Moreover, this title is also representative of one of the essential aspects of the work of Camera Austria.

Since 1974, the focus in Graz has been on contemporary photographic practice and particularly on "documentary" photography. One of the early friends of the project was American photographer Lewis Baltz, who was presented back in 1977 in the *American Photographers* exhibition for the steirischer herbst festival in Forum Stadtpark.[10] Five years later, in his contribution to the fourth symposium, he compared his series "Park City" and "San Quentin Point" to one another and expounded in the discussion on his view of the documentary approach: "I don't think of documentation as 'mere.' … I would think that documentation implies a high degree of objectivity. … Criticism suggests that one already understands the problems and has a solution in mind. I prefer to think of the "Park City" photographs as a questioning."[11] This perspective combines Baltz's own artistic ideas with the experimental setup envisaged by Christine Frisinghelli, Seiichi Furuya, and Manfred Willmann, the founders of Camera Austria: the questioning of the medium from an interdisciplinary perspective.[12]

In the early stages in particular, opinions were expressed by artists whose interests were largely identical to those of the Graz team and who also encouraged a discursive approach to photography that transcended existing boundaries. Baltz examined the effect of urbanization on the changing American landscape, while Luigi Ghirri[13] took as his subject his home region Emilia-Romagna. With the soft coloring typical of his work, he is regarded as one of the precursors of a European style of color photography. In 1982, he presented his series *Still Life: Modena 1978–1980* and *Topography – Iconography* at the third Symposion and, in his work as author and curator, pursued the question of whether it is possible to think in pictures: "Photographs refer to other, already familiar photographs, thus becoming fluctuating images, like the images of our own thoughts." Ghirri writes about the idea of the actively indeterminate, the undefined, although this contradicts some of the key characteristics of photography. He regards photography not as "a mere duplication of the world or the eye stopwatch that freezes the physical world, but rather the language in which the difference between reproduction and interpretation, albeit minimal, exists and gives rise to infinite imaginary worlds."[14]

At roughly the same time, William Eggleston was working on his *Louisiana Project*, which was presented in *Camera Austria International* in 1983, and to which Ghirri contributed the essay.[15] In Graz the subject was *Living with a City*[16], as exemplified by Seiichi Furuya's AMSterdam project in 1980. "The only remaining 'taboo' subject in photography is the ordinary and the only mysteries left are the quotidian mysteries. Only the everyday remains hidden because we choose to hide it from ourselves, and photography is the most marvelous medium ever devised for parting that veil."[17] This kind of visual documentation and the subjective view of the world correspond to the idea of contemporaneity as formulated by Frisinghelli and Willmann for Camera Austria. It is a concept that is comparable to Ghirri's formulation of the admittance of possibilities, one that does not impose limits but that can be interpreted as an open principle and hence can be cited as a fundamental quality of the Graz program.

Dialogue and Continuity – On the Structure
of the Exhibition

Exhibitions, symposia, and the magazine are different formats that have been, and still are, understood as a sanctuary for experimental, radical projects or for positions that are ahead of their time. The magazine, as a medium, promises continuity on the one hand, with each issue building upon the previous one, while on the other, it also requires being able to stay abreast of the times. This is a principle to which *Camera Austria International* has diligently applied itself, as shown in issue 100, from the year 2007: "In our anniversary issue Camera Austria No. 100 we intentionally want to refrain from looking back on our own history, and decided to look to the future instead. We dedicate this issue – that accompanies the exhibition of the same name – to the Market Photo Workshop founded by David Goldblatt in Johannesburg at the end of the 1980s. This issue thus picks up one of our magazine's main programmatic threads: to reflect on the social usages of photography, directly to support artistic production, and to offer a platform particularly fort he youngest movements in contemporary photography and media art."[18]

The interesting thing here is that the issue not only honors individual artists but also reveals the presence of direct institutional networks and continuities.[19] The Workshop in Johannesburg comes across as a sister institution of Camera Austria and points toward one of the thematic emphases of the Graz Forum, with its very early highlighting of non-European photography. Besides Japan (from 1975) and America (from 1976), there has been a clear focus on northern and southern Africa since the mid-1990s.[20]

From time to time, this continual forward-looking perspective is interrupted, and political positions are adopted, as demonstrated in issue 140 from the year 2017, whose cover was completely black, like a fade-to-black, a photographic failure. This can be seen as a direct critical commentary on the elections to the Austrian National Council in October 2017, when the right-wing populist Freedom Party of Austria (FPÖ) achieved a majority together with the conservative Austrian People's Party (ÖVP), enabling them to form a coalition government.[21]

The exhibition at the Museum der Moderne Salzburg makes use of the interplay of dialogue and continuity and is divided into eight sections, in which pioneers from the early years of Camera Austria are juxtaposed with contemporary positions. The results can be seen in the visual discourses on photography that have been conducted in Graz since the 1980s and which retain their relevance today. The exhibition is not a retrospective, but rather an opportunity to update certain historical aspects of the institution. The first thematic field, "Topography and Landscape," develops visual connections between the works of Robert Adams, Lewis Baltz, William Eggleston, Luigi Ghirri, Joachim Koester, and Lieko Shiga. The section on "Image and Identity" brings together works by Hans-Peter Feldmann, Sanja Iveković, Zanele Muholi, and Jo Spence, while "Habitat and Representation" develops a dialogue around works from the projects and series by Seiichi Furuya, Einar Schleef, Michael Schmidt, Manfred Willmann, and Tobias Zielony. The section "Composition and Deconstruction" presents the works of Michael Schuster and Hartmut Skerbisch, Josif Király, Zofia Kulik, Jörg Schlick, and Christian Wachter as image processes and commentaries on descriptions of reality. The dialogue on "Image and Politics" is developed as a response to the works of David Goldblatt, Susan Meiselas, Walid Raad, and Ahlam Shibli. This section is closely related to the "Research and Archive" section, which places works by Anna and Bernhard Blume, Annette Kelm, Tatiana Lecomte, and Peter Piller in relation to one another. "Image Politics and Science" presents the positions of Sven Johne, Darcy Lange, Allan Sekula, Sabine Bitter, and Helmut Weber. The boundaries between "Privacy and Public Image" are discussed in the concluding dialogue with works by Nobuoyshi Araki, Lamia Joreige, Petar Dabac, and Nan Goldin. As a supplementary feature, the work of the selected artists is accompanied by all the previous issues of *Camera Austria International* with the aim of visualizing the concept of contemporaneity in a spatial way. In addition, an illustrative choice of video and audio recordings from the photography symposia allow us to hear from artists and authors who are no less important, but whose own works could not be exhibited. The archived volumes covering the period from 1974 to 2003,[22] which have been scanned by Viennese artist duo Nicole Six & Paul Petrisch, give exhibition visitors a behind-the-scenes view of the networks and relationships that have been generated and woven over the years. This is, so to speak, the DNA of the institution, of an association that continues to have a seminal influence on our discourses on and with photography.

Christiane Kuhlmann

1   Christine Frisinghelli and Manfred Willmann, preface to *Camera Austria International* 19–20 / 1985, 3.
2   Reinhard Braun, "Arbeit an den Bildern," in *Österreich: Fotografie 1970–2000,* ed. Walter Moser, exh. cat. Albertina, Vienna (Cologne: Walther König, 2018), 221.
3   These photographers are the members of the photographic department of the Forum Stadtpark, from which the association Camera Austria emerged. The structures of the association have been retained to this day, with changing board members and responsibilities.
4   Breicha was editor of Protokolle: *Wiener Jahresschrift für Literatur, bildende Kunst und Musik* from 1966 to 1997. From the first issue of the magazine onward, Breicha published the work of contemporary photographers, and the journal reflected his great interest in modern art and photography; see also Otto Breicha, ed., *Kreative Fotografie aus Österreich,* exh. cat. Kulturhaus der Stadt Graz (Graz: Kulturhaus, 1974).
    This was the first exhibition in which Breicha presented traditional photographic positions such as those of Herbert Bayer, alongside those of new photographers who had yet to make a name for themselves, like Friedl Bondy (now Friedl Kubelka vom Gröller) and Otmar Thormann.
5   See Christiane Kuhlmann, "Die Sammlung und das Sammeln," in Moser, *Österreich* (see note 2), 227–33.
6   Manfred Willmann, preface to *Camera Austria International* 1 / 1980: 1.
7   For the association's members, it was important to clear away the vexatious question concerning the artistic value of photography and to investigate theoretical questions in addition to their own artistic practice. This was why they also discussed the exhibition *Photographie als Kunst 1879–1979 – Kunst als Photographie 1949–1979,* which was curated by Peter Weiermair, and which, after opening in Innsbruck, toured throughout Austria, also stopping in Graz. Weiermair, who was Otto Breicha's successor as director of the Museum in Salzburg from 1998 to 2001, described his curatorial approach to this important exhibition in *Camera Austria International* 2 / 1980, 13–18.
8   See further interactions in the chronology listed in this book.
9   Robert Adams, in Archiv Camera Austria, correspondence 1995
10 In the 1960s, Graz became the epicenter of Austria's literary avant-garde, and the artists' association at Forum Stadtpark was an important location for interdisciplinary discussions in many different areas of artistic practice. The establishment of the photography department within this context defines the main direction to be taken: a path that led toward conceptual photography, as is evident in the initial responses to the work of Lewis Baltz.
11 Lewis Baltz, in *Camera Austria International* 11–12 / 1983, 5.
12 This gears Camera Austria's orientation to the artistic aspirations of the Forum Stadtpark in Graz. The debates that have been conducted there since 1958 on contemporary literature and visual art have set standards in terms of quality. See Christine Frisinghelli, "Forum Stadtpark: Referat/Programm Fotografie," in *Styrian Window,* exh. cat. Neue Galerie Graz am Landesmuseum, 1995. At the same time, the conceptual media debate was certainly the most influential one in Graz in the early 1970s, even for the technical medium of photography. On this, see Sabine Breitwieser, ed., *RE-PLAY: Anfänge internationaler Medienkunst in Österreich,* Vienna: Generali Foundation, 2000.
13 Luigi Ghirri's first individual exhibition outside of Italy took place at the Forum Stadtpark in 1976 and was curated by Willmann.
14 Luigi Ghirri, "Still Life: Modena 1978–1980," *Camera Austria International* 7 / 1981, 32.
15 Luigi Ghirri, "Endless Worlds," *Camera Austria International* 13 / 1983, 35–36.
16 *Leben mit einer Stadt. Ergebnisse der Grazer Fotoworkshops 1975 und 1976,* exh. cat. Kulturhaus der Stadt Graz, 1977. But even before the workshops initiated by Breicha, it was Erich Kees (1916–2006) who demonstrated new ways for photographers to interact with place and landscape. Within the context of the photographic group TVN (Friends of Nature), he encouraged the use of photo collections, as he termed them, that led away from individual images toward authorial photography. Kees's work formed an important foundation for the early works of the generation of photographers around Branko Lenart and Manfred Willmann.
17 Baltz (see note 11), 14.
18 Christine Frisinghelli, Maren Lübbke-Tidow, and Manfred Willmann, preface to *Camera Austria International* 100 / 2007, 10.
19 The situation is similar for exhibitions devoted to individual countries and the editions of *Camera Austria International* that focused on specific cultures, such as the Netherlands, England, etc. (see chronology in this volume).
20 Issue 46 / 1994 contains an article by featured artist David Goldblatt, a format that was to be repeated many times in subsequent issues.
21 The cover is a reference to the "black issue," number 69, designed by Graz artist Jörg Schlick, which, for its part, was also a critical comment by the Camera Austria editors on the governing ÖVP/FPÖ coalition in the year 2000.
22 In 2017 Camera Austria delved into the archives maintained for the association and institution and presented all the material in two exhibitions. Nicole Six & Paul Petritsch developed a publication concept for the archives, which were made available as a set of reference books in the Camera Austria Library after the exhibitions. This collection is now also on display as part of the present exhibition at the Museum der Moderne Salzburg.

The Editorial Office as a Place for Discussion, the Magazine as Room for Debate

"The cultivated person ought to be: one who knows how to choose his company, among men, among things, among thoughts, in the present as well as in the past."

from: Hannah Arendt, "The Crisis in Culture: Its Social and Political Significance," in *Between Past and Future: Eight Exercises in Political Thought* (London: Faber and Faber, 1961), 226.

Dear Christine,

Today an artist friend of mine, Katja Eydel, informally asked me if I could recommend a photographer she could invite to give a workshop at her academy (in Helsinki), where she herself teaches). The workshop will take place in the context of a seminar devoted to the topic of "intimacy." She is looking for artists who have taken a very personal approach to their artistic work and have been able to translate it into an artistic position. Her question was: "What does it take to make an initially personal concern relevant to others as well, and to thus expand the scope of a work of art?"

Embarrassingly, I could think of only three artists on the spot, all of them male. Two of them, Michael Schmidt and Einar Schleef, are deceased. As far as the third candidate, Seiichi Furuya, is concerned, I was unsure whether he would necessarily be overjoyed at being invited to Helsinki at short notice.

I briefly wondered why I had been unable to reel off a whole list of younger artists or female artists on the spot. Could it be that today, a photographic approach no longer takes the personal as its point of departure (even though Facebook, Instagram, etc., are full of —indeed, overflowing with—personal snapshots)? In a similar vein, Manfred [Willmann] once told me that younger photographers should perhaps best start off by photographing their personal surroundings in order to understand themselves and find out who they are. Only then can something like an approach or an oeuvre emerge: a photographic oeuvre, but also one that assumes relevance beyond a fixation with the merely personal.

Later on, I was able to make a recommendation after all: Akinbode Akinbiyi. Not young. Not female. But he seemed a fitting choice: over the decades, he has doggedly and emphatically built up a body of photographic work that he has formalized, so to speak, through the conceptual framework in which he has embedded his pictures. Apart from that, I could still remember a simple yet resonant text on his oeuvre by Bonaventure Soh Bejeng Ndikung. It accompanied work from Akinbiyi's *Passageways* at documenta 14, the exhibition held in Athens and Kassel: "He … seeks something long ago lost but extremely familiar, essential, innocent. He has described this search in the following terms: 'Over the past years I have realized that I am looking for my childhood, that kind of innocence and childlikeness that I had growing up in London and Lagos, and which I feel is no longer there. Whenever I find such moments—fragments of this lost innocence—I take photographs. At the same time, I try to understand what's happening today in the cities I document." In a very simple and clear way, Akinbiyi's work combines personal experiences, including those associated with his own migration history, with the social and political changes he observes in cities.[Fig. 1]

Happy to be able to recommend someone to Katja Eydel for her workshop, another idea occurred to me: there are some works (such as the work of Akinbiyi) that I come across on repeated occasions without feeling the need to do anything with them: to write

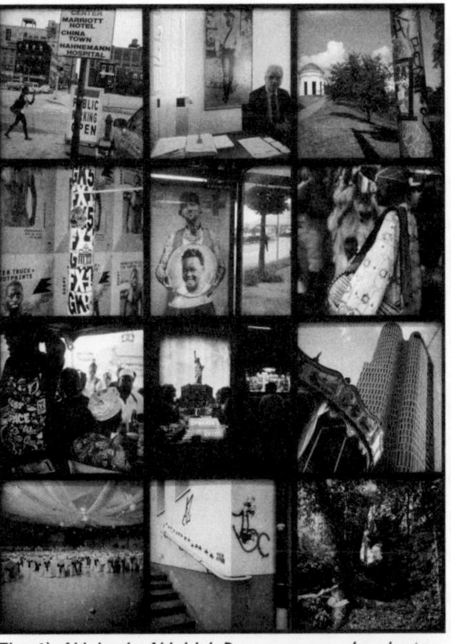

Fig. 1) *Akinbode Akinbiyi, Passageways, Involuntary Narratives, and the Sound of Crowded Spaces*, 2015–2017, documenta 14, Ottoneum Kassel, 2007

about them, exhibit them or—in the years when I worked as an editor—solicit contributions about them. They accompany me silently on the margins. A shift in perception often only comes about when these artists are given an opportunity to create a different presence for themselves—through a big exhibition, for example. With Akinbiyi, my change in perception mainly had something to do with the fact that his conceptual precision and coherence only became apparent once a body of work had taken shape. After all, the works of abiding interest are often those that captivate the viewer through a precision and persistence in their artistic practice. They frequently stand opposed to the fleetingness of our (or, rather, my) reception.

Warmly, Maren

P.S. Is there any truth to the old Camera Austria rumor that Akinbode Akinbiyi was the first-ever subscriber to *Camera Austria International*? Or was it just that his name was the first to appear in alphabetical order?

———————————————————————

Dear Maren,

The question "What does it take to make an initially personal concern relevant to others as well, and to thus expand the scope of a work of art?" invites reflection on a whole series of artistic ideas. Narrowing the focus to works of photography, the idea of "intimacy" naturally soon brought to mind the work of Nan Goldin. At the same time, however, I also thought of Wolfgang Tillmans' first large-scale exhibition at the Kunsthalle in Zurich in the early 1990s. In the mid-1980s, Nan Goldin's *Ballad of Sexual Dependency* revealed the most private and intimate matters—first as a slide show with a musical soundtrack in various New York clubs, in places where the people portrayed were often identical with the public viewing the work, then as a book with an unprecedentedly high print run on the German-language market. Yet even the voyeurism of spectators, their glimpse of a socially marginalized and endangered group, seemed (at the time) in no way detrimental to the truthfulness of the photographer's concerns, her solidarity and even complicity with the protagonists of her photographs. A great deal has changed since then, not least through the commercialization of the art world and the attendant commodification of authenticity and privacy in photography. One result of the enormous impression made by this exhibition was that Goldin's way of working inspired a whole generation of young photographers to take their own experience as the point of departure for their work.

Tillmans' work seemed far more enigmatic in comparison, yet I came away from the Zurich exhibition with the impression of having gotten closer to the meaning of his work through the *relation* of pictures to each other in the exhibition space—even if their meaning to the artist may have remained obscure to me. At the time, Tillmans' (published) work had already been familiar to me for several years, and we had repeatedly discussed the possibility of a publication in *Camera Austria International*. But it was not until years later that we finally were able—through your initiative—to get him to contribute to the magazine. This was followed by an exhibition that you yourself curated.

I think that Manfred Willmann's recommendation (or stipulation?) to young photographers to start out by finding where they personally stand, address their immediate surroundings and make this the subject of their work, reflects the mentoring role he has taken on for himself. I don't think his advice is about cultivating a subjective gaze. On the contrary, it's about knowing your own position in a social environment, reflecting on it, and deriving from it an urgency or even necessity for your work. Manfred's work itself stands for such a position. Even if artistic works can be read autobiographically, positing a quasi-natural (here: photographic) "self-expression" that disregards the material, conceptual and formal decisions made in the process of realization would be a naïve (mis) understanding of the artistic process. In the end, as you say, it is a matter of expanding "the scope of a work of art."

A further thought: the 1990s seem to me to have been *the* decade for interrogating identity: the end of the Cold War after 1989 and the associated debate on postcolonialism; newly independent or emerging nation-states; the breakup of Yugoslavia and the almost decade-long war in this region; the hopes and fears that came with economic globalization. Philosophical debates about identity were taken up in numerous artistic projects and reflected in curatorial practice. I'm thinking of Catherine David's documenta X from 1997; the exhibition *Mistaken Identities* by Abigail Solomon-Godeau, which we put on in 1992, [Fig. 2] and the thematically related Symposion on Photography from the same year; the first Austrian Triennial for Photography in Graz, on the topic WAR, which I curated with Werner Fenz in collaboration with the Neue Galerie Graz in 1993; as well as our conference on this topic (at which Susan Meiselas spoke about the beginning of her work on a national archive for Kurdistan; much later, in 2006, we published excerpts from this project, with an introduction by Allan Sekula, in *Camera Austria International*). [Fig. 3, Fig. 4]

Photography and video, and documentary approaches in general, were accepted in the 1990s in a way that seemed almost "natural," whereas in the 1980s, muse-

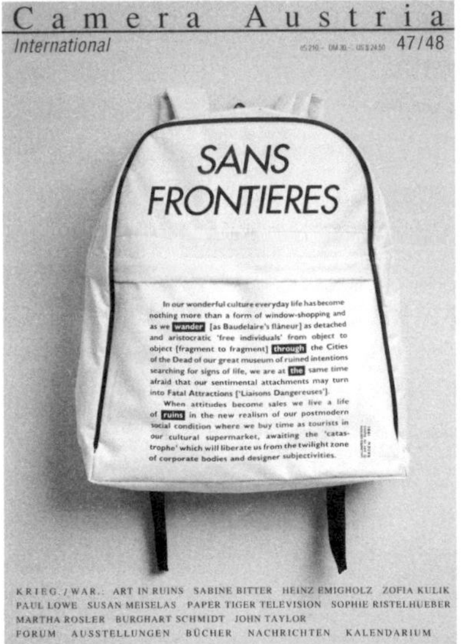

Fig. 2) *Mistaken Identities*, University Art Museum, University of California, Santa Barbara (US), edited in collaboration with Museum Folkwang, Essen (DE), Forum Stadtpark Graz (AT), Neues Museum Weserburg, Bremen (DE), Louisiana Museum of Modern Art, Humlebaek (DK), 1992, cover

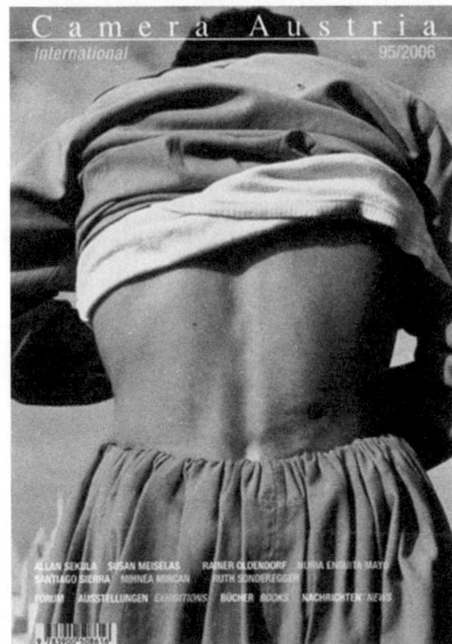

Fig. 3) *Camera Austria International* 47–48/1994, cover: Art in Ruins, *Sans Frontières*, 1991

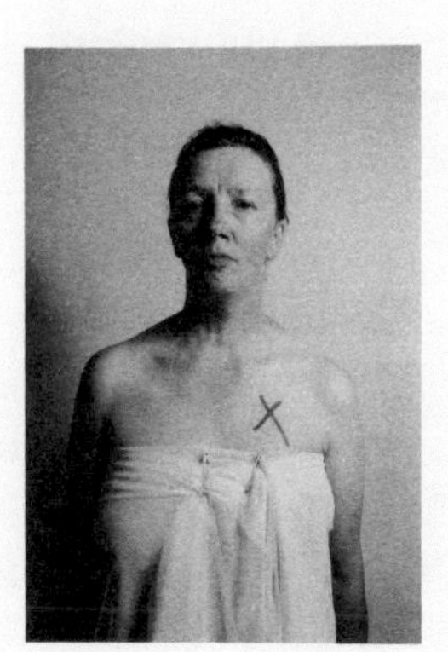

Fig. 4) *Camera Austria International* 95/2006, cover: Susan Meiselas, *Arbil, Northern Iraq, December 1991. Taymour Abdullah, 15, the only survivor of a village massacre, shows his wound*

ums and galleries still often questioned the artistic credentials of "pure" photography. Against this backdrop, too, the impact of Nan Goldin's work from 1985 is remarkable.

Regarding your question whether "today, a photographic approach no longer takes the personal as its point of departure:" I think that even so hermetic and analytic a work as Mary Kelly's *Post Partum Document* (which dispenses with photography altogether, using everyday objects, remnants and descriptions instead) has to take the personal as its point of departure to do justice to its own bid to establish a distance from the thematic center of the work. Precisely its almost scientific stance, its avoidance of any description of an authentic experience of motherhood, and its rejection of an essentially feminine viewpoint, are what make this work so personal: the artist puts her own experience on display, but she observes and describes herself as well in a process extending over many years. The work of Jo Spence, which radically challenged the formal conventions of photography from the 1970s onward, can in my view be perceived as similarly "personal." In 1992, the year in which Mary Kelly spoke about her own work at our Symposion on Photography, "So oder so nicht sein / Identities," we showed Jo Spence's *The Picture of Health* and Rosy Martin discussed her collaboration with the artist, who had passed away the previous year. *The Picture of Health* deals with the experience of illness and the loss of responsibility for one's own body as soon as the health system takes charge of methods and procedures for treating it. Jo Spence thematizes her own illness in this work, and her *Picture of Health* shows her own body: mercilessly, without drama or sentimentality, she makes it visible in all its vulnerability and debility—yet this very directness and harshness allows something like warmth and intimacy to emerge. ^{Fig. 5}

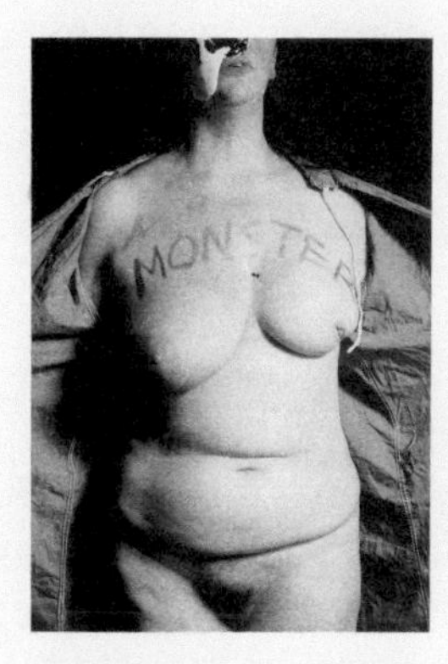

Fig. 5) Jo Spence (with Rosy Martin, Maggie Murray, Terry Dennett), from "The Picture of Health?," 1982–1986, *Camera Austria International* 94/2006

It was one of the most astonishing experiences of my working life when a women's self-help group told us that they "needed" this exhibition: they wanted to present it for a limited time at a women's health center in Graz to support their counseling activities and, above all, to help women empower themselves. We were happy to oblige. It happens all too rarely, after all, that a work of art is "needed" in this way and the activist, sociopolitical intention of a work is so closely linked to an artistic conception based on personal experience.

Akinbode Akinbiyi is a good choice, even if his work is rooted in a different, more subjective kind of experience. He was indeed our first-ever subscriber—he appears first alphabetically, too, but I have always been particularly pleased that the first subscriber of a magazine that bears its national origin in its title happened to be a photographer from Africa. That's why we invited him to join us in Graz in 2007 to celebrate the 100th issue of *Camera Austria International*. We have never published or exhibited his work—just as many other projects have remained unrealized.

We got to know Akinbode in Düsseldorf in 1980. Manfred, Seiichi and I had traveled to the 1st Düsseldorf Photo-Symposium. We had previously successfully held our first Symposion on Photography in the steirischer herbst (styrian autumn) festival of 1979. The articles had been published in a bilingual edition, but sales were terrible for lack of a marketing and distribution network. Manfred was the courageous one who decided we needed a magazine of our own as a forum in which the proceedings of future conferences could be published. Through subscriptions and regular communications, we hoped to find readers for the high-profile papers delivered at our symposia. The first issue appeared shortly before the summer of 1980. We thus came to Düsseldorf flushed with the success of our first Symposion and met Akinbode. We must have been very convincing, because he subscribed to a magazine that still existed only as an idea—the work we had done up to that point had presumably given him confidence in our venture.

Warmly, Christine

———————————————————————

Dear Christine,

It is certainly true that, as you put it, Nan Goldin's *Ballad of Sexual Dependency* "inspired a whole generation of young photographers to take their own experience as the point of departure for their work." In an interview I conducted with Joachim Brohm in 2014, "On Teaching Photography," he recalled how Nan Goldin's invitation to his academy [the Academy of Fine Arts in Leipzig] in the early 1990s threatened to overturn the conventional wisdom about working with the medium of photography—and not just among students. And it would definitely be interesting to ask an artist like Wiebke Loeper, who studied under Arno Fischer and Joachim Brohm at the time, whether Goldin's work played a role in her own artistic development—even if her work owes no obvious debt to Goldin in either form or content. But Loeper's *Moll 31* is, as far as I can tell, one of the first works in which an artist of her generation has very personally come to terms with the changes in Germany since the fall of the Berlin Wall in 1989, even if she's taken a drier, more conceptual approach to her material* and—an important consideration, in my view—has also published this work.[Fig. 6]

More and more works are now emerging from the archives which take the time around the fall of the Wall as their topic. The book *Irreguläre Tage* (Irregular Days), for example, published by Spector Books in 2013 with texts and photos by the late artist and author Michael Schade, is situated in just this period of transition between the last years of the GDR and the first of the new republic—a period during which Schade was enrolled in Leipzig as a student with an East German background. It is a personal and disturbing document that makes the artist's inner turmoil tangible in the social contexts of the time. I was also impressed by the new artist's book by Falk Haberkorn, *After the Gold Rush: Journey to Eastern Germany*, Fall 2004. It appeared only recently, in 2018. It's a kind of road movie through the new federal states following the "sell-off of the east." With its English title, the book also looks to America, and it would certainly be worthwhile to compare Haberkorn's black-and-white pictures, all shot from a moving vehicle, with similar images by Robert Frank. The pictures themselves—for all the apparent casualness with which, like Frank, they capture the atmosphere and social context of the time—stand in stark contrast to the promises made by Helmut Kohl in the summer of 1990, in the course of establishing the currency union. There would soon be "flourishing landscapes" in eastern Germany, the conservative chancellor pledged. The book speaks a different language, showing how, fifteen years after reunification, the country was still in a state of transition, but also how structural change had done significant damage to its infrastructure.

I must admit that Nan Goldin no longer appears on my inner radar, even though I fully appreciate her historical achievement and the changes she initiated. It never ceases to amaze me how deeply attitudes to specific works can be transformed by the passage

*   Here Loeper revisited her childhood home: a evacuated building in the former eastern part of the city, on Mollstraße in the Mitte district, which was about to be demolished. She has combined the photographs taken there with images from her family album.

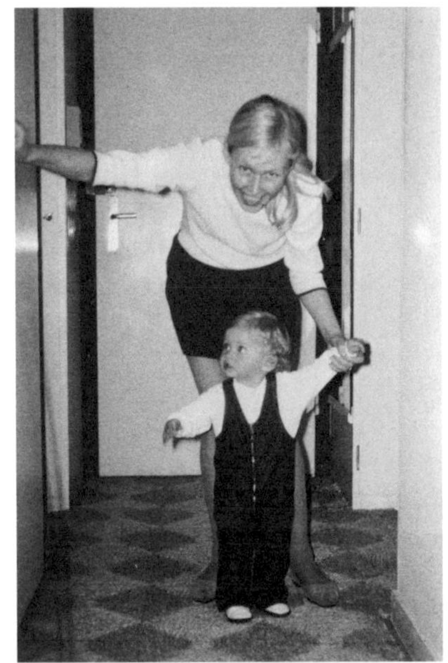

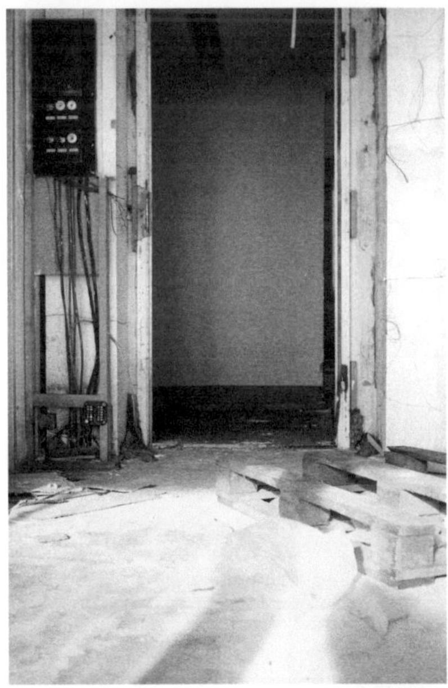

Fig. 6) Wiebke Loeper, from *MOLL 31*, book with chromogenic prints and metal type, edition: 9 + IV, Edition Liane, Berlin, 1995

of time. Even if it now detracts from her nimbus, and my criticism possibly—probably—is untenable: with Goldin I simply no longer get a sense of her specific formal aesthetic. Maybe that will change again.

I did not attend Wolfgang Tillmans' 1995 Zurich exhibition, and it is not documented online. However, his first book was published in the same year by Taschen in Cologne. To this day, I find his conception of photography as material far more rewarding for analysis: his continually innovative and experimental approach to photography, as reflected in forms of exposure, assignment of tonal values, developing (on different kinds of paper and using different procedures) and hanging, strikes me as extraordinary. Through such innovations, he is constantly sparking debate on the status of photography as a technically induced imaging medium. In my view, he is someone worth listening to: not just because he knows his own substan-

tial body of work in intimate detail and always reflects on and justifies his finely calibrated technical decisions, but also because—as a sought-after artist with an impressive résumé of exhibitions—he simply has a wealth of experience that others (unfortunately) often lack. On the other hand, I get irritated by the concepts of "youth culture" or "the nineties" that are trotted out whenever his work, particularly his early work, is discussed—not least because Tillmans has, in my opinion, not yet found the right wording for what he was up to in these photos, instead constantly explaining them with reference to his intuition, his "vision:" a way of speaking that often results in sweeping, purely emphatic gestures. These famous photos are "good pictures," to be sure—but they also invite a form of narcissistic (self-)identification that I find problematic. In the exhibition we put on together in Graz in 2007, it quickly became clear, partly for this reason, that the focus should lie on the then-new "paper drop" images. [Fig. 7]

However: your lines reminded me of an artist who perhaps adopts a position formally akin to Tillmans'—and who makes the switch to the present day. Ketuta Alexi-Meskhishvili is a young Georgian artist who came to New York as a child and who—along with fellow artists Walead Beshty, Liz Deschenes, Eileen Quinlan and Lucas Blalock, all of whom pursue a similar artistic agenda in their photographic works—studied at Bard College with Stephen Shore. She now lives in Berlin. An article on her work can be found in a recent issue of *Camera Austria International* 133 / 2016. The lightness and visual persuasiveness of her work strongly remind me of Tillmans, as do her formal solutions. She goes a step further here, not just by technically presenting her pictures as images which offensively operate on the threshold from the analog to the digital (such as when she photographs computer screens with a large-format camera and the pixels that hold together the information on the monitor begin to interfere with the image-generating grain of the analog print) [Fig. 8], but also by continually finding

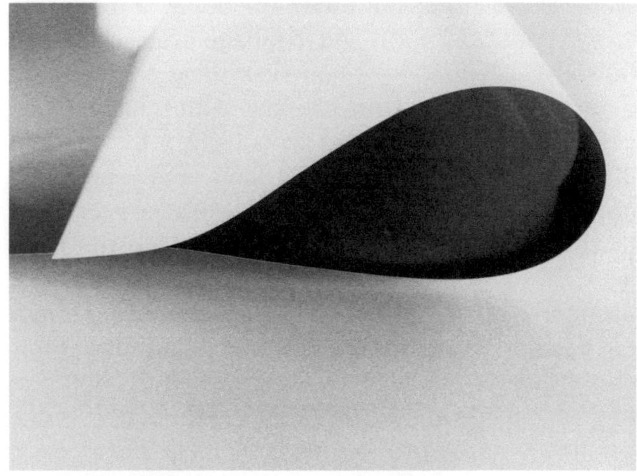

Fig. 7) Wolfgang Tillmans, *paper drop (rainbow)*, 2006

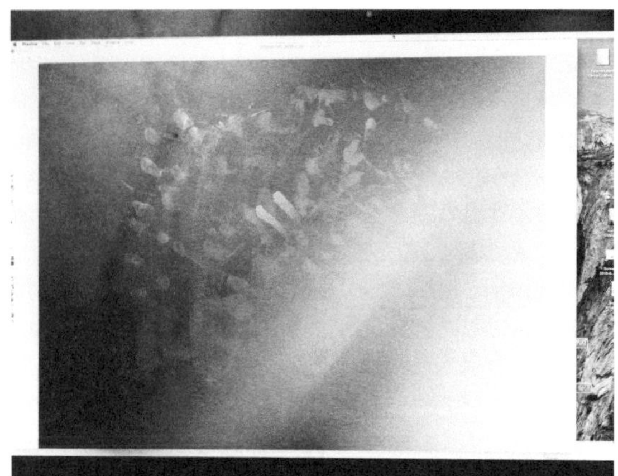

Fig. 8) Ketuta Alexi-Meskhishvili, *Monitor Large,* 2016

new substrates—textiles, for example—for her photographic images. Her motifs are drawn from negatives from her family's photographic archive, among other sources, or they depict the journeys she often makes back to her home town of Tiflis.

On a different topic, I wanted to discuss another recent issue of *Camera Austria International* 140/2017, [Fig.10] which I perused over the Christmas break. The cover of this new issue is entirely in black, thus referencing No. 69/2000. [Fig. 9] That "black issue" had been designed for us by Graz artist Jörg Schlick. The background to the invitation was the fact that in 2000, the far-right, nationalist FPÖ (Freedom Party of Austria) took part for the first time in forming a coalition government in Austria. This called for a break with tradition. Schlick responded to our own distress, which went hand in hand with our adamant determination to take a stand, with a rigorous gesture: he recommended that we not only blacken the issue's cover but extend the pall to the inside of the volume as well. Only the words *Austria 2000* would appear on each page. Schlick and Camera Austria thereby delivered a caustic commentary on Austria's political situation. So you want art and culture? The outlook is bleak.

I can well remember the productive tension in the editorial team during the making of this issue: for was this decision not also an admission of the paralysis we were all feeling at the time? For us, as a magazine, to surrender our form and language precisely in this outrageous situation, when everything cried out for a response, seemed questionable. Our refusal to provide pictures and text was like a blackout, to remain in Schlick's diction. Or was it, conversely, perfectly correct to transfer responsibility at this very moment to those who, we were convinced, held the right instruments for commentary in their hands: in this case, an artist who did not shirk from making a radical gesture? I was not the only one who thought this conflict insoluble, I believe—even when the decision had been made and No. 69/2000 was already in press. We finally agreed to include a slip of paper in each issue calling on readers to contribute to the debate:

"to counter the illegitimacy of the language of extreme right-wing politics in Austria with powerful words and images." [Fig. 11]

We were thus unwilling to lay down all our editorial tools. Otherwise, the issue itself was realized entirely in accordance with Schlick's specifications. Besides the slogan "Austria 2000," Schlick wanted no text whatsoever to appear in "his" issue, which thus turned into an artist's book. We were both surprised and delighted by the flood of reactions to this edition of *Camera Austria International.* For the rest of 2000, we could establish a platform for all the contributions sent to us in response to the issue as well as the political situation in Austria, and we documented these reactions in the following issues. No. 69 / 2000 was soon out of stock.

Not least, the forum for debate that arose thereafter also marked the beginning of our collaboration with Pierre Bourdieu, who came to Vienna with *raisons d'agir* shortly after the formation of the new govern-

Fig. 9) *Camera Austria International* 69/2000, cover: Jörg Schlick: *Österreich 2000*

Fig. 10) *Camera Austria International* 140/2017, cover

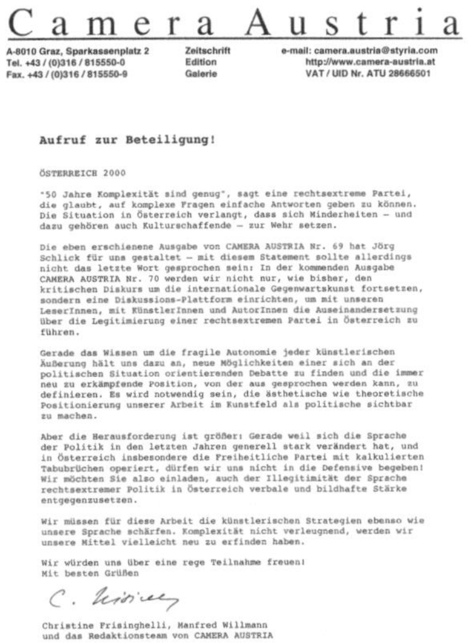

Camera Austria

A-8010 Graz, Sparkassenplatz 2 Zeitschrift e-mail: camera.austria@styria.com
Tel. +43 / (0)316 / 815550-0 Edition http://www.camera-austria.at
Fax. +43 / (0)316 / 815550-9 Galerie VAT / UID Nr. ATU 28666501

Aufruf zur Beteiligung!

ÖSTERREICH 2000

"50 Jahre Komplexität sind genug", sagt eine rechtsextreme Partei, die glaubt, auf komplexe Fragen einfache Antworten geben zu können. Die Situation in Österreich verlangt, dass sich Minderheiten – und dazu gehören auch Kulturschaffende – zur Wehr setzen.

Die eben erschienene Ausgabe von CAMERA AUSTRIA Nr. 69 hat Jörg Schlick für uns gestaltet – mit diesem Statement sollte allerdings nicht das letzte Wort gesprochen sein: In der kommenden Ausgabe CAMERA AUSTRIA Nr. 70 werden wir nicht nur, wie bisher, den kritischen Diskurs um die internationale Gegenwartskunst fortsetzen, sondern eine Diskussions-Plattform einrichten, um mit unseren LeserInnen, mit KünstlerInnen und AutorInnen die Auseinandersetzung über die Legitimierung einer rechtsextremen Partei in Österreich zu führen.

Gerade das Wissen um die fragile Autonomie jeder künstlerischen Äußerung hält uns dazu an, neue Möglichkeiten einer sich an der politischen Situation orientierenden Debatte zu finden und die immer neu zu erkämpfende Position, von der aus gesprochen werden kann, zu definieren. Es wird notwendig sein, die ästhetische wie theoretische Positionierung unserer Arbeit im Kunstfeld als politische sichtbar zu machen.

Aber die Herausforderung ist größer: Gerade weil sich die Sprache der Politik in den letzten Jahren generell stark verändert hat, und in Österreich insbesondere die Freiheitliche Partei mit kalkulierten Tabubrüchen operiert, dürfen wir uns nicht in die Defensive begeben! Wir möchten Sie also einladen, auch der Illegitimität der Sprache rechtsextremer Politik in Österreich verbale und bildhafte Stärke entgegenzusetzen.

Wir müssen für diese Arbeit die künstlerischen Strategien ebenso wie unsere Sprache schärfen. Komplexität nicht verleugnend, werden wir unsere Mittel vielleicht neu zu erfinden haben.

Wir würden uns über eine rege Teilnahme freuen!
Mit besten Grüßen

C. Frisinghelli

Christine Frisinghelli, Manfred Willmann
und das Redaktionsteam von CAMERA AUSTRIA

Fig. 11) Facsimile "Aufruf zur Beteiligung," supplement to *Camera Austria International* 69 / 2000

ment. We invited him to contribute to the magazine. It was only by sending him the issues of *Camera Austria International* featuring Cathren Müller's interview with him, and then his essays, that Bourdieu gradually came to understand where exactly he was publishing in Austria. He eventually approached us, through Franz Schultheis, to inquire whether Camera Austria could provide him with a venue for his earliest work, the photos he had taken in Algeria as a young man.

What are your memories of the period when No. 69 / 2000 appeared? What kinds of conversations did you have back then with Jörg Schlick when he dropped by the old editorial office at Sparkassenplatz Schlick's eccentric manner did not inspire in me the absolute confidence I would have wished for in bringing to press what was probably the most radical and provocative issue of *Camera Austria International*. What was your relationship with him like, and what gave you confidence, not just in Jörg Schlick as the artist entrusted with the task, but also in yourself and Manfred as the ones who ultimately bore responsibility for the issue?

The editorial by Reinhard [Braun] and the *Camera Austria International* team in the recent number 140 / 2007 strikes me as very clear and powerful: "'There are people who want the past to be repeated, so they ensure that we cannot remember it,' as Priya Basil notes in *Lettre International* no. 118, citing Paul Krugman. I can hardly imagine a more apt description of the consolidation of reactionary political powers, now playing out in Austria as well on the heels of the most recent national parliamentary elections. Such politics are increasingly moving towards a sealed-off, ethnically pure dream [of a] present that reflects the past, with its force rooted in the repression of memory of the region called Europe—constantly in flux, immersed in change, social blending, dissolution, and reinvention."

That reads like a manifesto. At the same time, it disturbs me that the current far-right nationalist government clearly no longer provokes storms of outrage and that the art scene today—unlike eighteen years ago—has failed to present a united front. That, it seems to me, made many things easier back then: rebellion was in the air. For that very reason, I applaud the stoic gesture with which *Camera Austria International* 140 / 2017 cites the old edition (No. 69 / 2000). While skeptical at first, I now find it more and more convincing. Not just because it is needed, but also because it shows that in producing a magazine, we have powerful instruments at our disposal that should not just be nostalgically recalled from time to time but should be deployed, now as then, in the face of all obstacles—and they have increased considerably in the intervening years. And sometimes, the gesture of refusal is simply the strongest—provided, of course, that it comes with a call to arms, which is why I want to transcribe the concluding sentence from this recent editorial: "Therefore, in this foreword, we call upon you to give your full attention and support to artistic and cultural initiatives in your immediate vicinity. They are especially deserving of such support in view of the transformed political hold on their deviant, marginal, minority, abstruse, idiosyncratic, autonomist, and possibly all but incommunicable themes, formats and content—otherwise, they may well vanish altogether."

Warmly, Maren

Dear Maren,

You write about *Camera Austria International* 69 / 2000—the "black" issue—and the reference by Reinhard Braun in No. 140 / 2017 to the formation of a new Austrian government in 2018. I find the link by Braun both salutary and important! I can only underscore his concluding sentence, which you quote at the end of your letter. Yes, the party-political constellation Austria decided on in 2017 is comparable to the situation back then: once again, the Freedom Party of Austria has formed a government in coalition with the Austrian People's Party (ÖVP).

Apropos Austria in 2000: I remember the evening in February when the announcement was made that the ÖVP would be forming a government with the FPÖ. We were doing the rounds of the galleries that line the Schleifmühlgasse in Vienna when the news reached us between the galleries of Georg Kargl and Christine König. The collective shock made any other topic of conversation seem trivial in comparison. Everyone sensed that, in light of this fact, any publicly visible work—both artistic and institutional—would henceforth be understood in terms of critical resistance or tacit submission.

In the previous decade, contemporary art had repeatedly come under attack from the FPÖ, led by Jörg Haider at the time. Everyone in this country remembers the poster campaign in the 1995 Vienna municipal elections with slogans denouncing artists and liberal politicians involved in the arts: "Do you love Scholten, Jelinek, Häupl, Peymann, Pasterk—or art and culture?" and "Artistic freedom, not socialist state artists."

Much of the drama in 2000 was also due to the situation of the media in Austria, where the most widely distributed print medium (the *Kronen Zeitung*) dominated the discourse and was thus able to steer public perceptions of art. Unfortunately, contemporary art is often conceded a place in the public sphere only when it gives rise to scandal. Indeed, derogatory and instrumentalizing arguments directed against it are perhaps characteristic of the self-declared *Kulturstaat* ("cultural state") of Austria under conditions allowed by the media. The "cultural state" derives its legitimacy precisely from such media-driven scandals. I had firsthand experience of this—and gained a certain expertise in crisis management—as director of the steirischer herbst festival from 1995 to 1999. Time and again, I had to ward off covertly ideological or overtly political attacks on the work of artists and institutions, even as the media ritually invoked each scandal as evidence of the festival's continuing sociopolitical relevance.

The political situation facing us in 2000 directly challenged us to take a stand. We were acutely aware of the responsibility that any expression of political protest would bring with it. What was decisive in the end, however, was the confidence that artists, authors, and readers had shown in our work through their often years-long collaboration, interest and solidarity. It seemed only fitting to use *Camera Austria International*, a magazine with an international audience and reputation, to make our political position clear, given that our ongoing efforts since the 1970s had made us part of a cultural and political public sphere.

In the first place, though, there was a difficulty to confront: how were we to deploy the editorial and aesthetic apparatus at our disposal, which had originally been developed to realize artistic projects adequately in magazine format, in a strategically correct way? The reticence we had always imposed on ourselves as editors proved unsuitable when it came to making a grand gesture. For our friend Jörg Schlick, on the other hand, provocation had long been a means of choice: as an artist and curator, he has set out time and again to ruffle feathers. Starting from the second half of the 1980s, he had led the visual arts section at Forum Stadtpark, and he was also responsible for developing public-relations strategies during my years at *steirischer herbst*. Never one to shy away from making enemies, and admirably equipped with the self-assurance needed to run the risk of public embarrassment, he cultivated his alter ego as *agent provocateur* with fine self-irony and steadfast support from his friends in the artistic community. The idea for the first issue of 2000 came from him. *Camera Austria International* 69 / 2000 featured paper printed entirely in black. In keeping with the magazine's usual layout, two types of paper were used: glossy and matte, corresponding to the artistic and editorial contributions. The heading "Austria 2000" would appear in Helvetica (Schlick's favorite typeface) at the top of every right-hand page in the type area. We instinctively accepted the audacity of this proposal as an artistic gesture and set about implementing it without hesitation.

We were nonetheless determined to keep a single "text page," the imprint detailing the magazine's ownership structure and acknowledging the support of various public bodies. In addition, each volume was sent out with a letter signed by Manfred Willmann, myself, and the editorial team (which you and I spent a long time redrafting), personally addressing all our subscribers and inviting them to take a position and send in their contributions. We received an extraordinary number of reactions, many positive, some negative; several subscriptions were canceled, but many new readers came our way. What was especially interesting was the political reaction to the issue's imprint: the legitimacy of a publicly funded institution taking a critical stand was called into question, and state subsidy of our work became a topic of debate in both the Graz municipal council and the Austrian national parliament.

With the publication of No. 69 / 2000, the year 2000 had gotten off to a highly emotional and polarizing start. There followed a period of intense exchange with artists and readers. In retrospect, I think we had visibly taken a stand here, as both citizens and editors, which had perhaps not previously been associated with us and our work by some members of the public.

In general, the significance of art as *socially necessary* work must continually be reemphasized. In keeping with this, photography dedicated to observing and describing social facts can be supported, even if too pronounced a relation to reality often works to its detriment: too much "middle-brow art," to quote Pierre Bourdieu's investigation of the social uses of photography from the 1960s [English: 1990]. As *un art moyen* (*an illegitimate art*, as the German translation puts it), Bourdieu takes photography's democratic accessibility to be its essential characteristic: an art that is practiced by everyone and can therefore only be defined through its social function. On the other hand, he concludes that photography, even where it is deployed as an artistic instrument or material, must be characterized as a *different* practice, a difference that is more sociological than aesthetic in nature. This statement is based on the observation that photography has no aesthetic norms of its own but "borrows" them instead from the other arts. Expressiveness, originality, singularity—all these aesthetic categories originate in other art forms and cannot be applied to photography owing to its mechanical nature.

Over the course of our work we have constantly run up against this question: How can a work of photography be brought to presence in an artistic context if it simultaneously represents this "different practice," and if institutions that bestow importance and status disregard this practice and its history? In the end, the division of the field into *Photography as Art—Art as Photography* (the title of two big exhibitions in the 1970s, whose wording says a great deal about the status of the debate at the time)[Fig. 12+13] can still be observed today.[Fig. 14+15] John Baldessari, who collaborated with us on a number of projects, began his address to our 1984 Symposion on Photography by demanding that the history of photography be ab-

sorbed into art history in general. By contrast, Allan Sekula—to Camera Austria, a hugely important thinker, artist, and author—maintains that "I find the endlessly repeated mantra that photography has finally, or yet again, arrived at the status of a fine art to be completely beside the point.—What is much more interesting is the modesty of this medium, and the radical wisdom that follows from close and sustained attention to observation."

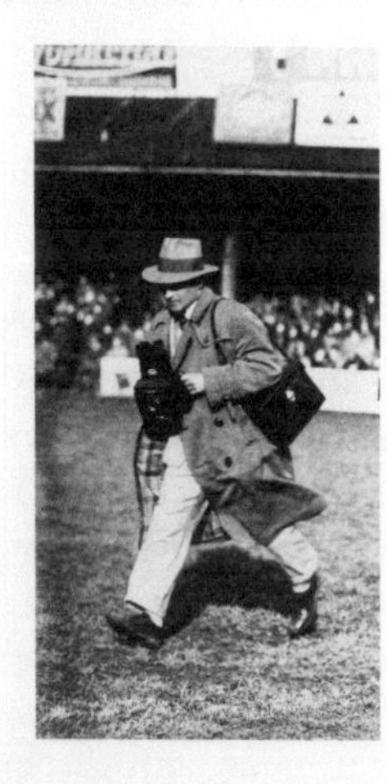

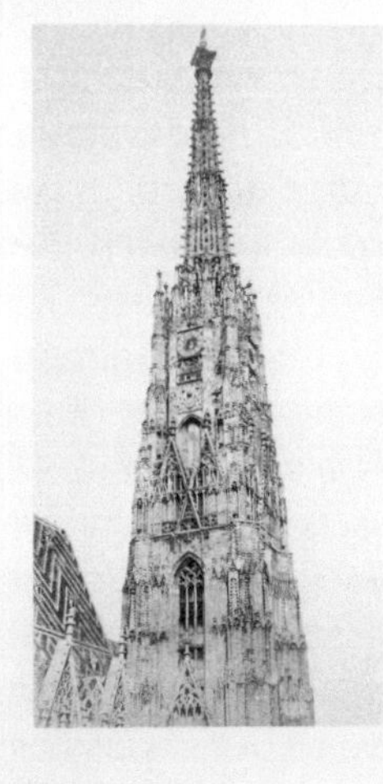

Fig. 14+15) Verein zur Erarbeitung der Geschichte der Fotografie in Österreich ed., *Geschichte der Fotografie in Österreich*, Bad Ischl: 1983, cover

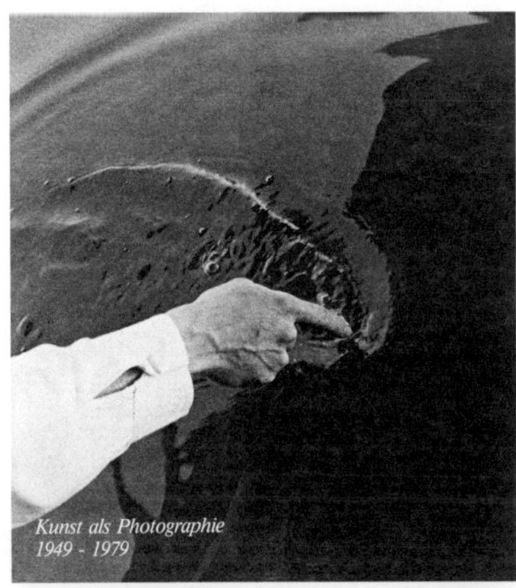

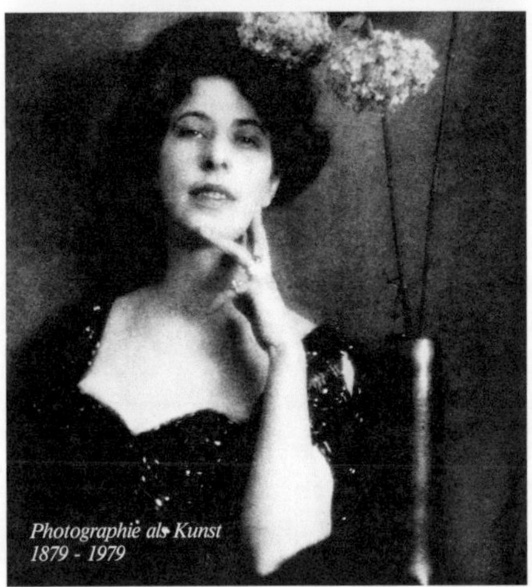

Fig. 12+13) Peter Weiermair ed., *Photography as Art 1839–1979. Art as Photography 1949–1979*, Innsbruck: Allerheiligenpresse, 1979, two covers

Our exhibiting and publishing activities have constantly been challenged by these two positions. In connection with AUSTRIA 2000, we—you and I—also approached Pierre Bourdieu to contribute something to the Austrian debate. As you have already pointed out, he came to know our work only gradually, a process that eventually led him and Franz Schultheis to ask us whether we were interested in the photos he had taken when carrying out his sociological and ethnographic research in Algeria. At that time, we were not the only ones unaware that the sociologist and activist Bourdieu was himself a practiced photographer as well as the author of the previously mentioned study on the social use of photography. Bourdieu had used this stock of photographic material (700 negatives, along with another 300 negatives and 300 or so prints that fortuitously turned up in early 2018) almost exclusively as an aide-mémoire. Only a few served as illustrations in publications, while three were used as book covers. In *Camera Austria International* 75 / 2001 we were able to show a first selection of these photographs in the context of a conversation with Franz Schultheis in which Bourdieu discussed his experiences in Algeria. That was the beginning—with you, Manfred, Seiichi, Anja Rösch and Franz Schultheis from the Fondation Bourdieu—of our work on an exhibition and book project. Unfortunately, Bourdieu passed away in 2002, so we could only share with him our initial ideas for the book and exhibition. This work allowed us to immerse ourselves in the investigations of a young philosopher who came to Algeria in 1954 as a simple soldier and critic of French colonial policy. Following the end of his military service, he decided to stay on in Algeria to study the effects of an almost decade-long war of liberation and colonization that had been going on for some 130 years. Above all, Bourdieu wanted to describe the reality in Algeria to his compatriots in metropolitan France. Photography served him as just *one* means for recording his findings in this "social laboratory." Through interviews, statistical data and the scientific methods he developed in the field and in confrontation with a disturbing reality, he endeavored to describe a society with a ruined economy and broken-down solidarity structures. The photographic result are images that are already "framed"—historically, but also in the writings of the author: his first book, the study *Une sociologie de l'Algérie,* appeared in the series "que sais-je?" You initially expressed skepticism about showing Bourdieu's photos in the context of an artistic institution. As a political scientist, you feared that opening up the relevant contexts for reception might prove all but impossible. And yes: finding the right form for these photographic studies was a challenge. Discussions about how best to contextualize this work have continued to this day as the exhibition has been lent to numerous other institutions. Fig. 16, Fig. 17

"See in order to understand; show in order to make comprehensible" was one of Pierre Bourdieu's principles. And he had this to say about his use of photography as a medium: "Photography, you see, is a manifestation of the distance of the observer who collects his data—and is always aware that he is collecting data—but at the same time, photography also assumes the complete proximity of the familiar … and a sensitivity with regard to even the least perceptible of details. Details the observer can only understand and interpret thanks to his familiarity… . But photog-

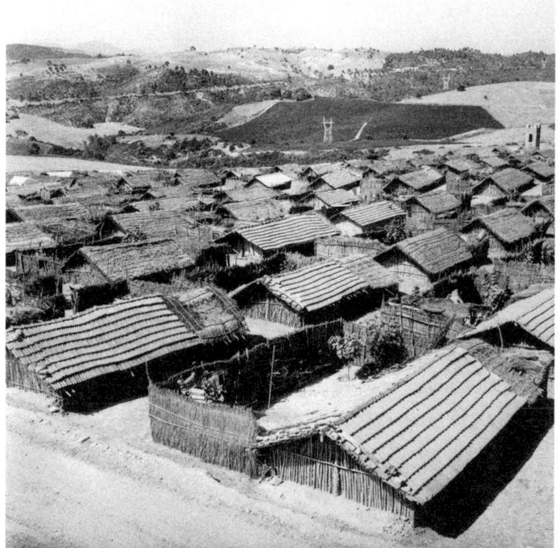

Fig. 16) Pierre Bourdieu, *Resettlement Camp, Djebabra, Chélif*

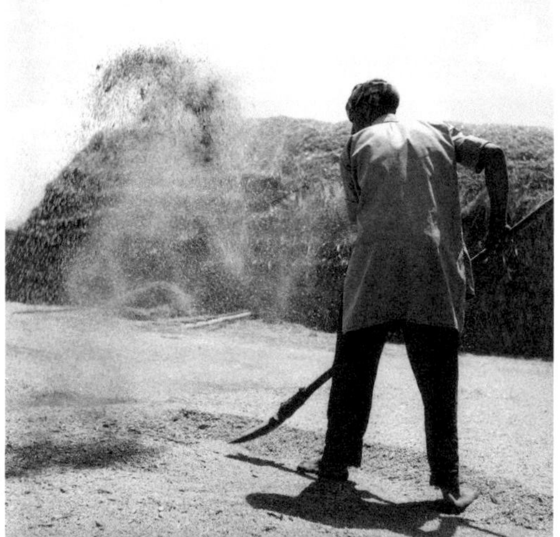

Fig. 17) Pierre Bourdieu, *Cheraïa,* N 8/6, published as cover image of the book *Le Sens pratique*

raphy itself is equally interwoven with the relationship I have had to my subject at any particular time, and not for a moment did I forget that my subject is people, human beings whom I have encountered from a perspective that—at the risk of sounding ridiculous—I would willingly refer to as caring, often touched."

Warmly, Christine

Dear Christine,

From today until March, Michael Schmidt's *Waffenruhe* (Ceasefire) will be projected each evening onto the façade of the Volksbühne at Rosa-Luxemburg-Platz in Berlin. Fig. 18

Schmidt's pictures are interrupted by sentences from Einar Schleef's text "Zigaretten" (Cigarettes). There are fourteen sentences in all, which also featured in the Michael Schmidt exhibition held in 1987 in the Martin-Gropius-Bau at the initiative of Janos Frecot, the then-director of the photographic collection of the Berlinische Galerie. The exhibition moved to

MoMA in New York a year later. The 1987 volume has been reissued to coincide with the projection onto the façade of the Volksbühne. I got hold of the last copy of the 100 books that Koenig Books had brought along—quite a success for an artist's book. [Fig. 19]

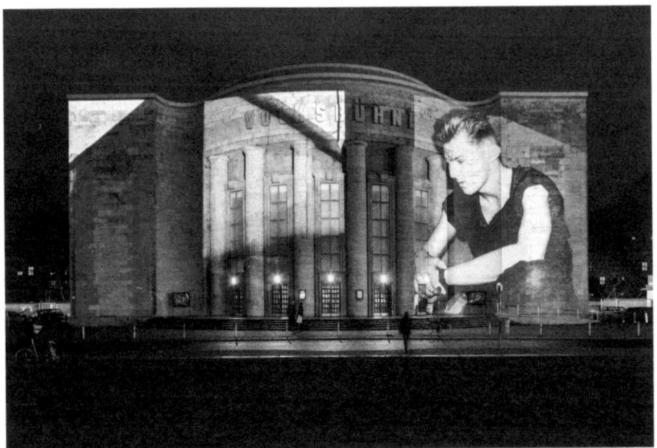

Fig. 18) Michael Schmidt, untitled, from *Waffenruhe* (Ceasefire) 1985–1987, Volksbühne Berlin, projection, 2018

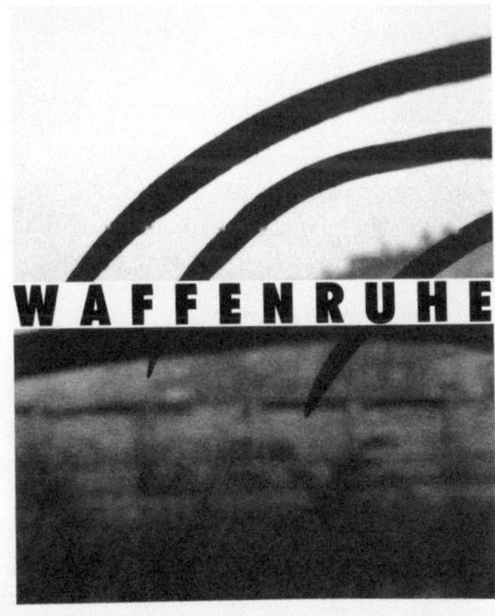

Fig. 19) Einar Schleef, Michael Schmidt, *Waffenruhe*, (Ceasefire) Berlin: 1987, cover

Of course, this work cannot be seen in isolation from the ongoing political intrigues surrounding the (old and new) directorship of the Volksbühne. Or can it? Chris Dercon, at any rate, expressed his hope at the opening evening event that, with *Waffenruhe*, a fitting parable for the current situation at the Volksbühne had perhaps been found... This is a pious wish, to be sure: not just with respect to the situation at the Volksbühne, but also with regard to Schmidt. For Schmidt would never have let himself be politically instrumentalized. At least as I came to know him in the last years of his life, he never rolled over and did what the institutions told him. On the contrary, he was always up for a fight. Whenever possible, he made the institutions work for him, frustrated their plans, and stuck to his guns. For this very reason, it is important to ask whether it is acceptable for this old work by Michael Schmidt to be shown thirty years later in such a radically altered form (and/or whether it does not contribute to the "event culture" the "new" Volksbühne is accused of promoting)—and it was interesting to observe how sharply opinions were divided on this point on that night. I have to say: my qualms are fairly limited. Not just because the archive is in the hands of Laura Bielau and Thomas Weski, who surely thought long and hard about this decision, but above all because Schmidt himself constantly recast his photographic images in new formats. The large-format posting of images from the series *Frauen* (Women, 1997–1999) throughout the city on the occasion of the sixth Berlin Biennale (2010) is a good example of this. This decision, and others like it, make clear that Schmidt was no less afraid of taking fresh approaches to his work than he was of making grand gestures. From my perspective, the projection was a success. Taking the West Berlin districts that Schmidt had combed through with his camera in the 1980s across town and now projecting them onto this building in East Berlin felt right to me. I was especially touched by the portraits from *Waffenruhe*, which stood in stark contrast to the harshness of the pictures of the then-divided city. The incredible fragility of human existence put on display here both moved me and evoked a strange feeling of connection. I was reminded of a passage from the new book by Didier Eribon that I'm reading at the moment. Referring to André Gide, he writes there about literary influences: "Books are 'mirrors' for us in which we don't see what we effectively already are but rather what we still want to become. Understood in this way, an influence entails a 'discovery' and 'awakening' of the self through the feeling of a 'rediscovered affinity.' The feeling is an entirely personal one, but it is also collective in the sense that it is shared by a community of readers transcending geographical space and historical time. This community of readers who discover themselves in a book, in a work, in the efforts of an author, form a public in the strong sense of the work: their complicity is based as much on emotions and sensations as on the intellect." The evening was pervaded by precisely this complex moment of contact that Eribon calls complicity, a moment in which emotion, sensation and intellect all flow together—at the point where every visitor stood alone in the dark on this enormous Rosa-Luxemburg-Platz (now without the wheel by Bert Neumann) in front of this newly "naked, dead building of striking ugliness" (Frank Castorf) and looked at Schmidt's projection. A provocative moment—actually the ideal moment—for us to take in a work of art (and write about it) is when it proves resistant to a purely intellectual view, or when this approach on its own does not suffice to open up a work.

But I'm actually writing for a different reason: Thomas Weski mentioned during the discussion afterwards that you brought together Michael Schmidt and Einar Schleef in Graz in the 1980s, thereby making it possible for Michael Schmidt's pictures and Einar Schleef's text "Cigarettes" to appear autonomously, side by side, in *Waffenruhe*. Their collaboration was never to be repeated. Dercon wanted to know what Schleef was doing in Graz at the time and mentioned the photo symposia initiated by you and Manfred for the steirischer herbst festival. But no one there knew how and why Schmidt and Schleef first met. Could you shed some light on this? And perhaps share a little about your own work with Schmidt and Schleef.

Warmly, Maren

Dear Maren,

I can well imagine that an outdoor projection raises questions about an appropriate way to present such a thematically and aesthetically rigorous work as *Waffenruhe*. With *Waffenruhe*, Michael Schmidt took what is surely the most striking step in his oeuvre while still retaining Berlin as the setting, subject, and object of his work. Relinquishing the claim to social documentary that had dictated proximity and distance to the protagonists and architectures of his previous book, *Berlin-Kreuzberg. Stadtlandschaften und Menschen* (Berlin-Kreuzberg: Urban Landscapes and People), Schmidt arrives in *Waffenruhe* at a form that allowed him to give aesthetic expression in his photography to his own experiences, honed by the unique geopolitical situation of the divided city, but also to the legendary or mythical character of this city. "Mythical images are perhaps the most untrustworthy," Lewis Baltz writes in his discussion of *Waffenruhe* in *Camera Austria International* 26 / 1988, the year the work first appeared. In *Waffenruhe*, however, Schmidt opened up a space for himself within photographic strategies and conventions that lent authority to him and his work while at the same time leaving him vulnerable to attack (and he often wrestled and quarreled with photography). Almost exactly a decade before *Waffenruhe*, in 1978, Michael Schmidt had taken the first step: in a letter to Manfred Willmann, he introduced us to the Werkstatt für Photographie (workshop for photography) he had set up in Berlin and initiated an exchange regarding our work at the Fotogalerie (photo gallery) at Forum Stadtpark. In 1977, three years after Manfred Willmann had started exhibiting the work of Austrian and international photographers, we had organized our first international collective exhibition with *American Photographers*, bringing out an exhibition catalogue as well. [Fig. 20]
Our goal at the time was not just to familiarize ourselves with the latest positions in US photography in the form of publications, but also to come into contact with their underlying ideas and modes of presentation through the original works themselves. By early 1977, we had (with Ralph Gibson and Mary Ellen Mark) [Fig. 21] initiated a series of workshops that continued until the mid-1980s. They made it possible for many photographers associated with Forum Stadtpark to acquire practical and theoretical experience of a kind offered by no other educational institution in the country at the time.

Lewis Baltz
Lee Friedlander
Ralph Gibson
Les Krims
Mary Ellen Mark
Duane Michals
Stephen Shore
Neal Slavin

AMERICAN
PHOTOGRAPHERS

Fig. 20) Manfred Willmann ed., *American Photographers*, Graz: Fotogalerie im Forum Stadtpark, 1977, cover

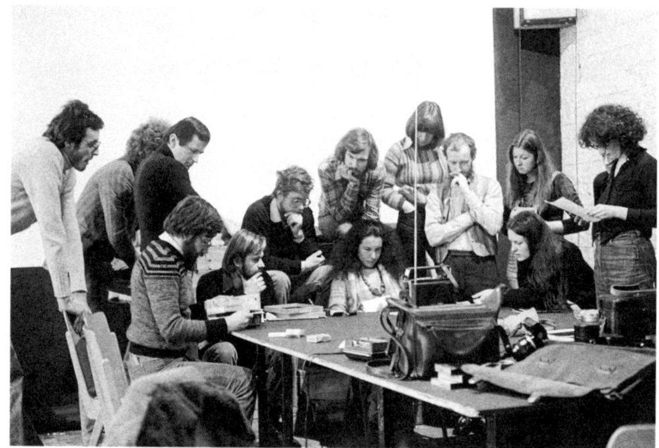

Fig. 21) Margherita Spiluttini, workshop with Mary Ellen Mark, Forum Stadtpark, Graz, 25–30 October 1978

Comparable goals, similar strategies and challenges thus animated Manfred Willmann in Graz and Michael Schmidt in Berlin, ultimately defining Willmann's friendship and collaboration with him (and subsequently with Wilmar Koenig and Gosbert Adler as well). Beyond considerations of photographic praxis, it was a question of establishing a contemporary culture of photography, elaborating upon its concepts, strategies, and content, and giving it an institutional foundation. This work could have an educational focus for the public, as was the case with the Berlin "workshop," integrated into a community college

(*Volkshochschule*)—or it could take place in the context of contemporary art, film, and literature, as was characteristic of our own work at the artists' association, Forum Stadtpark. Lectures and workshops with international photographers helped create a discussion forum and training ground for photographers, while exhibitions and publications brought the claims of an emerging photography scene to broader public attention.

Why am I dwelling at such length on this seminal period for our work, the mid- to late 1970s and early 1980s? Because what emerged then was the artistic field in which we wanted to see photography discussed: these projects were sustained by a new self-assurance on the part of photo artists who—unafraid of international competition—had to create a viable institutional and discursive context for producing and distributing their own work. The fact that so many journals and galleries were founded by photographers in the 1970s points to a widespread institutional deficit.

Einar Schleef made his literary debut in 1980 with the first volume of his novel *Gertrud*. The second volume followed in 1984. In between, in 1981, he published the photo book *Zuhause* (At Home), the visual background to *Gertrud*: ^{Fig. 22} pictures from the town of Sangerhausen, where he had spent his childhood and where his mother lived until her death in 1993, while he himself had left East Germany in 1976.

Written as an unrelenting internal monologue, this novel paints a harsh yet sentimental portrait of a family whose fraught relations reflect the drama of East and West German history. Schleef worked as a director, writer, painter, photographer, actor, and set designer. In each of these areas, he attained an intensity that often provoked and polarized his audience. "There have only been two geniuses in Germany since the war, Faßbinder in the West, Schleef in the East," Elfriede Jelinek declared after his death. We first got to know Schleef when he gave a reading at Forum Stadtpark in 1980, and in November 1983 we showed photos from *At Home* as an exhibition; Schleef read from his novel *Gertrud* at the vernissage.

By late 1983, we had long been friends with Michael Schmidt. He had regularly visited our symposia on photography and in 1983, together with Franco Vaccari, Hiromi Tsuchida, Christian Boltanski, and Cindy Sherman, among others, he had participated as a speaker and discussed his work [*Camera Austria International* 15–16 / 1984]. In December of that year, he was scheduled to give a talk that happened to coincide with Einar Schleef's exhibition *At Home*. I can no longer recall the details of our conversations, but I know that Schmidt was much taken with Schleef's rough, unembellished photographs, which completely eschewed the aesthetic conventions of the social-documentary photography in vogue at the time.

With Schleef, too, we soon found ourselves on a friendly footing. When visiting Berlin, we regularly paid visits to two apartments: Karin and Michael Schmidt's in the Wartenburgstraße in Kreuzberg and Einar Schleef's in the Nußbaumallee in Berlin-Westend, where he lived with his partner, Gabriele Gerecke. The two men first got to know each other when we brought Schleef along to introduce him to Schmidt and his family. I will never forget that afternoon, not least because Schmidt and Schleef both showed off their considerable talent for rock and roll dancing. After that, they seem to have reached a certain level of familiarity, which is probably how their collaboration on *Waffenruhe* came about. We stayed out of the conflict that later broke out between them—we held them in equally high regard (although both were very disputatious friends!). In 1997, Schleef and I planned to stage a Nestroy play for the steirischer herbst festival, but it had to be cancelled when Schleef pulled out of the project. Seiichi Furuya took the stage photos when he attended the first rehearsals in Graz, the two men got to know each other, and Schleef heard

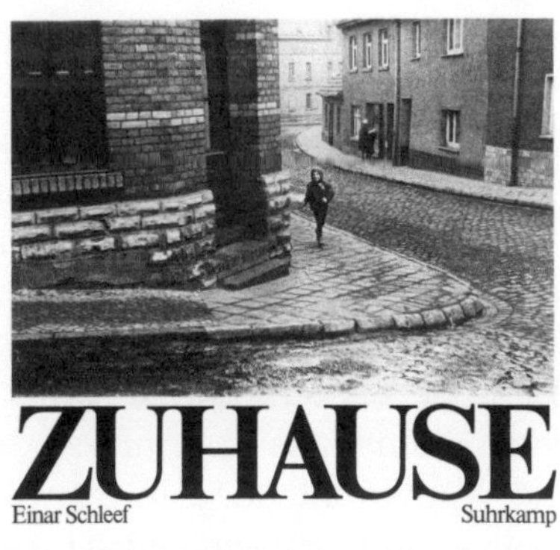

Fig. 22) Einar Schleef, *Zuhause*, Frankfurt a. M., 1981, cover

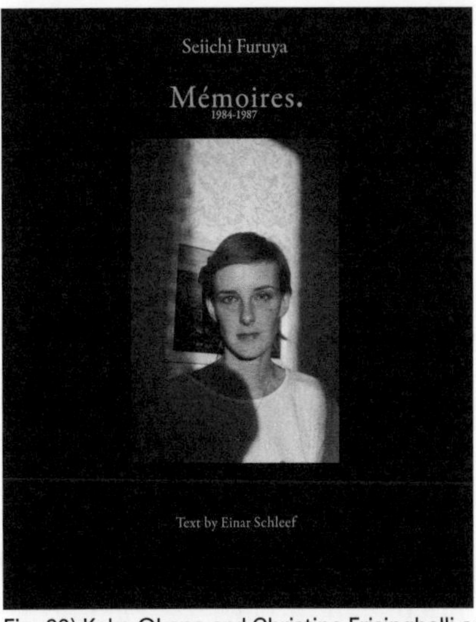

Fig. 23) Koko Okano and Christine Frisinghelli eds, *Seiichi Furuya: Mémoires. 1984–1987*, Graz: Edition Camera Austria, 2010, cover

of Furuya's experiences in East Germany in the 1980s. The result was the text "Schwarz–Rot–Gold" ("Black–Red–Gold"), published years later in 2010, after Schleef's death, in the final version of *Mémoires*.[Fig. 23] In fact, we only came across the text, which Furuya had thought lost, through the retrospective *Einar Schleef: Kontaktbögen* (Contact Sheets), put on by the Berlin Academy of Arts. We brought the retrospective to Graz in 2006. In 2002, a year after Schleef's death, the Kestner Society in Hannover had published this text (here understood as Schleef's reckoning with the GDR) in the catalogue to a Schleef exhibition. Only in the original context of Furuya's *Mémoires* did the images that surface in the text become comprehensible: "October 7. Anniversary of the Republic. She jumps out the window. A sea of flowers. Thousands cheer. The ambulance doesn't arrive till two hours later. It was held up by the demonstration. If when why."

Warmly, Christine

Dear Christine,

Do you still remember Marianne Wex? In the 1990s/2000s I once put her name forward as a possible contributor to *Camera Austria International*. Her book *Männliche und weibliche Körpersprache als Folge patriarchaler Machtstrukturen* (Male and Female Body Language as a Result of Patriarchal Structures) had appeared in 1979: a compendium made up of hundreds of photos of men and women intended to demonstrate Wex's argument, already spelled out all too clearly in the title. Her book was an important reference point for emerging feminist art studies in the 1970s and 80s. With the arrival of Judith Butler's *Gender Trouble* in the early 1990s and the ascendancy of gender theory, the terms of the debate shifted and her work went through a long period of neglect. In the end, we decided the time was not yet ripe to present this work in a larger context, and Wex appeared only sporadically as a somewhat distant but (to me, at least) obvious reference point in the context of Camera Austria.

In 2012 I stumbled across an exhibition announcement from the Badischer Kunstverein in Karlsruhe: this old work by Marianne Wex was now going to be presented in a solo exhibition.[Fig. 24] We reviewed the exhibition in *Camera Austria International* 119/2012. Although I did not realize it at the time, Mike Sperlinger had already shown the work in the UK at Focal Point in Essex. But from the Karlsruhe exhibition onwards, I started keeping an eye out. In 2016, for example, Ruth Buchanan, a New Zealand artist living in Berlin, invited Marianne Wex (who had with-drawn from the art scene to work as a healer after her book had been published) and Judith Hopf to exhibit jointly at the Adam Art Gallery in Wellington, New Zealand. And shortly before that, the Berlin gallerist Tanya Leighton had issued a press release announcing she had taken the work of Marianne Wex under contract. It is also interesting that a younger generation of artists has begun drawing explicitly on Wex: Andrzej Steinbach, for example, describes her work as a "modular system" from which he draws the poses for developing the figures in his photographic projects.

Be that as it may: in early January, a Marianne Wex exhibition was held at Tanya Leighton's gallery. I made a pilgrimage there. This work is truly multifaceted. For one thing, it became clear to me for the first time —no longer merely leafing through the long-familiar book but seeing her plates exhibited in the original—just how much time has gone by. The work is not just a photographic study of "male and female body language as a result of patriarchal structures." With its pictures taken partly from magazines, it allows viewers to soak up the atmosphere of postwar West Germany with its everyday life, its fashions, its figures from

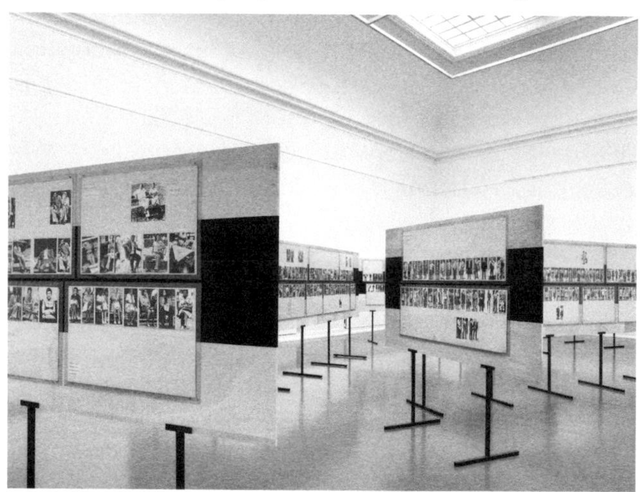

Fig. 24) Marianne Wex, *"Weibliche" und "männliche" Körpersprache als Folge patriarchalischer Machtverhältnisse, 1972–77*, Badischer Kunstverein, Karlsruhe, 2012, exhibition view

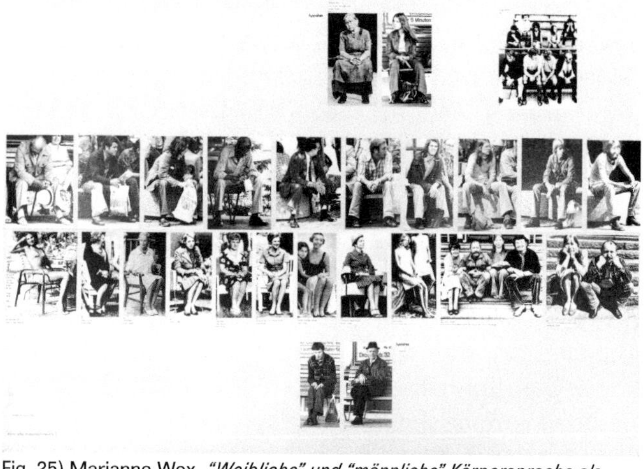

Fig. 25) Marianne Wex, *"Weibliche" und "männliche" Körpersprache als Folge patriarchalischer Machtverhältnisse, 1972–77*, detail

politics and the economy and its public social life. ^{Fig. 25} Only one aspect among many. I was impressed by how precisely and stoically Marianne Wex has pushed ahead with her own photographic practice and worked on her plates: in her sourcing of motifs, in her choice of excerpts and formats, in her uniformly black-and-white development—a dimension of the project becomes apparent here that is almost inconceivable today. Search engines like Google could perhaps, simply by being fed the right search terms, automatically generate everything that Marianne Wex set out to document in such fastidious detail. But the haptic quality of Wex's plates has stood the test of time. By deciding to show the work now, was Tanya Leighton seeking to comment on the #MeToo phenomenon? The extensive reception the exhibition is currently experiencing, which seems to read Marianne Wex solely from this angle, would suggest as much. A deeper engagement with and more nuanced contextualization of this work than has thus far occurred still strikes me as promising.

At Camera Austria, we have also repeatedly dedicated ourselves to "forgotten" positions. Sometimes we could introduce a relevant position at the right time and chime in with emerging debates: for example, when the work of Bas Jan Ader underwent a sudden revival and was discussed everywhere. We happened to publish an article on him at exactly the right moment (in *Camera Austria International* 71 / 2000), when approaches to conceptual practices began changing fundamentally. Keyword: *Conceptualism with a Splash of Cranberry*, to cite the title of a text by Martin Prinzhorn about a young conceptual artist from Los Angeles [Dean Saneshima]. It appeared in the same issue as Jan Verwoert's reappraisal of the historical position of Bas Jan Ader, who suddenly became a role model for the "new conceptualists."

The impetus behind your work for the magazine, it seems to me, was not just presenting contemporary works but also looking out for those who had fallen into oblivion, as well as shining a light on artists who simply persisted at their craft without necessarily gaining fame and fortune. Yayoi Kusama and Anna Oppermann, whose work we showed at a very early point in time, spring immediately to mind, as does Jo Spence before the posthumous hype set in. You thought very highly of other artists who, as far as I can see, have yet to receive the recognition they deserve: you initiated and also risked a great deal to publicize the work of Darcy Lange, for example. ^{Fig. 26}

You recently supported me in finally devoting a longer essay (in *Camera Austria International* 134 / 2016) to the work of Annette Frick, to which Katharina Sykora had drawn our attention years ago and which we had tried to keep track of ever since. I'm very happy with the decision, since Frick's work and its setting in the

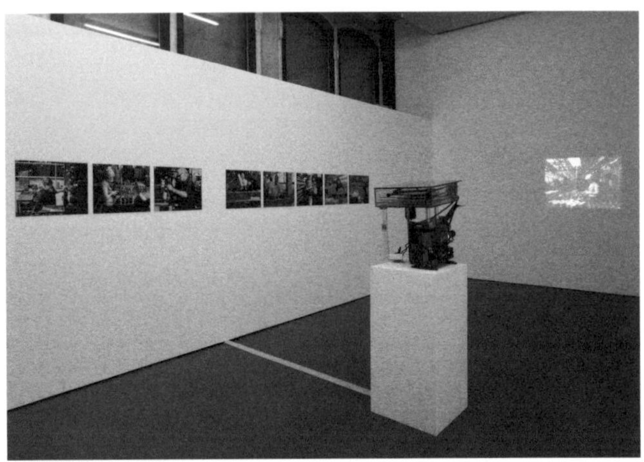

Fig. 26) Darcy Lange, *A Documentation of Bradford Working Life, UK, 1974*, Camera Austria, Graz, 2010, installation view

German underground is simply unique—even if the article, which arose in intensive collaboration with the artist, seems to have done nothing to change her status as an outsider. Her work exudes such an incredible sense of immediacy and delight, bringing still-existing subcultural contexts into the debate in a way that—with all respect—no conceptual artistic practice will ever be able to match. ^{Fig. 27, Fig. 28}

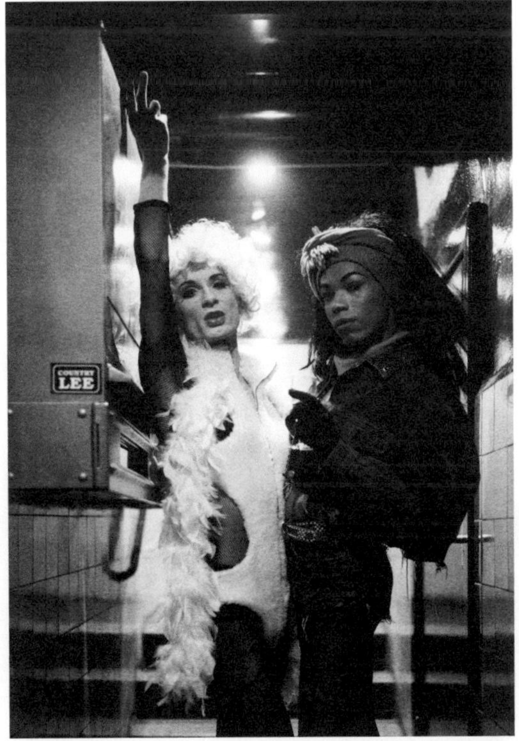

Fig. 27) Annette Frick, *Kaspar Kamäleon und ZeZe im Dschungel*, 1993

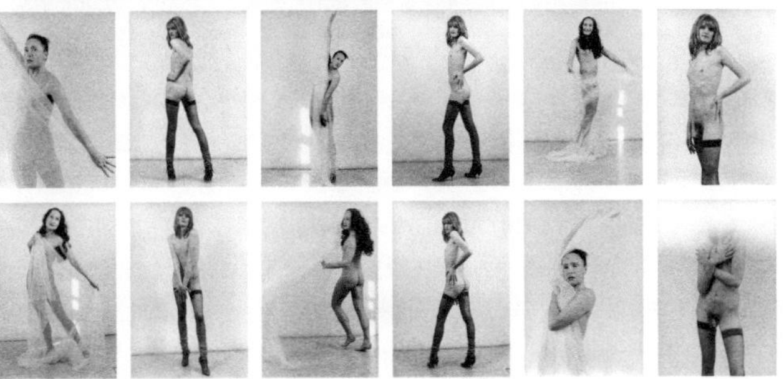

Fig. 28) Annette Frick, *Juweila und ZsaZsa im Studio*, 2000

Can one—can you—describe how interest dawns in a work, how it seizes hold of you and refuses to let go, until you finally decide to publish the work or put it on show, despite the risk that no one—or only a few people—will understand why? After all, our projects haven't always met with a euphoric reception, even when we were convinced of the positions in question. Sometimes, however, our tactics paid off and we were able to make the right mark at the right time.

Warmly, Maren

Dear Maren,

I remember your proposal that we dedicate an article to Marianne Wex in *Camera Austria International*, and also that the article never came about—although later, in your text on Ulrike Lienbacher [*Camera Austria International* 75 / 2001], [Fig. 29] you drew upon Wex as a historical reference point for Lienbacher's *Pin Up Übungen* (Pin-Up Exercises). We also published an image illustrating her work. I think that Wex's comparative work struck me back then as too schematic, too black-and-white: the male/female dichotomy running through the work seemed overly deterministic and restrictive, particularly given the pluralist concepts of identity that confronted us in the 1990s.

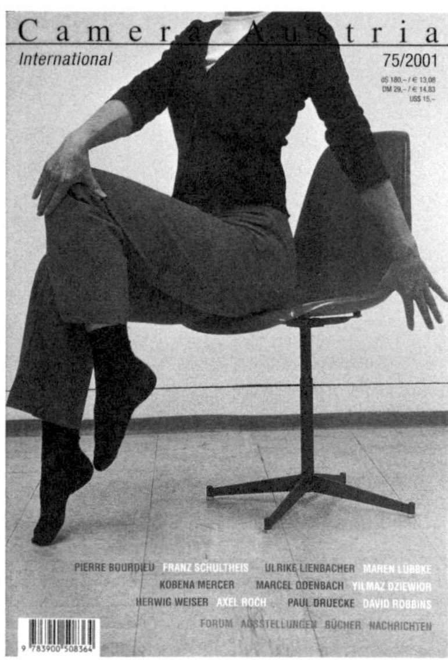

Fig. 29) *Camera Austria International*, 75 / 2001, cover: Ulrike Lienbacher, from "Pin Up Übungen / Pin Up Exercises," 2001

Interestingly, it is precisely the work's painstaking seriousness (which from my 1990s viewpoint was perhaps its weak point) that in hindsight constitutes my renewed fascination with it. I had seen only the book at the time—alerted by your letter, I have now looked at the views of the exhibition and have thus been able to get a sense of the work in its physical presence. The quasi-scientific madness that is such a distinctive feature of the work is something that has always attracted me: the artist's privilege would accordingly be to dedicate herself so intensely to the subject at hand that any other strategy—whether artistic, career- or market-driven, or concerning the technicalities of publication and exhibition—necessarily fades into the background. The uncompromising obsessiveness with which the artist devotes herself to her work, notwithstanding the superabundance of her material and the impossibility of doing it justice within a reasonable time frame, adds several layers (and hence also interpretative possibilities) to the "pure" collection of materials.

Perhaps so unconditional a dedication to the subject is one of the qualities that led us to several of the works we wanted to show and publicize—irrespective of their standing in the art market or any other institutional backing. In addition, in the 1960s and 70s, our years of apprenticeship, an appreciation for works and positions was formed less via the market than through books, exhibitions and personal exchange. We were equally well aware that an artistic career unaccompanied by success was far from unusual, nor did it diminish the significance of a work, provided it was "carried" by a community of kindred spirits or initiates (this was how many works that are now part of the status quo "survived," supported by new institutional possibilities in the 1990s and 2000s, and were integrated into a new, globally defined art history).

Through our discussion of Marianne Wex, I came across a review comparing her work to Chauncey Hare's. I thought of Lewis Baltz, who often referred in conversation to this "undoubtedly most contradictory contemporary American photographer," as he put it in his 1985 address to the Europe-America symposion. Over the years, Chauncey Hare* had disappeared from view, and I think we partly have Lewis Baltz to thank for the revival in our understanding and appreciation of his work.

To a certain extent, Camera Austria has always been a participative project, since artists, authors and colleagues have helped define the magazine's content and the institution's direction through their critical support. Their suggestions have challenged us and broadened our horizons. Another example: with the work *Bouquet for Bas Jan Ader and Christopher D'Arcangelo*, Christopher Williams dedicated his contribution to the 1994 Symposion on Photography to two artists, both gone and largely forgotten, who in their own unique way had called into question the increasing institutionalization of the art scene in the mid- to late 1970s. This gesture subsequently led to the publication of works by Bas Jan Ader in *Camera Austria International* 71 / 2000. [Fig. 30, Fig. 31]

* https://www.afterall.org/online/two-slight-returns-chauncey-hare-and-marianne-wex

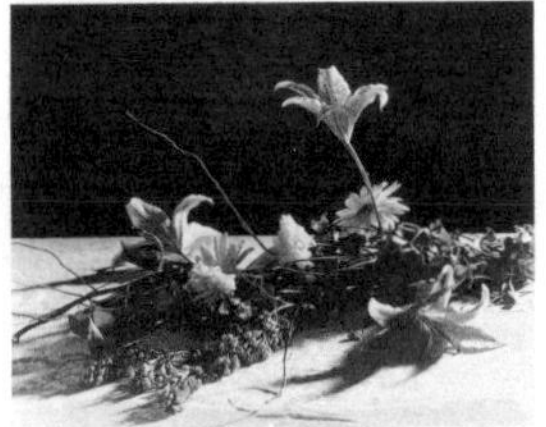

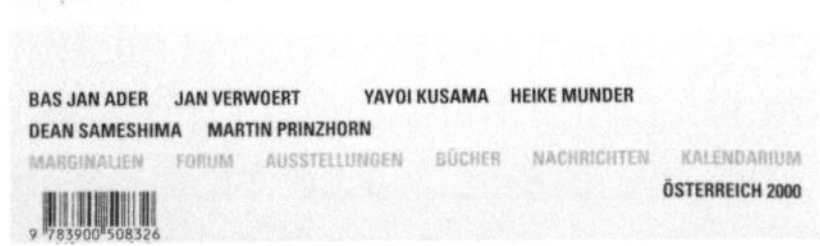

Fig. 30) *Camera Austria International*, 71 / 2000, cover: Christopher Williams

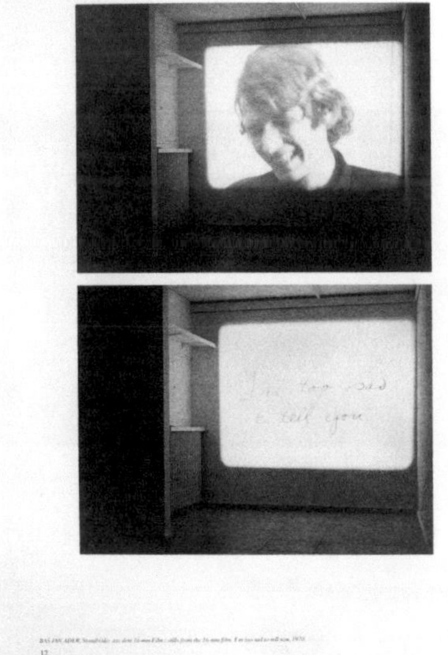

Fig. 31) *Camera Austria International*, 71 / 2000, Bas Jan Ader, *I am too sad to tell you*, artist contribution

It was the right moment, as you say, for Ader's ideas and approach to be taken up by a younger generation of artists. The thread was spun further: in 2006 you invited Christopher Williams to show this work at the two-part exhibition you curated with Reinhard, *First the artist defines meaning*, before inviting him back a second time in 2009 for *Then the work takes place: On the Paradigm of the Conceptual in Contemporary Photography*. The story would not be complete without mentioning that in 2000, the first comprehensive Bas Jan Ader exhibition was put on in Münster by Carola Grässlin, who also assisted us with visual material for the publication.

Incidentally, I visited this exhibition together with William Eggleston and Wilmar Koenig on a day trip from Hannover, where Eggleston was involved in the *How you look at it* exhibition and I was chaperoning him a little during his stay. Eggleston, too, was barely known in the European art market until he took part in documenta. By contrast, photographers had become aware of his work much earlier. They had also had an opportunity to get to know him personally at the workshops he gave at the Werkstatt für Photographie in Berlin and with us in Graz in 1983, and not least through his legendary appearance at our Photography Symposion in 1985. From early on, we provided artists with a forum for expressing their mutual awareness and esteem, particularly evident in Luigi Ghirri's wonderful article on William Eggleston, "Worlds Without End," which we were able to publish in *Camera Austria International* 13 / 1983. This text documents a European reception of Eggleston's work. The text, like Ghirri's work as a whole, barely made an impression in the USA: Ghirri's contribution to the history of photography in the twentieth century has received international recognition only fairly recently. Through Ute Ekildsen and Timm Rautert, we were introduced to Allan Sekula and Sally Stein. In 1986 Ute gave me a copy of *October* No. 39, containing Sekula's incredibly knowledgeable text, "The Body and the Archive." In 1988 the Museum Folkwang lent us the work *Sketch for a Geography Lesson* and we showed it for the first time in Austria. There followed a long-lasting collaboration with Sekula, who challenged and inspired us as a thinker, author, artist, and teacher until his death. His friendship and solidarity meant a great deal to us. We were similarly provoked by our collaboration with Jo Spence, whose uncompromising work we showed for the first time in 1987 in the context of an exhibition on contemporary British photography—a context in which she had not been perceived in the UK until then. We published the works featured in this exhibition in *Camera Austria International* 25 / 1988. We became aware of Spence through the important (although little-known in German-speaking countries) photography and theory magazine *TEN8*: John Taylor, its editor, was twice a guest at our Symposion on Photography. We were able to publish another article in *Camera Austria International* 84 / 2006 on the occasion of the retrospective curated by Jorge Ribalta. This ultimately led to the photographer-activist's posthumous participation in documenta.

We have just returned from Paris, where the first David Goldblatt retrospective in Europe was held at the Centre Pompidou. We were constantly asked how Camera Austria came into contact with him so early —back in 1994, [Fig. 32] we published texts and photos from his eminently important work *The Structures of Things Here*, the product of over a decade's labor, which appeared in book form following the end of apartheid as *The Structures of Things Then*. It was Chris Killip who, during a trip I made to Newcastle in the early 1990s to visit him and Graham Smith (another

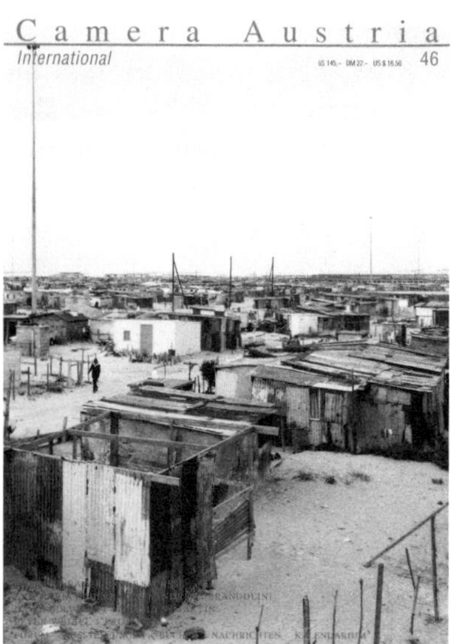

Fig. 32) *Camera Austria International* 46/1994, cover: David Goldblatt, *Flushing Meadows, Site B / Areal B, Khayelitsha, Cape Town, October 11, 1987*

photographer whose work has suffered from comparative neglect; see *Camera Austria International* 25 /1988), thrust a copy of the tenth-anniversary edition of the British literary magazine *Granta* [No. 28/1989] into my hands with the words: "Do you know this man? You should know him!" That was how I came across the work of David Goldblatt, leading to David's first publication with us. He later took part in the 1994 Photography Symposion on the topic of "the archive." He was subsequently awarded the Camera Austria prize in 1996, and finally we were able to devote an exhibition (which traveled from Graz to Munich, Prague, and Johannesburg) and the anniversary issue *Camera Austria International* 100/2007 to the Market Photo Workshop, the photography school for socially disadvantaged youth set up by Goldblatt at the end of the 1980s which now—partly thanks to our exhibition and the issue—enjoys an international reputation. I could write a whole chapter just on our exchange with Japanese photographers. Of crucial importance here were the efforts of Seiichi Furuya in helping to overcome the language barrier, but institutional independence and direct collaboration between artists also enabled a special relationship to emerge. We were thus able to realize the first retrospective solo exhibitions outside Japan for Daido Moriyama (1980), Shomei Tomatsu (1984) and Nobuyoshi Araki (1992). Fig. 33, Fig. 34 Numerous projects were introduced at our symposia, including by Tsuneo Enari, who grapples with Japan's wartime history and its effects to this day, Hiromi Tsuchida and his *Hiroshima* project, and Miyako Ishiuchi, whose work describes his own biography in postwar Japan. In 2003 we opened our new home in the Kunsthaus Graz with an exhibition of the younger generation of Japanese photographers and a symposion.

In Camera Austria's publication and exhibition history, the main role has always been played by individuals and their stance on societal facts. As a result, I have always been drawn to artists who take an investigative, exploratory, observational approach to reality. In addition, we have always been interested in works that fall outside the institutionally or formally defined parameters of so-called "photographic art" (although standards of judgment have changed over the nearly forty years we have been working in the field). We never wanted to preclude in advance heterogeneous modes of practice, whether conceptual, documentary, or poetic. By directly confronting different practices, aesthetics, and generations, the work of artists and authors was often placed in new and unforeseen contexts. Broader public appreciation could be a long time coming, and sometimes it never came at all, but at least we succeeded in continually challenging and surprising readers and the public, since they could never know for sure what awaited them with each new issue of our magazine.

Warmly, Christine

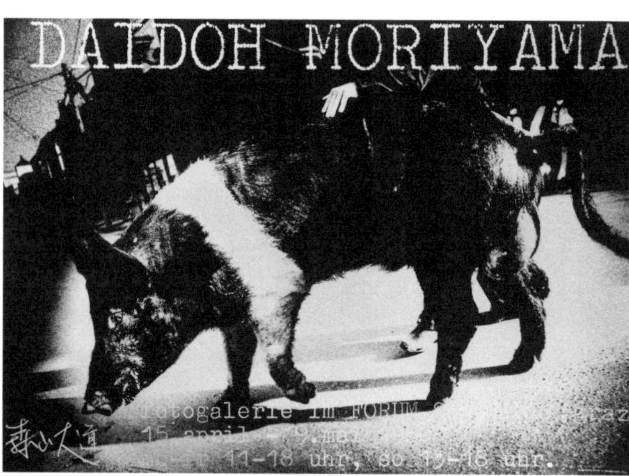

Fig. 33) Daidoh Moriyama, *Das ist Japan*, Fotogalerie at Forum Stadtpark, Graz, 1980, exhibition poster

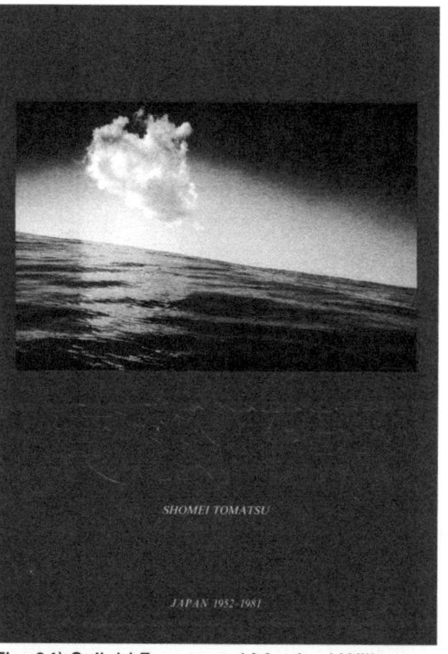

Fig. 34) Seiichi Furuya and Manfred Willmann eds, *Shomei Tomatsu, Japan 1952–1981*, Graz: Edition Camera Austria, 1984, cover

Dear Christine,

In your last letter, you again delved into the history of Camera Austria, exploring what the project means to you with respect to a specific way of dealing with artists and the stance you've taken from it. My collaboration with you and Manfred, and later with Reinhard, began sometime in the mid-1990s, before Reinhard and I assumed joint editorial control in 2011 (until my departure in 2014). How can we succeed in drawing out the elements that connected your work and mine? In your first letter, you write about the commercialization of the art scene, while in your last you describe, conversely, how personal contact and exchange within a long-marginalized coterie of artists provides an important framework for your work, regardless of market considerations. Among other things, this reflects your opinion that the forms in which artists collaborate today have changed; but so, too, perhaps, have the ways in which works become known. With regard to the wealth of material currently available, it could probably be said that personal contact is no more a prerequisite for an intensive engagement with a work than is the access to (artists') books you referred to. (Although the work of the Dutch-born, Brazil-based artist Erik van der Weijde, for example, had been confined to book format until we exhibited him in Graz in 2014 and we had previously only encountered his work in the forty-plus publications he had brought out to that point—just as the artist's book not only seems to be the ideal platform for photographers but has even undergone something of a renaissance over the past decade, due in part, I think, to the diversification of the art scene.) [Fig. 35]

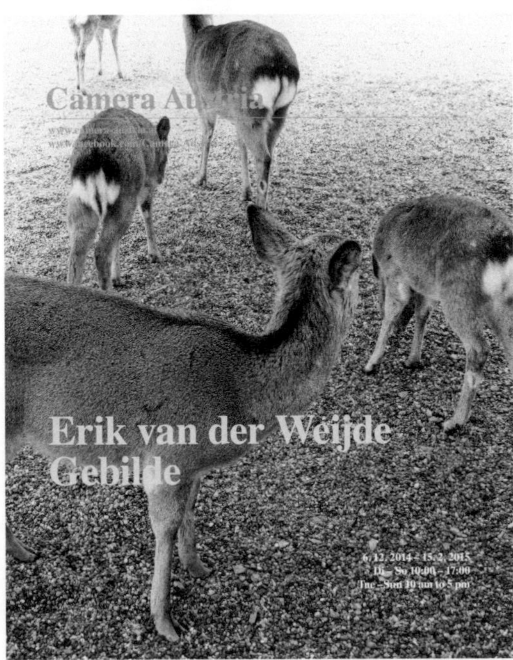

Fig. 35) Erik van der Weijde, *Gebilde*, Graz: Camera Austria, 2014–2015, exhibition poster

In addition, the situation of photographic art is surely no longer as precarious as you make out. Here, many of the obstacles standing in the way of an adequate reception have been cleared, even if others remain. When you speak of an indisputable commercialization of the art scene which can be inferred from a transformed approach to presentational modes (including those of photography), I would respond by suggesting that the task of making and publicizing art has by no means become any easier today. On the contrary. The scope for distributing art is narrowing. This is something we have been forced to experience firsthand at Camera Austria in recent years. But in order not to descend into a lament about our own (or my temporary) work area, let me briefly quote from a press release about the situation facing artists in Berlin which landed in my inbox back in April and has remained there ever since (some things simply cannot be deleted). It is just one example among many showing what the real situation is like in Berlin—and surely not just in Berlin. The summary of results from an ISFE survey notes, among other things: "The so-called gender pay gap in the Berlin art world lies at 28% and thus exceeds the general average of 21%. These figures conceal the real scandal, however: the average annual income for artists is 9,600 euros, while half of all artists earn less than 5,000 euros. Whereas men earn an average of 11,662 euros per annum, women earn only 8,390. Most artists therefore have to rely on other sources of income. Eighty percent make a financial loss from their artistic work. In total, only 10% derive their entire annual income from their artistic work, 13% men and 8% women. The study also shows that 90% of artists cannot subsist on their pension later in life. The average expected pension for artists is 357 euros, while for over half of all artists it amounts to less than 280 euros."

Even if the commercialization of the art scene dominates public perceptions and debate, I would thus want to draw attention to the downside: many artists still cannot—or in the current situation, can no longer—live off their artistic work. You could always reply that, when you talk of commercialization, you are thinking less of the actual sums in circulation than of the mechanisms for evaluating works of art. But money is becoming ever more topical in our precarious working environment, since on the one hand there is more money than ever before (in art) while, on the other, there is too little for almost everyone. Artists, too, are increasingly thematizing money in their work; here, works by Moyra Davey, Annette Kelm, and Eiko Grimberg have recently caught my attention. [Fig. 36, Fig. 37]

All this notwithstanding, the struggle to have one's own (photographic) work seen and recognized has not, I would claim, changed structurally, even if we find ourselves bombarded with information today.

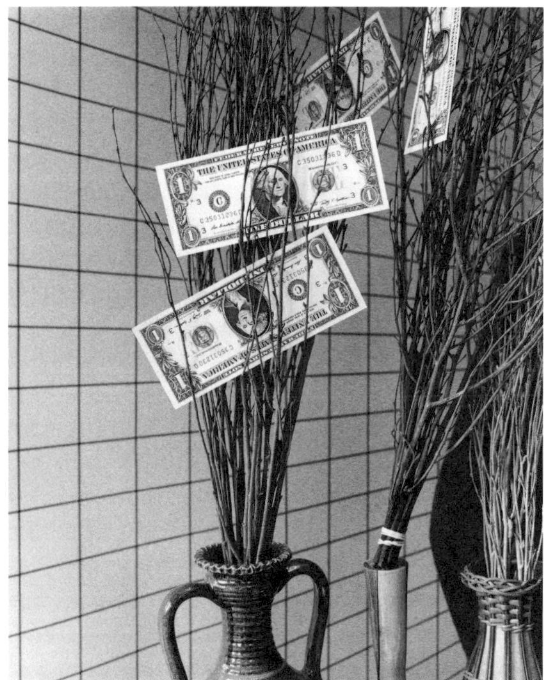

Fig. 36) Annette Kelm, *Money / Grid*, 2015

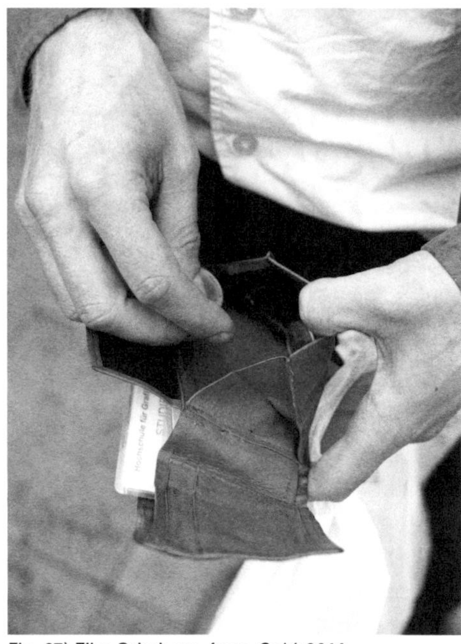

Fig. 37) Eiko Grimberg, from *Geld*, 2014

But to strike a more positive note, I would prefer to speak less of commercialization in regard to our sharply delimited field of work (for all that it may have been commercialized through and through) than of internationalization. I think this idea may take us further in describing changes to our work practices. This internationalization—hard won through initiatives like Camera Austria—is a positive development. To be sure, what facilitators such as yourself have helped establish as the basis for a forward-looking, photography-specific discourse on which a younger generation could build has continued to diversify. What I really want to say is this: the fact that we have both focused on a particular medium in our work has allowed us to retain an overview of these areas. Cer-

tainly, much escapes our notice—or mine, at any rate. And yet I would contend that the core of my work is quite clearly based on firsthand observation, concrete exchange, and the transfer of information from person to person. And this exchange definitely includes the many artists and facilitators whose work does not necessarily get the attention it deserves, given the seriousness with which they persist in their endeavors, just as it includes those whose work we thankfully—and often finally!—get to experience today in big overview exhibitions (which do not guarantee these artists financial security or a lasting reputation, by the way). In any case, I would say of my own work, and the work of many others who do not work freelance but advocate within institutions for often marginal positions, that here, the market does not—as it so often seems to do—represent the be-all and end-all. There are just as many good and bad, interesting and uninteresting, important and unimportant works there as anywhere else art may be found. But the market naturally also forms a frame of reference for my own work, not just to sharpen my antennae but also for whenever, as in Berlin, public institutions do not (or cannot) show enough contemporary art and this task falls to the galleries instead. How else, for example, could such diverse figures as the internationally renowned artist Walead Beshty, represented by some of the top galleries and with an impressive list of exhibitions behind him, and Stefanie Seufert, who lacks access to such cultural capital, come together in No. 115 / 2011? Both transcend the photo frame and disclose space in a way that made including them side by side in the same issue seem rewarding to us. ^{Fig. 38, Fig. 39}

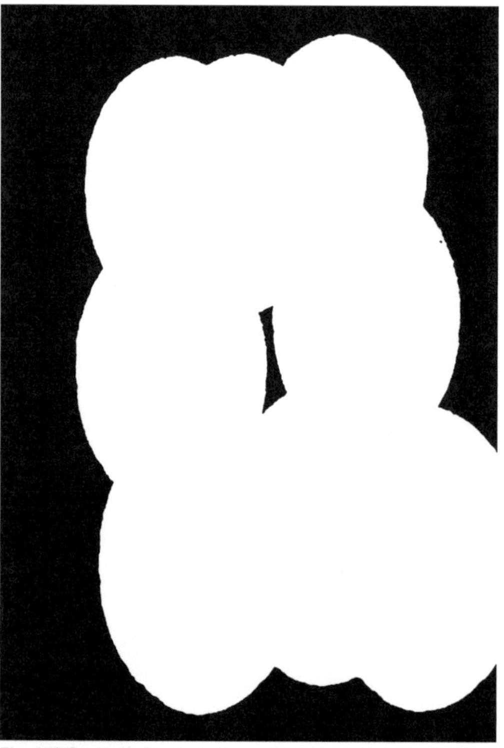

Fig. 38) Stefanie Seufert, *figure #1*, from *Inflatable*, 2017

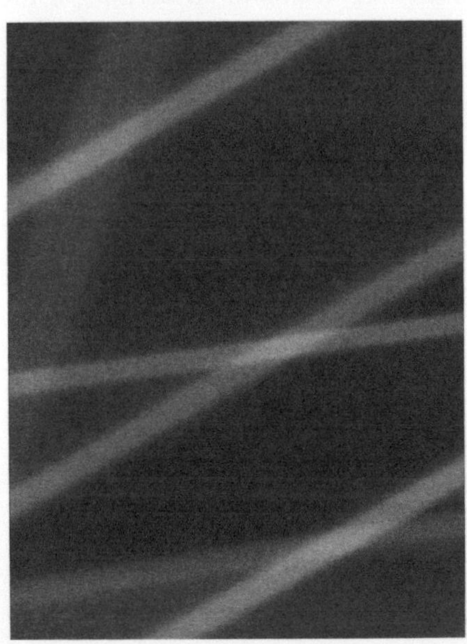

Fig. 39) Walead Beshty, *Transparency (Negative) [Kodak Portra 400NC Em. No. 3161: April 22–24, 2010 LAX/SFO SFO/LAX]*, 2011

Needless to say, we should do our best to bridge this very divide, and insist on monitoring contemporary artistic practices as closely as possible—regardless of whether these occur in a national gallery or in a niche. I chose Beshty and Seufert almost at random; countless other issues could be cited. There—between the covers of the magazine—we have often seen that it is not so much the positions that are disparate as the contexts in which the works are received. In this regard, I'm thinking in particular of an issue I recently edited in which I sought, among other things, to bring together Isa Genzken and Annette Frick. Both are constantly expanding the scope of their work and hence the scope in which we see art, leading in both cases to a shift in the idea of what constitutes a work. They are nonetheless diametrically opposed in their reception: recent years have seen a clear upturn in the reception of Genzken's oeuvre, widely celebrated today following some earlier hatchet jobs. Frick, on the other hand, is not only located in the *underground*; her work is subsumed under this category as well— a category that, as far as I can see, has yet to secure a fixed place in art. ^{Fig. 40, Fig. 41 a, b, c}

And this interest in the margins—wherever you happen to find them and wherever you draw the lines— has, I think, defined the magazine from its inception right down to the present day. One difference alone is striking—and difficult to "evaluate:" precisely on account of the plethora of international positions that are relevant today, a magazine such as *Camera Austria* can only hope to cover a small fraction of what is going on. The "old issues," by contrast, are perhaps more representative for a specific discourse. In hindsight, they are more representative because they could be.

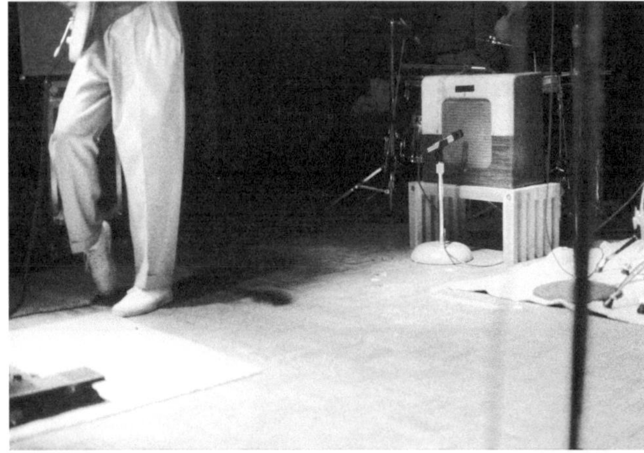

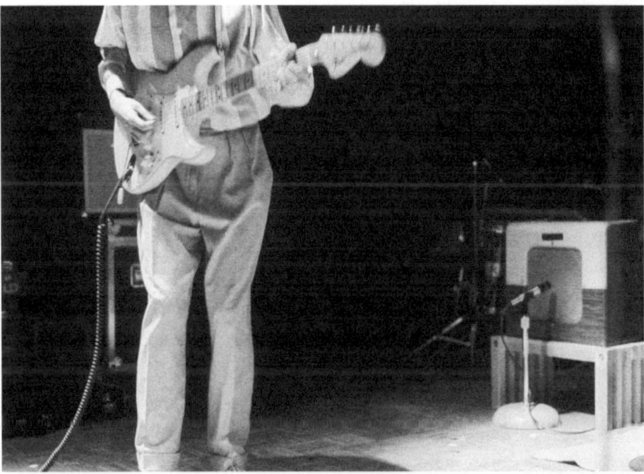

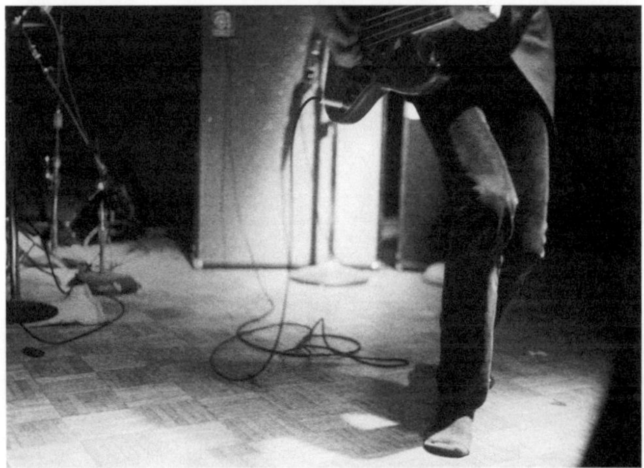

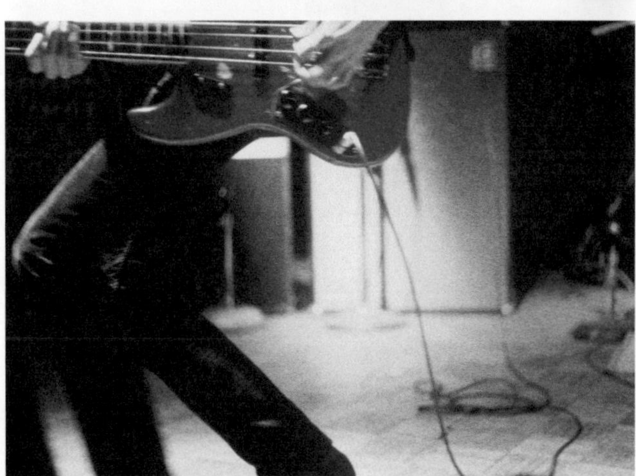

Fig. 40) Isa Genzken, from *New York*, 1981

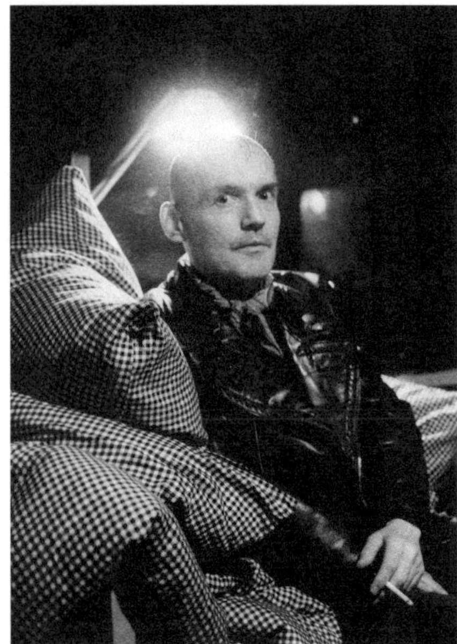

Fig. 41 a) Annette Frick, *Napoleon Seyfarth*, 2000

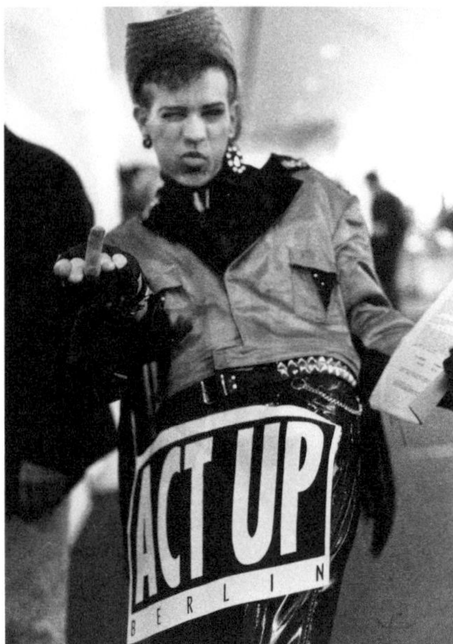

Fig. 41 b) Annette Frick, *Bev Stroganov*, Berlinale, 1992

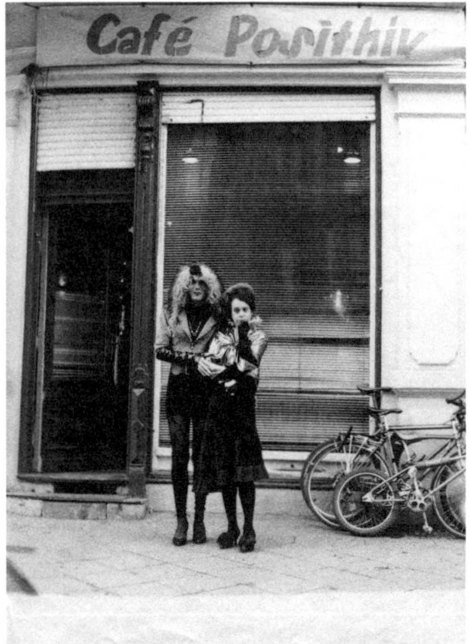

Fig. 41 c) Annette Frick, *Tina and friend in front of Café Posithiv*, Berlin, 1994

Whether this claim can and should be upheld today, or whether we should instead push much more strongly for something that has, in my view, always defined our work on the magazine—that is, productively applying the knowledge that the autonomy of editorial or curatorial activity is especially great when the niche is small—would have to be discussed further. In any case, this has been—as far as I can see—a constant.

Warmly, Maren

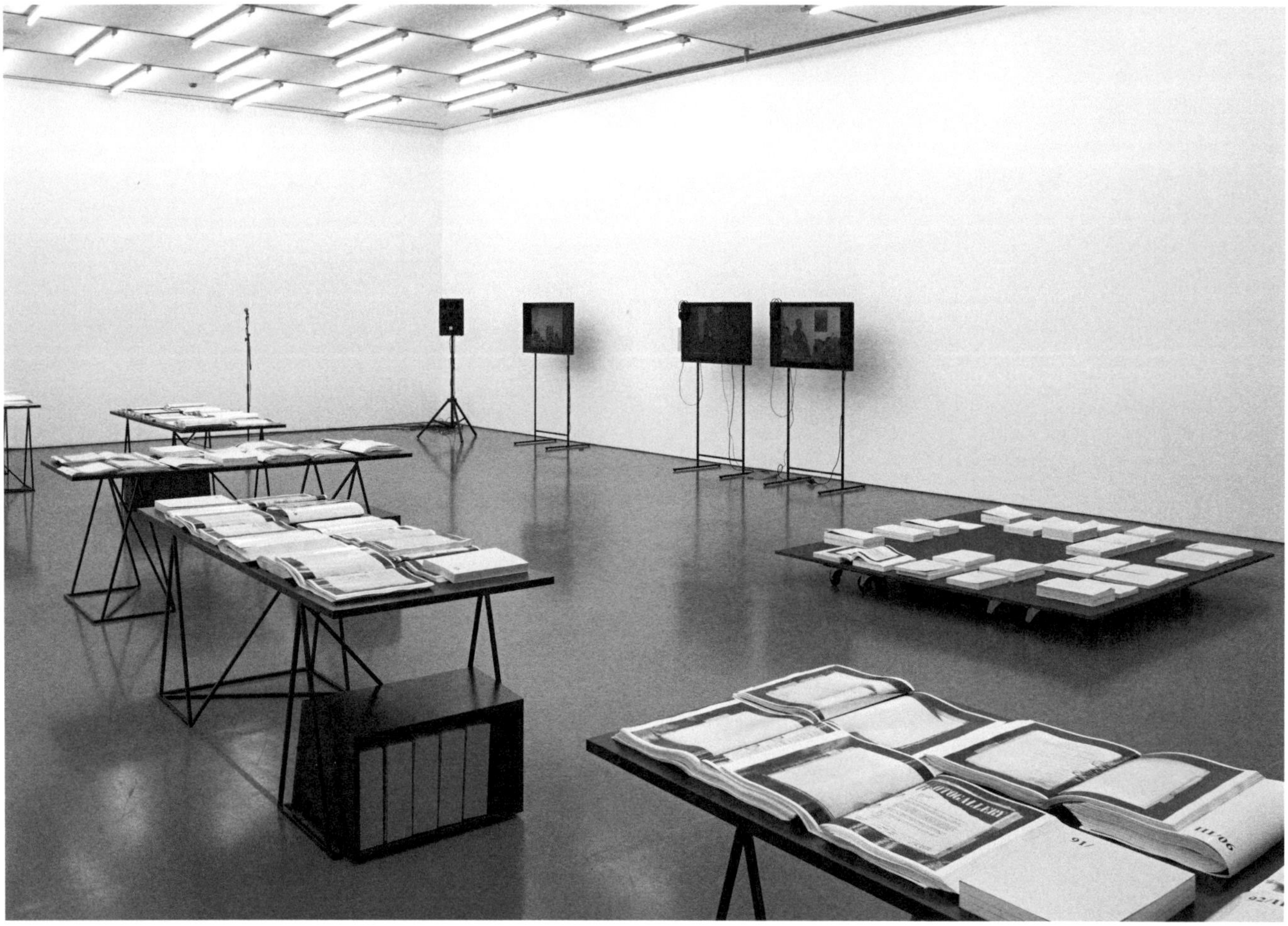

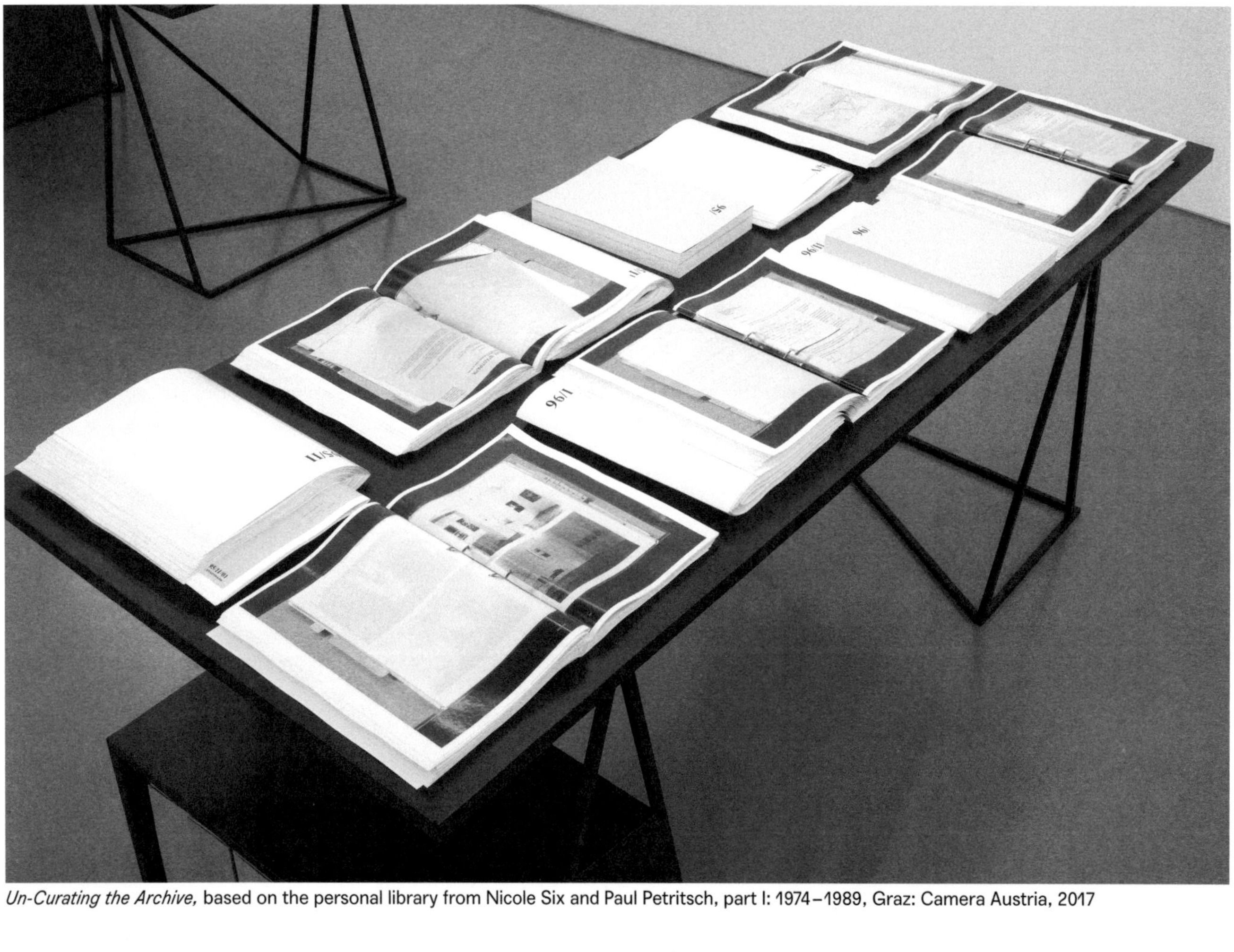

Un-Curating the Archive, based on the personal library from Nicole Six and Paul Petritsch, part I: 1974–1989, Graz: Camera Austria, 2017

The Ambivalence of the Archive as the Ambivalence of an Institution*

Even after almost 40 years, the history of an institution such as Camera Austria still manifests itself as something resilient, enduring and coherent, and the archive, with all its documents, texts, images, and so on, seems to confirm and corroborate this. Indeed, the manifold threads of the networks of people, ideas, associations, justifications, and conclusions that artistic and theoretical practices have been linked to, juxtaposed with or arranged in compositions with, can still be detected, pressed back into use, and added to. They have been materialized in and through the archive, and have created deposits. The work itself has been its own recording.[1] The archive seems to confirm this interwoven fabric of interests, uses, statements, criticisms, interpretations, opinions and assumptions. Not only that, it also seems to historicize it, provide proof of it, and make it narratable, i.e. transform it into a story, a development—with the exception, of course, of those lacunae that are contained and concealed in every archive.

And yet the institution and the archive are more fragile than one might think. Their history is rather one that is full of uncertainties, with its "episodes" taking place in leaps and starts, the whole thing much less straightforward and with many more unenvisaged twists and turns than it might seem at first sight to us, the archive's audience, or addressees. That does not necessarily mean that it was built on coincidence, even though coincidences also played their part, or that there were no plans, concepts or interests. It only, initially, means that the continuity of the archive cannot provide any evidence about the manner in which this continuity was created and fought for, or about the way in which it was ultimately possible for this continuity to be asserted and maintained. This is the first "power" of the archive: the fact that it seems to confirm what emerges in the reading of it. And this is the blind spot of every archive: the delicate basis of its very creation. Of course, the archive could never comprise the entirety of its own history, and those institutions and protagonists who were involved in the manifold contexts of Camera Austria's projects are always depicted only in their relation to these specific projects in this specific archive, which is to say that even though they may have left behind very identifiable traces, they are by no means adequately described by those traces and cannot be adequately reconstructed from them. This may seem like a banal thing to say, but it is also fundamentally true, because it illustrates the limited nature of the archive (of every archive?), which in a certain respect only ever makes it possible to talk about the archive when one is in the archive.

And yet an archive also offers the possibility of taking these threads, these twists and turns, and connecting them, interpreting them, in a new way. The possibility of looking at things in this way is something which the democracy of the archive itself promotes: "Real democratization is always measured by this essential criterion: the participation in and access to the archive, its constitution and interpretation."[2] However, this democracy also requires that the archive should be extended, supplemented, exceeded, or even left behind, or at the very least that one should write a way out of the archive, or write a continuation of the archive. "Proceeding from the assumption that the archive is not only a place of conservation, but also a place of production, in which our relation to the past is materialized and our present is written into the future, I regard the archive as a place of negotiation and a place of writing."[3] If the history of the institution itself is fragile, then is not the archive itself more fragile than it might seem at first sight? Is it then the archive in its very fragility that questions and subverts the robustness and the durability of an institution? Is it not precisely this function that the archive must adopt in order to expose and unleash the power over the document, its possession and interpretation? Is "everything" explicitly available in an archive? Has "everything" been said in an archive? Where would that leave the archive's unconscious, which Derrida would have us consider?[4] Should the archive therefore be less read and reread, and become more the subject of analysis? "The archive works always, and a priori, against itself."[5] How is that to be understood?

---

* This text is related to two other essays on the subject of the archive and the history of Camera Austria: Reinhard Braun, "Arbeit an den Bildern" in *Österreichische Fotografie 1970–2000*, ed. Walter Moser, exh. cat. Albertina, Vienna; Cologne: Walther König, 2017, "Post-Scriptum" in *Camera Austria International* 139/2017. See also Reinhard Braun, "Wer schießt eigentlich auf wen?" in *Culture is Our Business (Notes on Archives 2)*, ed. Ines Schaber, Berlin/Graz: Archive BOOKS in partnership with Edition Camera Austria, 2018.

One possible approach would be to ask what is missing from the archive, what happened and how much of what happened is even capable of being archived—what was, and still is, never capable of being archived? What remains of the telephone calls, conversations, those unarchivable things that were spoken or debated outside of the institutional context, all those things that are not to be found in any document or recording, because they were never intended for any kind of recording, and yet still happened, still existed, still had some kind of effect—are we talking here about the ghosts in the archive, or simply about those activities that have always negated, always exceeded the boundaries of the institution itself? Does the archive thus always confirm itself as the institution of an institution, in such a way "that the so-called archival technique no longer merely determines the moment of the conserving documentation, but also defines the institution of the archivable event"?[6] But how can it work against itself? Or does working against itself consist precisely of hiding and suppressing the area outside of the archive? Which experiences and memories does the archive exclude because its structures are incapable of encompassing them, because it cannot represent memories, but (only?) a kind of documentation? And how is it possible to give the archive its voice back, to let it speak, to imagine it as a space for action, to let it appear as a place of production and transformation—as a laboratory, acting as a point of reference for the exhibition at the Museum der Moderne in Salzburg?

By way of preparation for a two-part exhibition project by Camera Austria in 2017 and 2018 entitled *Un-Curating the Archive*, the archive was sorted, ordered chronologically and scanned. The entire project was realized by the two Vienna-based artists Nicole Six and Paul Petritsch, who were chosen for a number of reasons. On the one hand, Camera Austria itself arose from an artists' initiative, which is why even the theoretical work on contemporary photography since the 1970s can hardly be described as academic. Rather, the artistic practice itself is always also understood as a form of theory production, or at the very least as a form of knowledge production and the formulation of a political position (in the broadest sense of the word). This used to be known as attitude. On the other hand, in recent years a number of contributions have been presented in the exhibitions and in the magazine that were based on various different kinds of archive. These included works by Sven Augustijnen, Eric Baudelaire, Martin Beck, Peggy Buth, Peter Friedl, Maryam Jafri, Tatiana Lecomte, Ines Schaber, and Ala Younis, to name but a few. The questions that arose in connection with these projects—particularly those relating to what archives suppress or repress, what kind of suppressed or even illegitimate knowledge needs to be squeezed out of them—have sharpened our awareness for our own archive. Furthermore, it should also be mentioned that the overall political climate—not just in terms of cultural policy—certainly gives the impression of promoting a new kind of anti-intellectualism and a concomitant tendency towards more mass-audience event formats, hence raising the specter of institutions like Camera Austria becoming marginalized once again. Is it therefore possible for our examination of the archive's contents to produce something that not only reconstructs a particular form of dialogue between artistic practices and theory but also provides evidence of a different possible form of dialogue between art and its institutions, as well the general public and the world of politics? What spaces for social possibilities existed in which an institution like Camera Austria was able to remain active for a very long time and, at least during a certain period, was indeed able to expand and extend its activities? What kind of cultural policies can be detected within the archive or can be reconstructed from it? In what terms were negotiations conducted about art and culture? Are they the same as those we use today? This also implies that Camera Austria's archive also contains traces of changes in language, changes in ideas about the defining characteristics of works of art and photography, about image politics, about terms such as authenticity, subjectivity, and ultimately also about politics.

In the end, Nicole Six and Paul Petritsch decided to publish the entire archive, in order to pursue these and other questions and changes. They did not want to create the impression that it was the interests of the institution itself that determined publication. To a certain extent, the artists started by relieving Camera Austria of its own archive, and ended by giving it back to them. Without changing the structure of the archive, all of the material—invitations, posters, postcards and dozens of folders—was scanned and subsequently collated, by year, into a varying number of unbound books. These were then presented to the two exhibitions and displayed on tables in the exhibition room. The unbound books are a reference to the circumstance that the archive remains unprocessed, that it will quite possibly always be something provisional, incapable of conclusion, or at least will always remain transmutable, as if the pages of the books could be reordered in a completely different way. To a certain extent, this form of presentation makes it possible to undermine the archive's authority—it is not the archive which brings order to the story, but rather the uses that have been made of the archive which give form to the story and make it—at least potentially—capable of quite different interpretation and conception. The archive is openly accessible and

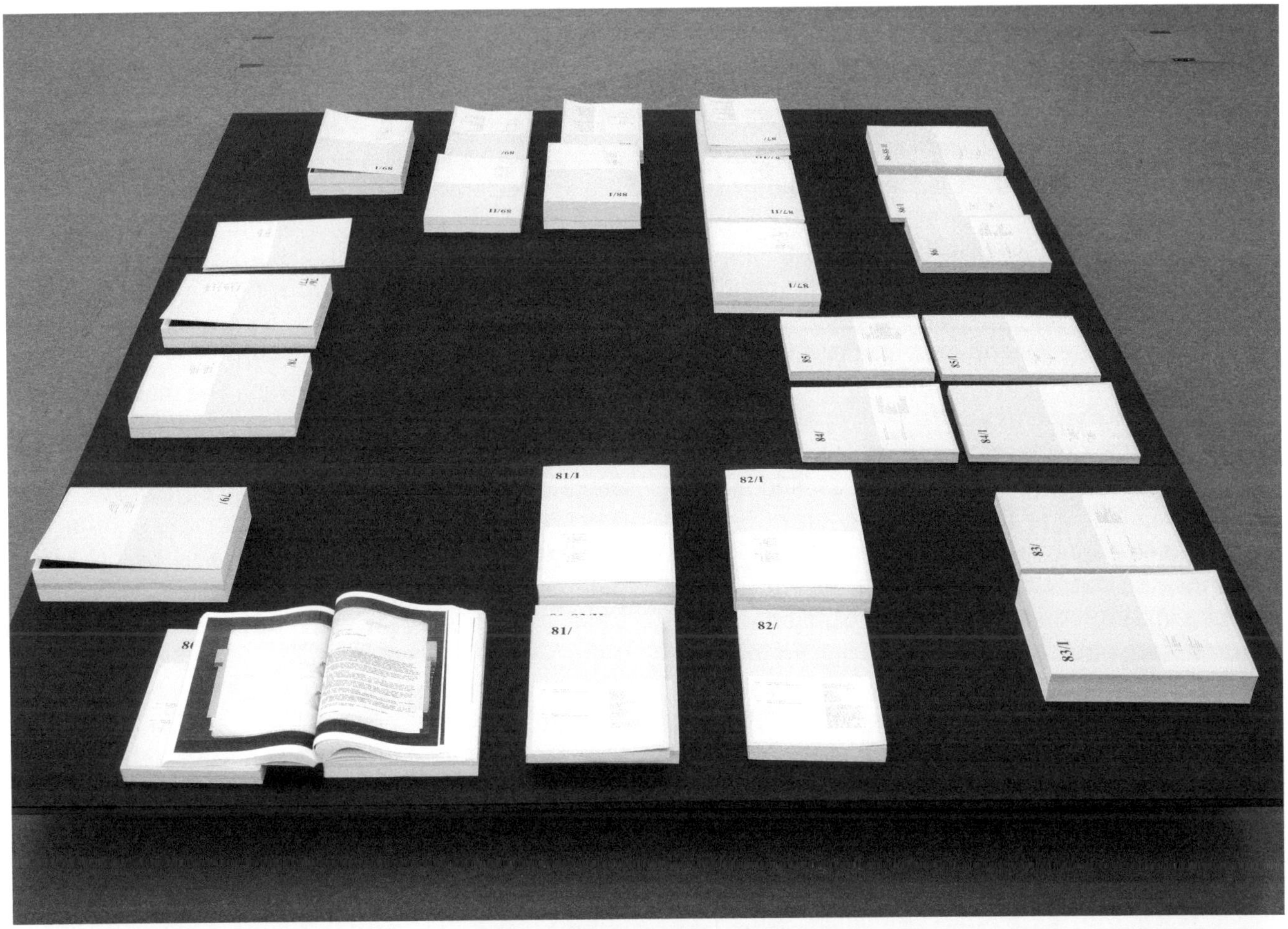

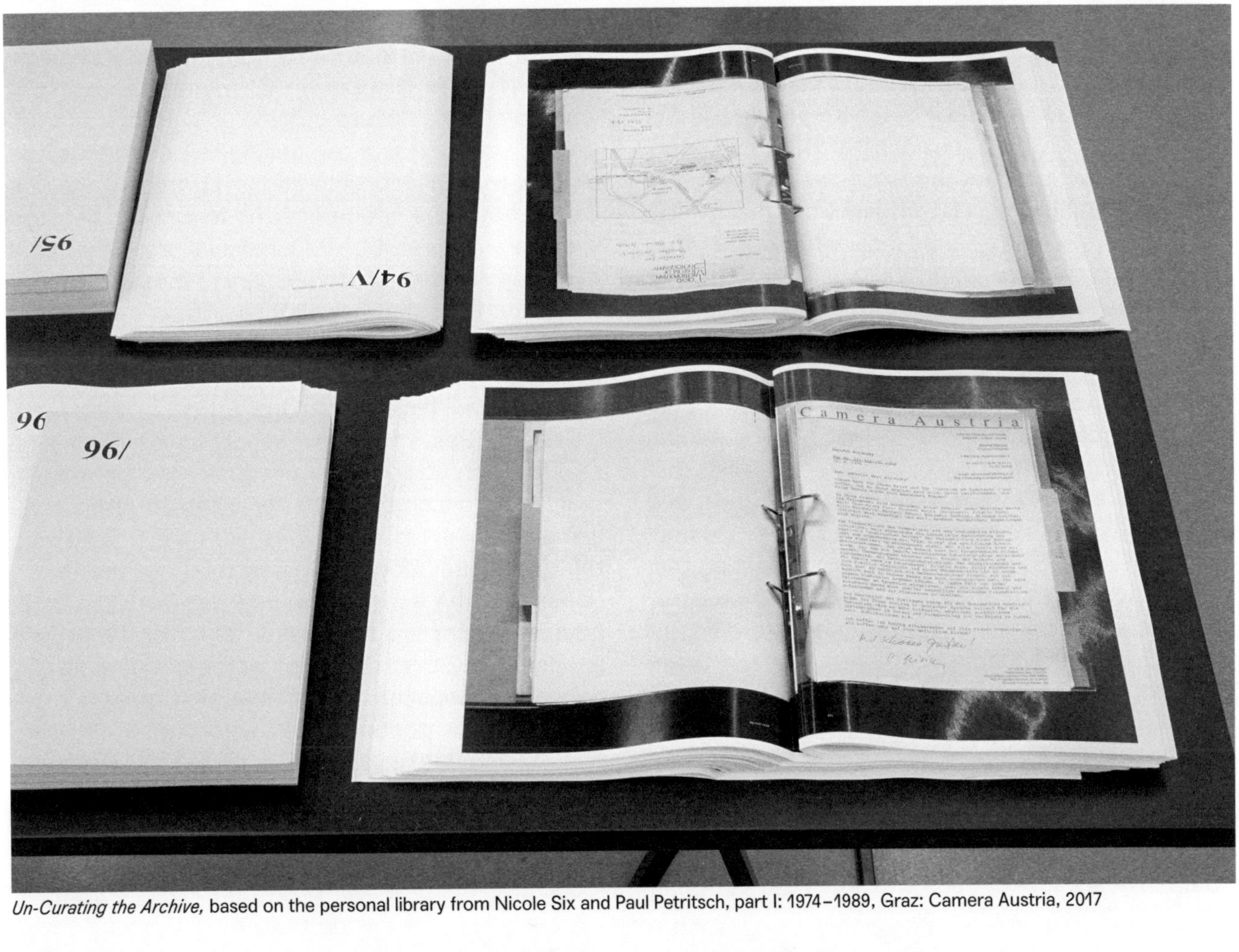

Un-Curating the Archive, based on the personal library from Nicole Six and Paul Petritsch, part I: 1974–1989, Graz: Camera Austria, 2017

makes itself available, rather than locking itself away. Care has also been taken to avoid the impression that the archive itself has turned into a kind of work of art, a fate that befalls most objects in the exhibition context. Fundamentally it was not really an exhibition, but no more and no less than the presentation of the archive itself.

Another part of this archive consists of audio, and later, video recordings of the symposia on photography from 1979 onwards. These recordings were also digitized and spliced together in unedited form. Each section of the recording was subtitled with the appropriate year and the names of the participants, and the final result was displayed on three monitors in the exhibition room. In a certain way, these videos reference the spaces, times, events and actions that the archive itself cannot reach, the transient nature of meetings, the impression made by a speech, the discussions and arguments. Although the majority of the lectures were published in the magazine, in that context they appear in edited, corrected, revised, and supplemented form, with all errors expunged, so to speak. And yet would not such an archive of errors, inaccurate quotes, mistaken identities, ambiguously used terms—an archive of errata and corrections— also be an essential part of every reconstruction? Some folders, for example, contain texts transmitted only as faxes, with corrections written on them. However, the ink on the paper has completely faded away; all that is still legible today are the corrections that read like concrete literature on empty pages. Although the texts can usually be attributed to specific authors, it is no longer possible to reconstruct their contents. Apart from the fact that this is a good image for the gaps in the archive, it is also evidence of a mechanism that applies to archives in general, which is that they are reluctant to reveal things, in whatever form, that have not been authorized. Yet the step that Nicole Six and Paul Petritsch have chosen, leads in precisely this direction, and shows the archive as something that has not always enjoyed "authorized" status. In addition, the videos play an important role by adding voices to the silent archive of documents, voices that in a way were spoken from out of the archive and back into it, and that are still speaking today. So how can the archive let itself be shown as something that aims to permanently change reality, to permanently revise and rethink it and represent it in a different light? How can an emphasis be placed on these changes, rather than on acts of confirmation or certification? Do these empty pages with their scattered corrections not also bear witness to this constant work?

Nicole Six and Paul Petritsch have also tried to elaborate a kind of image for the archive. The material from the years 1974 to 1989 was exhibited as bound volumes in the second part of the exhibition on an improvised podium made of tabletops: the varying thicknesses of the books produces in itself a topology of the projects, the work, the material, the sheer abundance, the unequal possibilities and energies, the imponderable external influences, and changing sources of funding. The current exhibition at the Museum der Moderne in Salzburg is also the first time that the archive material from 1974 to 2002 has been on display in its entirety in the form of bound volumes (in 2003, Camera Austria moved to its current location in the Eisernes Haus in Graz). The material is also available in this form as part of Camera Austria's research library in Graz.

Beyond the realm of the bookshelf, however, there emerges another form, another image, another "architecture" of documents, which are open to many different forms of interpretation or extrapolation— a kind of professionalization and expansion of the networks with an increase in the amount of correspondence, and insurance and transportation paperwork. Does this also already result in a kind of hierarchy? One that seems to contain the more extensive activities of certain years, as opposed to others? What kind of hierarchization (of the history of the institution) does this image create? What hierarchies does it confirm? Should we not also be concerned with leveling out these hierarchies? But why were certain projects not always more important than others? What, therefore, were the reasons for realizing the other projects at all? We must recognize that the archive is a long way from being able to provide us with this information—because it is often unable to depict these decisions, reasons, considerations, strategies, etc., because they were not committed to writing, because they, too, form part of the unofficial archive of arguments exchanged, of a movement of thought, speech, and arguments that have left their traces within the archive, but that are not depicted (or that cannot be depicted) within the archive.

When can the history of an institution, beyond mere dates and facts, invitations, openings, exhibitions, be said to begin at all? How long does a project remain precarious, uncertain, unstable, endangered, until one can start to speak of its consolidation? It is striking that hardly any documentation exists of the exhibitions from the early years until the early 1980s. In addition, there are hardly any texts on the artistic positions, but a lot of commentaries from local and national newspapers. What does that mean for the institution's perception of its own work? What is the context that it takes place in, and can this context be adequately reconstructed from the archive?

Is, therefore, the history of an institution such as Camera Austria not necessarily also a retrospective? A retrospective of surprises, of astonishment about the way that such fragility could be transformed into a continuity? What unlikely convergences needed to happen for us to be able to speak today of the history of an institution and to think not only about its archive, but also, and above all, about its significance? What needed to happen for us to be able to examine this archive in its relation to this history? But does not the archive's seductiveness consist precisely of the way in which it uses its presence to suggest that it has at its disposal a concept of the archive, a certainty of the documents, and hence a certainty with regard to its history, a history that can be reactivated? Is this not the deceptive certitude that the archive impresses, or even imposes, onto the documents via its own authority? And perhaps this applies not just to the documents, but also to the statements and comments, to the memories themselves, which at some time must ultimately also submit to the law of the archive and can only be rearticulated through it? Should we not feel obliged to break out of the archive, to reject it, as a power, as law, as authority, or simply as facticity, in order to be able to construct our own histories from scratch, outside of the archive, ever new, as something that we did not always know, but which first had to be written anew in a movement of reconsideration? And is this exhibition in the Museum der Moderne Salzburg not the first step to go beyond the archive, and by the same token to confront it with that to which it owes its existence, namely artistic work? For the first time the possibility exists, here in Salzburg, to compare these artistic works with what can be found about them in the archive. The archive's other: is that not art itself?

Reinhard Braun

1   Parts of the history of Camera Austria and its protagonists are presented in another text in this catalog.

2   Jacques Derrida, "Dem Archiv verschrieben," in Knut Ebeling, Stephan Günzel, eds, *Archivologie. Theorien des Archivs in Philosophie, Medien und Künsten,* Berlin: 2009, 34.

3   Ines Schaber, from unpublished project papers.

4   Derrida, "Dem Archiv verschrieben," 29.

5   Derrida, 38.

6   Derrida, 39.

Camera Austria:
A Bridge between Italy and Europe

The first time I heard about Camera Austria was in 1983. I was on the editorial board of two Italian photo magazines, *Progresso fotografico* and *Zoom* (the Italian edition of the French magazine), both of which were published by Editrice Progresso Fotografico. This time-honored Italian publishing house, founded in 1894 by Rodolfo Namias, a chemist and inventor of color photography techniques, specialized in the field of photography. When I started there in 1976, I was finishing my studies in art history at the University of Milan. The years I spent there, up until 1983, were my first experience in photography.

In the late 1970s, I met Luigi Ghirri quite often. Back then, he was very active not only as an artist, but also as a curator of significant projects on landscapes. Thanks to his great intellectual liveliness, his ability to think strategically, and his desire to make Italian photography a part of the culture and to place it in the realm of international dialogue, he was in fact an architect of contemporary Italian photography.

The group project he was working on in particular was *Viaggio in Italia*, which was destined to become the starting point of the now internationally known Italian school of landscape photography. Being very interested in this project, I wanted to publish it in *Progresso fotografico*, so I met Ghirri several times at his house while he was busy collecting photographs by numerous Italian photographers. In the end, there would be twenty of them: Olivo Barbieri, Gabriele Basilico, Giannantonio Battistella, Vincenzo Castella, Andrea Cavazzuti, Giovanni Chiaramonte, Mario Cresci, Vittore Fossati, Carlo Garzia, Guido Guidi, Luigi Ghirri himself, Shelley Hill, Mimmo Jodice, Gianni Leone, Claude Nori, Umberto Sartorello, Mario Tinelli, Ernesto Tuliozi, Fulvio Ventura, and Cuchi White. (Three of these were not Italian, but they were very close to Italian culture, and Ghirri's friends.) The idea was to refound the image of the Italian landscape—the landscape of the famous and beloved "Beautiful Country," as Italy is often called—freeing it of stereotypes and typical tourist motifs, while at the same time refounding Italian photography. Back then, the latter was very isolated from the international context. It was still tied very strongly to the traditional reportage model, or it engaged in shy attempts at artistic creativity in an attempt to enter the art mar-

ket. Ghirri's idea of working on the Italian landscape was a winning idea. Moreover, the group work composed by so many photographers created a climate of collaboration and exchange that had never occurred before, and that effectively raised the level of Italian photographic culture.

Ghirri was looking for a venue for the exhibition and a publisher for *Viaggio in Italia*, both of which were very difficult to find. Despite the enthusiasm ignited by the great Venetian event *Venezia '79. La fotografia* —an event that originated in the United States, with exhibitions, workshops, and conferences with photographers from all over the world[1]—the Italian situation was still a very difficult one for photography, which was not yet considered an art: a typical Italian problem. I recall that in 1983, at one of the meetings at Ghirri's home in Formigine, with the photographs scattered on his table, Ghirri told me that this photographic project on Italian landscapes might be exhibited in Graz, Austria. The location was the photo gallery founded in 1975 at Forum Stadtpark; the title of the exhibition was *Penisola: Appunti per un viaggio in Italia*. This was a great opportunity for Italian contemporary photography to overcome its shyness.

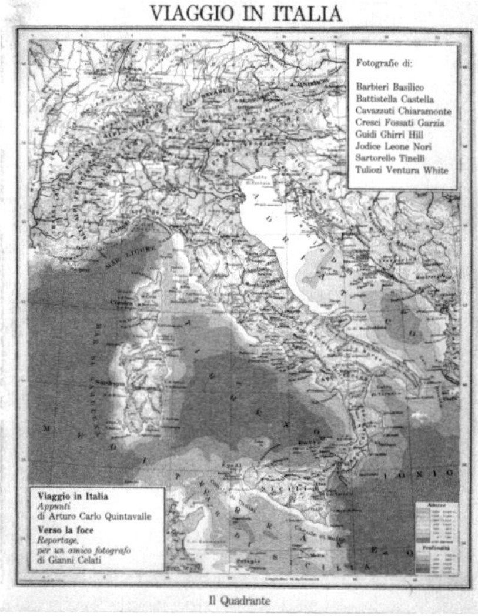

Fig. 1) L. Ghirri, G. Leone, E. Velati eds, *Viaggio in Italia, Il Quadrante*, Alessandria, 1984

The following year, on the pages of *Camera Austria International*, the works of the eleven photographers included in the exhibition (Vittore Fossati, Vincenzo Castella, Guido Guidi, Luigi Ghirri, Mario Cresci,

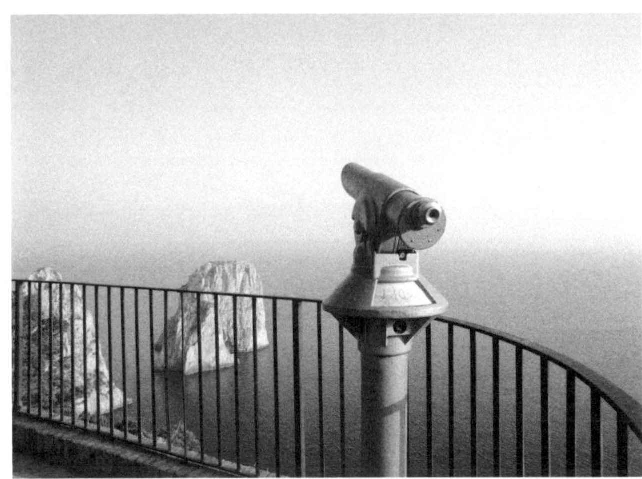
Fig. 2) Luigi Ghirri, *Capri,* 1982

Giannantonio Battistella, Giovanni Chiaramonte, Olivo Barbieri, Mimmo Jodice, Ernesto Tuliozi, and Fulvio Ventura) were published with an introduction by art historian Arturo Carlo Quintavalle. Quintavalle was a great friend of Ghirri's who, like me (but with much more authority than I had, as I was still young), was following Ghirri's project with great interest.[2] Quintavalle later wrote a longer essay for the Italian catalog of the exhibition, alongside a text by author Gianni Celati, when the exhibition *Viaggio in Italia* was presented in Italy at Bari's Pinacoteca Provinciale in 1984. The texts were published by Il Quadrante, a small publishing house in Alessandria.[3]

Camera Austria International was so necessary to Italy, which in those years had had only two legitimate magazines, *AFT* and *Fotologia,* once *Progresso fotografico,* starting in 1983, changed its focus and became more commercial and amateur-oriented. Neither *AFT* nor *Fotologia* was open to the international and contemporary scene, choosing instead to address mainly Italian historical matters.[4] Thus, *Camera Austria International* was absolutely a point of reference for the international photographic culture that was developing.

Luigi Ghirri established an important collaboration with this magazine,[5] in which he published his photographs and also his essays. For example, he presented, between 1982 and 1984, his photographs from the series "Still Life" and "Topografia-Iconografia," along with the work of William Eggleston,[6] one of the greatest and most innovative American photographers he was interested in.[7]

The influence of American photography on European photography in the 1980s was analyzed and discussed in a lively manner, and, as far as we were concerned, the influence on Italian photography was strong. It was an important theme. The kind of photography in question was landscape photography, which investigated the changes taking place in the contemporary environment: that which the historic exhibition of the *New Topographics* referred to as "a man-altered landscape."[8] To the photographers, landscapes were a mirror of society and at the same time a mirror of themselves: an idea discovered then and since unsurpassed in its importance.

Viaggio in Italia not only came shortly before another important European exhibition about urban landscapes held in Barcelona in 1985—*La ciudad fantasma*[9]—but was also held in the same year in which the Mission Photographique de la DATAR started up, with Italian photographer Gabriele Basilico taking part.[10] Since then, many exhibitions and publicly commissioned projects on landscapes have been held in Italy. This is a theme to which I have dedicated myself more and more. The landscape and the link between landscape photography and institutions have been a very important theme of study to me, then and now.[11]

In 1985, at the Forum Stadtpark, Camera Austria organized the Symposion on Photography VII, entitled *Europa – Amerika. Hello – Good Bye*, in which Luigi Ghirri took part.[12] I was present as well, with a presentation dedicated to the influence of American photography on Italian photography. On that occasion I met, very excited, Robert Frank, silent and lonely, Lewis Baltz and William Eggleston.[13] I felt like Alice in Wonderland. Regarding the relationship between American and European photography, an exhibition held in Venice in 1987 turned out to be a point of reference in Italy. *Nuovo paesaggio americano. Dialectical Landscapes* was curated by Paolo Costantini, who introduced for the first time in Italy the works of great contemporary American photographers Robert Adams, Lewis Baltz, William Eggleston, John Gossage, and Stephen Shore.[14]

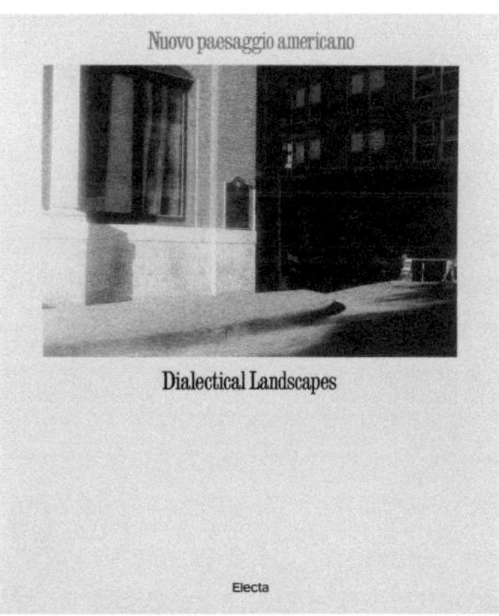

Fig. 3) P. Costantini, S. Fuso, and S. Mescola eds, *Nuovo paesaggio americano. Dialectical Landscape,* Milan: Electa, 1987

In Italy, in those years, there were no occasions for discussing contemporary photography, photographic languages, or conceptual projects. More accurately, the occasions were very rare, and they were not international in nature at all. The only moments of discussion and exchanges of ideas on the theme of the landscape, in which only a few Italian photographers and critics were interested, didn't involve the world of photography at all. Exceptions (though not symposia) were found in the portfolios of interesting European and American contemporary photographers that Roberto Salbitani had published in *Progresso fotografico* in the mid- to late 1970s and, certainly, the exhibition in Rimini as well as the book edited by Giovanni Chiaramonte in 1983, *Immagini della fotografia europea contemporanea*.[15]

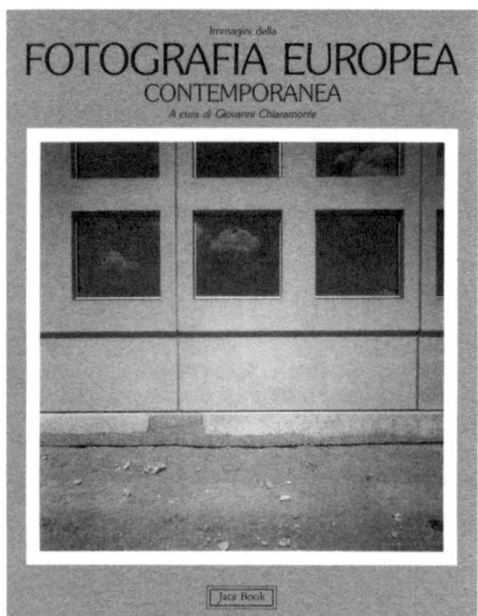

Fig. 4) G. Chiaramonte, ed., *Immagini della fotografia europea contemporanea*, Milan, 1983

Photojournalists and professional photographers literally hated landscape photographers, whom they wrongly regarded as producers of aesthetic and non-engaged photographs. That is why the two symposiums in Graz on the Europe-America relationship and those two important issues of *Camera Austria International* were of fundamental importance, even though only the small "cultured" Italian community linked to the question of the landscape was interested in them. Even Luigi Ghirri's project *Viaggio in Italia* had involved and interested but a few people. Only in recent times, since the exhibition *Racconti dal paesaggio. 1984–2004 A vent'anni da Viaggio in Italia* was held at Museo di Fotografia Contemporanea[16] and the photographs were added to the museum collection, has the project become somewhat legendary. Now young people study and write theses on it, and historians of photography refer to it in their essays as a turning point in Italian contemporary photography.

In 1988, I published an article in *Camera Austria International* about Gabriele Basilico,[17] who was the other great innovator and master of Italian photography, alongside Luigi Ghirri, Guido Guidi, and Mimmo Jodice. My next appointment with the magazine was in 1993. After Ghirri's sudden and premature death in February 1992, a great anthology of the artist's photographs taken in Emilia was presented at the Galleria d'Arte Moderna of Bologna. A large catalog edited by his widow, Paola, and Ennery Taramelli,[18] which I reviewed, offering a sad homage to the great master who had left us.[19]

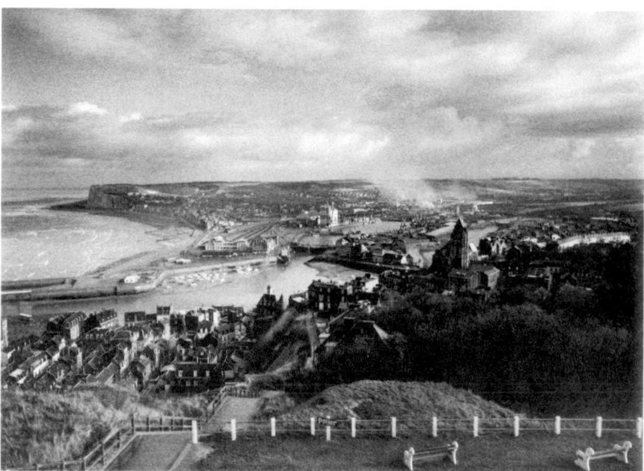

Fig. 5) Gabriele Basilico, *Le Tréport*, 1985

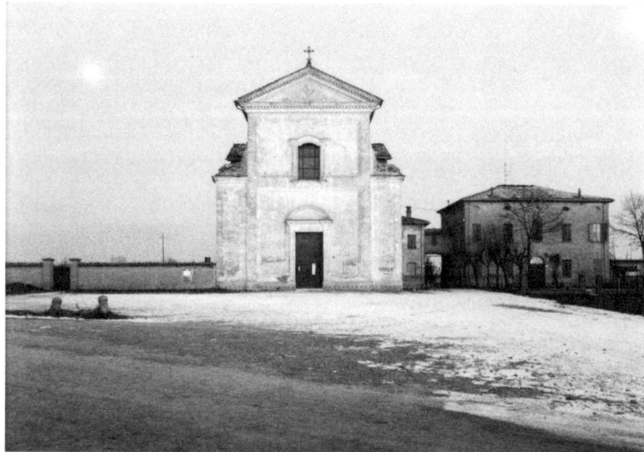

Fig. 6) Luigi Ghirri, *Cittanova di Modena*, 1985

I remember that, to me, writing on the pages of *Camera Austria International* meant having the opportunity to speak to the European public. That seemed so important to me, as Italian photography was still quite separated from the international context, even though we had many valuable artists who deserved to be much better known.

Camera Austria further promoted Italian photography—once again, landscape photography—on at least three important occasions, in 1993, 2004, and 2009. In 1992, the Symposion on Photography XIII was devoted to the issue of Identities. Two Italian photographers, Marina Ballo Charmet and Luca Campigotto, attended, along with a photographer-curator, William Guerrieri, director of Linea di Confine, Rubiera. Their contributions were published in the magazine the following year.[20]

In 2004 and 2009, the magazine hosted two significant group photographic projects commissioned by Italian public institutions. This confirmed on the one hand that the profound interest shown by Italian photographers in the changes taking place in the anthropic environment really constituted a point of strength, and on the other hand that the public sphere was an important context within which photography could flourish as an artistic project. This happened all over Europe; in his book *La photographie contemporaine*,

44

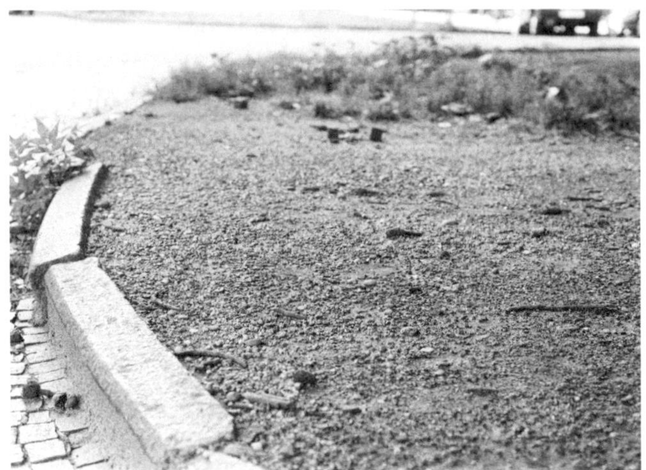

Fig. 7) Marina Ballo Charmet, *Con la Coda dell'Occhio*, 1995

Michel Poivert writes about "institutionalization of photography" in the 1980s and 1990s.[21]

In 2004, Thilo Koenig published an interview with me concerning *Archivio dello spazio*,[22] the most important long-term publicly commissioned photographic project in Italy, which I had the honor of curating.[23] Promoted by the province of Milan and lasting ten years (1987–1997), it involved fifty-eight Italian photographers—almost all the authors of *Viaggio in Italia* and all the prominent landscape and architecture photographers, including many young ones. Some eight thousand photographs were produced.

The project was part of a larger project of cataloguing the historical forms of architecture in the area around Milan. The photographers were asked to "document" in a personal way the relationship between the historical forms of architecture and the strongly industrialized and post-industrial landscapes where they were situated. The project was a huge, long workshop (exhibitions, lessons, conferences, Symposion, and books) that promoted relationships between art, photography, architecture, town planning, literature, psychology, and sociology. Its popularity motivated the province of Milan to decide that *Archivio dello spazio* was a starting point for establishing a center for photography. This museum project began in 1996, and the museum opened in 2004 as the Museo di Fotografia Contemporanea.[24]

In 2009, Thilo Koenig again published a text about two projects, *Atlante 003* and *Atlante 007*, dedicated to the state of landscape photography and promoted by the Italian Ministry of Culture. The title of Koenig's text was "Atlante italiano: A State-Commissioned Project on the Trail of DATAR".[25] With a significant delay compared to the French government (the Mission photographique de la DATAR had taken place from 1984 to 1989), the Italian government commissioned works on landscapes to photographers in the new millennium.[26] While the French project had tried to consider "the state of things," the Italian one reflected on the risks to the landscape: the beautiful Italian landscape almost completely destroyed, to be honest, because of construction speculation going on for years.

The last important example that I would like to mention is no longer the landscape, but the work of Franco Vaccari, a great artist and ingenious theorist of photography, who was the first of these to write about Ghirri's work in the early 1970s. Camera Austria immediately grasped the importance of his thoughts and his work, inviting him to speak at the Symposion on Photography in 1983 and publishing his essay titled "The Technological Unconscious and Photography" in 1984.[27] More recently, on the occasion of his exhibition *Franco Vaccari. Esposizoni in tempo reale* at the Spazio Oberdan in Milan and the release of the small volume Feedback. *Scritti su e di Franco Vaccari*[28] in 2007, *Camera Austria International* published some of his work, with a text by Antonello Frongia that describes Vaccari's work as a space-based practice, dealing with the possibilities of presentation and participation between the production and the reception of contemporary works of art.

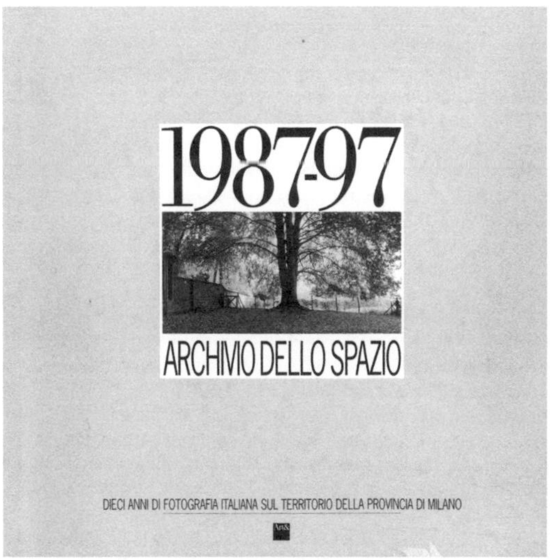

Fig. 8) Achille Sacconi and Roberta Valtorta eds, 1987–1997, *Archivio dello spazio. Dieci anni di fotografia italiana sul territorio della provincia di Milano,* Udine, 1997

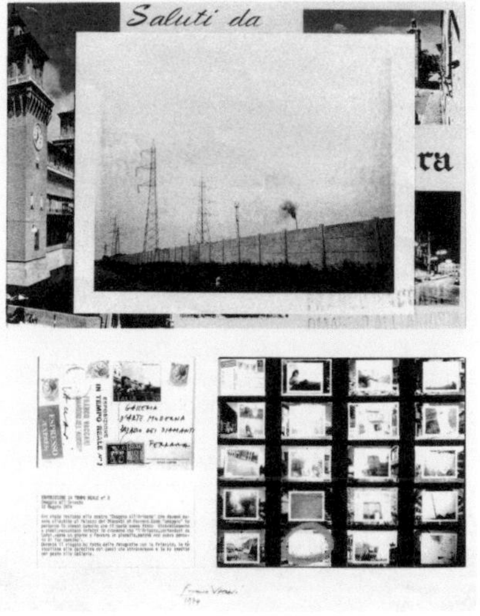

Fig. 9) Franco Vaccari, *Esposizione in tempo reale,* No. 8, Omaggio all'Ariosto, 1974

I have tried to give a few examples of the times that Camera Austria has dealt with Italian themes, bringing them to the international scene. It must, however, be emphasized that *Camera Austria International* has been operating for years as a tool for keeping Italian curators, critics, historians, and teachers up to date. Not widely known to the public—though its contents have always been about the most cultured, refined, and avant-garde areas of photography—and circulated only by subscription, it has in any case been present in the libraries of universities, academies, cultural centers, and schools of photography.

Roberta Valtorta

1   *Venezia '79. La fotografia,* exh. cat. (Milan: Electa, 1979).
2   Arturo Carlo Quintavalle, "Penisola: Appunti per un viaggio in Italia," in *Camera Austria International,* 14/1984.
3   Luigi Ghirri, Gianni Leone, and Enzo Velati, eds, *Viaggio in Italia* (Alessandria: Il Quadrante, 1984).
4   The other important magazines were the German *European Photography,* the Dutch *Perspektief,* the Spanish *Photovision,* the French *Photographies* and *La recherche photographique* and the American *Afterimage.*
5   Manfred Willmann had first presented Ghirri's work at an exhibition in Graz as early as 1976. There was a continuous exchange between Manfred Willmann, Christine Frisinghelli, and Luigi Ghirri. For the *Via Emilia* project, Ghirri invited Willmann to participate, and both were involved in the participating *Arc Lémanique* project. Ghirri and Willmann shared their position and took on the responsibilities of photographers, curators, and editors, which was quite typical for that time.
6   Ghirri's essay on Eggleston was commissioned by Camera Austria. Eggleston's *Kenya Project* exhibition and Ghirri's workshop at Fotogalerie im Forum Stadtpark were to coincide, and on this occasion the decision was taken that Ghirri would write about Eggleston. Ghirri was in Graz at that time to prepare the *Penisola: Appunti per un viaggio in Italia* exhibition.
7   Luigi Ghirri, "Still Life and Topografia-Iconografia," in *Camera Austria International* 7/1982; Luigi Ghirri, "William Eggleston," in *Camera Austria International* 13/1983/1984.
8   William Jenkins, ed., *New Topographics: Photographs of a Man-Altered Landscape,* exh. cat. (Rochester: International Museum of Photography at George Eastman House, 1975).
9   Marta Gili, ed., *La ciudad fantasma* (Barcelona: Fundaciò Joan Mirò, 1985).
10 François Hers and Bernard Latarjet, eds, *Paysages Photographies. La Mission Photographique de la DATAR. Travaux en cours 1984/1985* (Paris: Hazan, 1985); François Hers and Bernard Latarjet, eds, *Paysages Photographies. En France les années quatre-vingt* (Paris: Editions Hazan, 1989).
11 Among the many books about Italian landscape photography I've written or curated, the most important is: Roberta Valtorta, ed., *Luogo e identità nella fotografia italiana contemporanea* (Turin: Einaudi, 2013).
12 *Camera Austria International,* "Symposion on Photography VII, Part I. *Europa–Amerika. Hallo–Good Bye,*" 21/1986.
13 *Camera Austria International,* "Symposion on Photography VII, Part II. *Europa–Amerika. Hallo–Good Bye,*" 22/1987.
14 Paolo Costantini, Silvio Fuso, and Sandro Mescola, eds, *Nuovo paesaggio americano. Dialectical Landscapes* (Milan: Electa, 1987).
15 Giovanni Chiaramonte, ed., *Immagini della fotografia europea contemporanea* (Milan: Jaca Book, 1983).
16 Roberta Valtorta, ed., *Racconti dal paesaggio. 1984–2004 A vent'anni da Viaggio in Italia* (Milan: Lupetti, 2004). See http://www.mufoco.org/collezioni/fondo-viaggio-in-italia/.
17 *Camera Austria International,* 27/1988.
18 Paola Ghirri and Ennery Taramelli, eds, *Luigi Ghirri. Vista con camera* (Milan: Motta, 1992).
19 *Camera Austria International,* 42/1993.
20 *Camera Austria International,* 43/44/1993.
21 Michel Poivert, *La photographie contemporaine* (Paris: Flammarion, 2002).
22 *Camera Austria International,* 85/2004.
23 Achille Sacconi, Roberta Valtorta eds, *1987–1997, Archivio dello spazio. Dieci anni di fotografia italiana sul territorio della provincia di Milano,* (Udine: Art&, 1997); F. Gierstberg, ed., *SubUrban Options: Photography Commissions and the Urbanization of the Landscape* (Rotterdam: Nederlands Foto Instituut, 1998); https://journals.openedition.org/inha/4421; see http://www.mufoco.org/collezioni/archivio-dello-spazio/.
24 Roberta Valtorta ed., *Il museo, le collezioni,* (Milan: Tranchida, 2004); Roberta Valtorta, ed., *Il museo, le collezioni 2* (Cinisello Balsamo: Silvana Editoriale, 2009); Roberta Valtorta, ed., *2004–2014 Opere e progetti del Museo di Fotografia Contemporanea* (Cinisello Balsamo: Silvana Editoriale, 2014); see http://www.mufoco.org.
25 *Camera Austria International,* 107/2009.
26 Margherita Guccione, María Rosaria Nappi, Mosè Ricci eds, *Atlante italiano 003. Ritratto dell'Italia che cambia,* (Milan: Mondadori Printing, 2003); Francesca Fabiani, ed., *Atlante 007. Rischio paesaggio* (Milan: DARC/ Electa, 2007); see: http://www.maxxi.art/collezioni-di-fotografia/.
27 *Camera Austria International,* 15–16/1984.
28 Franco Vaccari, *Esposizioni in tempo reale/Exhibitions in Real Time* (Bologna: Damiami, 2007); Nicoletta Leonardi, ed., *Feedback. Scritti su e di Franco Vaccari* (Milan: Postmedia Books, 2007).

Learning from Graz

The place where I spent my formative years in my profession is one that cultivates a specific attitude towards photography—an attitude that does not pay enough attention to the continuity of critical, theoretical, and curatorial "tools" that are indispensable when stepping out of one's comfort zone. It may therefore be appropriate to begin this text with the situation in the mid-1970s, when Camera Austria was established and several projects were launched on the Croatian scene. This formative period will allow us to consider the similarities (as well as today's differences) between the institutional circumstances in Croatia and Austria as an aspect that contributed to the development of contemporary photography.

In 1973, the Centre for Photography, Film, and Television (CEFFT) was established as part of the Zagreb Galleries and the Gallery of Contemporary Art (GSU).[1] The Centre was a separate organizational unit created to promote through its programs new policies of collecting and presenting art; these policies focused on research and documentary-conceptual tendencies in photography, animated and experimental film, and television. The structure of CEFFT followed the principle of an open-type institution, contrary to the traditional notion of a museum.

In those years, GSU organized four exhibitions on *New Photography*[2] in collaboration with the Museum of Contemporary Art Belgrade and the Rotovž Salon at Art Gallery Maribor, which presented new views on non-aesthetic photography and trends outside of so-called "photographers' photography."

The photography magazine *SPOT* (1972–1978) emerged at a time of significant changes in art, especially regarding its modes of activity, the broadening field of interest, and the forms in which artistic content was manifested and mediated—changes that were partly a consequence of the political and social circumstances of the late 1960s. The magazine was founded by Radoslav Putar, director of the Gallery of Contemporary Art Zagreb, who was aware of the need to promote the culture of visual communications.[3] Putar perceived photography as a specific form of expression, documentation, and communication by means of images, a view that would be endorsed by GSU's curators, Davor Matičević and

Želimir Koščević, who were particularly dedicated to this medium. Another important figure promoting photography in the same decade was Petar Dabac, who founded the TD Archive (1978–98) as the only gallery in Zagreb specialized in photography and a site of numerous collaborations and encounters. Pero's Archive was frequented by, among other individuals, Albert Goldstein, one of the rare theoreticians of photography in Croatia, who also collaborated with Camera Austria.[4]

The synergy resulting from these initiatives, which were unfortunately and irretrievably discontinued, was closely related to the early days of Camera Austria and the perspectives initiated by Christine Frisinghelli, Manfred Willmann, and Seiichi Furuya. Thus, as a person who could not draw upon local "sources of youth" in contemporary photographic processes in 1970s Croatia, I owe most of what I have achieved in the medium to none other than Camera Austria.

The 1970s were the temporal framework of various initiatives in photography launched in various parts of the world. Experimental, critical, conceptual, and neo-avant-garde practices were adopting different formats—exhibitions, symposia, lectures, and magazines—with an increasing range of institutions specializing in photography. Here as well, Camera Austria played a crucial role, especially for all of us who (historically, geographically, and culturally) gravitated towards Austria.

Since I approached the photographic heritage of my local setting a few years after meeting Christine and Manfred, in the mid-2000s I perceive my position as a consequence of a reversible relationship, based on discovering traces of networking reaching back to the second half of the 1970s. Probably for a reason, it was Christine and Manfred who named *SPOT* as one of their sources of inspiration, while Dabac's gallery functioned as a small-format test area for individual photographic practices, inaugurated at the time through Camera Austria's exhibition program and magazine.[5]

Conceptual tendencies in photography, and digressions[6] on the consequences of photography for the culture and art of the 1970s, were presented at the exhibition with an accompanying catalogue called

Innovations in Croatian Art during the 1970s. Ten years later, there was another synthesis, this time of postwar photography in Croatia: the exhibition *Croatian Photography since the 1950s* made it possible for several generations of experts and audiences to gain insight into the events, tendencies, and authors' positions, both amateur and artistic.[7] The exhibition (and the text of the catalogue) reflected two visions that recalled the topics addressed in a review published in the first issue of *Camera Austria International*: photography as art and art as photography. Thus, it is also in this segment that one sees how, in those years, similar interests and ways of conceptualizing photographic practice were emerging in different settings.

While writing this text, I am recalling my first encounter with Camera Austria. In 1986, I visited steirischer herbst for the first time, but that was primarily for a symposion on architecture and talks by several genuine celebrities of postmodernism. I was not aware of another symposium taking place at the Forum Stadtpark, *Das Bild – Der Text,* which Camera Austria held only a few days after the architectural one. Nor do I recall exactly the first exhibition I saw of theirs, but what I do remember is the uncertainty it made me feel, which would evolve for years to come. Namely, our university lectures in Croatia taught us almost nothing about photography, and almost no theoretical literature existed in translation. For this reason, I still believed in the unquestionability of the photographic image, and would only later arrive at the many layers of meaning in its background (and its surroundings).

Even though memory is an unreliable phenomenon, the uncertainty concerning what I saw is something I do remember very well. The mechanical process with a series of (subjective and individual) choices in its background caused a series of mentally tectonic shifts, which made me aware of the fact that photography is "hardly ever a dispositive only of images."[8] These "petrified memories" hardly seem inspiring, and may even seem unimportant, but in fact they led to the project *Staying or Leaving* (*Bleiben oder gehen*), curated by Christine Frisinghelli with my assistance. It was this exhibition that helped me make the right decision. While in the exhibition context the decision was about the reasons why people chose to migrate, with photography as the medium used to identify one's "question of identities, a form of permanent surveying and exploration of the cultural territory,"[9] my personal decision concerned what photography revealed about the world order, about social cohabitation in terms of what Maria Papadimitriou, along with the other authors, revealed to the Zagreb audience. Her exhibition/participation "construct" referred to a condition that was to become fully revealed in

the present day, dramatically marked by migrant crises; she referred to "the social unknowable" as an outcome of the fact that society had (in the meantime) ceased to exist.[10] The way the exhibition space was constructed, in which photography was not only a visual-descriptive mode of presentation, but had become part of the construction of complex relations (in Sekula's case, these relations revealed exploitation, and with Papadimitriou it was unplanned, temporary "settlements") left a deep impression on me and influenced my further understanding, experience, and interpretation of photography.

The premise of the social unknowable, albeit not expressed in those very words, was in the background of my interpretation of Mladen Stilinović's works presented at the same *Bleiben oder gehen* exhibition, which I revisited in 2006 in my first extensive paper for *Camera Austria International*.[11] Besides his cream cakes, potatoes, and buried pain,[12] it was important to indicate Stilinović's peculiar way of reacting to the perceived and intellectually processed reality, the social divisions and injustice, the story of a man selling an empty wallet next to a footpath on the periphery of Zagreb (whom Stilinović did not photograph). Stilinović's view of everyday life, his attraction to "great subjects" such as political ideologies as well as to the transitory nature of everyday scenes, prepared me for photographs that were anything but "pretty pictures": those showing the body and disease. Thus I also became acquainted with Jo Spence, owing to an exhibition and book by Camera Austria, since they informed me about the Photo Workshop and the Women's Photo Association of Hackney Flashers. Its structure and impact have been of particular interest to me lately for my research on women who were active in Photo Club Zagreb in the past, but whose lives and work remain largely unknown. In Croatia, we won't encounter social activities such as those initiated by Jo, but her methods of constructing social identity as well as ways of using popular visual content, especially through montages of images and texts that are associative and at the same time critically intoned, are also somewhat reminiscent of the practice inaugurated in the Croatian context by Sanja Iveković.

Even though the context of social issues as presented in the Market Photo Workshop (Johannesburg) is different from that addressed by the Hackney Flashers, I link it to my experiences during the symposium and exhibition marking the 100th issue of *Camera Austria International* in 2007. Initiatives such as the Market Photo Workshop, intended for all ethnic groups in the Republic of South Africa and dedicated to various topics from social and political life, sum up what photography does, teaches us about, or mediates. We may once have believed that countries heavily burdened by their political legacy, race issues, prejudice related to gender or religion, or irreconcilable class differences are distant places, yet reality has shown that this is not so. Clichés that once helped us structure our knowledge and convictions about the world have in the meantime collapsed, and the cracks thus created teach us that the West has not been spared either. Unfamiliar gender-related, national, religious, and political sentiments and freedoms are no longer something happening on the other side of the globe, but across the street. Insights such as these have led to the participation of Ahlam Shibli at the exhibition titled *Seeking for a Place of Oblivion,* which I organized in Zagreb in 2008. In her photographs, a peculiar "landscape" is formed by collapsed buildings and devastated towns; this is a consequence of territorial control and a belief in the possibility of social utopias as they exist in memories that cannot be suppressed or limited.

Owing to the many texts and exhibitions in Camera Austria's production, it is now possible to see that which is (apparently) familiar, has regained visibility, or has become visible in a different way. What we see are actual spaces, as well as others whose reality depends on the archival order or scenario, and the need to continuously use them in a filmic context. Such places have been filmed by Karina Nimmerfall, who has been exploring the American architectural heritage of modernism, to which European architects have contributed with their ideas of socially aware and healthful housing, as well as architecture created for the needs of the film industry. Owing to Camera Austria, Croatian audiences could also get acquainted with the strategies of using archival photographic materials, namely through the work of Sabine Bitter and Helmut Weber.[13] A complex set of decisions on what remains invisible in photography or is found in documents, carefully archived (or even more carefully omitted from the archiving procedure) is only a part of a specific practice that, among other things, comments on the "crisis of the documentary image."[14] The artistic strategy of Tatiana Lecomte, whom we have also presented in Zagreb, partly results from the hiatus between the found and its construed meaning: it depends on evidence—someone's waste—that is used to explore the relationship between truth and reality.

Owing to Camera Austria, we can now investigate and build upon the photographic concepts based on the constitutive foundations of conceptual art; we are informed about and adopt analytical actions that precede or run parallel to shooting; we are interested in researching different positions, meanings, and relations, subjective statements, registers, and archives. We are getting acquainted with the work of artists who are also biologists, former students of German literature, or onomatologists.

Personally, I have found it important to venture into understanding the documentary-conceptual current. Besides visual content, I have need of text, information, reasons, historical details, and the subsequent constructions that might eventually challenge all of these. I remember the exhibition of Sven Johne, the rippled sea and the starry skies, large black formats with details that I can no longer recall. However, what remain are stories that take place under our common sky, documents of a world that keeps changing out of necessity.

I remember "banal" images lined up on a long table that had the same shape as the exhibition room, where the photographs of Erik van der Weijde (whose poster I still covet) started talking only after repeated readings, telling interest in a specific particular place, which he had arrived at through meticulous research. And I haven't forgotten how Camera Austria was transformed into a dark space filled with flickering images for Artur Żmijewski's exhibition *Democracy.* His work, characterized by a radical documentary quality, spoke of various forms of political declarations that European and Middle Eastern countries use to impose their own ideas and legal regulations on others.

I learned a lot from *Milk Drop Coronet: 30 Exhibitions on the Virtuosity of Thingness,* not only on about Harold Edgerton's photography, but also about the possibilities of philosophical speculations on art and reality. I was intrigued to see how a shot documenting the state between motion and stillness can be used to speak about delay, and how we define or at least try to understand the relationship between stable and unstable, material and invisible.

In addition to these exhibitions, symposia, texts, and the library, I also learned from Christine, Manfred, Seiichi, Reinhard, and Maren. Once I proposed placing a photograph by Jochen Lempert on the cover page and it was decided otherwise. But I was happy when a work by Chrystel Lebas ended up there, a strange scene shot at some museum of natural history as the ultimate arcadia that, while being looked at, produced a feeling of insecurity, uneasiness, and immobility.[15] I also remember feeling disturbed when the cover page once appeared completely black, summing up a state of mind that cannot be either described or visualized.[16] I love titles that span three years (*First the artist defines meaning; Then the work takes place*) and that glass ball by Joachim Koester, that has been mirroring different spaces and times.

For some texts and artists, I must still "exert myself," knowing that photographs sometimes miss their mark and that the artists are not necessarily interested in creating their own photographic images.[17]

Fortunately, there is still enough room for movement, both around the *House* of Manfred Willmann[18] and beyond the *Border* of Seiichi Furuya.[19] Among all those, there are meanings and knowledge that Camera Austria continues to convey.

Sandra Križić Roban

1   Today's Museum of Contemporary Art (MSU), Zagreb.
2   *Nova fotografija 1 / New Photography 1,* "Vidici i usmjerenja / Views and Trends," 1973–1974; *Nova fotografija 2 / New Photography 2,* "Fotografija kao umjetnost / Photography as Art," 1976; *Nova fotografija 3 / New Photography 3,* 1979–1980; *Nova fotografija 4 / New Photography 4,* "Fotografija osamdesetih / Photography from the 80s," 1984.
3   There were curators and photographers on the editorial boards (Petar Dabac, Enes Midžić, Dimitrije Bašičević, Marijan Susovski, Jozo Četković, Nenad Gattin), and the collaboration with other republics was also crucial: with Slovenian photographers and theoreticians (Zmago Jeraj, Mitja Koman) as well as theoretician Ješa Denegri from Belgrade.
4   He participated in the *Symposion on Photography II,* Forum Stadtpark, Graz, 1980. Published in "Zu einigen unscharfen Begriffen, die Fotografie betreffend / Some Comments on a Number of Blurred Concepts in Photography," *Camera Austria International,* 4/1980: 33–37.
5   Archive TD hosted the exhibitions of Max Aufischer, Manfred Willmann, Seiichi Furuya, and Branko Lenart, among others.
6   I am referring here to Dimitrije Bašičević, "Konzekvence fotografije. 11 digresija o kulturi i umjetnosti sedamdesetih godina" [Consequences of Photography: Eleven Digressions on Culture and Art in the 70s], in Marijan Susovski, ed., *Inovacije u hrvatskoj umjetnosti sedamdesetih godina* (Zagreb: Gallery of Contemporary Art, 1982), 83–91.
7   Curated by Davor Matičević, the exhibition took place in 1993 at the Gallery of Contemporary Art, Gallery of Primitive Art, and the Old Town Hall in Zagreb. The catalogue was likewise edited by Matičević and published posthumously in 1997.
8   Reinhard Braun, "Introduction" ("Vorwort"), in *Archives, Re-assemblances, and Surveys*, exh. cat. (Zagreb: Camera Austria and Croatian Photographic Union, 2014), 7.
9   Christine Frisinghelli, "Bleiben oder gehen / Staying or leaving," in *Bleiben oder gehen / Staying or leaving*, exh. cat. (Zagreb: Croatian Photographic Union, 2004), 5.
10 Compare Allan Sekula, "On 'Fish Story': The Coffin Learns to Dance / Über 'Fish Story:' der Sarg lernt tanzen," in *Camera Austria International,* 59–60/1997: 49. I am referring here to the titles of specific works by Mladen Stilinović.
11 Sandra Križić Roban, "Mladen Stilinović: 63 Meter Schmerz/ 63 Meters of Pain," in *Camera Austria International* 93/2006: 30–40.
12 I am referring here to the titles of specific works by Mladen Stilinović.
13 *Archives, Re-Assemblances, and Surveys,* an exhibition curated by Reinhard Braun and Sandra Križić Roban, a production of Camera Austria and the Croatian Photographic Union, Zagreb and Osijek, 2014.
14 Maren Lübbke-Tidow, "Archiving and Processing Dispositifs: Five Positions from Archives, Re-Assemblances, and Surveys/ Archivierungs- und Weiterverarbeitungsdispositive: Fünf Positionen aus Archives, Re-Assemblances, and Surveys," in *Archives, Re-assemblances, and Surveys,* (Zagreb: Camera Austria, and Croatian Photographic Union, 2014), 19 (German version: 20).
15 *Camera Austria International* 110/2010.
16 *Camera Austria International* 140/2017.
17 As Maren Lübbke-Tidow observed in "Archiving and Processing Dispositifs: Five Positions from Archives, Re-Assemblances, and Surveys / Archivierungs- und Weiterverarbeitungsdispositive: Fünf Positionen aus Archives, Re-Assemblances, and Surveys," 13.
18 I am referring here to Manfred Willmann, *Das Haus / The House*, 1993.
19 I am referring here to Seiichi Furuya, *Staatsgrenze / Border*, 1981–83.

The Topology, the Edges, and the Islands of Contemporary Japanese Photography

A society is like a living fabric. On the underside of this fabric—imperceptible from the outside—there is a mesh of distinct threads that only becomes visible at the outmost edges of the fabric. If we examine these edges more closely we come to see what elements make up the fabric. Just as we can recognize the interweave of warp and woof by the hem, so too can we discern the forces that go to make up a society by looking at its periphery. So where would this put the periphery of modern Japanese society? And what indication could we find at the edges of the conflicting forces? Discovering these edges is perhaps the most important task to be fulfilled by contemporary photography. Yet these edges do not manifest themselves in the form of a contrast between the center and the periphery or border area. Potentially, these edges exist everywhere, and very specific actions are required to bring them to the surface. An action creates an edge in a particular place, and the next action at this edge creates another edge.

The exhibition by Camera Austria: *Keep in Touch: Positions in Japanese Photography* 2003 was an attempt by a younger generation of photographers to investigate the various forces that are seen at the edges—we will concentrate here on just three among these positions. The three female photographers set out to plumb the signs that become visible at these edges with diverse methods and approaches. One edge, for example, is found in Okinawa. The geopolitical location of the islands of Okinawa at the border between Japan and the Asian continent is seen as a key military and political position. This gives rise to a complex structure of dominating and being dominated, discriminating and being discriminated against. The contemporary history of Okinawa is thus characterized by military concerns that totally disregard the will of the local population. However, Okinawa is not only a hub of international politics but is also the place where the memory of traditional Japanese culture is still alive today, a culture that has grown there since ancient times. In a way, the social, political, and psychological changes that Japan has undergone in the course of modernization are revealed in Okinawa raw and unadorned, like geological yield lines.

Mao Ishikawa focuses on the edges that have been ripped open in the last almost fifty years since Oki-nawa has belonged to Japan again (between 1945 and 1972 Okinawa was occupied by the US), working tirelessly and intuitively on making them visible. She conducts in-depth discussions with the population affected by the problems of the American military bases, e.g. the prostitutes at the disposal of the American soldiers, the dock workers employed by the army, the actors from Okinawa's traditional theatre, or the Japanese militiamen, and, on the basis of her own

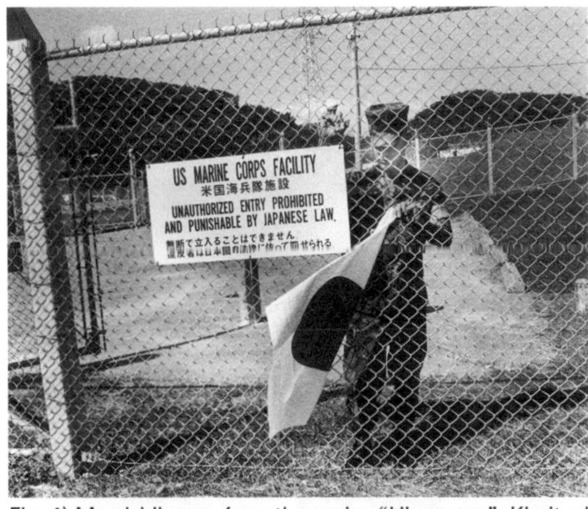

Fig. 1) Mao Ishikawa, from the series "Hinomaru": Kimitoshi Takanashi (21), a Japanese from Hiroshima, joined the US Marine Corps because he wanted to prove himself in the world's most powerful fighting force. "You can say what you want, but Hinomaru is our national flag, and we should be proud of it." After his release from the USMC, he now works in a private company in Hiroshima. (On a US Naval Base in Okinawa, October 14, 1995)

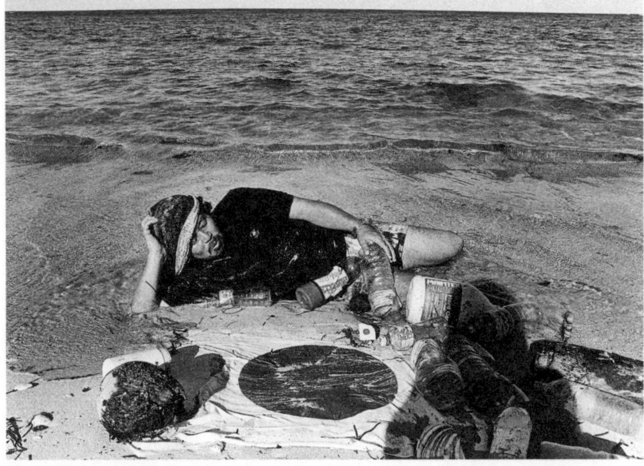

Fig. 2) Mao Ishikawa, from the series "Hinomaru": Tomohiro Sunagawa (42), cartoonist. "Various things from Taiwan, China and South Korea are washed up on the beach. By setting them up around the Hinomaru, I express that Japan is not a racially homogenous nation. The hermit crab, which must carry the Hinomaru on its back, stands for the Okinawa resident. I wonder if he feels at home. If Hinomaru really is our flag, we should be able to do whatever we want with it." (Miyako Island, Okinawa, 20 August 1995)

experience—the grief and pain that has arisen as a result of co-existing with these people—creates series of photos to document her own feelings. Hence, her work cannot be classified as part of a political activism, nor as photojournalism, although in exploring her feelings, she is necessarily faced with these questions.

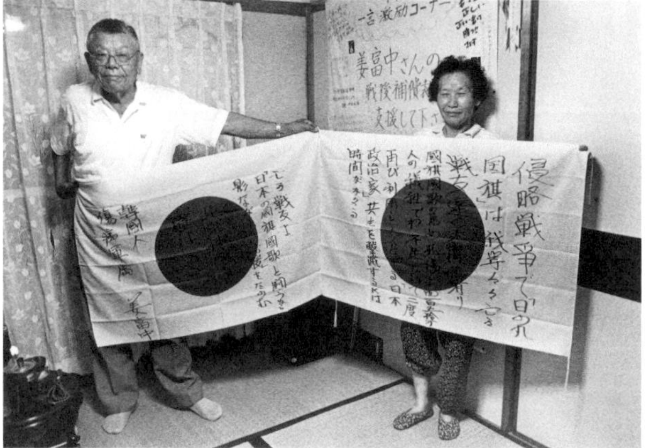

Fig. 3) Mao Ishikawa, from the series "Hinomaru": Kan Pu Jun (79) was a civilian Korean worker in the war industry who was wounded in World War II and now lives in Japan. He was forced to work by the Japanese navy and lost his right eye and right arm. "Every time I see the Hinomaru, all my hair stands on end. This flag is the arch enemy. Bullshit!" With his wife Li Kei Sun (72). (Shiga, August 14, 1999)

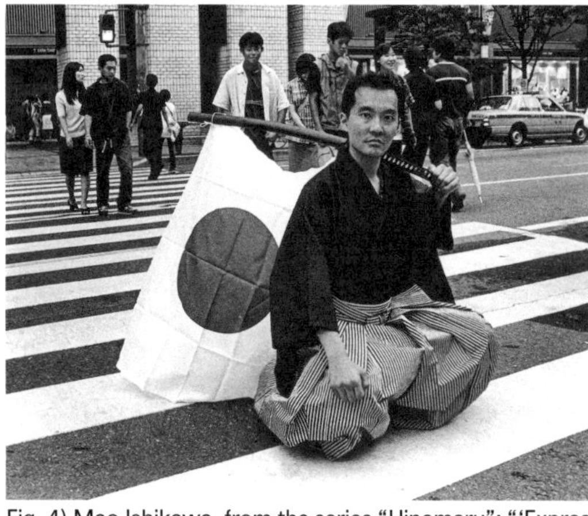

Fig. 4) Mao Ishikawa, from the series "Hinomaru": "'Express yourselves more forcefully' – That's what I want to say to the people of my generation when I walk across the zebra crossing dressed this way with the Hinomaru in my hand. When travelling in other countries, you notice that you are Japanese, even if you don't like it. I want the self-confidence. And I believe that beyond 'Japan', 'state' and 'nation' there is a world waiting," said Seiji Sano (29). (Fukuoka, August 15, 1999)

The two series *Omiai*, 2001, and *Cover*, 2002 by Tomoko Sawada, comprising studio-style engagement photos and photos from print club booths, could also perhaps be referred to as peculiar photographs of a "living room called Japan." On the one hand, Sawada uses the type of studio portraits that women have taken of them in their best clothes for the traditional Japanese form of matchmaking, and, on the other, so-called print club photos that are taken in simple, fully automatic photo studios and which have come to be a new form of communication tool among young people. On the basis of her personal percep-

tion of reality, Sawada, a master of disguise (she is impersonating all the poses), uses the medium of photography to create totally bizarre desires and lusts within Japan's highly developed consumer society. Unbiased by existing concepts of value and style, her point of departure lies in the embodiment of perception and consciousness of her own personality. At a deeper level, we see a determined approach with which she enacts her ideas on a grand scale.

The work of Mika Ninagawa "A Piece of Rainbow," 2001—2003 exhibits the same resolute-nonchalant attitude that is characteristic of young female Japanese photographers, although in her case I would particularly like to emphasize her garish colors. In a way they are filled to the brim with a peculiar atmosphere produced by the gravitational field that is Japan. What these colors signal is a kind of intangible atmosphere which, depending on the particular motif, covers the entire image. Detached from reality, weightless and insubstantial, everything that would assist perception vanishes. Ninagawa's loud, chemical and artificial chromatics evoke the feeling of a drug rush. Her technique of taking pictures produces the effect of blending with the object being photographed, and eliminates the borderline between the Self and the Other. In this way, the consciousness of a Japan imbued with speed and information becomes manifest.

The work of photographers of this generation not only differs in terms of subject and methodology, but also in terms of the narrative mode and expression. Having grown up in the period of the Japanese economic boom, they began to express themselves artistically, when images and media were just undergoing a process of homogenization. Subsequently they lived through times of great economic and social disorder. Under the influence of photographers from the previous generation, who were persistently challenging the conservative nature of Japanese society, but also in conscious contrast to them, they attempt to escape from the stereotype image of Japan and enter new spheres. They search for real things in the urban environment which is totally pervaded by a capitalist system that has passed its zenith and has now become vulnerable. They address the difficult problems of impoverished rural regions, and they observe the imperceptible progress of the crisis of culture and tradition. Without being able to elude the feelings of insecurity and tension, they continue their photographic activities.

Everything is in vertiginous motion, new phenomena are incessantly emerging. But in every era there is something that distinguishes this epoch, just as there must be common traits shared by their photos. The people who live in a certain epoch embody the various peculiarities that characterize their everyday life and thus communicate at a level far deeper than con-

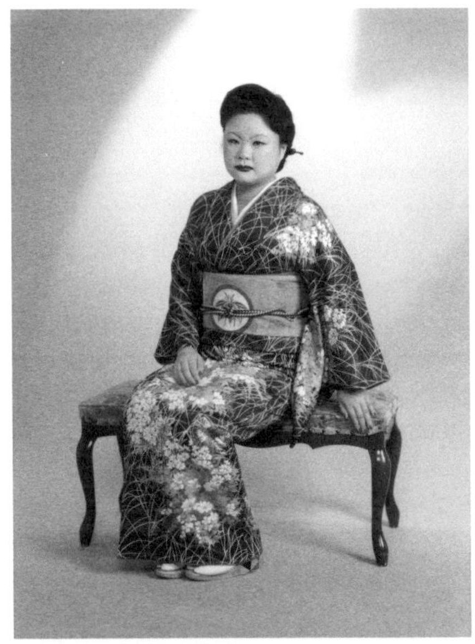

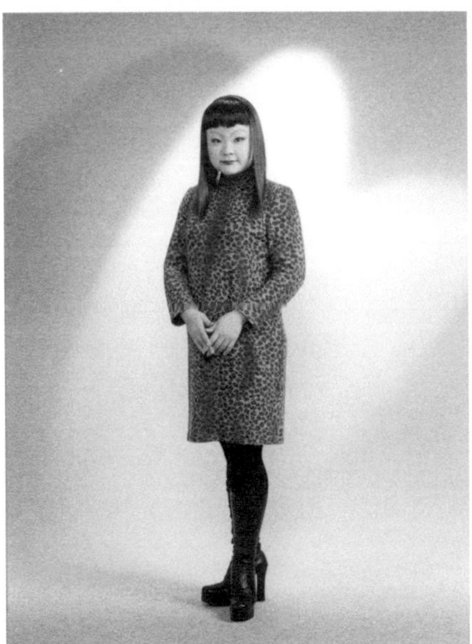

Fig. 5 + 6) Tomoko Sawada, from the series "Omiai," 2001

being a publicist to photographer after meeting Tomatsu, also visited Okinawa for the first time in 1971 to support a young man who had been wrongly arrested on the strength of newspaper photos. He condemned all photos that served the purpose of social justice as fraud and even criticized Shomei Tomatsu. He later suffered a sudden loss of memory, his participation in the symposion in Okinawa was his first public appearance in thirty years.

Tomatsu's original interest in Okinawa was in the Americanization of Japan and the problem of the local American military base, but during his visits to the various islands of Okinawa he also encountered the oldest layers of Japanese culture, which left a lasting impression on him. At the same time, he came across the photographs of Taro Okamoto, which also profoundly inspired him. Okamato had visited Okinawa in 1959, afterwards writing his cultural history treatise entitled *Forgotten Japan: A cultural history of Okinawa*. Before the war, he had worked as a painter in Paris

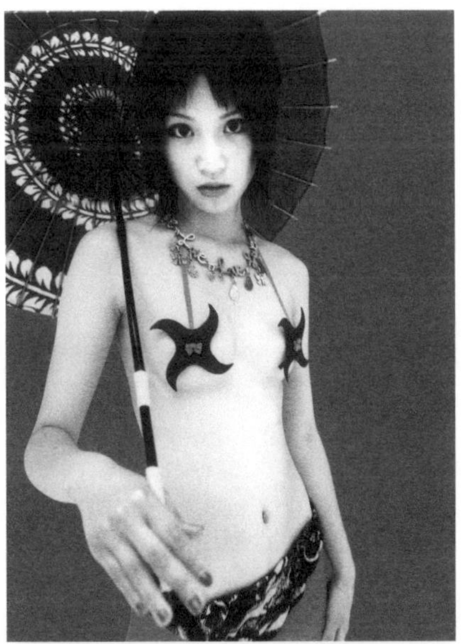

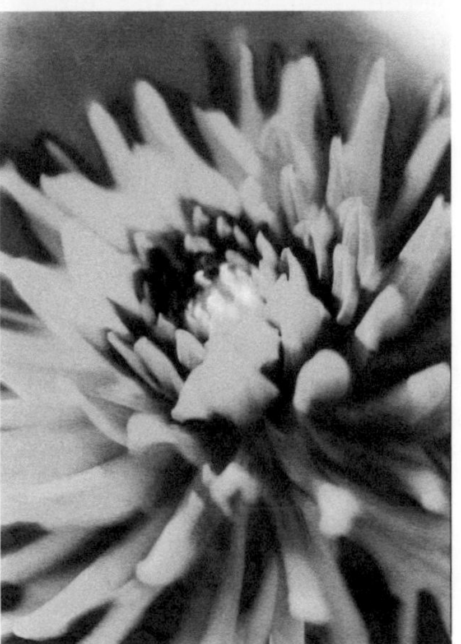

Fig. 7 + 8) Mika Nigawaga, from the series "A Piece of Rainbow," 2001–2003

scious reason. Things that appear to be totally contrary in fact reflect each other in some way or another. This is precisely why it is necessary—on the basis of the coexistence or fusion of the phenomena and expressions pushing in all directions—to identify a concealed framework that permits this diversity.

In the summer of 2002 there was a highly interesting symposion and exhibition in Okinawa featuring photographers from the generation preceding the artists presented here, including Shomei Tomatsu, Daido Moriyama, Takuma Nakahira, Nobuyoshi Araki; the symposion was entitled *Photographic Documentation–Photographic Creation* and the exhibition *Photonesia–Memories of Light, Fruits of Time*. Shomei Tomatsu first came to Okinawa in 1969, at a time when the conflict for reintegration into the Japanese state was seething, and moved there for almost two years in 1972. On the basis of this experience, together with Moriyama and Araki he founded a school offering photography workshops in 1974. Nakahira, who had gone from

53

and studied under the ethnologist Marcel Mauss. After World War II, he travelled all over Japan with his camera, intending to discover Japan anew, and finally ended up in Okinawa. What particularly impressed Okamoto about Okinawa were the so-called utaki, sacred groves deep in the forests to which the gods descend. Utaki are quite simply empty places in the forest, but an incredible force settles over these places. Okamoto was overwhelmed by the edge that arises out of this emptiness. For the first time he discovered the edge of Japan in all its clarity. At this edge he found himself facing the latent currents of Japan, a brute resistance of space and time. In Okinawa at the time there still existed a native religion similar to the ancient Japanese Shinto. The utaki were deeply imbued by these atmospheres. The rites of Okinawa that were performed around the utaki were originally linked to the customs of Pacific islanders. What fascinated Okamoto was the cluster of forces and energies that were adopted at irregular intervals from these islands. The name of the exhibition, *Photonesia,* also combines *photos* and *nisos,* i.e. photography and island, and thus alludes to Okinawa.

When we talk about the Ryukyu archipelago, i.e. the islands of Okinawa that link Japan to the Asian mainland, the very word—with its soft, flowing rhythm—already reflects the will to change the current condition of Japan that is characterized by centralist politics and a materialistic consciousness. Concealed within is the view of a conglomerate called Japan that is not the product of a linear historical evolution, as the Tenno system would seem to embody, but rather arisen from the succession and coexistence of different ethnic groups who all influenced each other.

Japan is essentially an archipelago, the chain of islands extends from Okinawa, that adjoins southeast Asia and Taiwan, through Kyushu, Honshu and Hokkaido, to Sakhalin and from there to the Eurasian continent. These are islands that have nothing to do with the rigid systems and ideological seclusion of the continent. But this peculiar feature of Japan has been lost in the twentieth century. Although the Japanese are physiologically and psychologically attached to the archipelagos, their consciousness and their thoughts were shaped by a continental view of the world and values, modernized to western standards, and led to a history of colonizing other Asian nations. The coexistence of these contradictory trends has led Japan into a kind of schizophrenia, breaking it in many ways.

In the works of Japanese photographers also are reflect the characteristics of such an existence charged with tension. Do their pictures not perhaps suggest the will to revive a new archipelago? The secret intention to wander from island to island, discovering new connections all the while? In a condition of Japanese culture in which history, ethics, aesthetics, memory and dreams have been lost, in which everything is mixed and deformed on a smooth surface, the experiments of the artists assembled here would seem to be gaping fissures that reveal things that have hitherto lain beneath the surface of everyday life. At the edges of the fissures, which only seemingly look like fine cracks, they lie in wait of things that may break free. Assuring themselves of their position in the ambivalent time we call the present, groping their way from fissure to fissure, as if ferrying from one island to the next, there slowly emerges a new horizon that was previously unseen.

Toshiharu Ito

Edited version of the essay in *Camera Austria International,* Issue 84/2003. Translation of the original German text by Richard Watts.

Collaboration Japan – Graz

In the exhibition *Camera Austria International: Laboratory for Photography and Theory,* the special relationship between Camera Austria and Japan is documented only by references to two artists: Nobuyoshi Araki, whose first series in color, "Shikikei," was shown at our *Akt Tokyo* exhibition, and Lieko Shiga, with an excerpt from her work *Rasen Kaigan*. We've published Shiga's work only once within the scope of the Forum, in *Camera Austria International.* For many young artists, however, such publication marked the beginning of a long-term collaboration with Camera Austria.

The exchange between Camera Austria and photographers and institutions from Japan has a long and special history, which is closely linked to the collaboration between Seiichi Furuya (who moved to Graz in 1975) and Manfred Willmann. It began as a dialogue between photographers, and with growing trust and mutual appreciation, a basis for exhibitions and publications was created in collaboration with Japanese photographic artists, institutions, publicists, and curators. In the summer of 1975, Willmann invited Furuya to show his photographs at the very last exhibition held by his Fotogalerie im Schillerhof before he was able to continue the exhibition program via the Artist's association Forum Stadtpark.

With Furuya's help, it was possible over time to present the most influential Japanese photographers in monographic exhibitions, often for the first time outside Japan: Daidoh Moriyama with *Das ist Japan* (This Is Japan) in 1980 (see *Camera Austria International* 2/1980); the comprehensive retrospective on the work of Shomei Tomatsu in 1984; and last but not least the legendary exhibition *Akt Tokyo* by Nobuyoshi Araki in 1992. Tsuneo Enari (1981), Hiromi Tsuchida (1983), and Miyako Ishiuchi (1992) were lecturers at our Symposia on Photography. Issei Suda (with Robert Mapplethorpe, 1981) and Masahisa Fukase (in "The Revenge of Recollection," 1988) took part in exhibitions that meant a lot to us. With the 2003 exhibition and symposion *Keep in Touch: Positions in Japanese Photography,* we introduced a younger generation of photographers. That project, which also inaugurated our new location in the Iron House, was made possible within the context of "Graz 2003—European Capital of Culture" and with the support of EU-Japan Fest. All of these presentations were accompanied either by catalogues or by publication in the magazine *Camera Austria International.*

Toshiharu Ito was involved in many of these projects: with essays in publications, such as the exhibition catalogues of Shomei Tomatsu in 1984 and Nobuyoshi Araki in 1992; as a consultant and generous host; and as the curator of an extensive exhibition project he realized for the Kunsthaus Graz in collaboration with Camera Austria: *Chikaku—Time and Memory in Japan / Zeit der Erinnerung in Japan* (2005). The following essay by Toshiharu Ito is an edited version of his essay for the Symposion on Photography 2003, "Keep in Touch" (see *Camera Austria International* 84/2003). We would like to thank Toshiharu Ito for his support of our work over many years and for his willingness to allow us to publish excerpts of this essay here to illustrate a specific part of Camera Austria's history.

Christine Frisinghelli

Dialog 1

Topography & Landscape

Camera Austria International

1982   "The Concern," Michael Köhler in an
interview with Robert Adams,
text contribution / artist contribution,
Camera Austria International 9 / 1982
1984   Robert Adams, "Michael Schmidt.
Berlin-Kreuzberg. Stadtbilder," exhibition
review, *Camera Austria International* 14 / 1984
1985   Lewis Baltz, "Robert Adams, Our Lives and
Our Children, New York, 1983," book review,
Camera Austria International 18 / 1985
2005   Thomas Weski, "Robert Adams:
Die Suche nach Frieden ist eine lange Reise,"
text contribution / artist contribution and
cover, *Camera Austria International* 89 / 2005
2010   Philipp Freytag, "Robert Adams," Hasselblad
Center, Göteborg Museum of Art, Göteborg,
exhibition review, *Camera Austria
International* 109 / 2010
2013   Andreas Prinzing, "The Place We Live,
Josef Albers Museum Quadrat, Bottrop,
Jeu de Paume, Paris; Fotomuseum
Winterthur," exhibition review,
Camera Austria International 124 / 2013

Exhibition

1995   *Listening to the River,* solo exhibition

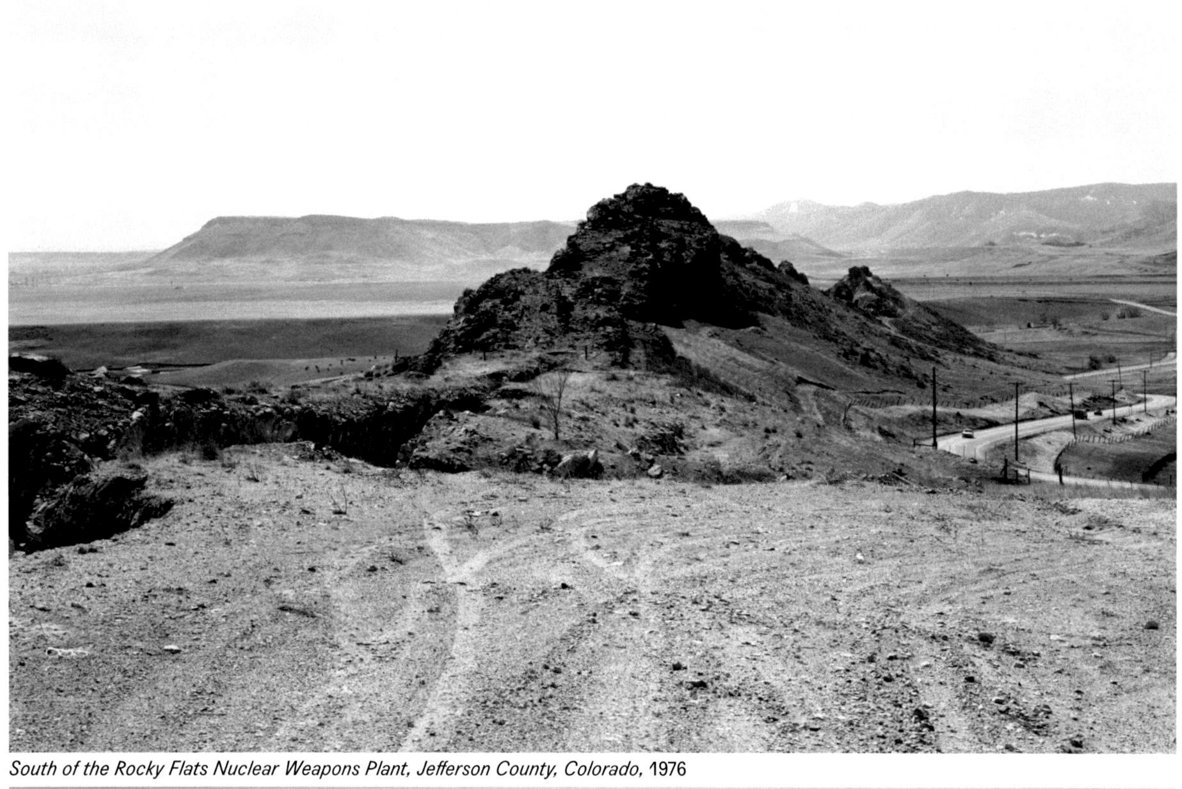

South of the Rocky Flats Nuclear Weapons Plant, Jefferson County, Colorado, 1976

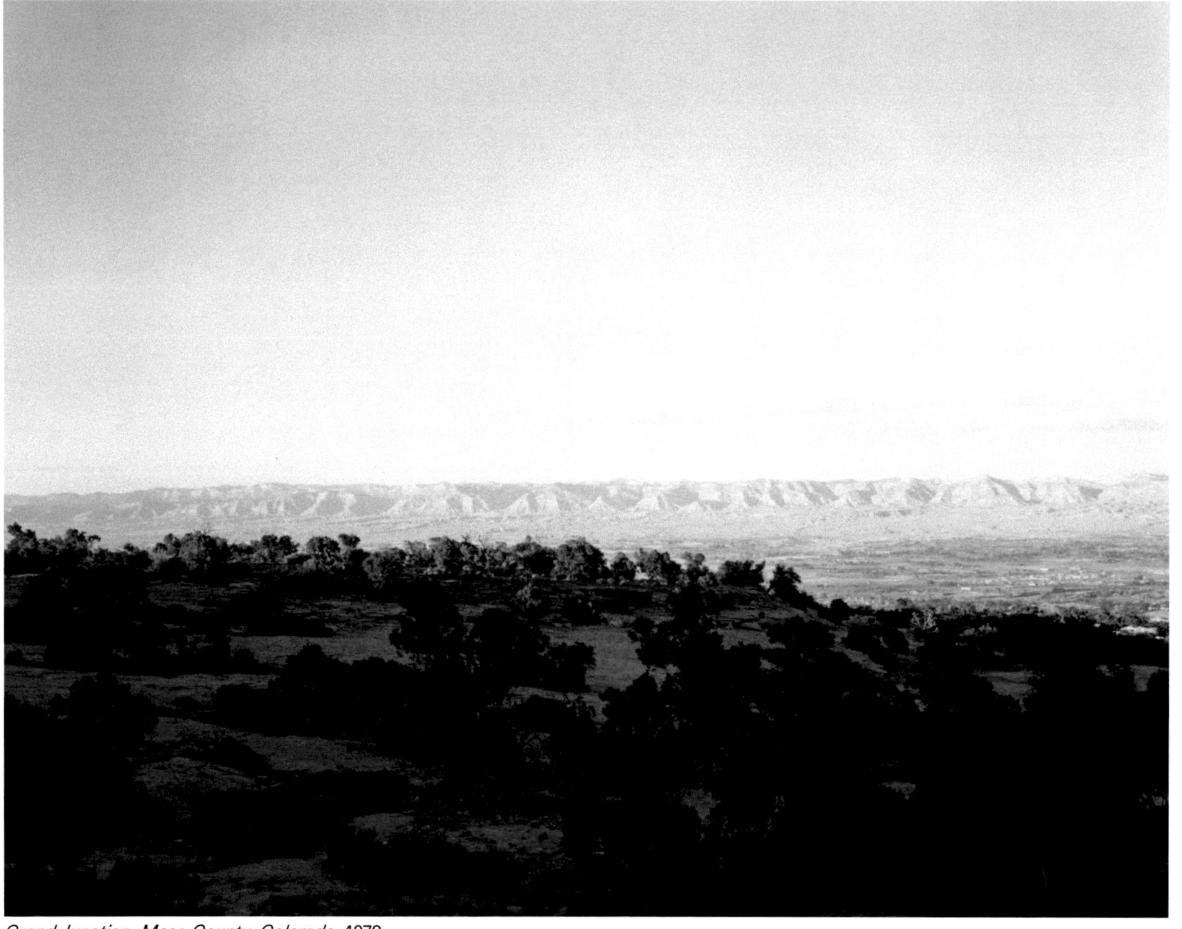

Grand Junction, Mesa County, Colorado, 1978

Robert Adams

I was raised here in Colorado. I went to school in southern California, and when I came back to Colorado I found it had become like California. There were suddenly freeways and smog. It was a deep shock to me, because I had spent my years as a boy mountain-climbing, camping and running rivers; and later I had worked for the Forest Service and the Park Service—it was a lot of my life. So to come back and find almost the end of that world was a terrible shock. As I began to teach in Colorado Springs then, I found I had an emotional and intellectual problem to solve: how was I going to continue to enjoy life here? I had to reach some sort of reconciliation with the landscape I thought I no longer loved. Slowly photography has enabled me to do that, to discover a way past the nihilism that I had begun to feel. I guess—although I didn't know it at first—what I was looking for was a way to take pictures that would enable me to tell the truth about what had happened here, but also, having told the truth, finally to reach an affirmative position towards it. Degas wrote somewhere that what he was after was a way "to lend enchantment to truth." That's not a bad phrase. It's not too hard to tell the truth, but it's very, very hard to find a way to affirm it. So, in the first years the effort was to discover a style that would enable me somehow to step back from the disaster that's going on…to be truthful about it, but nonetheless to bring to it a larger perspective. […]

Excerpt from: "'The Concern'. Michael Köhler in Conversation with Robert Adams," in *Camera Austria International* 9/1982: 2–16.

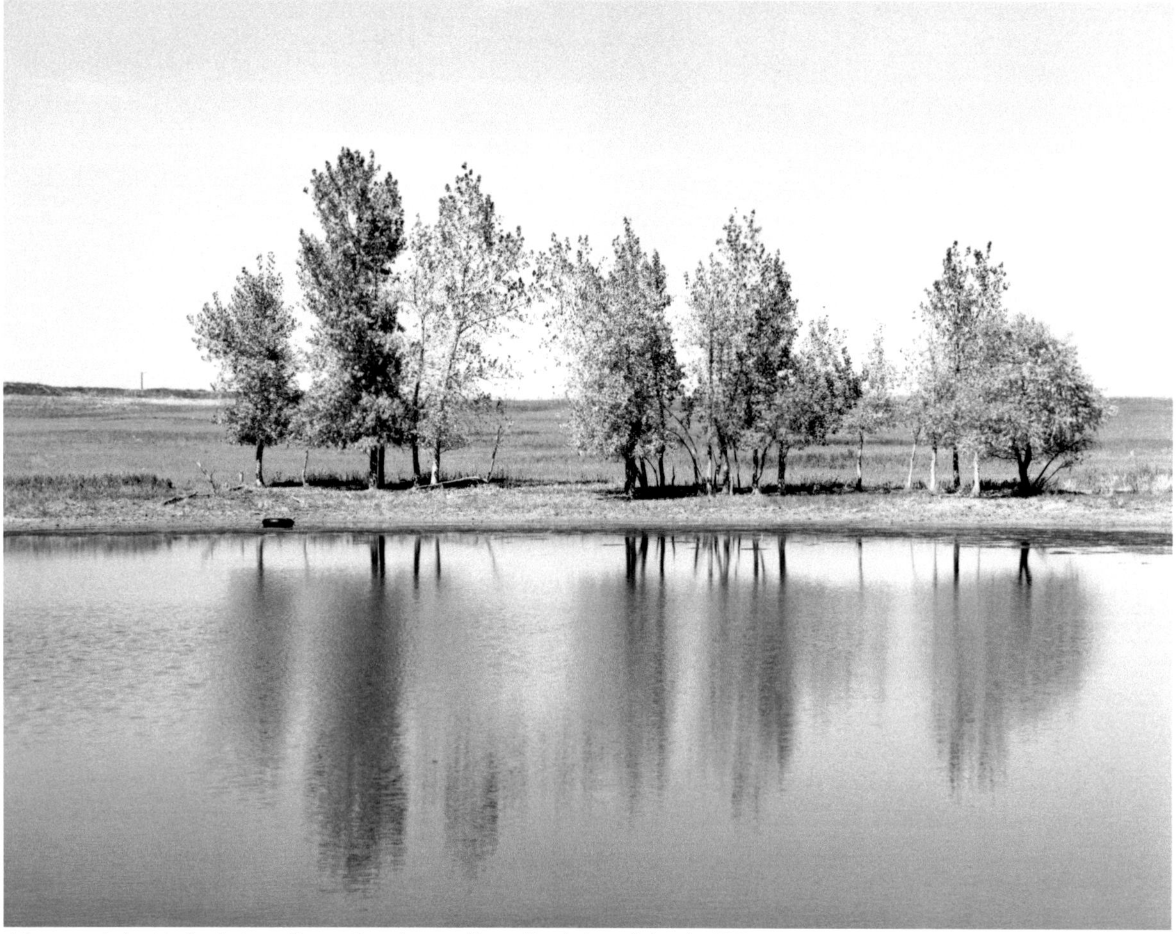

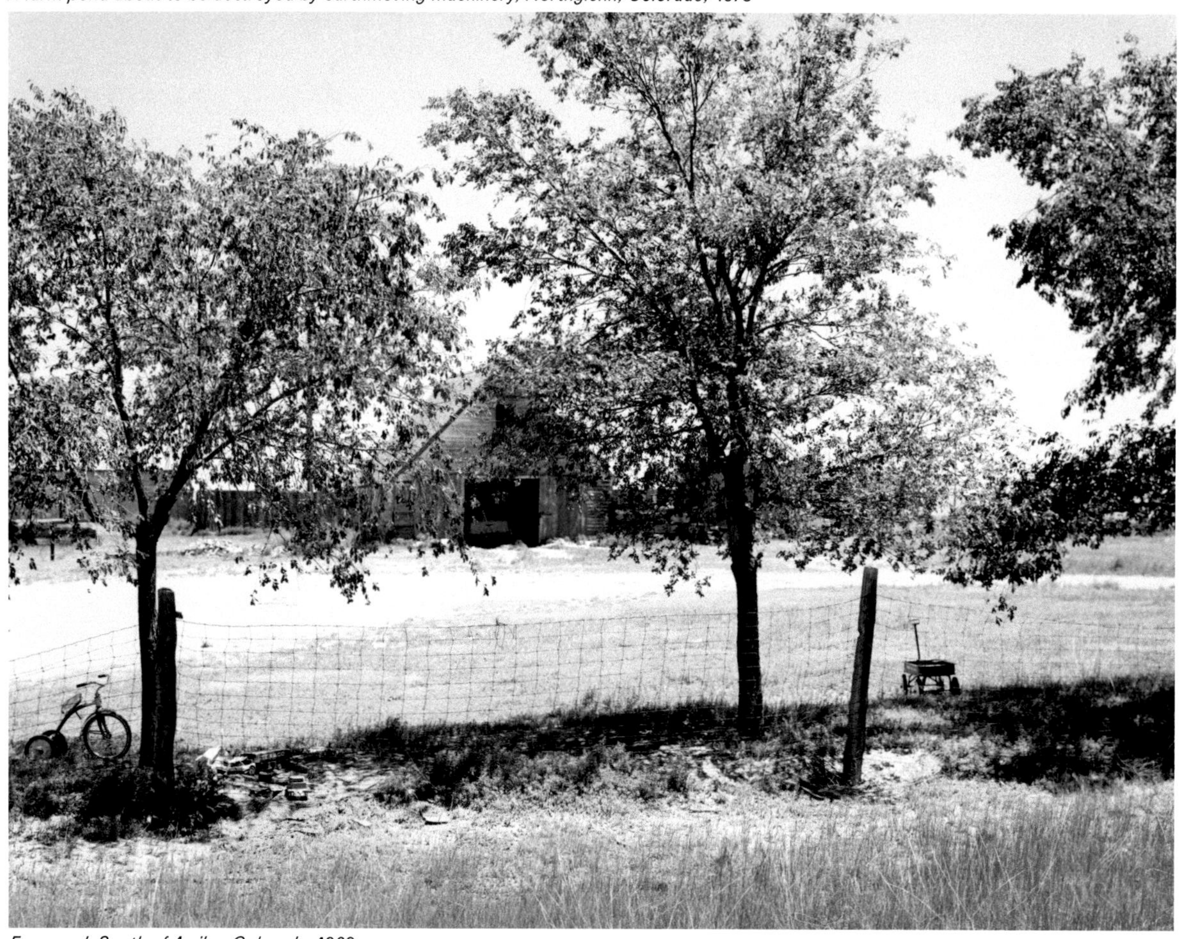

A farm pond about to be destroyed by earthmoving machinery, Northglenn, Colorado, 1973

Farmyard. South of Arriba, Colorado, 1969

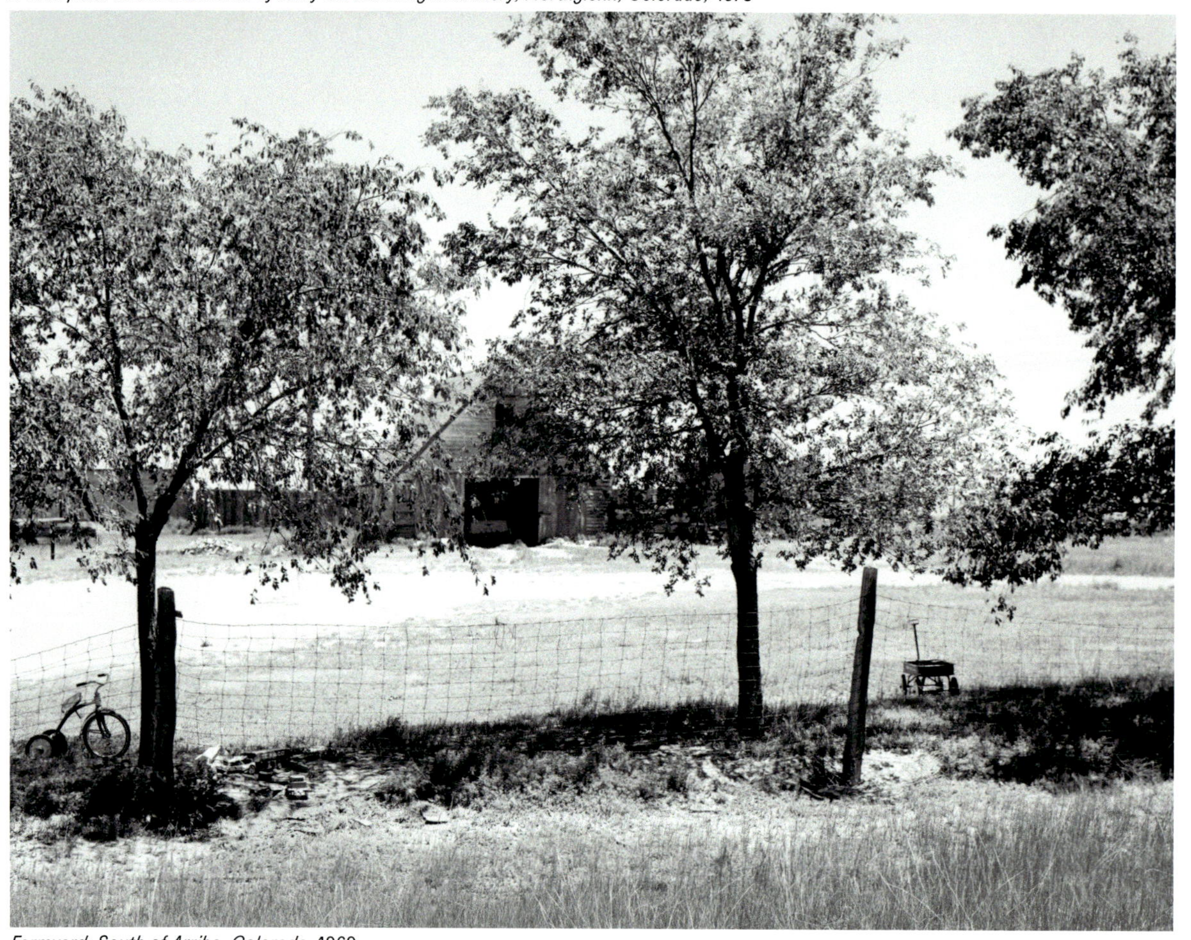

Farmyard. South of Arriba, Colorado, 1969

Camera Austria

International € 14,– **89/2005**

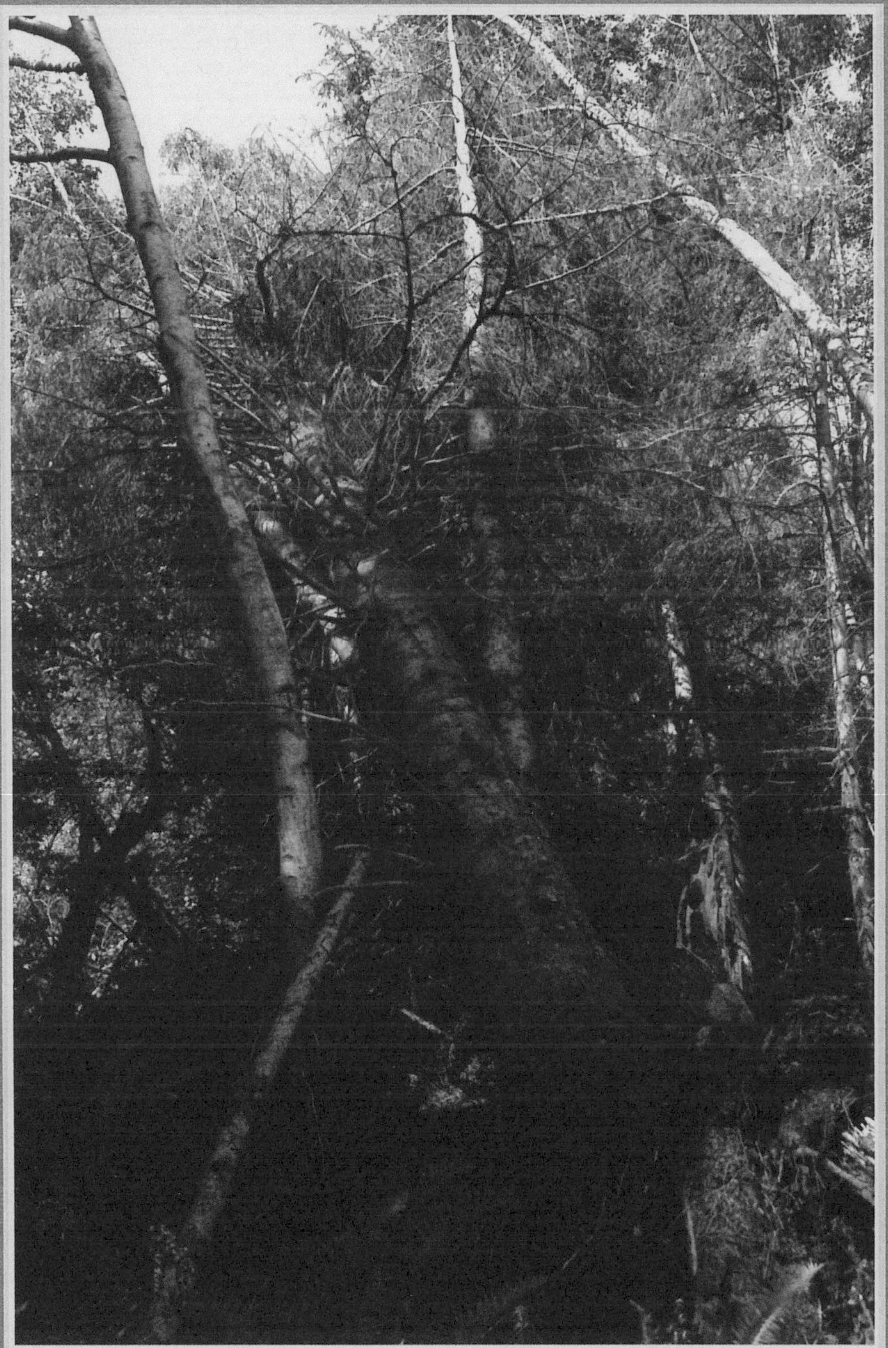

ROBERT ADAMS   THOMAS WESKI   PETER PILLER   MANISHA JOTHADY

INGEBORG STROBL   WOLFGANG KOS   PIOTR UKLAŃSKI   DANIEL BAUMANN

TOM HOLERT   **SEIICHI FURUYA**   HERTA WOLF

FORUM   AUSSTELLUNGEN / EXHIBITIONS   BÜCHER / BOOKS   NACHRICHTEN / NEWS

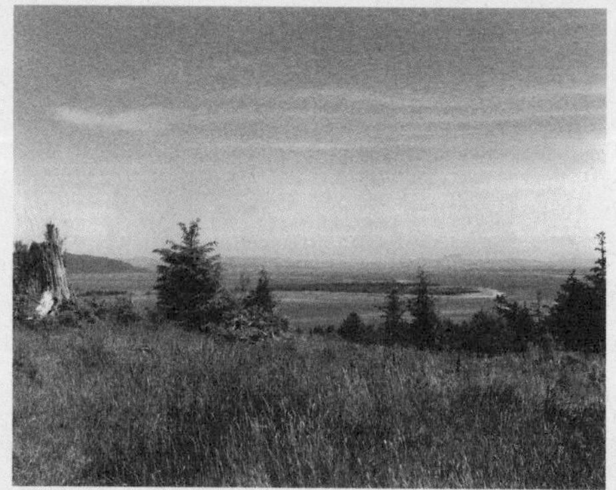

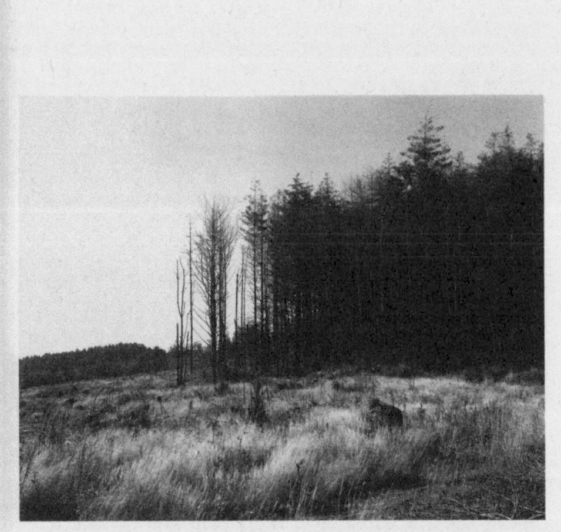

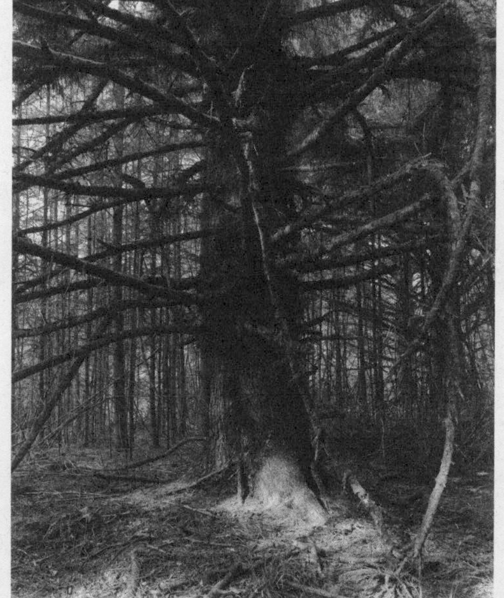

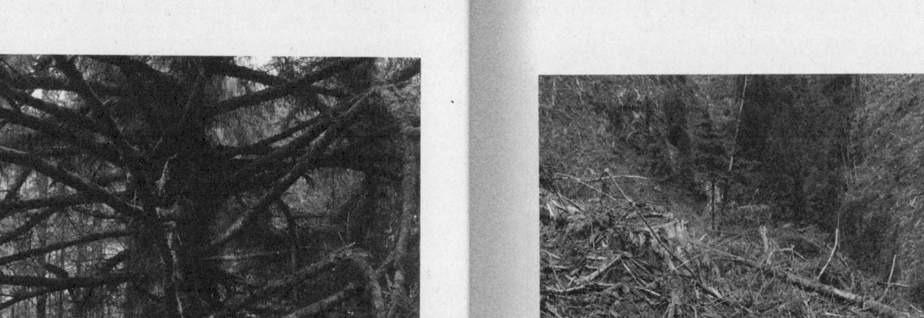

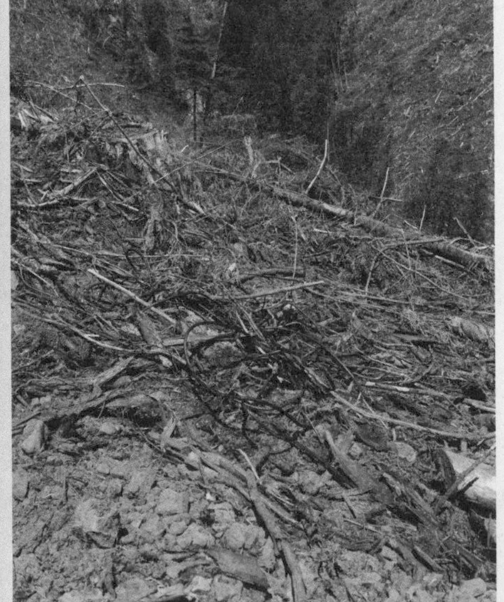

64

Lewis Baltz

Participation at Symposia

1982   Symposion on Photography IV,
17 – 19 October 1982, lecturer

1985   Symposion on Photography VII:
"Europa – Amerika. Hello – Good Bye,
Good Bye – Hello," 4 – 6 October 1985,
concept, lecturer

Camera Austria International

1981   Harald Strobl, "Lewis Baltz," text contribution, Lewis Baltz, "Park City," artist contribution, *Camera Austria International* 5 / 1981

1983   Lewis Baltz, text contribution / artist contribution (journal of Symposia), *Camera Austria International* 11 – 12 / 1983

1985   Lewis Baltz, "Konsumterror," text contribution, Lewis Baltz, "Robert Adams, Our Lives and Our Children," New York, 1983, book review, *Camera Austria International* 18 / 1985

1987   Lewis Baltz, text contribution (journal of Symposion), *Camera Austria International* 22 / 1987

1988   Lewis Baltz, "Notizen zu Waffenruhe," book review, *Camera Austria International* 26 / 1988

1992   "Lewis Baltz. Five Projects 1983 – 1988, Stedelijk Museum, Amsterdam, 1992," book review, *Camera Austria International* 39 / 1992

2012   Mario Pfeifer, "Lewis Baltz, Kunstmuseum Bonn," exhibition review, *Camera Austria International* 119 / 2012

2013   Nora Theiss, "Lewis Baltz," Kestnergesellschaft, Hannover; Albertina, Vienna, exhibition review, *Camera Austria International* 122 / 2013

Exhibitions

1977   *American Photographers*, Galerie im Taxispalais, Innsbruck (AT), Museum des 20. Jahrhunderts, Vienna (AT), exhibition participation

1979   *5 Jahre Fotogalerie im Forum Stadtpark*, exhibition participation

1982   *Fotografie 1982*, exhibition participation

1985   *Europa – Amerika: Hello – Good Bye, Good Bye – Hello*, exhibition participation

Publication

1977   Manfred Willmann, ed., *American Photographers,* Graz, Fotogalerie im Forum Stadtpark, 1977

Workshop

1980   26 – 28 September 1980

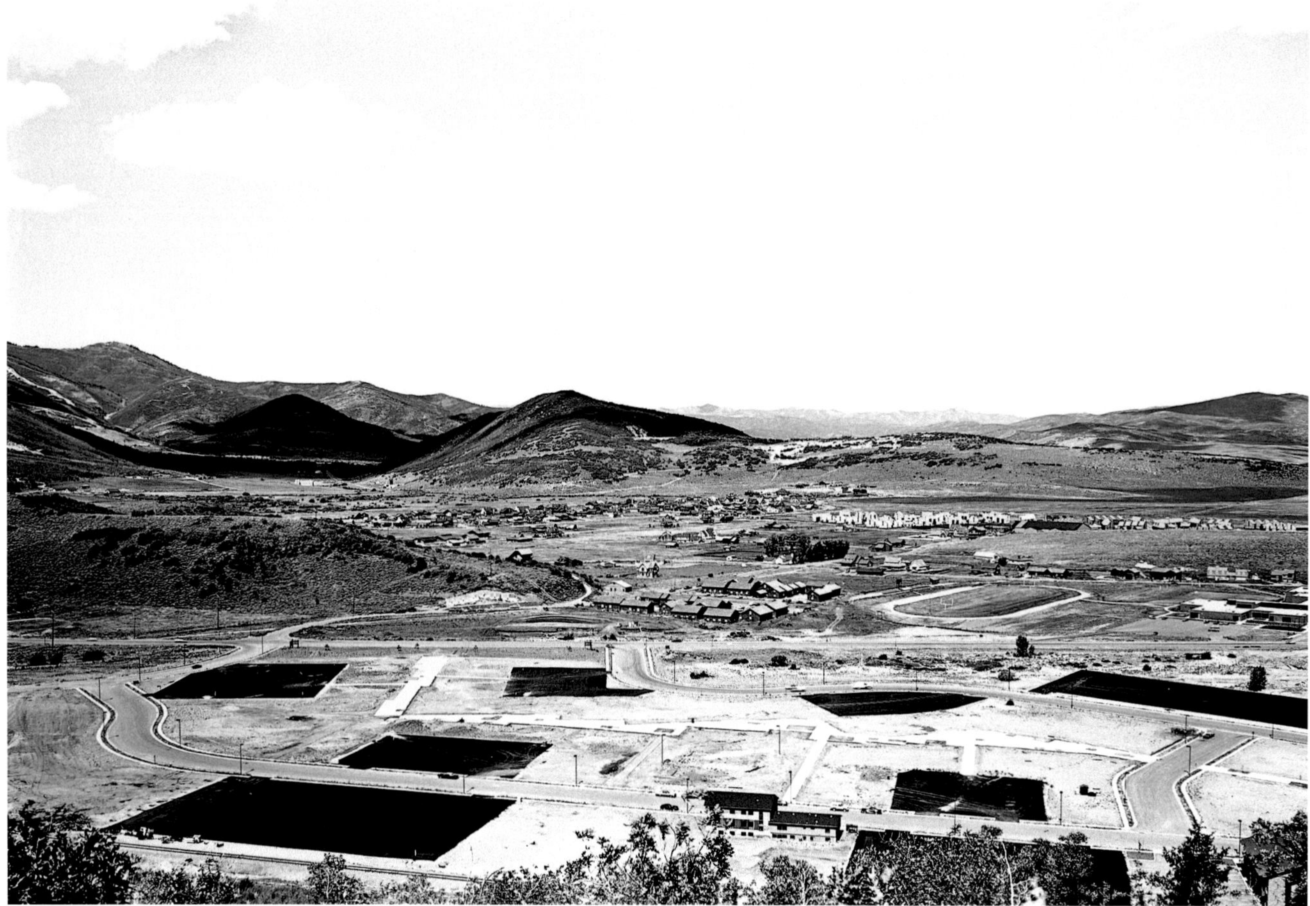

Looking North from Masonic Hill toward Quarry Mountain. In foreground, new parking lots on land between West Sidewinder Drive and State Highway 248. In middle distance, from left: Park Meadows, Subdivisions 1, 2 and 3; Holiday Ranchette Estates; Racquet Club Estates. At far distance on left, Parkwest Ski Area.

From the series "Park City," 1978–1980

Lewis Baltz

Notes on "Park City"

[…] When I first saw Park City it was the land, rather than the structures, that held my interest. Other than in films and photographs of natural catastrophes—or in disaster movies—I had never seen a landscape so bleak, blasted and chaotic. Much of the land was churned and pocked, littered with fragments of wood, twisted wire, rusted metal and broken glass, and supported only the sparsest vegetation. The appearance of "matter out of place" was only partly attributable to the detritus of mining and, later, construction; even the land that had thus far escaped both waves of development looked preternaturally silent and dead. The overall impression was one of purposeless, violent, destruction. During the two and one half years that I worked in Park City that impression never wholly left me and much that I saw later reinforced it. […]

In "Park City," as in most of my previous works, the series and not the individual image is the unit of work. Working in series allows points to be raised, asserted through repetition, critiqued, restructured into subcategories; a visual syntax can be evolved to show a number of facets of the same subject. The effect is comparable with non-narrative film, a "paper movie," to use Larry Sultan's phrase. And, while one "frame" might be more interesting, or esthetically appealing, than another, each is of equal importance and each relies on the context of the total work to achieve significance. The individual image, removed from its context in the group, is a fragment.

Ideally in such a project, the photographer should be invisible and the medium transparent, and I aspire to that level of objectivity. I intend that this work be neutral and uninflected and as free as I can make them from esthetic and ideological posturing. The photographs in "Park City" are made to conform to the conventions of ordinary seeing. I do this in the hope that the works will be seen as factual statements about their subject rather than expressions of the artist's attitudes.

Each image is titled with its exact location, an implicit invitation to a viewer to visit the scene and judge its veracity for him or herself.[1] Equally, the viewer is invited to consider the context from which the image was taken, as much significant information is about what takes place outside the borders of the image. My technique is based on the idea of showing the subject with the maximum possible precision and clarity. In many of the "Park City" images important information exists in small details, or is seen at a distance, which is the reason for my choice of high-definition image. I attempted to give equal emphasis to each area of image, privileging no one area at the expense of another, to permit the viewer to select from an array of democratically rendered information, rather than have the emphasis pre-selected.[2] […]

Excerpt from: Lewis Baltz, *Texts,* (Göttingen: Steidl Verlag, 2012).

1 As one artist and critic, Mario Pfeifer, recently did, not with "Park City," but with *The New Industrial Parks near Irvine, California.* Editor's note: See Pfeifer, *Reconsidering The New Industrial Parks near Irvine, California by Lewis Baltz,* 1974 (Berlin: Sternberg Press, 2011).

2 Joe Deal, several years later, coined the term "optical democracy." I wish I had.

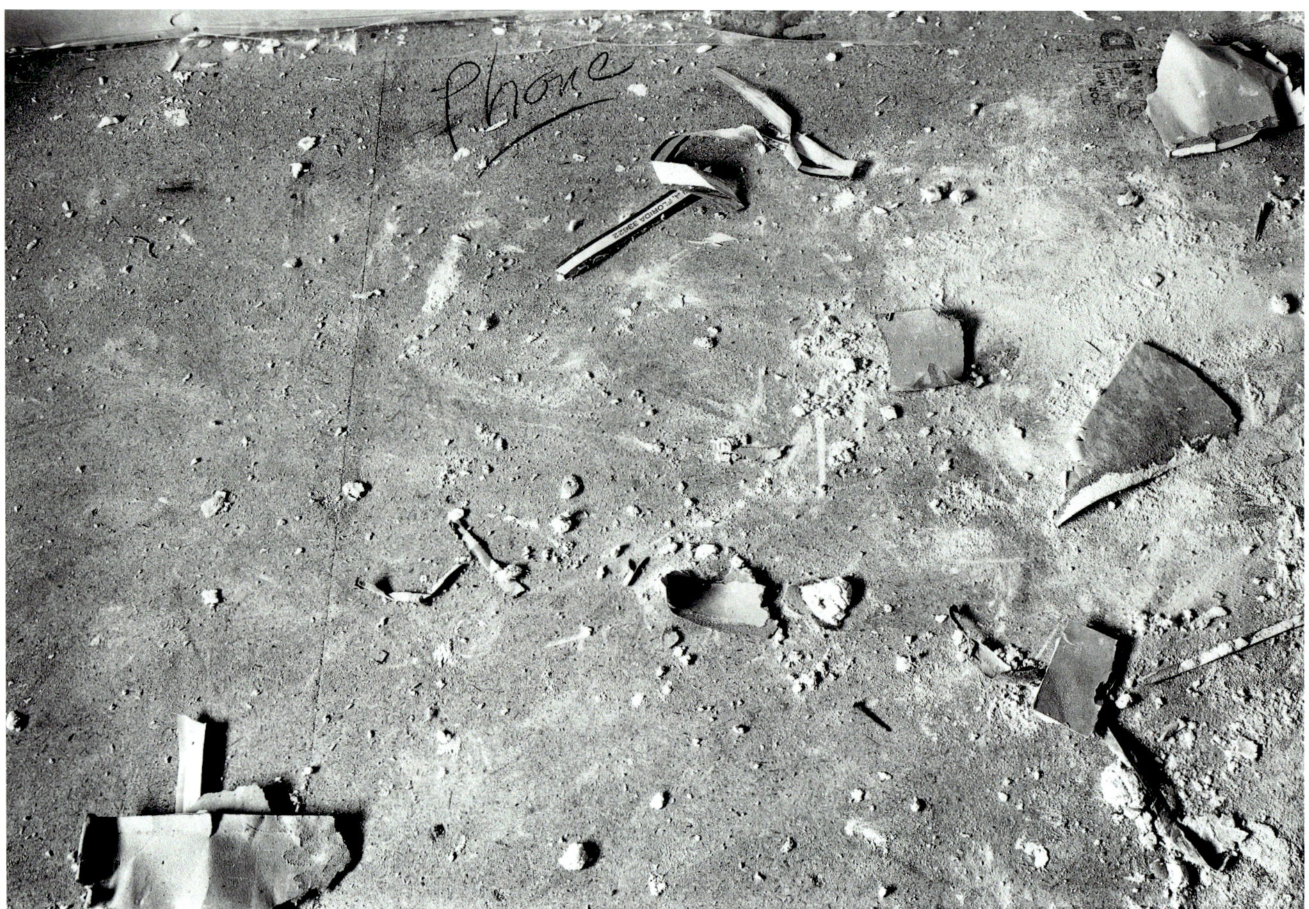

Park City, interior 17.

From the series "Park City," 1978–1980

LEWIS BALTZ: „PARK CITY"
oder „Landscape as real estate"

I

Im Rückblick erscheint manches klarer, als es eigentlich je war. So fällt es zum Beispiel nachträglich leicht, die Geburtsstunde der „Fotogalerie im Forum Stadtpark" aus der letztlich diese Zeitschrift hervorging, auf den Oktober 1974 festzuschreiben, auch wenn diese Stunde in der Außenstelle im Café Schillerhof schlug. Ebenso weiß man heute, daß selbige Galerie im Herbst 1977 aus den Kinderschuhen schlüpfte und daß damals Galerist Manfred Willmann gewissermaßen seine Reifeprüfung ablegte, als er erstmals eine große internationale Ausstellung organisierte, die er dann schlicht „American Photographers" nannte. Unter den acht Ausstellern gab es klingende Namen wie Duane Michals, Lee Friedlander oder Ralph Gibson. Die waren zu der Zeit selbst der unterversorgten österreichischen Fotoszene schon Begriffe. Neben diesen stellten aber auch Fotografen jüngerer Jahrgänge, denen kein Ruf vorauseilte, aus. Deren Aufnahmen, schien es, beeindruckten das Publikum aber nicht minder. Lewis Baltz war einer von diesen.

Sein Beitrag gehörte gewiß zu den stillsten, unaufgeregtesten der Ausstellung. Mit zehn Fotografien von Gebäuden, die leicht als Industriearchitekturen von der nobleren Sorte zu identifizieren waren, behauptete sich Baltz recht tapfer gegen die Phalanx seiner ungestümeren Kollegen. Die einigermaßen flach wirkenden, geradeheraus und ohne Firlefanz fotografierten Bilder, die – obwohl vom Kleinbild – durch technische Brillianz bestachen, gaben nicht vor, mehr sein zu wollen als eben Ansichten von Gebäuden. Und doch vermittelten sie neben jener kühlen Ästhetik, die Fotografien von Beton-, Stahl- und Glasfassaden fast immer ausstrahlen, noch etwas, wovon ich aber damals nicht mehr wußte und sagen konnte, als daß es mich anzog.

II

Zwei Jahre danach zierten wieder Fotografien von Lewis Baltz die Wände des Forum Stadtpark. Drei Bilder aus dem kleinen Portfolio „Nevada" hatte er zu der Sammelausstellung beigesteuert, mit der die Fotogalerie ihr fünfjähriges Bestehen feierte. Diesmal blieb der Eindruck schwächer, denn die Masse der damals ausgestellten Fotografien erdrückte reihum das jeweils einzelne Set jedes Fotografen und minderte es zu einem bloßen „Beitrag" herab.

Ein weiteres Jahr später bekam ich aber erneut Arbeiten von Lewis Baltz zu Gesicht. Nicht drei, nicht zehn oder vielleicht zwanzig, nein, über hundert. Und auch hingen sie nicht an den Wänden der Galerie, sondern lagen ausgebreitet auf einem ungeheuer langen Tisch. Lewis Baltz hatte sie selbst mitgebracht und dort – in drei Etappen – aufgelegt, als er im Herbst 1980 für eine Woche nach Graz kam, um zwei Workshops zu halten.

Was er damals in einem schweren Koffer von London über Zürich nach Berlin und von dort über Frankfurt nach Graz und ungefähr wieder zurück schleppte, war sein neuestes Portfolio „Park City".

III

Drei Tage dauerte der Workshop, den ich mitmachte. In dieser Zeit lernte ich nicht nur die neuen Bilder eines Fotografen kennen, sondern auch den Menschen, der sie hergestellt hatte. Das vage Bild, das seine Biografie in Form von Ortsnamen und Jahreszahlen hinterlassen hatte, wurde nun mit Leben aufgefüllt. Ich lernte den Fotografen Lewis Baltz kennen, wenigstens den öffentlichen Teil seiner Person, jenen Teil also, den er in seine Arbeit einbringt, und den diese wiederum freigibt. Und der ist freilich bei Lewis Baltz, wenn auch nicht sofort greifbar, doch recht beträchtlich.

18

Nochmal kurz zurück: Lewis Baltz fing 1967 als Kunststudent an einer kalifornischen Hochschule zu fotografieren an. Es sah bald ein, daß das Einzelbild seinen Absichten und Vorstellungen nicht gehorchte, also begann er mit Serien. Seine erste abgeschlossene Arbeit, das Portfolio „Tract Houses", legte er 1974 vor. Nüchtern und sachlich hielt er darin die landverschwenderische Zersiedelung seiner eigenen Heimat fest. Über die Gründe und den Anlaß dazu sagt er: „Jedermann, den ich kannte, auch ich selbst, war in so einem Haus aufgewachsen. Ich fand es erstaunlich, daß bei der großen Zahl von Fotografen in Kalifornien keiner es der Mühe wert hielt, etwas, das so allgegenwärtig war, zu fotografieren." Damit aber war die eine Hälfte des Weges, den der Fotograf Lewis Baltz gehen sollte, bereits abgesteckt. Er könne nur Dinge gut fotografieren, mit denen er vertraut sei, meint er, Dinge, die ihn unmittelbar berührten.

IV

Wachsamkeit und Empfindsamkeit der Umwelt – auch der unbelebten gegenüber – standen also am Beginn. Baltz war von Jugend auf betroffen von der Gewalt und der Gewissenlosigkeit, mit der der Mensch in die Natur eindringt, die ihm, wie er sagt, allmählich sogar in Haß auszuarten scheinen. Der Westen Amerikas, in dem er großgeworden ist, bot ihm dann auch zu Hauf Beispiele, wie rücksichtslos die Menschen mit ihrem Lebensraum verfahren. Lewis Baltz's Arbeiten legen beredtes Zeugnis dafür ab, wie diese Haltung Schule gemacht hat, und auch dafür, wie tief sie in ihm ... Wie er selbst zugibt, kenne seine Fotografie von Anfang nur das eine Thema: die Landschaft im Übergang von einer Naturlandschaft zu einer vom Menschen geschaffenen Landschaft. Und diese Veränderung schmerzt doppelt, weil sie nicht nur so gewaltsam, sondern geradezu planmäßig vorangetrieben wird, und weil sie meist in Zerstörung mündet. Diese aber ist immer unumkehrbar, also endgültig.

V

War es in der Serie „Tract Houses" die geschwürartige Ausbreitung der typisch westamerikanischen Einfamilienhäuser, die Baltz geflissentlich aufzeigte, so versuchte er in seinem zweiten großen Portfolio „The New Industrial Parks Near Irvine, California" die vom Reißbrett weg verordnete Verbauung eines Gebietes von der Größe Wiens, das einst der Zitrusgarten von Los Angeles gewesen war, fotografisch sinnfällig zu machen. Zwei wesentlich begrenztere Aufgaben, an denen Baltz in dieser Zeit arbeitete, führten ihn zwar aus seinem Heimatstaat heraus, nach Maryland und Nevada, sein Stil und die Thematik änderten sich jedoch nur wenig. Sein bislang letztes und umfangreichstes Projekt in Park City, Utah, ist dann nur die logische Folge der vorangegangenen Serien. Mehr denn je bleibt Baltz darin seinem selbstgewählten Auftrag verpflichtet. Zweieinhalb Jahre lang bearbeitete er so geduldig wie mechanisch, und doch scheinbar absichtslos, das neue Thema: das Vordringen des Menschen und seines zivilisatorischen Anhangs in die Landschaft. Während er jedoch früher nur den Endpunkt eines solchen Prozesses dokumentierte, zeichnete er in „Park City" die einzelnen Phasen des Vorgangs selbst auf. Zudem ist er in Park City noch eine dritte Schicht: die Überreste der Eingriffe in die Natur vor gut einem Jahrhundert, als in dem hochgelegenen Talbecken edles Metall gefunden wurde und die Minen buchstäblich aus dem Boden schossen. Der Boom, der Park City ergriff, dauerte gerade so lange, wie die Silberadern tief waren. Die folgende Abwanderung wurde erst in den letzten zwei Jahrzehnten ...

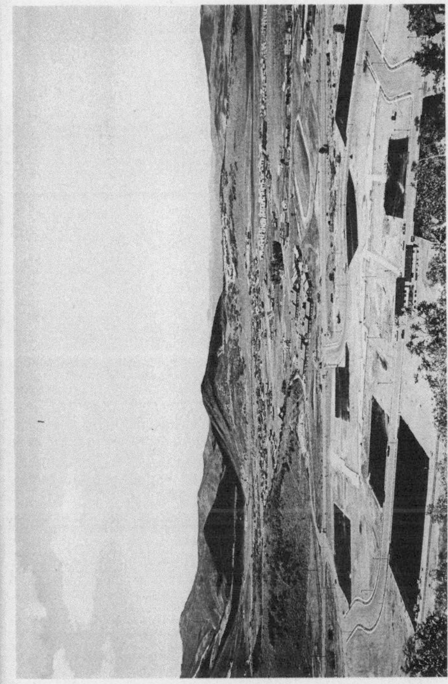

1. Looking North from Masonic Hill toward Quarry Mountain. In Foreground, new parking lots on land between West Sidewinder Drive and State Highway 248. In middle distance, from left: Park Meadows, Subdivisions 1, 2 and 3; Holiday Ranchette Estates; Racquet Club Estates. At far distance on left, Parkwest Ski Area.

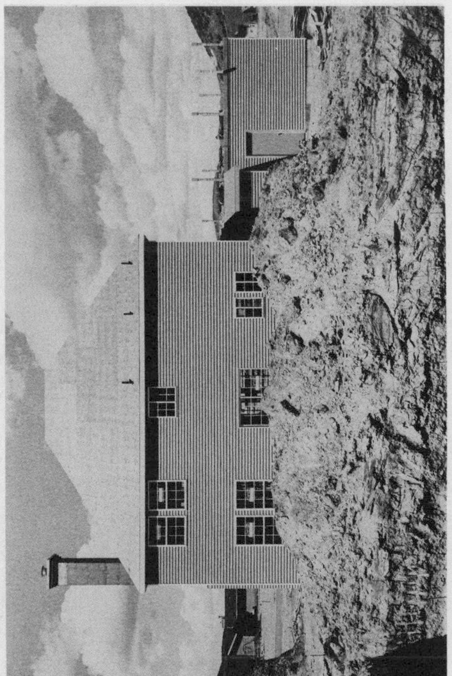

44. Prospector Park, Subdivision Phase III, Lot 123, looking North.

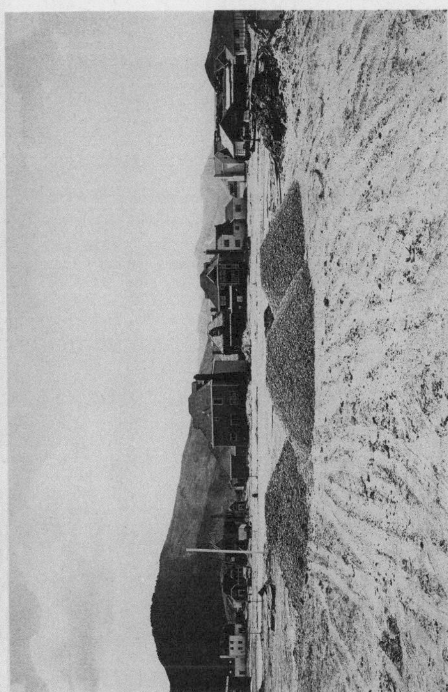

51. Prospector Park, Subdivision Phase III, Lot 160, looking West.

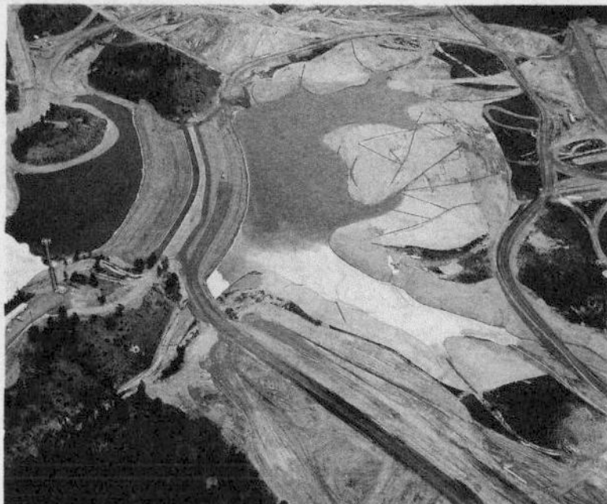

DAVID HANSON, *Excavation, deforestation and waste ponds. June 1984*
Ausschachtung, Rodung und Grundwasserseen. Juni 1984

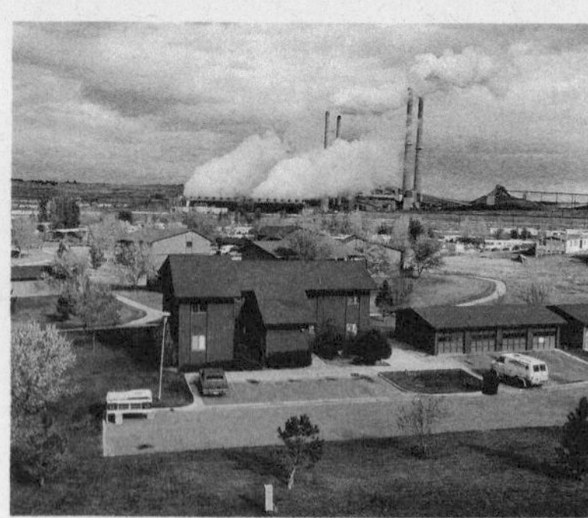

DAVID HANSON, *View from 1st Baptist Church of Colstrip; Company houses and power plant. October 1984.*
Blick von der 1st Baptist Church in Colstrip: Betriebsgebäude und Kraftwerk. Oktober 1984
Aus der Serie / *from the series:* Colstrip, Montana

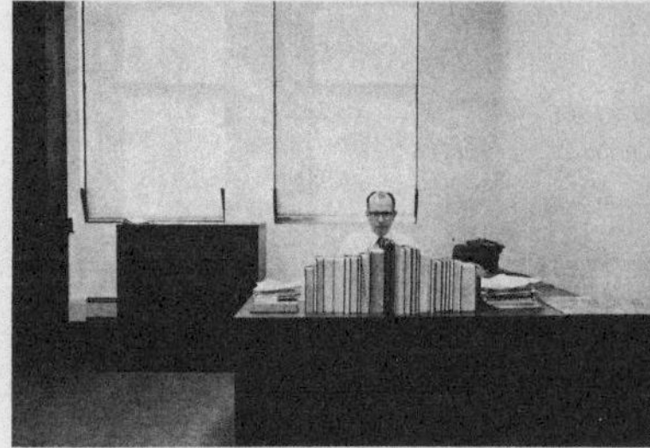

Lewis Mumford's image of the pyramid as a symbol of the megamachine ran through my head a lot in 1976 and 1977 when I photographed Standard Oil. Mumford is one of my heroes. He hypothesized that the pyramids were built block by stone block by masons who began their trade in early childhood. They learned from their fathers to chisel granite boulders by hand so that they would fit together and be level to within one quarter of an inch in one half a mile. The resigned acceptance of the precise machine-like activity of men was the norm while working at Standard. If your father is an engineer and you are an engineer, it's hard to know there is anything else to a work life other than just chipping away at what "they" give you to do.

In den Jahren 1976 und 1977, als ich Standard Oil fotografierte, ist mir oft Lewis Mumfords Bild der Pyramide als Symbol der Megamaschine durch den Kopf gegangen. Mumford ist einer von meinen Helden. Seine Hypothese war, daß Pyramiden Stein um Stein von Handwerkern gebaut wurden, die schon in früher Kindheit angelernt wurden. Sie lernten von ihren Vätern, wie man mit Handarbeit Bausteine aus großen Granitblöcken meißelt, so präzise, daß sie zu Mauern von einer halben Meile Länge zentimetergenau in der Waage gefügt werden konnten. Das resignierte Hinnehmen dieser präzisen, maschinenartigen Tätigkeit von Menschenhand war bei Standard Oil die Norm. Wenn der Vater Ingenieur gewesen ist und man selbst Ingenieur ist, kann man sich kaum vorstellen, daß es im Leben auch etwas anderes gibt, als das, was sie einem Tag für Tag zu tun geben.

CHAUNCEY HARE, aus / *from: This was Corporate America, 1984*

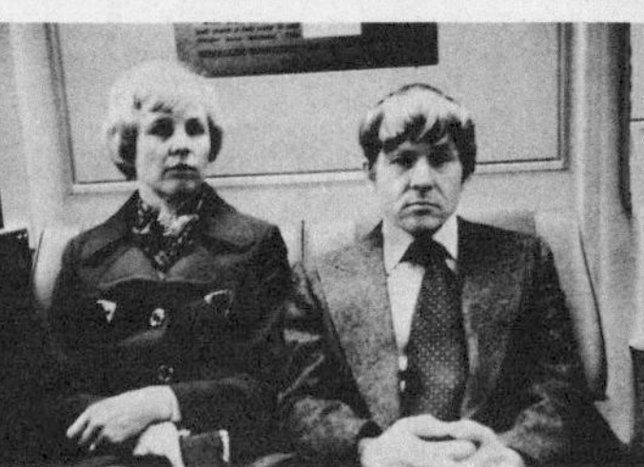

Late one afternoon I was making a photograph of the refinery from a hill in nearby Point Richmond where I live. Suddenly, through the miracle of imagination, I saw 500 years into the future. A National Park Service tour guide was describing the scene before me to an assembled group of tourists – of which I was one. "Here lies the largest collection of valves, pipes, compressors, distillation columns and furnace stacks remaining in the world," he said. "The gasoline and engine oil manufactured in this refinery was used to fuel and lubricate the automobiles that traveled the roads of the country that once was corporate America."

Einmal habe ich spät am Nachmittag die Raffinerie fotografiert, und zwar von einem Hügel bei Point Richmond, wo ich wohne. Plötzlich blickte ich 500 Jahre in die Zukunft – ein Wunder der Vorstellungskraft. Ein Führer des National Park Service beschrieb einer Touristengruppe, zu der auch ich gehörte, die vor mir liegende Szene. "Hier befindet sich die größte weltweit noch erhaltene Ansammlung von Ventilen, Rohren, Kompressoren, Destillationszylindern und Schloten", sagte er. "Mit dem in dieser Raffinerie hergestellten Benzin und Motoröl würden seinerzeit die Autos betrieben und geschmiert, die auf den Straßen eines von Konzernen und großen Firmen regierten Amerika unterwegs waren."

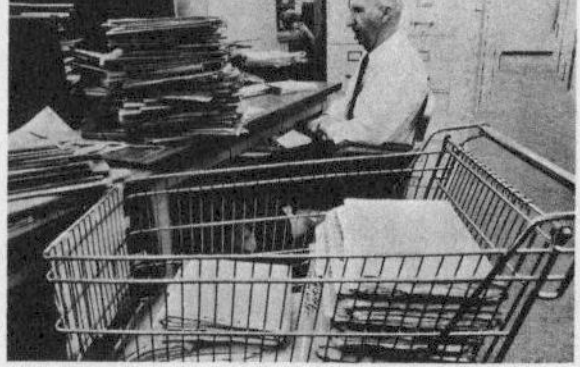

The thing that strikes you immediately about the jobs at the Social Security Administration is the boredom. Think about paging through manila file folder after manila file folder eight hours a day, five days a week, year after year. The file folders are contained in row after row of file cabinets – half a mile long. When I photographed at the Western Program Center in Richmond in 1978, I thanked my lucky stars I wasn't working there. Two years later I was paging through manila file folder after manila file folder in my new job at the Environmental Protection Agency.

Was einem bei den Jobs im Amt der Sozialversicherung sofort auffällt, ist die Langeweile, die da herrscht. Man stelle sich das vor: Akten und Akten durchblättern, acht Stunden am Tag, fünf Tage in der Woche, Jahr für Jahr. Die Akten werden in Reihen von Aktenschränken aufbewahrt, und so eine Reihe ist eine halbe Meile lang. Als ich 1978 im Western Program Center in Richmond fotografiert habe, war ich heilfroh, daß ich dort nicht arbeiten mußte. Zwei Jahre später habe ich selbst bei meinem neuen Job bei der Umweltschutzbehörde Akten und nochmals Akten durchgeblättert.

CHAUNCEY HARE, aus / *from: This was Corporate America, 1984*

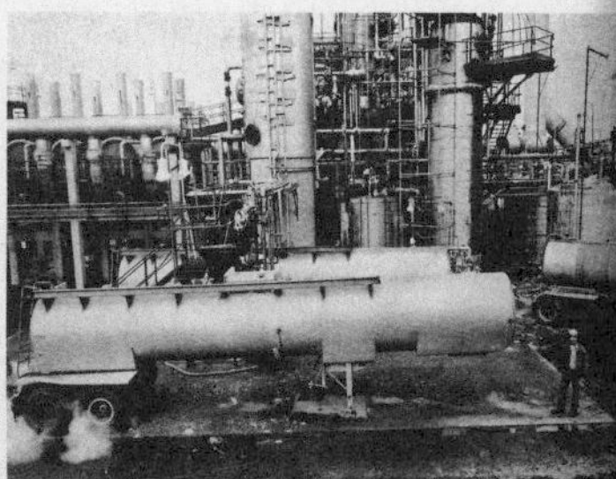

I helped design distillation columns to make gasoline and chemicals but I never had to operate these units until the refinery strike of 1969. I was assigned the job of lube oil pumper and the first thing I did was accidentally pump the wrong oil into the wrong tank ending up with 500 barrels of off-test lube oil. I have enormous respect for refinery shift workers who can line up in perfect order more than thirty valves on a lube oil line at 2:00 A.M. in the driving rain – and not one of the valves will be open to the wrong tank. One senior operator may be required to run an entire chemical unit by himself, including filling the tank trucks with the chemicals the plant produces. The imminent possibilities of fire and explosion, the responsibility for making on-test products, the constant exposure to chemicals and the shift schedule makes this job extremely stressful. It amazes me that some men have been refinery operators for more than thirty years and have lived to tell about it.

Ich hatte bei der Konstruktion von Destillationszylindern zur Herstellung von Benzin mitgearbeitet, aber solche Anlagen bis zum Raffineriestreik im Jahr 1969 nie selbst bedient. Ich wurde als Schmierölpumper eingeteilt, und als erstes pumpte ich gleich das falsche Öl in den falschen Tank und produzierte 500 Barrels minderwertiges Öl. Ich habe die größte Hochachtung vor den Raffineriearbeitern, die in Wind und Wetter um 2 Uhr morgens über dreißig Ventile an einer Schmierölleitung richtig bedienen, so daß kein Öl in den falschen Tank fließt. Es kommt vor, daß ein Vorarbeiter eine komplette chemische Anlage allein bedienen muß und die hergestellten Chemieprodukte auch noch auf Lastwagen verlädt. Die ständige Brand- und Explosionsgefahr, die Verantwortung, normgerechte Ware zu produzieren, die Tatsache, daß man Schadstoffen ausgesetzt ist und der Schichtbetrieb schaffen bei dieser Arbeit extremen Streß. Ich staune über die Männer, die seit dreißig Jahren in der Raffinerie arbeiten und noch am Leben sind und davon erzählen können.

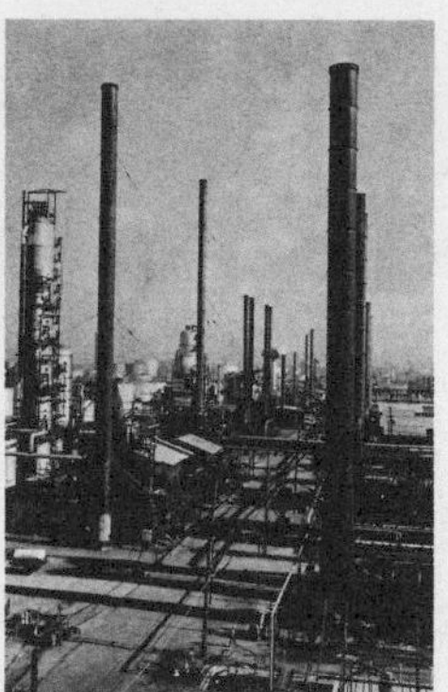

I was riding a Bay Area Rapid Transit train opposite a man and his wife who stared passively at me and my camera. I felt as though I were looking at myself and my ex-wife ten years earlier. The man's hair was combed forward like mine. He had a forlorn and helpless look about him – perhaps he was thinking about the pointless engineering routine he lived daily. As I pressed the shutter, I found I was angry at this man (myself) for waiting so long to do something that would finally break that routine! In 1983 when I look at the picture I made in 1978, I'm learning to accept both the man in the photograph and the photographer who angrily took the picture of the look-alike train rider.

Ich saß in einem Städteschnellzug in der Nähe von San Francisco einem Mann und seiner Frau gegenüber, die mich und meine Kamera passiv anstarrten. Mir war, als hätte ich mich selbst und meine Exfrau vor mir, wie wir zehn Jahre zuvor gewesen waren. Der Mann hatte, wie ich, das Haar in die Stirn gekämmt und einen verlorenen, hilflosen Ausdruck – vielleicht dachte er gerade an seine tägliche sinnlose Technikerroutine. Während ich auf den Auslöser drückte, war ich zornig auf diesen Mann (auf mich selbst), weil er sich so lange Zeit ließ, endlich etwas zu tun, um diese Routine zu unterbrechen! Wenn ich nun, im Jahr 1983, dieses Bild ansehe, das ich 1978 gemacht habe, lerne ich sowohl den Mann im Bild als auch den Fotografen zu akzeptieren, der zornig sein Konterfei im Zugabteil fotografiert hat.

CHAUNCEY HARE, aus / *from: This was Corporate America, 1984*

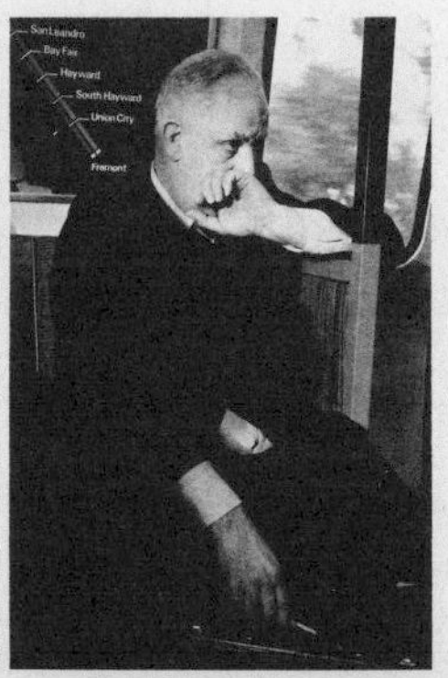

I made one photograph of a transit rider that I exhibited at the San Francisco Art Institute when I was a student there in 1979. It was the only picture stolen from the show. The photograph was of an elderly and successful business man with his chin resting defensively on one arm. I had a Charles Reich quote beneath the photo, "What corporate executives need is not more status symbols, not another Cadillac in the garage. What each of them needs is a hug." I like to think some students at the Institute walked off with the photo because it spoke to him about his father's predicament.

Ich habe ein Bild von einem Schnellzugpassagier gemacht, das ich am San Francisco Art Institute ausgestellt habe, als ich dort im Jahr 1979 studierte. Es war das einzige Bild, das aus der Ausstellung gestohlen wurde. Es zeigt einen älteren, erfolgreichen Geschäftsmann, der defensiv das Kinn auf den Arm stützt. Unter dem Bild stand ein Zitat von Charles Reich: "Die Manager der großen Konzerne brauchen nicht mehr Statussymbole, nicht noch einen Cadillac in der Garage. Vielmehr haben sie es nötig, daß jemand sie in die Arme nimmt." Ich stelle mir vor, daß irgendein Student das Foto geklaut hat, weil es ihm das Dilemma seines Vaters vor Augen geführt hat.

Participation at Symposion

1985   Symposion on Photography VII: "Europa – Amerika. Hello – Good Bye, Good Bye – Hello," 4–6 October 1985, lecturer

Camera Austria International

1983   Luigi Ghirri, " 'Endless Worlds' zu William Egglestons Arbeiten," text contribution, William Eggleston, "Louisiana Project," artist contribution, *Camera Austria International* 13/1983

1987   William Eggleston, "Democratic Forest," artist contribution (journal of Symposia), *Camera Austria International* 22/1987

1990   Joachim Brohm, "William Eggleston. The Democratic Forest," book review, *Camera Austria International* 31–32/1990

1992   Joachim Brohm, "William Eggleston. Ancient and Modern, Barbican Art Gallery, London," exhibition review, *Camera Austria International* 39/1992

2000   Christine Frisinghelli, "William Eggleston: Morals of Vision," text contribution, William Eggleston, artist contribution, *Camera Austria International* 72/2000

2002   Anne Bertrand, "William Eggleston, Fondation Cartier pour l'art contemporain, Paris," exhibition review, *Camera Austria International* 77/2002

2003   Magdalena Kröner, "William Eggleston: Los Alamos, Museum Ludwig, Cologne," exhibition review, *Camera Austria International* 82/2003

2004   Carolin Förster, "Double Exposure. William Eggleston & Wilmar Koenig, Neuer Berliner Kunstverein, Berlin," exhibition review, *Camera Austria International* 88/2004

2009   Maren Lübbke-Tidow, "William Eggleston: Democratic Camera. Photographs and Videos 1961–2008, Haus der Kunst, Munich," exhibition review, *Camera Austria International* 106/2009

Exhibitions

1983   *Kenia,* solo exhibition
1985   *Europa – Amerika: Hello – Good Bye, Good Bye – Hello*, exhibition contribution

Workshop

1983   7–8 May 1983

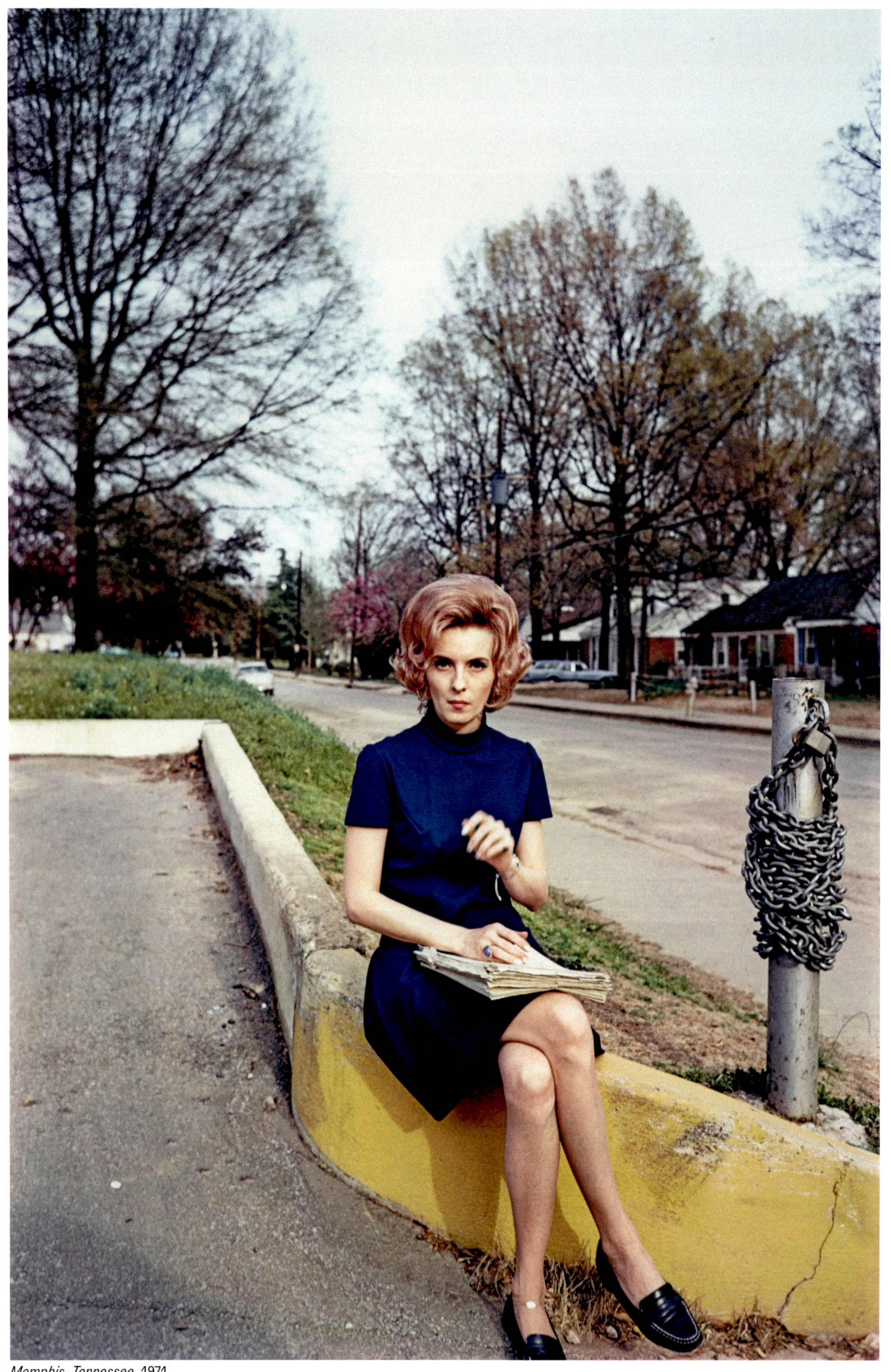

Memphis, Tennessee, 1971

William Eggleston

Lewis Baltz on William Eggleston

[…] Most writing on Eggleston's work has shown a preoccupation with two of its most obvious features, his southernness and his debt to the aesthetic of the color snapshot. Little more needs to be said on the topic of southernness; it is a simplistic and ultimately sterile approach to Eggleston's photographs. His appropriation of the traits of the color snapshot, however, is a more complex and, apparently, more contentious issue. The most persistent criticism that has followed Eggleston since his 1976 Museum of Modern Art exhibition and book has taken the tone that he has failed to improve upon his vernacular model, that his photographs are "merely" snapshots.[1]

To the extent that modernism required each artist to reinvent his medium, Eggleston reinvented color photography, using features of the color snapshot as his benchmarks, in much the same way that Stephen Shore restructured the conventions of commercial color photography into a serious instrument of contemporary expression.

Since the 1960s the snapshot has acquired an elevated status in the hierarchy of imagery. Enthusiastically extravagant claims have been put forward in its behalf: it is the most democratic instance of the most democratic medium yet devised by the mind of man; it is the perfect expression of the innocent eye. Whatever else, it has certainly been a superior vehicle of curatorial and critical hubris.

Unfortunately the qualities that sophisticated observers appreciate in snapshots are usually the very qualities that make them dismal failures in the eyes of their anonymous authors. "Successful" snapshots don't interest us very much: they too closely resemble the post cards, studio portraits, and magazine photos that they mimic. (So much for "the innocent eye.") The failed snapshot, however, earns our patronizing admiration by its surreal juxtapositions, touching clumsiness, and nostalgic content.

That most snapshots "fail" is no mystery; exactly how they do so is another matter, one whose implications escaped almost everyone except Eggleston, who learned, or intuited, how utterly alienating snapshots could be when they failed to close—visually and psychologically—with their nominal subject.

It is this awkwardly disengaged quality of the failed snapshot that Eggleston uses to supply his photographs with their tenseness and their ineluctable alienness. This "offness," to use Janet Malcolm's word, rescues Eggleston's best photographs from the vapid seductive glamour of photographic color, a glamour that in less intelligent hands transforms everything—especially the color photograph itself—into saccharine visual merchandise. When Eggleston is at his best, not even the cloying sweetness of photographic color can span the distance between the viewer and the subject. In that sense, though only in that sense, his work can be said to be impenetrable. And this device supports the central irony in Eggleston's photographs: images of the American home place, inviting on their surface and ice cold at their heart, like images from another planet.

Eggleston's other noteworthy attainment is more traditional in photographic practice. He has annexed more new territory into photography than any of his contemporaries with the obvious exception of Lee Friedlander. The newly identified subjects have usually vantage points: children's toys, Dymo labels, an airline cocktail in its distasteful plastic glass, an uncommonly ugly Venetian glass bowl: trivial stuff that other photographers have mistakenly found beneath their attention. Eggleston seems to pay rapt, if sporadic, attention to everything democratically.

There is a canny, knowing quality to this vein of Eggleston's work, yet the images seem, almost offhand, inviting that most unintentionally flattering criticism: "Why would anyone make a photograph of that?" […]

Excerpt from: Lewis Baltz, "Konsumterror: Late-Industrial Alienation," in *Camera Austria International* 18/1985: 16–27. This essay was delivered at Mills College, Oakland, California, in a slightly revised form, in November 1983.

1 The most literate and perceptive discussion to date of William Eggleston's work can be found in Mark Haworth-Booth's introduction to the Victoria and Albert Museum's exhibition catalog *William Eggleston, Colour Photographs from the American South* (London: 1983).

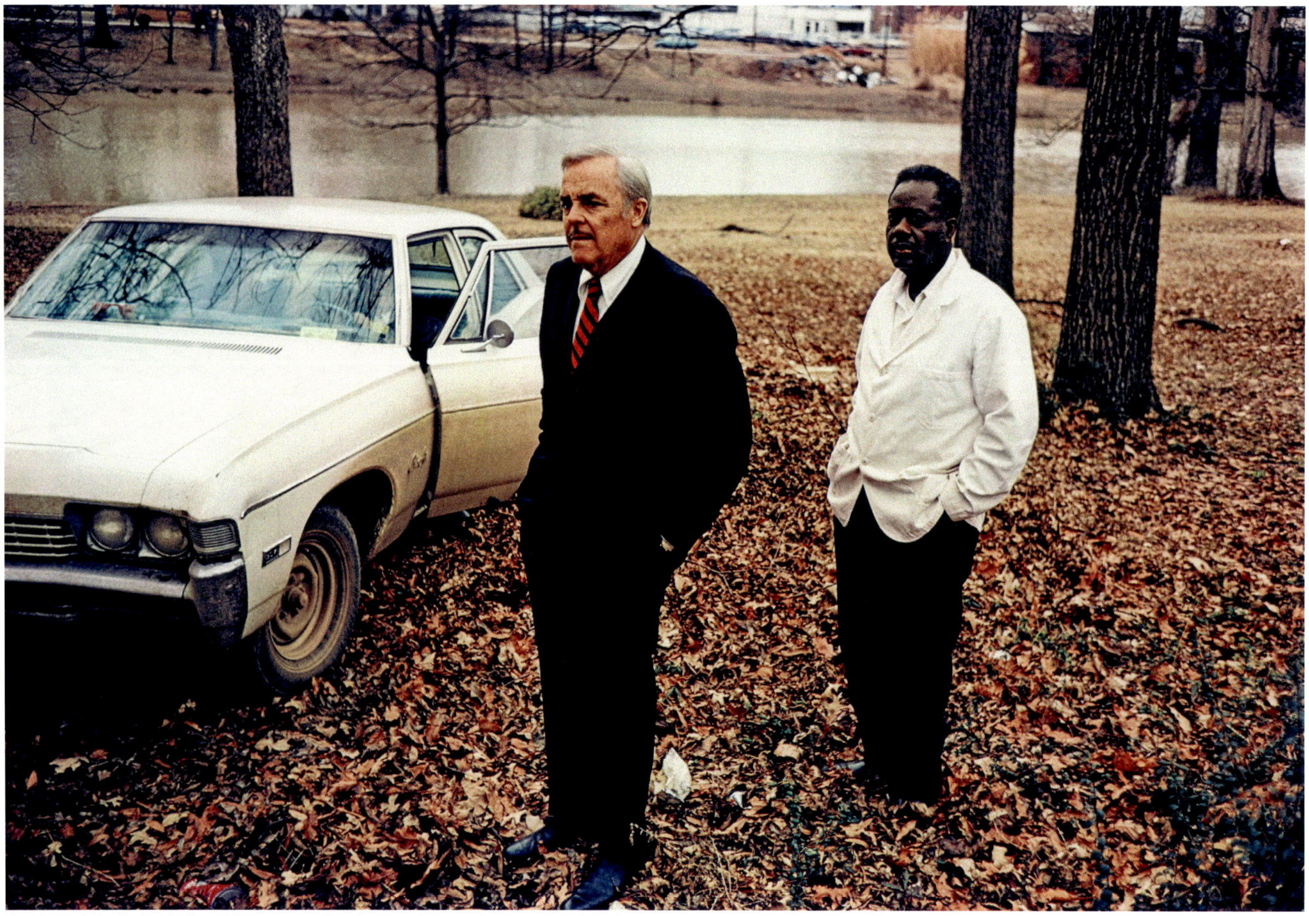

Sumner, Mississippi, Cassidy Bayou in background, 1971

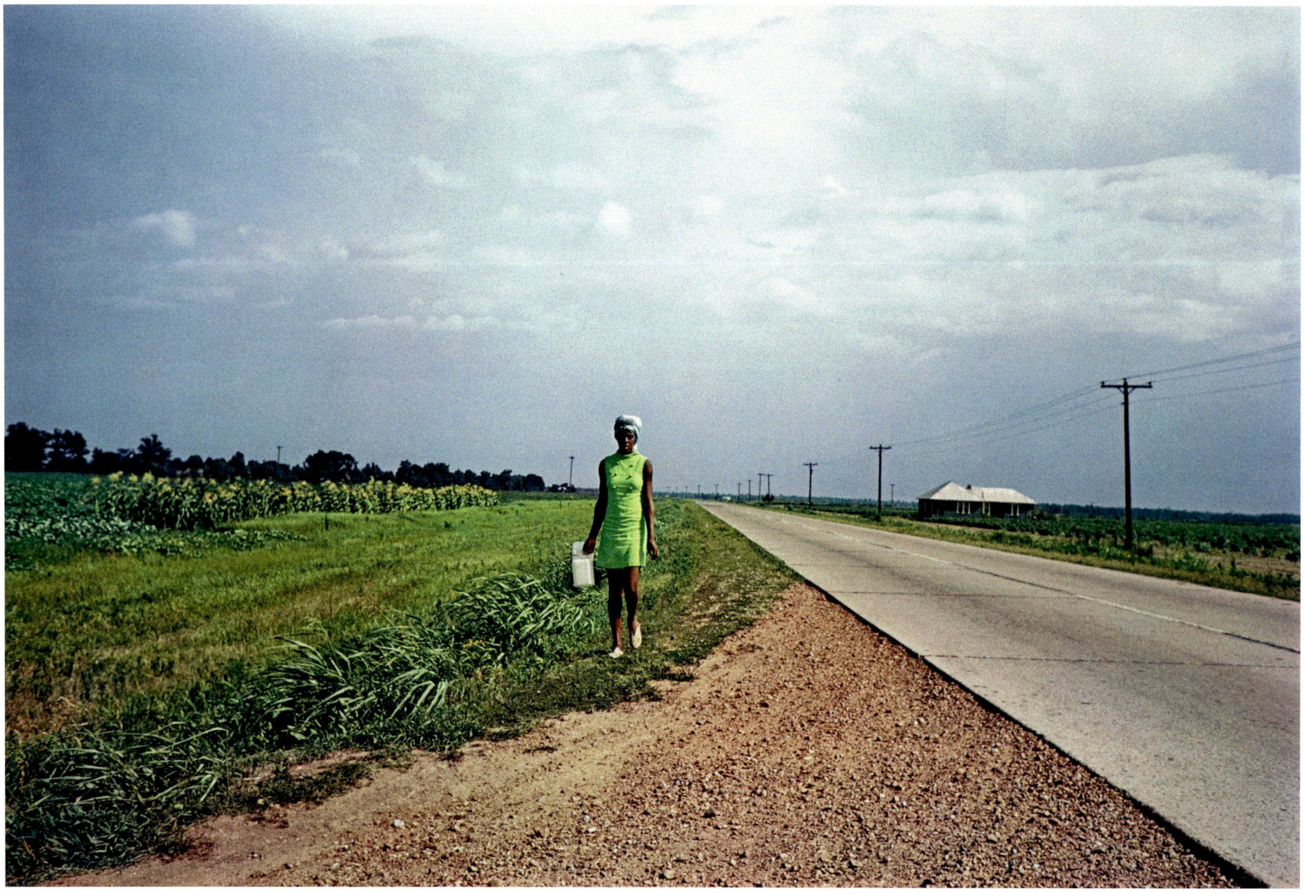

Near Minter City and Glendora, Mississippi, 1970

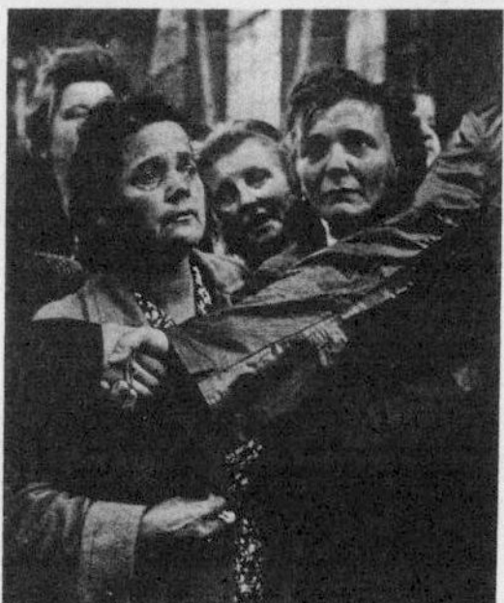

ERNST HAAS: Bildreportage über Kriegsheimkehrer, in der Zeitschrift „Heute", 1949

haben wir, den einzelnen Abschnitten entsprechende Bildbeispiele ausgewählt. Die hier gezeigten Arbeiten sind im Katalog nicht enthalten, in der Reihung folgten wir der Chronologie ihres Entstehens.

Christine Frisinghelli

Anmerkungen

1 *Wien:* Museum des 20. Jahrhunderts, 8. 12. 1983–26. 2. 1984. *Graz:* Neue Galerie am Landesmuseum Joanneum und Künstlerhaus, 17. 3.–17. 4. 1984. *Linz:* Neue Galerie der Stadt Linz, 3. 5.–24. 6. 1984. *Klagenfurt:* Galerie im Stadthaus und Künstlerhaus, 9. 8.–16. 9. 1984. *Salzburg:* Museum Carolino Augusteum und Salzburger Kunstverein 25. 9.–28. 10. 1984. *Innsbruck:* Landesmuseum Ferdinandeum, 16. 11.–31. 12. 1984.
2 Anna Auer, Fotografis Länderbank, Wien; Peter Dressler, Sammler, Wien; Dr. Monika Faber, Museum Moderner Kunst, Wien; Prof. Hans Frank, Photomuseum des Landes Oberösterreich, Bad Ischl; Christine Frisinghelli, Forum Stadtpark, Graz; Otto Hochreiter, Publizist, Innsbruck, Leopold Kandl, Sammler, Wien, Margarethe Kuntner, Höhere Graphische Bundes-Lehr- und Versuchsanstalt, Wien; Michael Mauracher, Fotohof, Salzburg; Timm Starl, Fotogeschichte, Frankfurt am Main, Peter Weiermair, Frankfurter Kunstverein, Frankfurt am Main; Manfred Willmann, Camera Austria, Graz.
3 Der Katalog (zwei Bände, 794 Seiten) ist an den jeweiligen Ausstellungsorten zum Preis von S 380,– erhältlich, bzw. im Museum Moderner Kunst, 1090 Wien, Fürstengasse 1, zu bestellen.

*

Eine ausführliche Besprechung der Ausstellung „Geschichte der Fotografie in Österreich" wird in Heft 14 von CAMERA AUSTRIA erscheinen.

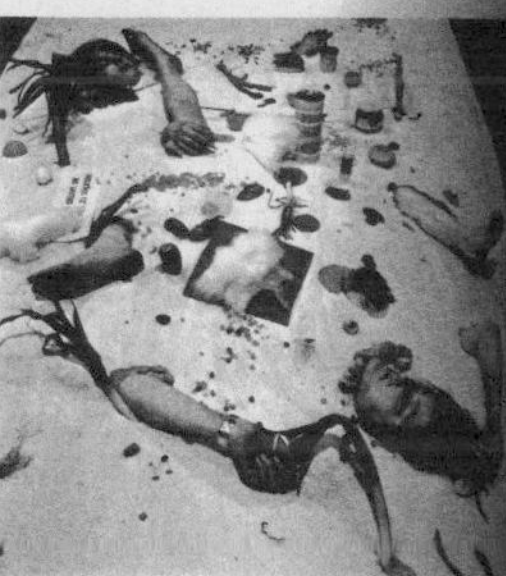

OTTO MUHL: „Nahrungsmitteltest", Aktion 26, 1966

series of later origin by *Leo Kandl* (wine houses, Vienna for example, *Seiichi Furuya* (Frontier), *Nikolaus Walter*, the Kleine Walsertal) show that the method of the photographic essay has a continous tradition in Austrian photography.

One subject on which particular emphasis is laid are Nudes (from artists' copies in the 19th century to the 1980's). In this field Rudolf Koppitz's motion studies are outstanding as well as the series from the studio Manassé of the 1930's made for picture postcards. Other important subjects are the ones of *"Fashion, Dance, Advertising"*, *"Photographs of the Working Class"*, and *"Photography in Rural Areas"*. The latter is particularly important for Austria where international comparison is concerned. It is particularly the Tyrolean photographers *Peter Paul Atzwanger, Adalbert Defner* and *Simon Moser* whose works show the photographers' preference for the rural way of life and the mountainous countryside in the time between Worldwar I and II.

Contributions on *amateur photography, art with photography,* and *photographs of authors* refer to the development of photography after 1945.

We have chosen examples from the large number of pictures of this show corresponding to the various sections. The works shown here are not contained in the catalogue. The order of the works presented is determined by the chronology of their creation.

Christine Frisinghelli

Notes

1 *Vienna:* Museum des 20. Jahrhunderts, 8. 12. 1983–26. 2. 1984. *Graz:* Neue Galerie am Landesmuseum Joanneum und Künstlerhaus, 17. 3.–17. 4. 1984. *Linz:* Neue Galerie der Stadt Linz, 3. 5.–24. 6. 1984. *Klagenfurt:* Galerie im Stadthaus und Künstlerhaus, 9. 8.–16. 9. 1984. *Salzburg:* Museum Carolino Augusteum und Salzburger Kunstverein 25. 9.–28. 10. 1984. *Innsbruck:* Landesmuseum Ferdinandeum, 16. 11.–31. 12. 1984.
2 Anna Auer, Fotografis Länderbank, Wien; Peter Dressler, collector, Wien; Dr. Monika Faber, Museum Moderner Kunst, Wien; Prof. Hans Frank, Photomuseum des Landes Oberösterreich, Bad Ischl; Christine Frisinghelli, Forum Stadtpark, Graz; Otto Hochreiter, journalist, Innsbruck, Leopold Kandl, collector, Wien, Margarete Kuntner, Höhere Graphische Bundes-, Lehr- und Versuchsanstalt, Wien; Michael Mauracher, Fotohof, Salzburg, Timm Starl, Fotogeschichte, Frankfurt am Main. Peter Weiermair, Frankfurter Kunstverein, Frankfurt am Main. Manfred Willmann, Camera Austria, Graz.
3 The catalogue (two volumes, 794 pages) can be bought at the price of AS 380,– at the respective places of the show or it can be ordered at the Museum Moderner Kunst, 1090 Wien, Fürstengasse 1.

*

A review of the show „Geschichte der Fotografie in Österreich" will appear in No. 14 of CAMERA AUSTRIA.

William Eggleston

WELTEN OHNE ENDE
Von Luigi Ghirri

Als ich im Grazer Forum Stadtpark die letzten Werke William Egglestons sah, gelang es mir nicht, einen Zustand des Unbehagens zu verbergen; der erste Eindruck war der des Staunens, vermischt mit nicht gerade glücklicher Überraschung. Eggleston ist einer der Autoren, die ich in der zeitgenössischen Fotografie besonders schätze und liebe, vielleicht gehört diese Liebe dem Ungenauen an und wird mit Argwohn und Mißfallen betrachtet, aber sie ist auch Zeichen eines tiefen und ehrlichen Interesses am Autor und an seinem Werk.

Das Unbehagen, das ich empfand kommt gerade aus diesem Bild, das ich von Eggleston hatte; ich bin und wir sind es gewohnt, uns ein Bild über „Bilder" zu konstruieren. Eggleston war in meinen Augen derjenige der Monographie des Museum of Modern Art.

Aber bei intensiverer Betrachtung entdeckte ich Zeichen und Andeutungen, die mir statt des bekannten Bildes ein anderes zeigten, eines mit undeutlichen Umrissen, aber sicherlich weniger streng und kodifiziert, und daher nicht greifbar. Der „Blick" von Eggleston in diesen Bildern enthüllte sich als anderer, eine Art zuvor ungekannter Verzauberung der Welt gegenüber.

Was ich vorfand, waren nicht die dem Autor seit je teuren Zeichen, Plätze und symbolischen Objekte, sondern oft ungenaue, verschwommene Bilder, mit manchmal auch ungenauen Fluchtpunkten und Perspektiven. Momente und Elemente der Diskordanz und des Unbehagens folgten aufeinander und suggerierten mir nicht nur die Begegnung mit einem Autor, dessen „Kennwort" ich nicht mehr kannte, sondern ließen mich langsam erahnen und definieren, was die Absicht von Eggleston war.

Immer zu Unrecht als Vorkämpfer des fotografischen Banalismus als Philosophie und Anschauung betrachtet, führt Eggleston in dieser Arbeit kein identisches Projekt weiter, kurz, er äfft sich nicht selbst nach; mit dem Verlassen der bekannten Regeln, mit der Freiheit der Erfindung versucht er vielmehr, die Idee einer Fotografie, die sich nicht wiederholt und die nur sie selbst sein soll, aufs Papier zu bringen.

Abseits der feinen Alchemie der „Prints", weit weg von den Halluzinationen und dem Schwindelgefühl der Genauigkeit, betraut er den Bereich der Auflösung und Bruchstückhaftigkeit mit der Aufgabe, ein früheres Bild zu zerstören.

Nicht mehr *ein* Weg, eine Welt aufzubauen, sondern verschiedene Wege, um verschiedenartige Welten aufzubauen.

Wenn sich die früheren Bilder Egglestons auf die figurative amerikanische Tradition zurückführen ließen, mit all ihren Fertigkeiten und sonstigen Bezugspunkten, und der Autor dieser auf wohlbekannten Pfaden schritt, so führt Eggleston in diesen neuen Bildern einen klaren Bruch herbei, er betritt die Welt der „Utopie", wie wir es nennen könnten, nicht als Projektion der Utopie, sondern als Anwendung der unbegrenzten Macht der Utopie.

Diese Veränderung erinnert mich an Handke, wenn er in seinem Buch „Das Gewicht der Welt" schreibt: „Plötzlich wieder, wie jetzt gegen Abend, von der Zeit freigelassen; mildes, seliges Freiheitsgefühl, wie nach einer tragischen Erfahrung, die man überstanden hat."

ENDLESS WORLDS
By Luigi Ghirri

When I saw William Eggleston's latest work at the Forum Stadtpark in Graz I did not succeed in hiding a state of unease; my first impression was a rather unhappy surprise mixed with amazement. Eggleston is one of those authors in contemporary photography who I particularly love and appreciate- maybe this love is vague and is considered with suspicion and displease, but it is also a sign of my deep and sincere interest in the author and his work.

The unease I felt derives exactly from the immage I had of Eggleston; I am and we all are used to constructing for ourselves immages of "immages". In my mind Eggleston was connected with that of the monography of the MOMA.[1]

But studying him more intensely I discovered signs and indications showing a different picture instead of the wellknown one. It was a picture with vague outlines, but it was certainly less rigid and codified and therefore less tangible. Eggleston's "view" in these pictures revealed itself as different, as a kind of unknown enchantment for the world.

I did not find the signs, places, and symbolic objects which had always been dear to the author, but frequently vague and blurred pictures, sometimes with wrong vanishing points and perspectives. Moments and elements of discord and unease succeded one another and did not only suggest to me the idea of meeting an author whose "code" I did not know any longer, but they made me slowly sense and define what Eggleston's intentions were.

Eggleston, who had always been wrongly considered the pioneer of photographic banalism as a philosophy and a point of view, does not continue an identical project in this work, in short, he does not copy himself. Abandoning the traditional rules and making use of the liberty of invention, he tries to put to paper the idea of photography which does not repeat itself and is supposed to be nothing but itself.

Far from the subtle alchemy of the "prints", far from the halluzinations and the dizziness of precision, he entrusts the sphere of dissolution and fragmentation with task of destroying a former picture.

It is no longer one way of constructing one world, but various ways of constructing various worlds.

Whereas Eggleston's earlier pictures could be traced back to the figurative American tradition with all its values and other reference points, and with the author thus striding along wellknown paths, Eggleston brings about a clean break in this new work; he enters the world of "utopia" as we could call it, not as a projection of utopia but as the application of the unlimited power of utopia.

This change reminds me of Handke, who writes in his book *Das Gewicht der Welt (The weight of the world),* "Suddenly again, like now, towards evening, I feel free from time. I have a mild and sweet feeling of liberty, as after a tragic experience one has made."

Thus Sally Eauclaire's idea of a romantic approach by Eggleston, which she describes in her beautiful book "New Colour Photography"[2] turns out to be correct. Ludwig Richter, a painter of that period, says, "I go on an adventurous journey into Romance, where man and nature are equally dominant, and each gives significance and interest to

So bestätigt sich die Ahnung von Sally Eauclaire, die in ihrem sehr schönen Buch „New Colour Photography"[2] von einer romantischen Betrachtungsweise Egglestons spricht. Ein Maler dieser Epoche, Ludwig Richter sagt: „Ich begebe mich auf eine abenteuerliche Fahrt ins Romantische, dort wo Mensch und Natur in gleicher Weise dominieren, und jeder dem anderen Bedeutung und Interesse verleiht." In dieser Suche nach der Symbiose zwischen Werk und Leben, zwischen Natur und Kultur, finden wir nicht nur einen „Topos" der gesamten romantischen Kultur, sondern auch eine Vertiefung seiner früheren Arbeiten. So erscheint zum ersten Mal, auf direkte und klare Weise das Thema der Sehnsucht, das in den früheren Fotografien nur angedeutet war, sich bis zum Leitmotiv des Gesamtwerkes steigert.

Was ist für Eggleston dieses Gefühl der Sehnsucht? „Ich spüre Sehnsucht nach diesen Dingen. Für viele ist ‚Sehnsucht' ein häßliches Wort, ein Zeichen für beschränktes Denken. Aber ich habe kein anderes Wort, um das auszudrücken, was ich nicht habe und das sich mir gleichzeitig als Befreiung präsentiert.

Ich habe Sehnsucht nach einem Fühlen, da es mir vorkommt, ohne Gefühle zu sein, die nicht schon von schlechten Gedanken verpestet sind.

Ich habe Sehnsucht nach einem Erzählstil, der mich mit den anderen verbindet, denn alles, was ich niederschreiben kann, sind Dinge, die vom Leben der anderen getrennt sind.

Das wahre und starke Gefühl, das am besten wiedergeben könnte, ist jenes, verloren zu sein. Nicht ich im besonderen, als Individuum. Es ist viel eher ein Zustand, den ich überall anzutreffen scheine. Und je mehr ich in einer Großstadt bin, in Paris zum Beispiel, desto mehr bin ich überzeugt, daß ich mir das nicht nur einbilde. Ich bin überzeugt, daß dieses Verlorensein das wahre Gefühl ist, das ich um mich habe, das Lebendigste, was existiert. Immer wieder lese ich Sartre, der sagt: ‚Nur die Dreckskerle fühlen sich nicht verloren!'" (Gianni Celati)

Und es gibt keinen Zweifel, daß uns Eggleston in dieser „unsicheren" Fotografie wie verloren erscheint, zwischen den Wegen und Straßen der Provinz und der wuchernden Natur Kenias.[3] Und was gibt es romantischeres, aber in neuem und befreienden Sinne, als sich verloren zu fühlen und die Natur und die Welt von ihrer „panischen" Seite wahrzunehmen?

Aber wenn der bekannte Autor Eggleston nicht sofort erkannt wird, können wir Eggleston als Individuum besser verstehen, das sich nicht versteckt, sondern uns vor allem seine Vielseitigkeit und Komplexität als Mensch entfaltet. Wahrscheinlich haben wir, wenn wir auch den Menschen nicht gefunden haben, den Autor sicherlich nicht verloren; denn wenn auch viele „schon wieder" diese Bilder als banal, überholt, schlampig und amateurhaft bezeichnen könnten, so könnte man sich bei Eggleston auch diesmal getäuscht haben. Kurz: Eggleston hat sich alles erlaubt, weil er vor allem William Eggleston „ist".

Geht es bei diesem Problem darum, die Identität zu erkennen und den Autor dabei zu vergessen? Mag sein.

Die zeitgenössische amerikanische Farbfotografie wie die von Shore, Meyerowitz, Sternfeld, um nur einige der wichtigsten Namen zu nennen, hat uns an eine Bildproduktion gewöhnt, die von halluzinatorischer und schwindelerregender Genauigkeit ist.

Verwirrend und an gewissen Stellen in ihrer diabolischen Kälte faszinierend, nehmen uns diese Bilder wie Blendwerke oder Gespenster gefangen, zwingen uns zu einer „Nulleinstellung" des Blicks, der seine Unfähigkeit, die Welt zu begreifen, weniger oft zu verbergen vermag, als sein Unvermögen, das fotografierende Individuum zu erfassen.

Vielleicht ist der Satz aus Shakespeares' Märchenspiel „Cymbeline": „Was für eine Ironie, eine so gute Sicht zu haben und sich in eine Sackgasse zu begeben", besonders geeignet, die amerikanische Fotografie, aber nicht nur diese, zu beschreiben, die paradoxerweise von der Realität immer dann besonders weit entfernt ist, wenn sie diese darzustellen vermeint.

Dieses Schwindelgefühl der Genauigkeit entspricht nicht mehr unserer Art, die Welt zu betrachten; die Auflösung

the other." In this search for the symbiosis between work and life, between nature and culture we do not only find a "topos" of the entire romantic culture but also a deepening of his earlier works. Thus the topic of nostalgia appears for the first time directly and openly, which had been only-suggested in the earlier photographs and is now being increased to become the "Leitmotiv" of the whole work.

What does this feeling of nostalgia mean to Eggleston? "I feel a nostalgic longing for these things. For many people "nostalgia" is an ugly word, a sign of narrow-minded thinking. But I cannot find another word to describe what I have not got and which at the same time presents itself as liberation to me. I have a longing for a feeling, since I seem to be without sentiments, which are not contaminated by bad thoughts.

I have a longing for a style of narration which links me with the others, for anyting I can write down are things which are separated from the lives of the others.

The true and strong feeling I could describe best is that of being lost. It is not me in particular, as an individual. It is rather a state of being which I seem to meet everywhere. And the more I am in a city, in Paris for example, the more I am convinced that I do not only imagine it. I am convinced that the feeling of being lost is the true feeling I have around me, the most lively that exists. Again and again I turn to read Sartre, who says, 'It's only the swine that don't feel lost.'" (Gianni Celati)

And there is no doubt that Eggleston seems to be lost in that "uncertain" photography, between the streets and the roads of the province and the exuberant nature of Kenia.[3] And what is there more romantic–but in a new and liberating sense of the word–than feeling lost and perceiving the world from its panic side?

But when the wellknown author Eggleston is no longer recognized at once, we can understand the individual Eggleston better, who does not conceal himself but reveals to us first of all his versatility and complexity as a human being. Even though we have not found the human being, we have not lost the author; for even if many people might call these pictures banal, outdated, careless, and amateurish "again", we could in one way have taken about Eggleston this time as well. In short, Eggleston has taken the liberty of doing anything because he "is" primarily William Eggleston.

Is it a question of revealing the identity and forgetting the author in doing so? Maybe!

The contemporary American colour photography, such as that by Shore, Meyerowitz, Sternfeld, to list some of the most important names, has got us used to a production of pictures which are characterized by hallucinatory and staggering exactness.

These pictures are confusing and in certain places fascinating because of their diabolic coldness; they grib us like mirages, phantasms and force us to use a "zero adjustment" of our view which can hide its inability of comprehending the world more frequently than its inability of getting hold of the individual who takes the photos.

Maybe the sentence from Shakespeare's *Cymbeline* "What an irony: having got such a good view and walking into a blind alley" is particularly suited to describe American and not only photography, which paradoxically seems to be particularly far from reality when it tries to represent it.

This vertigo of exactness no longer corresponds to our way of looking at the world; the dissolution of the real and of the glance which we observe the world with, has become irreversible by now. We cannot keep up the modules of the creative subjective photography as appropriate either, because they have used themselves up in a stupid and sterile way, in an unlimited repetition of themselves. The blind confidence in ingenuity as such and in creative photography has awfully failed. It has not only failed in the search for a personal interiority, but mainly and justly so in what we might call a total disinterest in culture, in a world of ideas, and in society; and thus the production of visible material, which rarely reaches an acceptable decorative level, has become doubly unbearable and inadmissable.

That is the problem of the numerous "producers of confetti and shooting stars", whether they like it or not. Even if

LOUISIANA-PROJECT

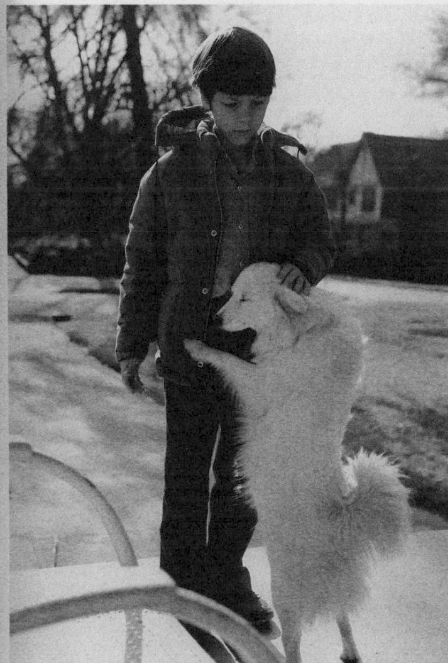

realm of "high-art". Hare broke with the powers in the photography, branding himself as an unstable ingrate, and returned to school, more to make contact with other photographic workers and seekers than to achieve a fixed academic goal. During this period his work was taken on board by the Marxist critics in a seemingly perfect marriage of convenience: Hare was a perfect "homo economicus", a man whose plight had been fashioned by oppressive capitalist structures, now aware of his subjugation and able to offer a criticism of his past circumstances in brilliant terms. Further, Hare's work filled a gap in the corpus of American Marxist criticism, which had shone brilliantly in the theoretical aspects of photography but was dismally weak in practice. Hare seemed to find this role limiting, however, and began to see more personal and spiritual solutions to his anguish.

Hare's work became widely known through the publication of his first book, "Interior America"7. Hare was ultimately dissatisfied with the book however as it treated his work more as an object of esthetic contemplation than as a statement of his own crisis, a crisis that he felt was shared by millions with whom he wished to communicate his suffering and the process of his liberation. The book I'm showing now, "This Was Corporate America" is Hare's own conception, photographs with accompanying text, also by Hare, telling of his struggle and offering it as a model for others seeking to find autonomy in a world and system that usurps it. There is neither praise or criticism to be made of this book, I believe; it stands as a personal statement of process whose conclusion is, in fact, the process itself. It is one person's hard-fought battle. Not every answer Hare finds is applicable to others, some not even to himself; each answer is tentative, a step on a path. If any judgement can be made it is one of admiration for the enduring courage of Hare's struggle, the courage of Hare's renunciation, and the courage, finally, of his will to continue.
Thank you.

1 cf. CAMERA AUSTRIA No. 8/1982, Symposion on Photography III, Graz 1981; Lecture by Joe Deal and reproductions referring mainly to his series "The Fault Zone", 1980
2 Robert Adams, From The Missouri West, Aperture, Millerton, New York, 1980
3 Robert Adams, Los Angeles Spring, Aperture, Millerton, New York, 1986; cf. also CAMERA AUSTRIA No. 9/1983, pp. 2–16, Robert Adams, Interview with Michael Köhler; CAMERA AUSTRIA No. 18/1985, p. 16, Lewis Baltz, Konsumerterror
4 John Gossage, The Pond, with an essay by Denise Sines, Aperture, Millerton, New York 1985; text by John Gossage and reproductions from "The Pond" in CAMERA AUSTRIA No. 19/20, 1985–86, Symposion on Photography VI, Graz 1984
5 "Rodeo Drive" is planned to appear as a book of its own in 1987; cf. also CAMERA AUSTRIA No. 18/1985, p. 16, Lewis Baltz, Konsumerterror
6 Chauncey Hare, This was Corporate America, Institute of Contemporary Arts, Boston 1984
7 Chauncey Hare, Interior America, Aperture, Millerton, New York 1978

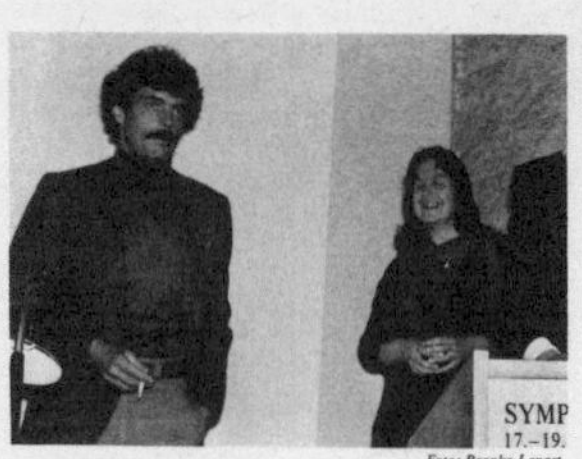
LEWIS BALTZ
born 1945; studied at San Francisco Art Institute and at Claremont Graduate School; photographer, teacher, lecturer; his most important publications are: "The New Industrial Parks Near Irvine, California", New York 1975; "Park City", New York and Millerton 1981; "San Quentin Point", 1986.
Foto: Branko Lenart

wurde. Hare brach mit den Mächtigen in der Welt der Fotografie, brandmarkte sich selbst als labilen, undankbaren Menschen und ging zurück an die Universität, nicht so sehr mit einem bestimmten akademischen Ziel vor Augen, sondern um Kontakt mit anderen Fotografen zu suchen, die ebenfalls arbeiten und auf der Suche sind. In dieser Zeit nahmen sich marxistische Kritiker seiner Arbeit an, und es ergab sich eine offenbar perfekte Zweckehe: Hare war der perfekte "homo oeconomicus", ein Mensch, dessen Dilemma auf die Unterdrückung durch kapitalistische Strukturen zurückzuführen war, der sich nun seiner Unterjochung bewußt und imstande war, an seinen früheren Lebensumständen in brillanter Weise Kritik zu üben. Außerdem füllte seine Arbeit eine Lücke im Gefüge der amerikanischen marxistischen Kritik, die, was die theoretischen Aspekte der Fotografie betrifft, geglänzt, aber in der Praxis wenig vorzuweisen hatte. Hare fühlte sich in dieser Rolle jedoch eingeengt und fand persönlichere, geistigere Auswege aus seinen Qualen.

Seine Arbeit wurde durch die Veröffentlichung seines ersten Buches, "Interior America"7, weithin bekannt. Hare war aber schließlich mit dem Buch unzufrieden, da seine Arbeit darin eher als Objekt ästhetischer Betrachtung und nicht als Ausdruck seiner Krise behandelt wurde, einer Krise, in der seiner Ansicht nach Millionen anderer Menschen stecken, die er an seinem Leid und an seinem Befreiungsprozeß teilhaben lassen wollte. Das Buch, das ich jetzt zeige – "This Was Corporate America" – ist von Hare konzipiert. Die Bilder begleiten einen Text, der ebenfalls von ihm stammt, sein Ringen schildert und es anderen als Modell anbietet, die autonom sein wollen in einer Welt und in einem System, wo Autonomie unterdrückt wird. Dieses Buch, finde ich, bedarf weder des Lobes noch der Kritik; es steht da als der persönliche Ausdruck einer Entwicklung, deren Ziel die Entwicklung selbst ist. Es handelt von dem mühsamen Kampf eines einzelnen. Nicht jede Antwort, die Hare findet, ist auch für andere anwendbar, manche nicht einmal für ihn selbst; jede Antwort ist provisorisch, ein Schritt auf einem Weg. Wenn ein Urteil überhaupt möglich ist, dann ist es Bewunderung für den Mut und die Ausdauer, mit denen Hare seinen Kampf geführt hat, für den Mut seiner Verweigerung und für seinen Mut, weiterzumachen.
Danke.

1 s. dazu CAMERA AUSTRIA 8/1982, Symposion über Fotografie III, Graz 1981; Vortrag Joe Deal und Abbildungen hauptsächlich zur Serie "The Fault Zone", 1980
2 Robert Adams, From The Missouri West, Aperture, Millerton, New York, 1980
3 Robert Adams, Los Angeles Spring, Aperture, Millerton, New York, 1986; zur Arbeit Robert Adam's s. auch die Veröffentlichungen in CAMERA AUSTRIA Nr. 9/1983, S. 2–16, Interview mit Michael Köhler; CAMERA AUSTRIA Nr. 18/1985, S. 16 ff., Lewis Baltz, Konsumterror
4 John Gossage, The Pond, mit einem Essay von Denise Sines, Aperture, Millerton, New York, 1985; Kommentar und Bildmaterial zu "The Pond" in CAMERA AUSTRIA Nr. 19/20 – 1985/86, Symposion über Fotografie VI, Graz 1984
5 "Rodeo Drive" soll auch als eigenes Buch herauskommen und ist bei Aperture, Millerton, New York für 1987 geplant; zu weiteren Arbeiten von Anthony Hernandez s. auch CAMERA AUSTRIA Nr. 18/1985, S. 16 ff., Lewis Baltz, Konsumterror
6 Chauncey Hare, This was Corporate America, Institute of Contemporary Arts, Boston, 1984
7 Chauncey Hare, Interior America, Aperture, Millerton, New York 1978

Übersetzung: Klaus Feichtenberger

LEWIS BALTZ
geboren 1945; studierte am San Francisco Art Institute und an der Claremont Graduate School; Fotograf, Lehrer, Vortragstätigkeit; seine wichtigsten Buchveröffentlichungen sind: "The New Industrial Parks Near Irvine, California", New York 1975; "Park City", New York und Millerton 1981; "San Quentin Point", 1986.

William Eggleston

DEMOCRATIC FOREST, 1984/85

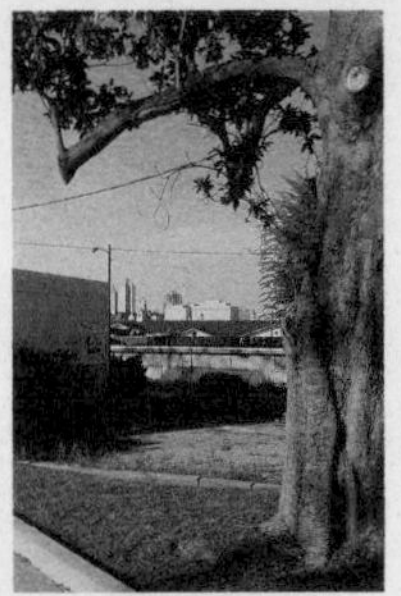
Nashville, das Heim der "Country" Musik

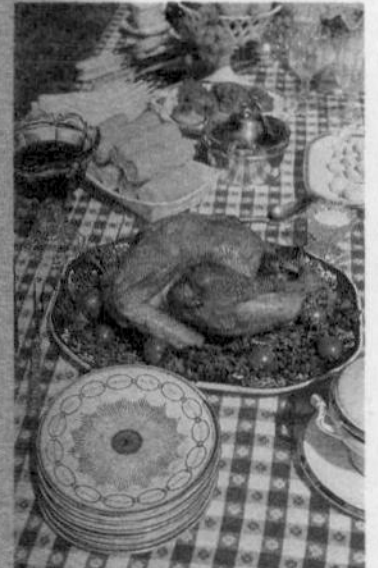
Der Ernst der Hausfrau

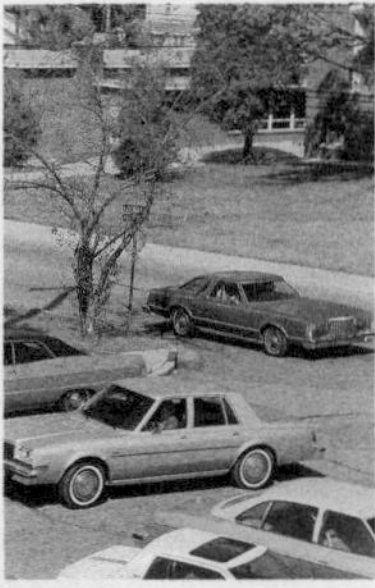
Gott macht die Bäume; der Mensch das Automobil

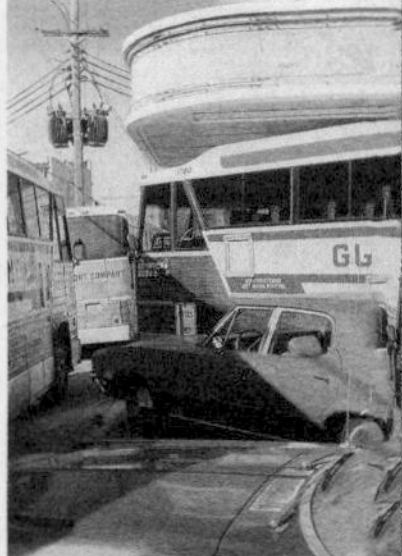
Wohin?

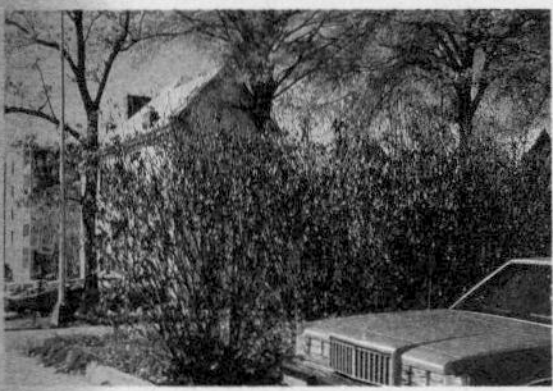
"Im Feuer des Frühlings", Omar Khayan

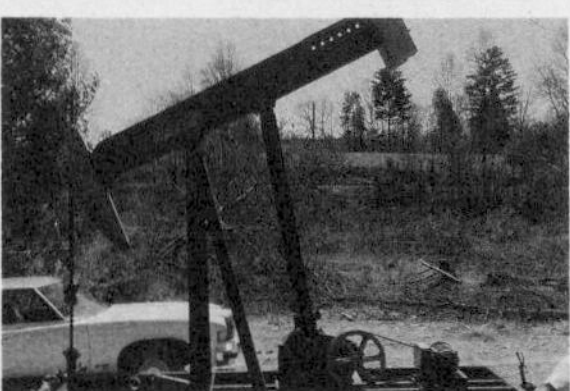
"Wildcutting" in den Bergen von Ost-Tennessee

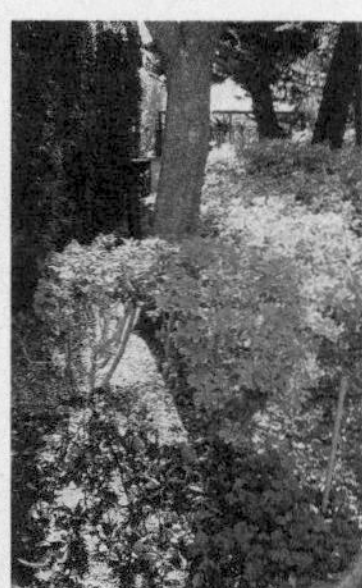
Die Schatten im Garten

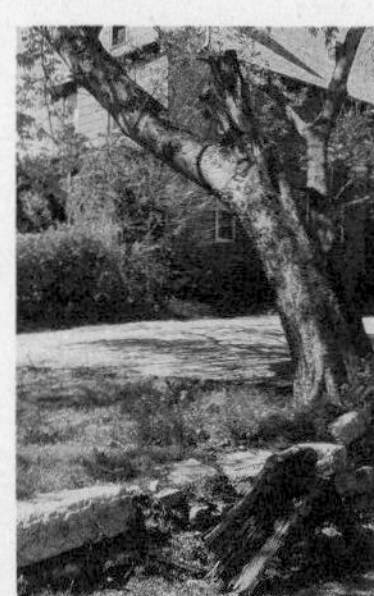
Der Tod als das Ende des Lebens

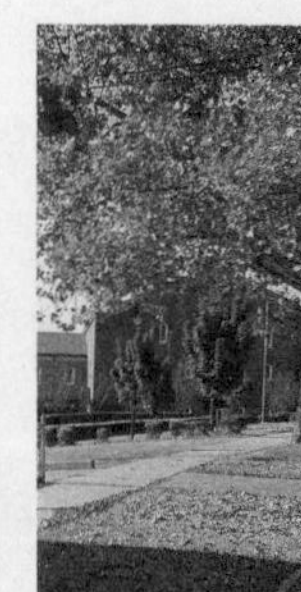
Der Tod und die Ewigkeit

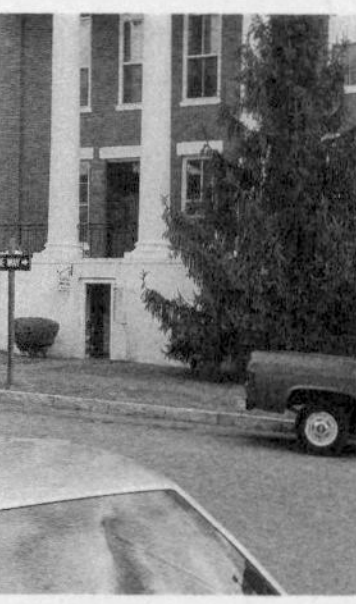
Der Tannenbaum

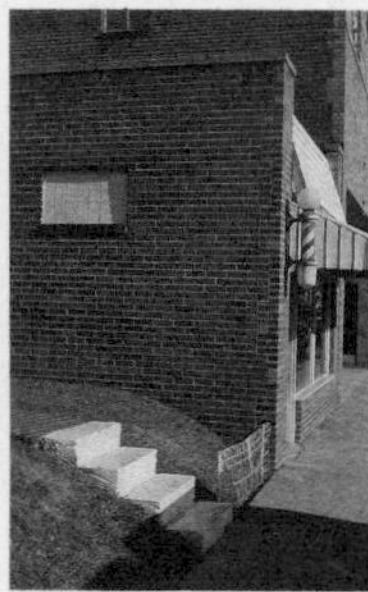
Der Friseur in Kingsport, Tennessee

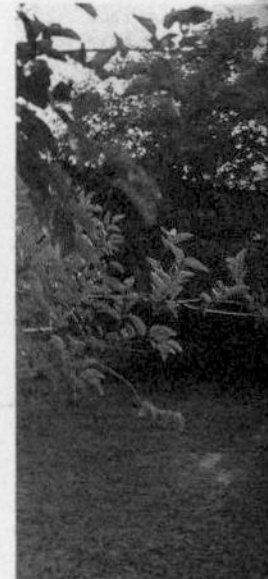
Ein Garten im Spätsommer in Memphis, 1985

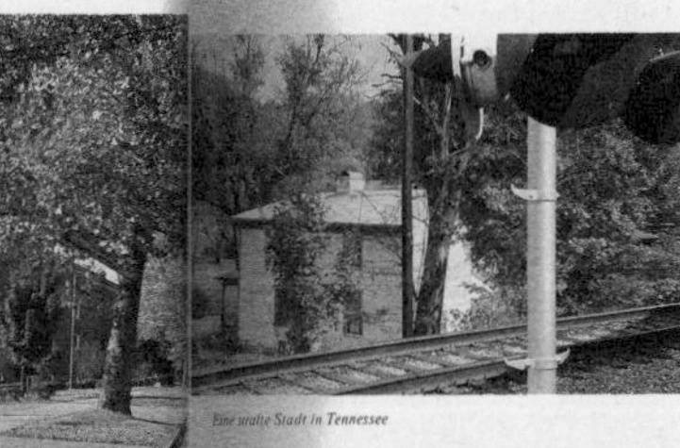
Eine wahre Stadt in Tennessee

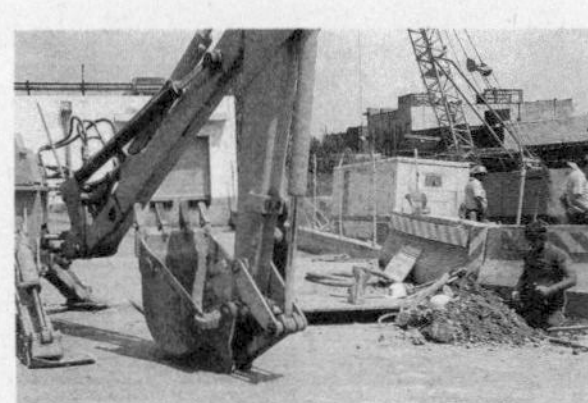
Der Mensch als Meister der Maschinen

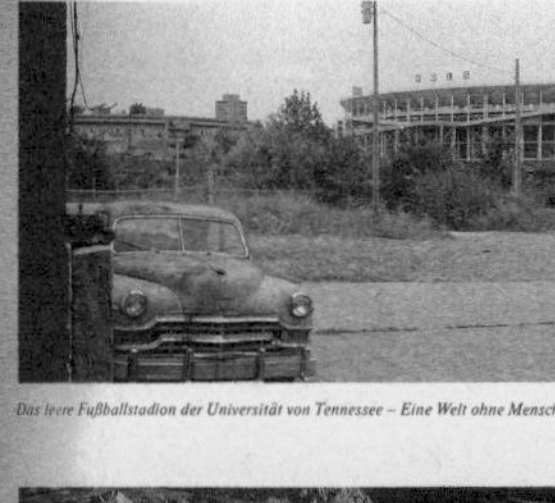
Das leere Fußballstadion der Universität von Tennessee – Eine Welt ohne Menschen

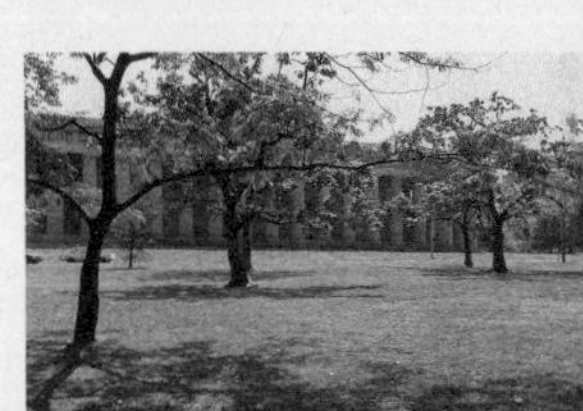
Der Parthenon im fremden Lande (Nashville, Tennessee, 1984)

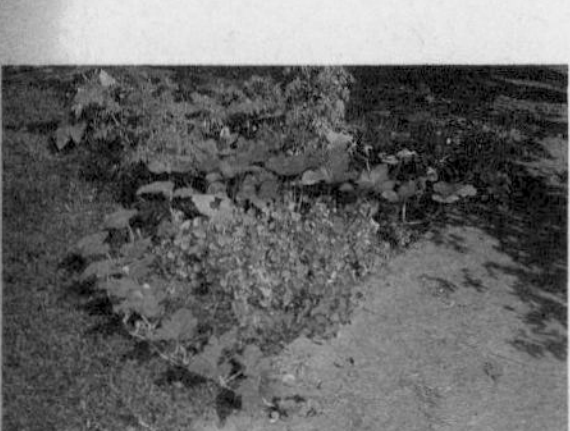
Ein Kohlgarten, verbunden mit Nasturtians

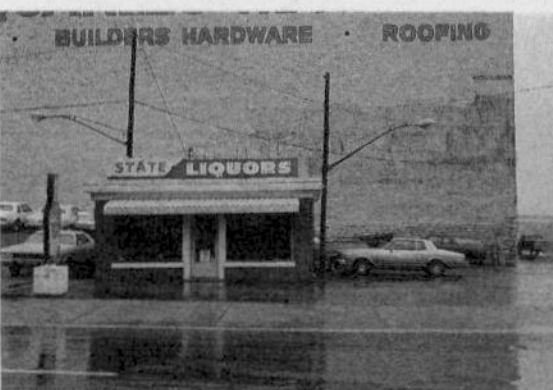
Eine Flasche Wein am Weg nach Hause an einem kalten, nassen Tag

Luigi Ghirri

Participation at Symposia

1981 Symposion on Photography III,
18–22 October 1981, lecturer
1985 Symposion on Photography VII:
"Europa–Amerika. Hello–Good Bye,
Good Bye–Hello," 4–6 October 1985,
lecturer

Camera Austria International

1982 Luigi Ghirri, "Topographie – Ikonographie,"
text contribution / artist contribution
(journal of Symposia), *Camera Austria
International* 7 / 1982
1983 Luigi Ghirri, "Endless Worlds,"
about William Egglestons works, text contribution, *Camera Austria International* 13 / 1983
1984 Arturo Carlo Quintavalle, "Penisola –
Appunti per un Viaggio in Italia," text contribution, Luigi Ghirri, artist contribution (with
Vittore Fossati, Vincenzo Castella, Guido
Guidi, Mario Cresci, Giannantonio Battistella,
Giovanni Chiaramonte, Olivo Barbieri,
Mimmo Jodice, Ernesto Tuliozi),
Camera Austria International 14 / 1984
1986 Luigi Ghirri, "Das Männchen am Rande des
Grand Canyon," text contribution / artist
contribution (journal of Symposia),
Camera Austria International 21 / 1986
1993 Roberta Valtorta, "Luighi Ghirri: Vista
con camera," text contribution, Luigi Ghirri,
artist contribution, *Camera Austria
International* 42 / 1993
2001 Julia Garimorth, "Luigi Ghirri: Zwischen alter
und neuer Welt," Patrimoine Photographique,
Hôtel de Sully, Paris: Fotomuseum
Winterthur, exhibition review, *Camera
Austria International* 74 / 2001

2012 Gabriele Francesco Sassone, "Luigi Ghirri:
Project Prints: An Adventure in Thinking
and Looking, Castello di Rivoli," exhibition
review, *Camera Austria International* 118 / 2012
2018 Radek Krolczyk, "Luigi Ghirri: Karte und
Gebiet, Museum Folkwang, Essen; Museo
Reina Sofía, Madrid; Jeu de Paume, Paris,"
exhibition review, *Camera Austria
International* 142 / 2018

Exhibitions

1976 *Luigi Ghirri,* solo exhibition
1979 *5 Jahre Fotogalerie im Forum Stadtpark,*
exhibition contribution
1983 *PENISOLA – Una Linea della Fotografia
Italiana a Colori,* exhibition contribution
and curator
1985 *Europa–Amerika: Hello–Good Bye,
Good Bye–Hello,* exhibition contribution
1989 *Arc Lémanique,* Musée de l'Elysée,
Lausanne (CH), exhibition contribution

Workshop

1983 4–5 June 1983

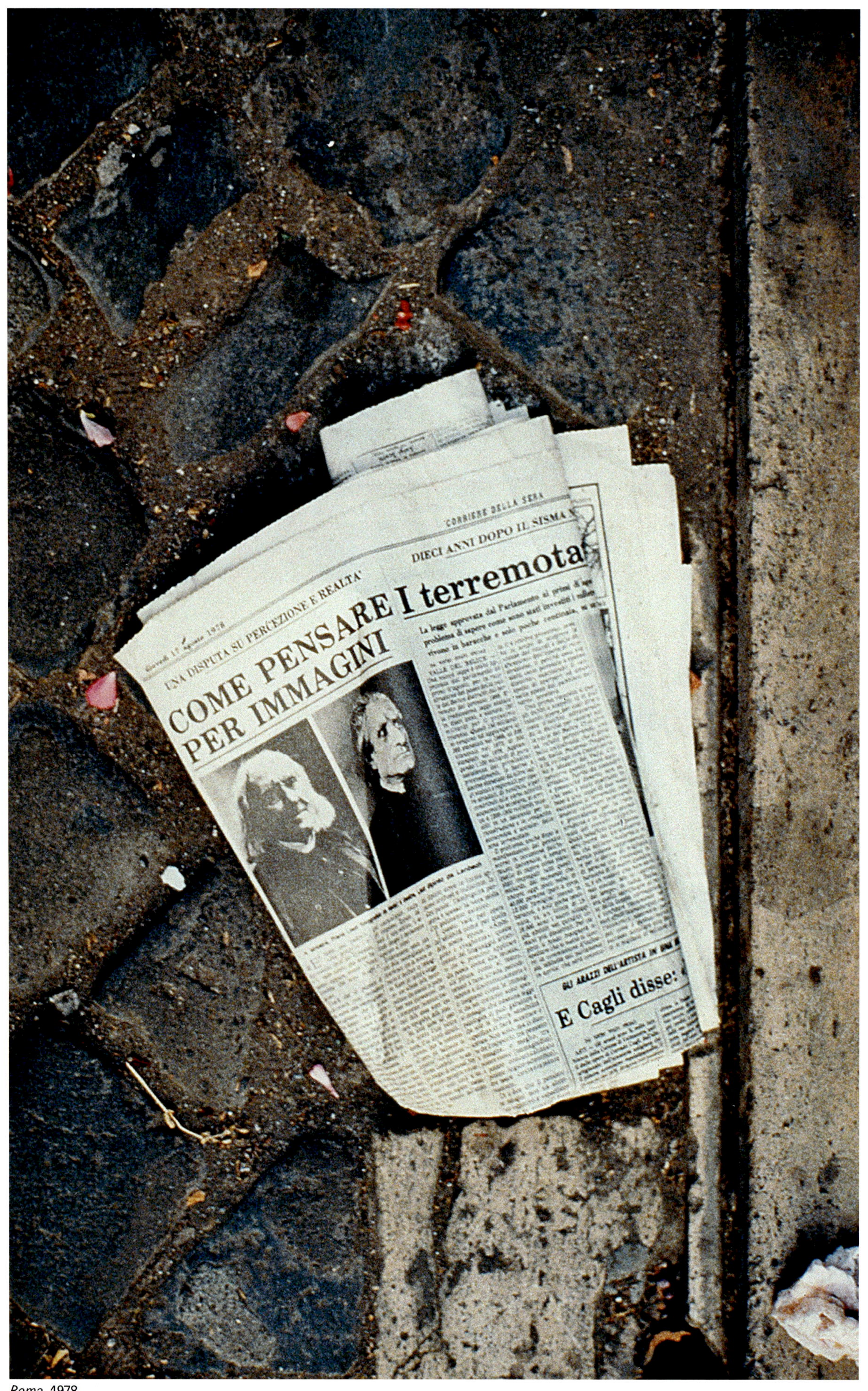
CORRIERE DELLA SERA
DIECI ANNI DOPO IL SISMA
UNA DISPUTA SU PERCEZIONE E REALTA'
COME PENSARE I terremota
PER IMMAGINI
E Cagli disse:

Roma, 1978

Luigi Ghirri

[…] In the course of my work I do not only deal with a reality that is easily identifiable or highly loaded with symbols, but also with thought, memory, imagination, the phantastic and estranged meanings.

On the other hand the possibility of seeing and penetrating the universe of reality pervades all representations and all cultural models known to us, which have been given to us as definite and decisive, our relation to reality and life and even the relationship of the picture of the satellite to the earth.

Thus photography with its indeterminateness becomes a privileged subject for being able to get outside the symbolism of definite representations; the value of truth is given to it.

The inherent capacity of photography to analyze in space and time the signs which form reality, and which have always slipped our comprehension in their entirety, thus permits the photograph—because of its *fragmentary* character—to get exceptionally close to things which cannot be delimited, and that is physical existence.

That is why I am not interested in the pictures and the *decisive* moments, the study or the analysis of language as an end in itself, aesthetics, the concept or totalizing idea, the emotions of the poet, the sophisticated quotation, the search for a new aesthetic creed, the application of a style. I am occupied with *seeing* clearly, that is why I am interested in all possible functions, without separating any single one from the whole; I absorb them in a total way in order to be able to see and to render recognizable from one time to the other the concealed hieroglyphs.

I have to add that I have always tried not to confine myself to one movement or one genre only; I did not want to create a style or brand of my own, rather I have followed different courses in a process of activating thought; I did not try to produce *photographs* but *maps* and *diagrams* which were at the same time photographs. For me photography is a sort of personal anthropology, portrait and self-portrait at the same time. […]

Originally published in italian: Luigi Ghirri, *Kodachrome* (Milan: Punto e Virgola, 1978). This text version is a reprint of the contribution by Luigi Ghirri to *Camera Austria International* 7/1982.

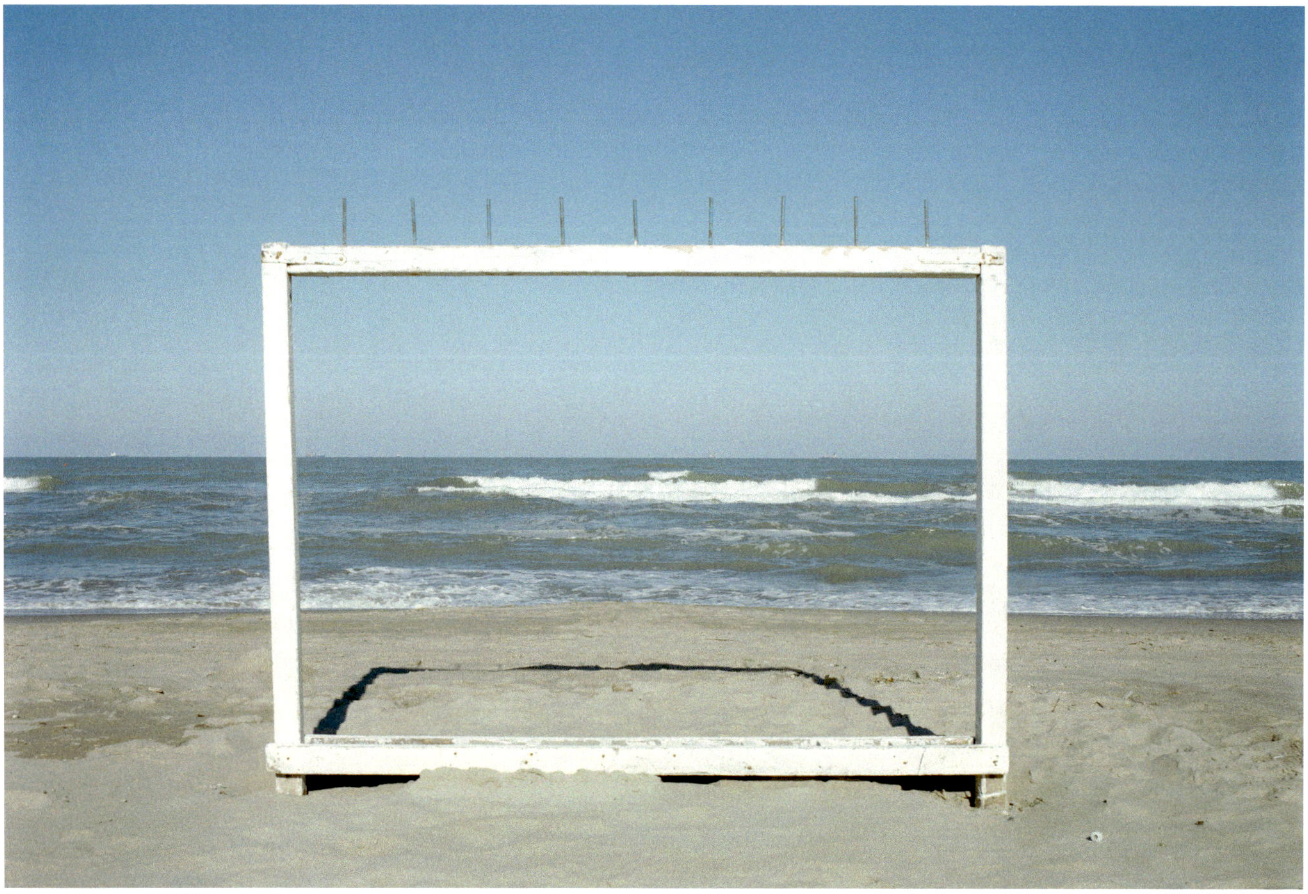

Marina di Ravenna, 1986

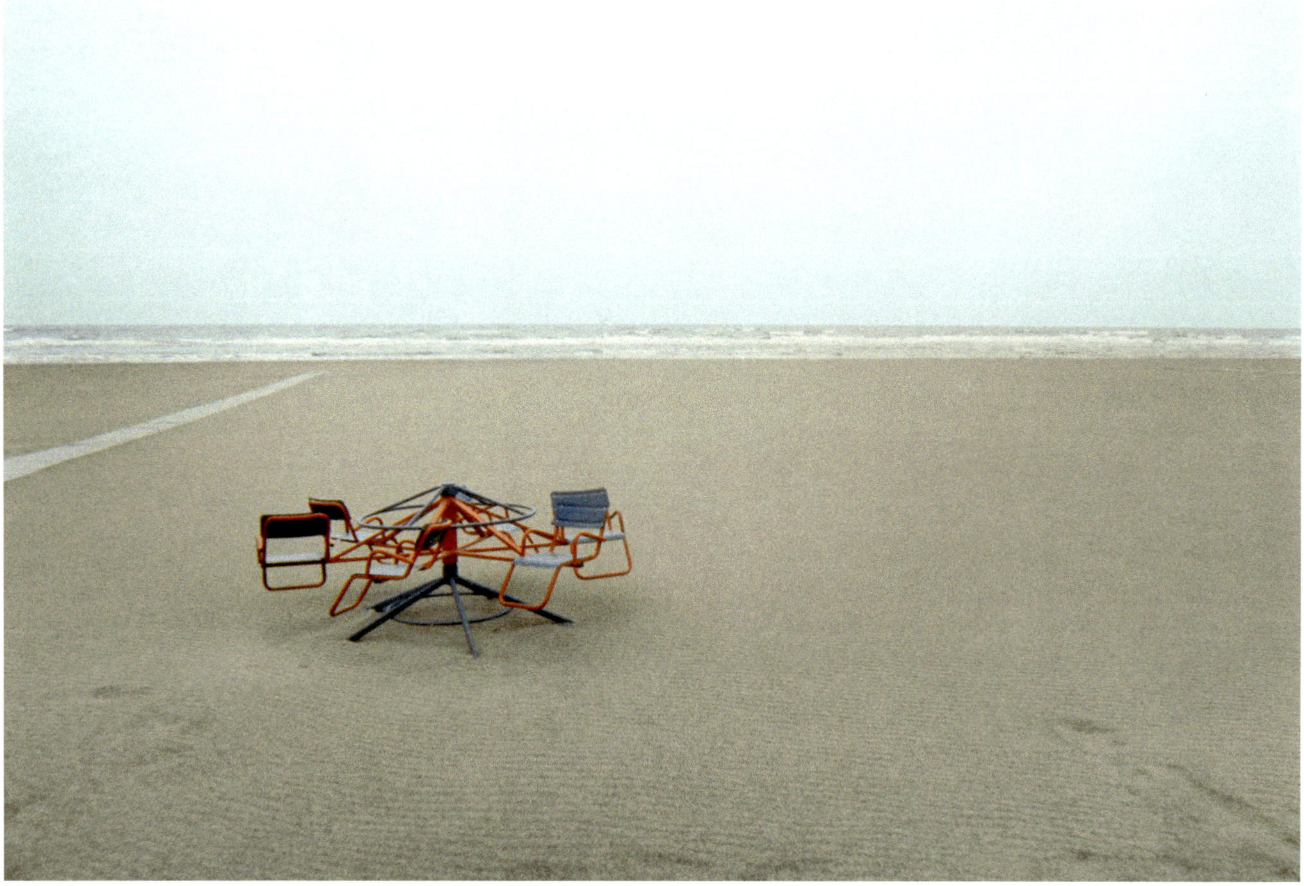

Lido di Spina, 1974

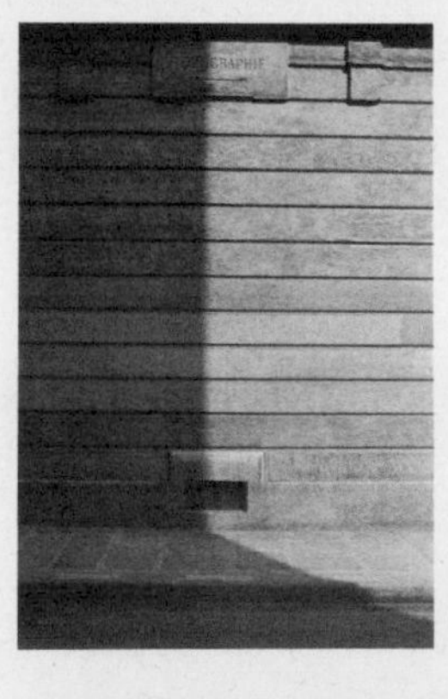
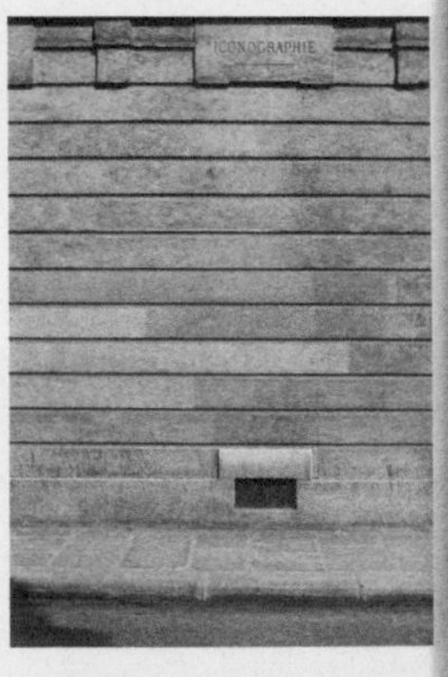
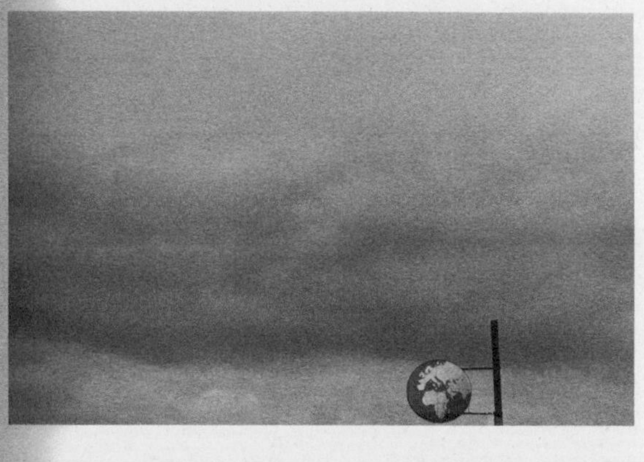
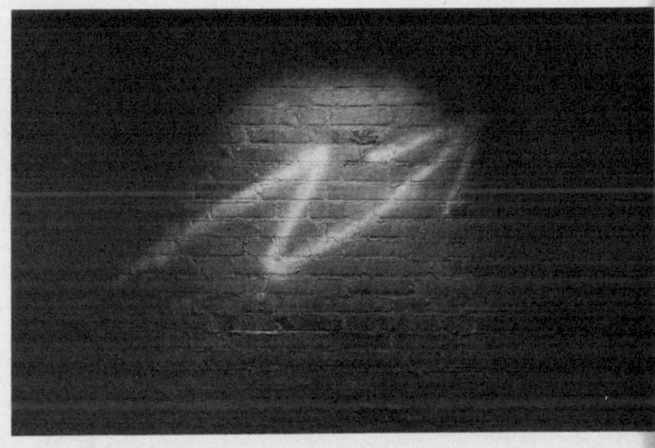
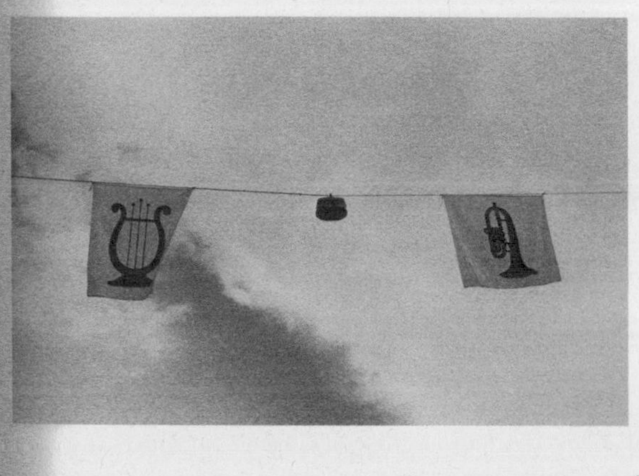

24

25

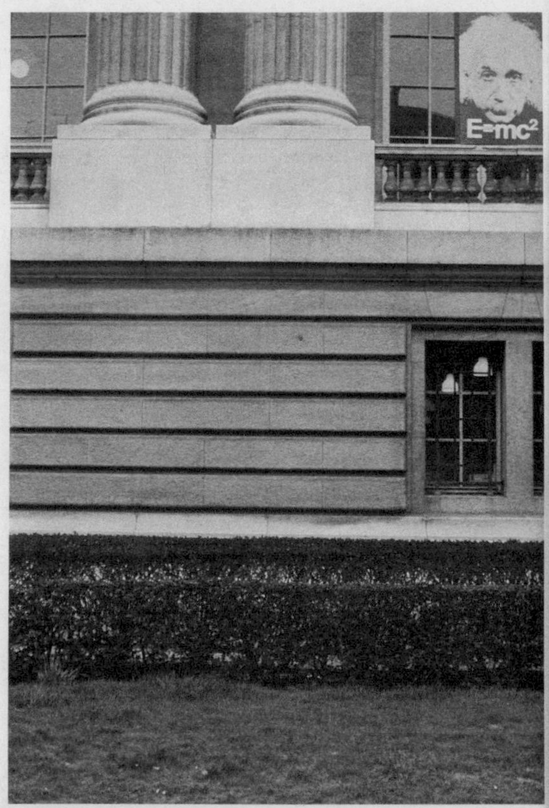
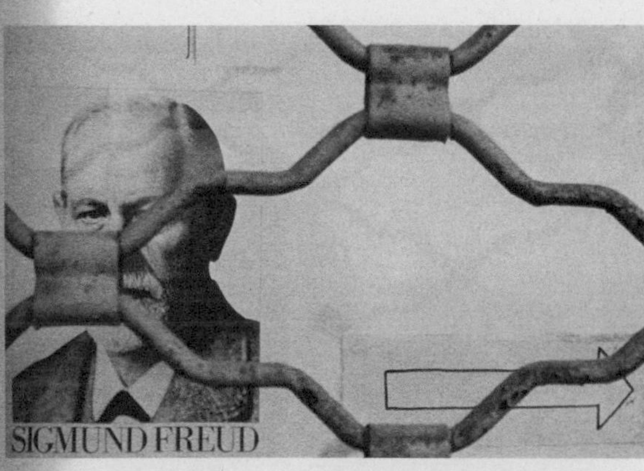

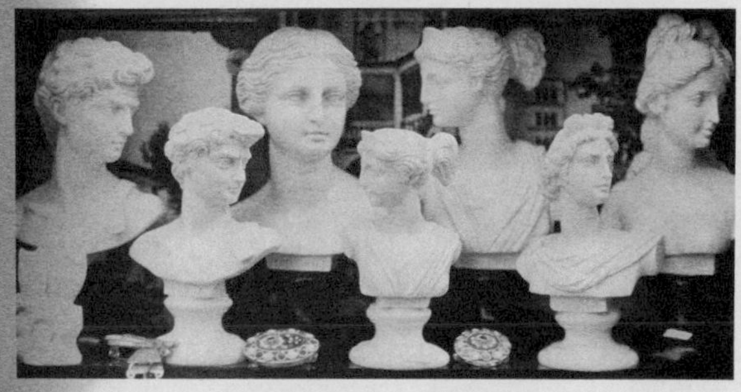

26

27

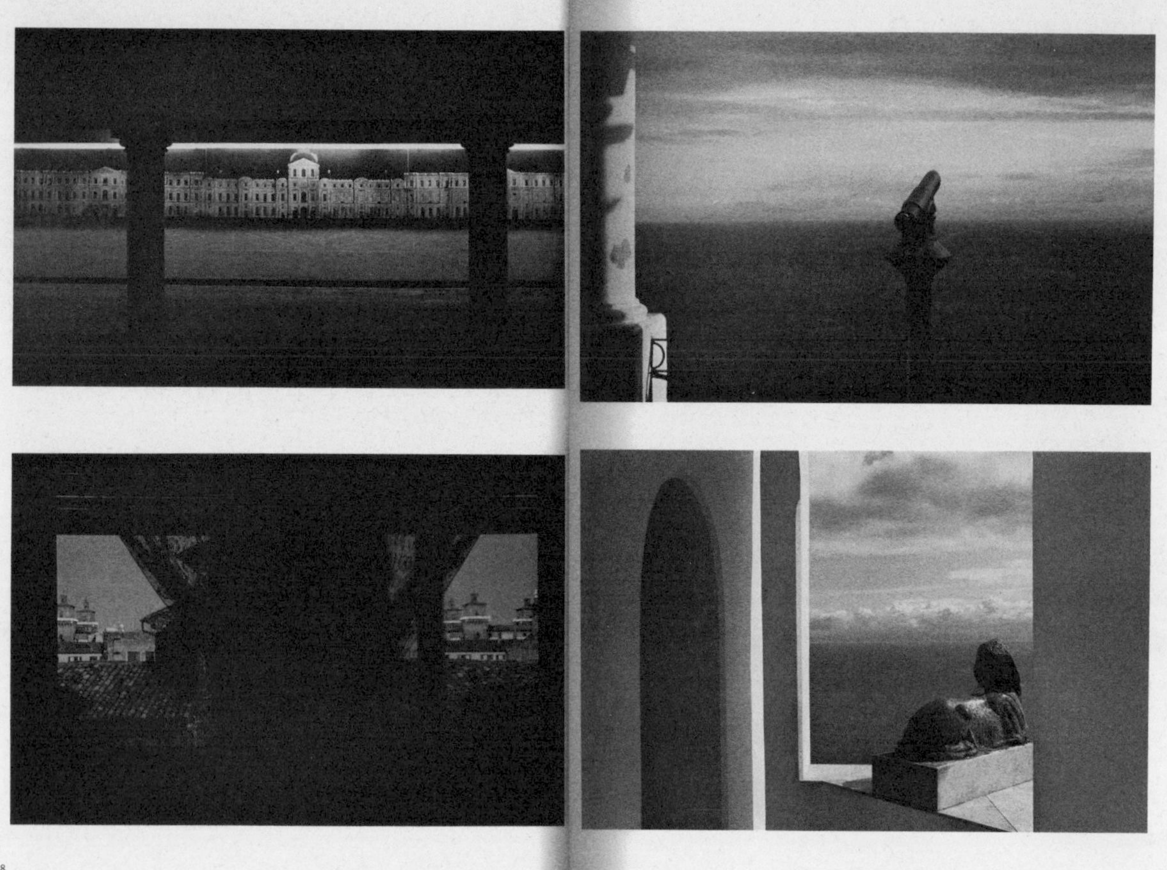

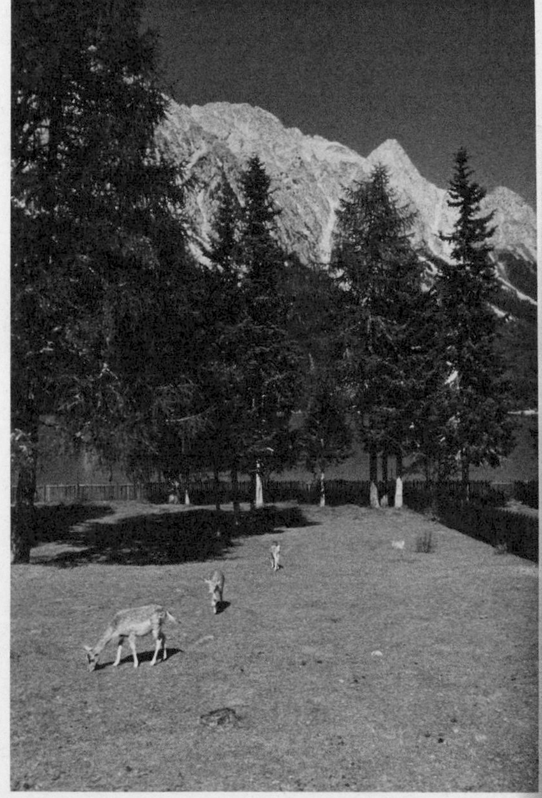

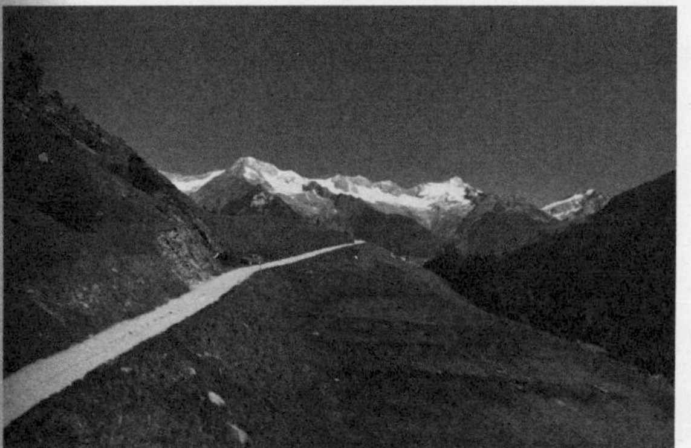

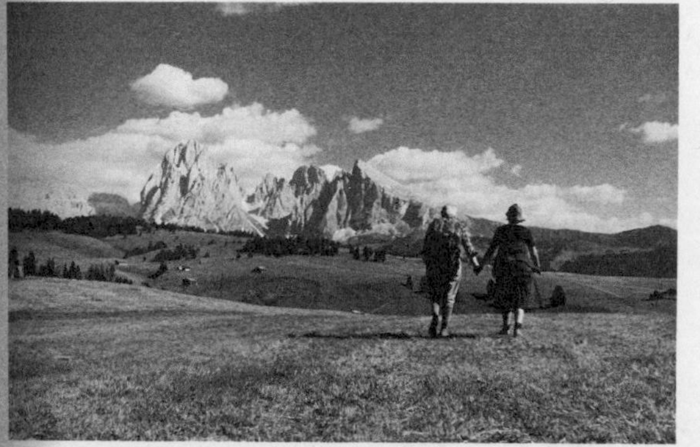

28

29

30

31

Camera Austria Award

2013   Camera Austria Award for Contemporary Photography by the City of Graz

Camera Austria International

1999   Maia Damianovic, "Interview with Joachim Koester," text contribution,
Catsou Roberts, "Joachim Koester: Blauer Schleier: Bilder aus einem kürzlich geträumten Traum," text contribution,
Joachim Koester, artist contribution,
Camera Austria International 66 / 1999

2006   Niels Henriksen, "Joachim Koester. Morning of the Magicians and Other Works, Galleri Nicolai Wallner, Copenhagen," exhibition review, *Camera Austria International* 94 / 2006

2013   Stefaan Vervoort, "Joachim Koester: Maybe One Must Begin with Some Particular Places, S.M.A.K., Ghent," exhibition review, *Camera Austria International* 121 / 2013

2014   Dan Byers, "Joachim Koester: Some Boarded Up Houses," text contribution, Joachim Koester, artist contribution and cover, *Camera Austria International* 125 / 2014

2017   Francesca Laura Cavallo, "Joachim Koester: In the Face of Overwhelming Forces, Camden Art Centre, London," exhibition review, *Camera Austria International* 137 / 2017

Exhibitions

2006   *First the artist defines meaning. On the Conceptual Paradigm,* exhibition contribution

2009   *Then the work takes place. On the Conceptual Paradigm in Contemporary Photography,* exhibition contribution

2014   *The Ghost Shop,* solo exhibition

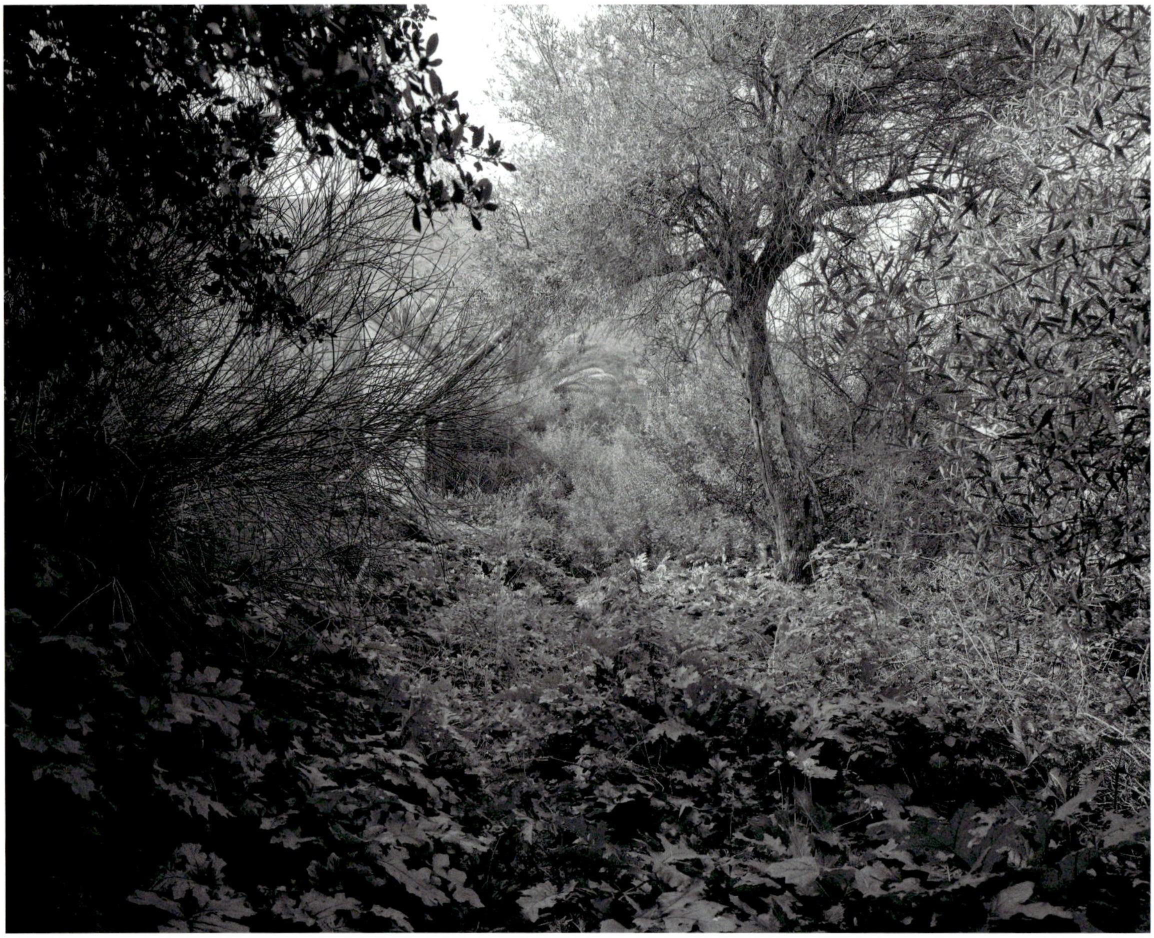

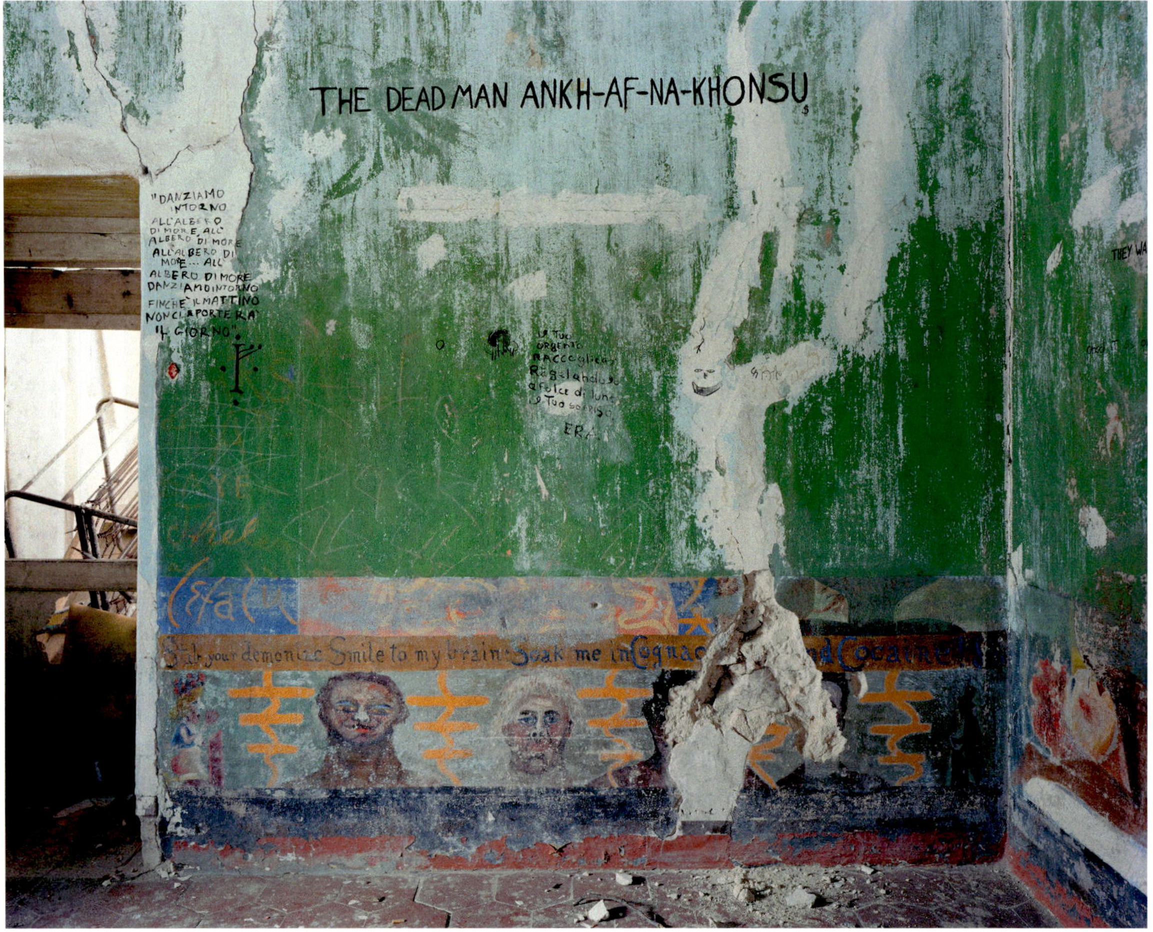

Morning of the Magicians, 2005–2006

Morning of the Magicians

The house and garden of the Abbey were completely overgrown in a strangely evocative way. As I walked the faintly visible path to what was once the main entrance, I was so overwhelmed by the scene's dormant qualities that I had to pause. It seemed to me as if sediments, pieces of leftover narratives and ideas from the individuals that once passed through this place had formed knots, as tangled as the bushes and trees that were now taking over, creating a kind of sleeping presence.

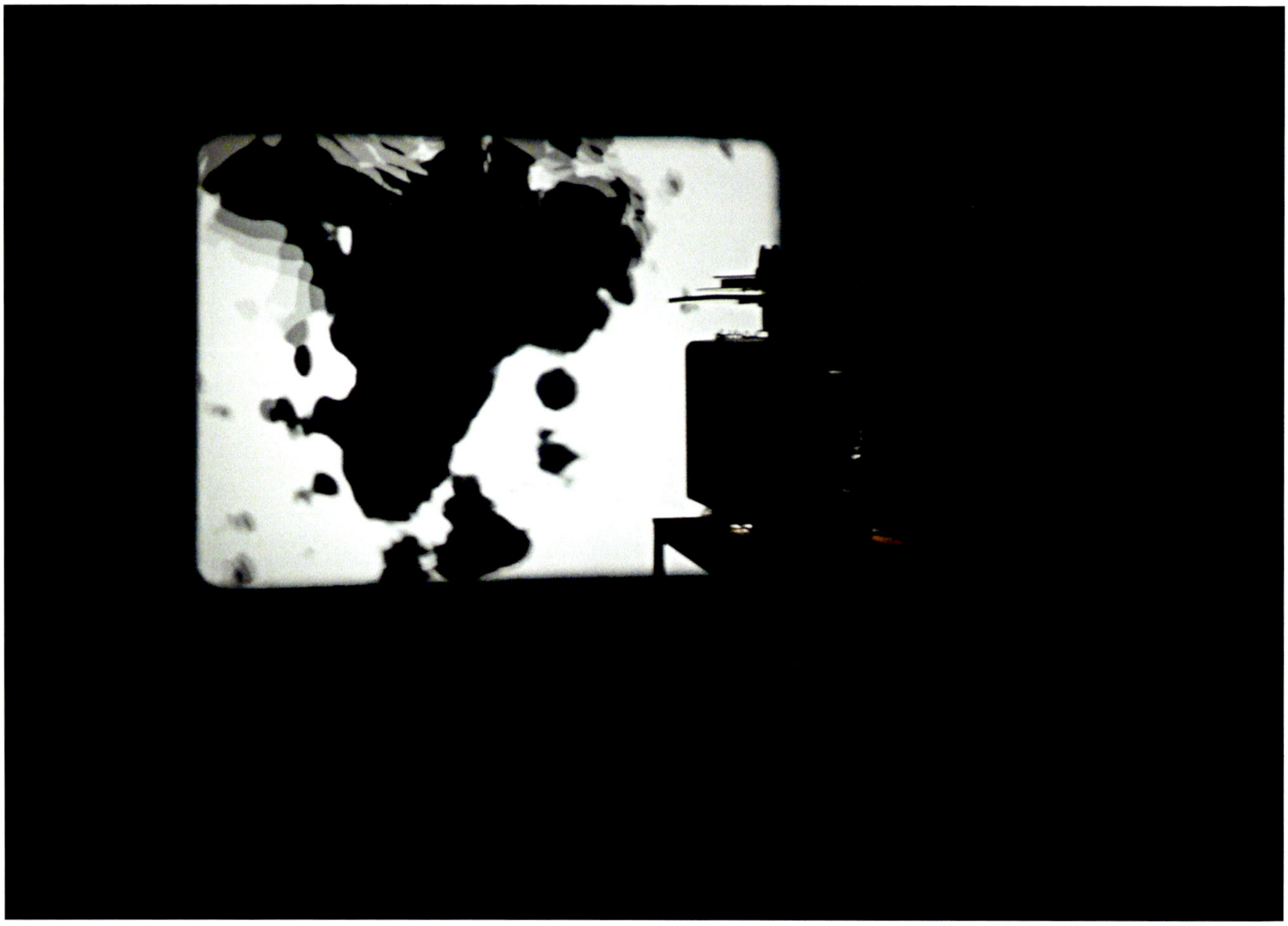

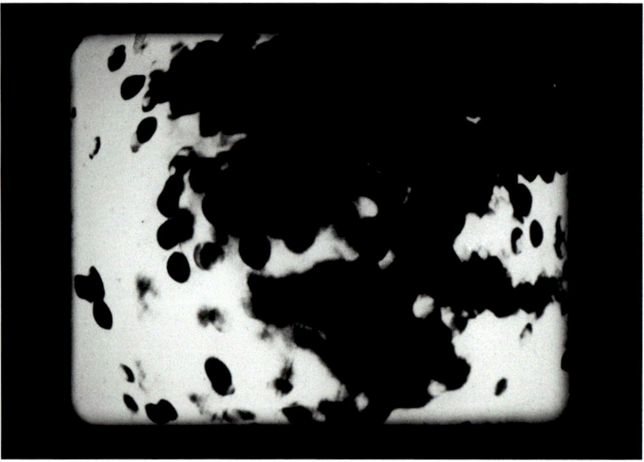
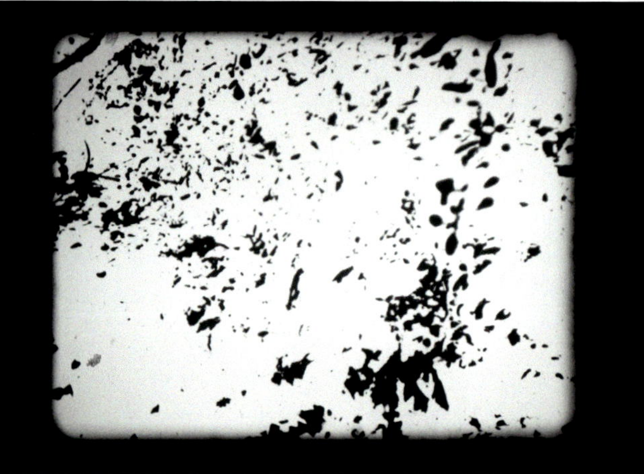
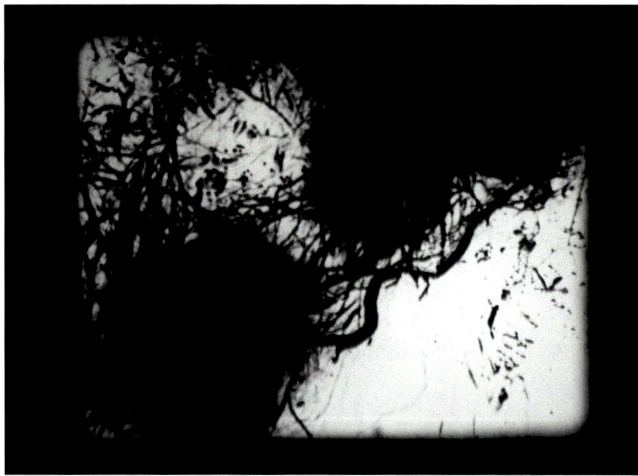
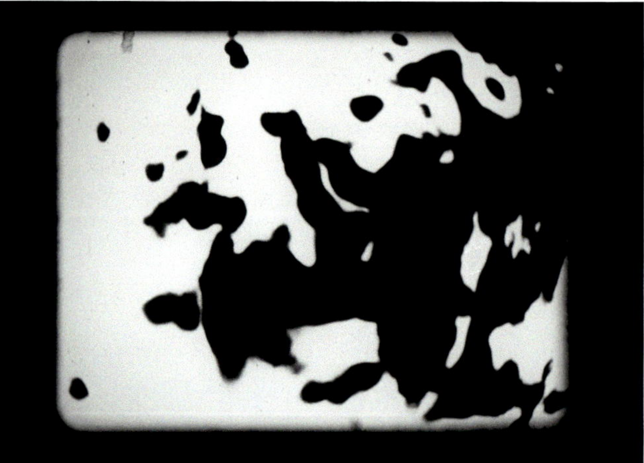

Morning of the Magicians, 2005–2006, installation view

86

Camera Austria

INTERNATIONAL

Zielony
... Lübbke-Tidow
...aucyila Brooke
Dan Byers
Alanna Lockward

CH
23,– sFr

Camera Austria International 125 / 2014. Cover

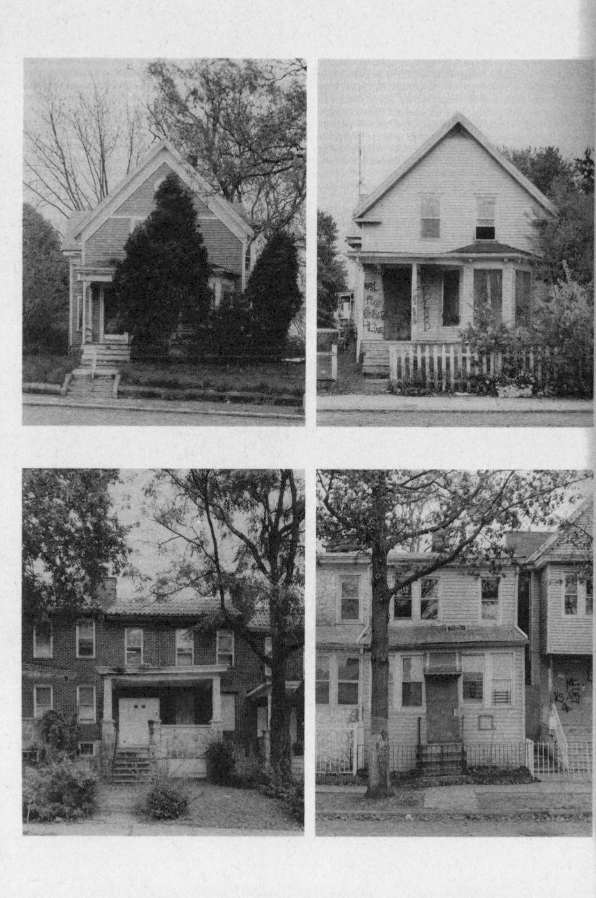
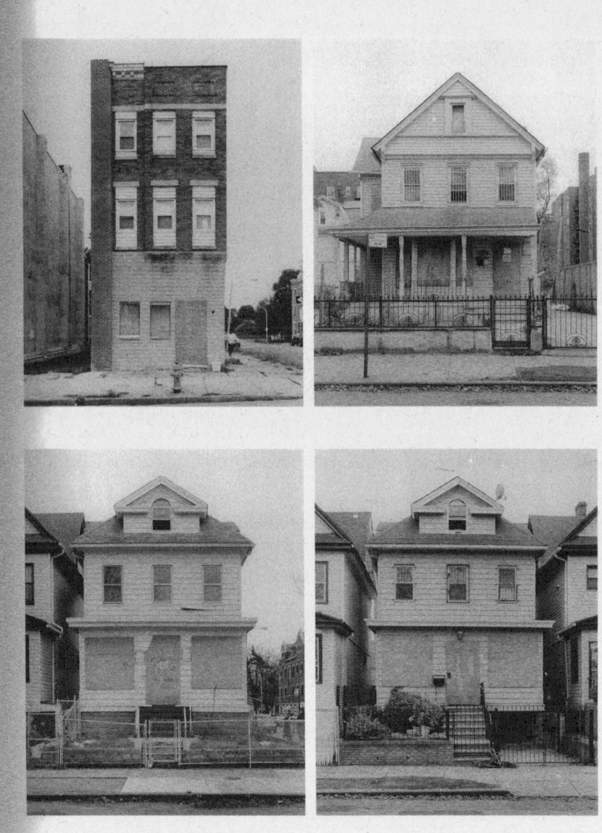
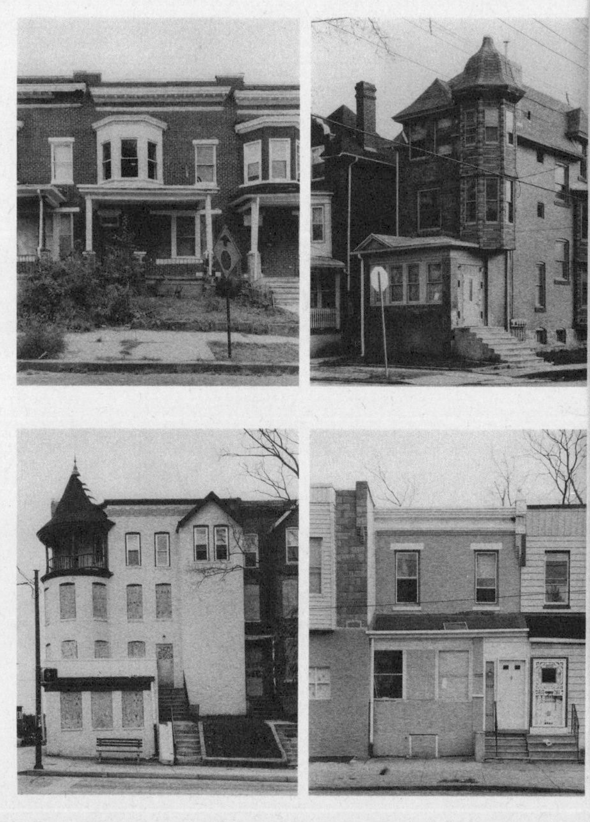
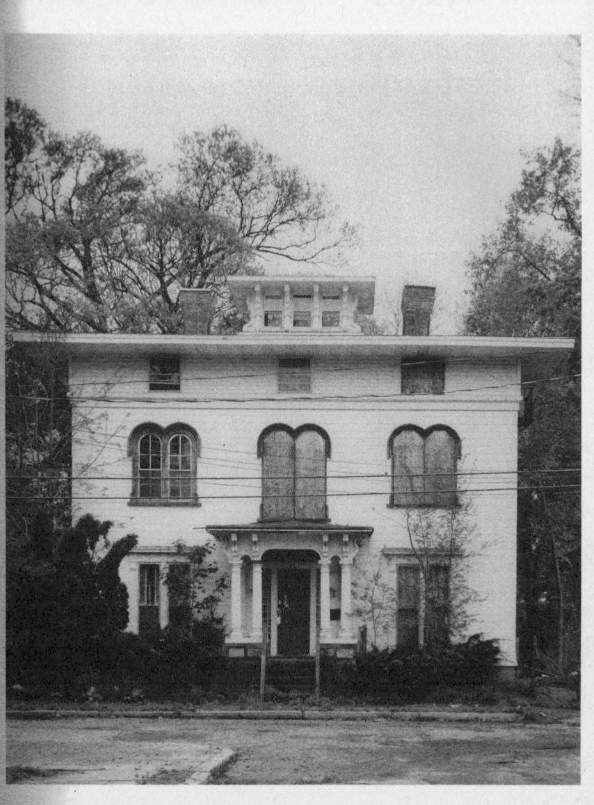

Lieko Shiga

Camera Austria
International

2008   Presentation at Forum, *Camera Austria International* 101 / 2008

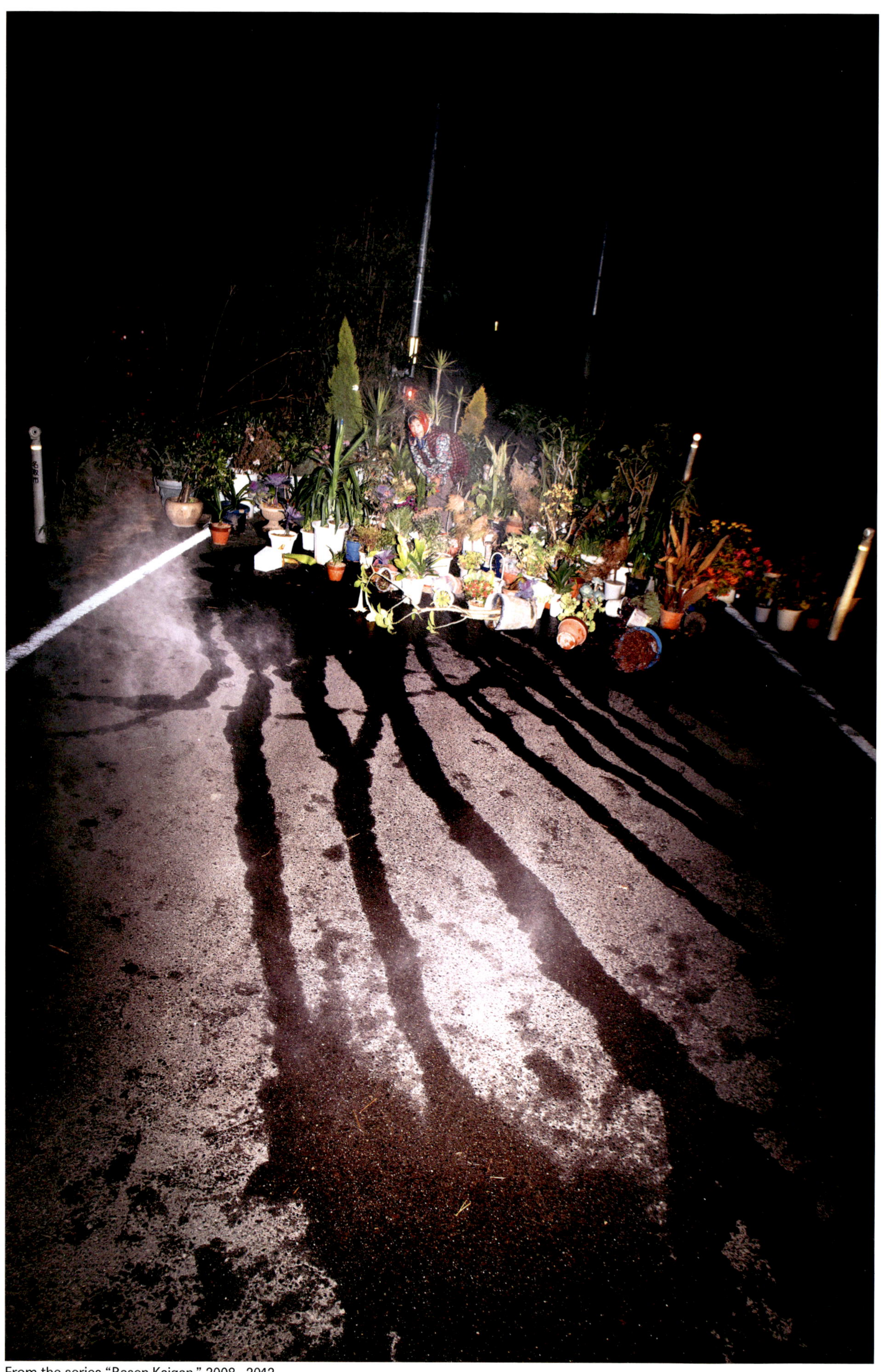

From the series "Rasen Kaigan," 2008–2012

Lieko Shiga

Rasen Kaigan

In winter 2008, I met a place called Kitagama, a village in northeast part of Japan, facing the Pacific Ocean. There, 372 lived in people with 107 houses. The "Rasen Kaigan" series consists of 250 pictures which were taken in this village, while I was living there as a resident photographer: documenting in photographs festivals, ceremonies, and every official activity of the village, collecting oral histories of the village to my body. These works were born in collaboration of the residents of Kitagama and me. The bodies of those residents who became subject of the works represent all the stories which are so delicate and invisible to be written as a history. Through the ritual of the shooting the photographs, their bodies unify to "the land." On the other hand I tried to photograph, through subsuming and reflecting the ritual of shooting photographs, my body experiences and traces which are related to the land of the Kitagama. The title "Rasen Kaigan" means "Rasen=spiral / helical morphology, Kaigan=coast" in direct translation but I also meant "Past, Present, or Future" with this title. In the space of photographs, there is no past, present or future: the value of the photographs swings from being treated as litter to having the same value as a living human being, or more, a subject for a prayer.

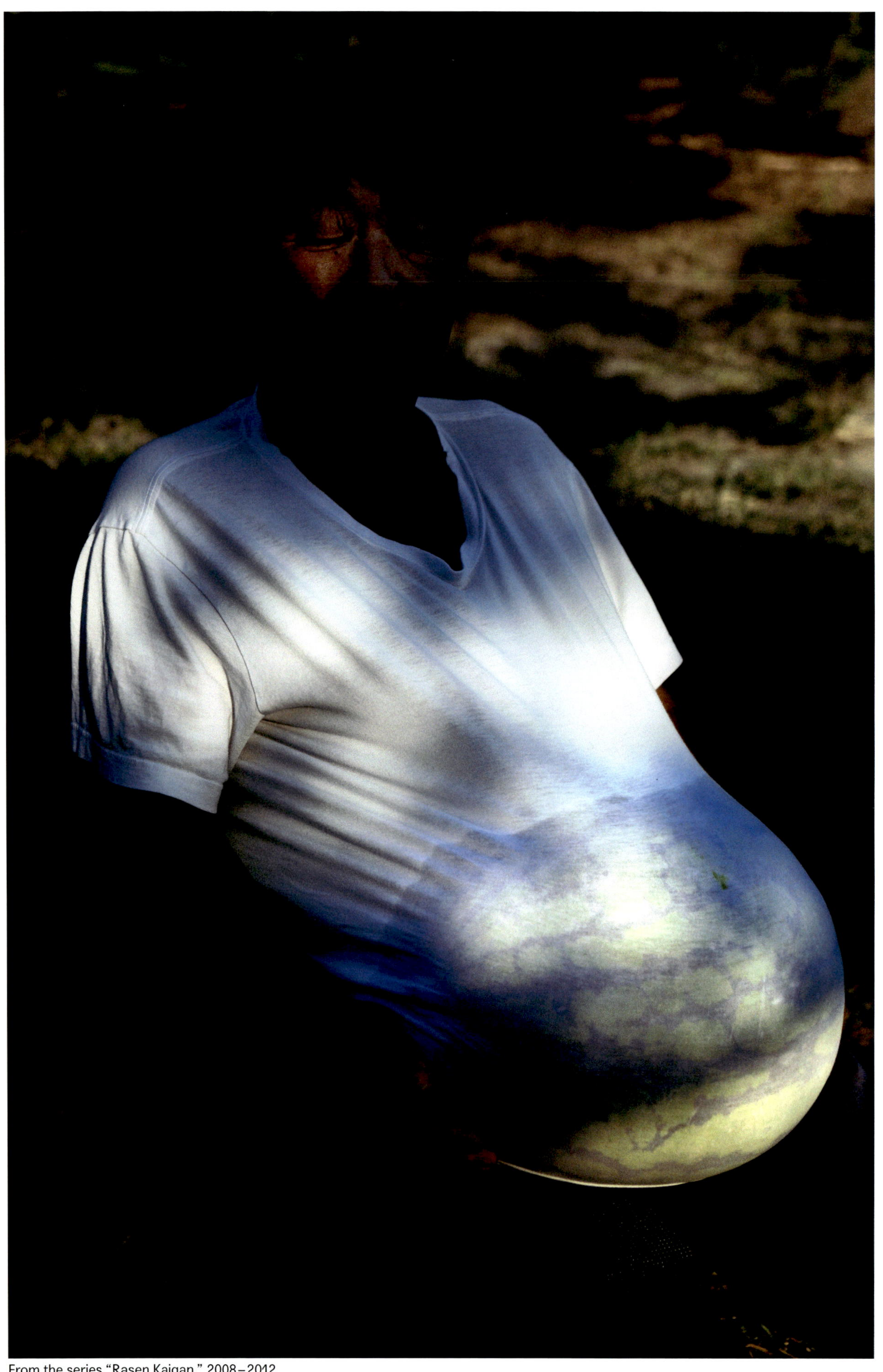

From the series "Rasen Kaigan," 2008–2012

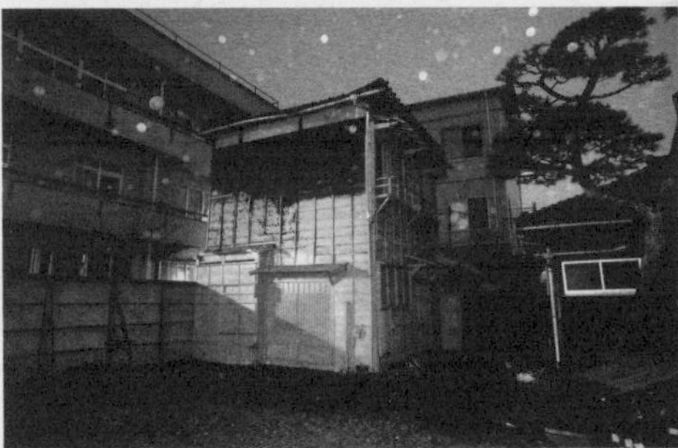

Pink House, 2006. C-print, 60 cm x 90 cm.

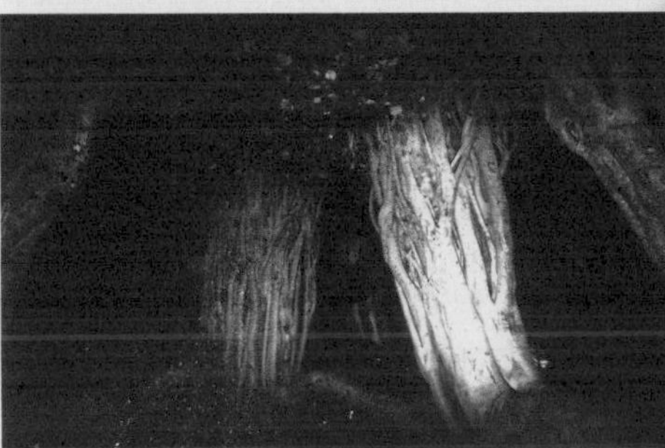

Forest of Figs, 2006. C-print, 60 cm x 90 cm.

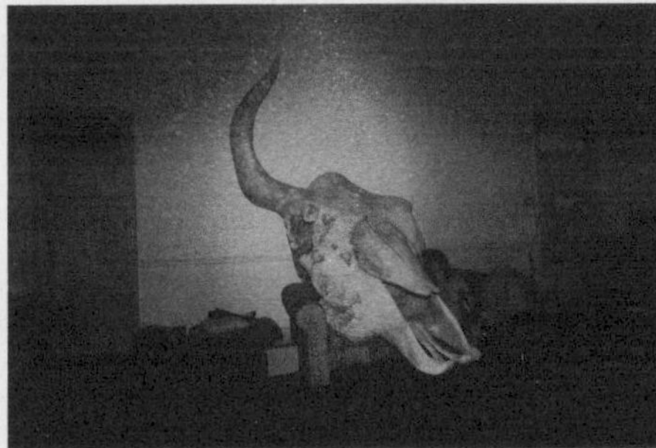

My Husband, 2006. C-print, 60 cm x 90 cm.

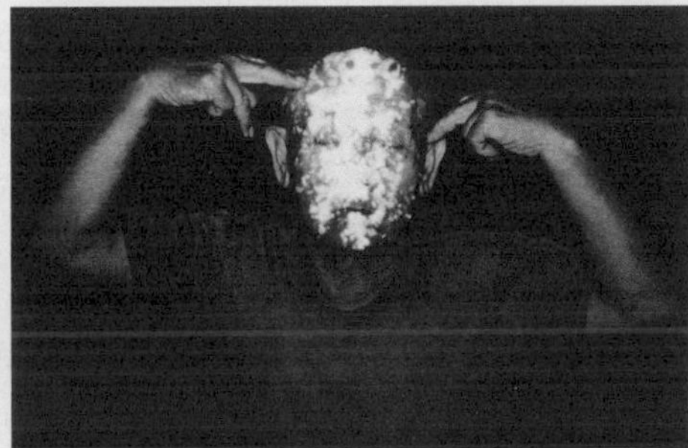

Remember that?, 2006. C-print, 60 cm x 90 cm.

DEATH BY SHOOTING

The photographic paper becomes evidence. The printed image appears before me, smelling strongly as though it were some kind of raw food. If the axis of time in this world also exists in the photograph, then I am completely out of range and trying to escape from the floating and ungraspable uncertainty that is the »present«; I'm desperately trying to get a grip on the axis that really exists.
Confronting the inevitability of my own death and the passage of time, the act of creating frozen time resembles that of prayer, and some images are imbued with strong emotions and desires that respond to my self-confrontation.
When taking photographs, I set up scenarios that will bring out the coincidental within the image, and allowing myself to lose control of the vision that I consciously hold in my mind, I wait for the unforeseeable results that will be captured by the camera. If »shooting« photographs is like an act of killing, then it is also as though I am being shot, and time is revived through this act. Together with that, the creative process disappears like a form of memory loss, and as though a defection to the other side is taking place, the events depicted on the photo paper slowly replace the memories in my mind.

[...] already see the image before I even encounter and photograph the people or the sceneries depicted. The time that exists before the [...] the photograph »shoots« me – me who is out of range – and it is revived. The body is the empty vessel and the medium through which [...] times pass.
What is memory?
The people and sceneries have been sacrificed by the photograph.
Look at what they have offered to that world.

Lieko Shiga, born in Aichi prefecture (JP) in 1980, lives and works in Berlin. Graduated at Chelsea University of Art and Design (BA Fine Art New Media), London (GB) in 2004. www.liekoshiga.de

Dialog 2

Image & Identity

Sanja Iveković

Camera Austria Award

2009 Camera Austria Award for Contemporary
Photography by the City of Graz

Camera Austria International

2001 Katy Deepwell, "Sanja Iveković: Personal Cuts,
Galerie im Taxispalais, Innsbruck," exhibition
review, *Camera Austria International* 75 / 2001
2005 Nataša Ilić, "Sanja Iveković: Die Politik
des privaten Lehren," text contribution,
"Sanja Iveković," artist contribution,
Camera Austria International 90 / 2005
2011 Tom Holert, "Sanja Iveković: On the Humming
of the Community. On the Barricades,"
text contribution, Sanja Iveković, artist contribution, *Camera Austria International* 113 / 2011
2012 Walter Seidl, "Sanja Iveković, Sweet Violence,
MoMA, New York," exhibition review,
Camera Austria International 117 / 2012

Exhibition

2011 *Communitas. The Unrepresentable Community*,
exhibition contribution

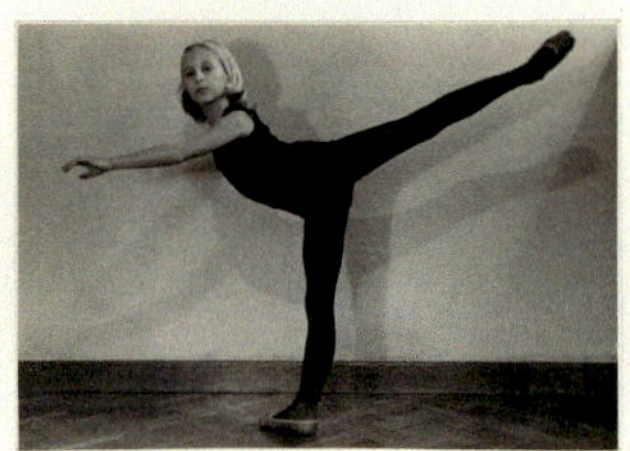

proljeće lo961.5. razred baletne škole.

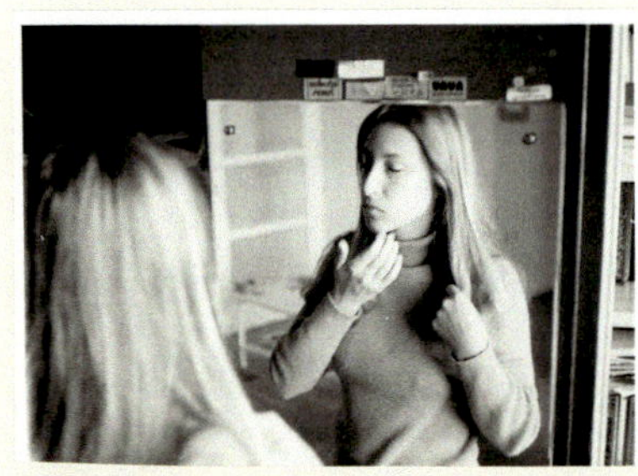

decembar 1975.Jutro pri stavljanju šminke.

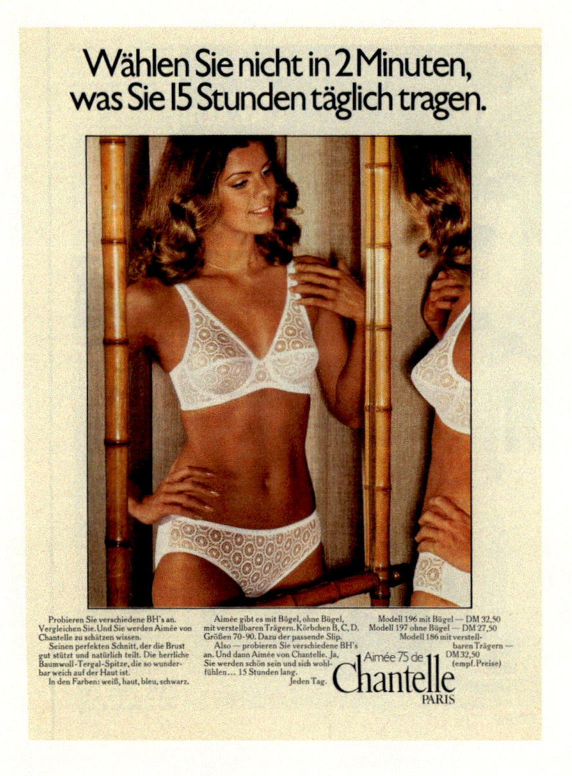

"BRIGITTE",novembar 1975.

From the series "Dvostruki Život," 1974–1975

Sanja Iveković

Dvostruki Život / Double Life

[…] In her early work, *Double Life* (1975), Iveković juxtaposed, in the form of an illustrated book, photos from the world of advertising with photos from her personal album. More recent artistic production was characterized by similar attempts to make a critical account of the manipulative role of advertising through achieving a parasitical relationship with the discourse of advertising and mass media. However, what is exceptional in Iveković's project is its *retroactive perspective.* Advertising imagery of women showing their bodies are not mimicked or re-enacted, but catapulted back to some personal memories recorded on old photographs. Paradoxically, this project is a double investigation: an investigation into the social condition of consumerism and its reflection in a socialist framework, but more importantly an investigation into a personal role as a woman in structuring social conditions. As opposed to a man on the similar task, Iveković's project is not a result of some public activity but a result of a very personal habit of glancing through fashion magazines and through her personal photo-album.

It is known too well that identities are constructed and imaginary. It is also the case that identities can be retroactive because they are always incomplete. To paraphrase Laclau and Zac, "every identification is constitutively incomplete and will have to be always re-created through new identification acts." Iveković, by identifying her own situations and postures from the past with advertising imagery, comes not just to her own "double life" but to a whole complexity of the ideological and gender issues of the Socialist Yugoslavia.

This is therefore not a double identity of any woman (and the generalized conclusion that her ego is not transparent and organized around a singular identity) but a double identity of the artist herself clutched between her critical public pursuits and personal desires and weaknesses.

Excerpt from: Branislava Andjelković, "How 'persons and objects' become political in Sanja Iveković's art?," in *Sanja Iveković Selected Works*, exh. cat., Barcelona: Fundació Antoni Tàpies, 2008.

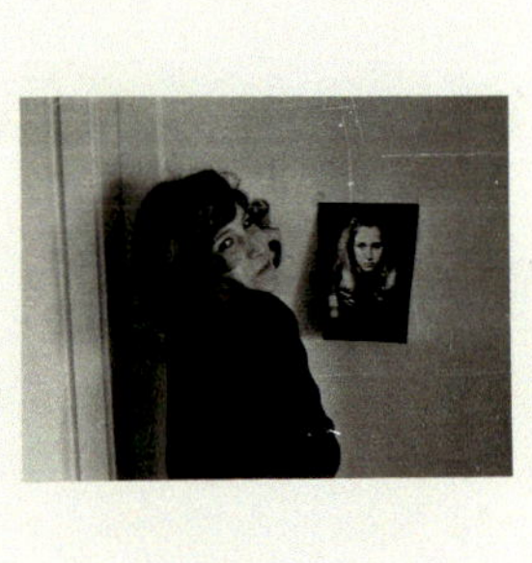

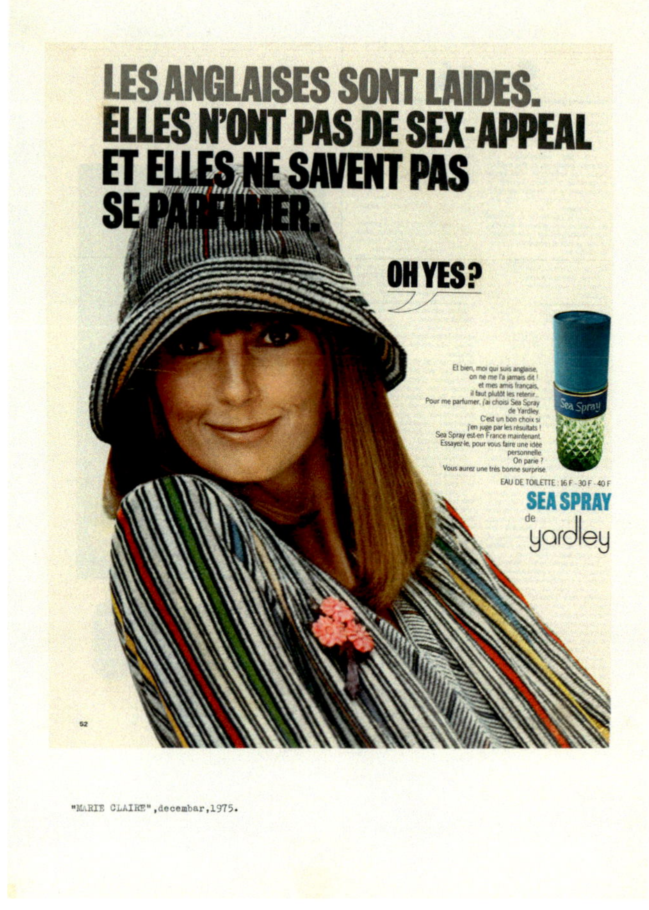

"MARIE CLAIRE",decembar,1975.

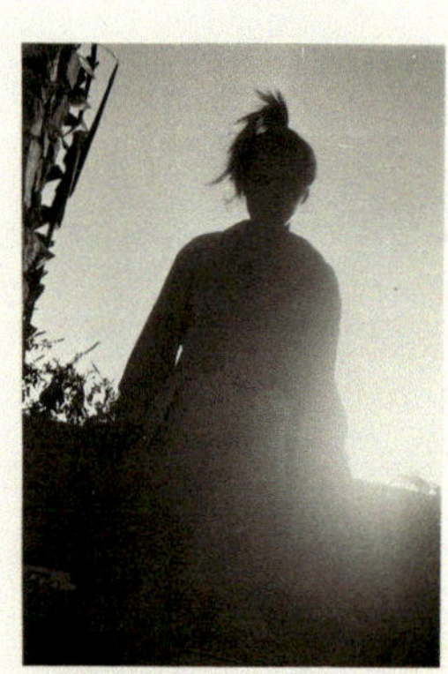

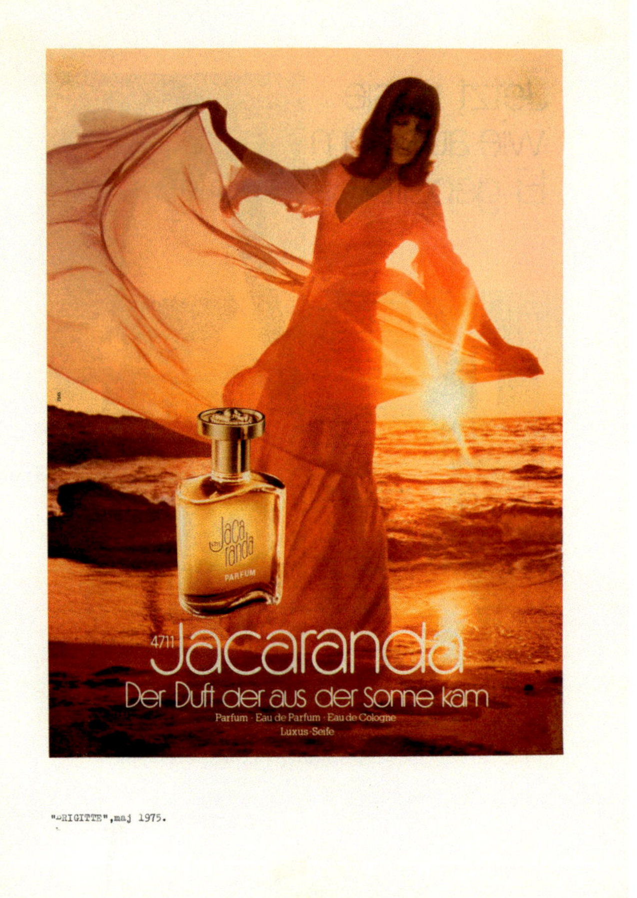

"BRIGITTE",maj 1975.

From the series "Dvostruki Život," 1974–1975

Life« (1975), where personal photos are paired with photos from the »crime« sections of newspapers.

Media coverage makes people and events appear appealing, interesting, dramatic, and desirable. On the pages of the mass media publications, the life of the artist comes across as almost glamorous and comprehensible. Yet Iveković – who as a protagonist of the so-called »New Art Practice« in Yugoslavia in the 70s[1] experienced the marginalisation of every artistic practice which departed from the classical divisions made by the media, i.e. into painting, sculpture and graphics – is actually dreadfully aware of the marginalised social position of artists and intellectuals understood as their »positionality in relation to capital circulation and accumulation«[2].

These works show how pervasive the textualisation of public life has become and how it works, but they also criticise the socialist regime. There are no artistic interventions in the images themselves, they are just ordered in pairs to reveal new meanings. These meanings do not refer only to gender construction in the proclaimed equality of the sexes under socialism, which, as described by Daša Duhaček, functioned as »a thin layer of ideologically-based egalitarianism superimposed on a stable patriarchy«[3], but also to the frustrations of the never satisfied longings of the socialist worker-consumer, whose striking propensity to consume was the declared difference between the Yugoslavian self-management model of socialism and the communist regimes of Eastern bloc countries. To put it simply, the media material used in these works implies that unlike other countries of the Eastern bloc, workers in Titoist Yugoslavia were not only seen as political subjects, but also as happy consumers in a welfare state. And it was exactly this discrepancy between the colourful and self-absorbed picture which society had of itself and projected onto reality, and the actual reality which continuously deepened social inequalities and conflicts – and in turn caused an aggravation which could only be resolved by a new nationalist self-absorption – that escalated so brutally with the war in Yugoslavia at the beginning of the 90s.

The juxtaposition of media and private images locates politics in media spaces and the private realm dominated by the media, thus revealing the way in which politics are always embedded in »ways of life« and »structures of feeling«.[4] The production and reception of critique took place in the public space of the gallery[5] and in the art world. It was exactly this framework that enabled a critical gaze and attention not usually dedicated to media images. This made it possible to recognise how the real is constructed in part through the media and reality in turn materially affected by media discourses; moreover, apparently immaterial and supposedly ahistorical phenomena like feeling, style etc. have direct political consequences.

In the 90s the site of critique shifted directly to media circulation. »Gen XX« is a work that was initially published in 1998 in the Croatian magazines »Arkzin«, »Kruh i Ruže« and »Zaposlena«. All these magazines were established within the so-called independent, alternative scene which arose during the 1990s out of a critique of nationalist politics and culture, state phantasms, and their ideological foundations and rhetoric. The work consists of textual interventions in advertising photos featuring famous fashion models. An image that is recognised as an advertisement by the average media

SANJA IVEKOVIĆ, from the series: Bitter Life / aus der Serie: Bitteres Leben, 1975. Photo collage, b/w newspaper photos including captions, b/w photographs from the artist's album / SW-Zeitungsfotos inkl. Bilduntershriften, 21 cm x 29,5 cm.

»Double Life« (1975) ist eine Serie von paarweise zusammenge-stellten Fotografien, die jeweils aus einem Zeitschriftenbefo... und einem Bild aus dem privaten Fotoalbum der Künstlerin beste... hen und inhaltlich und formal miteinander korrespondieren. Di... hervorgehobenen prätentiösen Ähnlichkeiten zwischen dem privat... ten Bild und dem Medienbild, die den Unterschied zwischen dem... Original und der Kopie, zwischen Modell und Darstellung, zwi... schen Vorher und Nachher zum Verschwinden bringen, verweisen... darauf, welchen Druck die Medien auf die Form privater Erfahrun... gen ausüben, wie sehr wir von Medien umstellt sind und dies... unsere persönliche Identität durchdringen. Ein ähnliches Verfahre... der Paarung von Medienbildern mit persönlichen Fotos benutzt... Iveković auch in Arbeiten wie »Swee... Life« (1975/76), in... sie Fotos und Bildfol... genden aus den Skan... dalspalten der Tages... zeitungen, oder »Bit... ter Life« (1975), wo... sie Fotos aus Zei... tungsberichten über... Kriminalfälle mit Bil... dern aus ihren priva... ten Fotoalben kombi... nierte.

Medienberichte machen Menschen und Ereignisse attrak... tiv, interessant, dra... matisch und begeh... renswert. Selbst das... Leben von Kunst... schaffenden erschein...

auf den Seiten der Massenmedien als eingängig und nahezu gla... mourös. Doch Iveković, die als Protagonistin der so genannten »neuen Kunstpraxis« im Jugoslawien der siebziger Jahre[1] erlebt hatte, wie jede künstlerische Praxis, die von der klassischen media... len Spartentrennung in Malerei, Bildhauerei und Grafik abweicht, marginalisiert wird, ist sich der randständigen Situation von Künst... lerInnen und Intellektuellen – im Sinne ihrer »Positionierung im Verhältnis zur Kapitalzirkulation und -akkumulation«[2] – nur zu schmerzlich bewusst.

Ihre Arbeiten zeigen, wie umfassend die Textualisierung des öffentlichen Lebens geworden ist und wie sie funktioniert, sie kriti... sieren aber auch das sozialistische Regime. Iveković nimmt keiner... lei künstlerische Eingriffe an den Bildern vor, sie werden lediglich in Paaren angeordnet, um neue Bedeutungen zu enthüllen. Dies... verweisen nicht nur auf die Konstruktion von Gender in der vom Sozialismus proklamierten so genannten Gleichheit der Geschlech... ter, die, wie Daša Duhaček geschrieben hat, als »dünne Schicht eines ideologisch begründeten Egalitarismus ein stabiles Patriarcha... überlagerte«,[3] sondern auch auf die Frustrationen nie befriedigter Konsumwünsche des sozialistischen Arbeiterkonsumenten, durch dessen ausgeprägte Neigung zum Konsum sich das jugoslawische blockfreie Selbstverwaltungsmodell des Sozialismus von den kom... munistischen Regimes der Ostblockstaaten abhob. Anders gesagt: ArbeiterInnen im titoistischen Jugoslawien im Gegensatz zu ande... ren Ostblockstaaten nicht nur als politische Subjekte, sondern auch als glückliche KonsumentInnen in einem Wohlfahrtsstaat gesehen wurden. Und es war genau diese Diskrepanz zwischen dem auf die Realität projizierten, selbstgefälligen Selbstbild der auf sich... Gesellschaft und der tatsächlichen Realität, in der sich die sozialen Ungleichheiten und Konflikte ständig vertieften und Spannungen

Opposite page / gegenüberliegende Seite

SANJA IVEKOVIĆ, from the series: Sweet Life / aus der Serie: Süßes Leben, 1975/76. Photo collage, b/w magazine photos, b/w photographs from the artist's album / Foto-collage, SW-Zeitungsfotos, SW-Fotografien aus dem Album der Künstlerin, 36 cm x 29,2 cm.

40

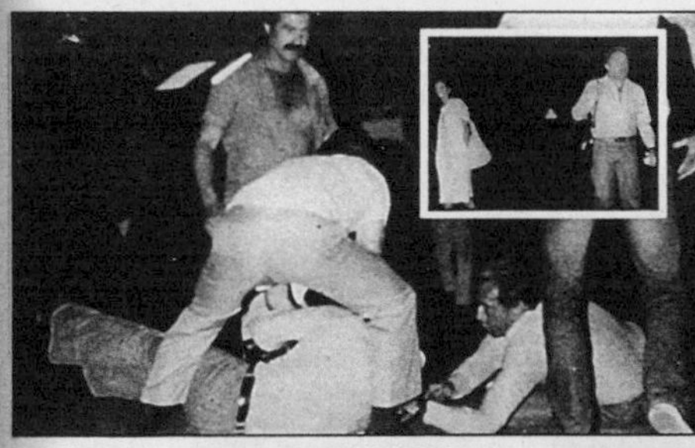
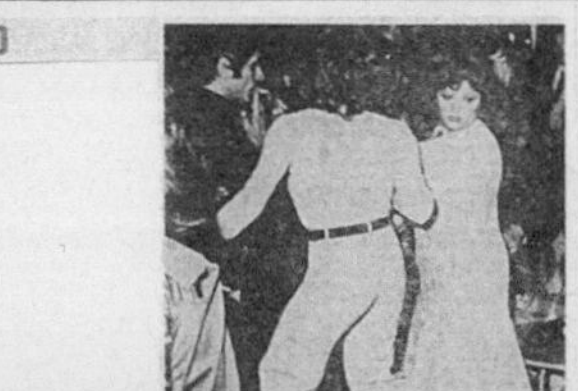
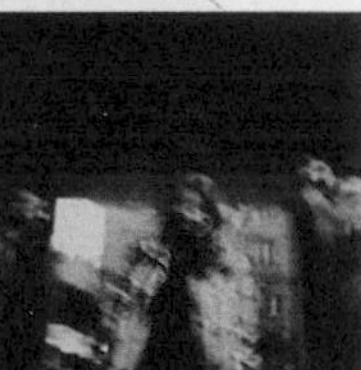
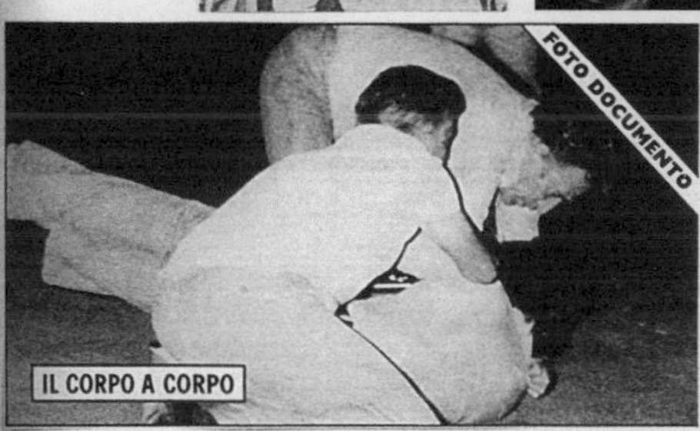

41

consumer is augmented by a text that introduces the model using the first name and surname of a national heroine from the anti-fascist struggle of World War II, along with her age at the time of her death. In the late 1980s, if not even earlier, the stories of national heroines (and the same goes for national heroes) had ceased to be an inspiration or role model for the younger generation of socialists, although the socialist state of Yugoslavia continued up until its very end to diligently commemorate its own foundations legitimised by national uprisings against the occupation during WWII, which under the leadership of the Communist Party developed into a revolution that overthrew the bourgeois regime. The system tirelessly proclaimed the continuity of the socialist revolution, but the cynicism of everyday life linked the names of these national heroes with institutions, factories and brand names rather than with the ideals of the struggle for social justice and equality for which people were willing to sacrifice their lives. But during the 90s, with society contaminated by nationalist ideology, war, the triumph of capitalism and the rediscovery of market economy, the struggle against the so-called left cultural hegemony – understood as a foreign, external element that threatened the purity of national identity – Croatia officially, albeit timidly, accepted its anti-fascist heritage, while in fact denying it by supporting the silent amnesia of the whole socialist era. In such a situation, presenting national heroines as advertisement models in the media is not only a cynical commentary on the ideology that promotes one thing and does another, but also a gesture endorsing human and social values denied by the system. The artist does not intervene in the images but, without deviating much from the aesthetics of advertising, changes the text and lets the images, in which the models are looking straight at the viewers, »seduce« the audience.

Iveković knows how visualisation operates in the dramatisation of politics, and that the creation and politicisation of readership is a key feature of politics in contemporary society. Thus by using the techniques employed in the symbolic construction of media readership, she transforms their usual political applications. The work advertises the values which national heroines stood for – dedication to the ideals of social justice and equality – but also the image of women who participate on equal terms in public affairs and politics, as opposed to the prevailing ideal of women in Croatia of the 90s, which stressed family values and motherhood as the only proper domains for women. Using her symbolic power as an artist, Iveković enters the media to deliver the message society had been silent about, allowing the media to do its job.

A similar strategy is employed by the artist in her media interventions around the »Women's House« project which she has been developing with women's non-governmental organisations since 1997. The project grew out of a series of workshops with women

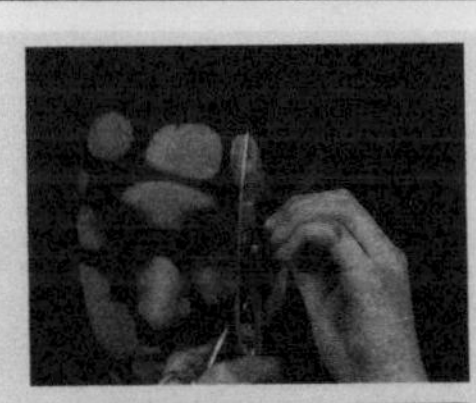
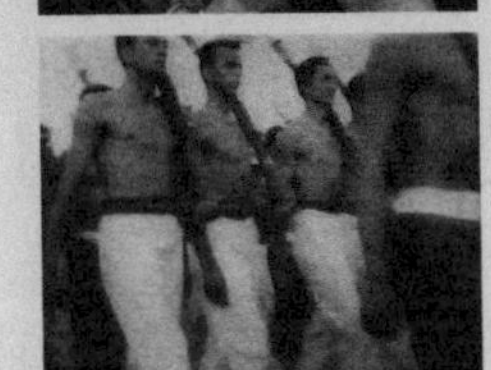

SANJA IVEKOVIĆ, top / oben: Still from / aus: Sweet Violence / aus: Süße Gewalt, 1974. Video. Below / darunter: Stills from / aus: Personal Cuts, 1982. Video.

hervorriefen, die ihrerseits n... durch eine neuerliche national... Selbstbezogenheit gelöst werde... konnten, welche Anfang der neu... ziger Jahre so brutal mit dem Krie... in Jugoslawien eskalierte.

Mit der Gegenüberstellung von Medienbildern und Privatbilder... wird Politik im Medienbereich un... in der von Medien dominierten Pri... vatsphäre verortet und zugleic... gezeigt, wie Politik stets i... »Lebensweisen« und »Gefühls... strukturen«[4] eingebettet ist. D... Produktion und Rezeption der Kri... tik fand im öffentlichen Raum de... Galerie[5] und im Umkreis der Kunst... welt statt. Genau in diesem Rahme... wurde es auch möglich, de... Medienbildern gegenüber einen kri... tischen Blick zu entwickeln, de... ihnen normalerweise nicht entge... gengebracht wird, und zu erkenne... dass die Realität etwas – zum T... durch die Medien – Konstruierte... und selbst wieder von Mediendis... kursen Beeinflusstes ist und da... scheinbar immaterielle und ver... meintlich ahistorische Phänome... wie Gefühl, Stil usw. unmittelba... politische Auswirkungen haben.

In den neunziger Jahren wur... der Ort der Kritik direkt in d... Medienwelt hinein verschobe... »Gen XX« (1998) ist eine Arbei... die ursprünglich in den kroatische... Zeitschriften »Arkzin«, »Kruh... Ruže« und »Zaposlena« veröffen... licht wurde, lauter Neugründunge... der so genannten unabhängige... Alternativszene, die in den neunzi... ger Jahren aus einer Kritik an de... nationalistischen Politik und Kul... tur, an Staatsphantasmen und der... ideologischen Grundlagen un... Rhetorik hervorgingen. Die Arbei... besteht aus Textinterventionen i... Werbefotos, auf denen berühmt... Models zu sehen sind. Bilder, di... von jedem durchschnittliche... Medienkonsumenten als Werbu... zu erkennen sind, werden durch einen Text ergänzt, der das Mode... mit dem Vor- und Nachnamen einer Nationalheldin des antifasc... stischen Kampfes im Zweiten Weltkrieg vorstellt und ihr Alter u... Todesdatum angibt. In den späten achtziger Jahren, wenn ni...

Following pages / folgende Seiten

SANJA IVEKOVIĆ, Gen XX (Nada Dimić), 1997/2001. Photo collage, digital print, 100 cm x 70 cm

SANJA IVEKOVIĆ, Women's House (AZKZ, Zagreb), 2003. Photo collage, digital print, 142 cm x 100 cm

SANJA IVEKOVIĆ, Women's House (UDI, Genova), 20... photo collage, digital print, 70 cm x 50...

SANJA IVEKOVIĆ, from the series / aus der Serie: Figure & Ground, 20... Photo collage, digital print, dimensions var...

42

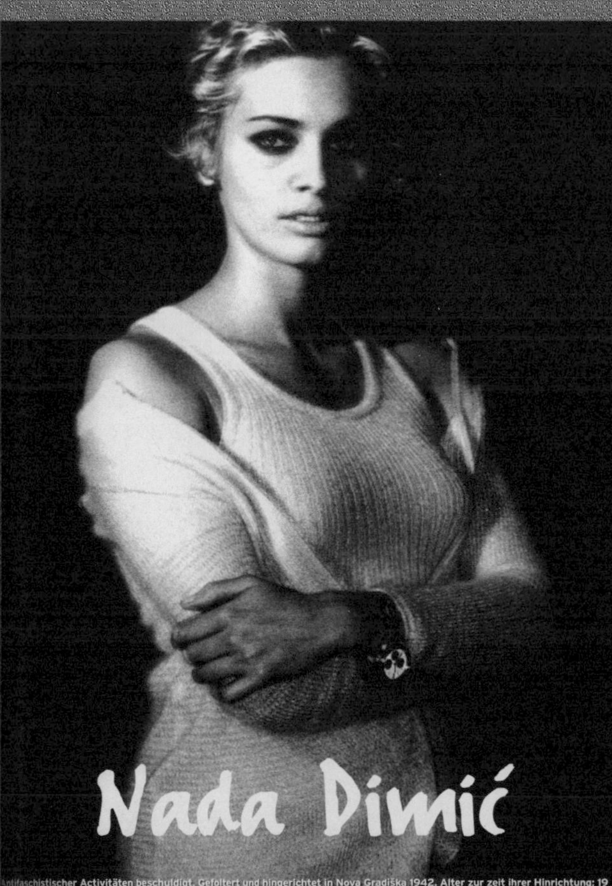

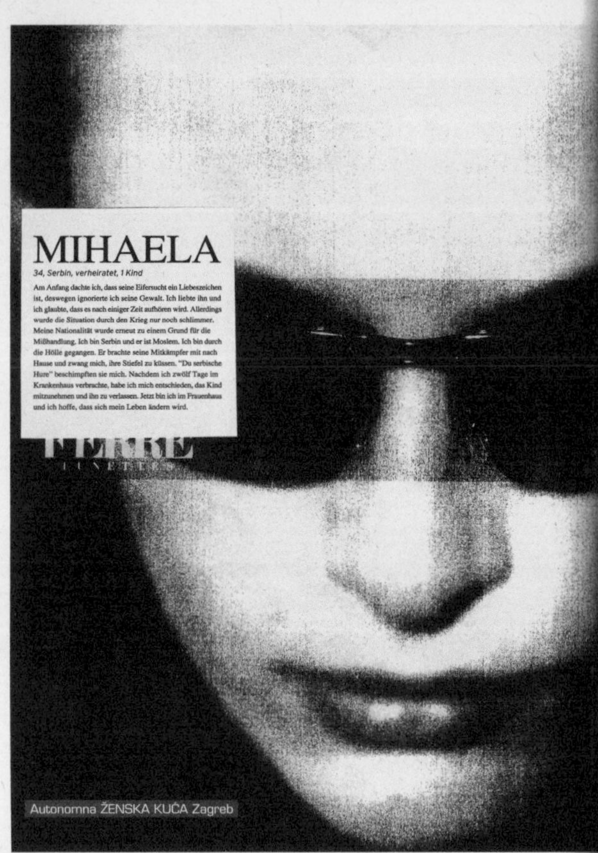

MIHAELA

34, Serbin, verheiratet, 1 Kind

Am Anfang dachte ich, dass seine Eifersucht ein Liebeszeichen ist, deswegen ignorierte ich seine Gewalt. Ich liebte ihn und ich glaubte, dass es nach einiger Zeit aufhören wird. Allerdings wurde die Situation durch den Krieg nur noch schlimmer. Meine Nationalität wurde erneut zu einem Grund für die Mißhandlung. Ich bin Serbin und er ist Moslem. Ich bin durch die Hölle gegangen. Er brachte seine Mitkämpfer mit nach Hause und zwang mich, ihre Stiefel zu küssen. "Du serbische Hure" beschimpften sie mich. Nachdem ich zwölf Tage im Krankenhaus verbrachte, habe ich mich entschieden, das Kind mitzunehmen und ihn zu verlassen. Jetzt bin ich im Frauenhaus und ich hoffe, dass sich mein Leben ändern wird.

FERRE
LUNETTES

Autonomna ŽENSKA KUĆA Zagreb

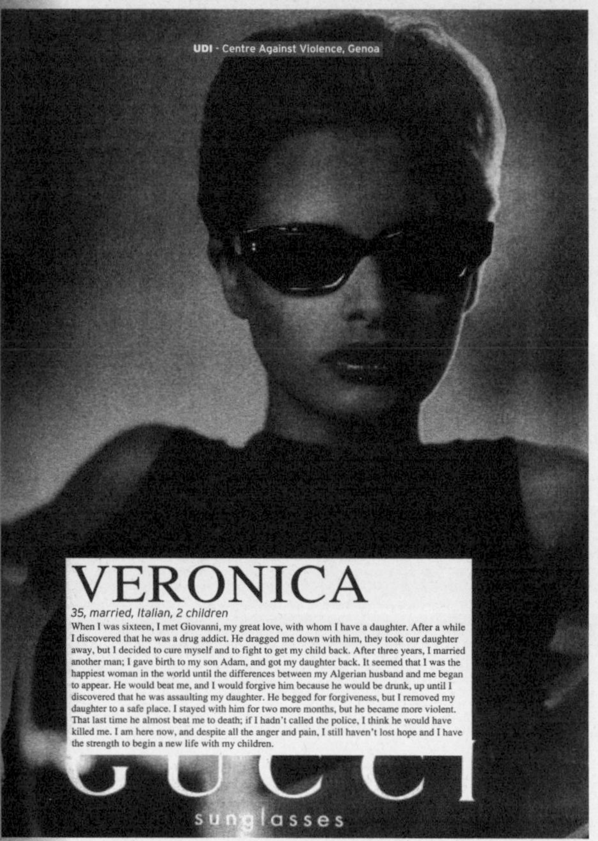

VERONICA

35, married, Italian, 2 children

When I was sixteen, I met Giovanni, my great love, with whom I have a daughter. After a while I discovered that he was a drug addict. He dragged me down with him, they took our daughter away, but I decided to cure myself and to fight to get my child back. After three years, I married another man; I gave birth to my son Adam, and got my daughter back. It seemed that I was the happiest woman in the world until the differences between my Algerian husband and me began to appear. He would beat me, and I would forgive him because he would be drunk, up until I discovered that he was assaulting my daughter. He begged for forgiveness, but I removed my daughter to a safe place. I stayed with him for two more months, but he became more violent. That last time he almost beat me to death; if I hadn't called the police, I think he would have killed me. I am here now, and despite all the anger and pain, I still haven't lost hope and I have the strength to begin a new life with my children.

GUCCI
sunglasses

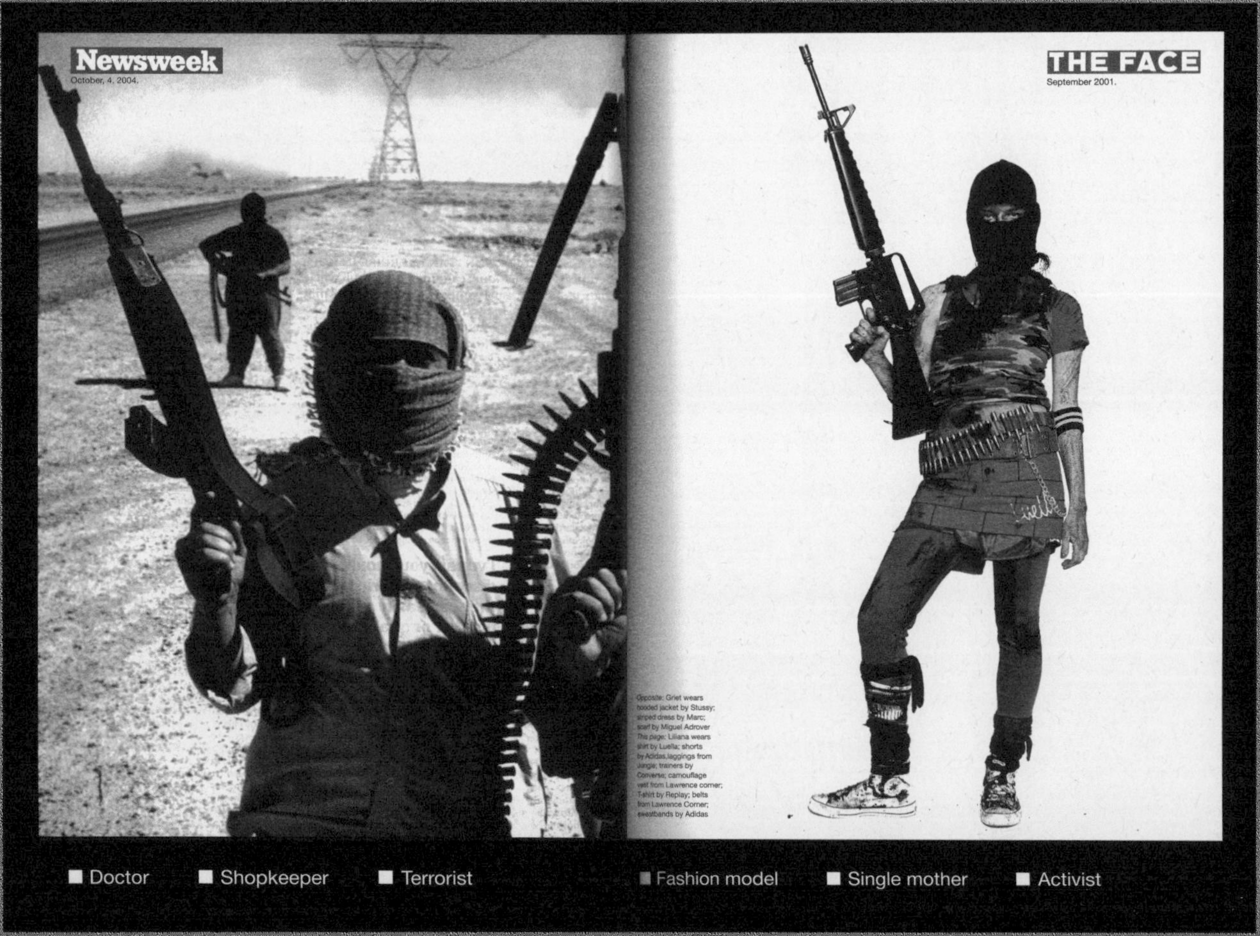

■ Doctor   ■ Shopkeeper   ■ Terrorist   ■ Fashion model   ■ Single mother   ■ Activist

Hans-Peter Feldmann

Camera Austria Award

1999 Camera Austria Award for Contemporary Photography by the City of Graz

Participation at Symposion

1994 Symposion on Photography XV: "The Archive"

Camera Austria International

1995 Hans-Peter Feldmann, "Der Kopf ist schon eine Maschine," artist contribution (journal of Symposion), *Camera Austria International* 51–52/1995

1999 Diedrich Diederichsen, "Fotografie und Gedenken: Feldmann, RAF, Schlick, Kippenberger usw.," text contribution, *Camera Austria International* 66/1999

2000 "Hans-Peter Feldmann," artist contribution, *Camera Austria International* 70/2000

2002 Manuel Olveira, "Hans-Peter Feldmann, Fundació Antoni Tàpies, Barcelona; Centre national de la photographie, Paris; Fotomuseum Winterthur, Winterthur; Museum Ludwig, Köln," exhibition review, *Camera Austria International* 78/2002

2005 Maren Lübbke-Tidow, "Hans-Peter Feldmann und Klaus Heilmann: Frauen im Gefängnis, Barbara Wien, Berlin," exhibition review, *Camera Austria International* 92/2005

2011 Alberto Martín, "Hans-Peter Feldmann: An Art Exhibition, Museo Nacional Centro de Arte Reina Sofía, Madrid," exhibition review, *Camera Austria International* 113/2011

2012 Ulrike Matzer, "Hans-Peter Feldmann, Serpentine Gallery, London; BAWAG Contemporary, Vienna; Deichtorhallen, Hamburg," exhibition review, *Camera Austria International* 119/2012

Exhibitions

1994 *The Archive,* exhibition contribution
1999 *Künstlerbücher,* solo exhibition
2003 *Graz,* solo exhibition
2011 *Milk Drop Coronet. 30 Exhibitions on the Virtuosity of Thingness,* exhibition contribution

Publication

2002 *Hans-Peter Feldmann. Graz,* Düsseldorf: 3 Möven Verlag, Edition Camera Austria, 2002.

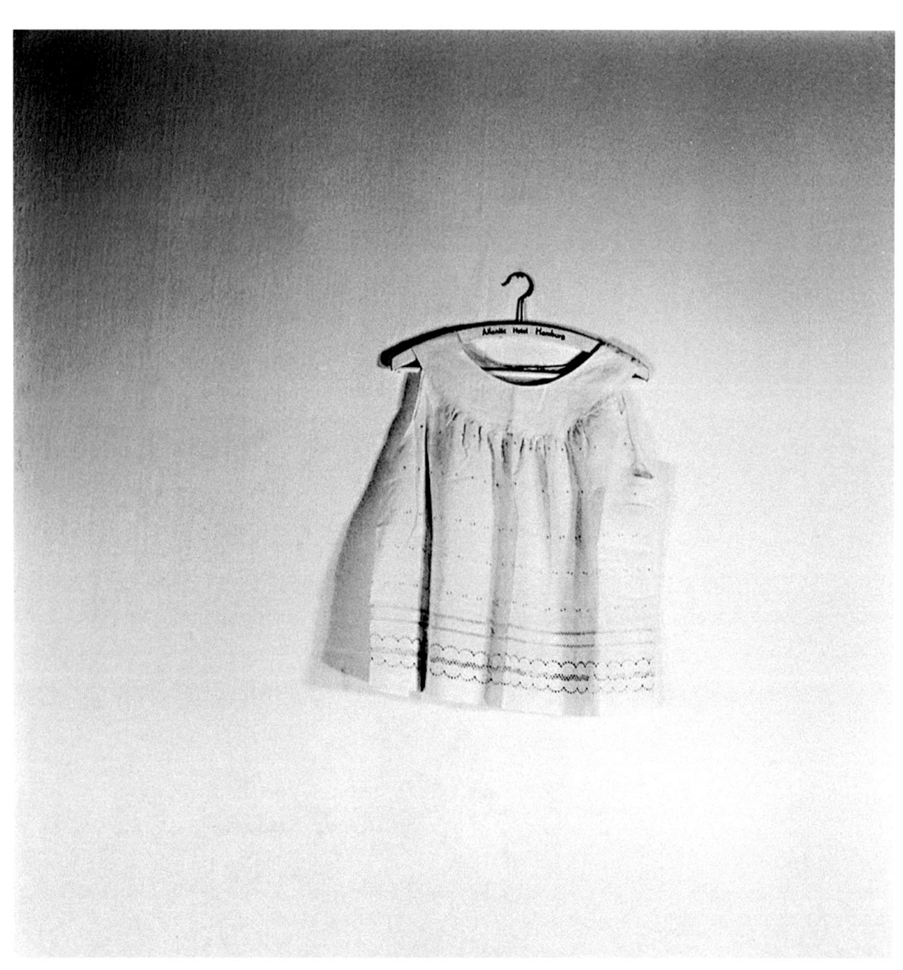

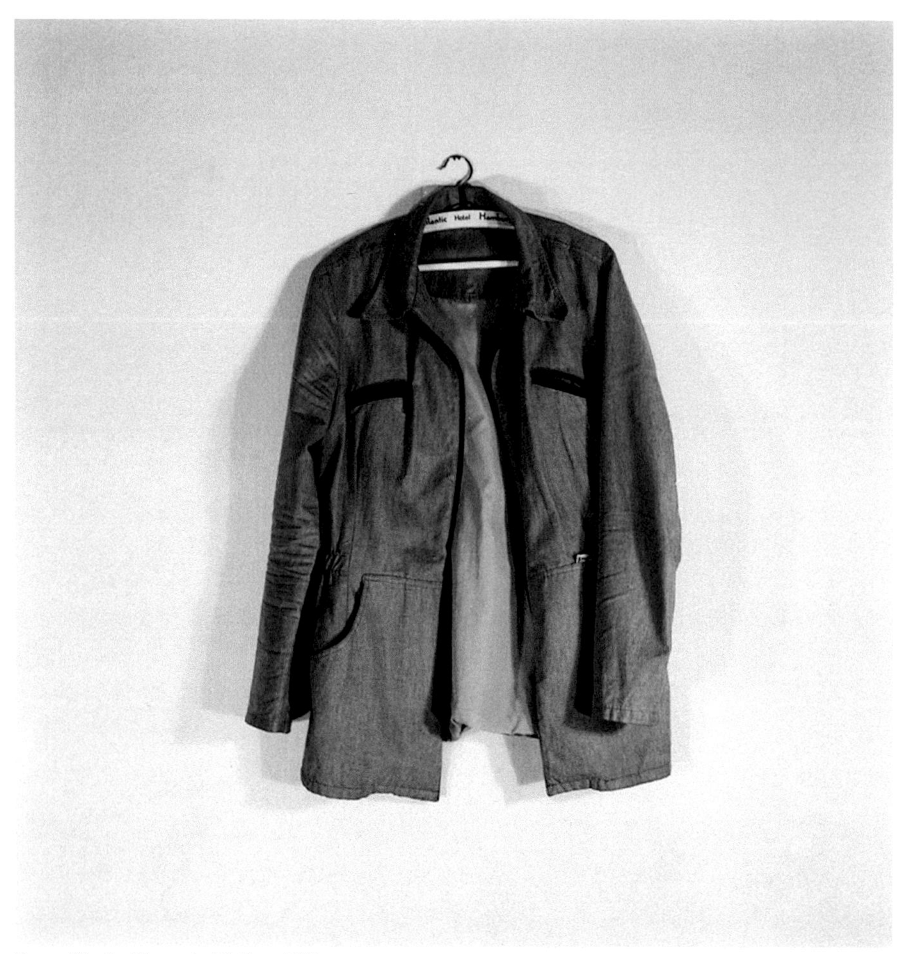

From *All of a Woman's Clothes*, 1975

Hans-Peter Feldmann

"I'm a camera with its shutter wide open, quite passive, recording, not thinking. Recording the man shaving at the window opposite and the woman in the kimono washing her hair. Some day, all this will have to be developed, carefully printed, fixed."

Quote from Christopher Isherwood's novel, *Good Bye to Berlin,* 1932 in *Hans-Peter Feldmann*, Graz: Edition Camera Austria, 2002.

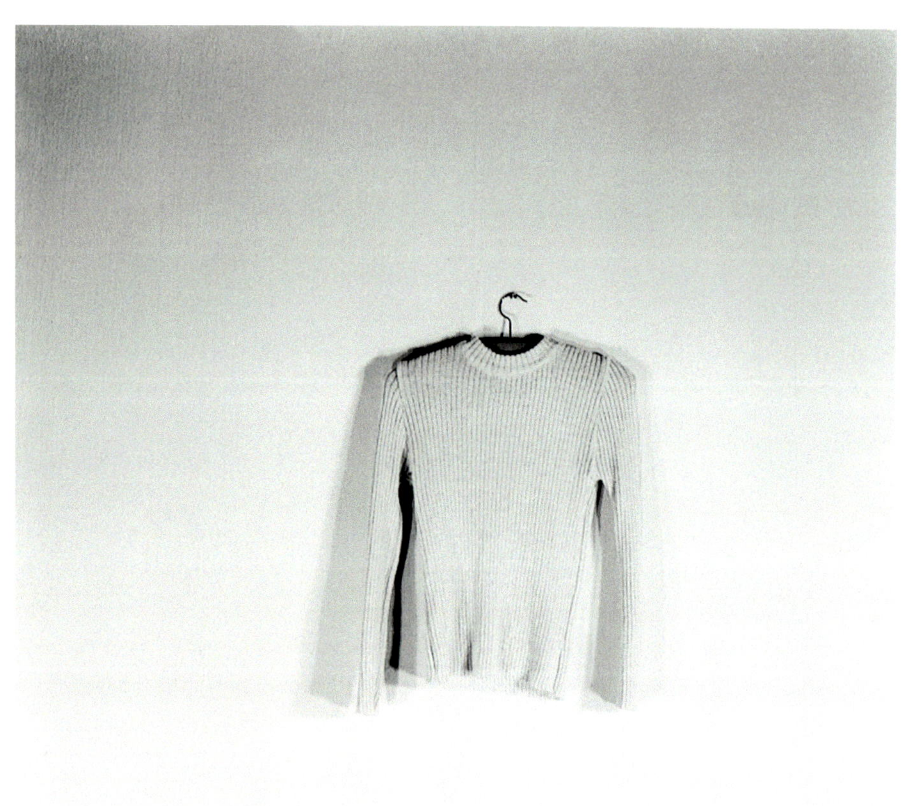

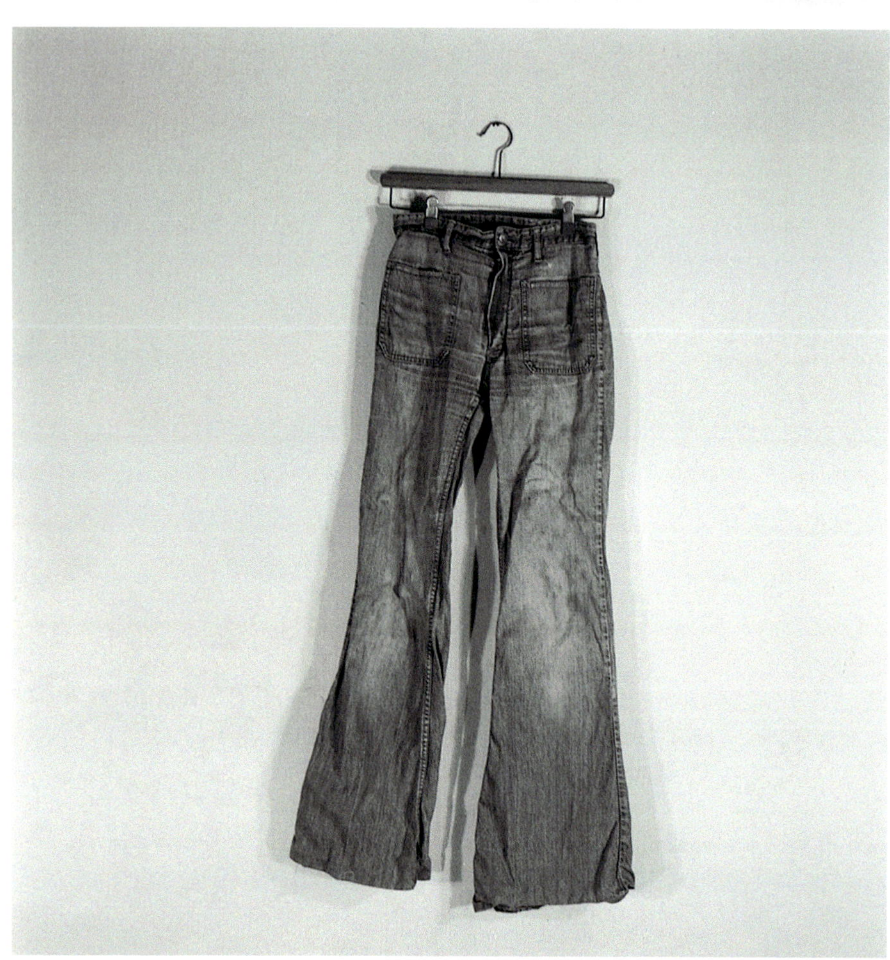

From *All of a Woman's Clothes*, 1975

Hans-Peter Feldmann

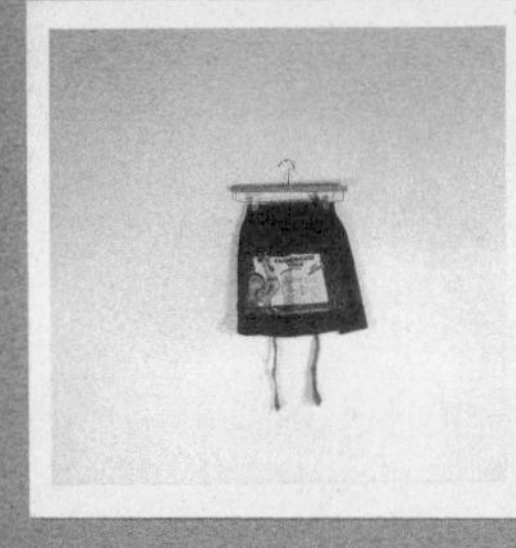
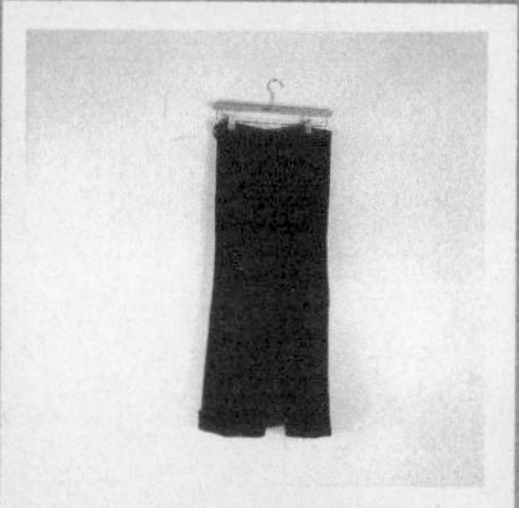
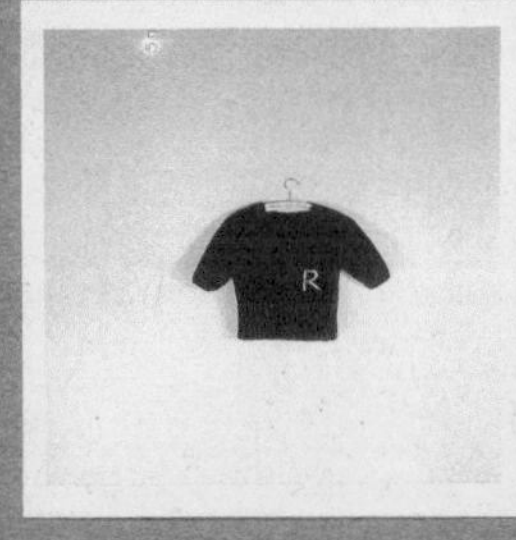
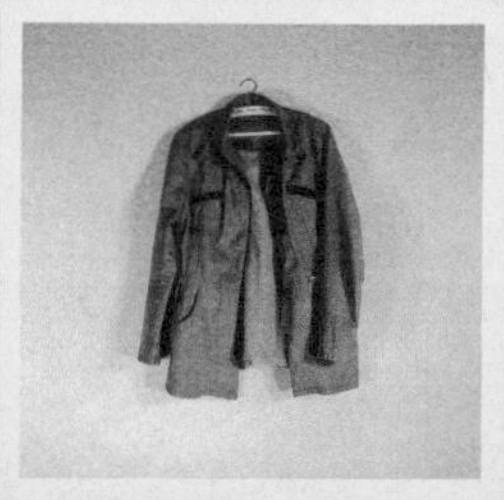
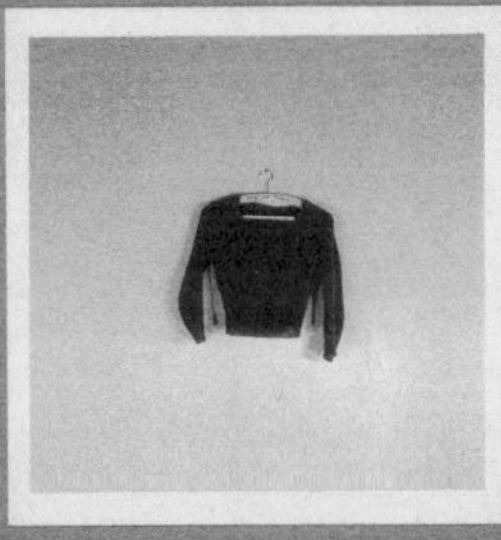
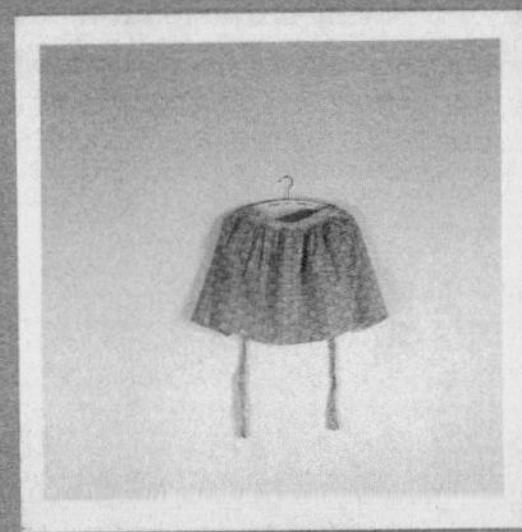

DER KOPF IST SCHON EINE MASCHINE[1]

Hans-Peter Feldmann hält als Beitrag zum Symposion über Fotografie keinen Vortrag im eigentlichen Sinn, er sieht sich auch nicht als alleiniger Initiator eines Gesprächs über Fotografie, zum Thema »das Archiv« oder was auch immer. Aber er provoziert dennoch ein solches Gespräch, indem er zunächst feststellt, er habe keine Theorie, an der entlang er seine Arbeiten entwickelt, sondern höchstens: jeden Tag neue Theorien, weshalb seine Antworten morgen ganz anders ausfallen könnten.

Er beginnt allerdings dennoch mit einigen Erklärungen seiner Arbeitsweise, vor allem in Hinblick auf all die Bilder, die während des Symposions präsent, oder zumindest potentiell gegenwärtig waren: an den Wänden, in Büchern. Jedes dieser Bilder repräsentiert für ihn eine Welt für sich, die Erinnerungen des Rezipienten evoziert – obwohl sie doch nur Farbe auf Papier sind, eine rein materielle Sache, von der wir glauben, daß sie in irgendeiner Weise die Welt repräsentiert. Für Hans-Peter Feldmann handelt es sich aber eher um Projektionen als um Repräsentationen, um ein Lesen der Bilder, das durch eigene Erfahrungen ergänzt wird. Dementsprechend sieht er seine eigene Arbeit als ein Sich-Selbst-Vorführen von Dingen, die er nicht versteht oder nicht einordnen kann, um sie auf diesem Weg für sich zu klären. Aus diesem Grund stellt er auch keine Einzelbilder her, sondern immer Serien, da ein einzelnes Bild total falsch sein kann – und er zielt mit seinen Serien auf den Durchschnitt. Und manche Bilder dieser Serien, die » zu gut« sind, werden dann aussortiert, da für ihn Ästhetik eine Sache für andere Berufe oder andere Zeiten ist.

Für seine Arbeit waren – und sind es zum Teil noch – die Klischeebilder, vor allem aus seiner Jugend, d. h. der Nachkriegszeit, prägend. Die Reisemöglichkeiten waren sehr eingeschränkt, es gab bei weitem nicht so viele Illustrierte und Unmengen von Werbebildern und außerdem – kein Fernsehen. Die vorhandenen – auch die öffentlichen – Bilder wurden sehr genau und auch viel länger angeschaut. Und sie prägten sich ein, vor allem jene, die etwas von der amerikanischen Kultur zeigten, aus dieser Welt, in der kein Krieg stattgefunden hatte, in der alles viel schöner, viel freier, viel offener zu sein schien. Diese Klischees gingen als Vorurteil den Bildern auch schon voraus, die Rezeption bestätigte und bekräftigte sie noch zusätzlich. Die »Bilder aus Amerika« zeigten Dinge, die es in Deutschland zu jener Zeit nicht gab. Und die deutschen Klischeebilder, die in den 50er Jahren entstanden, waren durch die Abkehr all der virulenten Probleme gekennzeichnet. Es bestand ein Bedarf an Bildern all jener Lebensinhalte, die bis jetzt gefehlt hatten – Friede, Familienglück, das heimelige Glück am eigenen Herd.

Seine Generation wuchs innerhalb dieses Vakuums auf, mit falschen Klischees, die ihr eigentlich nichts mitteilten. Und so kam es sehr bald zum Bruch dieser Generation mit diesen Klischees, da es ihr klar wurde, daß etwas mit all diesen Sachen nicht stimmt, die ihr angeboten wurden. In diese Zeit fiel auch die verstärkte Einflußnahme der amerikanischen Sub- und Pop-Kultur, etwa durch Jack Kerouac. Die nachfolgende Generation konnte dann schon wieder von völlig anderen Dingen ausgehen. Seine künstlerische Produktion kann also auch unter dem Aspekt einer Aufarbeitung, einer Revidierung dieser Bilder gesehen werden: eine Art Selbstbehandlung durch (neue) Fotos, um jene alten wieder auszulöschen bzw. zu relativieren.

Feldmann hat sich auch gerade über neue wissenschaftliche Entdeckungen die menschliche Wahrnehmung betreffend unterhalten. Das Auge nimmt nur ganz punktuell Eindrücke wahr, sehr schnell und sehr präzise – der Rest wird vom Gehirn aufgebaut und nicht wirklich optisch wahrgenommen. Wenn jemand eine Hausecke betrachtet, dann wird der Rest des Hauses gewissermaßen vom

46

ALREADY, THE HEAD IS A MACHINE[1]

As his contribution to the symposium, Hans-Peter Feldmann is not holding a lecture in the actual sense of the word, nor does he regard himself as the sole initiator of a debate about photography, with »the Archive«, or whatever, as a theme. He does, however, provoke such a debate by claiming, from the outset, that he has no theory along which he develops his work. At best, there are new theories every day, so that his answers may be quite different tomorrow.

But then he begins with some explanations of his working method, with particular reference to all the images that are – at least potentially – present at the symposium: on the wall and in books. To him, each of these images represents a world of its own, evoking memories in the recipient, although they are but color on paper, purely material things we believe to somehow represent the world. To Hans-Peter Feldmann, these images are projections rather than representations, being read, as they are, in the light of personal experience. Correspondingly, he sees his own work as a presentation of things to himself – things he does not understand or cannot fit into place – in order to gain clarity about them himself. For this very reason he never makes individual pictures but always series. A single image can be completely mistaken. His series aim at the mean value. And some pictures within a series that are, in a sense, too good, are then being sorted out, since he regards aesthetics to be a thing for other professions and other times.

The main influence on his work were, and partly still are, the cliché images of his youth, that is, of the post-war years. Travelling opportunities were limited, there were not half as many illustrated magazines and advertisements as today, and there was no television. The images that did exist – publicly, as well – were looked at much more carefully and longer. They made an impact, especially such images that showed something of American culture, of a world where there had been no war, where everything was so much more beautiful, free and open. Such clichés arrived, as prejudices, even before the images whose reception only confirmed and reinforced them. The »Images from America« showed things that did not exist in Germany at the time. And the German cliché images that appeared in the fifties were characterised by their avoidance of the virulent problems of the time. There was a demand for images representing the values of life that had been lacking – peace, family joys, contentedness at one's own hearth.

His generation grew up within this vacuum, with these false clichés that actually said nothing. And so his generation soon broke with these clichés since people realised that something was wrong with the promises made to them. This was the time when the American sub- and pop culture gained influence, for instance through Jack Kerouac. The following generation had a completely different base to build on. Feldmann's artistic production can thus also be seen under the aspect of confronting and reviewing these images, as a sort of autotherapy through (new) photographs in order to delete certain images or put them in perspective.

Feldmann also talked of new scientific discoveries about human perception. The eye only perceives very selectively, very quickly and precisely – all the rest is being built up by the brain and not really optically registered. When someone looks at the corner of a house, the rest of the house is quasi built up by the brain. So, already, the head

HANS-PETER FELDMANN, Alle Kleider einer Frau (All of a Woman's Clothes) 1974
70 SW-Polaroids / 70 bw-polaroids, je/each 9 cm x 8,8 cm.

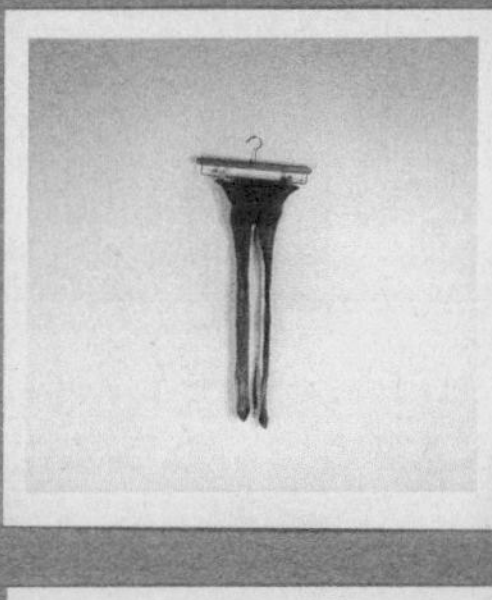
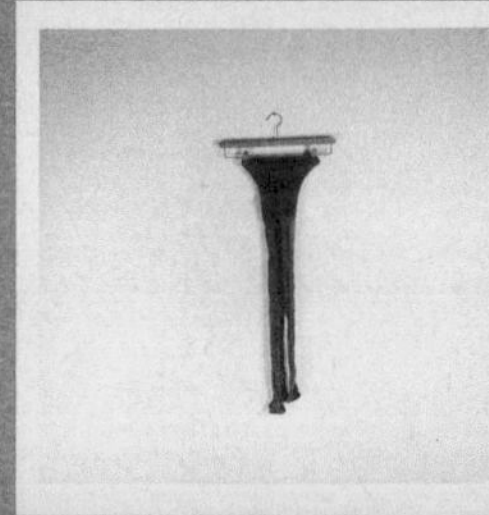
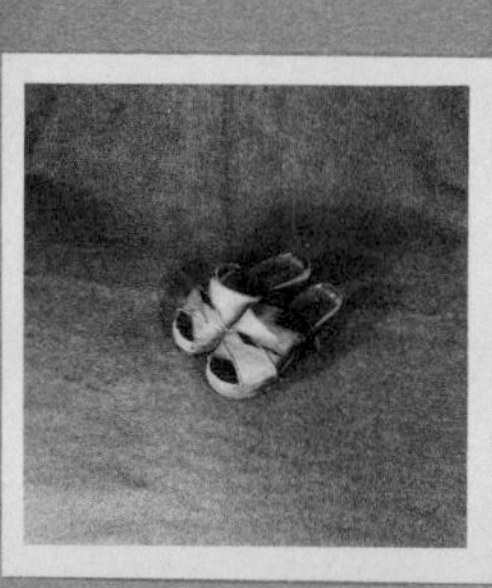
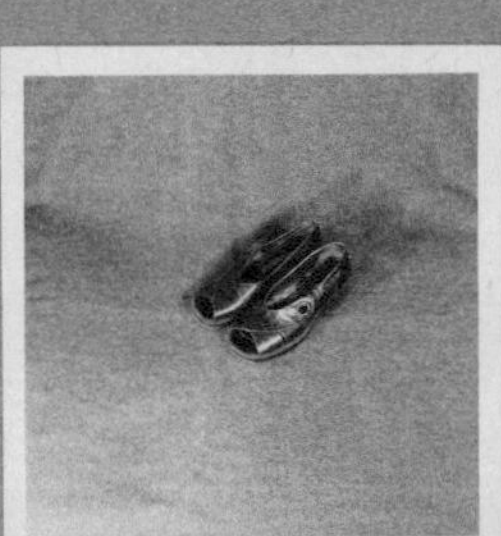
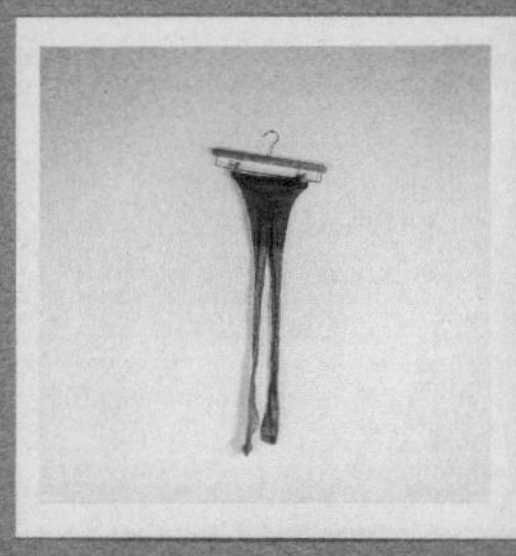
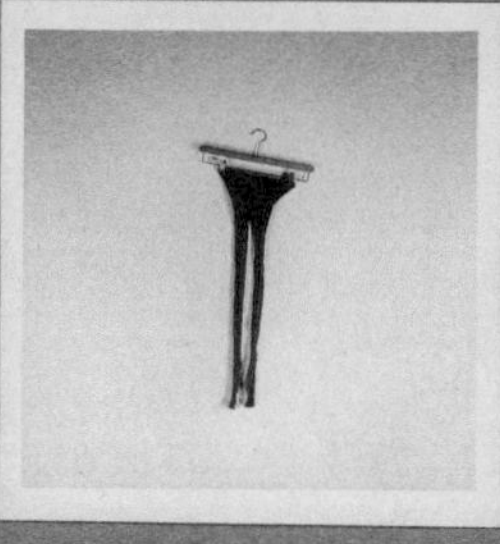
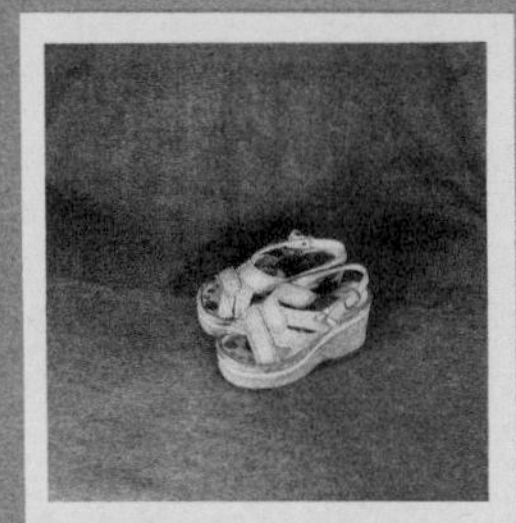
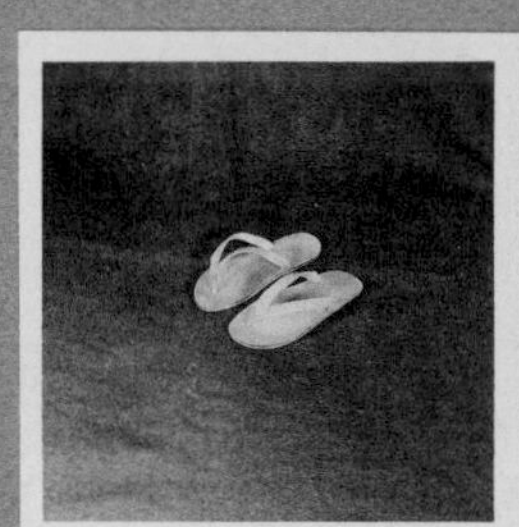
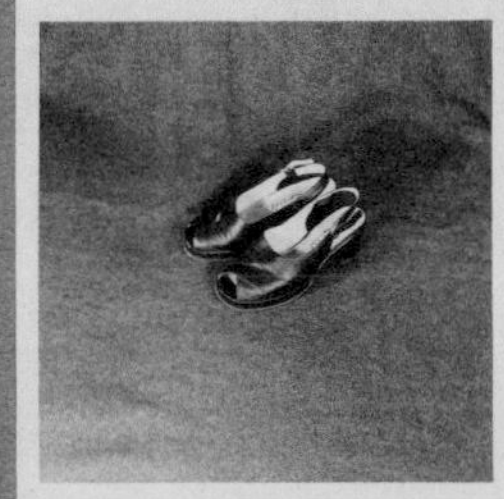
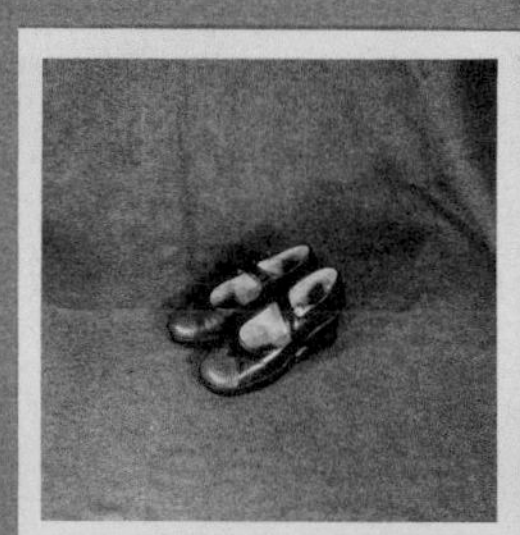
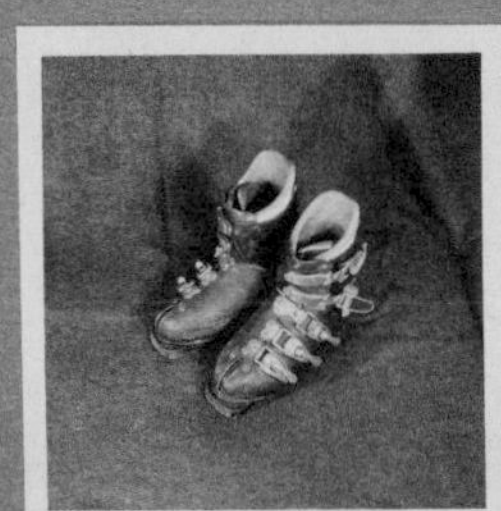
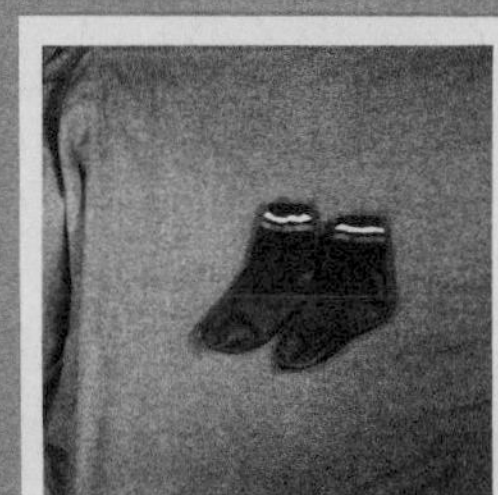

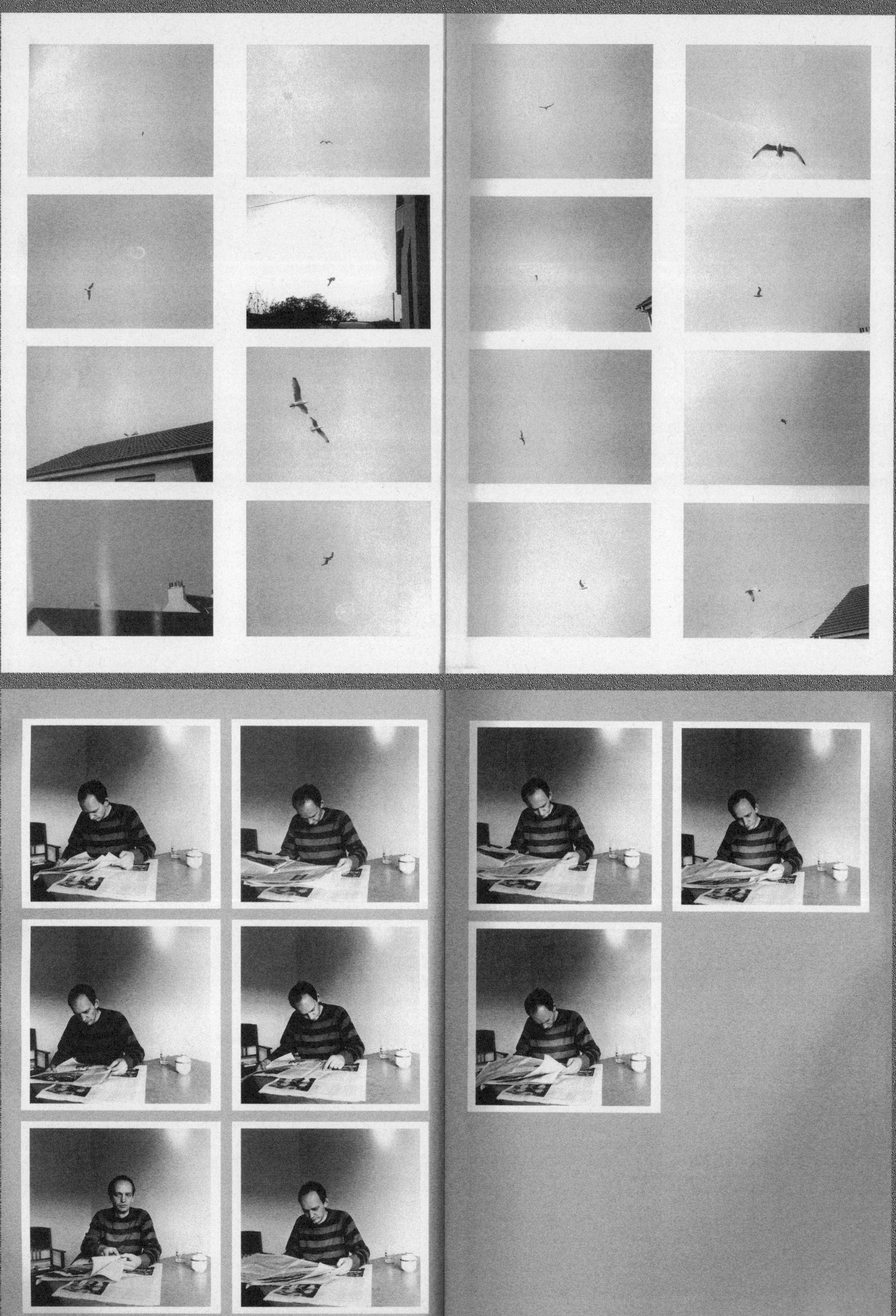

Camera Austria International

2007   Zanele Muholi, "Faces & Phases,"
text contribution / artist contribution,
Camera Austria International 100 / 2007

Exhibition

2007   *I am not afraid. The Market Photo Workshop,
Johannesburg,* exhibition contribution

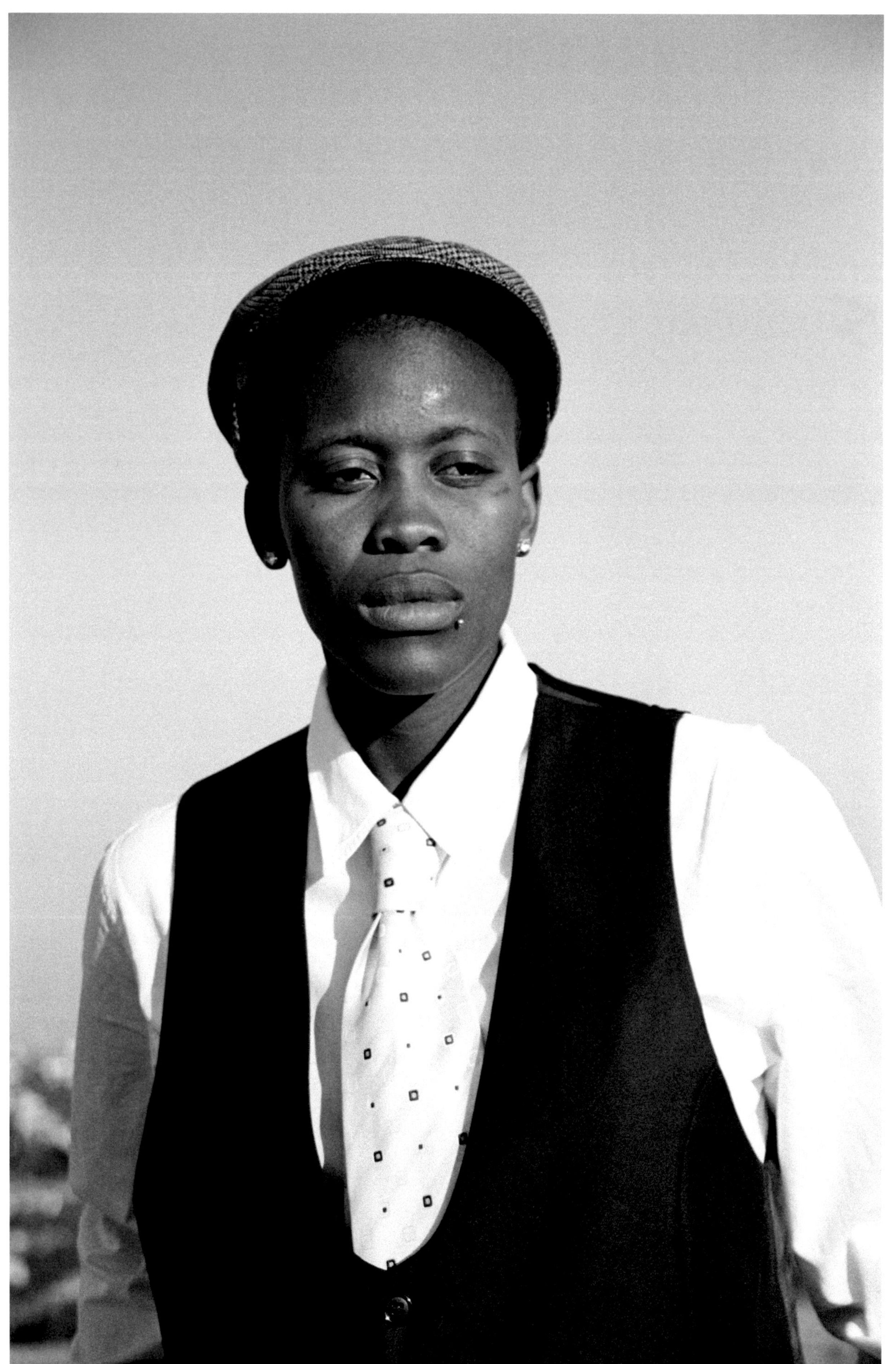

Dikeledi Sibanda, Yeoville, Johannesburg, 2007
All images from the series "Faces & Phases," 2006–ongoing

Zanele Muholi

Faces & Phases

There is a meaning or interplay to "Faces & Phases" and why the project focuses on these two words. I decided to capture images of my community in order to contribute towards a more democratic and representative South African queer and homosexual history. Up until 1994, we as black lesbians and trans people were excluded from participating in the creation of a formal queer movement and our voices were missing from the pages of gay publications, while white gay activists directed the movement and wrote about gay issues and struggles. Hence, few of us were present in the forefront, but many operated underground.

I embarked on a journey of visual activism to ensure that there is black LGBTQIA+ visibility, to showcase our existence and resistance in this democratic society and to present positive and representative imagery.

Aside from the dictionary definition of what a "Face" is (the front of the head, from forehead to chin), the face also expresses the person. For me, this means me, photographer and community worker, being face to face with the many persons I interacted with from different South African communities and beyond. In each of these locales there are queer people who are living openly regardless of the stigma and homophobia attached to their identity, whether masculine, feminine or non-binary. Being part of the LGBTQIA+ community is often seen as negative, as destroying the nuclear heterosexual family; the stigma around queer identity frequently arises from the fact that homosexuality is seen as un-African. For many African people assigned female at birth, the expectation is that they must have children and procreate with a male partner, who is considered the head of the family. That is part of the "African tradition". Failing to conform to these expectations, these individuals are perceived as deviants, needing "curative rape" to erase attitudes perceived as 'male'. The attempt is to make us into 'true women': mothers, men's property.

The individuals in "Faces & Phases" hold different positions and play many different roles within the black lesbian and trans community: we are soccer players, actresses, scholars, cultural activists, lawyers, dancers, filmmakers, human rights/gender activists. However, we are often depicted by outsiders as mere victims of rape and homophobia. Our lives are sensationalised, rarely understood. This is the reason for "Phases": our lives are not just what make the newspaper headlines every time one of us is attacked. We go through many stages, we express many "identities," which unfold as part of our existence.

From an insider's perspective, this project is meant as a commemoration and a celebration of the lives of the black lesbians and trans people I met in my journeys through the townships and beyond. Lives and narratives are told with both pain and joy, as some of these women, non-binary and transgender individuals were going through hardships and triumphs in their lives. Their stories caused me sleepless nights as I did not know how to deal with the urgent needs I was told about. Many of them had been violated. I did not want the camera to be a further violation; rather, I wanted to establish relationships with them based on our mutual understanding of what it means to be female, trans, lesbian, queer and black in South Africa today.

I call this method the birth of visual activism: I decided to use it to mark our resistance and existence as members of the LGBTQIA+ community in our country, because it is important to put a face on each and every issue.

"Faces & Phases" is about our histories, struggles and lives on this queer mother planet: we will face our experiences regardless what they'll be, and we will move on.

A previous version of this text feature appeared in *Camera Austria International* 100 / 2007: 64–71.

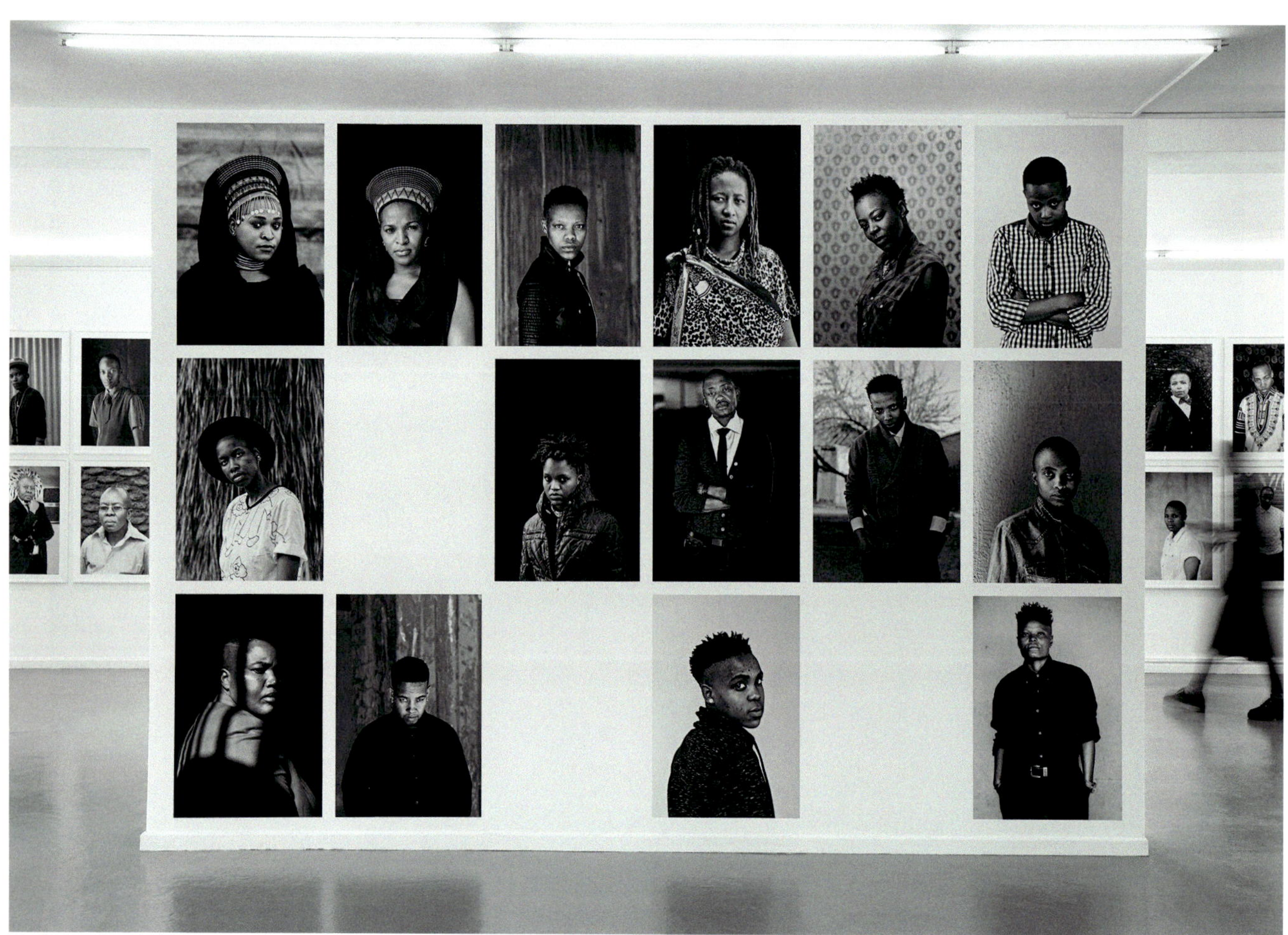

Zanele Muholi, Faces & Phases 10, Stevenson, Johannesburg (ZA), 2016, exhibition view

Zanele Muholi

FACES & PHASES

There is a meaning or interplay to »Faces & Phases« and why the project focuses on these two words.

I decided to capture images of my community in order to contribute towards a more democratic and representative South African homosexual history. Up until 1994, we as black lesbians were excluded from participating in the creation of a formal queer movement and our voices were missing from the pages of gay publications, while white gay activists directed the movement and wrote about gay issues and struggles. Hence, few of us were present in the forefront, but many operated underground.

I embarked on a journey of visual activism to ensure that there is black lesbian visibility, to showcase our existence and resistance in this democratic society, to present a positive imagery of black lesbians.

Aside from the dictionary definition of what a »Face« is (the front of the head, from forehead to chin), the face also expresses the person. For me, this means me, photographer and community worker, being face to face with the many lesbians I interacted with from different Gauteng townships such as Alexandra, Soweto, Vosloorus, Katlehong, Kagiso…

In each township there are lesbians who are living openly regardless of the stigma and homophobia attached to their lesbian identity, both butch and femme. Most of the time being lesbian is seen as negative, as destroying the nuclear heterosexual family; for many black lesbians, the stigma of queer identity arises from the fact that homosexuality is seen as un-African. Expectations are that African women must have children and procreate with a male partner, the head of the family. That is part of the »African tradition«. Failing to conform to these expectations, we are perceived as deviants, needing a »curative rape« to erase our male attitude and make us into true women, females, real women, mothers, men's property.

Individuals in this series hold different positions and play many different roles within the black lesbian community: soccer player, actress, scholar, cultural activist, lawyer, dancer, film maker, human rights/gender activist. However, each time we are represented by outsiders, we are merely seen as victims of rape and homophobia. Our lives are always sensationalised, rarely understood. This is the reason for »Phases«: our lifes are not just what makes the newspapers headlines every time one of us is attacked. We go through many stages, we express many »identities«, which unfold in parallel in our existence.

From an insider's perspective, this project is meant as a commemoration and a celebration of the lives of black lesbians that I met in my journeys through the townships. Lives and narratives are told with both pain and joy, as some of these women were going through hardships in their lives. Their stories caused me sleepless nights as I did not know how to deal with the urgent needs I was told about. Many of them had been violated; I did not want the camera to be a further violation; rather, I wanted to establish relationships with them based on our mutual understanding of what it means to be female, lesbian, and black in South Africa today.

I call this method the birth of visual activism: I decided to use it to mark our resistance and existence as black lesbians in our country, because it is important to put a face on each and every issue.

»Faces & Phases« is about our histories, struggles and lives on this queer mother planet: we will face our experiences regardless what they'll be, and we still move on.

FACES & PHASES

In »Faces & Phases« steckt ein Wechselspiel von Bedeutungen, darum zeigt sich in diesen beiden Wörtern der Fokus meines Projekts.

Ich beschloss, Bilder von meiner Community zu machen, um einen Beitrag zu einer demokratischeren und repräsentativeren queeren Geschichte Südafrikas zu leisten. Bis 1994 waren wir schwarzen Lesben vom Aufbau einer formellen Schwulenbewegung ausgeschlossen und unsere Stimmen fehlten in den schwulen Publikationen. Die Bewegung wurde von weißen Aktivist*innen gelenkt, und die waren es auch, die über die Probleme und Kämpfe von Schwulen schrieben. Infolgedessen standen wenige von uns im Rampenlicht, im Untergrund aber operierten viele.

Ich machte mich als visuelle Aktivistin auf, um etwas für die Sichtbarkeit des schwarzen Lesbentums zu tun, unsere Lebensweise und unseren Widerstand in dieser demokratischen Gesellschaft zu dokumentieren und ein positives Bild schwarzer Lesben zu zeichnen.

Abgesehen von seiner Wörterbuchdefinition als Körperteil (die Vorderseite des Kopfes von der Stirn bis zum Kinn), ist das Gesicht auch ein Ausdruck von Charakterzügen. Für mich als Fotografin und Community-Arbeiterin hieß das, von Angesicht zu Angesicht mit vielen Lesben aus verschiedenen Townships in der Provinz Gauteng, in Alexandra, Soweto, Vosloorus, Katlehong, Kagiso usw. zusammenzuarbeiten.

In all diesen Townships leben offene Lesben, trotz der Ächtung und Homophobie, der sie sich mit ihrem Lesbentum – egal ob Butch oder Femme – aussetzen. Lesbischsein wird meist als etwas Negatives, als Bedrohung für die heterosexuelle Kleinfamilie gesehen; für viele schwarze Lesben besteht das Stigma der queeren Identität zusätzlich darin, dass Homosexualität als unafrikanisch angesehen wird. Von afrikanischen Frauen wird erwartet, dass sie Kinder kriegen und sich mit einem männlichen Partner, dem Familienoberhaupt, fortpflanzen. Das gehört zur »afrikanischen Tradition«.

Da wir diese Erwartungen nicht erfüllen, werden wir als Abweichende eingestuft, die nur eine »gesunde Vergewaltigung« brauchen, um sie von ihrer männlichen Einstellung zu »kurieren« und sie zu richtigen Frauen, Müttern, zum Besitz eines Mannes zu machen. Die Personen in dieser Serie sind auf den unterschiedlichsten Gebieten tätig und spielen die verschiedensten Rollen in der schwarzen lesbischen Community: Fußballerin, Schauspielerin, Wissenschaftlerin, Kulturaktivistin, Anwältin, Tänzerin, Filmemacherin, Menschenrechts- oder Genderaktivistin. Wenn wir aber von Außenstehenden dargestellt werden, sind wir immer bloß Opfer von Vergewaltigung und Homophobie. Unser Leben dient immer nur der Sensationsmache, verstanden wird es kaum einmal. Deshalb auch die »Phasen«: unser Leben ist nicht nur, was in die Schlagzeilen gelangt, sobald eine von uns attackiert wird, sondern wir durchlaufen viele verschiedene Zustände, haben viele nebeneinander existierende »Identitäten«.

Von innen gesehen ist dieses Projekt als Feier und Andenken an das Leben der schwarzen Lesben gedacht, die ich auf meinen Reisen durch die Townships getroffen habe. Ihre Lebensgeschichten werden mit Schmerz und Freude erzählt, da einige dieser Frauen gerade schwere Zeiten durchmachten. Ihre Geschichten bereiteten mir schlaflose Nächte, weil ich nicht wusste, wie ich mit den Nöten, von denen sie mir berichteten, umgehen sollte. Viele von ihnen sind vergewaltigt worden; ich wollte sie mit der Kamera nicht noch tiefer verletzen, sondern eine Beziehung herstellen, die auf einem gegenseitigem Verständnis dafür beruht, was es heißt, im heutigen Südafrika eine Frau, eine Lesbe und eine Schwarze zu sein.

Ich nenne das die Geburt des visuellen Aktivismus: Ich beschloss, mit dieser Methode ein Zeichen für unseren Widerstand und unsere Existenz als schwarze Lesben in diesem Land zu setzen, weil es wichtig ist, jedem Problem offen ins Gesicht zu sehen.

»Faces & Phases« handelt von unseren Geschichten, Kämpfen und Leben auf diesem queeren Mutterplaneten: Wir werden uns unseren Erfahrungen stellen, wie immer sie aussehen mögen, und wir werden weitermachen.

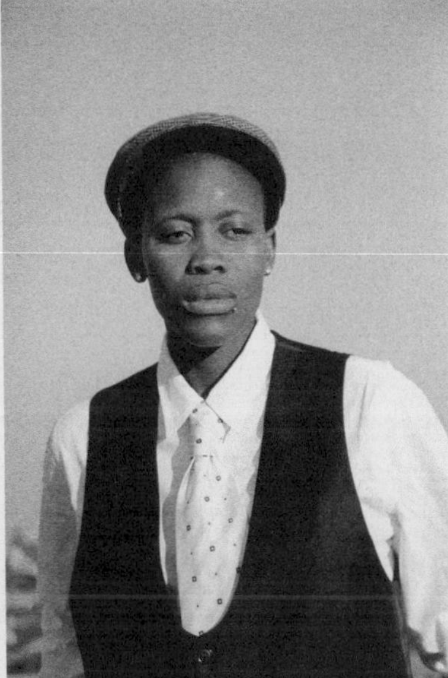

Dikeledi Sibanda, 2007.

Seite / pages 65–71: ZANELE MUHOLI, Faces & Phases, 2006 – 2007. Lichtahn silver prints, je / each 86 cm x 80 cm bzw. / resp. 80 cm x 86 cm. Courtesy Michael Stevenson, Kapstadt / Cape Town.

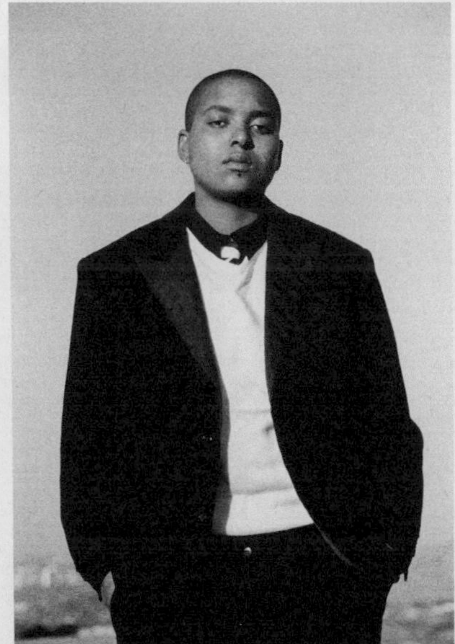

Tumi Mkhuma, 2007.

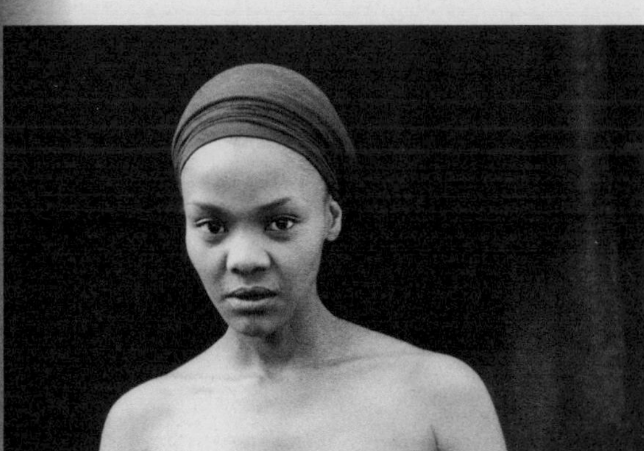

Rolinde Mhasi, 2007.

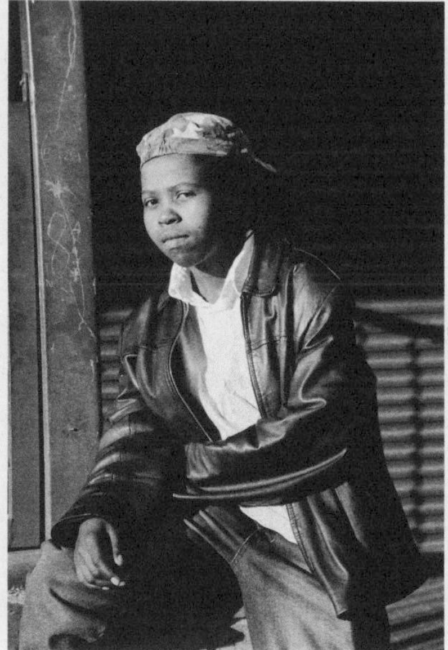

Nonzwakazi, 2007.

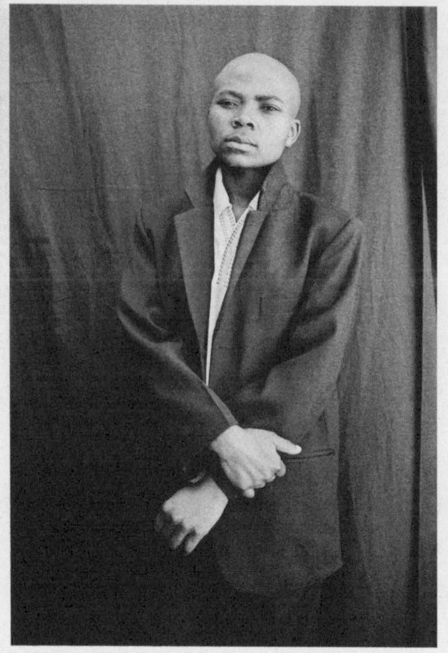

Nosipho Solundwana, 2007.

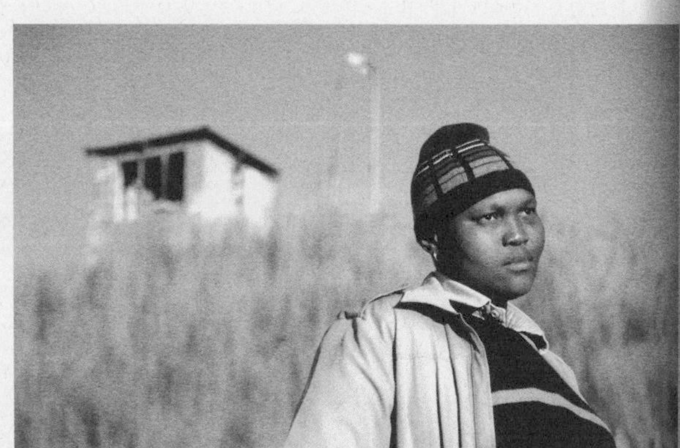

Busi Sigasa, 2006.

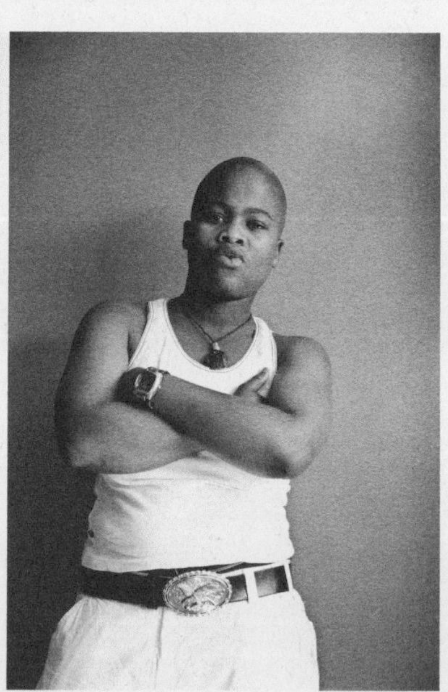

Thembi Nyoka, 2007.

Jo Spence

Camera Austria International

1987   Gisela Bartens, "Sich selbst ins Bild setzen. Jo Spence. Putting Myself in the Picture," book review, *Camera Austria International* 23/1987

1988   Jo Spence, "Fotografiegeschichte umgestalten: Eine Zusammenarbeit von zwei Fotografen," text contribution and artist contribution, Jo Spence, "Was mir mein Vater nie beigebracht hat …," text contribution, *Camera Austria International* 25/1988

1993   Rosy Martin, "Wir als Subjekt unserer Bilder. Die Arbeiten von Jo Spence," text contribution (journal of Symposion), Jo Spence, artist contribution, *Camera Austria International* 43–44/1993

2006   Jo Spence, "Die dokumentarische Praxis infrage stellen?," text contribution/artist contribution and cover, Jorge Ribalte, "Die anhaltende Relevanz von Jo Spence," text contribution, *Camera Austria International* 94/2006

2012   Martin Herbert, "Jo Spence: Work (Part I & II), [space], London; Studio Voltaire, London," exhibition review, *Camera Austria International* 119/2012

Exhibitions

1987   *Königreich. Fotoarbeiten aus Großbritannien,* exhibition participation

1992   *So oder so nicht sein/Identities,* exhibition participation

2006   Jo Spence, *Beyond the Perfect Image,* in collaboration with Jorge Ribalta and Terry Dennett, in cooperation with Museu d'Art Contemporani de Barcelona (ES), solo exhibition

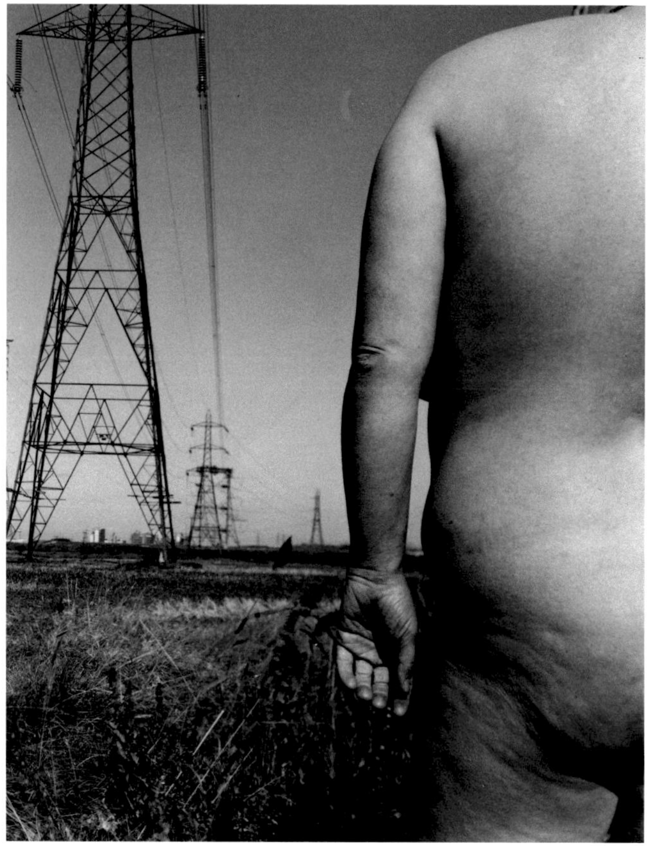
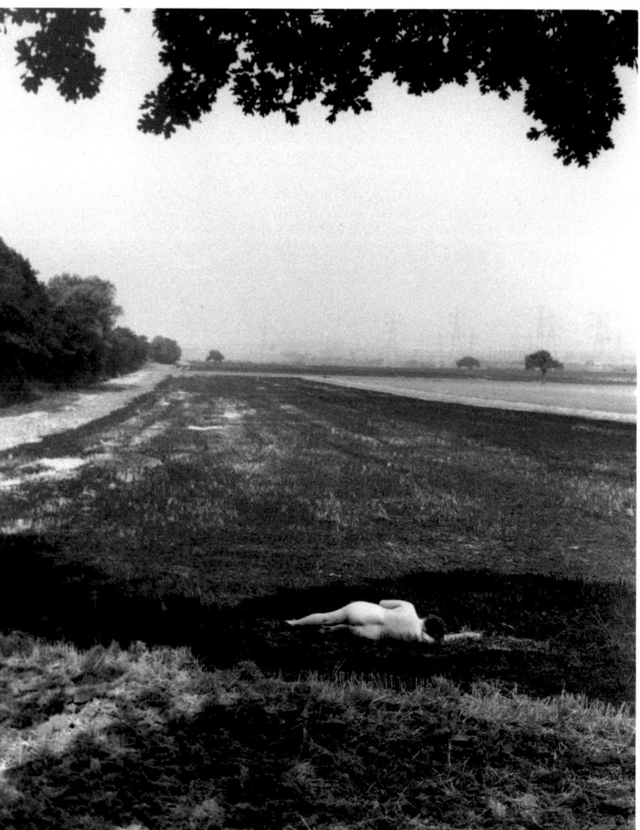

Industrialisation

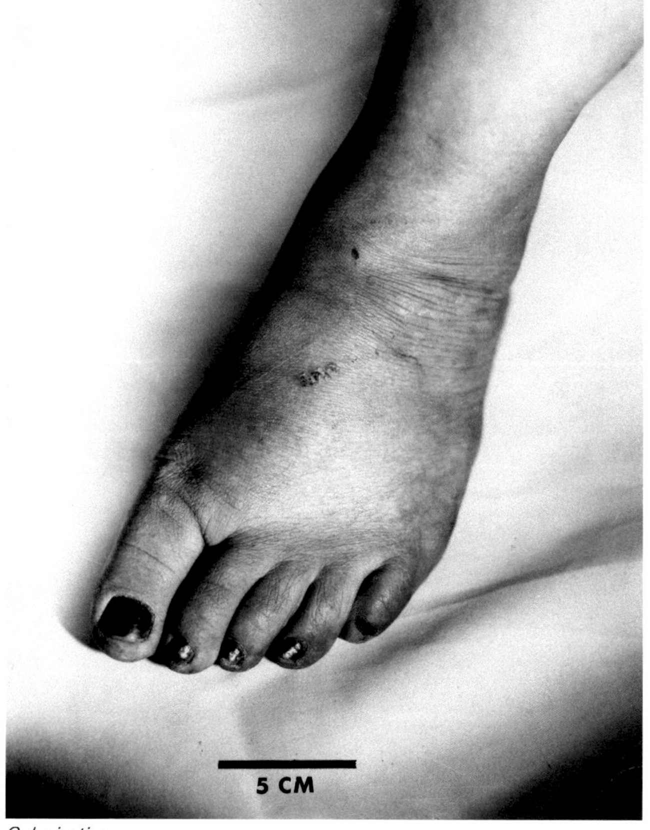

Colonisation

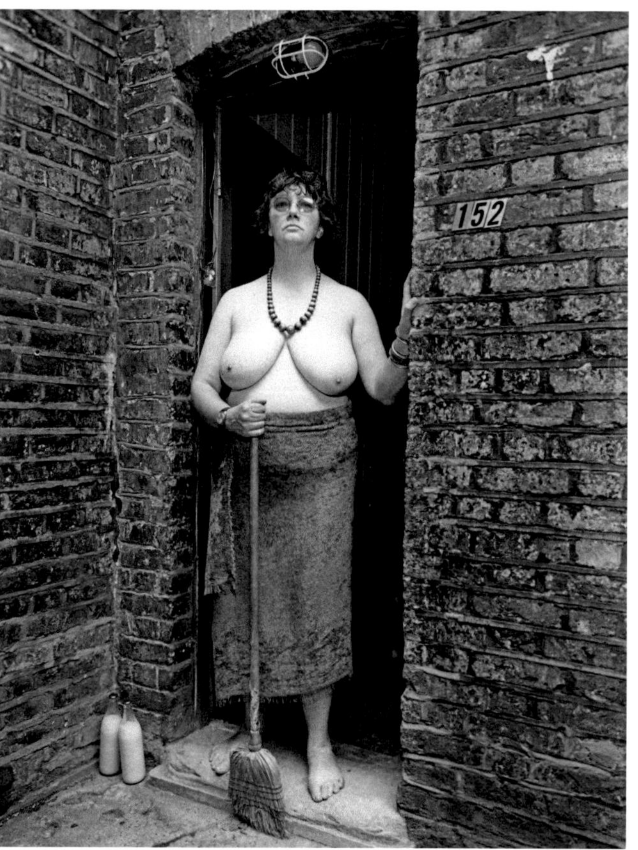

From the series "Re-Modelling Photo History," 1981–1982

Jo Spence

2.4

Jo Spence and Terry Dennett
Re-Modelling Photo History

For those of us who are photographic workers it is obvious that a vast amount of work still needs to be done on the socalled history of photography itself, and the function they have had in constructing and encouraging particular ways of viewing and telling about the world. The photo work which follows is an exploration of our attempts to work through some of this problem by "making strange" the everyday, normalized, institutional practices and codes of "the trade," re-ordered, re-modelled, re-invented, so that their commonsense, unquestioned notions become disrupted. We are not trying to show familiar objects in unfamiliar ways, but rather to denaturalize the genres of photography which already consist of fully coded visual signs. [...]

This piece of work is a very tiny statement which should be seen in the tradition of "worker photography"—our workplace being photography as a production process in which we are daily involved. As two working photographers, we have tried any number of ways of making and using photographs so that they do not merely parrot the dominant modes of visual representations of the left, centre, or right of cultural practices and politics but call such practices into question so that it begins to be easier to understand that the camera is not a window on the world, nor are meanings of pictures fixed, but that visual signs (in this case photographs) are in themselves sites of struggle. In trying to make a piece of work "about" photography, we are making a break with our former work, but as life-long photographers we feel it might be useful to look at the ways in which various institutions and apparatuses have used and validated photography, and to try, within that perspective, to make a visual/verbal statement on work and sexuality.

[...] Crucial to this project was the fact that we wanted to re-examine and re-work the model/photographer relationship, which is generally so one-sided. At the same time as we drew upon our own knowledge of the codes and signifying practices of portraiture, record, still life, documentary, fashion and "nude" photography, we also traversed what we knew of photo practices from within fine art, anthropology, news, advertising, science, law, medicine, welfare and charity institutions. We did not attempt the futile task of trying to invent another language, but tried rather to indicate how photographs which are usually given a currency and circulated within different (and apparently contradictory) spheres can, when brought together in this disruptive way, enable the viewer to make new and political connections.

Although "Re-Modelling Photo History," attempts to map out relationships between the apparatuses which use and straddle photography and the institutions which validate or teach photographic practices, we also wanted to indicate how this linked up with the placing of women within the family by showing that there is consistency between some of the ways in which oppressed women and other subordinated groups are represented. Though the project offers a starting point from within photography, it allows us to move beyond the eternal textual analysis to ask questions about what is not being shown or said; what cannot be said (what is visually unsayable); and what is being displaced or rendered structurally absent. In asking what is absent we enter the realm of the analytical, be it through psychoanalysis or historical materialism. The former engages with the construction of our gendered subjectivity, unconscious desires and pleasures, positioned as we are within familial relationships and within texts in specific discourses: the latter engages with the possibility of conscious scientific and socially useful historical knowledge and the possibility of political change. Both realms address memory – that which is considered unthinkable/unspeakable/unknowable, socially censored from consciousness, and that which in terms of class/power relations is rendered invisible, not named/discussed/shown and often actively suppressed.

Excerpt from: "Re-Modelling Photo History" in *Camera Austria International* 25/1988, 50–52, [first published in Screen, 23, 1/1982, *Jo Spence, Putting Myself in the Picture,* London: Camden Press, 1986, 118–133.]

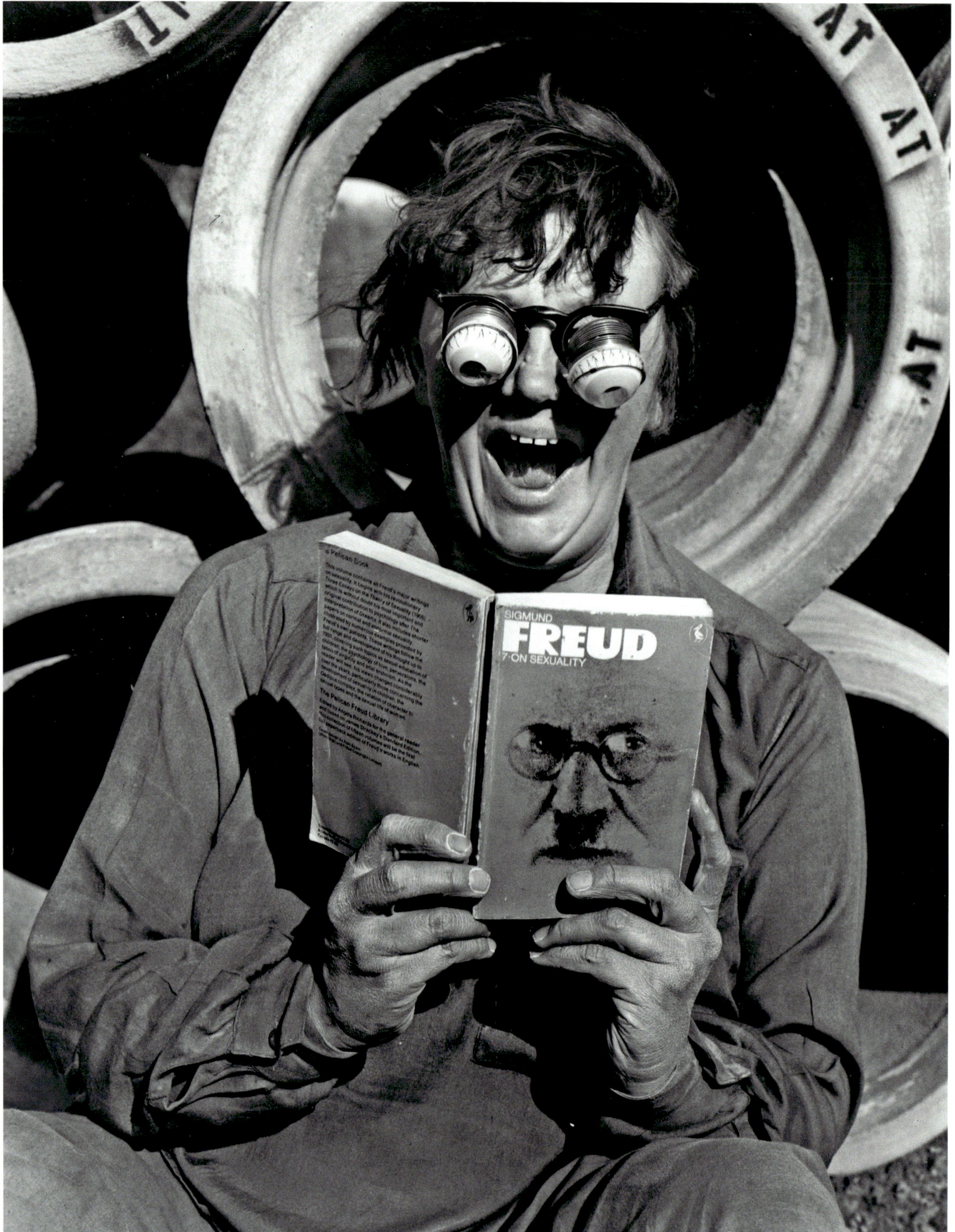

Revisualization

From the series "Re-Modelling Photo History," 1981–1982

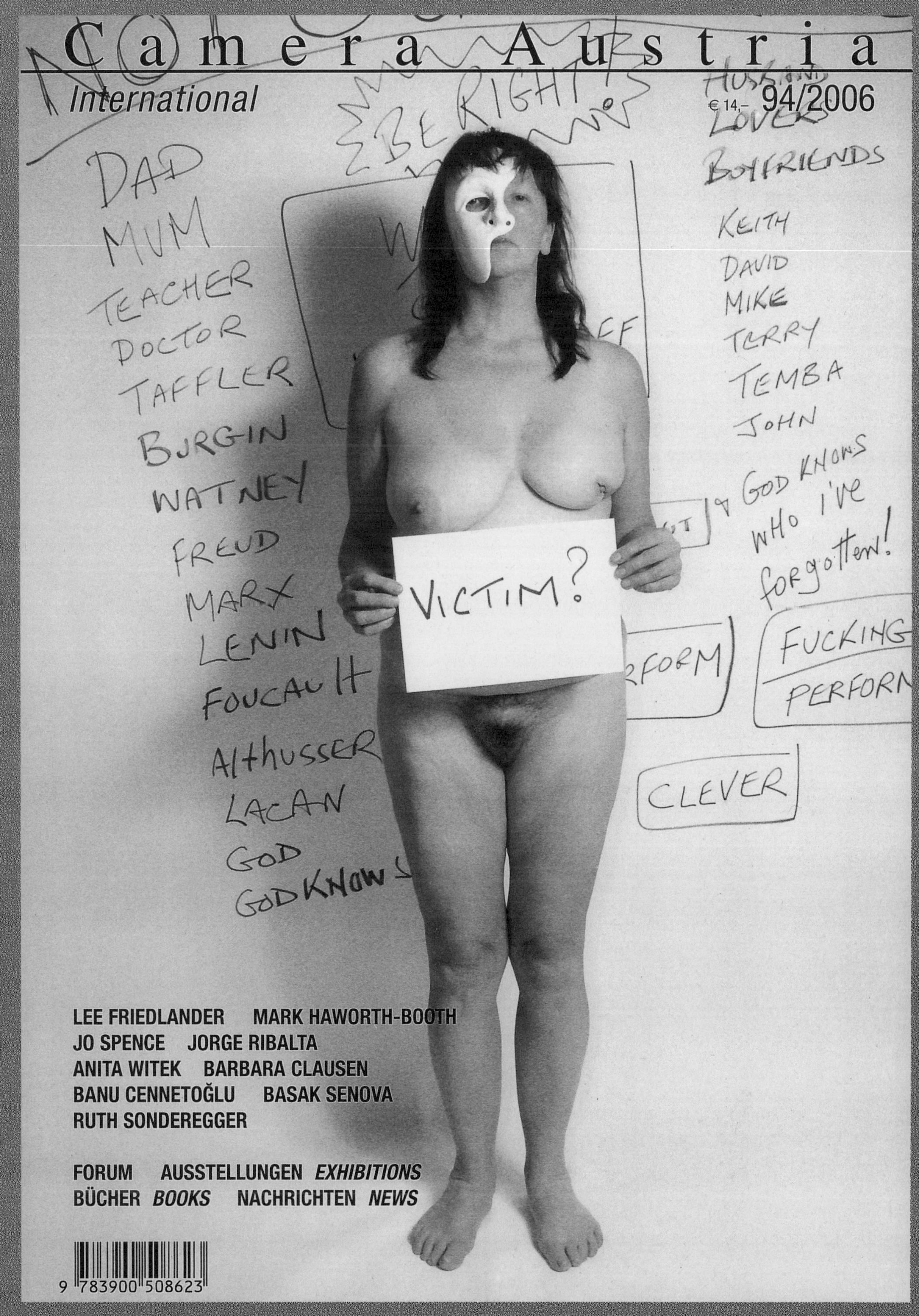
Camera Austria
International
€ 14,– 94/2006
DAD
MUM
TEACHER
DOCTOR
TAFFLER
BURGIN
WATNEY
FREUD
MARX
LENIN
FOUCAULT
Althusser
LACAN
GOD
GOD KNOWS
BE RIGHT
HUSBAND
LOVERS
BOYFRIENDS
KEITH
DAVID
MIKE
TERRY
TEMBA
JOHN
& GOD KNOWS
WHO I've
forgotten!
VICTIM?
PERFORM
FUCKING
PERFORM
CLEVER
LEE FRIEDLANDER   MARK HAWORTH-BOOTH
JO SPENCE   JORGE RIBALTA
ANITA WITEK   BARBARA CLAUSEN
BANU CENNETOĞLU   BASAK SENOVA
RUTH SONDEREGGER
FORUM   AUSSTELLUNGEN EXHIBITIONS
BÜCHER BOOKS   NACHRICHTEN NEWS
9 783900 508623

Jo Spence

REMODELLING PHOTO HISTORY:
A Collaboration Between Two Photographers

Terry Dennett and Jo Spence, 1981—1982

For those of us who are photographic workers it is obvious that a vast amount of work still needs to be done on the so-called history of photography, and on the practices, institutions and apparatuses of photography itself, and the function they have had in constructing and encouraging particular ways of viewing and telling about the world. The photo work which follows is an exploration of our attempts to work through some of this problem by «making strange» the everyday, normalized, institutional practices and codes of «the trade», re-ordered, re-modelled, re-invented, so that their commonsense, unquestioned notions become disrupted. We are not trying to show familiar objects in unfamiliar ways, but rather to denaturalize the genres of photography which already consist of fully coded visual signs. Much of our thinking on this has been influenced by reading and seeing the work of Brecht, and by the writings of Augusto Boal.

This piece of work is a very tiny statement which should be seen in the tradition of «worker photography» — our workplace being photography as a production process in which we are daily involved. As two working photographers, we have tried any number of ways of making and using photographs so that they do not merely parrot the dominant modes of visual representations of the left, centre, or right of cultural practices and politics but call such practices into question so that it begins to be easier to understand that the camera is not a window on the world, nor are meanings of pictures fixed, but that visual signs (in this case photographs) are in themselves sites of struggle. In trying to make a piece of work «about» photography, we are making a break with our former work, but as life-long photographers we feel it might be useful to look at the ways in which various institutions and apparatuses have used and validated photography, and to try, within that perspective, to make a visual/verbal statement on work and sexuality.

Above all, we wanted to get away from the dry didacticism which pervades so much worthy work on photographic theory and to provide instead a kind of «revolt» from within the ranks. In a funny sort of way this is a return to our class roots, where adversity and oppression are dealt with not only through comradely snuggles or learned exposition, but lived out through individual or group rituals like sarcasm or irony (what is commonly termed «taking the piss»). We aimed to produce something which was perhaps not quite in such «good taste» as is usually expected; something which tried to break down some of the sacred cows of photography and bourgeois aesthetics while daring to mention police photography and fashion photography in the very same breath, to indicate that perhaps they share some common formal features.

What we finally hit upon was a form of photo-theatre. Here we could use non-naturalistic modes of representation which allowed us to create a kind of hybrid «spectacle» whilst drawing upon and disrupting well-known genres of photography which have been concerned with the representation of aspects of the female body. Obviously this collaboration between two photographers, using themselves both as photographer and as photographic object, stems from our joint interests in photography and politics. So whilst attempting to engage with some of the current theories of visual representation, we are at the same time attempting to offer a critique of standard histories of photography, which still mostly exclude details of institutional, state, class or economic determinants, being grounded rather in «great inventions», «great names», «great companies» and «great themes». The work particularly allowed us to draw upon our separate experiences as a scientific photographer and photo historian (Terry) and as an ex-commercial and ex-portrait photographer now working on the visual/socio-economic history of the family (Jo).

We decided not to rely on what we could find to photograph (in the classic documentary sense), nor on montaging visual elements at the post-shooting stage, nor on «subversive» texts. We wanted to provide a twin performance — the staging and acting out of a tableau for the camera, done by us as social actor/s, and then a two dimensional signi-

fying performance on film and paper. Within this framework we had extended discussions in order to previsualize and script everything but still leave room for an element of spontaneity at the shooting stage. We did this work sporadically across several months, taking long weekends to drive around looking for props and locations, and to do the acutal shooting. Working mostly with large format cameras on tripods, we could economically re-shoot anything we were not entirely satisfied with. Drawing upon our long disused but internalized professional experience, we chose how to depict a range of styles and genres, both contemporary and historical. By adding a sparse text (what amounted to a recategorization process), we hoped the spectator could make new inferences.

Crucial to this project was the fact that we wanted to re-examine and re-work the model/photographer relationship, which is generally so one-sided. At the same time as we drew upon our own knowledge of the codes and signifying practices of portraiture, record, still life, documentary, fashion and »nude« photography, we also traversed what we knew of photo practices from within fine art, anthropology, news, advertising, science, law, medicine, welfare and charity institutions. We did not attempt the futile task of trying to invent another language, but tried rather to indicate how photographs which are usually given a currency and circulated within different (and apparently contradictory) spheres can, when brought together in this disruptive way, enable the viewer to make new and political connections.

Although »Remodelling Photo History« attempts to map out relationships between the apparatuses which use and straddle photography and the institutions which validate or teach photographic practices, we also wanted to indicate how this linked up with the placing of women within the family by showing that there is consistency between some of the ways in which oppressed women and other subordinated groups are represented. Though the project offers a starting point from within photography, it allows us to move beyond the eternal textual analysis to ask questions about what is not being shown or said; what connot be said (what is visually unsayable); and what is being displaced or rendered structurally absent. In asking what is absent we enter the realm of the analytical, be it through psychoanalysis or historical materialism. The former engages with the construction of our gendered subjectivity, unconscious desires and pleasures, positioned as we are within familial relationships and within texts in specific discourses; the latter engages with the possibility of conscious scientific and socially useful historical knowledge and the possiblity of political change. Both realms address memory — that which is considered unthinkable/unspeakable/ unknowable, socially censored from consciousness, and that which in terms of class/power relations is rendered invisible, not named/ discussed/shown and often actively suppressed.

Apart form hoping to give some critical pleasure to an audience, part of our project has been to find a pleasurable new way of working together. Previous collaborations between us have revolved around notions of photography for social and political action, and we wanted to do something which would allow us to explore our personal as well as our working lives and political relationships. Finally we wanted to pose questions beyond the scope of these images. Since we'd been working within a Brechtian tradition of distanciation, trying to transform feeling into thinking and questioning through a form of »educational entertainment«, we turned to Brecht's own writing. His questioning poem, coming from outside photographic discourse, seemed relevant to the overall problems of history — both of the individual gendered subject, and to our positioning within a hierarchical class society.

(Incidentally, what we can't or don't ask of most photographs is questions of t h e i r history...)

(From: Jo Spence, Putting Myself in the Picture, Camden Press, London 1986).

FOTOGRAFIEGESCHICHTE UMGESTALTEN:
Eine Zusammenarbeit von zwei Fotografen

Terry Dennett und Jo Spence, 1981—1982

Für diejenigen von uns, die Fotografiearbeiter sind, ist klar, daß noch eine Menge Arbeit zur sogenannten Geschichte der Fotografie zu leisten ist, zu den Praktiken, Institutionen und Apparaten der Fotografie selbst, wie zu deren Funktion für die Ausbildung und Förderung bestimmter Seh- und Erzählweisen der Welt. Die folgende Fotoarbeit ist eine Sondierung unserer Versuche, einen Teil dieses Problems durchzuarbeiten, indem wir die geläufigen, normalisierten, institutionellen Praktiken und Codes des »Gewerbes« verfremdeten, sie neu zusammenstellten, gestalteten, neu erfanden, um ihre selbstverständlichen, unhinterfragten Vorstellungen aufzubrechen. Es geht uns nicht darum, vertraute Gegenstände in ungewohntem Licht zu zeigen, wir versuchen vielmehr, die bereits aus voll codierten visuellen Zeichen bestehenden Genres der Fotografie zu denaturalisieren.

Diese Arbeit ist ein sehr kurzes Statement, das in der Tradition der »Arbeiterfotografie« zu sehen ist, wobei unser Arbeitsplatz die Fotografie ist, der Produktionsprozeß, mit dem wir Tag für Tag beschäftigt sind. Als Berufsfotografen haben wir die verschiedensten Möglichkeiten ausprobiert, Fotos so zu machen und zu verwenden, daß sie die herrschenden visuellen Darstellungsweisen in der kulturellen Praxis und Politik, sei's der Linken, des Zentrums oder der Rechten, nicht bloß nachäffen, sondern diese Praktiken in Frage stellen, sodaß es leichter wird zu verstehen, daß die Kamera nicht ein Fenster zur Welt ist, daß die Bedeutung der Bilder nicht fixiert ist, sondern daß visuelle Zeichen (in diesem Fall Fotos) selbst Orte der Auseinandersetzung sind. Mit dem Versuch eine Arbeit »über« Fotografie zu machen, brechen wir mit unseren früheren Arbeiten, aber als Menschen, die Zeit ihres Lebens Fotografen waren, erscheint es uns sinnvoll, die Art und Weise, wie verschiedene Institutionen und Apparate Fotografie verwendet und bewertet haben, einmal unter die Lupe zu nehmen, und im Rahmen dieser Perspektive ein visuell-verbales Statement zum Thema Arbeit und Sexualität zu versuchen.

Vor allem wollten wir weg von der trockenen Schulmeisterei, die so viele wertvolle Arbeiten zur Fototheorie durchzieht. Stattdessen wollten wir sowas wie einen »Aufstand« aus den eigenen Reihen heraus machen. Auf eine komische Weise ist dies eine Rückkehr zu unseren Klassenwurzeln, wo Not und Unterdrückung nicht nur durch kameradschaftlichen Streit und gelehrte Ausführungen bewältigt werden, sondern auch durch Einzel- und Gruppenrituale wie Sarkasmus und Ironie ausgelebt werden (was man gemeinhin »durch den Dreck ziehen« nennt). Unser Ziel war es, etwas zu machen, was vielleicht von nicht so »erlesenem Geschmack« ist, wie das gewöhnlich erwartet wird; etwas, das manche heilige Kühe der Fotografie und der bürgerlichen Ästhetik zu stürzen versucht, und es wagt, Polizei- und Modefotografie im selben Atemzug zu nennen, um anzudeuten, daß sie vielleicht ein paar formale Merkmale gemeinsam haben.

Worauf wir schließlich stießen, war eine Form von Foto-Theater. Dabei konnten wir nicht-naturalistische Formen der Darstellung verwenden, die es uns ermöglichten, eine Art hybrides »Spektakel« zu schaffen und uns dabei auf gut bekannte Genres der Fotografie, die sich mit der Darstellung von Aspekten des weiblichen Körpers beschäftigen, zu beziehen und diese zu untergraben. Es liegt auf der Hand, daß diese Zusammenarbeit zweier Fotografen, die sich nicht nur als Fotografen sondern auch als Gegenstand der Fotografie verwenden, aus unserem gemeinsamen Interesse an Fotografie und Politik hervorgeht. So ist also der Versuch, uns mit einigen aktuellen Theorien der visuellen Darstellung auseinanderzusetzen, gekoppelt mit dem Versuch einer Kritik der Standardgeschichte der Fotografie, die noch immer großteils die Einzelheiten institutioneller, staatlicher, klassenbedingter oder ökonomischer Determinanten ausgrenzt, und stattdessen lieber auf »große Erfindungen«, »große Namen«, »große Gesellschaften« und »große Themen« setzt. Diese Arbeit gestattete uns besonders, auf unsere jeweiligen Erfahrungen als Wissenschaftsfotograf und Fotohistoriker (Terry) bzw. frühere Kommerz- und Portraitfotografin, die jetzt an der

visuellen sozio-ökonomischen Geschichte der Familie arbeitet, (Jo) zurückzugreifen.

Wir beschlossen, nicht auf das zu setzen, was wir zum Fotografieren vorfinden können (im Sinn der klassischen Dokumentation), auch nicht auf die Montage von Bildelementen nach der Aufnahme oder auf »subversive« Texte. Wir wollten eine doppelte Darstellung — die Inszenierung und schauspielerische Darstellung eines Tableaus vor der Kamera mit uns selbst als soziale Darsteller und dann die zweidimensionale Deutung auf Film und Papier.

Auf unsere lange brachliegende, aber tiefsitzende Berufserfahrung zurückgreifend, wählten wir die Darstellung einer Reihe sowohl zeitgenössischer, als auch historischer Stile und Genres. Durch die Hinzufügung eines knappen Textes (der auf einen Prozeß der Umwertung hinauslief) hofften wir, daß der Betrachter neue Schlüsse ziehen könnte.

Ein wesentlicher Aspekt dieses Projektes war die Absicht, die in der Regel so einseitige Beziehung zwischen Modell und Fotograf einer Neubetrachtung und Neubestimmung zu unterziehen. Zusammen mit dem Rückgriff auf unsere Kenntnis der Codes und Sinnstiftungspraktiken von Portrait-, Erinnerungs-, Stilleben-, Dokumentations-, Mode- und Aktfotografie, durchforsteten wir auch, was wir über Fotopraktiken auf den Gebieten der Kunst, Anthropologie, Reportage, Werbung, Wissenschaft, Medizin, Recht, sowie der Sozial- und Wohlfahrtsinstitutionen wußten. Wir unternahmen nicht den fruchtlosen Versuch, eine andere Sprache zu erfinden, sondern versuchten vielmehr aufzuzeigen, wie Fotografien, die gewöhnlich in anderen (und scheinbar widersprüchlichen) Bereichen geläufig und verbreitet sind, den Betrachter in die Lage versetzen können, neue und politische Zusammenhänge herzustellen, wenn sie auf diese subversive Weise zusammengebracht werden.

Obgleich »Remodelling Photo History« die Beziehungen zwischen den Apparaten, die Fotografie benutzen und einzwängen, und den Institutionen, die fotografische Praktiken bewerten und lehren, auszuloten versucht, wollten wir auch darauf verweisen, wie dies mit der Position der Frau in der Familie zusammenhängt, indem wir zeigen, daß es eine Gemeinsamkeit zwischen der Darstellung unterdrückter Frauen und anderer unterprivilegierter Gruppen gibt. Auch wenn das Projekt seinen Ausgang von der Fotografie selbst nimmt, so gibt es uns doch die Möglichkeit, über die ewige Textanalyse hinauszugehen und die Frage aufzuwerfen, was gezeigt wird und was nicht, was gar nicht gesagt werden kann (was visuell unsagbar ist), was verdrängt oder strukturell abwesend ist. Mit der Frage nach dem Abwesenden betreten wir das Gebiet der Analyse, sei es nun Psychoanalyse oder historischer Materialismus. Die erstere beschäftigt sich mit dem Aufbau unserer geschlechtlich bestimmten Subjektivität, unserer unbewußten Wünschen und Begierden, eingeschrieben wie wir sind in Familienbeziehungen und den Kontext bestimmter Diskurse; der letztere beschäftigt sich mit der Möglichkeit bewußter wissenschaftlicher und sozial nützlicher historischer Erkenntnis wie der Möglichkeit der Veränderung. Beide zielen auf das Gedächtnis — was als undenkbar /unsag/unerkennbar gilt, sozial aus dem Bewußtsein verbannt, was im Hinblick auf Klassen-/ Machtverhältnisse unsichtbar gemacht, nicht benannt/besprochen/gezeigt und häufig aktiv unterdrückt wird.

Außer daß wir hofften, dem Publikum ein wenig kritisches Vergnügen zu bereiten, suchten wir mit unserem Projekt zum Teil auch für uns eine lustvolle neue Form der Zusammenarbeit. Frühere Gemeinschaftsarbeiten waren um die Idee einer Fotografie zur sozialen und politischen Aktion gekreist, und wir wollten etwas machen, was uns die Möglichkeit bot, unser persönliches Leben ebenso zu erkunden wie unser Arbeitsleben und unsere politischen Beziehungen. Schließlich wollten wir auch Fragen aufwerfen, die den Rahmen dieser Bilder sprengen. Da wir mit einer Brechtschen Form der Verfremdung gearbeitet hatten, mit dem Versuch, Gefühl durch eine Form »belehrender Unterhaltung« in Denken zu verwandeln, wandten wir uns Brecht selbst zu. Sein Gedicht »Fragen eines lesenden Arbeiters« schien von Bedeutung für die gesamte Grundproblematik der Geschichte — der des geschlechtlich bestimmten Subjekts ebenso wie der unserer Einschreibung in eine hierarchische Klassengesellschaft.

(Übrigens, worauf wir die meisten Fotos nicht befragen können oder einfach nicht befragen, ist *ihre* Geschichte...)

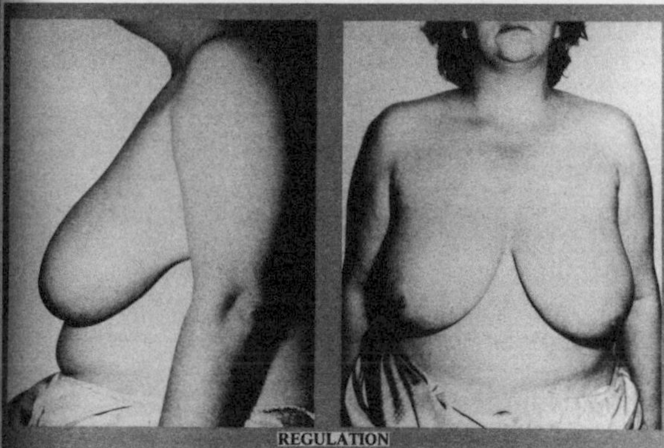

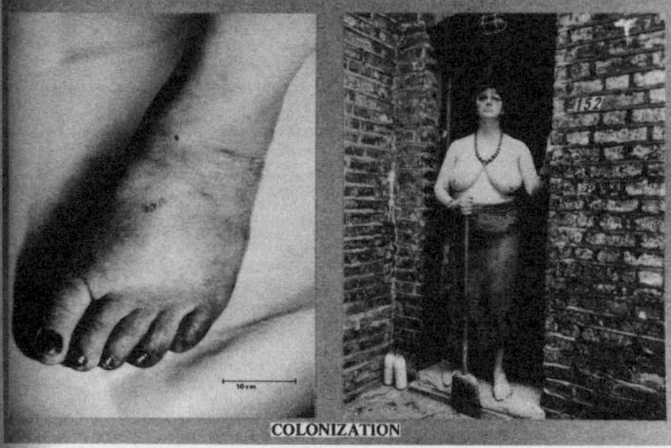

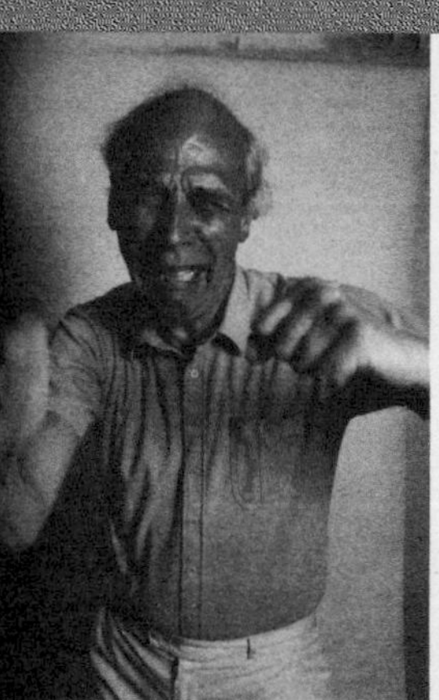

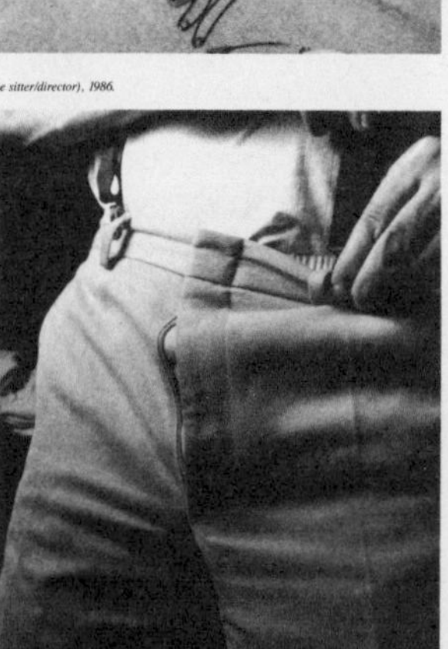

DAVID ROBERTS & JO SPENCE, from: Things My Father Never Told Me.
Collaboration work done by Jo Spence (as photographer/therapist), and David Roberts (as the sitter/director), 1986.

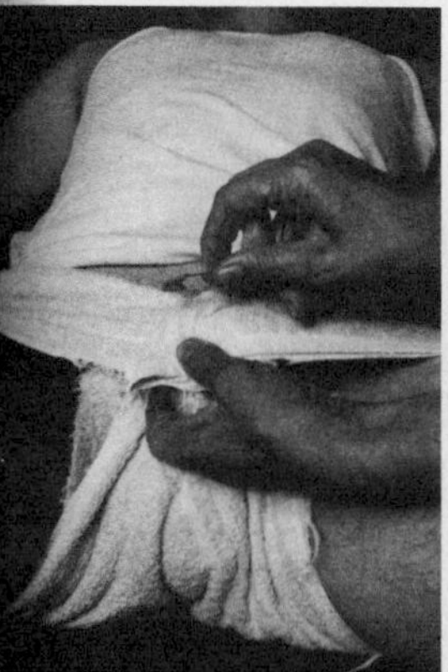

DAVID ROBERTS & JO SPENCE, aus: Was mir mein Vater nie beigebracht hat.
Gemeinschaftsarbeit von Jo Spence (als Fotograf/Therapeut), und David Roberts (als Patient/Regisseur), 1986.

(Original in Farbe / original in colour)

Dialog 3

Living Environment & Representation

Camera Austria Award

1993   Camera Austria Award for Contemporary Photography by the City of Graz

Camera Austria International

1980   Peter Tumer, "Seiichi Furuya," text contribution, Seiichi Furuya, "Portraits von Christine," artist contribution and cover, *Camera Austria International* 1/1980

1981   Seiichi Furuya, "Border," artist contribution, *Camera Austria International* 6/1981

1983   Peter Weiermair, "AMS + Schwarz und Gold," text contribution, Seiichi Furuya, "AMS," artist contribution, *Camera Austria International* 9/1983

1988   "Über-Lebens-Energie," artist contribution and cover, *Camera Austria International* 28/1988

1989   Christine Frisinghelli, "Die Rache der Erinnerung," text contribution, Seiichi Furuya, "Die Reise," artist contribution, *Camera Austria International* 29/1989

1990   Seiichi Furuya "Mémoires," artist contribution, *Camera Austria International* 31–32/1990

1995   Christine Frisinghelli, "Seiichi Furuya: Vertreiben – Flüchten," text contribution, Seiichi Furuya, "Vertreiben – Flüchten," artist contribution, *Camera Austria International* 50/1995

1996   Frits Gierstberg, "Mémoires," book review, *Camera Austria International* 55/1996

1998   Monika Faber, "Seiichi Furuya: Christine Furuya-Gössler. Mémoires, 1978–1985, Korinsha Press, Kyoto, 1997," book review, *Camera Austria International* 64/1998

2003   Sally Stein, "Seiichi Furuya: Last Trip to Venice," book review, *Camera Austria International* 81/2003

2007   Marie Röbl, "Seiichi Furuya: Mémoires 1983," book review, *Camera Austria International* 99/2007

2010   Walter Seidl, "Reclaiming the Personal. Seiichi Furuya: Mémoires, Tokyo Metropolitan Museum of Photography, Izu Photo Museum, Mishima, Contemporary Art Museum, Kumamoto," exhibition review, *Camera Austria International* 111/2010

2011   Carolin Förster, "Seiichi Furuya – Mémoires, Galerie Thomas Fischer, Berlin," exhibition review, *Camera Austria International* 116/2011

2014   Maren Lübbke-Tidow, "Staatsgrenze," text contribution, Seiichi Furuya, "Staatsgrenze," artist contribution, *Camera Austria International* 125/2014

2015   Falk Haberkorn, "Seiichi Furuya: Gravitation. Fotografien 1978–1994," Technische Sammlungen Dresden; Seiichi Furuya: Dresden 1984. Was wir sehen, Kunsthaus Dresden; Seiichi Furuya: Erinnerung – Kontrolle, Galerie für Zeitgenössische Kunst Leipzig, exhibition review, *Camera Austria International* 130/2015

Exhibitions

1975 *199 Fotos,* solo exhibition
1979 *5 Jahre Fotogalerie im Forum Stadtpark,* exhibition participation
1980 *Porträts von Christine,* solo exhibition
1980 *Europäische Fotografen, Teil 1: Steiermark,* exhibition participation
1981 *Dokumentation eines Workshops mit Peter Schlessinger,* exhibition participation
Neue Fotografie aus Österreich, exhibition participation
AMS, solo exhibition
Österreichische Fotografen, exhibition participation
1982 *Graz 1982,* Galerija Sinagoga, Maribor (SK), exhibition participation
1985 *Six Austrian Photographers,* Arbitrage Gallery, New York City (US), Municipal Art Gallery, Los Angeles (US), exhibition participation
1988 *Die Rache der Erinnerung,* exhibition participation
Questioning Europe, Photo Biennale Rotterdam (NL), exhibition participation
Über–Lebens–Energie, exhibition participation
Border and *Porträts von Christine,* Länderbank, Kapfenberg, in conjunction with *Über-Lebens-Energie,* results of the photo workshops "Über-Lebens-Energie," station, Kapfenberg, exhibition participation
1989 *Stadtpark Eins,* Kunsthaus Zug, Zug (CH), exhibition participation
1993 *Forum Stadtpark Graz, Austria,* Museum des Zentrums für Volkskunst, Kharkiv (UA), exhibition participation
WAR, I. Austrian Triennial for Photography, exhibition participation
1994 *Zuhause in Berlin-Ost,* solo exhibition
Three Photographers: Seiichi Furuya, Erich Lázár, Manfred Willmann, Stadtgalerie Bratislava (SK), European Month of Photography Bratislava, exhibition participation
1994 *siebzehn,* exhibition participation
1996 *Stadtpark Zwei,* Art Pavilion, Zagreb (HR), exhibition participation
2001 *Portrait,* solo exhibition
2002 *Seiichi Furuya, Portrait,* solo exhibition
2003 *Freundschaftsspiel,* exhibition participation
2004 *alive,* solo exhibition

Publications

1981 *Seiichi Furuya, AMS,* Edition Camera Austria, 1981
1982 Manfred Willmann, ed., *Graz 1982,* Graz, Fotogalerie im Forum Stadtpark, 1982
1984 Seiichi Furuya and Manfred Willmann, eds, *Shomei Tomatsu, Japan 1952–1981,* Graz, Edition Camera Austria, 1984
1989 Manfred Willmann, ed., *Stadtpark Eins,* Graz, Edition Camera Austria, 1989
1992 Seiichi Furuya and Manfred Willmann, eds, *Nobuyoshi Araki, AKT–TOKYO. 1971–1991,* Graz, Edition Camera Austria, 1992
1993 Werner Fenz and Christine Frisinghelli, eds, *WAR,* publication in two volumes for exhibition of the l. Austrian Triennial for Photography, Graz, Edition Camera Austria, 1993
1997 Manfred Willmann, ed., *Stadtpark Zwei,* Graz, Edition Camera Austria, 1997
2010 Koko Okano and Christine Frisinghelli, ed., *Seiichi Furuya: Mémoires. 1984–1987,* Graz/Mishima: Edition Camera Austria/ Izu Photo Museum, 2010

Workshop

1988 4–17 June 1988, Kapfenberg, in conjunction with *Über-Lebens-Energie*

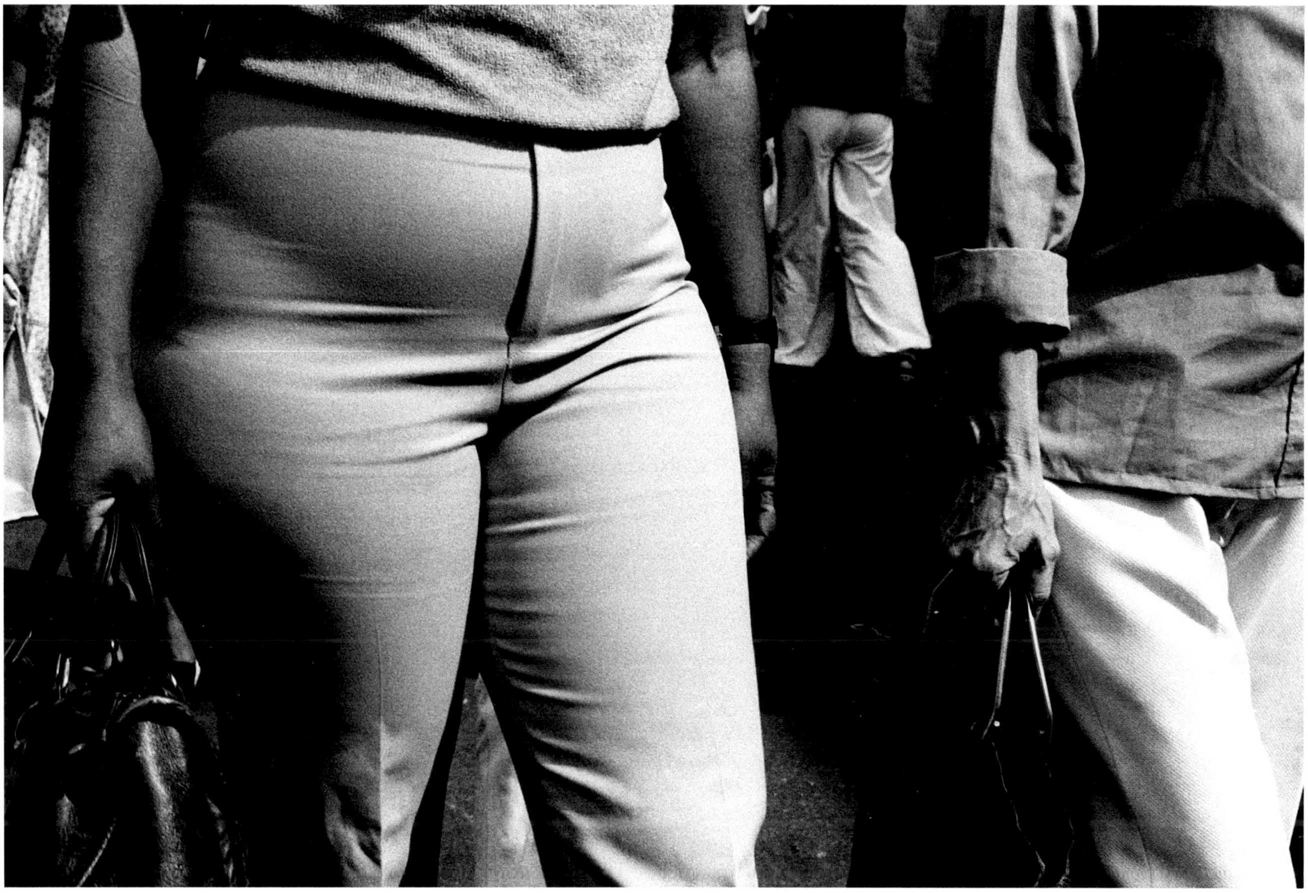

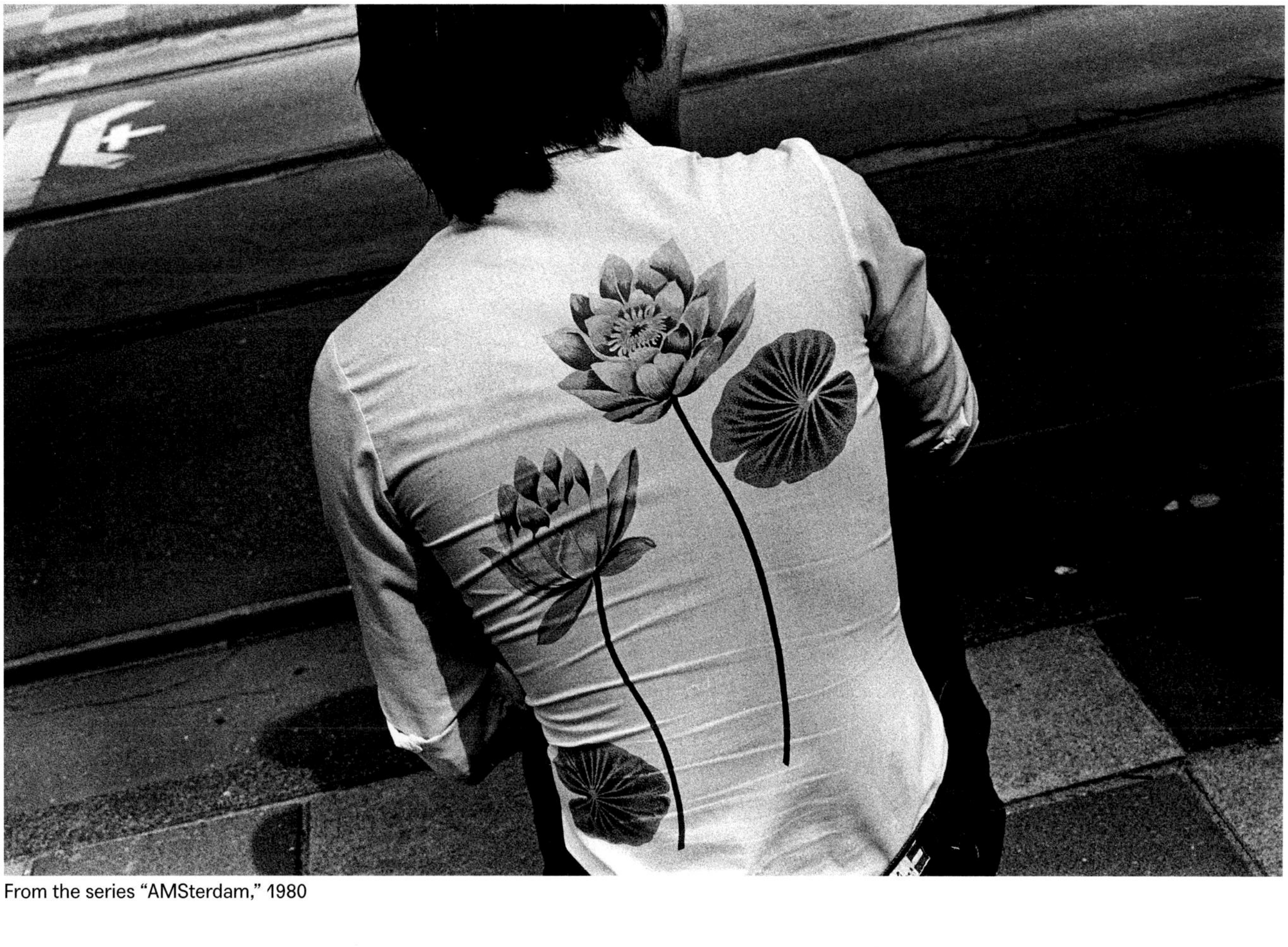

125

From the series "AMSterdam," 1980

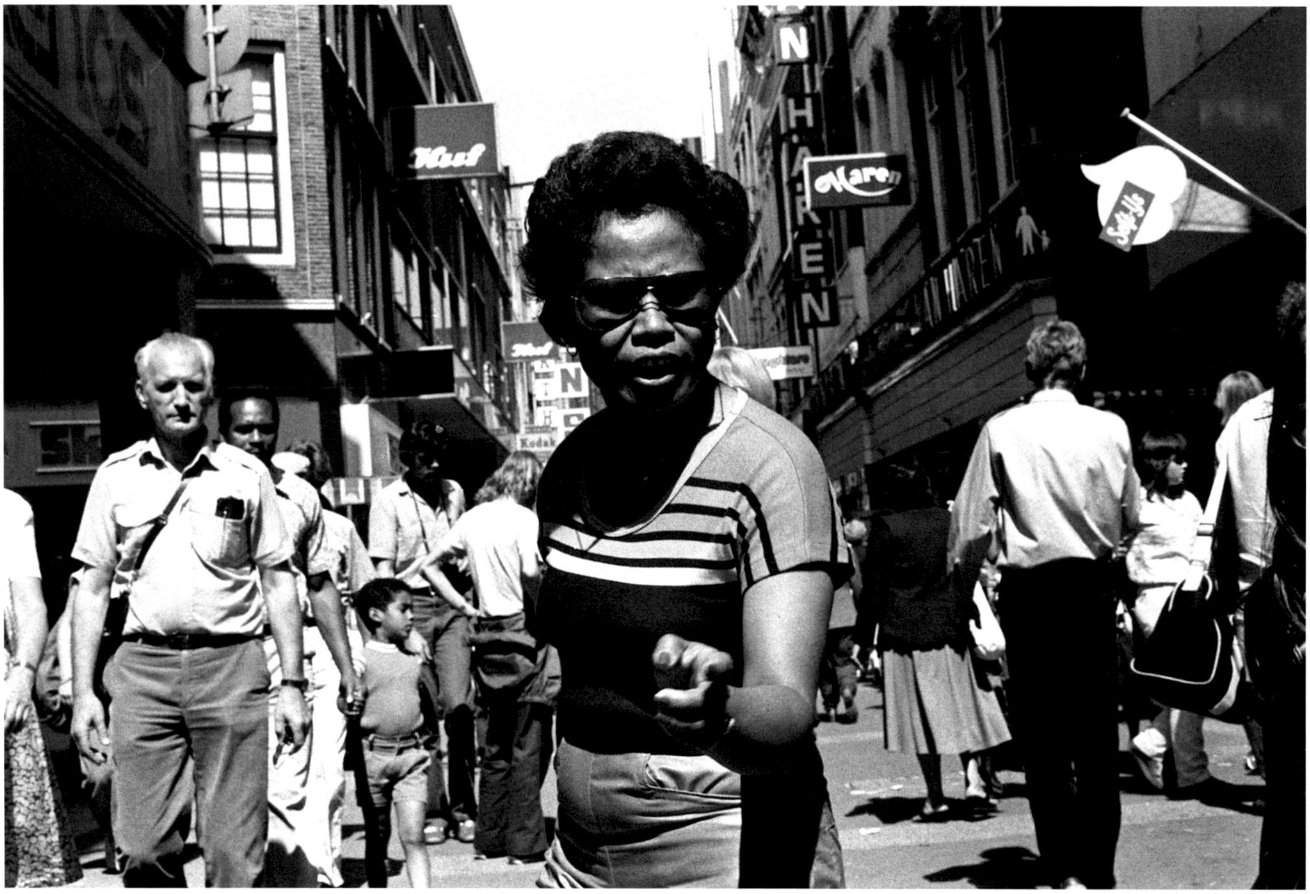

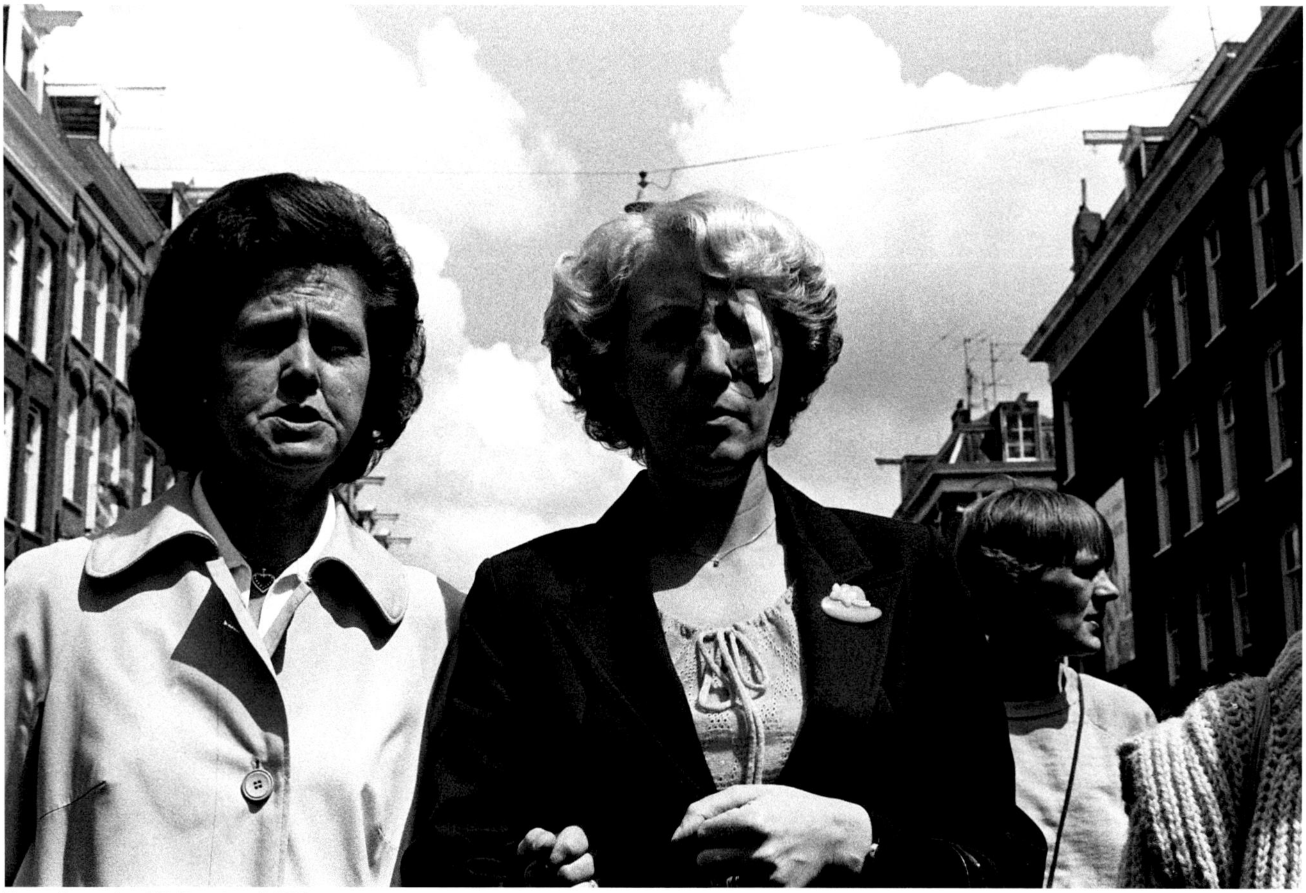

From the series "AMSterdam," 1980

Seiichi Furuya

Seiichi Furuya: In 1975 in Graz I was confronted with the enormous joy of taking photographs, the enthusiasm with which Manfred Willmann and his friends used the camera, and that impressed me very much. I was unable to share this unbroken pleasure, and still cannot to this day. Nonetheless my relationship with photography changed decisively at that time. The dynamic pace at which first a gallery, then a symposion and finally a magazine developed, was certainly unusual.

Monika Faber: Why were you not able to share your friends' enthusiasm for photography? At the time you almost never took any photos in the town you were living in.

Furuya: No, that is still the case. The town is so small, I feel a kind of shame when someone I know sees me taking pictures. For me, photography is a disreputable thing, like theft, not an intelligent pursuit at all. That is just one point among many. It is also a question of the challenge that I need in order to feel that I have to make a picture. In Amsterdam for instance it wasn't a problem: nobody knew me there, but I was fascinated by all the people and the completely different feeling in the streets. It was the first time since leaving Japan that I had been reminded of life in Tokyo. I am not the kind of photographer who really likes photos, but sometimes I feel an urge to take pictures. Suddenly a moment occurs when I see something that seems uncanny to me, and then I take a picture of it—but maybe it will take me years to finish working on it.

Faber: A lot of the characteristic features that later came to be associated with your work cannot be found in your early pictures, features like different moods, nature photography, details from daily life.

Furuya: No, that kind of world didn't exist within me. I didn't see those things at all. I think I lived in a different world. You have to go way back in my biography to really understand it. It is to do with the way I view the world, something which had already established itself during my childhood: The world is not beautiful, and people lie. I was already quite a negative person,

even at an early age. I did not attach any importance to beautiful things, and probably didn't even see them. And I was always mistrustful. I never tried to use a rush of energy or bravery to turn things around or change them. Somehow I always just accepted everything. Why shouldn't that be reflected in my pictures?

Excerpt from: "'Ich suche keine Antwort': Seiichi Furuya in conversation with Monika Faber" in *Seiichi Furuya: Mémoires*, exh. cat., Tokyo: Tokyo Metropolitan Museum of Photography, 2010.

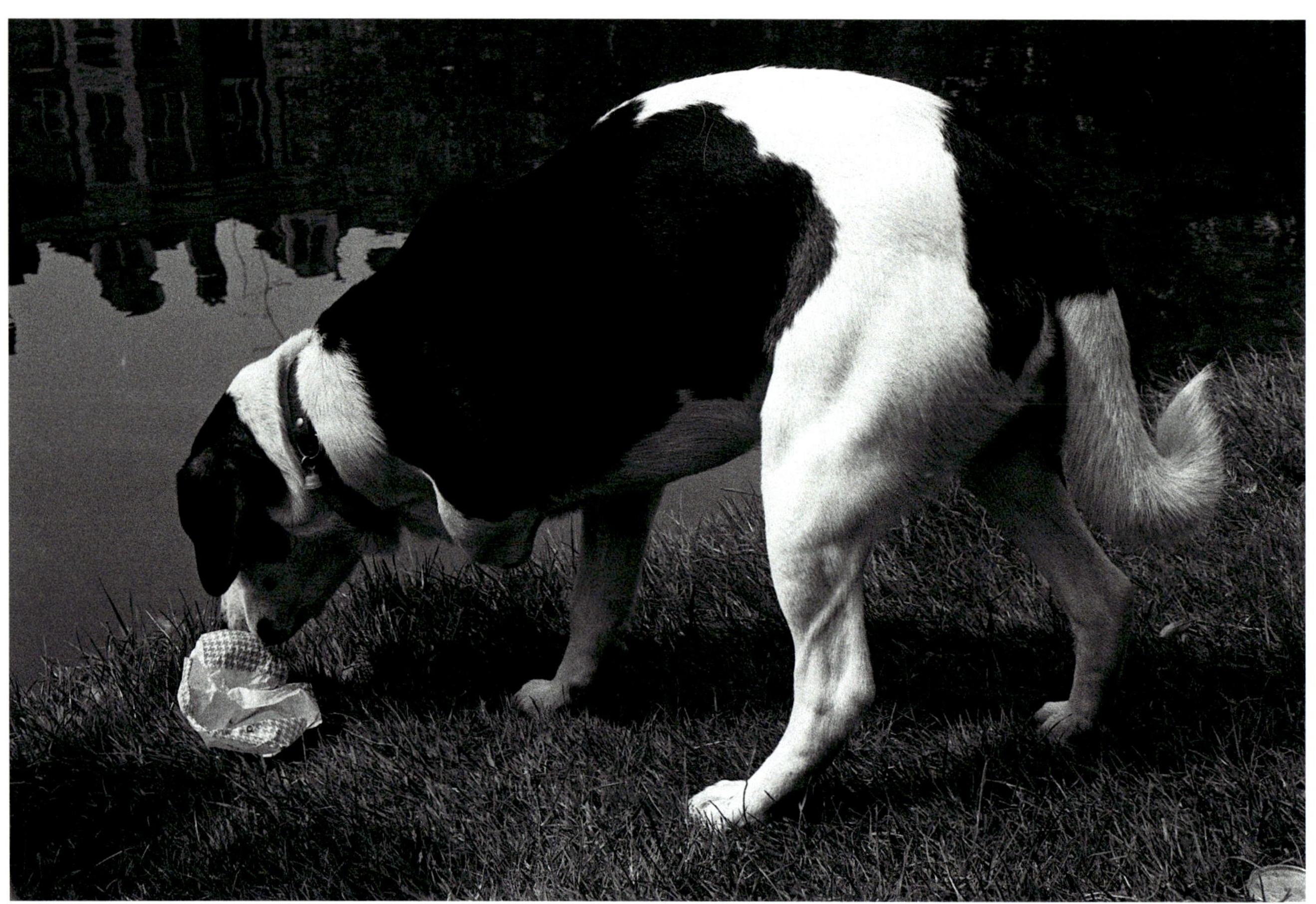

From the series "AMSterdam," 1980

PROJEKTARBEIT MIT: GOSBERT ADLER HERMANN CANDUSSI HEINZ CIBULKA SEIICHI FURUYA WILMAR KOENIG RICHARD KRATOCHWILL MICHAEL SCHMIDT CHRISTIAN WACHTER MANFRED WILLMANN ÜRSULA WÜST

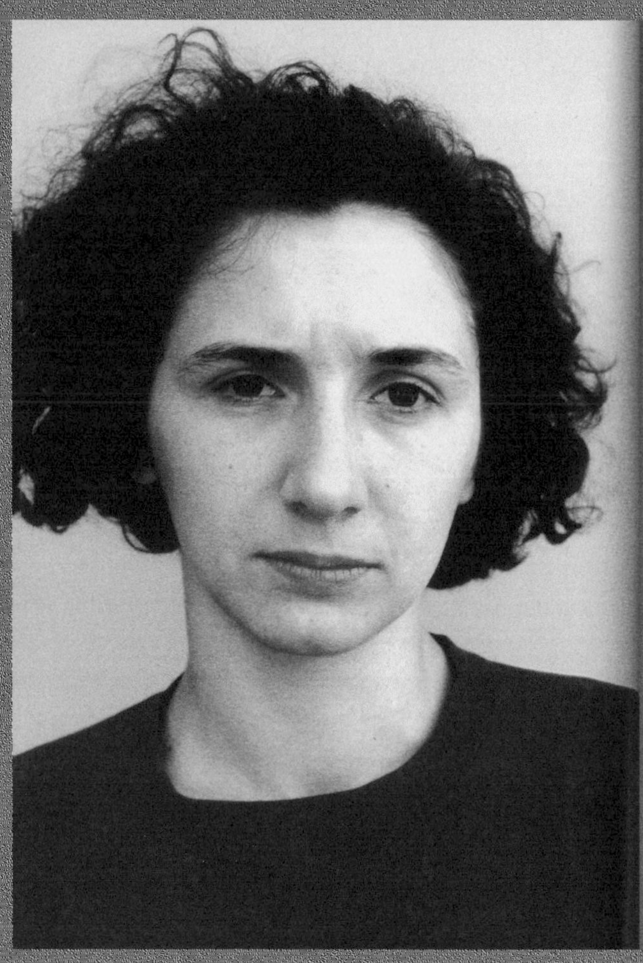
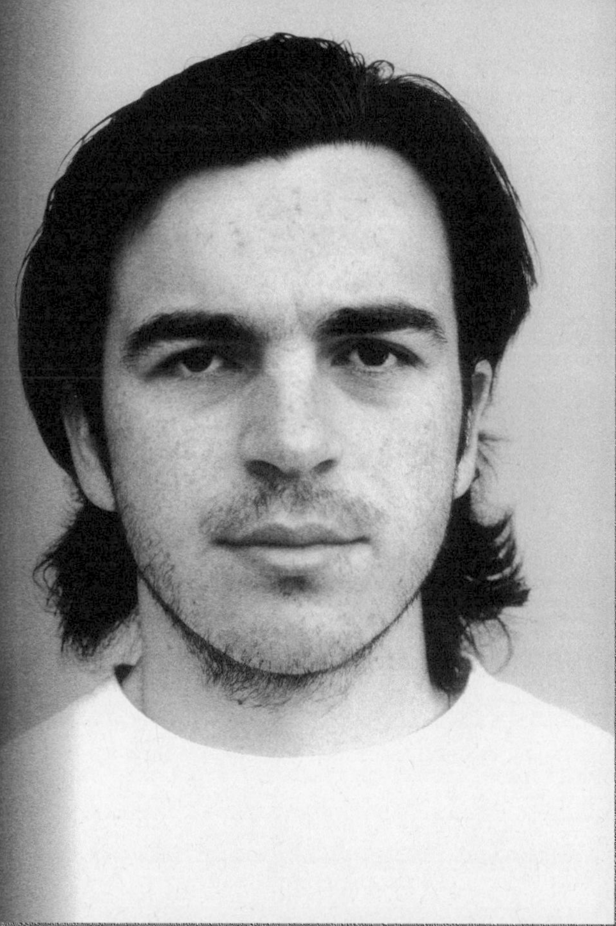
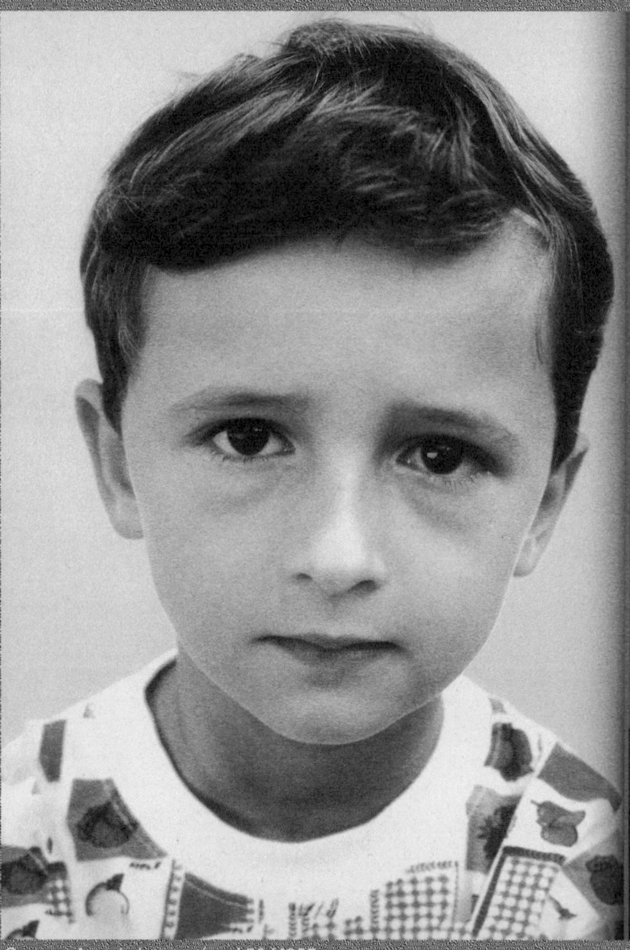
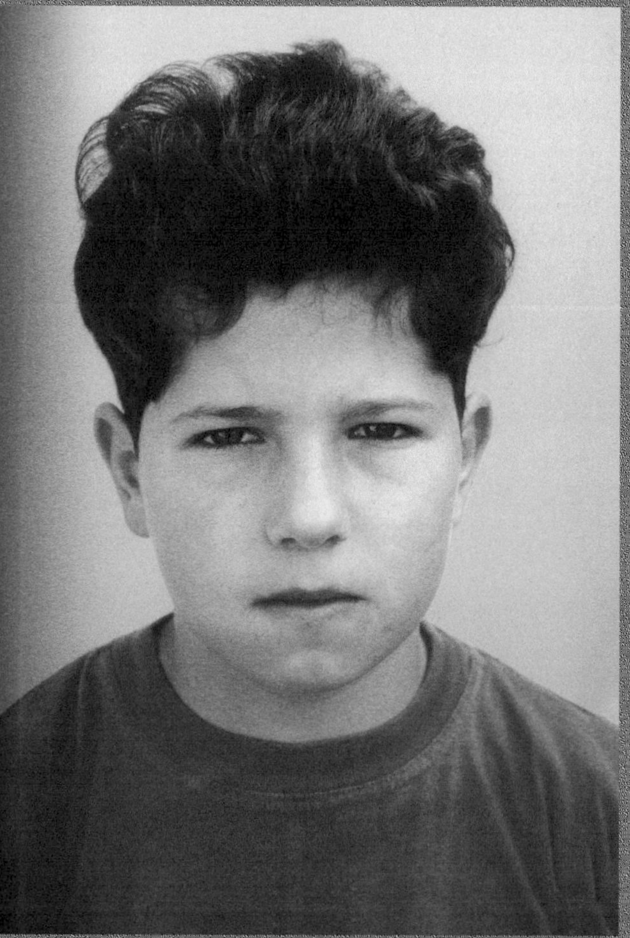

Einar Schleef

Camera Austria International

1988   Gisela Bartens, "Michael Schmidt, Einar Schleef. Ceasefire," book review, *Camera Austria International* 26 / 1988

2014   Jan Wenzel, "Das Stottern der Bilder. Über einige Doppelseiten in Fotobüchern von Einar Schleef und Michael Schmidt," in Einar Schleef, *Zuhause,* Frankfurt am Main, Suhrkamp Verlag, 1981, book review, *Camera Austria International* 128 / 2014

Exhibitions

1983   *Einar Schleef, Zuhause,* solo exhibition
1986   *Das Bild: Der Text,* exhibition participation
2007   *Einar Schleef, Kontaktbögen,* solo exhibition

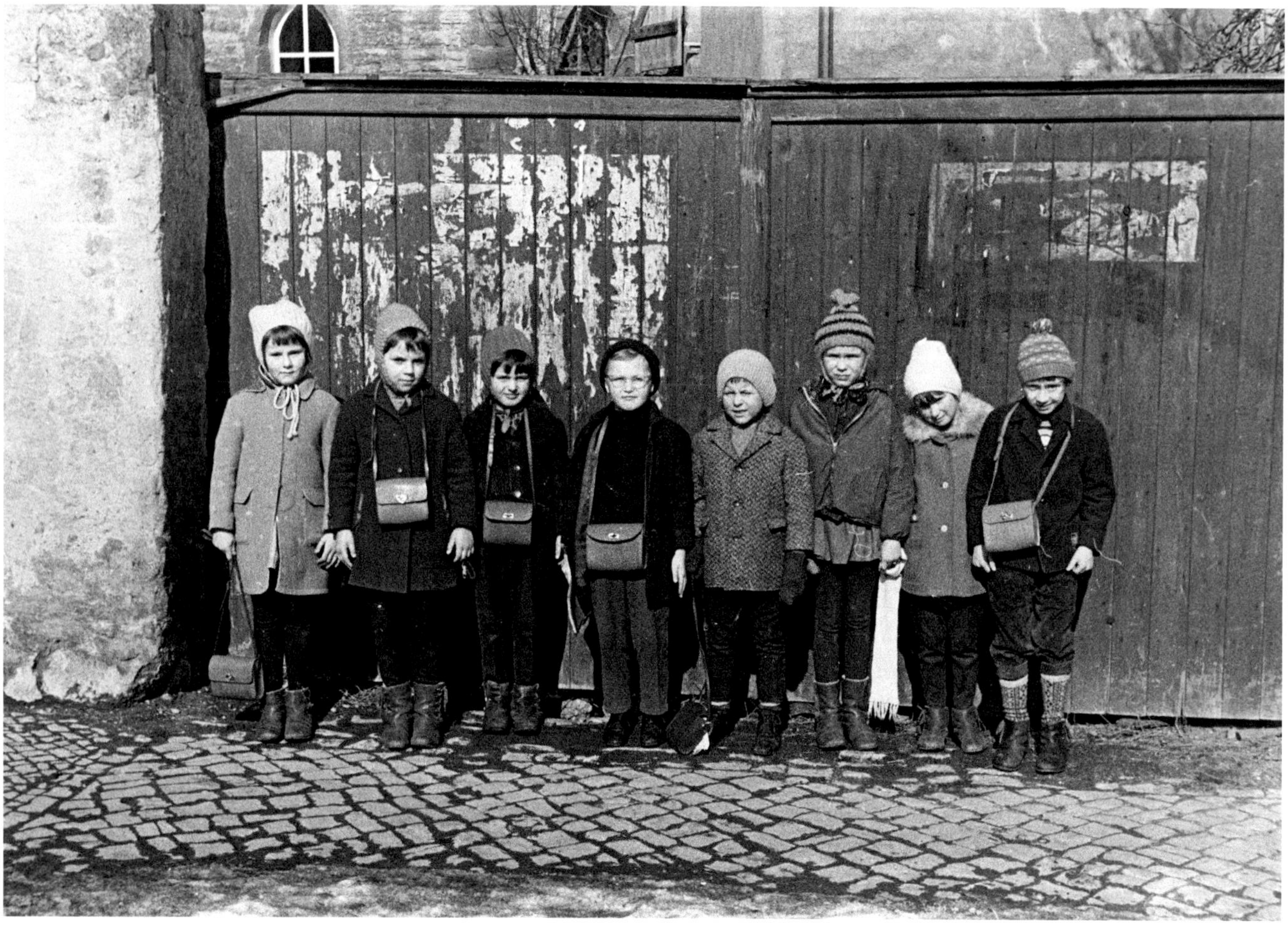

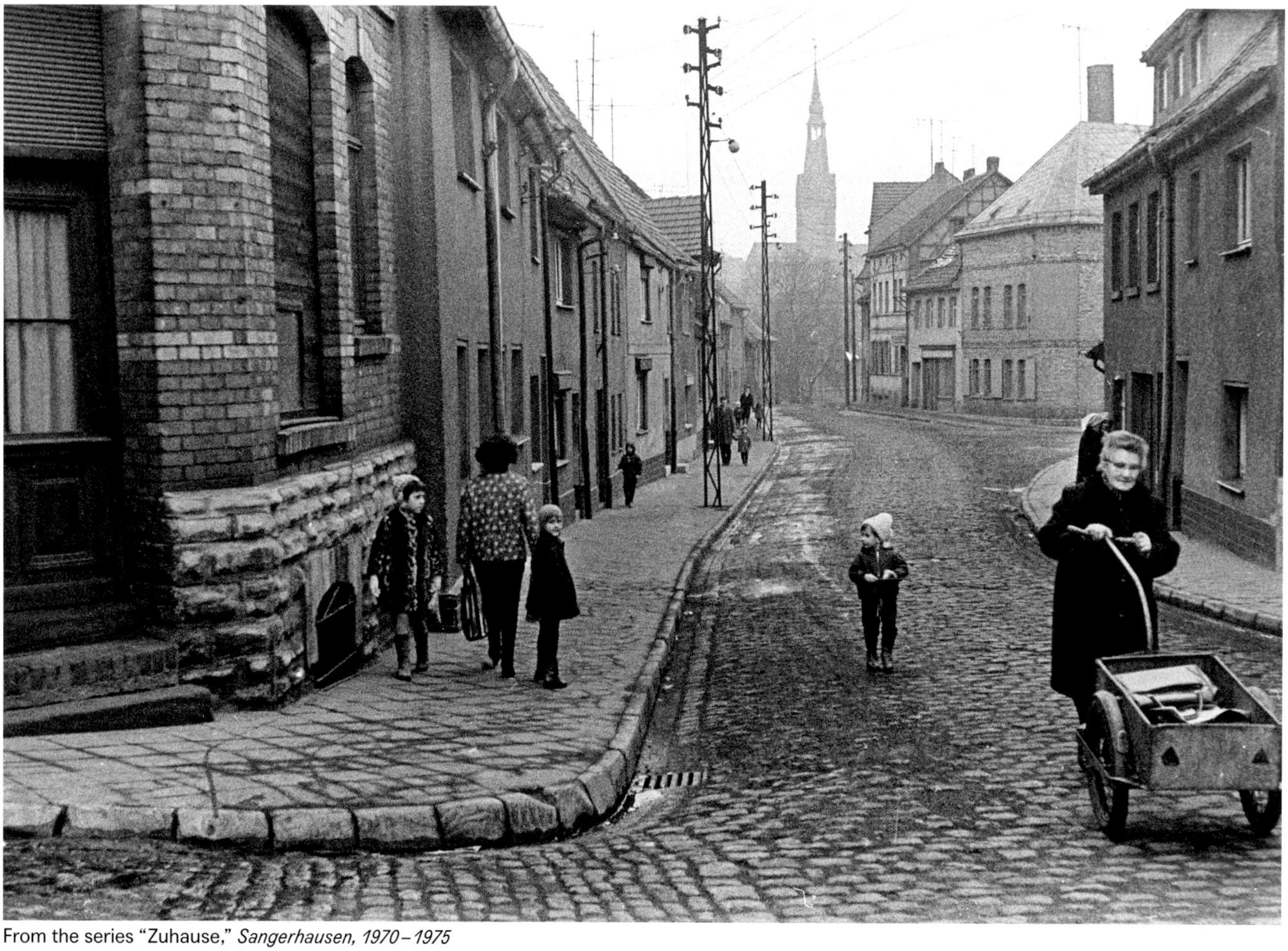

From the series "Zuhause," *Sangerhausen, 1970–1975*

Einar Schleef

Description of Sangerhausen and its Surroundings

When I was lying in bed I thought of the white hills in Ammendorf, the lake in Teutschenthal, the journey from Sangerhausen to Halle, with every station like a journey of love. I will describe them for mother. When I thought about the rendering plant, the railroad crossing, the road down to Riestedt, it calmed me down. Riestedt down in the valley, with the fields in between, the road with the poplar trees, then, over towards Blankenheim forest, the farmhouse among the fields: that's what it must look like in Italy, with the poplars, the half-timbered houses, the brown, almost red, earth. Then the forest and the tunnel. The way mother was shot at on the train and fled into the woods in the snow with aunt Hette. Us on a cross-country march with the Pioneers. When the train goes into the forest you can look back: there's Sanger-hausen back between the two bumps in the ground, a yellowish light, St. James' church, with the pyramid, the spoil heap, up on the right, on the crest of the wave. In the woods over to the left there's the branch line down to Hettstedt-Sandersleben, my line. Eis-leben. Dirt and slag heaps, the little church towers, the stretched-out factory wall with the party slogans facing the road. The hospital, the factory. Behind all the dirt the brightness of the Süße See. Mother swam across it, right across the whole lake. Seeburg. The castle. Our school outing. The old walls and tractors, the apprentices' combine, the waves of the lake reaching right up to the roadway. On the left, in the bend of the road, the swimming baths and the mead-ows. Childhood. The narrow road through the town, hill and village, two small lakes in the next hollow. You can't see it from the train. All the times I couldn't hitch a lift any further, had to climb the hill, through cherry trees and plantations, vineyards right there among all the dirt, three square kilometers of Italy, just like Purrmann's pictures of Ischia.

Einar Schleef, 22.2.1978, from: "Tagebuch 1978," in *Tagebuch 1977–1980*, Berlin: Suhrkamp Verlag 2007, 234.

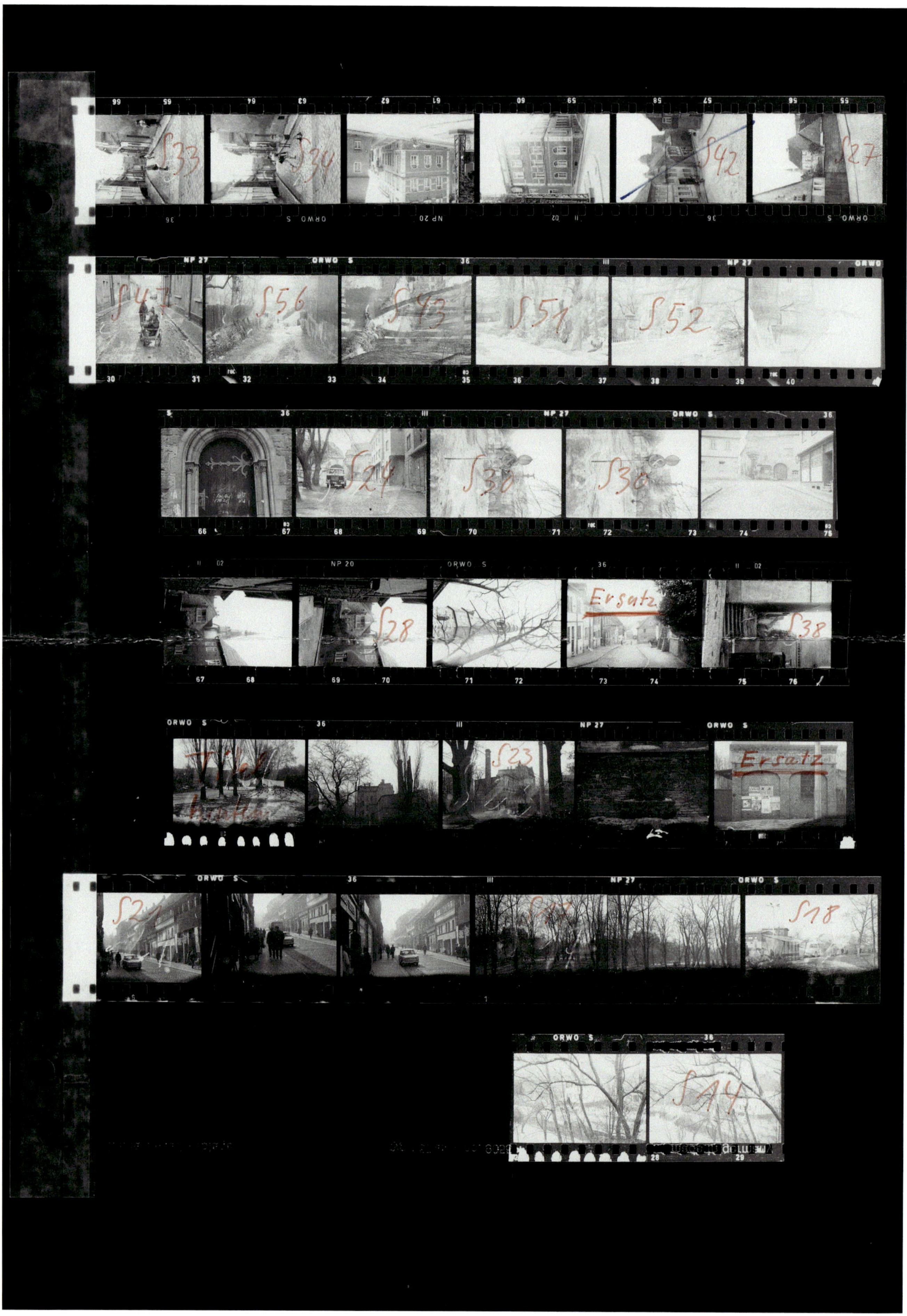

Liebe Frau Frisinghelli

So das Foto ist verpackt,dann kleb ich noch die Fahrkarten an,morgen
gehts dann zur Post.Heut ist der 6.I.,vielleicht gehts diesmal fixer.
Danke für die Gastfreundschaft,ich war sehr froh darüber.Es hat mir
sehr gefallen und ich muß mich bei den ganzen Fotoleuten bedanken,be-
sonders bei Ihnen.
Ich war ganz froh,nur nach dem Wetterumschwung hier,hab ich schlapp
gemacht,lag bis gestern,da ließ das Fieber nach,da schreib ich gleich.
Diesmal wars nicht so schlimm.
Das Plakat finden alle hier gut.Der Herr Kandussi soll ruhig alle Kri-
tiken dem Lektor schicken,vielleicht macht das den auch etwas munterer
bei dem Wetter.Ob ich sie auch bekommen kann.Im Radio war eine,erhielt
auch Kopie davon,aber so schlimm,man kanns nicht lesen,nur ahnen und
da sind viele Löcher drin.Ausfüllen möchte ich die nicht selber.

Hab mich auch gleich hingesetzt und 2 Bilder vom Pensionistenheim gemacht,muß aber eine größere Leinwand besorgen.Würde gern mal länger
nach G.kommen.

Jetzt muß der Katalog ja im Endlauf sein.Vielleicht erwische ich dann
irgendwo noch die Ausstellung.

         Mit herzlichen Grüßen und viellen Dank
             gleich mit Doppel L

Ein (Schmid)

Ob ich den Theatertext schicken
soll? Nur Frage. (Müßte sonst
Extrabrief an Herrn K. schicken.)

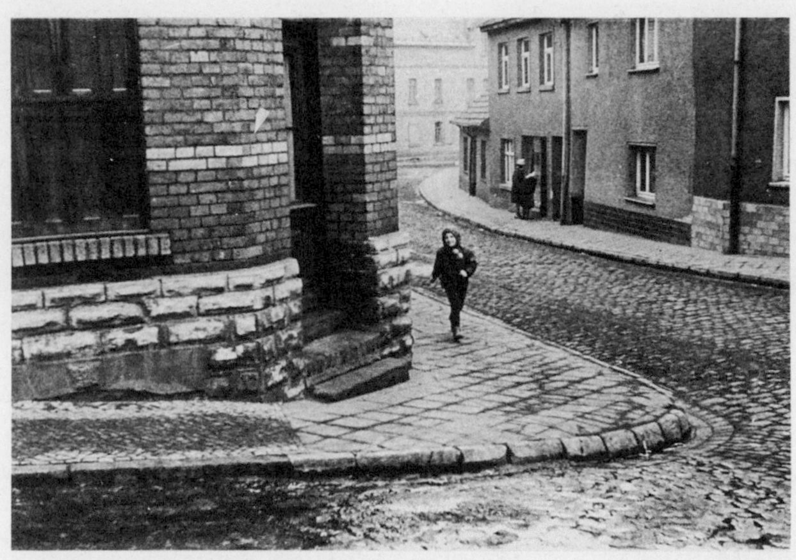

ZUHAUSE

EINAR SCHLEEF

fotogalerie im FORUM STADTPARK, Graz
24. 11. – 22. 12. 1983, Mo. – Fr. 11–18 Uhr
Eröffnung: Mittwoch, 23. 11. um 19.30 Uhr

Participation at Symposia

1983   Symposion on Photography V,
7–9 October 1983, lecturer

1985   Symposion on Photography VII:
"Europa–Amerika. Hello–Good Bye,
Good Bye–Hello," 4–6 October 1985,
concept, lecturer

Camera Austria International

1983   Harald Strobl, "Michael Schmidt. Benachteiligt," book review, *Camera Austria International* 13 / 1983

1984   Robert Adams, "Michael Schmidt. Berlin-Kreuzberg. Stadtbilder," book review, *Camera Austria International* 14 / 1984

1984   Michael Schmidt, artist contribution (journal of Symposion), *Camera Austria International* 15–16 / 1984

1987   Michael Schmidt, artist contribution, *Camera Austria International* 23 / 1987

1988   Gisela Bartens, "Michael Schmidt, Einar Schleef. Ceasefire," book review, *Camera Austria International* 26 / 1988
Michael Schmidt, "Über-Lebens-Energie," artist contribution, *Camera Austria International* 28 / 1988

1996   Christine Frisinghelli, "EIN-HEIT: Zu Michael Schmidts Buch-Arbeiten," text contribution, Michael Schmidt, "EIN-HEIT," artist contribution, *Camera Austria International* 54 / 1996

2006   Carolin Förster, "Michael Schmidt: Irgendwo," book review, *Camera Austria International* 93 / 2006

2010   Esther Ruelfs, "Langeweile als Methode. Michael Schmidt. Grau als Farbe. Fotografien bis 2009, Haus der Kunst, Munich,"exhibition review, *Camera Austria International* 111 / 2010

2011   Maren Lübbke-Tidow, Michael Schmidt, "Michael Schmidt: Mehr Fragen stellen als Antworten geben," text contribution, Michael Schmidt, artist contribution, *Camera Austria International* 114 / 2011

2012   Joachim Brohm, "Michael Schmidt: Lebensmittel," Snoeck Verlag, Köln 2012, book review, *Camera Austria International* 118 / 2012

2014   Jan Wenzel, "Das Stottern der Bilder. Über einige Doppelseiten in Fotobüchern von Einar Schleef und Michael Schmidt," Michael Schmidt: Lebensmittel, Snoeck, Köln 2012, book review, *Camera Austria International* 128 / 2014

2015   Annette Kelm, "Belichtung und Farbwerte / Exposure and Chromaticity," *Camera Austria International* 131 / 2015

2016   Falk Haberkorn, "Kreuzberg – Amerika. Werkstatt für Photographie 1976–1986," exhibition review, *Camera Austria International* 136 / 2016

2018   Maren Lübbke-Tidow, "Michael Schmidt: Ceasefire, Volksbühne Berlin," exhibition review, *Camera Austria International* 141 / 2018

Exhibitions

1982   *Michael Schmidt,* solo exhibition
1983   *Fotografie 1983,* exhibition participation
1985   *Europa – Amerika: Hello – Good Bye, Good Bye – Hello,* exhibition participation
1988   *Über-Lebens-Energie,* exhibition participation
2011   *Milk Drop Coronet. 30 Exhibitions on the Virtuosity of Thingness*, exhibition participation

Workshops

1982   17–18 April 1982
1988   30 April–13 Mai 1988, Eisenerz, in conjunction with *Über-Lebens-Energie*

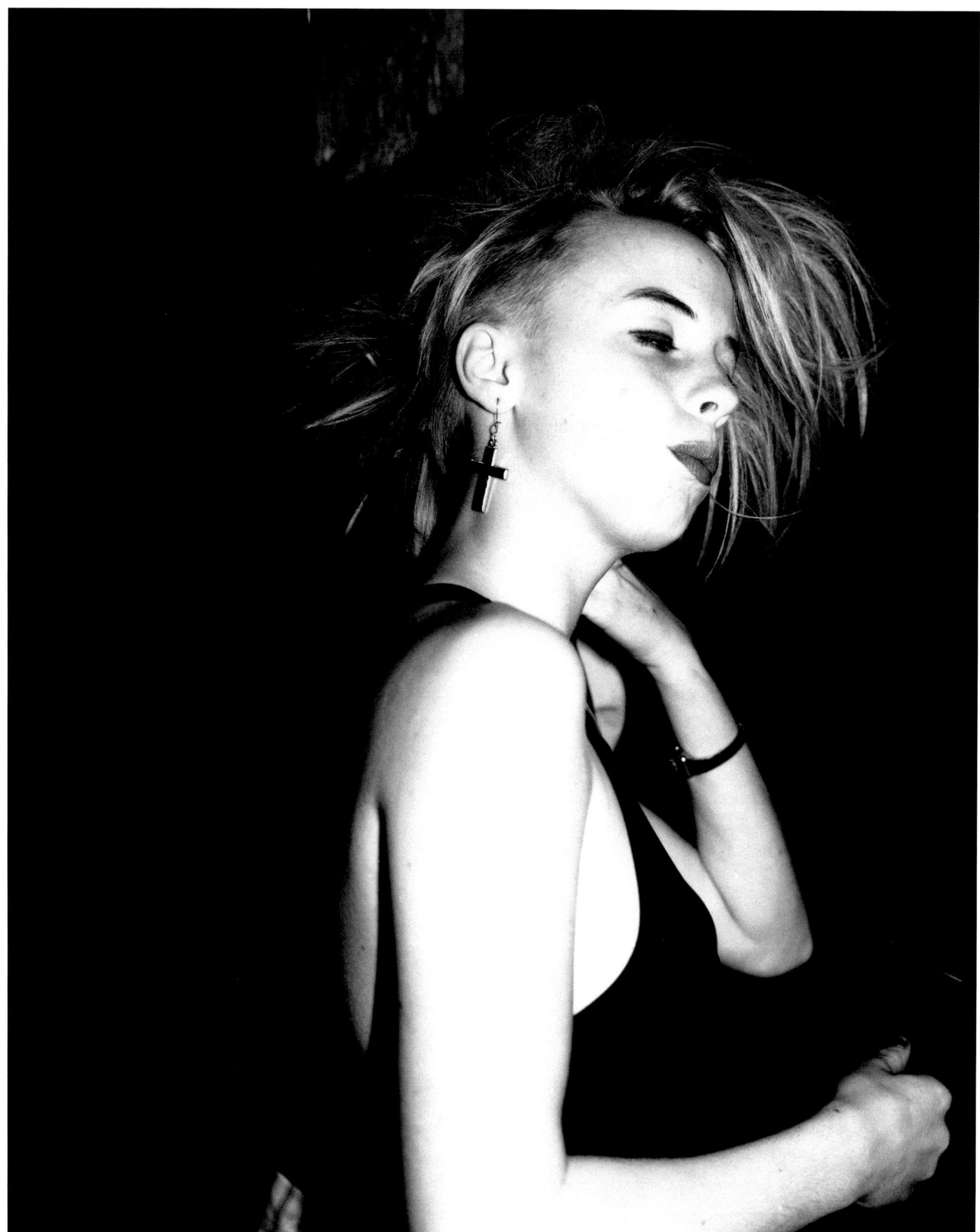

From the series *Waffenruhe*, 1985–1987

Michael Schmidt

Lewis Baltz
Notes on *Waffenruhe* (Ceasefire)

"A republic of images." It is early March 1988 and everyone who has ever had the intention to photograph Berlin has probably done this by now. In the last seven or eight years, the city has become established as a place for serious photographic work and it has attracted numerous interesting artists from Germany and abroad. And for a good reason: Apart from New York and its legend of ambition and success endlessly reproducing itself, Berlin is the last mythic city of the occident. If Berlin had not already existed, Calvino would have invented it.

London, Paris, Rome, have a history, but Berlin has a past. It is the Sodom of our century, destroyed for its sins and left like that as a dark memorial. Since the 1920s, Berlin has been a city approached through images: Döblin, Pabst, Isherwood; the vicious shrine of Nazism; the Year Zero; the Airlift, John Kennedy and the spies who came in from the cold; the generation of '68, the stylized desperation of the punk underground and angles you can touch, these are some of the images making the myth. Myths, however, do not only lend events a human dimension, they are also manufactured to mystify experiences. Mythic images are perhaps those you have to be most suspicious of. Yet the idea of a post-apocalyptic city captivates the contemporary spirit and images of it spring like mushrooms again. Berlin will soon be flooded with pictures as New York and Paris and the images of the city will have lost all their power, except to reflect and remind of each other.

The best photographer of Wartenburgstraße. Michael Schmidt was born in Berlin in 1945 and has photographed the city for nearly twenty years. Schmidt's work maintains a dialectic relation to Berlin; his photographs and the city explain each other. Of the thousand pictures populating Berlin, many of the most memorable are those by Schmidt. Schmidt continues the photograph Berlin and the viewer continues to see Berlin with his eyes. But now something new happens: Photographer and viewer see Berlin as if it was for the first time.

Schmidt is an artist of protean intellectual energies. Furthermore, he is an artist of the fragment, of complexity, of contradiction. His work is consistent and versatile. In *Waffenruhe* he is also passionate, which makes this collection of photographs his most intense and poignant to date. Not only does this mean that Schmidt is a better artist now, but also that he has become an entirely different artist. He has—except for the most rudimentary—cut all ties with the traditional documentary style and replaced it by an aesthetic of immediate experience. There is no confusion, no hide and seek in *Waffenruhe*. Schmidt's work is full of self-confidence and authority now.

Questions of space and time. The protagonist of *Waffenruhe* is the Berlin Wall or more precisely the city limits and some of the things happening within them. A fifth of the photographs show the Wall; another fifth alludes to its presence; almost all imply its existence. The Wall is Berlin's dark symbol of itself, the most representative landmark of the city, a kind of sinister Eiffel Tower. However, as the Eiffel Tower somehow "naturalizes" Paris (Barthes) the Wall reinforces Berlin's artificiality and elusiveness. The Wall is Europe's most atrocious landmark, yet it is also the one where use value and symbolic value are most closely linked. […]

Excerpt from: Lewis Baltz, *Texte*, Göttingen: Steidl Verlag 2013, 93–97, first published in *Camera Austria International* 26/1988.

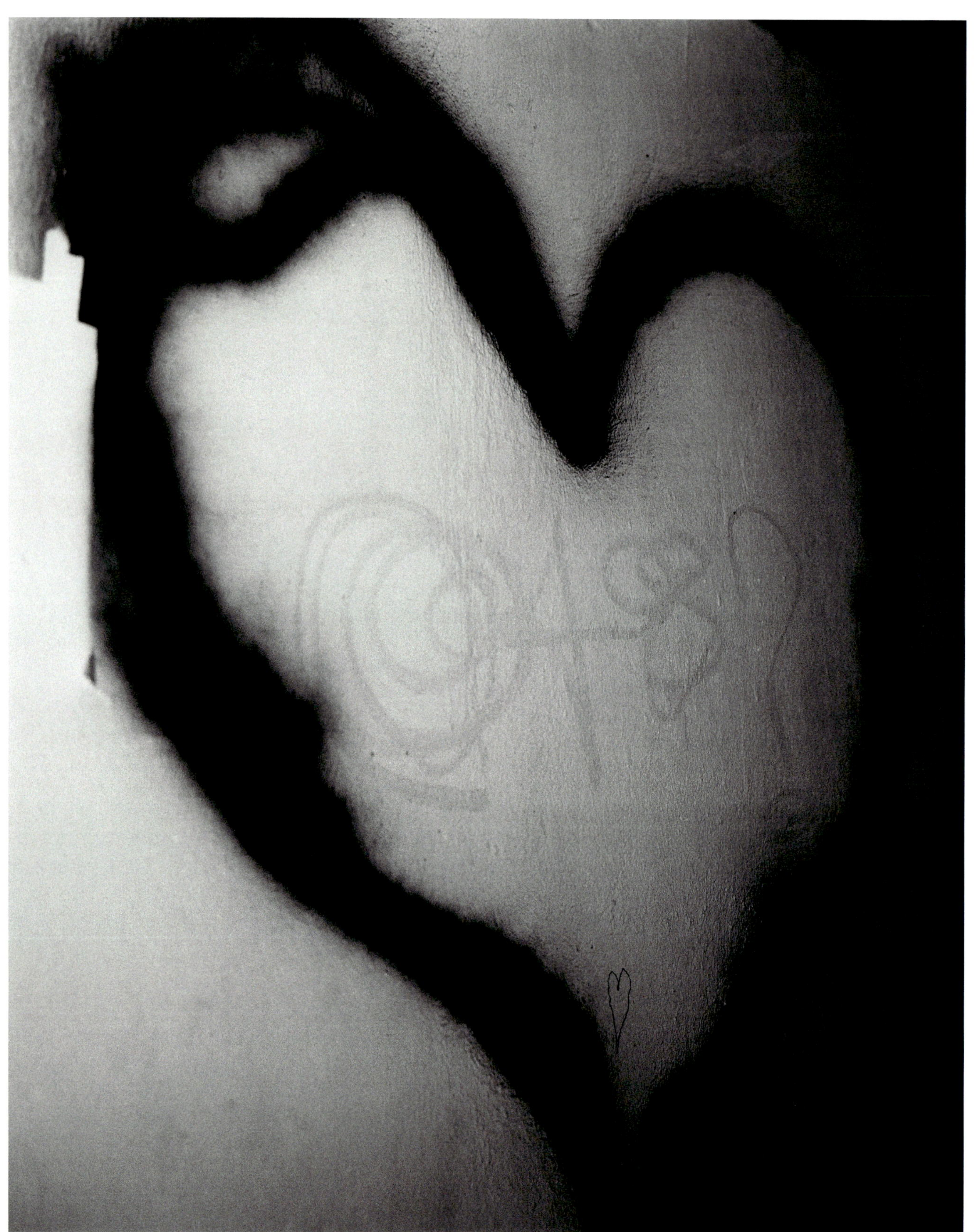

From the series *Waffenruhe*, 1985–1987

Michael Schmidt

141

Camera Austria International 15–16/1984

DISKUSSION

Frage: Du sagst, du fotografierst jetzt mehr mit Gefühl; welche Gefühle haben dich bewegt, deine Arbeitsweise zu ändern?
Michael Schmidt: Alle! Ich kann nicht meine Gefühle analysieren, ich wüßte nicht . . .
F.: Es gibt in deiner Arbeit einen Unterschied zwischen Landschaft und Menschen; die Distanz ist sehr unterschiedlich. Was sind das für Unterschiede?
M. S.: Wenn ich das richtig verstehe, würde ich sagen, ich bin innerlich nicht richtig gefestigt oder abgeschlossen genug, um mich jedem Menschen gleich zu nähern. Ich habe Phasen starker Verunsicherung und Angst, die ganz plötzlich da sind.
F.: Warum fotografieren Sie nicht in Farbe?
M. S.: Ich habe noch nie das Verlangen gehabt, in Farbe zu fotografieren, obwohl ich farbig sehe; aber vielleicht passiert es einmal.
F.: Mir ist aufgefallen, daß einige Architekturaufnahmen sehr gebaut, fast komponiert sind und andere wieder sehr sachlich, fast zufällig. Ist das bewußt, oder?
M. S.: Mir ist das noch nicht aufgefallen, deshalb kann ich dazu schwer etwas sagen, darüber muß ich nachdenken.
F.: Für mich ist der Großteil deiner Bilder so bedrückend kontrolliert. Ist das einfach das Ergebnis einer Umgebung, oder . . .?
M. S.: Ich muß mich kontrollieren, sonst kann ich nicht arbeiten. Aber vielleicht ist es durch das Milieu, von dem ich nicht emanzipiert genug bin.
F.: Was denken Sie jetzt über die objektive dokumentarische Richtung?
M. S.: Ich bin als Dokumentarist abgestempelt worden, aber als Dokumentarist in dem Sinne fühle ich mich nicht. Wenn ich jemals Dokumentarist im objektiven Sinne war, so war das eine Sackgasse, die für mich sehr befruchtend war, um die Fotos zu machen, die ich jetzt mache. Ich wäre zur jetzigen Arbeit nie gekommen, hätte ich die andere nicht gemacht. Heute würde ich sagen, daß Objektivität zur Entfremdung führt, aber ich mußte die Entfremdung durchmachen, um zu erfahren, daß es nicht mein Weg ist. Aber ich stehe voll und ganz zu dieser Arbeit und zu dem, was ich bislang dazu gesagt habe. Allerdings erhebe ich nicht meine eigenen Aussagen zum Dogma, ich bin doch nicht verrückt und mauere mich selber ein.
F.: . . .
M. S.: Dazu kann ich sehr wenig sagen, wenn du sagst, daß ich früher strenger gesehen habe. Ich bin etwas freier geworden. Gegen Strenge hab' ich nichts, aber gegen unerbittliche Härte.
F.: . . .
M. S.: Wenn ich dich richtig verstanden habe, meinst du, daß die Menschen, die ich fotografiert habe, ziemlich unfrei sind. Ja, sehe ich auch so.
F.: Heißt das, daß du dich freier fühlst als die Menschen, die du fotografierst?
M. S.: Manchmal ein bißchen, emanzipierter wäre richtiger.
F.: Wie fühlst du dich, wenn du Bilder außerhalb von Berlin machst?
M. S.: Wenn ich fotografiere, dann fühle ich mich nicht anders, egal wo. Für mich wäre es sehr schwierig, ständig in Graz zu fotografieren, weil das ganze Klima anders ist und die Reizschwelle eine ganz andere ist, längst nicht so hoch, hier wirkt alles viel ruhiger, und meine Bilder würden, wenn ich hier leben würde, sicherlich anders ausfallen. Ich lebe aber nicht hier, und zum anderen muß ich sagen, glaub ich, kann man am besten da arbeiten, wo man lebt. Ich könnte auch woanders arbeiten, aber ich wüßte nicht warum.
F.: Fotografierst du mit einer Reflexkamera oder mit einer Kamera, in die du hineinschaust – ich kenn' die Fachausdrücke nicht.
M. S.: Ich fotografiere mit einer Sucherkamera. Ich habe früher viel mit einer Spiegelreflexkamera fotografiert, nur dann sehe ich Bilder auf der Mattscheibe, und die Sucherkamera ermöglicht mir, das Bild oder die Situation viel physischer zu erleben, ohne daß ein Bild dazwischen geschaltet ist. Ich habe also nur das Gefühl, als ob ich eine Brille mit Fensterglas aufhätte. Meine Bilder entstehen also

DISCUSSION

Question: You say that more feeling is involved in your pre[sent] photography. What feelings have caused you to change [your] manner of working?
M. Schmidt: All of them! I cannot analyze my feelings, I just [don't] know . . .
Q.: In your work there is a difference between landscape and pe[ople], your distance is not the same. How come?
M. S.: If I understand you right, let me say that I am still i[n the] making and lack the inner security it would take to approach [every] person the same way. I experience phases of great insecurity [and] anxiousness that come very suddenly.
Q.: Why don't you photograph in color?
M. S.: I have never felt a desire to, although I see in color. [It] may well happen some day.
Q.: I have noticed that some architectural photographs seem [very] much constructed, almost composed, while others are [very] objective, almost accidental. Is that intentional?
M. S.: I'm not aware of that myself, so it's hard to make a comme[nt]. I've got to think about it.
Q.: Most of your pictures impress me as being controlled [in a] depressive way. Does that merely result from your environ[ment] or are there other reasons?
M. S.: I must control myself in order to be able to work. [And] perhaps the reason is in fact the environment. Perhaps I a[m not] sufficiently emancipated from that environment.
Q.: What do you think about objective, documentary photogra[phy]?
M. S.: I have been labelled a documentarist, although I d[on't] actually feel as one. If I ever was a documentarist in the obj[ective] sense, it was a dead-end street. However, it greatly inspi[red the] work I am doing now. Without it, I would not be doing wha[t I'm] doing now. Today I might say, objectiveness lead[s to] estrangement, but I had to experience estrangement in ord[er to] realize it's not my way. Yet, I fully acknowledge my former [work] and what I have said about it. I do not want to be dogmatic a[bout] what I say, and I'm not so crazy as to surround myself with a [wall].
Q.: . . .
M. S.: If you find my earlier vision stern, there is not much I ca[n do] about it. I feel more free now. I have nothing against stern[ness] but I object against merciless harshness.
Q.: . . .
M. S.: If I understand you correctly, you mean to say that the pe[ople] I have photographed are not very free. Yes, that's how I se[e it] too.
Q.: Does that mean you feel more free than the people [you] photograph?
M. S.: It would be more accurate to say: At times I feel [more] emancipated.
Q.: How do you feel when you take pictures outside Berlin?
M. S.: When I take pictures, it doesn't matter where I am. I d[on't] find it extremely difficult to work in Graz always, since the amb[ience] here is different and the stimulus threshold is not the same at all, as high as in Berlin, by far. Everything seems more tranquil [here]. If I lived here, my pictures would turn out rather differently, I['m] sure. But as it is, I don't live here. I also think that you [can] work best where you live. Of course I could work somewher[e else] as well, but why should I?
Q.: Do you work with a reflex camera or with the kind you [just] look into—I don't know the technical term . . .
M. S.: I use a camera with a view finder. Earlier, I often us[ed a] reflex camera, but then I see images on a screen, and the view fi[nder] enables me to experience a situation much closer to life, witho[ut the] image getting into the way. I merely feel like wearing glasses [with] plain glass. My pictures are not made on a screen, they are m[ade] in the situation I record. The camera merely serves to record [the] experience.
Q.: What about picture number 3? You haven't said anyt[hing] about it. It differs from the others. There is an A in the pict[ure] as in Austria.

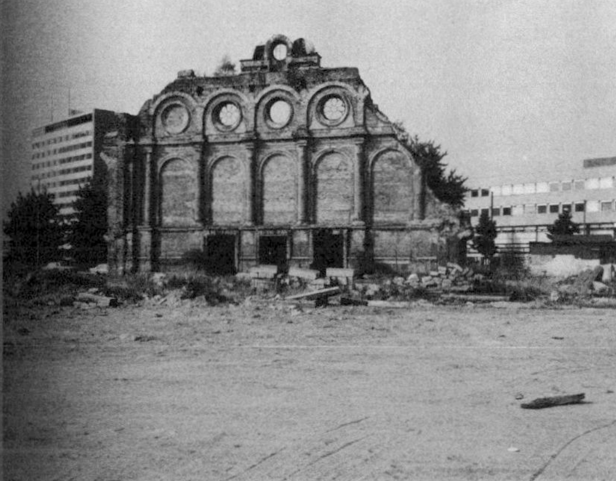

Berlin, 1983

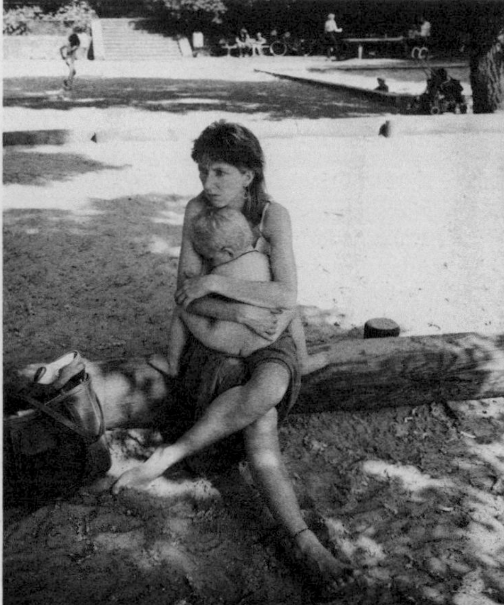

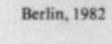
Berlin, 1982

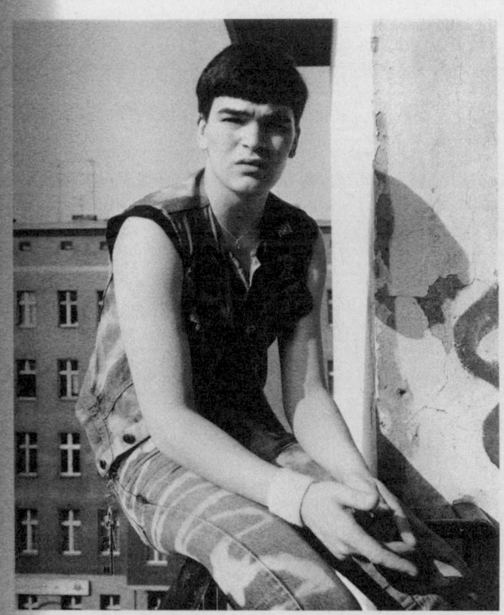

Berlin, 1983

"

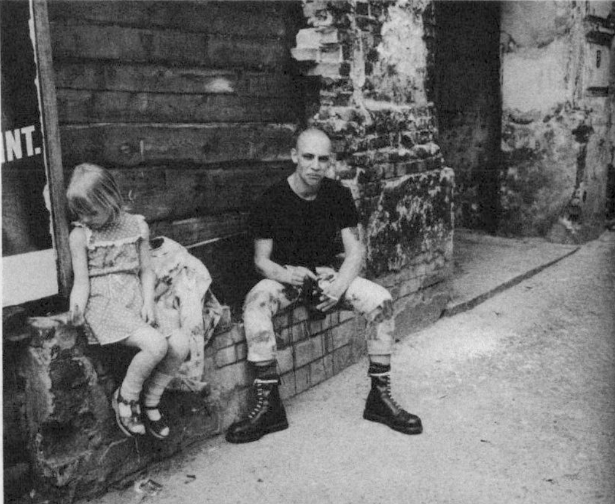

Berlin, 1983

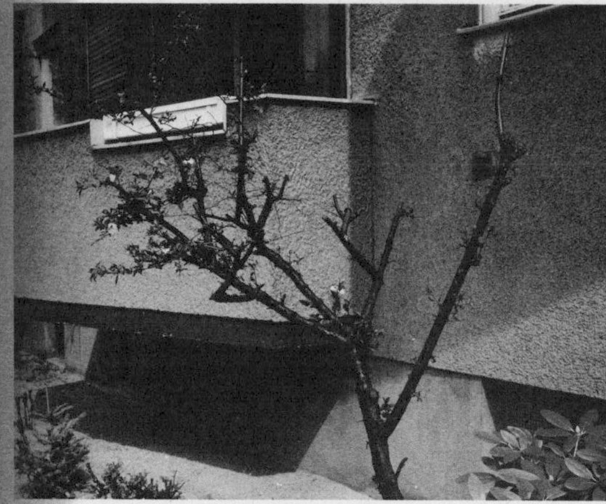

Berlin, 1982

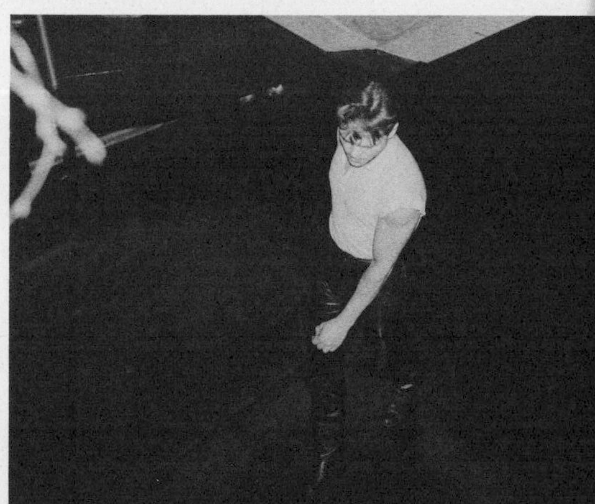

Berlin, 1983

nicht auf der Mattscheibe, sondern sie ergeben sich einfach aus Emotionen, und die halte ich fest. Die Kamera dient mir einfach zur Verankerung dessen, was ich erlebt habe.

F: Was ist mit dem Bild mit der Ziffer 3, dazu haben Sie nichts gesagt, es ist anders als die anderen, es hat auch ein A – wie Österreich.

M.S.: Also so sehr ich Graz schätze und Österreich auch, muß ich Sie leider enttäuschen, das A ist das Zeichen für Anarchie.

F: Der 3er ist für mich dominant, es hat einen bestimmten abstrakten Charakter. Es ist einfach abstrakt im Vergleich zu den anderen.

M.S.: Vielleicht habt ihr recht, es kann sein. Ich finde es nicht abstrakt.

F: Du sagst, daß du das fotografierst, was du wahrnimmst. Dazwischen liegt doch ein Unterschied. Wie überbrückst du diese Schwierigkeiten?

M.S.: Mein Problem ist jetzt, daß ich gar nicht den Unterschied sehe zwischen Wahrnehmen und Sehen. Für mich ist das alles ein bewußtes Sehen, und da unterscheide ich gar nicht. Was ist der Unterschied?

F: Ich möchte folgendes sagen: Das Sehen ist ein optischer Vorgang, das Registrieren aller Details, all dessen, was vor mir liegt, während das, was ich wahrnehme, über den Kopf geht, über meine Empfindungen, über meine Vorkenntnisse, über meine Assoziation usw., da bildet sich etwas ganz anderes heraus als das, was an Objekten wirklich vor mir liegt.

M.S.: Ich sagte, als ich die Bilder zeigte, daß ich nur das fotografiere, was mich irgendwo innerlich berührt, und das ist dann wahrscheinlich die Wahrnehmung.

F: Könnte man sagen, daß du früher mehr gesehen hast und jetzt mehr wahrnimmst?

M.S.: Das ist möglich.

F: In den vergangenen Jahrzehnten ist die Dokumentarfotografie zu einem sehr starken Anspruch an ihre politische Relevanz gemacht worden, ist dieser Aspekt für dich und deine jetzige Arbeit noch wichtig?

M.S.: Eben wollte ich noch ganz glatt nein sagen, aber ich bin mir jetzt nicht so ganz sicher. Aber Tagespolitik wollte ich nie machen. Eine sozial dokumentarische Fotografie, würde ich sagen, ist es nicht, eine sozial dokumentarische Fotografie hätte mehr damit zu tun, so wie ich das verstehe und so wie ich sie kenne, daß man ganz bestimmte Gruppen herausgreift und über sie berichtet. Und wenn die Bilder gut sind, dann haben sie einen starken aufwieglerischen Aspekt oder einen starken mitreißenden Aspekt, währenddessen meine Bilder mehr alle Menschen zeigen. Also keine FSA-Fotografie.

F: Ich habe dich vorhin nach deinen Gefühlen gefragt, und jetzt möchte ich gern noch einmal nachfragen...

M.S.: Ich kann jetzt auch schwer was sagen, wenn du sagst, da sind Bilder dabei, die dich begeistern und andere, die platt sind und keine Aussage haben, was soll ich da sagen, ich kann am besten sagen, daß ich manchmal auch platt bin. Aber das macht nichts. Du bist ja auch nicht immer auf der Höhe deiner geistigen Kraft, sondern manchmal fehlt da irgend etwas.

Sind noch irgendwelche Fragen, sonst machen wir Schluß!
Ich bedanke mich recht herzlich, daß Sie so aufmerksam waren!

M. S.: As much as I love Graz and Austria, I have to disappoint you. The A stands for anarchy.
Q.: Picture number 3 seems dominant to me, there is a certain abstract character to it. It is plainly abstract, as compared to the other pictures.
M. S.: You may be right, perhaps that is so. I don't find it abstract, though.
Q.: You say you photograph what you experience. There is a difference, isn't there? How do you bridge the gap?
M. S.: My problem presently is that I just don't see the difference between perception and seeing. For me it is all conscious seeing, and I don't differentiate. What is the difference, anyway?
Q.: Seeing is an optical process, a registering of all details, of everything in your view, whereas perception goes via the head, it's emotional, previous knowledge is involved, associations are made etc. The result is entirely different from what actually lies before me.
M. S.: When I showed the slides I said I only photographed things that somehow touch me inwardly. Probably that is what you mean by perception.
Q.: Would it be accurate to say that formerly you saw more and now you perceive more?
M. S.: That is possible.
Q.: During the past decades documentary photography was made with a strong claim on its political relevancy. Is that aspect still important to you and to your work?
M. S.: Just this moment I wanted to respond in the definite negative, but now I am not so sure. I was never interested in day-to-day politics. Neither would I call my work social documentarist photography. As I know and understand social documentation, it focuses on definite social groups and reports about them. And when the pictures are good quality, they tend to incite and to rouse. My pictures, in contrast, show all kinds of people. It is no FSA-photography.
Q.: In the beginning, I asked you about your feelings—now let me ask once more.
M. S.: Even now it is hard for me to say anything. You claim my work includes pictures that excite you while others seem shallow and lacking expression. What can I say? Sometimes I am shallow, I guess—so what? You are not always in spiritual top shape, sometimes there is something lacking.

Any more questions? If not, let's come to an end!
Thank you very much for your kind attention!

MICHAEL SCHMIDT
geboren 1945 in Berlin, lebt und arbeitet in West-Berlin. Begann 1965 zu fotografieren, seit 1973 freischaffender Fotograf; unterrichtete ab 1969 an der Volkshochschule Berlin künstlerische Fotografie, 1976 Gründung der Werkstatt für Photografie an der VHS Kreuzberg. Publikationen: „Berlin-Kreuzberg", 1973; „Berlin Stadtlandschaft und Menschen", 1978; „Berlin-Wedding", 1978; „Benachteiligt", 1981; „Berlin-Kreuzberg, Stadtbilder", 1984.

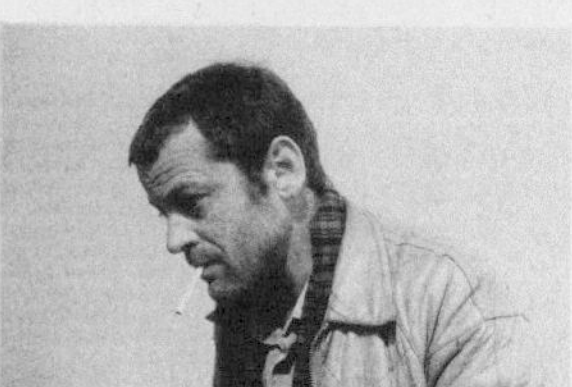

Foto: H. Tezak

MICHAEL SCHMIDT
Born in Berlin in 1945, lives and works in Western Berlin. In 1965 he began to photographs, since 1973 he has been a free-lance photographer; he has been teaching artistic photography to adult classes at the Volkshochschule Berlin since 1969; in 1976 he founded the workshop for photography at the Volkshochschule Kreuzberg. Publications: "Berlin—Kreuzberg", 1973; "Berlin Stadtlandschaft und Menschen", 1978; "Berlin—Wedding", 1978, "Benachteiligt", 1981; "Berlin—Kreuzberg", Stadtbilder, 1984.

Participation at Symposion

1979 Symposion on Photography I,
29 September – 2 October 1979,
artist contribution

Camera Austria International

1980 Manfred Willmann, "New York," artist
contribution, *Camera Austria International* 1/
1980

1981 Manfred Willmann, "Volkmarweg 36,"
artist contribution, *Camera Austria
International* 6/1981

1982 Manfred Willmann, text contribution,
Camera Austria International 10/1982

1984 Manfred Willmann, "Interview mit Klaus
Honnef zu: The Power (and the Glory) of
Photography," text contribution (journal of
Symposion), *Camera Austria International*
15 – 16/1984

1987 Manfred Willmann, "Wie interessant ist
die Fotografie in Österreich?," text contribution, *Camera Austria International* 22/1987

1987 Manfred Willmann, artist contribution,
Camera Austria International 23/1987

1988 Manfred Willmann, "Über-Lebens-Energie,"
artist contribution, *Camera Austria
International* 28/1988

1989 Manfred Willmann, "Die Sieger," artist
contribution, *Camera Austria International*
29/1989

1993 Christine Frisinghelli, Manfred Willmann,
"Eine Art ungeschützter Schmerz. Im
Gespräch mit Boris Mikhailov," text
contribution, *Camera Austria International*
42/1993

2002 Martin Prinzhorn, "Manfred Willmann:
Ideologiekritik," text contribution,
Manfred Willmann, artist contribution,
Camera Austria International 77/2002

2006 Reinhard Braun, "Die Wirklichkeit durch-
arbeiten. Manfred Willmann. Werkblick.
Neue Galerie am Landesmuseum Joanneum,"
Graz; Manfred Willmann. Das Land.
Photo España 2006, Círculo de Bellas Artes,
Madrid, exhibition review,
Camera Austria International 94/2006

2010 Herta Wolf, "Der Rotklee-Bläuling.
Für Manfred Willmann," text contribution,
Manfred Willmann, artist contribution,
Camera Austria International 109/2010

2011 Sandra Križić Roban, "Manfred Willmann:
Arbeit," exhibition review, *Camera Austria
International* 114/2011

2012 Presentation to the Forum (with Christine
Frisinghelli), *Camera Austria International*
117/2012

2018 Jens Asthoff, "Manfred Willmann: Blitz &
Enzianblau, Fotohof edition, Salzburg 2017,"
book review, *Camera Austria International*
124/2018

Exhibitions

1979 *New York,* exhibition contribution
5 Jahre Fotogalerie im Forum Stadtpark,
exhibition contribution

1980 *Europäische Fotografen, Teil 1: Steiermark,*
exhibition contribution

1981 *Dokumentation eines Workshops mit Peter
Schlessinger,* exhibition contribution
New Photography from Austria, exhibition
contribution

1982 *Graz 1982,* Galerija Sinagoga, Maribor (SI),
exhibition contribution

1985 *Six Austrian Photographers,* Arbitrage Gallery,
New York City (US), Municipal Art Gallery,
Los Angeles (US), exhibition contribution

1986 *Self-Images / World-Images,* exhibition
contribution

1987 *Fotografie in Österreich,* Museum Folkwang,
Essen (DE), exhibition contribution

1988 *Arc Lémanique,* Musée de l'Elysée,
Lausanne (CH), exhibition contribution
Die Rache der Erinnerung

exhibition contribution
Questioning Europe, Photo Biennale
Rotterdam (NL)
Über–Lebens–Energie, exhibition contribution
results of photo workshop "Über-Lebens-
Energie," station, Leoben, exhibition
contribution
1989 *Die Sieger,* solo exhibition *Stadtpark Eins,*
Kunsthaus Zug, Zug (CH), exhibition
contribution
1993 *Forum Stadtpark Graz, Austria,* Museum
des Zentrums für Volkskunst, Kharkiv (UA),
exhibition contribution
WAR, I. Austrian Triennial for Photography,
exhibition contribution
1994 *Another Continent,* Tokyo Metropolitan
Museum of Photography (JP), exhibition
contribution
Alle haben Alles gesehen, Modena per la
Fotografia 1994, Palazzo Comunale, Modena
(IT), exhibition contribution
*Three Photographers: Seiichi Furuya, Erich
Lázár, Manfred Willmann,* Stadtgalerie
Bratislava (SK), European Month of Photography Bratislava, exhibition contribution
siebzehn, exhibition contribution
1996 *Stadtpark Zwei,* Art Pavilion, Zagreb (HR),
exhibition contribution
2003 *Freundschaftsspiel,* exhibition contribution
2007 *What We Bought,* exhibition contribution

Publications

1977 Manfred Willmann, ed, *American Photographers,* Graz, Fotogalerie im Forum Stadtpark,
1977
1978 Manfred Willmann, ed, *Reportage Fotografen,*
Graz, Fotogalerie im Forum Stadtpark, 1978
1980 Christine Frisinghelli and Manfred Willmann,
eds, *Symposion on Photography,* Graz, Fotogalerie im Forum Stadtpark, 1980
1981 *Manfred Willmann,* "Schwarz und Gold,"
Graz, Edition Camera Austria, 1981
1982 Manfred Willmann, ed., *Graz 1982,* Graz,
Fotogalerie im Forum Stadtpark, 1982
1984 Seiichi Furuya and Manfred Willmann, eds,
Shomei Tomatsu, Japan 1952 – 1981, Graz,
Edition Camera Austria, 1984
1984 *Helmut Tezak, DAKAR,* Graz, Edition Camera
Austria, 1984
1987 Manfred Willmann, ed., *Hans Frank, Hinter
den Kulissen,* Graz, Edition Camera Austria,
1987
1989 Manfred Willmann, ed., *Stadtpark Eins,* Graz,
Edition Camera Austria, 1989

1992 Seiichi Furuya and Manfred Willmann, eds,
Nobuyoshi Araki, AKT–TOKYO. 1971 – 1991,
Graz, Edition Camera Austria, 1992
1993 Werner Fenz and Christine Frisinghelli,
eds, *WAR,* publication in two volumes for
exhibition of the I. Austrian Triennial for
Photography, Graz, Edition Camera Austria,
1993
1997 Manfred Willmann, ed., *Stadtpark Zwei,*
Graz, Edition Camera Austria, 1997
2006 Max Aufischer, Werner Fenz, and Manfred
Willmann, eds, *Erich Kees, in mir,* Graz,
Edition Camera Austria, 2006
2007 Manfred Willmann, ed., *Camera Austria
International: Index Nr. 1 | 1980 – 100 | 2007,*
edited by Heidi Oswald and Anja Rösch,
Graz, Edition Camera Austria, 2007

Workshop

1988 6 – 23 September 1988, Leoben, in
conjunction with *Über-Lebens-Energie*

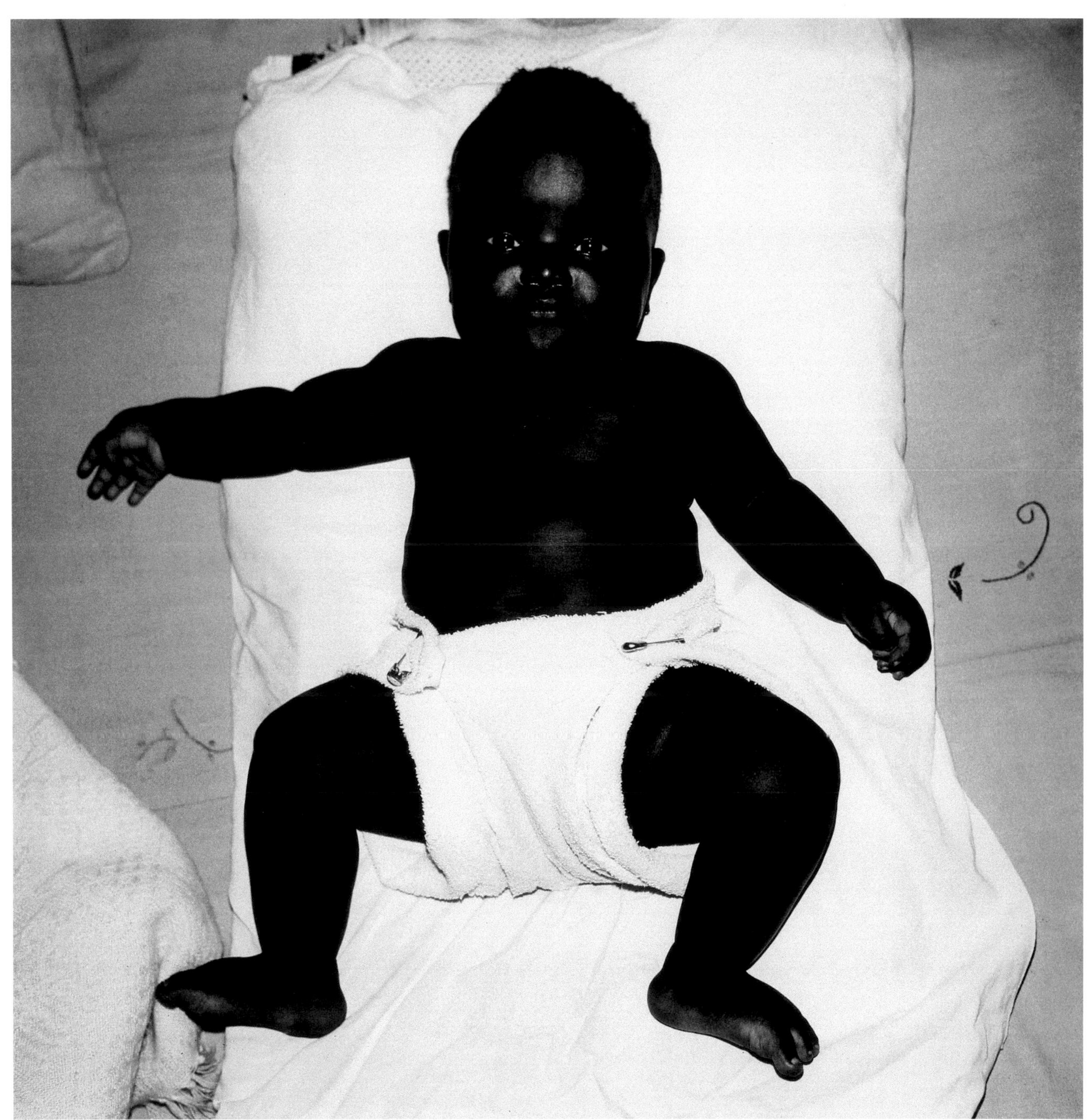

145 From the series "Schwarz und Gold," 1979–1981, part 3, *Ich träume nie!*

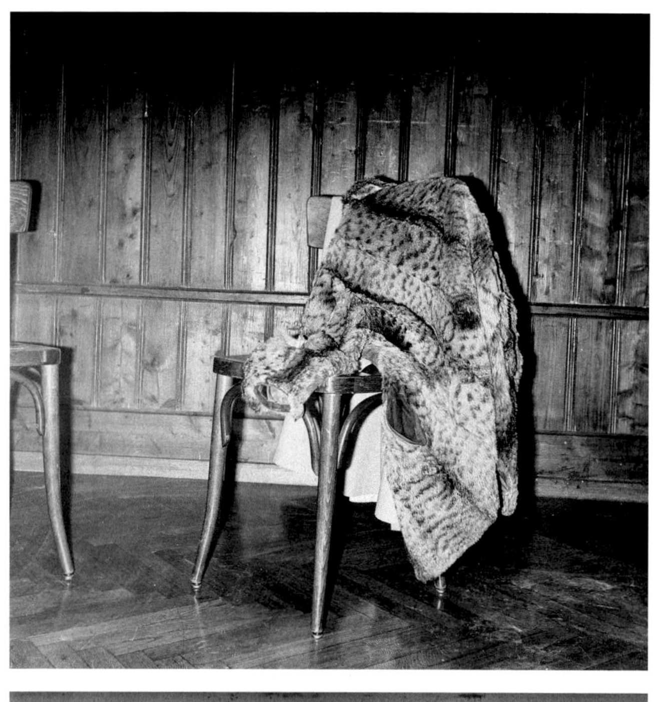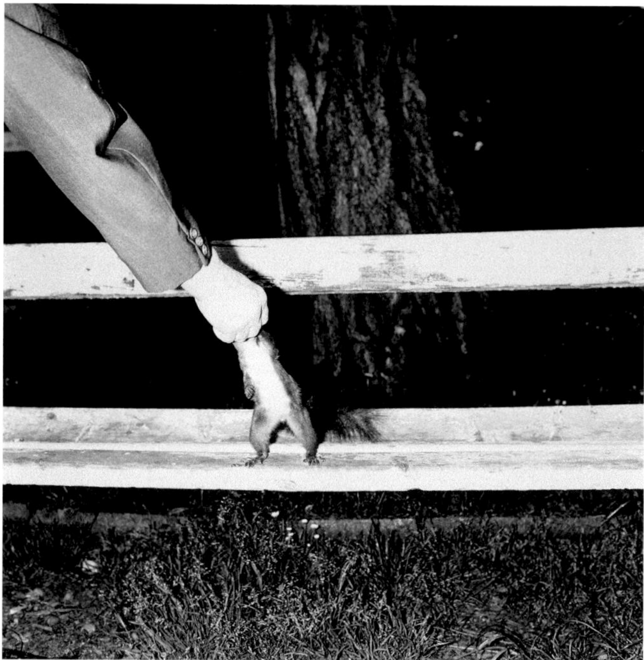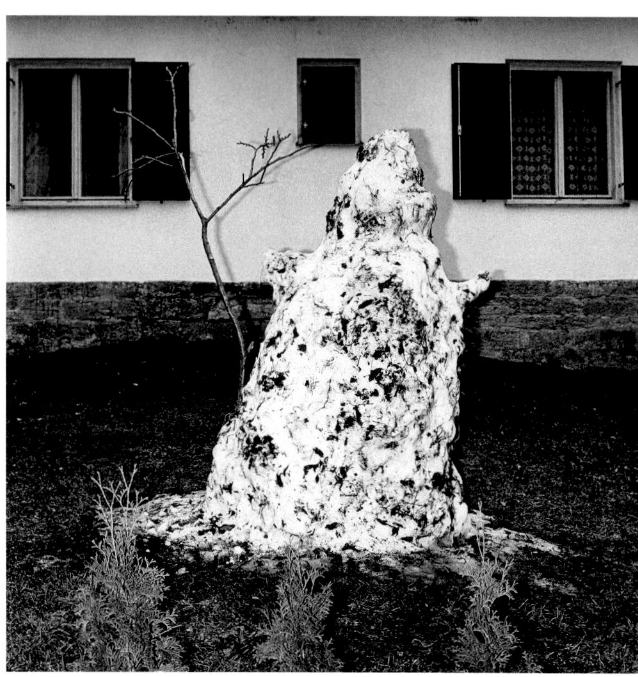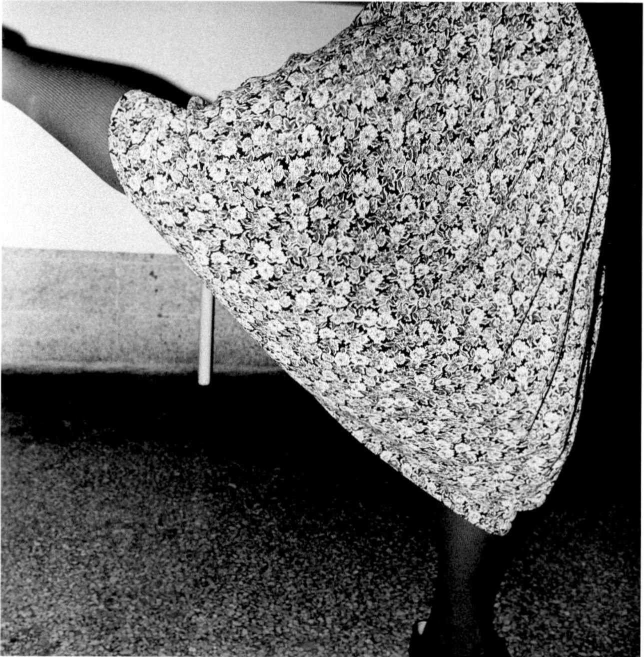

From the series "Schwarz und Gold," 1979–1981, part 3, *Ich träume nie!*

Manfred Willmann

Excerpt from: Georg Schöllhammer, "The World is Beautiful?," in *Manfred Willmann, Werkblick*, Cologne: published by Verlag Walther König, 2005.

It is visual thinking, in which the word "conceptual" is not related to something abstract but hits on a specific sensory form, a thinking that forms sentences in Willmann's series and constellations of pictures that reciprocally comment on each other. In the arrangements and long-term studies of the last decades it is the after-images of a situation that remain permanently fixed. The memory of a social experience is recorded that would remain excluded from visual space if it were not imprinted in the memory with precisely the details and incidentals that photography fixes. An unending supply of mostly trivial and boring objects and shapes, average faces and ordinary social behaviour are constantly recurring elements of this photography. Willmann's genius lies in bringing together an idea, a concept of the social element, with a way of looking at it, in the way pictures of everyday links between things and people can become an instrument for understanding arrangements and phenomenologies, the micropolitics of local connections in all their contradictoriness. Willmann does it with a wonderfully mischievous sensitivity and a sharp eye for the textures and effects of the semiotic relationships between things and living beings.

Precisely because he wants to know how the abstractions of photography work in the representation of tangible life, how its idiom helps to shape our view of the world, his photography of these years is not content with working off various formal registers of pictures, nor with the knowledge of how photography plays with reality, darkens it, lightens it or uncovers it, or behaves subversively vis-à-vis the presumptions of reality, nor does it remain content with a reference to its mediality and the ease with which it can be circumvented. Willmann is much more interested in what way the constellation of principal and ancillary things can be depicted so as to show how social relationships hang together, precisely and tangible, explicitly—and not just how one might happen to observe them. He photographs such constellations time and again, expressing his view on formal similarities and more remote links.

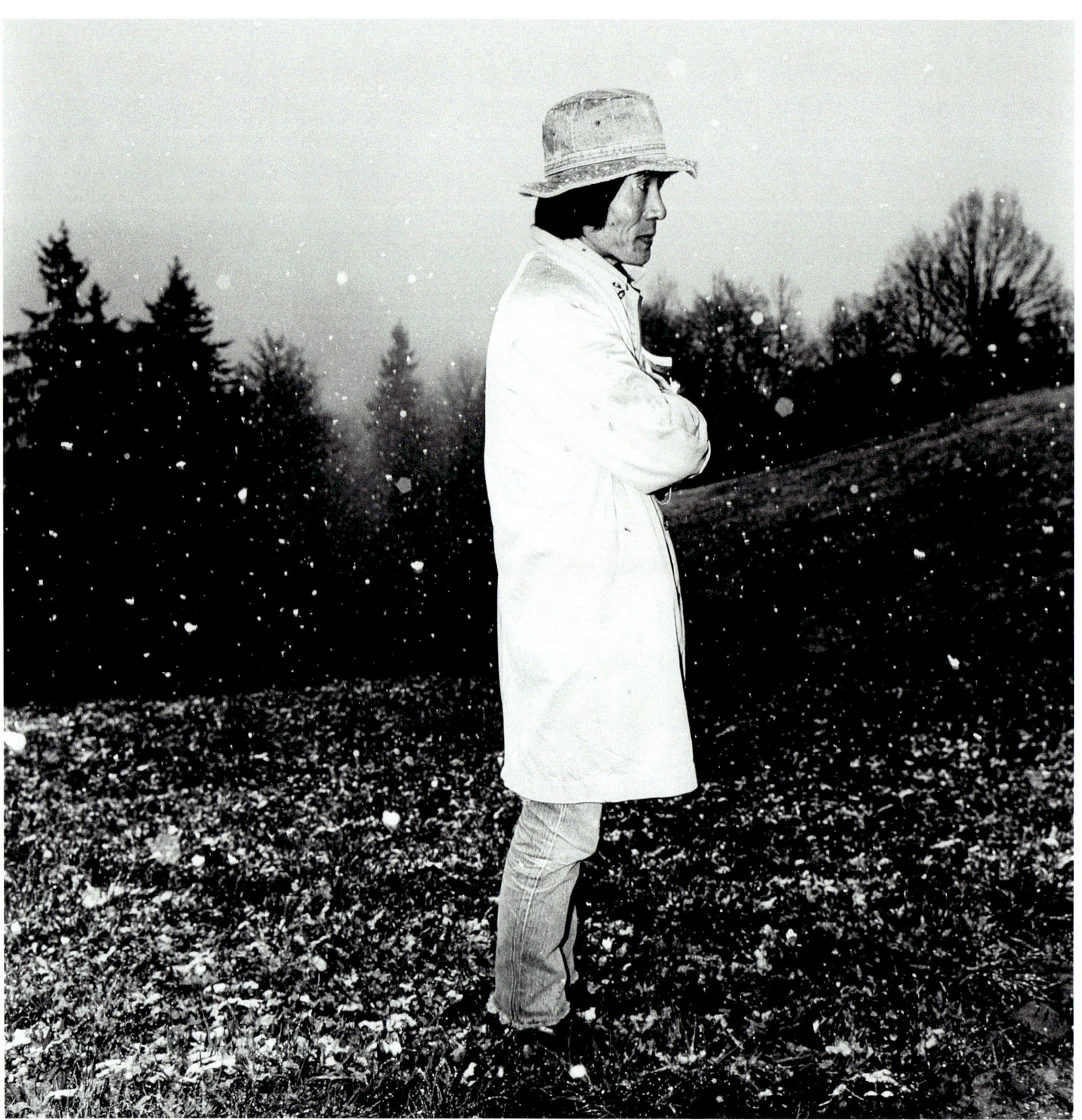

From the series "Schwarz und Gold," 1979–1981, part 3, *Ich träume nie!*

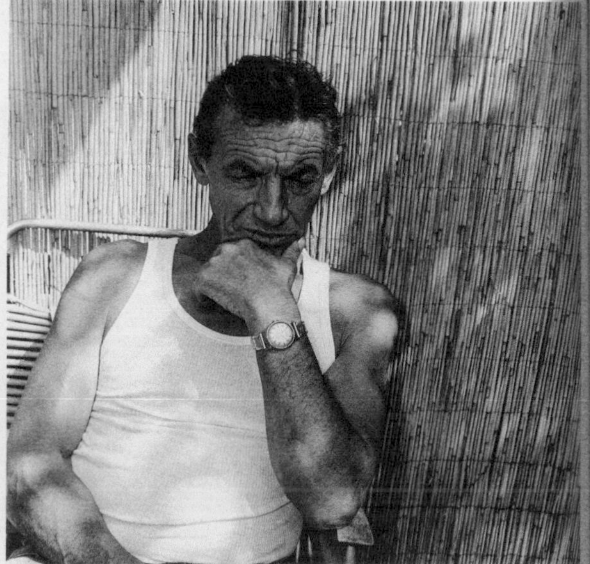

MANFRED WILLMANN, aus „Volkmarweg 36" (mein Vater), 1979

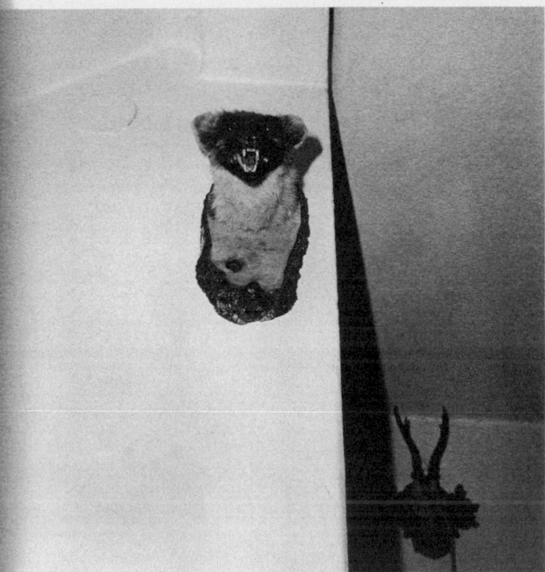

MANFRED WILLMANN, aus „Volkmarweg 36", 1979

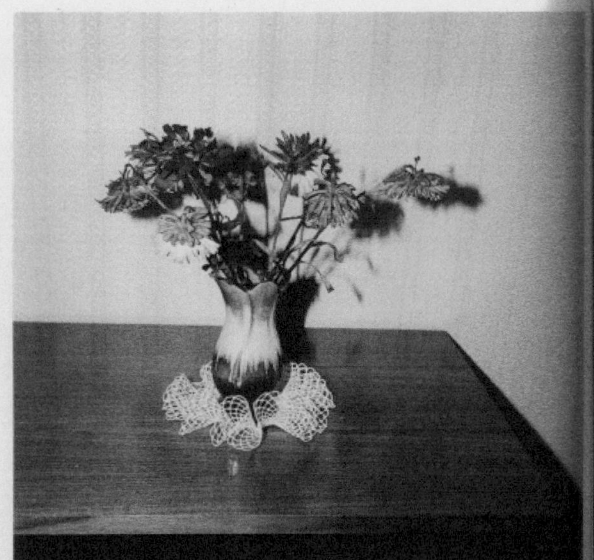

MANFRED WILLMANN, aus „Volkmarweg 36", 1979

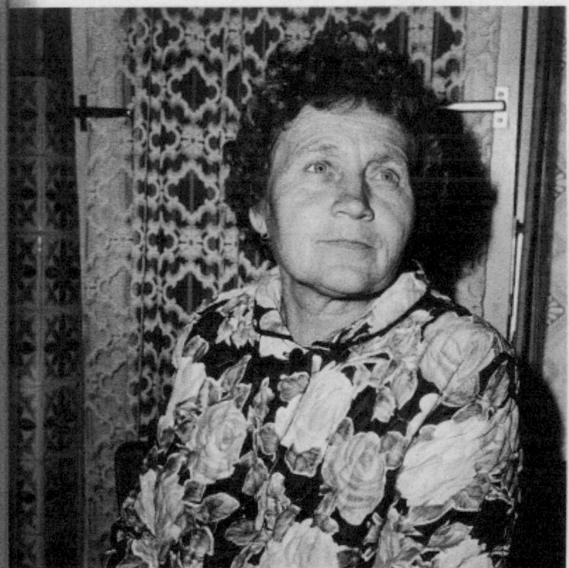

MANFRED WILLMANN, aus „Volkmarweg 36" (meine Mutter), 1979

Is the leg supported by the pipe? Shadows from the flash
make the room look so shallow that for a moment we believe leg
and pipe might touch, and that the figure might be as immobile
as a statue. But the illusion, once we understand it, directs
us to the truth: the woman is dancing as joyously as Lartigue's
cousin Simone turned somersaults. The figure and dress are
alive, changing shapes. And one then notices that the little
flowers seem vaguely to derive from the aggregate in the hard,
modern floor--as remarkable a transformation as any bacchante
or photographer could wish.

                    Robert Adams
                    Longmont, U.S.A., 1989

Tobias Zielony

Camera Austria International

2009   Stefanie Loh, "Tobias Zielony: Story /
No Story," exhibition review, *Camera Austria
International* 105 / 2009

2011   Guest editor, text contribution / artist contri-
bution and cover, Reinhard Braun, Maren
Lübbke-Tidow, Tobias Zielony, "Tobias
Zielony: I Don't Believe They Will Disappear,"
Tobias Zielony, Paul Graham, "Paul Graham:
Die Frage neu ins Bild setzen 'Wie ist die
Welt?,'" text contribution, Tobias Zielony,
Laurence Bonvin, "Laurence Bonvin: Leb-
ende Geisterstädte," text contribution,
Tobias Zielony, Thomas Ruff, "Thomas Ruff:
Optische Prothesen," text contribution,
Tobias Zielony, Timm Rautert, "Timm Rautert:
Teilnehmendes Interesse," text contribution,
Tobias Zielony, Uchihara Yasuhiko, "Uchihara
Yasuhiko: Die nicht gemachten Fotos,"
text contribution, *Camera Austria
International* 114 / 2011

2013   Estelle Blaschke, "Tobias Zielony: Jenny
Jenny, Berlinische Galerie," exhibition review,
Camera Austria International 123 / 2013

2014   Tobias Zielony, "Nan Goldin: A Conversation,"
text contribution, *Camera Austria
International* 125 / 2014

Exhibitions

2011   *Manitoba,* solo exhibition

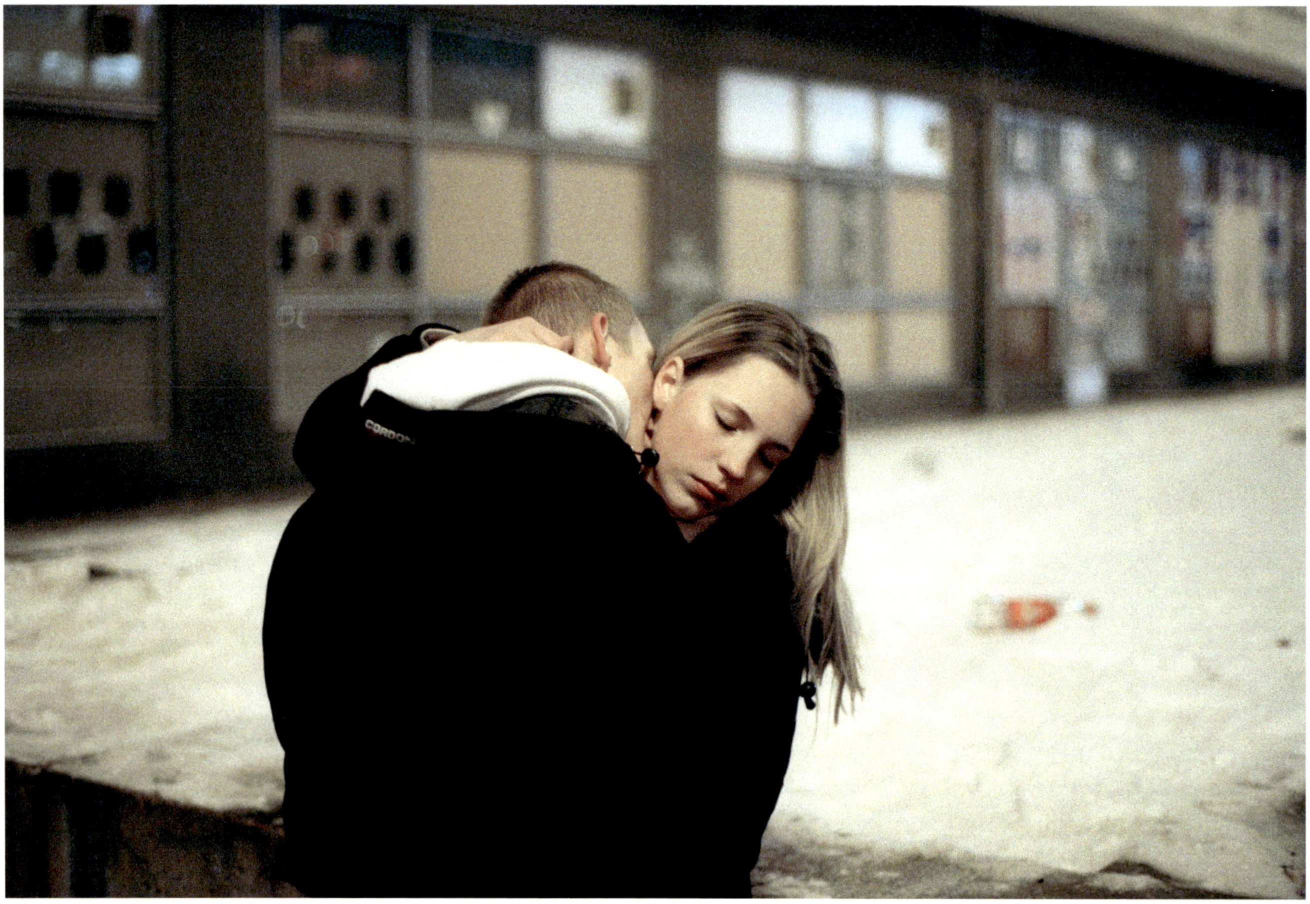

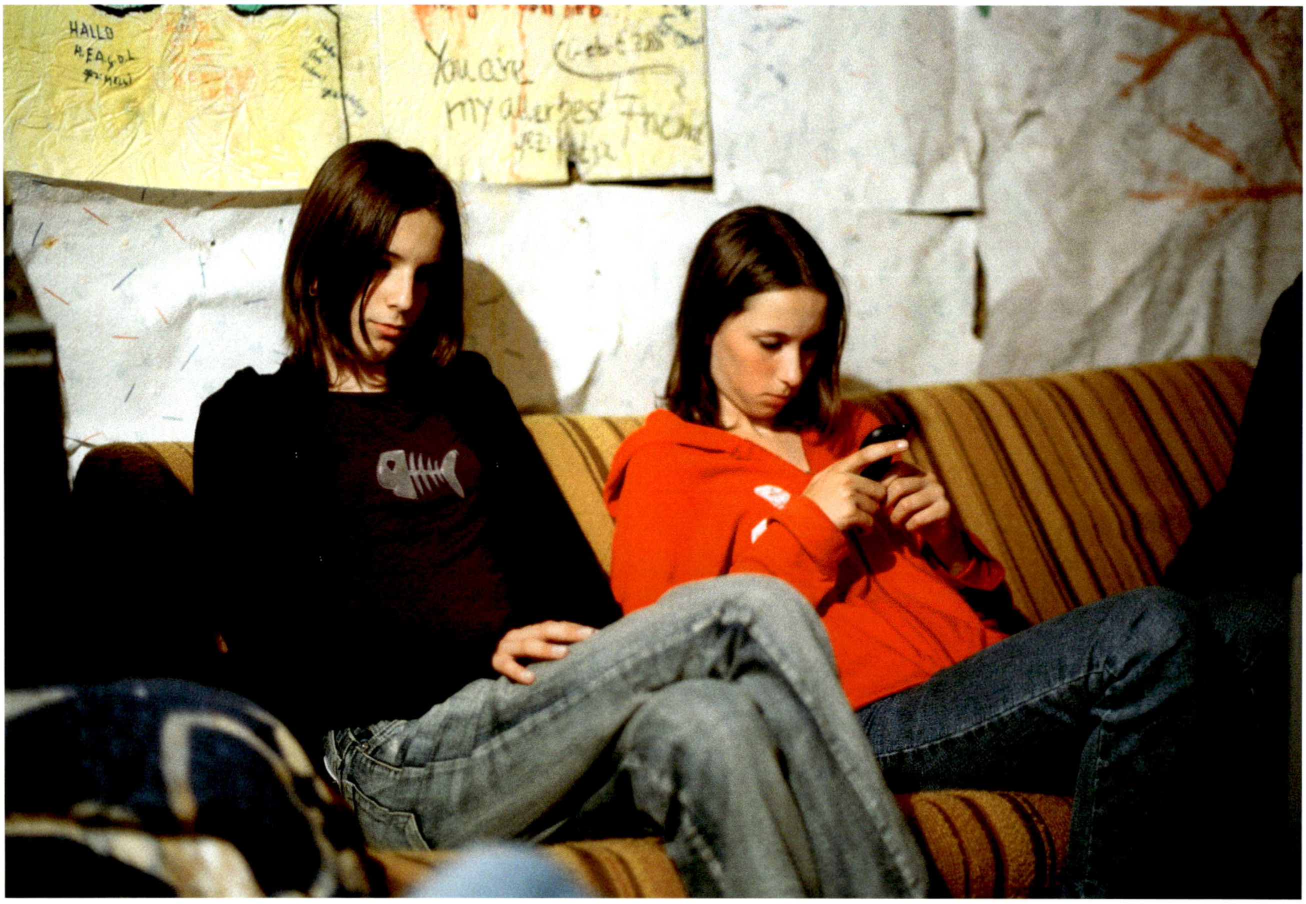

Haus der Jugend, 2017

Tobias Zielony

3.5

Reinhard Braun and Maren Lübbke-Tidow
in conversation with Tobias Zielony
I Don't Believe They Will Disappear …

[…] Braun / Lübbke-Tidow: An important point in the debate about the documentary is the criticism of classical journalistic work, picking out places and also producing victims through the images in these places: victims of natural disasters, of political unrest (as currently in Egypt and Libya), or also victims of social conditions. Therefore, perhaps it is also a matter of this border on which you work with your projects—to what extent are your protagonists specifically not the subject of an investigation and thus also not "victims," what is their share? Your protagonists are probably well aware of the image of them that circulates in society …

Zielony: […] Not necessarily; often they are people who have the feeling there are no images of them at all. In the beginning I had the impression that people were just happy that finally someone was looking more closely. But naturally it is the case that when you are working in Germany, many people have RTL broadcasts in mind and the images that television produces. But about the first part of your question: I studied documentary photography in the UK, a very traditional education. But we started working and photographing with an awareness of this whole problematic issue from the beginning. Even when you are a student, the question arises: Can you even do that? Do I even want to do that? You can hardly escape from this entanglement. For me, it was a conscious decision to say I want to continue elements from this tradition exactly for that reason and continue working on political issues also in the broadest sense, on which documentary photographers have already worked before, with people who are socially excluded or have problems participating. The question for me, however, was how can I do it so that it fits for me and for the people I am photographing, and not always repeating the view from above and the production of victim roles. For me, typical reportage images are not representative of what I experienced in Wales, for instance. These images don't help in telling what is important to me and what per-haps marks the everyday life of the people. So this raises the question for me, to which images do I refer, when I take pictures myself: broken panes of glass, wide angle, flash? We can call up all these images, maybe they are not even wrong or right in a narrow sense, but we read them the way we are supposed to read them, and then that's it. You look as though looking at a surface. […]

Excerpt from: *Camera Austria International* 114 / 2011: 14.

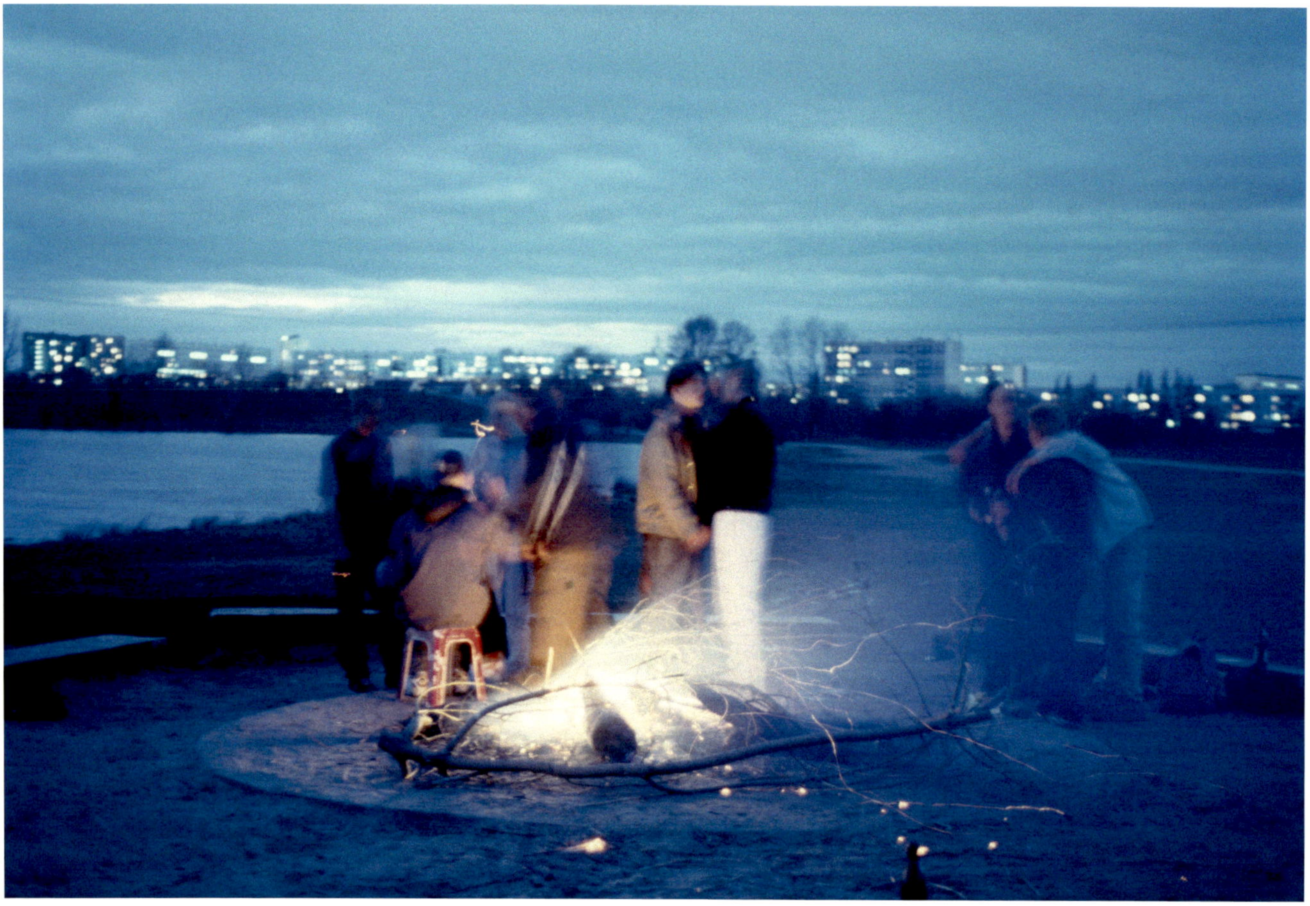

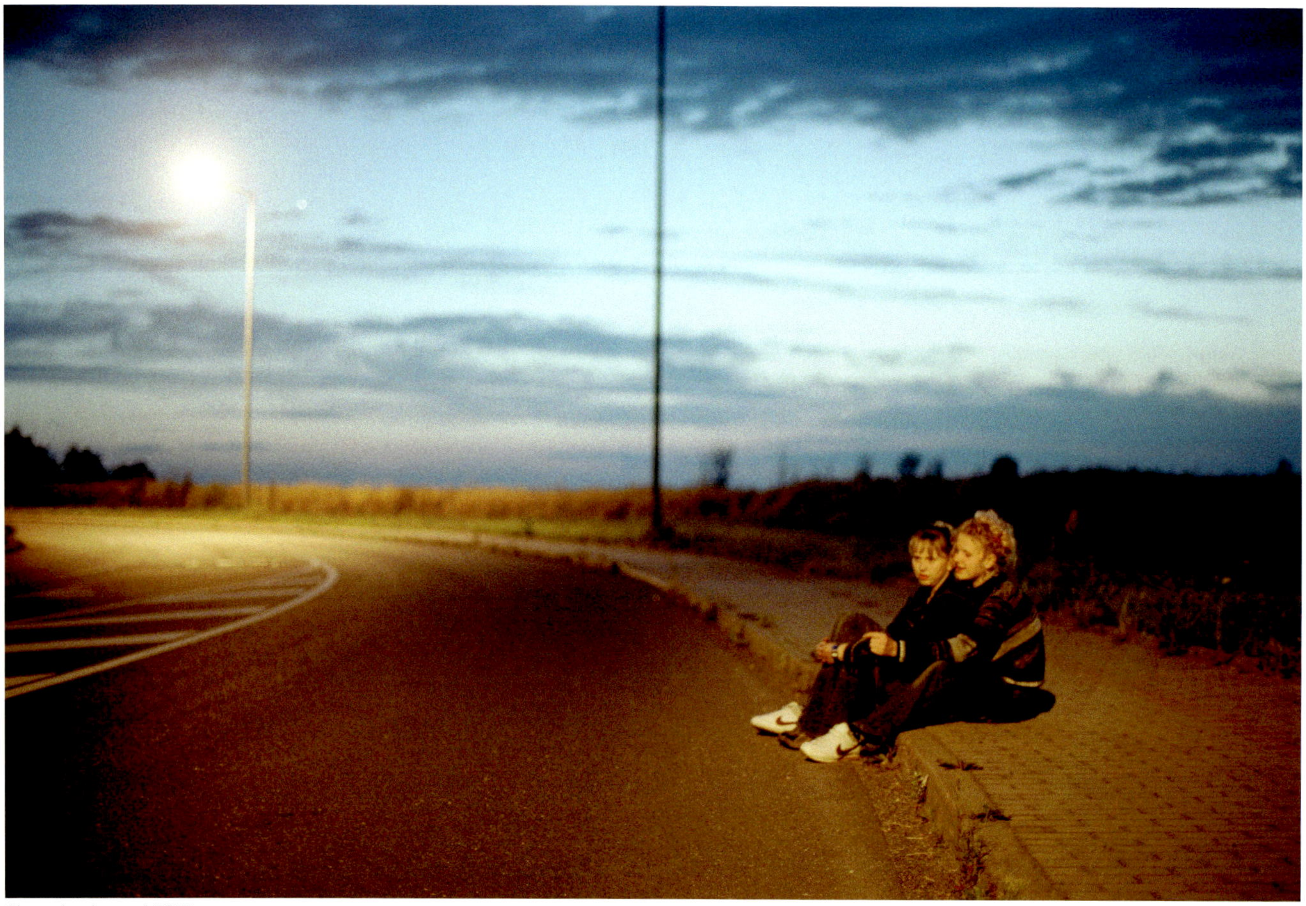

Haus der Jugend, 2017

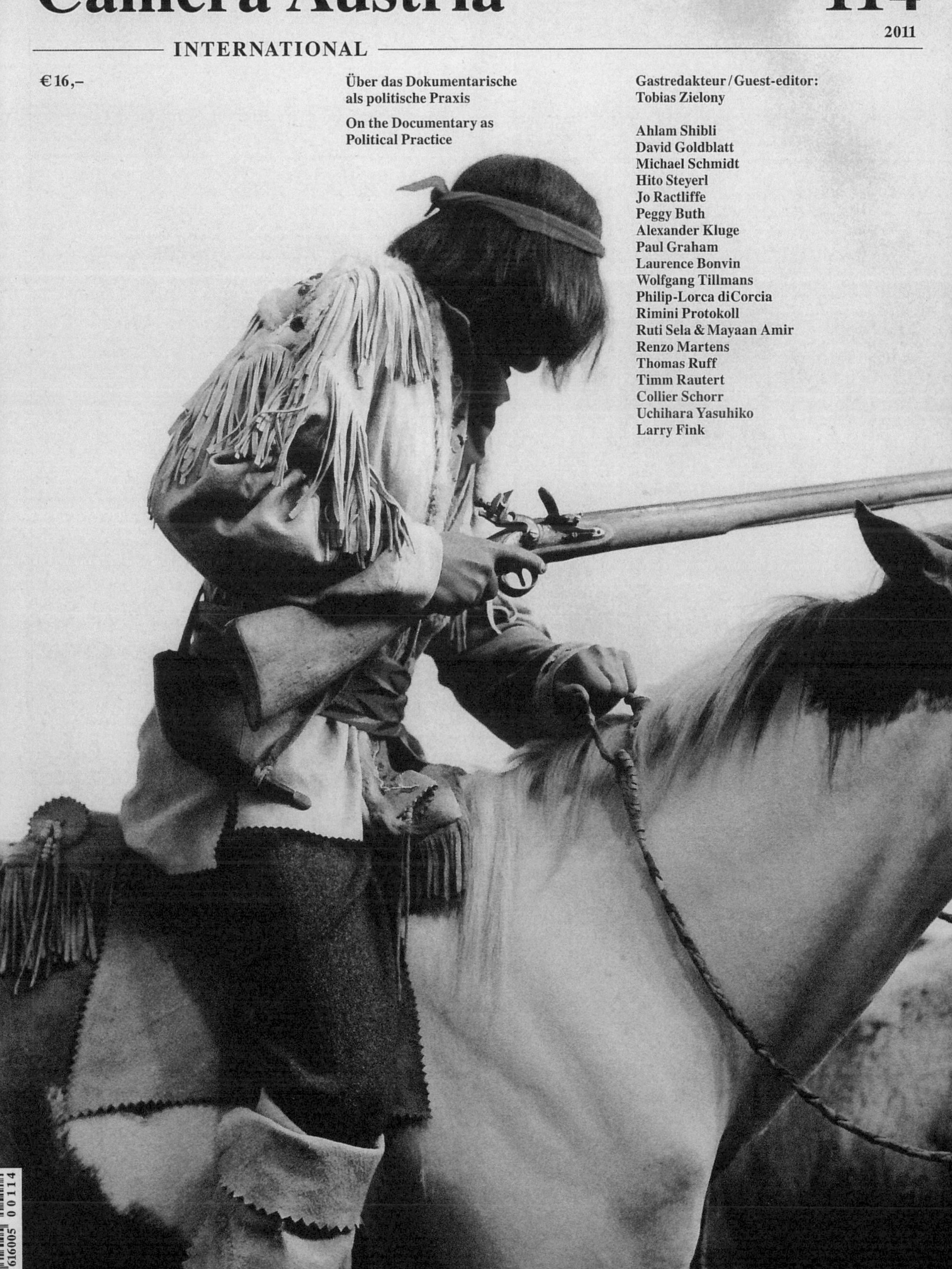

Camera Austria

INTERNATIONAL

114

2011

€ 16,–

Über das Dokumentarische als politische Praxis

On the Documentary as Political Practice

Gastredakteur / Guest-editor:
Tobias Zielony

Ahlam Shibli
David Goldblatt
Michael Schmidt
Hito Steyerl
Jo Ractliffe
Peggy Buth
Alexander Kluge
Paul Graham
Laurence Bonvin
Wolfgang Tillmans
Philip-Lorca diCorcia
Rimini Protokoll
Ruti Sela & Mayaan Amir
Renzo Martens
Thomas Ruff
Timm Rautert
Collier Schorr
Uchihara Yasuhiko
Larry Fink

that. But there is rarely an arrangement, more something like an unspoken agreement or a balancing of ideas, possibilities or images. I also set something off, when I show up there, sometimes resistance, but also a kind of desire to become an image or to be shown in a certain way.

Q An important point in the debate about the documentary is the criticism of classical journalistic work, picking out places and also producing victims through the images in these places: victims of natural disasters, of political unrest (as currently in Egypt and Libya), or also victims of social conditions. Therefore, perhaps it is also a matter of this border, on which you work with your projects—to what extent are your protagonists specifically not the subject of an investigation and thus also not "victims", what is their share? Your protagonists are probably well aware of the image of them that circulates in society …

A … Not necessarily; often they are people, who have the feeling there are no images of them at all. In the beginning I had the impression that people were just happy that finally someone was looking more closely. But naturally it is the case that when you are working in Germany, many people have RTL broadcasts in mind and the images that television produces. But about the first part of your question: I studied documentary photography in the UK, a very traditional education. But we started working and photographing with an awareness of this whole problematic issue from the beginning. Even when you are a student, the question arises: Can you even do that, do I even want to do that? You can hardly escape from this entanglement. For me, it was a conscious decision to say I want to continue elements from this tradition exactly for that reason and continue working on political issues also in the broadest sense, on which documentary photographers have already worked before, with people who are socially excluded or have problems participating. The question for me, however, was how can I do it so that it fits for me and for the people I am photographing, and not always repeating the view from above and the production of victim roles. For me, typical reportage images are not representative of what I experienced in Wales, for instance. These images don't help in telling what is important to me and what perhaps marks the everyday life of the people. So this raises the question for me, to which images do I refer, when I take pictures myself: broken panes of glass, wide angle, flash? We can call up all these images, maybe they are not even wrong or right in a narrow sense, but we read them the way we are supposed to read them, and then that's it. You look as though looking at a surface.

Q It seems important to you to evade collective attributions. Your protagonists appear both profane and special to an equal extent … they may stand in for a group that can certainly be found through a recurrent outfit, through recurrently repeated gestures, but they are also individualised, which has to do not only with a rhythmising, but also with lighting, and this brings us to the theme of film …

A I find it principally interesting that classical image reportage functions similarly to a sequencing of film stills. Jumping from close-up to long shot, from landscape to group. There is an idea of a possible narrative that is evoked in this way. If you look more closely, you wonder what is really being narrated here. There are hardly any conjunctions, except that the images come together. You don't even know what the people have to do with one another, whether everything has really been photographed in one place. This is where imagination or fictionalisation sets in. What is interesting is the image of the protagonist, similar to that of an actor, which is recognisable and remains individual at the same time, but also dissolves in certain roles of a film or a play.

Q Thinking of specific stylistic devices, it is conspicuous that you often take photographs in semi-darkness, where the light sources specify the possibilities for designating the persons, letting them become visible. This is also reminiscent of filmic strategies, which engender a glorification of the individual.

A I principally work only with the existing light. There is only one series where I used a flash. There is no film set where I set up lighting. Nevertheless, film also does nothing other than to imitate light.

F In der Vorbereitung haben wir das Dokumentarische als politische Praxis betont, das Fotografieren selbst als Praxis. Du arbeitest zunächst vor Ort, zeigst deinen ProtagonistInnen mitunter bereits Bilder, die du zuvor woanders aufgenommen hast, wodurch sie sich schon klar darüber sind, wo ihre Repräsentationen landen. Würdest du das auch so beschreiben wollen, dass du mit deinen ProtagonistInnen bis zu einem gewissen Grad die Autorenschaft teilst?

A Die Bilder werden ja gemacht, dazu gehören auch die Leute, die ich fotografiere. Es ist aber eine Absprache, mehr so etwas wie eine unausgesprochene Übereinkunft oder ein Abgleichen von Ideen, Möglichkeiten oder Bildern. Ich löse auch etwas aus, wenn ich da auftauche, manchmal Widerstand, aber auch eine Art Sehnsucht danach, ein Bild zu werden oder in einer bestimmten Art gezeigt zu werden.

F Ein wichtiger Punkt in der Debatte um das Dokumentarische ist die Kritik an der klassischen journalistischen Arbeit, Orte auszusuchen, und an diesen Orten über die Bilder Opfer zu produzieren: Opfer von Naturkatastrophen, von politischen Unruhen (wie aktuell in Ägypten und Libyen), oder auch Opfer von sozialen Verhältnissen. Deswegen geht es auch um diese Grenze, an der du mit deinen Projekten arbeitest – inwiefern sind deine ProtagonistInnen gerade nicht Gegenstand einer Untersuchung, und also keine »Opfer«, worin liegt ihr Anteil? Deinen ProtagonistInnen ist wahrscheinlich auch sehr bewusst, welches Bild von ihnen in der Gesellschaft zirkuliert …

A … Nicht unbedingt; oft sind es auch Leute, die das Gefühl haben, es gibt gar keine Bilder von ihnen. Am Anfang hatte ich den Eindruck, dass die Leute froh sind, dass endlich jemand genau hinsieht. Aber es ist natürlich schon so, dass, wenn man in Deutschland arbeitet, viele Leute die RTL-Sendungen im Kopf haben und die Bilder, die das Fernsehen produziert. Aber zum ersten Teil deiner Frage: Ich habe in Großbritannien Dokumentarfotografie studiert, eine sehr traditionelle Ausbildung. Aber wir haben von Anfang an mit dem Bewusstsein für diese ganze Problematik begonnen zu arbeiten und zu fotografieren. Schon als Student stellt sich die Frage: Kann man das überhaupt noch machen, möchte ich das überhaupt machen? Man kommt fast gar nicht aus diesem Gestrüpp raus. Für mich war es eine bewusste Entscheidung zu sagen, gerade deshalb möchte ich Elemente aus dieser Tradition weiterführen und auch im weitesten Sinn an politischen Fragestellungen weiterarbeiten, an denen auch vorher schon Dokumentarfotografen gearbeitet haben, mit Leuten, die gesellschaftlich ausgeschlossen sind oder Probleme haben, teilzuhaben. Die Frage für mich war allerdings, wie kann ich das so machen, dass es für mich und für die Leute, die ich fotografiere, stimmig ist und nicht immer diesen Blick von oben und die Produktion der Opferrollen zu wiederholen. Die typischen Reportagebilder sind für mich nicht repräsentativ für das, was ich etwa in Wales erlebt habe. Mit diesen Bildern kommt man nicht weiter, um das zu erzählen, was für mich wichtig ist und vielleicht auch den Alltag der Leute prägt. Deshalb stellte sich für mich die Frage, auf welche Bilder beziehe ich mich, wenn ich selbst Bilder mache: kaputte Glasscheiben, Weitwinkel, angeblitzt? Wir können diese Bilder alle abrufen, vielleicht sind sie auch gar nicht in einem engeren Sinn falsch oder richtig, aber wir lesen sie so, wie wir sie lesen sollen, und dann war's das. Man schaut wie auf eine Oberfläche.

F Dir ist es wichtig, aus kollektiven Zuschreibungen herauszukommen. Deine ProtagonistInnen wirken gleichermaßen profan wie besonders … sie mögen stellvertretend für eine Gruppe sein, durch das immer wiederkehrende Outfit, durch die immer wiederkehrenden Gesten, die aufzufinden sind, die aber auch individualisiert werden, was nicht nur mit einer Rhythmisierung zu tun hat, sondern auch mit einer Lichtführung, und damit sind wir auch beim Thema Film …

A Ich finde es grundsätzlich interessant, dass die klassische Bildreportage ähnlich funktioniert wie eine Aneinanderreihung von Film Stills. Das Springen von Nahaufnahme und Totale, von Landschaft auf Gruppe. Es gibt die Idee einer möglichen Narration, die dadurch bereits hervorgerufen wird. Wenn man genau hinsieht, fragt man sich, was hier eigentlich erzählt wird. Außer, dass die Bilder zusammen kommen, gibt es ja kaum Zusammenhänge. Man weiß ja gar nicht, was die Leute miteinander zu tun haben, ob wirk-

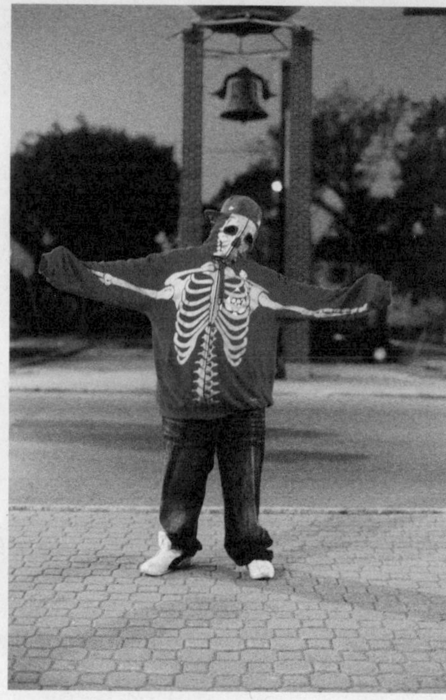

Tobias Zielony, Ghost, 2009. Aus der Serie / from the series: Manitoba. Winnipeg, CAN, 2009.

lich alles an einem Ort fotografiert ist. An diesem Punkt setzt eine Imagination oder Fiktionalisierung ein. Interessant ist das Bild des Protagonisten, es ist so ähnlich wie das eines Schauspielers, das gleichzeitig erkennbar und individuell bleibt, aber auch in bestimmten Rollen eines Films oder Theaterstücks aufgeht.

F Wenn man an konkrete Stilmittel denkt, ist besonders auffallend, dass du oft im Halbdunkel fotografierst, wo die Lichtquellen die Möglichkeiten vorgeben, die Personen zu kennzeichnen, sichtbar werden zu lassen. Das erinnert ebenso an filmische Strategien, die eine Überhöhung des Individuellen erzeugen.

A Grundsätzlich arbeite ich nur mit vorhandenem Licht. In einer einzigen Serie habe ich eine Blitz benutzt. Es entsteht kein Filmset, an dem ich Lampen aufstelle. Trotzdem macht der Film nichts anderes, als Licht nachzustellen. Ich glaube tatsächlich, dass ich durch die Dunkelheit und das Licht, das ich vorfinde, viel stärker Dinge hervorheben oder auch verschwinden lassen kann, dass ich also mehr Einfluss darauf habe, etwas zentral im Bild sichtbar zu machen oder auch wegzulassen, wie etwa den Kontext der Aufnahme. Das scheint mir eine filmische Strategie zu sein.

F Im Gespräch, das du mit Christian Petzold im Katalog Story/No Story[1] führst, verständigt ihr euch teilweise über bestimmte Filmszenen, die die Leseweise der Serien bestimmt oder den Blick, den du vor Ort auf die Situation wirfst oder darauf, was du in den Serien letztendlich konstruierst. Bleiben die Protagonist in diesem filmischen Raum nicht auch gefangen? Wo sind die Momente, wo du in der Konstruktion der Serie sie wieder aus diesem filmischen Blick entlässt?

A Ich glaube, wir bewegen uns hier an der Grenze zur Idee des Dokumentarischen. Meine Erfahrung ist, dass mir nicht vorgeworfen wird, alles wäre nur gestellt, ich würde die Unwahrheit erzählen, eine Foto-Love-Story nachstellen, so tun, als sei alles nur ein Film. Es gibt tatsächlich etwas, das man als Glaubwürdigkeit bezeichnen könnte, ein Vertrauen in mich oder diese Bilder. Welche Bilder wären besser oder echter oder korrekter in Bezug auf die Wirklichkeit der Leute, die ich fotografiere? Ich glaube, diese Frage betrifft tatsächlich einen Grenzbereich. Interessanterweise haben in den USA viel mehr Leute vermutet, meine Bilder wären gestellt, als das in Europa der Fall war, weil sie sich nicht vorstellen konnten, dass diese ohne Verabredung entstehen können, dass derartige Bilder »echt« sein können. Ich denke schon, dass das den Kern dokumentarischer Praxis betrifft, dass man zurzeit noch glauben kann, dass es »echte« Bilder gibt. Dass es Elemente in den Bildern gibt, in denen die Individualität der Personen, die Charakteristik der Orte durchschlagen, genauso wie die Intentionen des Fotografen, der Fotografin.

F In unserem Gespräch wurde erkennbar, dass sich deine Arbeit an der Grenze zwischen dem Dokumentarischen und einem Moment der Fiktionalisierung bewegt. Was bedeutet das für unser Thema des Dokumentarischen als politische Praxis – angesichts der totalen visuellen Durchdringung unserer politisch-sozialen Gegenwart, in der sich Bild und Wirklichkeit permanent gegenseitig zu errichten und zu kommentieren scheinen?

A Ich glaube, die Arbeit funktioniert deshalb, weil dieser Moment des Fotografischen noch wahrgenommen wird. Auch, wenn die Leute nicht mehr fest daran glauben, steckt diese Annahme noch in den Köpfen, dass ein Foto noch eine Referenz der Wirklichkeit aufweist, von dem Ort und dem Zeitpunkt, an dem das Foto gemacht worden ist. Es kann natürlich sein, dass sich das im Laufe der Zeit verschleift, durch immer mehr gestellte Bilder, durch manipulierte Bilder. Ganz habe ich allerdings diese Hoffnung noch nicht aufgegeben. Fotografie war von Anfang an eine Konvention zwischen den ProduzentInnen und den BetrachterInnen. Wenn man die Bilder aus Libyen oder Ägypten ansieht, kann man natürlich an all diesen Bildern zweifeln, warum wurden sie gemacht, mit welcher Absicht, sind sie echt oder nicht, was bedeutet überhaupt echt? So, wie mit diesen Bildern gearbeitet wird, wo sie auftauchen, welche politischen Entwicklungen sie auslösen, sind sie aber immer noch von entscheidender Bedeutung. Wir müssen uns nur von der Idee der Objektivität endgültig verabschieden. Die Konventionen werden sich ändern, aber ich glaube nicht, dass sie verschwinden werden.

In fact, I believe that I can emphasise things more strongly or even let them vanish through the darkness and the light, so that I also have more influence over making something centrally visible in the image or leaving it out, such as the context of the shot. That seems to me to be a filmic strategy.

Q In the conversation you have with Christian Petzold in the catalogue Story/No Story[1], you partly communicate through certain film scenes, or the memory of films which determines the way the series are read, or even the gaze that you cast on the situation on site or on what you ultimately construct in the series. Don't the protagonists also remain captured in this filmic space? Where are the moments in which you release them again from this filmic gaze in the construction of the series?

A I think we are moving here along the border to the idea of the documentary. My experience is that I'm not accused of having staged everything, of telling an untruth, imitating a photo love story, pretending it is all just a film. There is something that could be called credibility, a confidence in me or these images. Which images would be better or more genuine or more correct in relation to the reality of the people I photograph? I think this question actually applies to a border area. It is interesting that many more people in the US suspected my images were staged than this was the case in Europe, because they couldn't imagine that these photos could be made without prior agreement, that images like this could be "genuine". I do think this relates to the core of documentary practice, that people can still believe at this time that there are "genuine" images. That there are elements in the images, in which the individuality of the persons, the characteristics of the places come through, just like the intentions of the photographer.

Q It has become evident in our conversation that your work moves on the border between the documentary and a moment of fictionalisation. What does that mean for our theme of the documentary as political practice—in light of the total visual penetration of our political-social present, in which image and reality permanently seem to be mutually setting up and commenting on one another?

A I think the work functions because this moment of the photographical is still perceived. Even if people no longer firmly believe in it, there is still this assumption in their minds that a photo exhibits a reference to reality, to the place and the point in time when the photo was made. Of course, it may be that this wears down over the course of time, due to more and more staged images, manipulated images. However, I have not yet entirely given up this hope. From the beginning, photography has always been a convention between the producer and the viewer. If you look at the images from Libya or Egypt, naturally you can doubt all these images, why they were made, with which intention, whether they are genuine or not; what does genuine even mean? So the way in which these images are worked with, where they show up, which political developments they trigger, always still has a crucial significance. We must let go of the idea of objectivity once and for all. The conventions will change, but I don't believe they will disappear.

1 Maik Schlüter, Florian Waldvogel and Jan Wenzel (eds.), Tobias Zielony: Story/No Story (Ostfildern: Hatje Cantz Verlag, 2010).

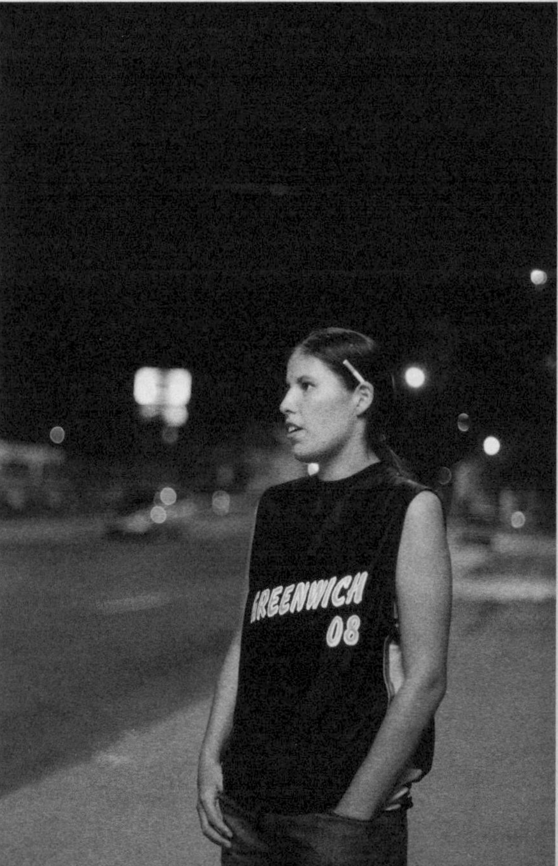

Tobias Zielony, Greenwich, 2009. Aus der Serie / from the series: Manitoba. Winnipeg, CAN, 2009.

Dialog 4

Composition & Deconstruction

Iosif Király

Camera Austria
International

2008   Rolf Sachsse, "Iosif Király: Tinseltown
           Buzescu," text contribution,
           Iosif Király, artist contribution, *Camera*
           Austria International 102 / 2008

Exhibitions

2010   *Iosif Király, Reconstructions,* solo exhibition
           (with Christian Wachter, *Impressions*
           D'AFRIQUE)
2012   subREAL (Călin Dan, Iosif Király,
           Dan Mihălţianu), exhibition contribution

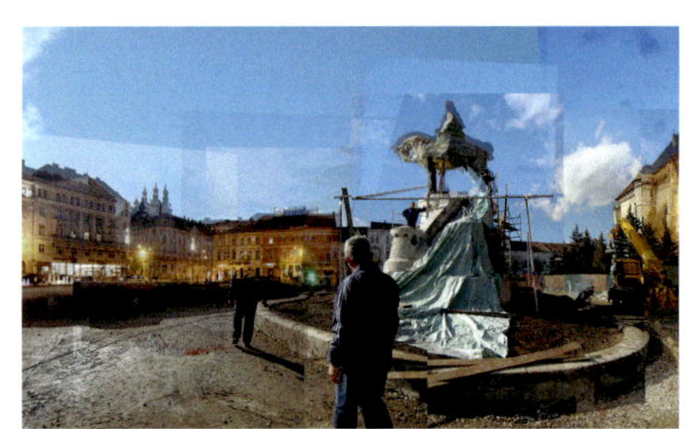

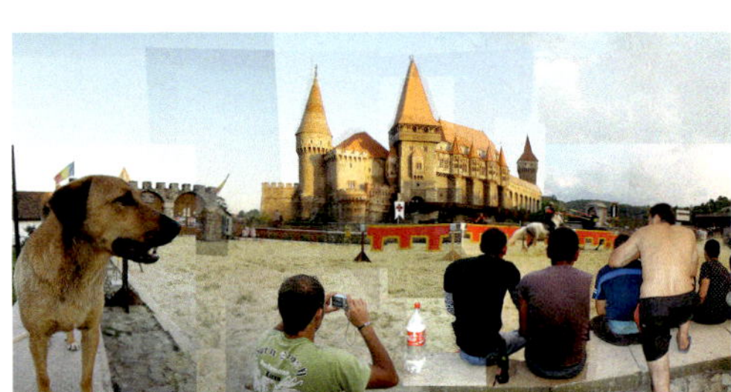

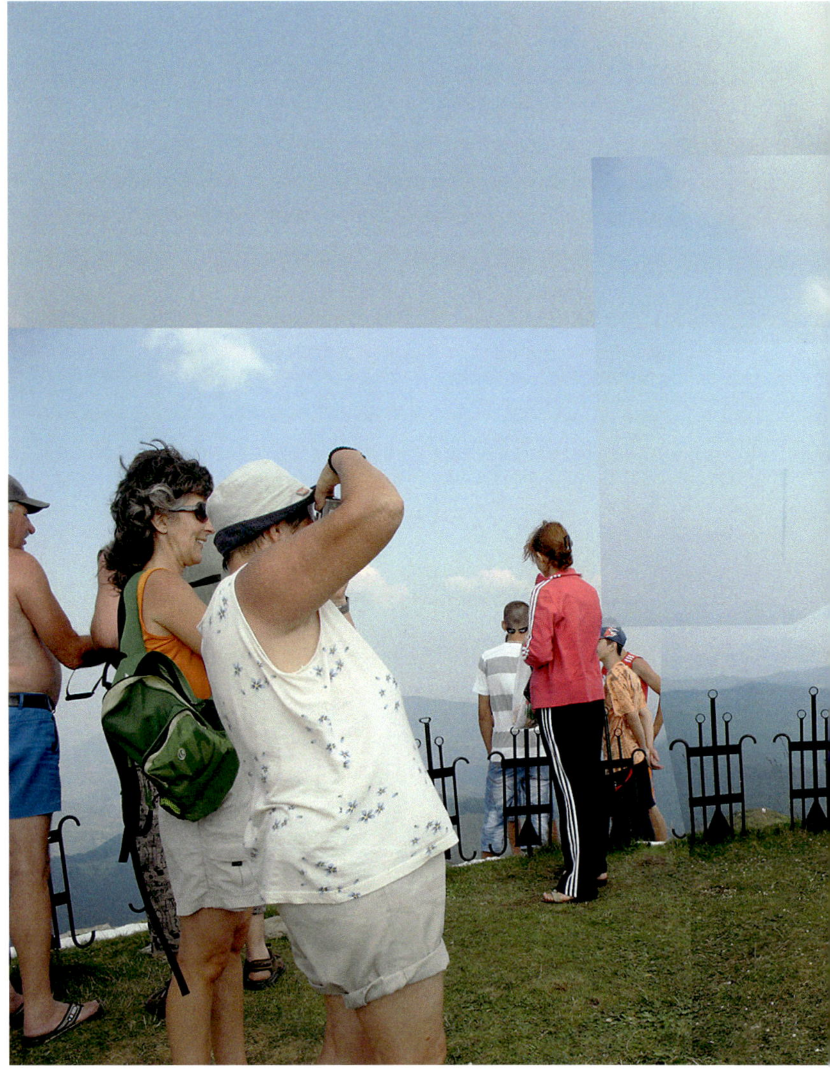

Idols were human beings too. From the series "Sinapses" (Mogoşoaia, Găina Mountain, Piatra Neamţ, Roman, Huneodoara, Văratec, Berlin), 2006–2017

Iosif Király

Reconstructions

The series of photos installations called Synapses points out the connections and synchronisations that can sometimes appear among people, things, and events. They are built around images from the series "Reconstructions," which investigate, through photography, the problem of time and of memory, the way in which we can forget and remember.

The "Reconstructions" are polyperspectival compound images in which each constitutive photo acts like an information-and-memory bit. The fact that these snapshots are taken of more or less the same place, yet at different times (after some minutes, days, months, years), confers on the final image a spatial coherence and a temporal discontinuity.

The whole ensemble aims to reconstruct certain contexts and personal experiences that played out in the past in order to create some puzzles which can sometimes break qua "time windows" pointing to other horizons.

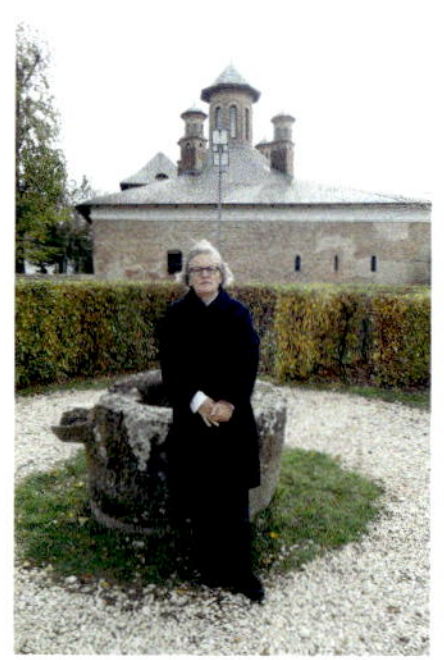

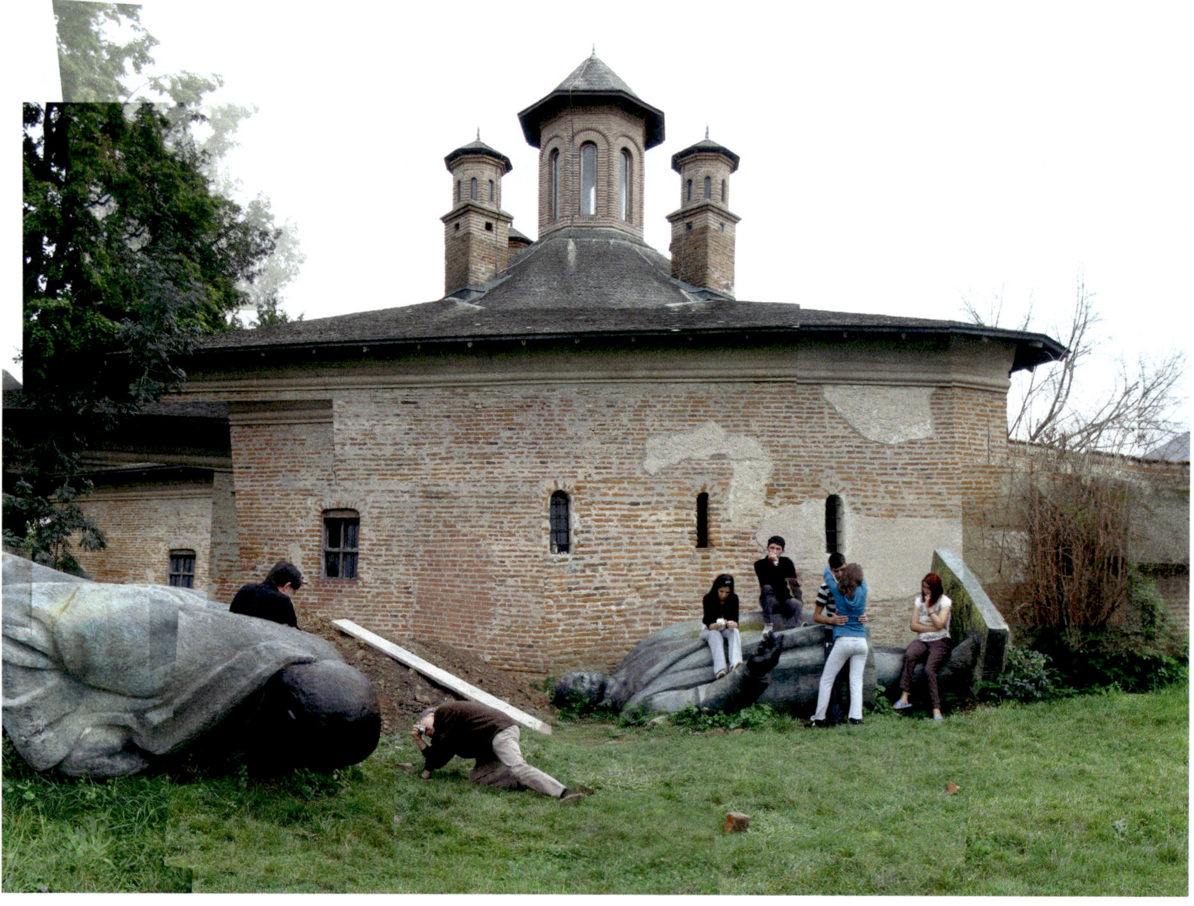

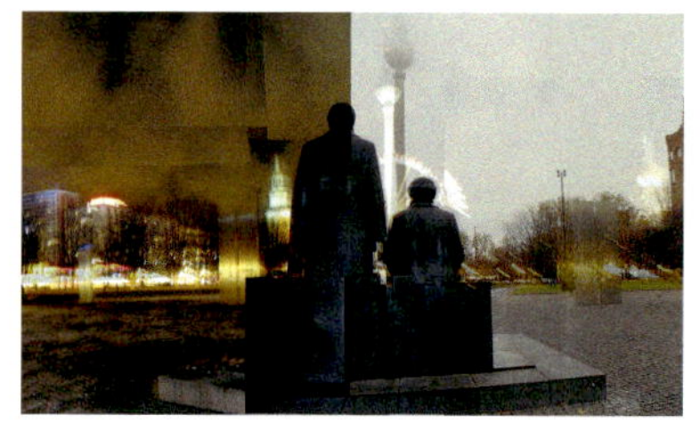

Idols were human beings too. From the series "Sinapses" (Mogoşoaia, Găina Mountain, Piatra Neamţ, Roman, Huneodoara, Văratec, Berlin), 2006–2017

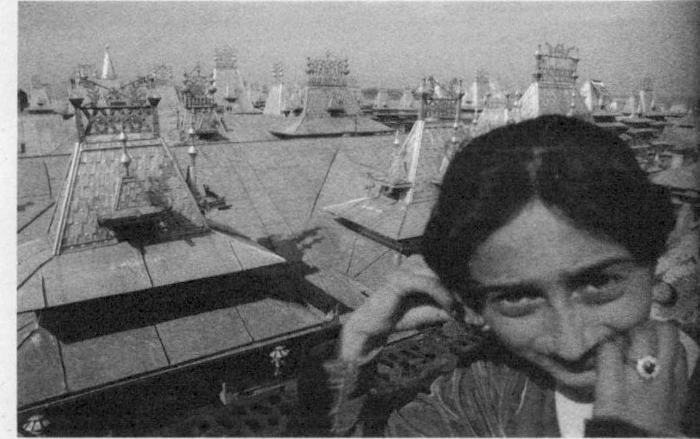
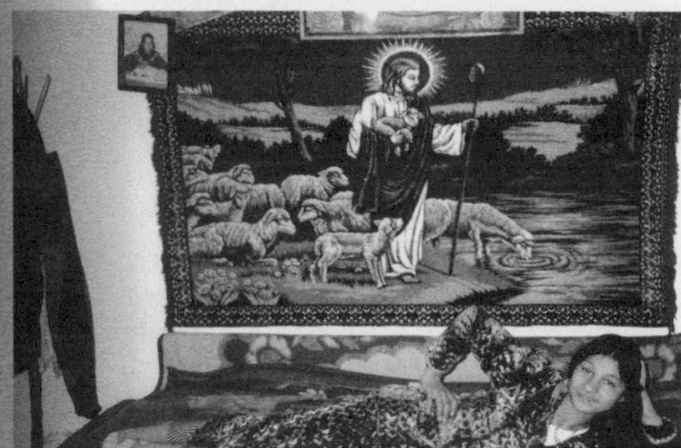
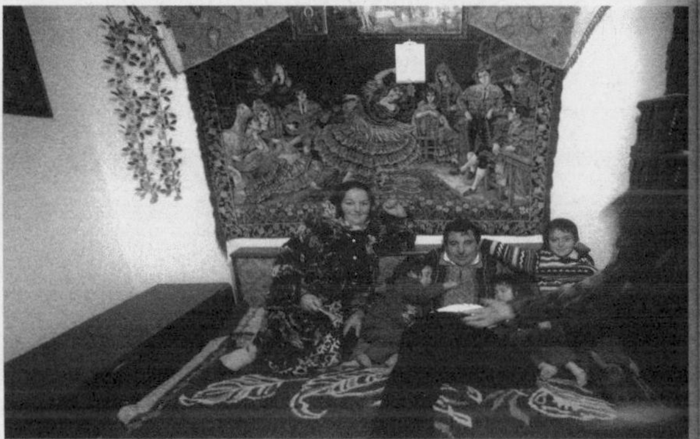
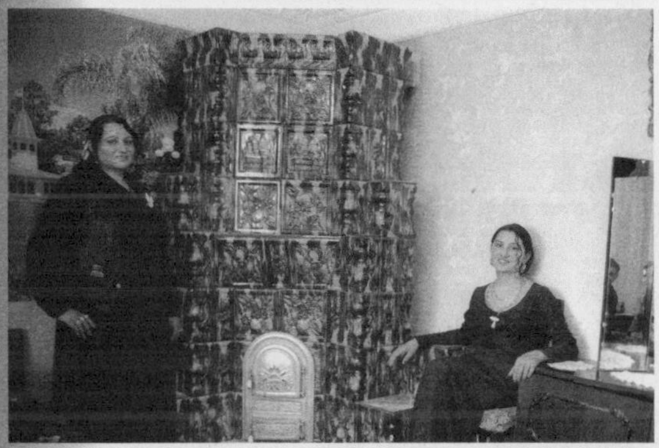

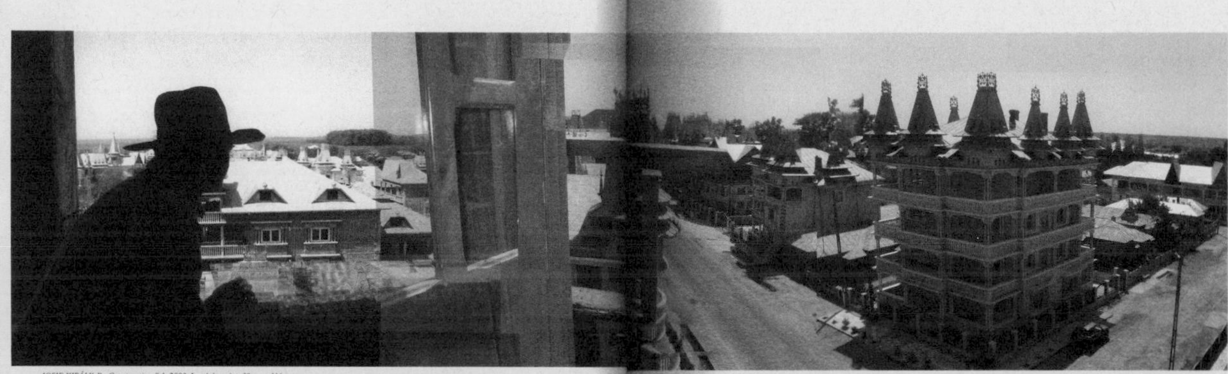

IOSIF KIRÁLY, Re-Construction # 1, 2003. Lambda-print, 30 cm x 116 cm.

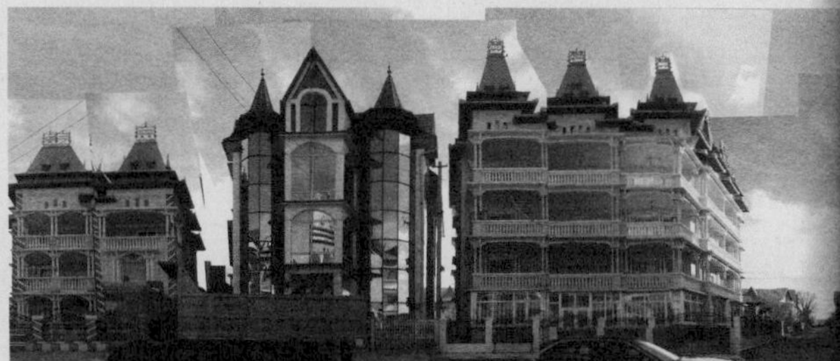
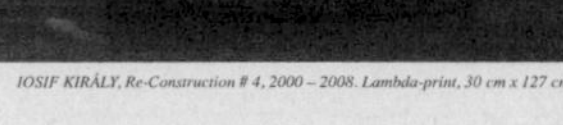
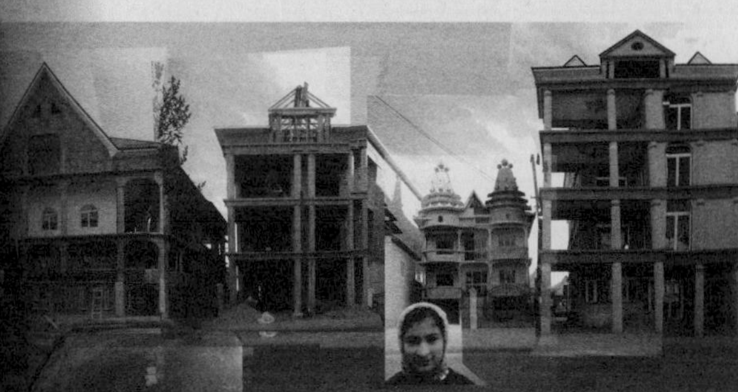

IOSIF KIRÁLY, Re-Construction # 4, 2000 – 2008. Lambda-print, 30 cm x 127 cm.

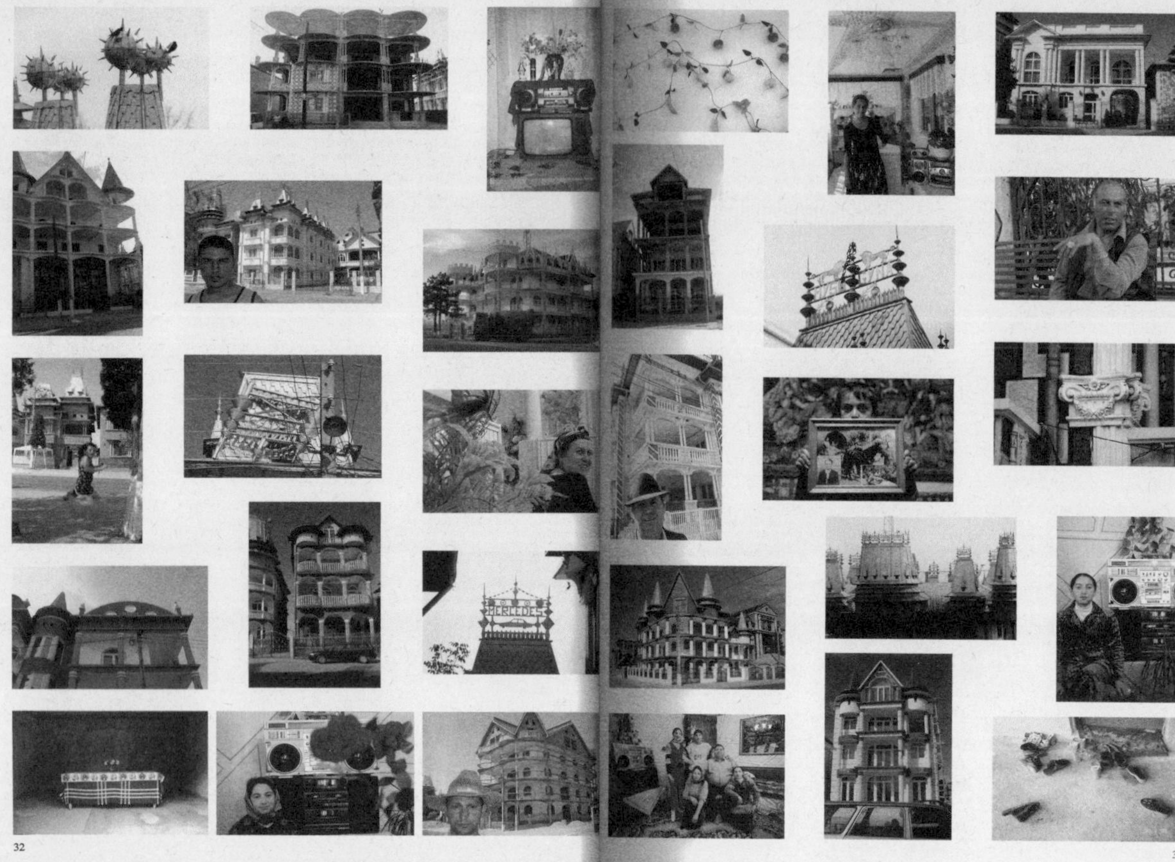

bauten Straßenzügen stehen dann einzelne Panoramen der Dachlandschaften, die zudem das Drinnen und Draußen der Bauten thematisieren wie im »Marlboroman«. Die hiermit doppelte Brechung der medialen Amerikanismen im Blick auf die Häuser von Buzescu – zum einen durch die Farbe, die es so nur in den *gated communities* der weißen Oberschichten auf dem amerikanischen und afrikanischen Kontinent gibt, zum anderen durch die Nutzung einer Montagetechnik der Post Pop Concept Art – sollte genug deutlich machen, dass es dem Künstler Iosif Király bei seiner Annäherung an diesen Ort mindestens genauso viel um seine Arbeitsweisen zu tun ist wie um den voyeuristischen Blick auf die Bauten, den er locker uns Lesern und Bildbetrachtern unterstellen kann. Gerade weil die Perfektion der Fotomontagen diejenige der Häuser konterkariert – hier die fragilen Säulenreihen und Vordächer, dort die vermeintlich zusammengeklebten Bildchen in bestem Photoshop-Finish – spielt Iosif Király eher mit den Verhaltenserwartungen der Bildbetrachter als mit dem Gegenstand seiner Arbeit.

Die zweite und dritte Ebene der Annäherung wird von der Begegnung mit den Menschen markiert. Zum einen fotografiert Iosif Király die Frauen und Kinder der in Buzescu Wohnenden vor den Gebäuden, und bei manchen hat er es sogar geschafft, im Haus Aufnahmen zu machen. Die Außenaufnahmen mit Menschen vor den Häusern, Straßenzügen, Eingängen und Pflanzen sind sehr ähnlich aufgebaut: Die Person vorne und unten am Bildrand, meist leicht angeblitzt, dahinter ein kaum erkennbarer Mittelgrund aus Straße oder Vorplatz und dahinter ein Gebäude. Unmittelbar wird ein Zusammenhang zwischen Person und Haus hergestellt, doch sicher ist dieser nicht: Eigentlich liegen die abgebildeten Gebäude auf der anderen Straßenseite, in einem fremden Territorium, jenseits einer unsichtbaren Grenze. Fast immer bauen sich die Porträtierten in einer Weise vor der Kamera auf, die sie als würdevoll interpretieren, doch sie werden dadurch selbst zur Sache, zum Fetisch des fetischisierten Hauses im Hintergrund. Iosif Király, mit allen Wassern der Fotogeschichte gewaschen, referiert mit diesem Aufbau und den Haltungen sowohl Vor-Bilder aus der Farm Security Administration Campaign der 1930er Jahre als auch aus der ethnografischen Fotografie des 19. Jahrhunderts. Kinder agieren in diesem Setting weitgehend unbefangen, manche halten Bilder in der Hand, die auf Abwesende verweisen – nach Jay Ruby in der Fotografie ein deutlicher Verweis auf Tote. Die Porträts auf der Straße und vor den Bauten vermitteln genau die Melancholie des konsumistischen Hintergrunds von Buzescu: Die Traumhäuser sind errichtet, und der realisierte Traum stimmt in seiner grotesken Perfektion einfach nur noch traurig.

Die Porträts im Innenraum sind durchwegs von großer gegenseitiger Zuneigung getragen; ganz offensichtlich ist es Iosif Király gelungen, bei einigen Familien so viel Vertrauen zu gewinnen, dass er sie in ihren Häusern fotografieren durfte. Auch hier gibt es das Bild im Bild, wenn etwa ein Kind einen großen Rahmen mit Porträts längst Verstorbener hochhält. Aber meist zeigen sich die Menschen als stolze Besitzer von Sachen, legen festtägliche Kleidung an und lagern sich auf den großen Sofabetten, die es genauso im Orient und in Zentralasien gibt. Überhaupt sind die Frauen fast immer üppig geschmückt und bis zu einem gewissen Alter auch geschminkt; die Kinder tragen Pullover und Hemdkragen, die jungen Männer Jacketts und oft auch Hut, die alten ohnehin. Auch hier betont Király die schwierige Kommunikation zwischen Fotograf und Fotografierten durch die Positionierung seiner Protagonisten an Bildrändern, durch kräftige Blitzbeleuchtung oder das Warten auf eine zögerliche Geste – der Akt des Fotografierens wird immer in die Aufnahme integriert, quasi als Maßnahme gegenseitiger Distanzierung. Die Zimmer sind meist mit Wandteppichen oder floralen Arrangements geschmückt, überall finden sich Blumen und kleine Rahmen mit Familienbildchen. Möbel wie Tische und Schränke folgen ähnlichen Konventionen wie die Häuser, wirken in ihrer Ambitioniertheit billig folkloristisch und doch so fehl am Platz wie die ganze vorgetragene Sesshaftigkeit des Ambientes.

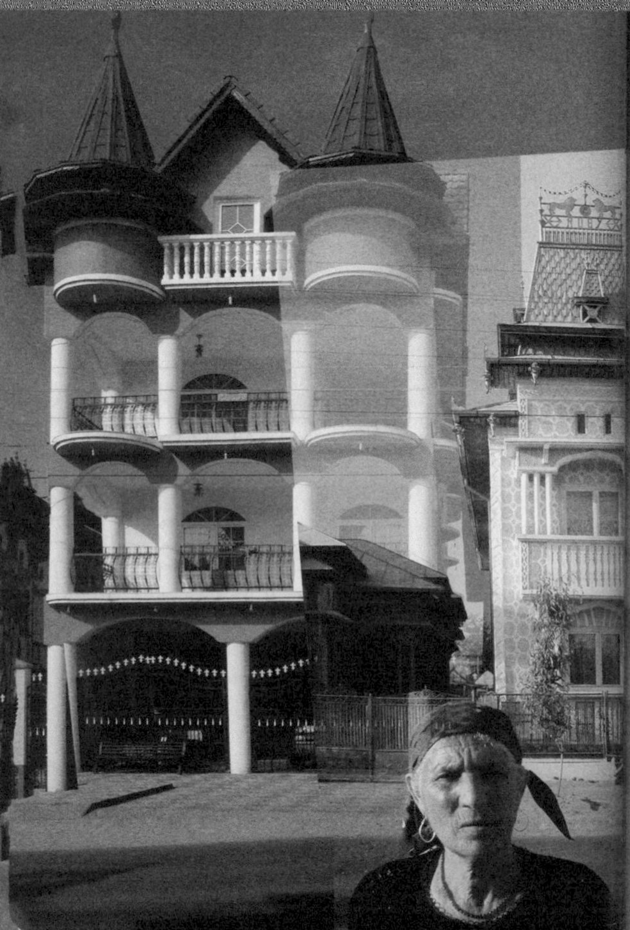

IOSIF KIRÁLY. Detail aus / from: Re-Construction # 5, 2003–2008. Lambda print, 30 cm x 45 cm.

ficiently clear that, in his approach to this place, the artist Iosif Király is just as much concerned with his work methods as with the voyeuristic view of the buildings that he can safely impute to us readers and viewers. Precisely because the perfection of the photomontages counteracts that of the houses – on the one hand the fragile rows of columns and canopies, on the other the little pictures presumably glued together with a perfect Photoshop finish – Iosif Király plays with the viewer's expectations rather than with the object of his work.

The second and third layer of the approach is the human encounter. On the one hand, Iosif Király takes photos of the wives and children of the residents of Buzescu outside their homes, and sometimes even managed to take pictures inside the houses. The outdoor shots with people in front of the houses, streets, doorways and plants are very similarly structured: The person in front, at the bottom edge of the picture, usually with a slight glare, a barely perceptible middle ground of street or forecourt behind, and a building beyond. You immediately link the person and the house, but this link is by no means certain: The buildings in the picture are in fact on the other side of the road, on foreign territory, beyond an invisible border. In almost all cases, the portraitees take up a pose in front of the camera that they see as dignified, but which in fact makes them an object themselves, a fetish of the fetishised house in the background. With this composition and these poses, Iosif Király, well versed in the history of photography, makes reference to original pictures from the Farm Security Administration Campaign of the 1930s as well as to the ethnographic photography of the nineteenth century. The children in this setting behave fairly naturally, some are holding pictures of absent people in their hands – which in photography is, according to Jay Ruby, a clear indication of someone who has died. The portraits on the street and in front of the buildings convey the very melancholy of the consumerist background of Buzescu: The dream homes have been built, and the grotesque perfection of this dream come true is nothing but sad.

The indoor portraits all exhibit a strong sense of mutual affection; obviously Iosif Király managed to gain enough trust of some families that they allowed him to take pictures inside their homes. Here again we see the picture in a picture, for instance when a child holds up a large frame with portraits of the long deceased. But the people usually present themselves as proud owners of things, wearing their Sunday best and sitting on the big sofa beds that are just as common in the Orient and in Central Asia. Indeed, the women are almost always decked out with jewellery and, up to a certain age, also wearing make-up; the children are wearing pullovers and shirt-collars, the young men jackets and often hats, the old men always. Here again Király emphasises the difficult communication between the photographer and the portraitees by positioning his protagonists on the edges of the pictures, by means of a strong flash, or by waiting for a hesitant gesture – the act of photographing is always integrated into the photo, as a measure of mutual disassociation, as it were. The rooms are generally decorated with tapestries or floral arrangements, with flowers and little frames with family snapshots everywhere. Furniture such as tables and cupboards obeys similar conventions as the houses, appearing cheap and folksy in its aspirations and yet as much out of place as the whole sense of settledness of the ambience.

The fourth layer of representation can be found in the still lifes inside the houses: We see media equipment, television sets and stereo systems, often gigantic ghetto blasters. Iosif Király reported that all of the indoor photos were taken amidst deafening noise from these machines, usually in the form of the same pop folklore that assaults the ears in restaurants and shops on every corner of Bucharest. The still lifes show nothing of this, rather they are like the arrangements that they depict, meticulously composed, axially symmetrical like the roof ornaments, and as colourful as the façades. The last picture in the series could just as well be the first: the collection of children's shoes outside the door on garishly patterned tiles.

The whole »Tinseltown« series originally consists of some sixty pictures, is set out in the style of a book, and jumps to and fro

35

Zofia Kulik

Participation at Symposion

1982   Symposion on Photography XIV: "WAR," lecturer

Camera Austria International

1994   Zofia Kulik, text contribution / artist contribution (journal of Symposion), *Camera Austria International* 47–48 / 1994

Exhibitions

1993   *WAR*, I. Austrian Triennial for Photography, exhibition participation
1994   *Another Continent,* Tokyo Metropolitan Museum of Photography (JP), exhibition participation

Publications

1993   Werner Fenz and Christine Frisinghelli, eds, *WAR*, publication in two volumes for exhibition at I. Austrian Triennial for Photography, Graz, Edition Camera Austria, 1993

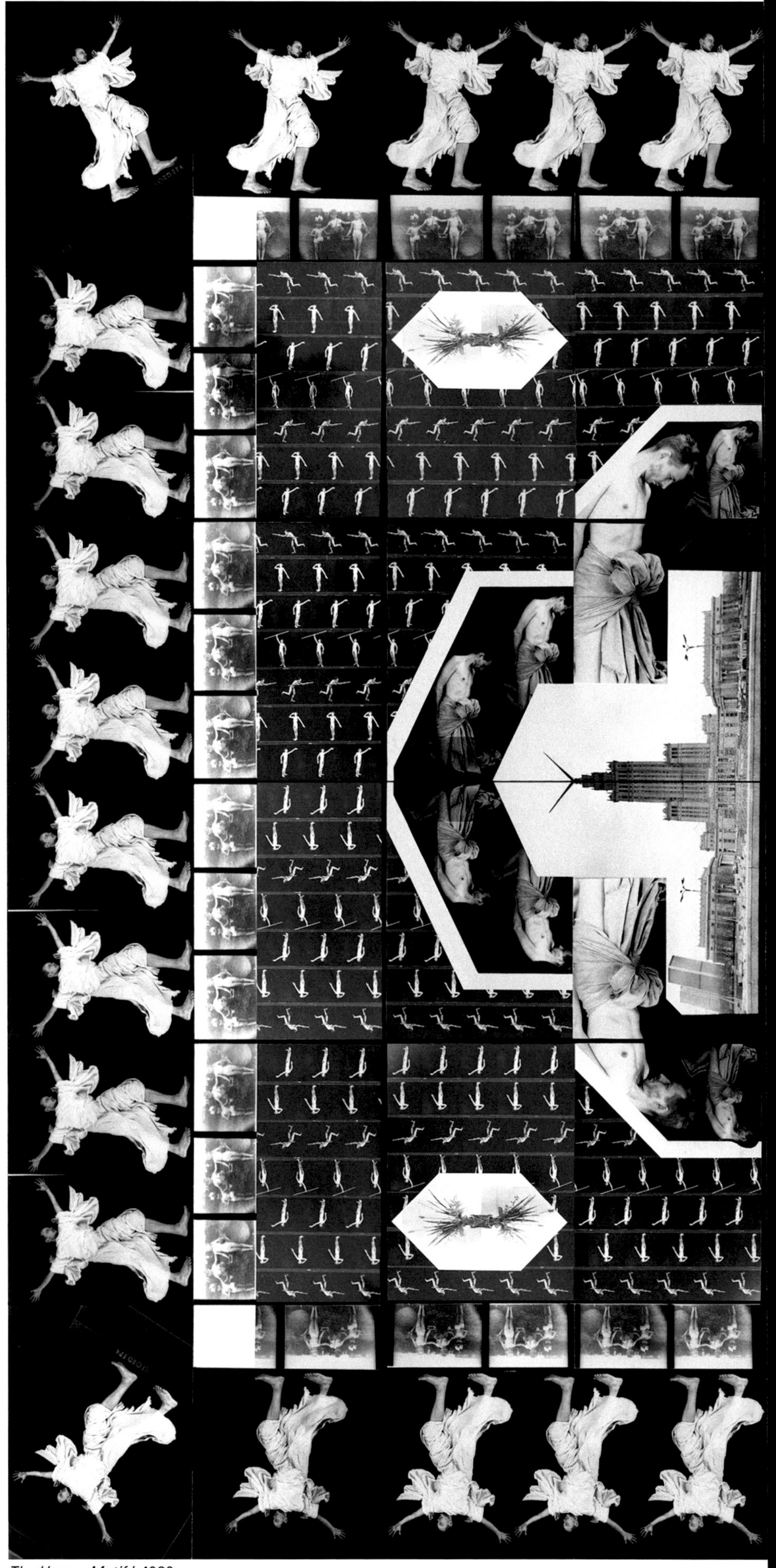

The Human Motif I, 1989

Zofia Kulik

[…] My mother is a dressmaker. In our house there were always piles of cloth—silk, cotton, linen—and everywhere there were patterns for suits. Almost daily, women would come to be measured for suits, costumes, skirts, jackets, blouses or coats. They had been looking at fashion journals and ladies' magazines, and they talked, talked, talked about pleats, tucks, décolletés, collars, belts and pocket flaps.

My father, who is now retired, was a colonel in the People's Army of Poland and, as I suspect, he was in the Propaganda Department. Until I was fourteen I lived in military quarters. Until 1956 (I was eleven, then) nobody from the street could come to the building I was living in. All visitors had to ask for a permit, and you can imagine the grotesque situations when all the women coming to see my mother first had to go to the permit office.

From my window I could see an oval field surrounded by curbstones painted white. There was a small stone monument to the right of it, and to the left a red-brick building where the military command was based.

Day after day I would see soldiers and officers walking or marching to and fro; I saw military ceremonies, the changing of the guard, the raising of the flag, and there were commands and salutes.

Mother in the house and father outside the window. […] I would now like to quote some passages from texts I have written about my artistic work.

"I am interested in building structures, composing more complex wholes. I am fascinated by closed forms, centricity, symmetry, multiplication, order, figural ornament, imposing upon myself certain already existing patterns of structures that I try to fill with my own madness [I wrote this in 1989; now I feel it should be a different word]—these are my form-shaping rules of composition."

"[…] First, I search for a pattern, and then while composing according to that pattern I begin to feel the sense of what I am doing […]."

[…] About my work *All the Missiles Are One Missile*, […] I wrote, "The whole composition has the form of a carpet, a photographic carpet, as it were. Its 'decorativeness' is built up of photographic images chosen from my collection of b/w negatives. These include images of socialist monuments, cemeteries, landscapes, photo still lives composed by me, human gestures performed by my models, and 'real' events taken from TV—wars, protest marches, executions, marches past, riots, etc. I copy the images from the negatives onto the surface of the photographic paper by covering and uncovering different parts of the surface, according to plans and stencils I have made before. The complete work is made up of a number of photographic sheets 60 cm by 50 cm in size. […]"

Excerpt from *Camera Austria International* 47–48/1994. Excerpt from a transcription of a Symposion lecture in conjunction with the Austrian Triennial for Photography, Neue Galerie am Landesmuseum Joanneum und Forum Stadtpark, Graz, 17 September – 31 October 1993.

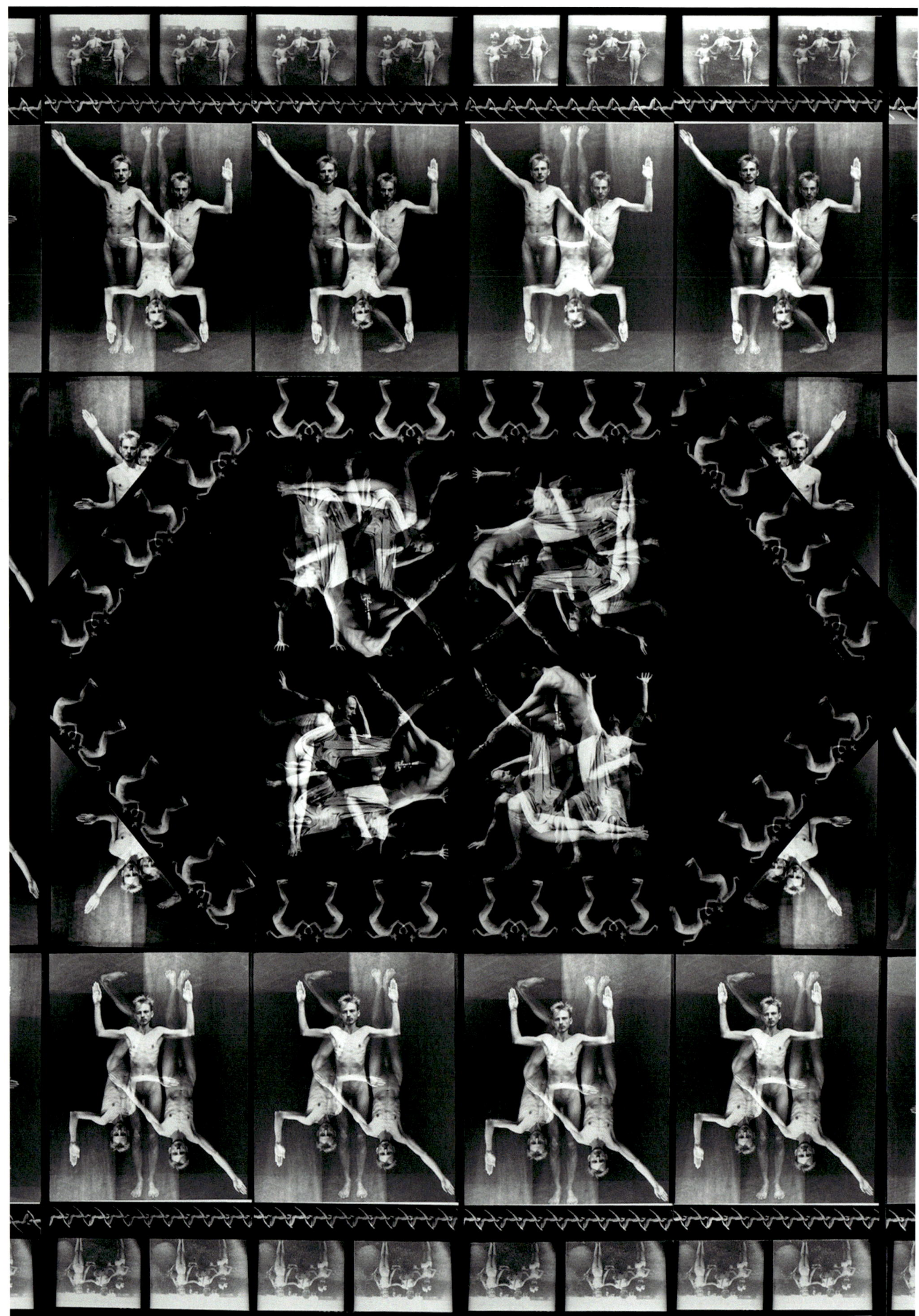

Detail from: *The Human Motif I*, 1989

Zofia Kulik

In 1987 I decided to produce art that could be framed and hung on the walls of galleries and, better still, museums. I wanted my work to exist and function without my explanations, without my comments, without my presence. Now, for this symposium, I have decided to break my resolution. I will try to explain something about my work. These will be fragments of explanations, in a collage made up of different parts.

My mother is a dressmaker. In our house there were always piles of cloth – silk, cotton, linen – and everywhere there were patterns for suits. Almost daily, women would come to be measured for suits, costumes, skirts, jackets, blouses or coats. They had been looking at fashion journals and ladies' magazines, and they talked, talked, talked about pleats, tucks, décolletés, collars, belts and pocket flaps.

My father, who is now retired, was a colonel in the People's Army of Poland and, as I suspect, he was in the Propaganda Department. Until I was fourteen I lived in military quarters. Until 1956 (I was eleven, then) nobody from the street could come to the building I was living in. All visitors had to ask for a permit, and you can imagine the grotesque situations when all the women coming to see my mother first had to go to the permit office.

From my window I could see an oval field surrounded by kerbstones painted white. There was a small stone monument to the right of it, and to the left a red-brick building where the military command was based.

Day after day I would see soldiers and officers walking or marching to and fro; I saw military ceremonies, the changing of the guard, the raising of the flag, and there were commands and salutes.

Mother in the house and father outside the window.

I have no personal experience of war. I was brought up in the shadow of World War II, under the strong pressure of the »propaganda truth« that there would never again be war near our homes. No war – thanks to the October Revolution that brought us peace and justice, thanks to the Allies and the »peace-loving« powers united in the Warsaw Pact, thanks to our wise and »peace-loving« leaders, and thanks to our »peace-loving« brother in the east, the Soviet Union.

Now it is 1993, and the only thing I can say about war is that I am afraid of it. What for us is a nightmare vision, is reality for others. Even the most important quote from the wisest of books is worthless when you are confronted by an enemy, someone who treats you as the enemy, that is.

I would now like to quote some passages from texts I have written about my artistic work.

»I am interested in building structures, composing more complex wholes. I am fascinated by closed forms, centricity, symmetry, multiplication, order, figural ornament, imposing upon myself certain already existing patterns of structures (...) that I try to fill with my own madness [I wrote this in 1989; now I feel it should be a different word] – these are my form-shaping rules of composition.«[1]

»Their purpose is to humiliate 'the spectator' and bring him to his knees. But for whom are you to humble yourself today? There is no god, no leader, no mystery. So whom are you to serve? That is a question. I am afraid of myself – that I can feel and visualize subordination so well. I do not show an individual man; the man is a splinter which I can divide and multiply at will and then build a composition of it. But it is neither free nor fanciful (...). First, I search for a pattern, and then while composing according to that pattern I begin to feel the sense of what I am doing (...). Do I appreciate and praise 'subordination' by depicting it, or do I deride and refute it? Having accepted 'subordination' as my problem and motive, but being fearful and hateful of the situation marked by compulsive subordination, I take my artistic revenge by grabbing every symbolic and formal weapon that has been used against me. I love the grass which I love to cut down.«[2]

36

Im Jahr 1987 beschloß ich, solche Kunst zu machen, die gerahmt in Galerien, oder besser noch in Museen, ausgestellt werden kann. Meine Arbeiten sollten ohne meine Erklärungen und meinen Kommentar, ohne meine Gegenwart bestehen können. Von diesem Vorsatz gehe ich ab, wenn ich heute versuche, Ihnen meine Arbeit etwas zu erklären, in Form einer Collage aus verschiedenen Elementen.

Meine Mutter ist Schneiderin. In unserer Wohnung hatten sich stapelweise Stoffe – Seide, Baumwolle, Leinen – und überall Schnittmuster. Beinahe täglich kamen Kundinnen, um sich ein Kleidungsstück anmessen zu lassen – Kostüme, Röcke, Jacken, Blusen, Mäntel. Sie hatten sich Modejournale und Frauenzeitschriften angesehen und unterhielten sich nun endlos über Falten, Abnäher, Ausschnitte, Gürtel, Krägen und Taschenklappen.

Mein Vater, er ist schon pensioniert, war Offizier in der polnischen Volksarmee. Ich vermute, daß er für die Propagandaabteilung arbeitete. Bis zu meinem vierzehnten Lebensjahr wohnten wir im Kasernengelände. Bis 1956, ich war damals elf, konnte niemand zu uns nach Haus kommen, ohne sich vorher einen Passierschein zu holen. Sie können sich die grotesken Situationen vorstellen, wenn alle Kundinnen meiner Mutter erst in das entsprechende Büro gehen mußten, um sich dieses Papier zu holen.

Wenn ich aus dem Fenster sah, blickte ich auf einen ovalen Platz, eingefaßt mit weißen Steinen. Rechterhand stand ein kleines Steindenkmal, linkerhand ein roter Ziegelbau, in dem das Heereskommando untergebracht war.

Tagaus, tagein sah ich die Soldaten und Offiziere hin- und hergehen oder marschieren. Ich sah Militärfeiern, Wachablösen, Fahnenappelle, hörte Befehle und Salutieren.

Zuhause, da war meine Mutter, und draußen, vor dem Fenster, mein Vater.

Ich habe Krieg nie selbst erlebt. Ich wuchs im Schatten des zweiten Weltkrieges auf, unter dem Einfluß des »propagandistischen Versprechens«, daß es in unserer Heimat nie wieder Krieg geben wird. Nie wieder Krieg, dank der Oktoberrevolution, die uns Frieden und Gerechtigkeit gebracht hatte, dank der Alliierten und der »friedliebenden« Mächte des Warschauer Paktes. Nie wieder Krieg, dank unserer weisen, »friedliebenden« Führer, und unseres »friedliebenden« Bruders im Osten, der Sowjetunion.

Heute, im Jahr 1993, kann ich über den Krieg nur sagen, daß ich ihn fürchte. Was für uns eine Schreckensvision ist, ist für andere Realität. Wenn man einem Feind gegenübersteht, das heißt, jemandem, der einen als Feind betrachtet, hilft auch die größte Weisheit aus dem klügsten Buch nicht mehr.

Ich zitiere nun einige Passagen aus Texten über meine Arbeit.
»Mir geht es um das *Schaffen* von Strukturen, die Komposition komplexer Gefüge. Mich faszinieren geschlossene Formen, Zentrierung, Symmetrie, Multiplikation, Systematik, figurale Elemente, die Unterwerfung unter vorgegebene Strukturmuster (...), die ich mit meinem Wahnsinn fülle [das war 1989; heute würde ich einen anderen Begriff wählen] – dies sind die formgebenden Prinzipien meiner Kompositionen.«[1]

»Ihr Zweck ist, 'den Betrachter' zu demütigen, ihn in die Knie zu zwingen. Aber wem soll man sich heute unterwerfen? Da ist kein Gott, kein Führer, kein Mysterium. Wem also dienen? Das ist ein Problem. Ich habe Angst vor mir selbst – der Tatsache, daß ich mich in die Unterordnung so gut einfühlen, sie mir so gut vorstellen kann. Wenn ich einen Mann zeige, geht es nicht um das Individuum. Der Mann ist wie ein Splitter, den ich nach Belieben zerteilen und vervielfältigen kann, um daraus meine Komposition aufzubauen. Aber diese ist weder frei noch beliebig (...). Zuerst suche ich ein Muster, und indem ich das Muster umsetze, beginne ich allmählich den Sinn meines Tuns zu spüren (...). Ist meine Darstellung der 'Unterwerfung' Ausdruck lobender Bestätigung oder höhnischer*

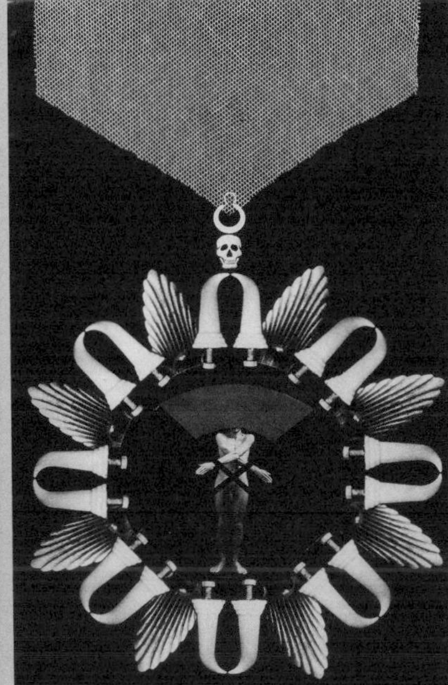

ZOFIA KULIK, from the series »Medals« / aus der Serie »Ehrenzeichen«, 1989, 50 x 33 cm.

37

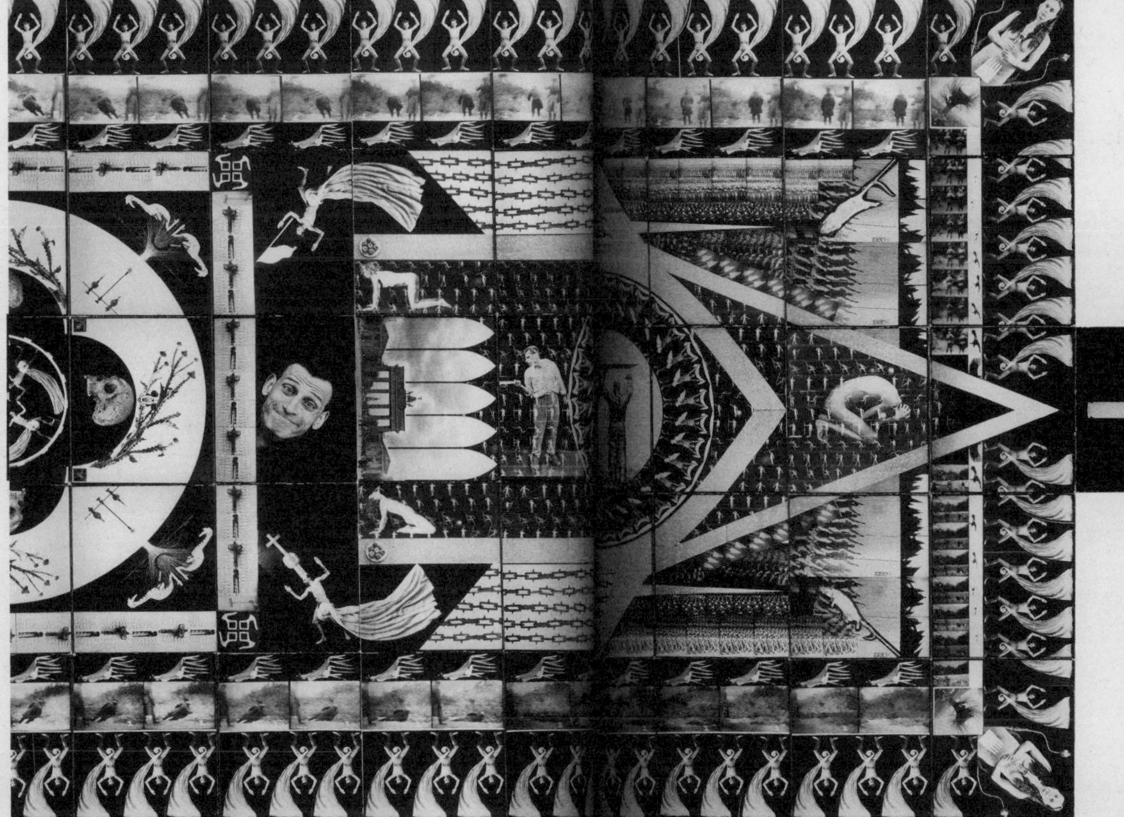

43

169

ZOFIA KULIK, *Square of Palaces / Quadrat aus Palästen*, 1990, 240 x 150 cm.

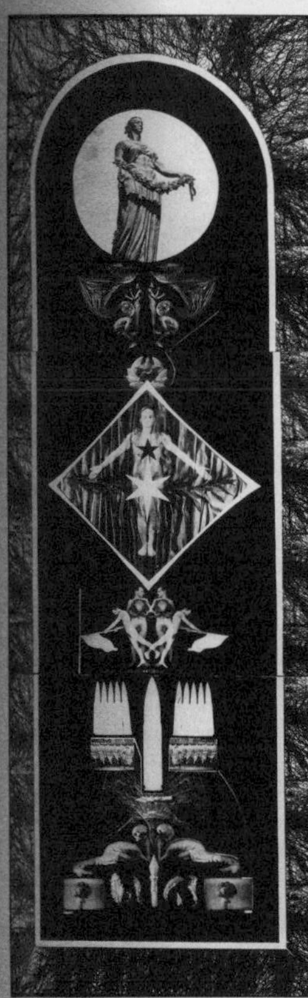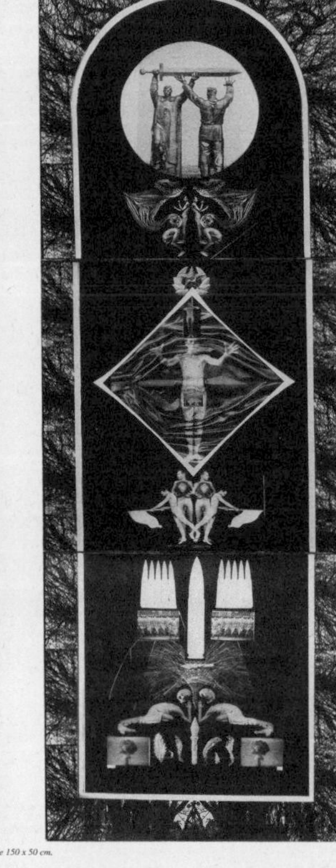

ZOFIA KULIK, *from the series »Columns« / aus der Serie »Säulen«*, 1992, each / je 150 x 50 cm.

In a letter to Christine Frisinghelli about my work »All the Missiles Are One Missile«, which is shown in the Neue Galerie in Graz[3], I wrote, »The whole composition has the form of a carpet, a photographic carpet, as it were. Its 'decorativeness' is built up of photographic images chosen from my collection of b/w negatives. These include images of socialist monuments, cemeteries, landscapes, photo still lifes composed by me, human gestures performed by my models, and 'real' events taken from TV – wars, protest marches, executions, marches past, riots, etc. I copy the images from the negatives onto the surface of the photographic paper by covering and uncovering different parts of the surface, according to plans and stencils I have made before. The complete work is made up of a number of photographic sheets 60 cm by 50 cm in size.

Entwertung? Ich habe 'Unterwerfung' als mein Problem und [als] künstlerisches Motiv akzeptiert, aber zugleich fürchte und ha[sse ich] diese Situation zwanghafter Unterwerfung. So räche ich m[ich als] Künstlerin, indem ich mir jedes Symbol, jedes formale Eleme[nt, das] je gegen mich verwendet wurde, zu eigen mache. Ich liebe da[s ...], das ich immer wieder beschneide.«[2]

Über die Arbeit »All the Missiles Are One Missile«, die [in der] Neuen Galerie in Graz zu sehen ist[3], schrieb ich an Chr[istine] Frisinghelli: »Die ganze Komposition hat die Form eines Te[ppichs,] eines Fototeppichs. Ihr dekorativer Charakter stellt sich [aus] fotografischen Bildern her, die ich aus meiner Samm[lung von] Schwarzweißnegativen ausgewählt habe. Dazu gehören Bild[er von] sozialistischen Monumenten, Friedhöfen und Landschaften, v[on mir] komponierte Fotostilleben, Modelle, die bestimmte Gesten [ausführ]ren, sowie 'wirkliche' Ereignisse aus dem Fernsehen – K[riege,] Demonstrationen, Exekutionen, Aufmärsche, Unruhen usw. [Ich ko]piere diese Bilder vom Negativ auf das Fotopapier, indem ich [nach] vorher angefertigten Mustern und Schablonen bestimmte Be[reiche] abdecke bzw. belichte. Die ganze Arbeit besteht aus einer Anz[ahl von] Blättern im Format 60 x 50 cm.«

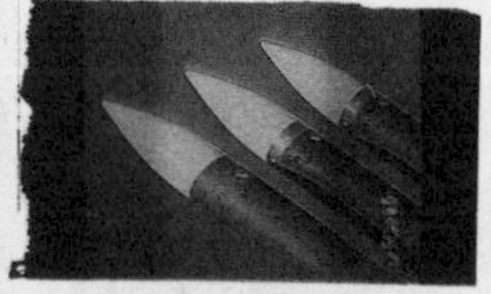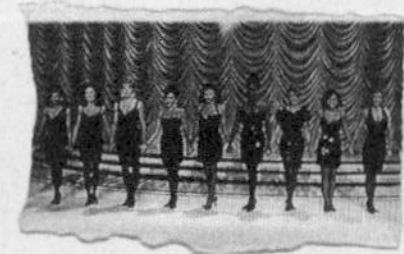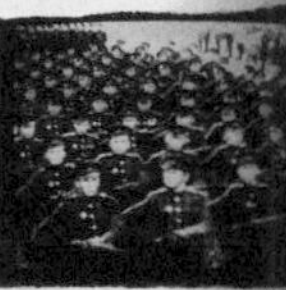
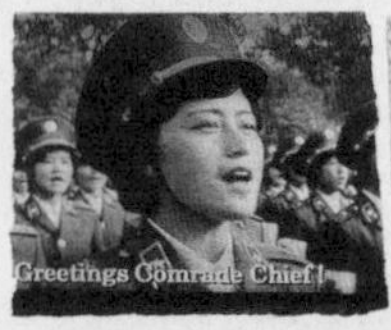

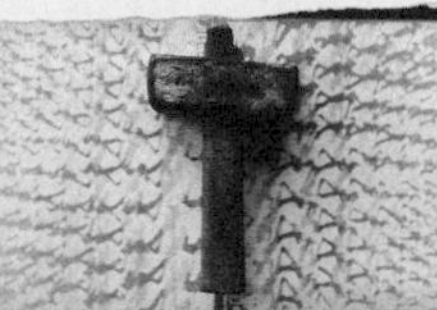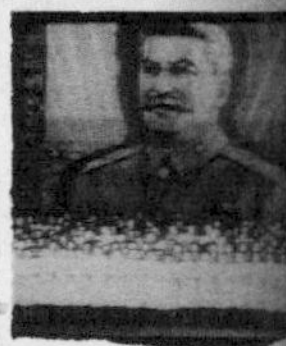

Material used for »All the Missiles Are One Missile«, 1993 / Material, das für die Arbeit »Alle Geschoße sind ein Geschoß« (1993) verwendet wurde.

In the second letter to Christine Frisinghelli I wrote, »When you look at all these real and definite things in the photographs, remember that they show not only real and definite things and events but that they can be seen without their background – they show what they show.« So, in the work in the Neue Galerie, you have on the left a monument from Leningrad, entitled »Fatherland – Mother«, dating from 1960, and on the right, the monument »Back and Front«, erected in Magnitogorsk in 1979. In the first case, what you see is a woman wearing a garland, in the second case, a man with a sword.

Zofia Kulik concluded her presentation with a video showing, among other things, details of a concurrent exhibition of her work in Poland.

(Edited by Bärbel Fink)

In meinem nächsten Brief an Christine Frisinghelli schrie[b ich]: »Wenn Du all die realen, konkreten Dinge in den Fotos sie[hst, erinnere Dich,] nicht, daß sie sich nicht nur auf eine konkrete Wirklichkeit [beziehen,] sondern auch unabhängig von ihrem Zusammenhang geseh[en werden] können – sie stellen vor, was sie vorstellen.« Die Arbei[t in der] Neuen Galerie zum Beispiel zeigt links ein 1960 errichtetes D[enkmal] aus Leningrad mit dem Titel »Vaterland – Mutter«, und [rechts das] Denkmal aus Magnitogorsk mit dem Titel »Vorne und Hinte[n«, 1979] errichtet. Was Sie bei ersterem vor Augen haben, ist eine b[ekränzte] Frau, bei letzterem einen Mann mit einem Schwert.

Zofia Kulik setzte Ihren Beitrag mit einem Videofilm fort, [der unter] anderem eine zur gleichen Zeit in Polen laufende Ausstellung [ihrer] Arbeiten zeigte.

(Übersetzung: Bärbel [Fink])

1 Zofia Kulik, »Kwiekulik«, in: Exit. Nowa sztuka w Polscie (New Art in Poland), no. 5, January – March 1991, p.161.
2 Ibid.
3 Contribution to the »Austrian Triennial on Photography 1993, Neue Galerie am Landesmuseum Joanneum and Forum Stadtpark, Graz, 17. 9. – 31. 10. 1993, see: Werner Fenz, Christine Frisinghelli (ed.), WAR., Austrian Triennial on Photography 1993, exhibition catalogue, 2 vol., Edition Camera Austria, Graz 1993, vol. 1, p. 97, vol. 2, p. 18.

1 Zofia Kulik, »Kwiekulik«, in: Exit. Nowa sztuka w Polscie (Neue Kunst in Polen), Nr. 5, Januar – März 1991, S. 161.
2 Ebda.
3 Beitrag zur »Österreichischen Triennale zur Fotografie 1993«, Neue Galerie am Landesmuseum Joanneum und Forum Stadtpark, Graz, 17. 9. – 31. 10. 1993, siehe: Werner Fenz, Christine Frisinghelli (Hg.), KRIEG., Österreichische Triennale zur Fotografie 1993, Ausstellungskatalog, 2 Bd., Edition Camera Austria, Graz 1993, Bd. 1, S. 93, Bd. 2, S. 18.

Paul Lowe

WITNESS OF EXISTENCE

Some notes on Bosnia

... along with a large group of other journalists, TV crews, [and photographers], to go and see a massacre. We are lined up, as if [at the start] of some macabre race, held back by a young sergeant [from] the British Army, whilst a delegation from the United Nations in Geneva is taken on a guided tour of a village ahead of us where dozens [of Muslim civilians] have been burnt alive by Croats. Suddenly, the [pack breaks] out, carried along by our desire to be the first to get there, [and we] begin to run up the hill. At first, it is like some game, a [children's] race, except that we are festooned with cameras, and [sweating] in our flak jackets. But our initial enthusiasm begins to wane [as we] enter the village and see bloated cows lying dead in the fields, [destroyed] houses, a bicycle lying in the road. By the time we get to the [scene] of the atrocity, a grim silence has descended on the small group [who have] taken the lead. We find one of the houses, a burnt out [shell, and] cautiously enter. It's dark, and at first hard to see what has [happened]. But then, we realise that there are three or four bodies, it's [hard to tell] how many exactly, lying charred beyond recognition, on [the floor]. I realize that I have almost stepped on one in the gloom. [Recoiling,] feeling sick, I try to make a picture. A hand sticks up, like [a claw,] reaching out to accuse its killer. After a few moments, I leave, [feeling like] a grave robber.

Outside, a group has formed, all trying to get inside the house. And [in their] midst, like some gameshow host from a tacky TV programme, [wearing] a slick suit and shiny shoes, is a special representative from [the UN in] Geneva, holding a clipboard and trying to give sound bites [to anyone] who will listen. »Come on down, the massacre's on [primetime!«] I burst out laughing at this ridiculous man, the giggling [a release] from the horror at what is inside the house. My pictures of [that] day never get used, but the atrocity is widely reported, and helps [turn] opinion against the Croats.

Why photograph war? I am continually asked why go there, what [makes] you want to put yourself at risk, aren't you some kind of [adrenalin] junkie? But I don't consider myself a »war photographer«, [rather a] photographer of extreme situations, of ordinary people in [extraordinary] circumstances. A group of Sarajevan artists formed [themselves] into a collective called »Witnesses of Existence«, I adopted [their] name and spirit.

The historical moment is too important to be ignored, to be [conceptualised] out of existence. Edo Numankadic, an old artist, [a friend,] with gentle eyes, like some great wise owl, makes me believe [that being] there, that witnessing existence, is vital, that without that [record nothing] will be remembered. He tells me that for him, »Just to [be here] in Sarajevo, to survive, is an act of art, fighting for life itself [... By my] sheer survival I am defending the values that I believe [in ... My] belief in humanity. Art is my way of fighting in this war, fighting for civilisation, for the [quality of] life. My answer to destruction is construction. Art lasts for [generations,] this war lasts just a second. Art will remain a witness to [what happened here].«

As I write this I have just finished seeing Gilles Peress' new work [on Bosnia], and I am overwhelmed, almost brought to tears, carried [along] by the emotional intensity of the experience, by the loss of [life,] by the loss of home, family, life. No conceptual piece removed [from the scene] could carry such intensity, such depth, and still retain [such an] overriding sense of being there, of actual experience. No [other medium] could convey the sense of chaos, confusion, and horror [...] of Capa's pictures of the D-Day landings, or the evilness of the [military machine] in Philip Jones Griffith's »Vietnam Inc.«.

EXISTENZZEUGE

Anmerkungen zu Bosnien

Gemeinsam mit einer großen Gruppe anderer Journalisten, Fernsehteams und Fotografen warte ich auf den Zutritt zum Schauplatz eines Massakers. Wir stehen in einer Reihe, wie am Start irgendeines makabren Rennens, zurückgehalten von einem jungen Sergeant der Britischen Armee, während eine Delegation der Genfer UNO-Behörde an einer Führung durch das Dorf teilnimmt, das vor uns liegt. Kroaten haben hier ein Dutzend moslemischer Zivilisten bei lebendigem Leib verbrannt. Plötzlich stürmt die ganze Meute los, jeder getrieben von der Gier, der erste zu sein, und wir rennen den Hang hinauf. Zunächst wirkt es wie ein Spiel, ein Kinderwettlauf, nur daß wir, statt mit Papierschlangen, mit Kameras behangen sind und in unseren Flakjacken schwitzen. Unser anfänglicher Enthusiasmus schwindet, als wir in das Dorf kommen und die aufgeblähten Rinder auf den Wiesen liegen sehen. Die Häuser sind zerstört, auf der Straße hingeworfen ein Fahrrad. Wir haben den Ort der grauenvollen Tat erreicht. Schauderndes Schweigen hat sich über die kleine Gruppe der Erstankömmlinge gesenkt. Wir nehmen uns eines der Häuser vor, eine ausgebrannte leere Hülle, und treten vorsichtig ein. Es ist finster, und im ersten Moment ist kaum zu erkennen, was geschehen ist. Aber dann stellen wir fest, daß auf dem Boden drei, vier Leichen liegen, bis zur Unkenntlichkeit verkohlt, die Anzahl ist nicht genau auszumachen. Beinah wäre ich auf eine getreten und zucke zurück. Mir ist übel. Ich versuche, ein Bild zu machen. Eine Hand ragt in die Luft wie eine Klaue, wie eine Anklage gegen den Mörder. Ein paar Augenblikke später entferne ich mich. Ich komme mir vor wie ein Grabräuber.

Draußen kommt es zu einer Ansammlung. Alle wollen in das Haus. Mitten unter ihnen, wie der Moderator einer abgeschmackten TV-Show, im eleganten Anzug und mit glänzenden Schuhen, ein Sonderrepräsentant der UNO aus Genf. Er hat eine Schreibunterlage und jedem was zu sagen, der zuhören will. »Hereinspaziert – das Massaker läuft im Hauptabendprogramm!« Ich muß loslachen über diesen lächerlichen Typ, mein Kichern ist ein Ventil des Grauens, das ich drinnen gesehen habe. Die Bilder, die ich an diesem Tag gemacht habe, werden nie gedruckt, aber über die Greueltat wird ausgiebig berichtet. Das trägt dazu bei, die öffentliche Meinung gegen die Kroaten zu wenden.

Warum Krieg fotografieren? Ich werde ständig gefragt, warum ich hinfahre, warum ich das Risiko auf mich nehme, ob ich nicht ein Adrenalin-Junkie sei. Dabei sehe ich mich gar nicht als Kriegsfotograf, eher als Fotograf von Extremsituationen, von gewöhnlichen Menschen in außergewöhnlichen Umständen. Eine Gruppe von Künstlern aus Sarajevo hat ein Kollektiv gebildet und sich »Existenzzeugen« genannt. Ich habe diesen Namen und auch ihren Geist übernommen.

Der historische Moment ist zu wichtig, um ignoriert, aus seiner Existenz fortkonzeptualisiert zu werden. Edo Numankadic, ein alter Künstler, ein Freund mit sanften Augen wie eine große, weise Eule, macht mich glauben, daß es lebenswichtig ist, dabeizusein, als Augenzeuge des Seins, und daß ohne Aufzeichnung alles vergessen wird. »Für ihn«, sagt er, ist »das Leben in Sarajevo, das bloße Überleben hier, ein Kunstwerk. Um das Leben an sich zu kämpfen – das ist Kunst. Allein durch mein Überleben verteidige ich die Werte, an die ich glaube. Was ich im Kopf habe, mein Glaube an die Menschheit, das ist meine Waffe. Ich kann mich an diesem Krieg nur durch Kunst beteiligen – ich kämpfe um Zivilisation, um die Qualität des Lebens. Meine Antwort auf destruktives Handeln ist konstruktives Handeln. Die Kunst wird bestehen – als Zeugnis dessen, was hier geschehen ist.«

Jörg Schlick

Camera Austria International

1999   Diedrich Diederichsen, "Fotografie und
        Gedenken: Feldmann, RAF, Schlick,
        Kippenberger usw.," text contribution,
        Camera Austria International 66 / 1999
        Martin Prinzhorn, "Einige kognitions-
        psychologische Präliminarien zur Arbeit
        von Jörg Schlick," text contribution,
        Jörg Schlick, artist contribution,
        Camera Austria International 67 / 1999
2000   "Österreich 2000," (black edition, design),
        Camera Austria International 69 / 2000
2006   Christine Frisinghelli, "Jörg Schlick:
        1951–2005," text contribution
        Jörg Schlick, artist contribution,
        Camera Austria International 93 / 2006

Exhibitions

2001   *Poésie Noire. Für Elisabeth Printschitz,*
        solo exhibition
2003   *Freundschaftsspiel,* exhibition contribution

Jörg Schlick

Monika Pessler
Jörg Schlick: Poésie Noire

DNA consists of four "letters" or bases: A, T, C and G (adenine, thymine, cytosine and guanine). These letters are arranged in pairs – A with T and C with G – that you can imagine like rungs on a ladder. Human DNA is made up of 3.2 billion of these base pairs, which are joined together to create a twisted helix structure. The Human Genome Project aims to chart the exact arrangement of these 3.2 billion pairs.

The identification of these genetic combinations forms the basis for the artistic concept. The 3.2 billion possible genetic combinations are translated into artistic representations.

Jörg Schlick transposes art into the system of biological rules: four views of a found (everyday) object are recorded photographically and each assigned to one base. The serial arrangement creates tableaux of 24 photo elements whose order is based on the clear-cut sequence of nitrogen bases—e.g. A A T C T G … .

The content of the documented object by no means relates to the message of the manufactured art product. The selected object appears to be divested of its identity, for the views of the object serve neither to describe its function nor to underscore its importance.

Only the structuring of the object obtained in the photographic depiction is of relevance to the work. The specific manifestations of the motifs—be they geometrical forms of an interior view or the organic vocabulary of a depiction of nature—are the parameters with the aid of which the complex make-up of genetic information is represented. Detached from representation, the structural make-up of the pictorial elements is reflecting the programmatic draft of life.

Whereas the selection of the object and the angle of viewing are subjective decisions, the act of photographic documentation subsequently initiates a process of objectification that culminates in the mathematical stringency of biochemical formulae.

Photography is relieved of its conventional function in these visualisations, the single image disappears as artistic value. The conceptual use of the medium makes the photo a constitutive component of the semantics of the work. The realisation of the artistic "composition" is also geared to the result of biotechnology research and is subordinate to the mathematical laws of lived nature.

From: "Jörg Schlick, 'Poésie Noire,'" in *To Live in Forests Like Timid Deer,* Cologne: Verlag Walther König, 2001.

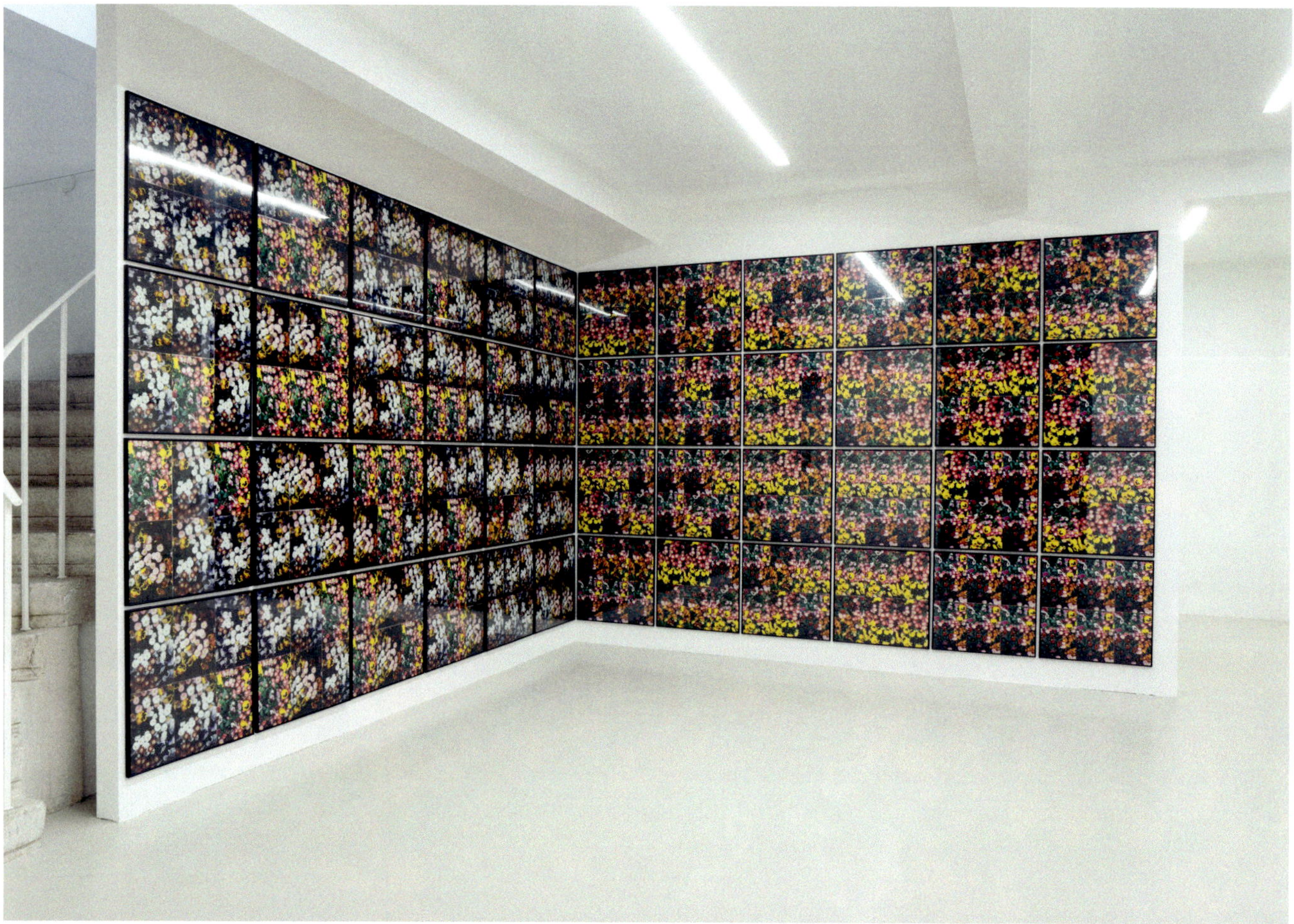

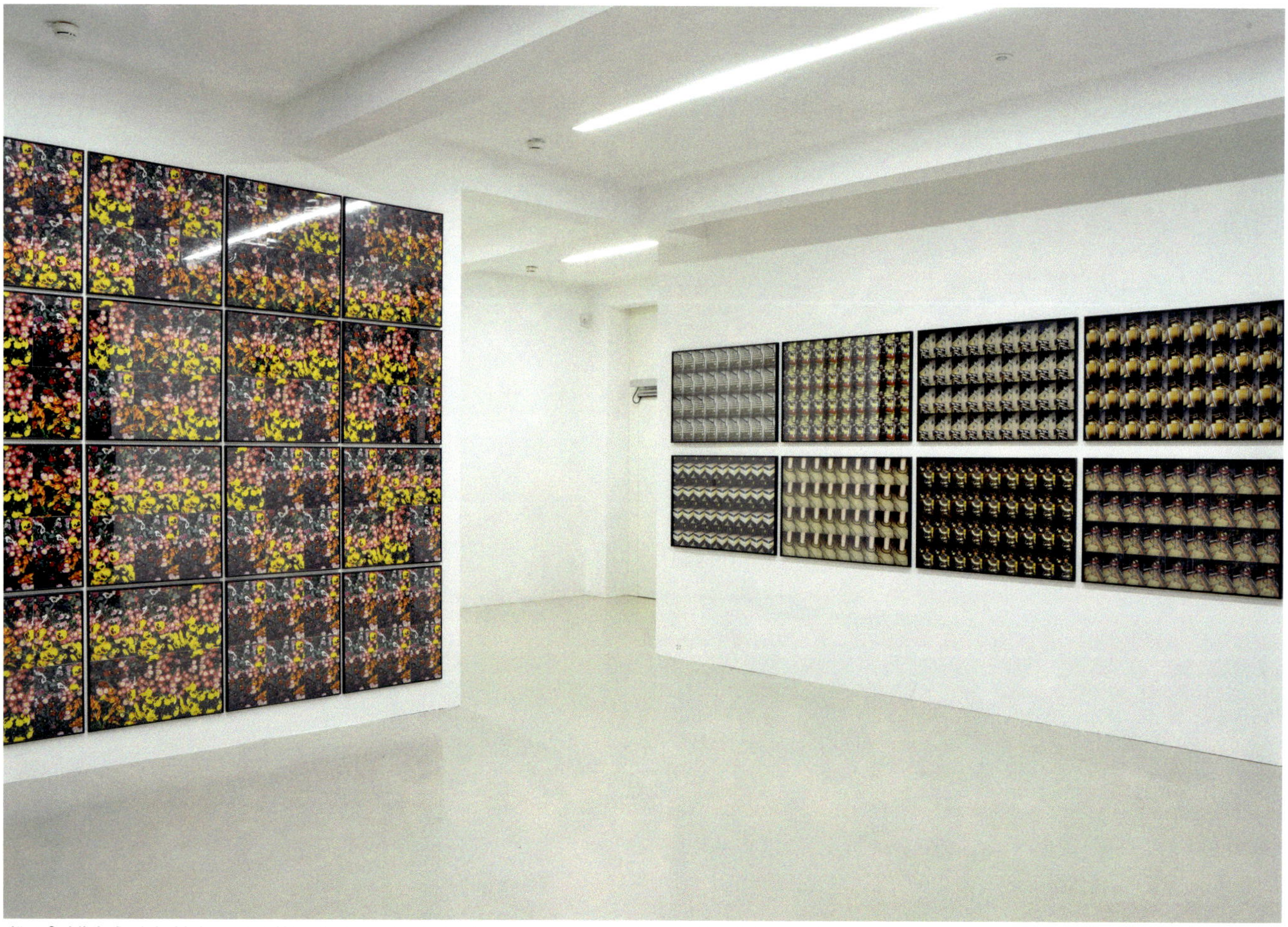

Jörg Schlick, Poésie Noire, 2001, Künstlerhaus, Halle für Kunst und Medien, Graz (AT), 2015, exhibition view

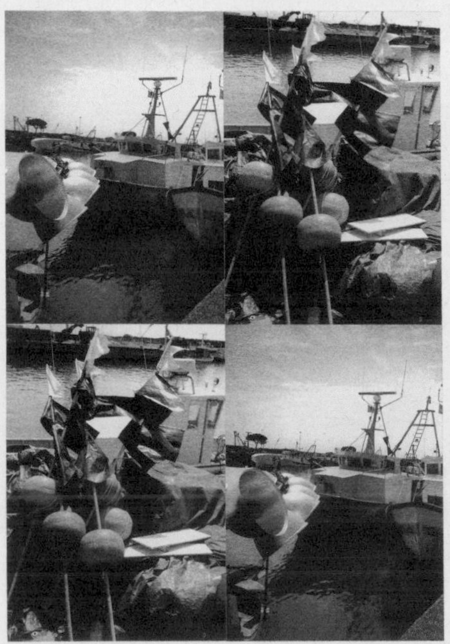

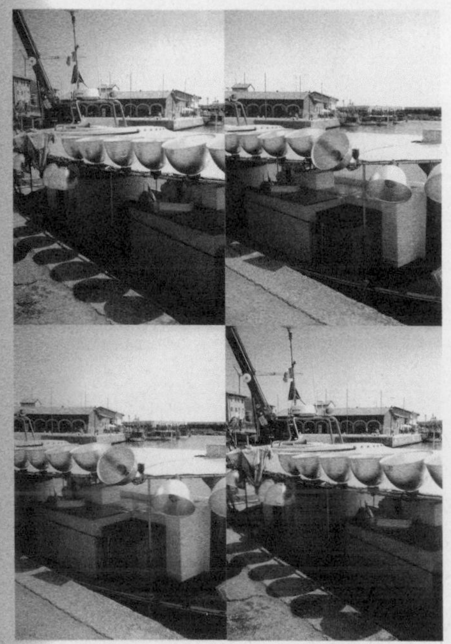

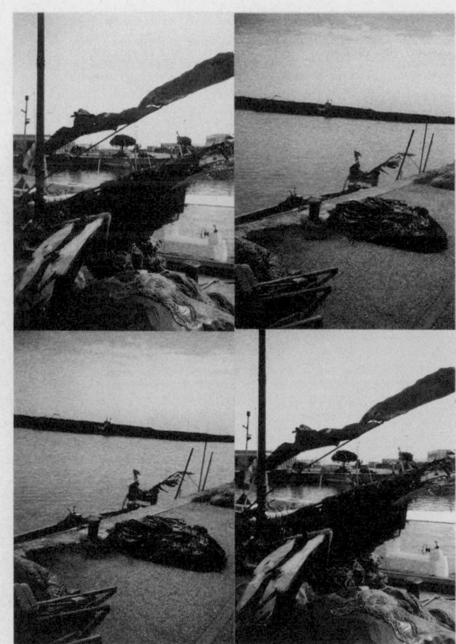

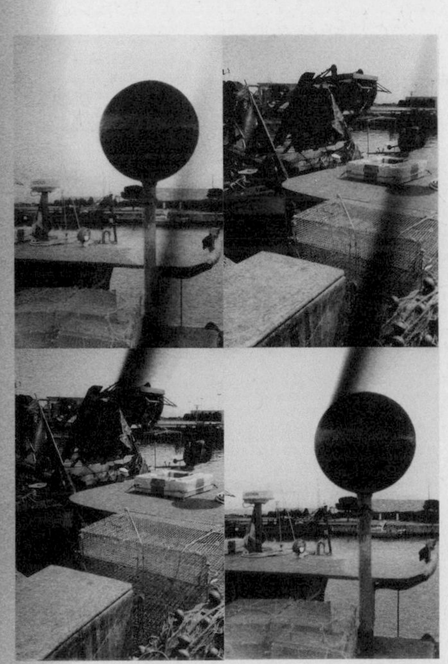

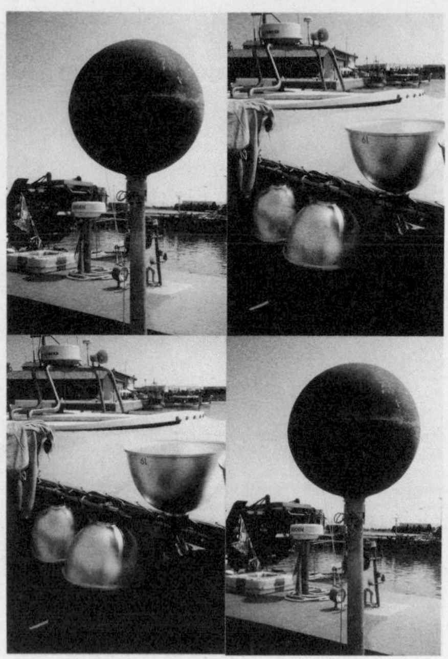

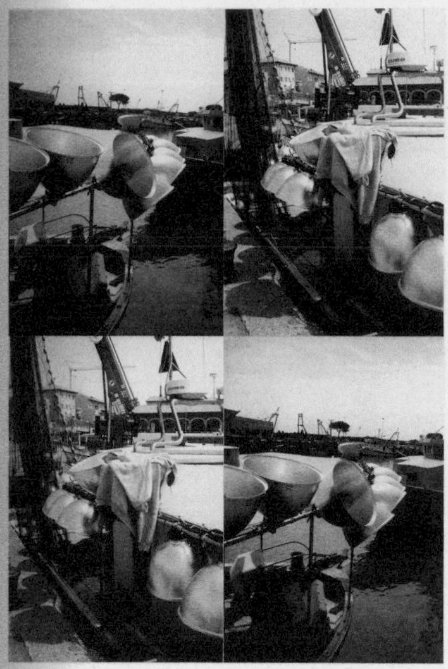

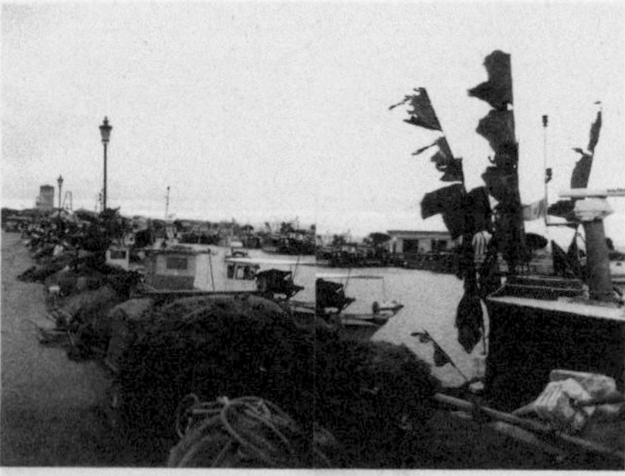

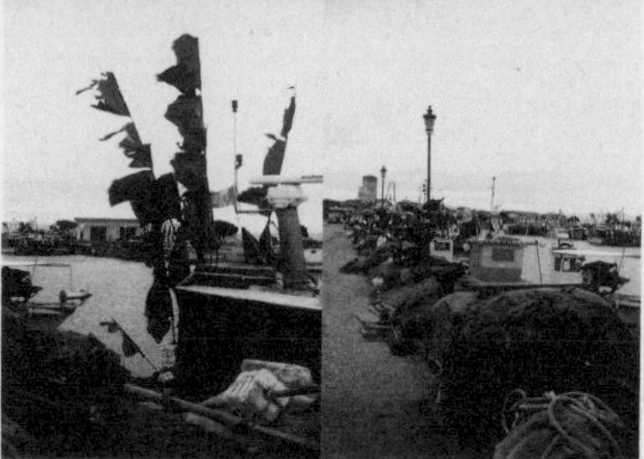

JÖRG SCHLICK: 1951 – 2005

Ich habe Jörg Schlick Anfang der 1980er Jahre kennen gelernt. Er war damals – wie bis über die Mitte der 1990er Jahre hinaus – Erzieher in einem Lehrlingsheim, ein Brotberuf, der ihm seine Unabhängigkeit als Künstler sicherte. Zu der Zeit hatte er gerade Lehrlings-Kulturtage organisiert, um den Lehrlingen Zugang zur zeitgenössischen Kunst zu ermöglichen, aber schließlich auch, um künstlerische Arbeit außerhalb der Institutionen der Kunst zur Diskussion zu stellen. Dieses Anliegen würde sich durch sein ganzes Leben ziehen, und zeigt den Ernst seines künstlerischen Ansatzes ebenso wie sein politisches Denken. Sichtbar wird hier aber auch – bereits sehr früh – seine Entscheidung, in dieser Stadt – Graz – lokal verankert zu bleiben und die Vermittlung von Kunst gleichbedeutend neben die eigene künstlerische Arbeit zu stellen. Ein paar Jahre später, im steirischen herbst 1983, erinnere ich mich an die Aufführung seiner symphonischen Komposition »Besser als Ludwig Van«, in der er die Struktur und klangliche Intensität der vier Sätze der Eroica-Symphonie Beethovens identisch nachbaute und – für jeden Satz ein eigenes Instrument wählend, nachspielte. Diese Performance – im Kontext eines Avantgarde-Festivals aufgeführt, dessen Anspruch zugleich herausfordernd wie ironisch kommentierend – bildete, zumal mit ihrem anmaßenden Titel – gleichsam das heroische andere Ende der Skala künstlerischer Ermächtigungs-Gesten.

Kunst stand für Jörg Schlick niemals außerhalb des gesellschaftlichen Kontextes, und seine Beschäftigung mit der Rolle des Künstlers in unserer Gesellschaft bildet so etwas wie das zentrale Motiv seiner Arbeit, seines Lebens. Die Idee des Werkes war für ihn deshalb auch umfassender als das allein materielle Ergebnis künstlerischer Arbeit, schloss soziale und politische Entscheidungen ebenso ein wie sie an viele außerkünstlerische Bereiche anknüpfte. Er hat in manchen Werken, einem Wissenschaftler gleich, seine Bildfindungen als Modulation von Versuchsanordnungen durchgespielt – auch wenn, wie wir seit 2001 nunmehr betriebenen Vorhaben zeigt, er für die bild-künstlerische Darstellung von 3,2 Milliarden genetischen Kombinationsvarianten 10.000 Jahre seiner Lebenszeit gebraucht hätte. Seine Faszination für wissenschaftliche Rationalität bildet wohl die konzeptuellen Grundlagen solcher Arbeiten, niemals jedoch wird das Geheimnis ihrer künstlerischen Wahrheit zur Gänze preisgegeben, wie es der Satz von Mallarmé ausdrückt, den er als Titel einer seiner letzten Ausstellungen wählte: »Ein Würfelwurf niemals je auslöschen wird den Zufall!«

Seine vielfältigen und internationalen künstlerischen Partnerschaften haben ihm wohl am meisten bedeutet – rückblickend können sie einen erweiterten Kontext bilden, in dem sein Werk gelesen wird. Für ihn waren die damit verbundenen Freundschaften Schutzschild gegen das Philistertum, Möglichkeit zur Selbst-Vergewisserung, sie boten ihm wohl auch Momente des Aufgehoben-Seins, als Person und als Künstler – um in Graz, in Österreich, in den letzten dreißig Jahren, auszuharren.

Ich hatte das große Privileg, mit Jörg Schlick zu arbeiten, und mit ihm befreundet zu sein. 1987 bis 1992 war er Leiter des Referates bildende Kunst im Forum Stadtpark, wo auch unsere Arbeit für/um zeitgenössische Fotografie Mitte der 1970er Jahre begonnen hatte. Von 1995 bis 1999 hat Jörg Schlick, während meiner Intendanz des Festivals »steirischer herbst« die Öffentlichkeitsarbeit neu definiert und das Festival dem jungen Publikum neu erschlossen; 2000 hat er für Camera Austria die Nummer 69, das »schwarze Heft« gestaltet, das unsere Positionierung in der politischen Debatte forcierte.

Jede seiner Arbeiten und Tätigkeiten hat er mit dem ihm eigenen Ernst erfüllt, hat sich mit seinem enormen Wissen, seinem Verantwortungsgefühl und seiner so besonderen Fähigkeit zur Analyse von Beziehungen und Gegebenheiten allen seinen Aufgaben gewidmet: als Künstler, Gestalter und Kurator ebenso wie in seiner Lehrtätigkeit, als Freund und Berater. Wie unglaublich scharf war seine Diagnose wenn es darum ging, Dummheit, Opportunismus, Anmaßung und Feigheit bloßzulegen, und wie sehr konnte man sich auf sein Urteil verlassen. Seine Großzügigkeit, seine Strenge, seine Eleganz und Diskretion, nicht zuletzt die Facetten und Schattierungen seines Lachens haben unsere Freundschaft geprägt. Welches Beispiel konnte er uns sein. Wie sehr wird er uns allen fehlen.

I met Jörg Schlick at the beginning of the 1980s. At the time – and until after the mid-1990s – he was a youth care worker in an apprentice's hostel, a bread and butter job that allowed him his independence as an artist. He was organising culture days for apprentices at the time, with the aim of enabling apprentices to get into contemporary art, but ultimately also to focus the discussion on artistic work outside the art institutions. This goal would run through his whole life and demonstrates the seriousness of his artistic approach as well as his political thought. But it also evidences his decision – taken at a very early stage – to stay locally entrenched in this city – Graz – and to pursue art education on an equal level with his own artistic work. A few years later, at steirischer herbst 1983, I remember the performance of his symphonic composition »Besser als Ludwig Van« (better than Ludwig Van), in which he identically reproduced the structure and tonal intensity of the four movements of Beethoven's Eroica symphony, playing each movement with a different instrument. Particularly in view of its presumptuous title, this performance – given in the context of an avant-garde festival, challenging and ironically commenting on its aspirations – formed the heroic other end of the scale, as it were, of gestures of artistic empowerment.

For Jörg Schlick, art was never detached from the social context, and his examination of the role of the artist in our society forms a kind of central theme of his work, and indeed of his life. To him, then, the idea of the work was more extensive than the solely material result of artistic work, embracing social and political decisions as much as linking up with many extra-artistic spheres. In some works, like a scientist, he would play through his visualisations in the manner of a modulation of experimental set-ups – even if he needed 10,000 years of his lifetime for the pictorial-artistic representation of 3.2 billion genetic combinations, as demonstrated by one project that he had been pursuing manically since 2001. His fascination with scientific rationality most likely forms the conceptual foundation of such works, but never did he completely reveal the secret of their artistic truth, as expressed by a Mallarmé quotation that he chose as a title for one of his last exhibitions: »A roll of the dice will never abolish chance!«

His manifold and international artistic partnerships were presumably most important to him – in retrospect they may be said to form an extended context in which to interpret his work. For him, the friendships involved were a shield against philistinism, and an opportunity of self-assurance; they probably also offered him moments of security, as a human being and as an artist – to hold out in Graz, in Austria, in the last thirty years.

I had the great privilege of working with Jörg Schlick and of being friends with him. From 1987 to 1992, he headed the visual arts section of Forum Stadtpark, where our work for (in the cause of) contemporary photography had begun in the mid-1970s. From 1995 to 1999, during my term as director of the »steirischer herbst« festival, Jörg Schlick redefined PR work and made the festival accessible to young people; in 2000 he designed number 69 of Camera Austria, *the »black issue«, that echoed and amplified our position in the political debate.*

He executed every one of his works and activities with characteristic seriousness, devoting himself to all of his tasks with his vast knowledge, his sense of responsibility, and his very special capacity of analysing relationships and situations: as an artist, designer and curator as well as in his capacity as teacher, as a friend and adviser. How incredibly astute was his analysis when it came to unmasking stupidity, opportunism, arrogance and cowardice, and how safely could you rely on his judgement. His generosity, his strictness, his elegance and discretion, and, last but not least, the facets and shades of his laughter, all left their mark on our friendship. What an example he was to us. How badly we will all miss him.

Christine Frisinghelli

17

Michael Schuster/ Hartmut Skerbisch

Participation at Symposia

1982   Symposion on Photography IV,
1–19 October 1982, lecturer
1989   Symposion on Photography X:
"Das Neue Konzept,"
10–12 November 1989, lecturer

Camera Austria International

1981   Michael Schuster/Hartmut Skerbisch,
"Szene aus dem gleichnamigen Stück.
Dokumentation," text contribution/
artist contribution, *Camera Austria
International* 5/1981
1982   Michael Schuster/Hartmut Skerbisch,
"All Has Been Seen By All," text contribution/
artist contribution, *Camera Austria
International* 11–12/1982
1990   Michael Schuster/Hartmut Skerbisch,
"All Has Been Seen By All III," text contribu-
tion/ artist contribution, *Camera Austria
International* 33–34/1990

Exhibitions

1980   *Europäische Fotografen, Teil 1: Steiermark,*
exhibition participation
1982   *Fotografie 1982,* exhibition participation
1989   *Das Neue Konzept,* exhibition participation
1994   *All Has Been Seen By All,* Modena per la
Fotografia 1994, Palazzo Comunale,
Modena (IT), exhibition participation

Michael Schuster / Hartmut Skerbisch

4.4

All Has Been Seen By All
Szene aus dem gleichnamigen Stück
(Scene from the play of the same name)

To introduce this work I would like to present a few thoughts as point of reference—I could entitle them: The state/condition/circumstance *All Has Been Seen By All* and where do we go from here?
Just as the events of the Revelation could already be of the past or be happening at this very moment, and we merely believe they are yet to come, in the same way we could already be in the situation *All Has Been Seen By All* and for whatever reason—in this case be it just because cameras do exist—take photos and show them to the others, even though, as said, *All Has Been Seen By All,* and the photos with an existence of their own exert such a strong attraction to us, that the avalanche carries us away, and we produce photo after photo, a whole work of pictures, and once our imagination has been inflicted, it lives intensively in this new picture-world, one more time forgetting that *All Has Been Seen By All.*
If out of a picture-world in which we all share, we isolate single images by using apparatuses, which by being singled out take on an importance, such an off-balance can be re-adjusted, by returning the photos, as untouched as possible, back to where they came from—so to say, keeping it confidential. If I were to take such photos and were to have them on me now, I would pass them out to you here at the symposium, irrelevant to if I got them back again—most important being, getting rid of them, and that no superfluous meaning be attached to the act. With the idea of the state/condition/circumstance *All Has Been Seen By All* I would, however, also like to point out, that in fact an apparatus-world has been created, which without our aid registers all possible images of the world, and reproduces them in all possible ways, on screen, prints or whatever, in such variety and quantity and of such self-suffenciency, almost as if human consciousness weren't needed at all.
At the crucial point "Szene aus dem gleichnamigen Stück" takes over. The title of this work could be seen in what photography does: With each photo a scene of a play is produced, which is in the end the

events of this world perceived merely as a scene, even then when the play is only the existence of the earth's passive surface, as Lewis Baltz showed us with great intensity right at the beginning of this symposion. Following are reproductions from this work up till NOW.

Symposion on Photography IV, Forum Stadtpark Graz, October 1982, published in *Camera Austria International* 11–12/1983, 85–86.

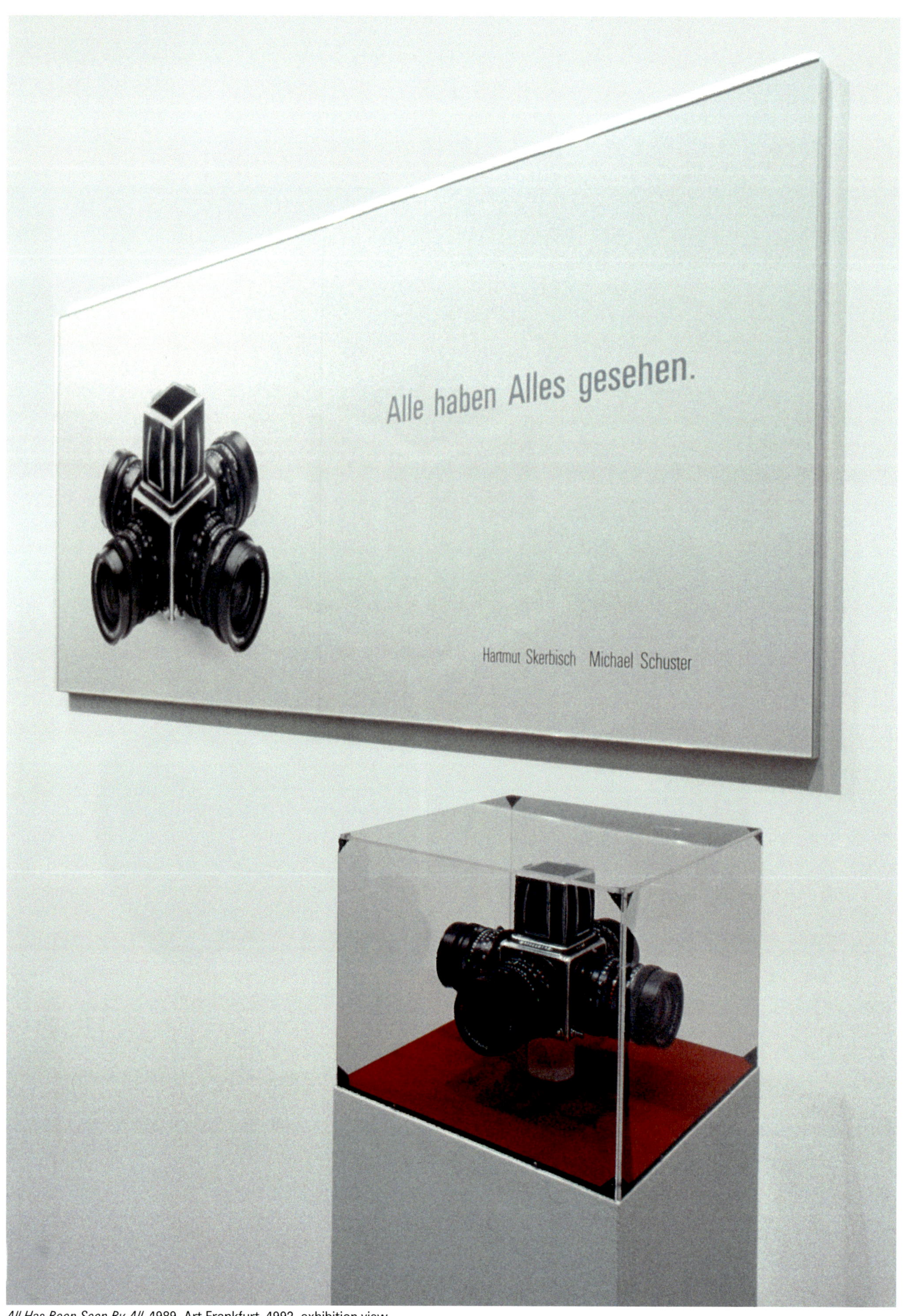

All Has Been Seen By All, 1989, Art Frankfurt, 1992, exhibition view

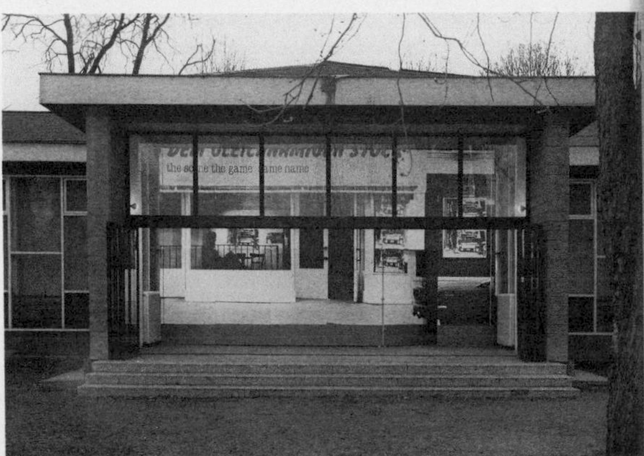

Situation ‚Durchgehen durch eine Fotografie' / Ausstellung ‚Szene aus dem gleichnamigen Stück' / Forum Stadtpark Graz, März 1981

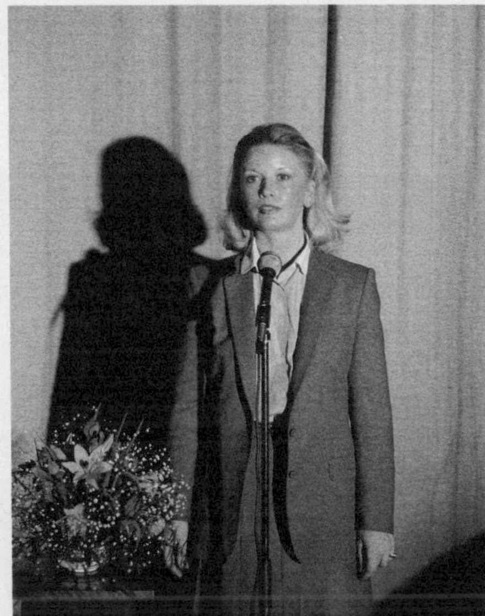

♫ – Sprechprobe – Szene aus dem gleichnamigen Stück – Szene aus dem gleichnamigen Stück ________
_________________________ Sprechprobe – Szene aus dem gleichnamigen Stück – Szene aus dem gleich-
namigen Stück – Szene aus dem gleichnamigen Stück _______________________________________
____
____ Sprechprobe – Szene aus dem gleichnamigen Stück –
Szene aus dem gleichnamigen Stück – Szene aus dem gleichnamigen Stück ________________________
____ Sprech-
probe – Szene aus dem gleichnamigen Stück ____
____
_______________________________________ Sprechprobe – Sprechprobe – Szene aus dem gleich-
namigen Stück ______________________________ ♫ ____________________________________
____
____
_________ Szene aus dem gleichnamigen Stück

Situation ‚Eva Maria Illinger – Eva Maria Illinger spricht' / Ausstellung ‚Szene aus dem gleichnamigen Stück' /
Forum Stadtpark Graz, März 1981

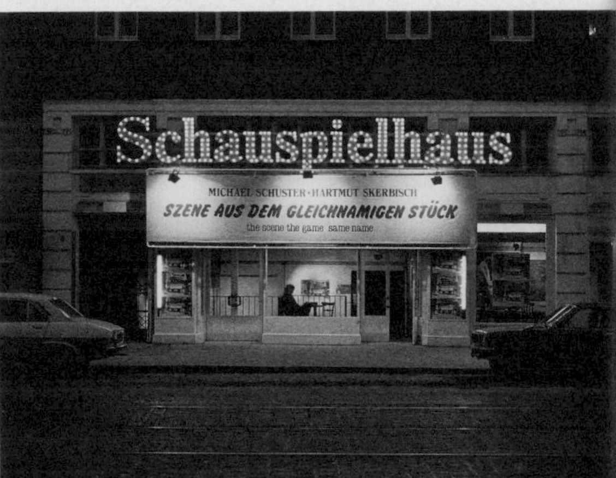

Situation ‚Szene aus dem gleichnamigen Stück' / Schauspielhaus Porzellangasse 19 Wien, Jänner 1981

SZENE AUS DEM GLEICHNAMIGEN STÜCK

Augenscheinlich könnten wir davon erfahren durch ein fotografisches Bild oder diese Zeichen. Das Stück könnte im Schauspielhaus spielen und ‚Szene aus dem gleichnamigen Stück' heißen. Die Szene aus dem gleichnamigen Stück könnte ‚Kino-Ausgang' ‚Schauspielhaus' heißen. Das Stück könnte ‚Szene' heißen. Die Szene könnte die gedruckt wiedergegebene Erscheinung eines Diapositives sein. Das Stück das gespielt wird könnte die Welt sein. Das Stück könnte sein daß es fortlaufend als Szene aufgefaßt wird. Die Szene könnte die Erscheinung der Hausfassade sein. Das Stück könnte gerade jetzt spielen. Das Stück könnte um 5 h 04 eine fotografische Aufnahme lang gespielt haben. Das Stück könnte solange spielen wie das reproduzierte fotografische Bild hält. Das Stück könnte einen englischen Untertitel tragen. Das Stück könnte im Bewußtsein des Betrachters spielen. Das Stück könnte von Michael Schuster / Hartmut Skerbisch sein. Das Stück könnte von **Kodak** sein.

MICHAEL SCHUSTER, geb. 1956, lebt in Graz. Fotografische Konzepte / Dokumentarische Dialektstudie vom Fersental bis Garmisch-Partenkirchen / Phono, Photo, Film / in Zusammenarbeit mit Norbert Brunner / Präsentationen: Biennale für Grafik und visuelle Kunst, Wien 1979 / galerie H, 1980 u. a.

HARTMUT SKERBISCH, geb. 1945, lebt in Neuhof/Übelbach. Kommt über die fotografische Dokumentation seiner oft nur kurzfristig existierenden Arbeiten zu rein fotografischen Arbeiten: 12 x 4 Reproduktionen auf Cibachrome aus einer endlosen Serie, 1979 / Teile daraus präsentiert in der Ausstellung „Österreichische Künstlerfotografien 1965–80" Galerie Krinzinger/Nächst St. Stephan, Basel, New York, Innsbruck, Wien 1980 / Galerie Pakesch, Wien 1981 u. a.

Memories, Anete & Inga Humpe 1985

66

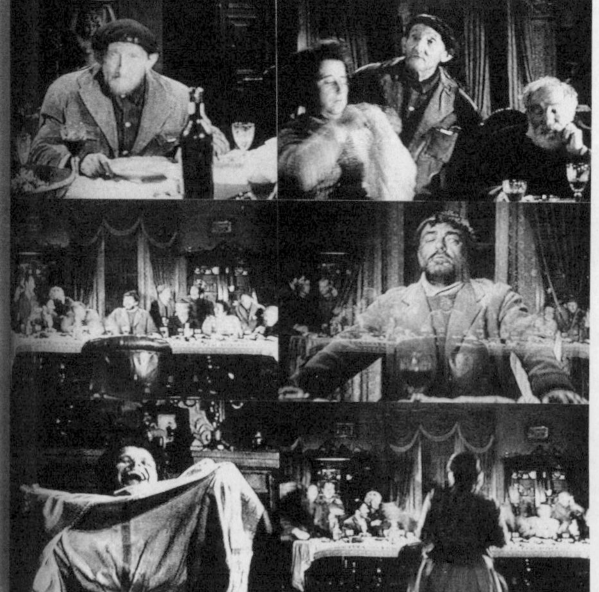

Mann A	Theresina.
Th.	Ja.
Mann A	Jetzt?
Th.	Jetzt!
Mann A	Ja. Theresina macht jetzt ein Foto von uns zur bleibenden Erinnerung.
Mann B	Mit welchem Apparat?
Th.	Mit dem den ich mitgekriegt hab.
Mann B	*lacht.*
Mann A	Ihr müßt alle auf die andere Seite. Na los. Ihr müßt auch rüber!
Th.	Los los, nicht so faul. Sonst mach ich keine Aufnahme von euch. Schneller, schneller!
Frau	Was soll denn der Quatsch!
Th.	Wenn ich sage 'Jetzt' bewegt sich keiner. Ruhe! *Hahn kräht. Theresina hebt den Rock. Gelächter.*
Th.	Ätsch, reingeflogen. *Gelächter.*

Man A	*Theresina.*
Th.	*Yes.*
Man A	*Now?*
Th.	*Now!*
Man A	*Right. Theresina will now take a photo of us, something to remember.*
Man B	*With what camera?*
Th.	*The one I was given.*
Man B	Laughs.
Man A	*You all must stand over there! Come on! You too, over there!*
Th.	*Come on, come on, move, or I won't take a picture of you. Hurry up!*
Woman	*What's all this nonsense?*
Th.	*When I say "now", don't move! Quiet!* Rooster crows. Theresina lifts her skirt. Laughter.
Th.	*Ha-ha, got you!* Laughter.

Bunuel/Viridiana 1h 11min 51sec to 1h 12min 57sec

68

69

Camera Austria International

1984   Presentation of Forum, exhibition review,
       Camera Austria International 14/1984
1987   Christian Wachter, artist contribution,
       Camera Austria International 23/1987
1988   Christian Wachter, "Über-Lebens-Energie,"
       artist contribution, *Camera Austria
       International* 28/1988
1997   Birgit Flos, "Lesearten und Spielformen,"
       text contribution/artist contribution,
       Camera Austria International 57–58/ 1997
2007   Michael Ponstingl, "Christian Wachter:
       Impressions D'AFRIQUE," book review,
       Camera Austria International 99/2007
2010   Ruth Sonderegger, "Impressions
       D'AFRIQUE. A Not At All Personal (Travel)
       Story," text contribution,
       Christian Wachter, artist contribution,
       Camera Austria International 111/2010
2012   "Christian Wachter: ABPOPA/AURORA,
       MUSA, Vienna," exhibition review,
       Camera Austria International 117/2012

Exhibitions

1984   *Wiener Porträts,* solo exhibition
       (with Gerhard Jurkovic, *–ich– ist ein anderes*)
1986   *Self-Images / World-Images,* exhibition
       participation
1987   *Fotografie in Österreich,* Museum Folkwang,
       Essen (DE), exhibition participation
1988   *Über–Lebens–Energie,* exhibition
       participation
1988   Photographies, Gemeindhaus, in conjunction
       with *Über-Lebens-Energie,* solo exhibition
1988   results of the photo workshop "Über-
       Lebens-Energie," station, Neuberg/Mürz,
       exhibition participation
1989   *Stadtpark Eins,* Kunsthaus Zug, Zug (CH),
       exhibition participation
1990   *ABPOPA/AURORA*, solo exhibition

1993   *Forum Stadtpark Graz, Austria,* Museum
       des Zentrums für Volkskunst, Kharkiv (UA),
       exhibition participation
1995   *Netz und Knoten,* solo exhibition (with
       Yve Lomax, *Sometime(s)*)
1996   *Stadtpark Zwei,* Art Pavilion, Zagreb (HR),
       exhibition participation
1997   *Im Referenzmeer tauchen …,* solo exhibition
       (with Herwig Kempinger, *The World Is Half
       Night*)
2003   *Freundschaftsspiel,* exhibition participation
2010   *Impressions D'AFRIQUE,* solo exhibition
       (with Iosif Király, *Reconstructions*)

Publications

1989   Manfred Willmann, ed., *Stadtpark Eins,*
       Graz, Edition Camera Austria, 1989
1990   Christian Wachter, *ABPOPA / AURORA,*
       Graz, Edition Camera Austria, 1990
1997   Manfred Willmann, ed., *Stadtpark Zwei,*
       Graz, Edition Camera Austria, 1997

Workshop

1988   14–27 May 1988, Mürzzuschlag,
       in conjunction with *Über-Lebens-Energie*

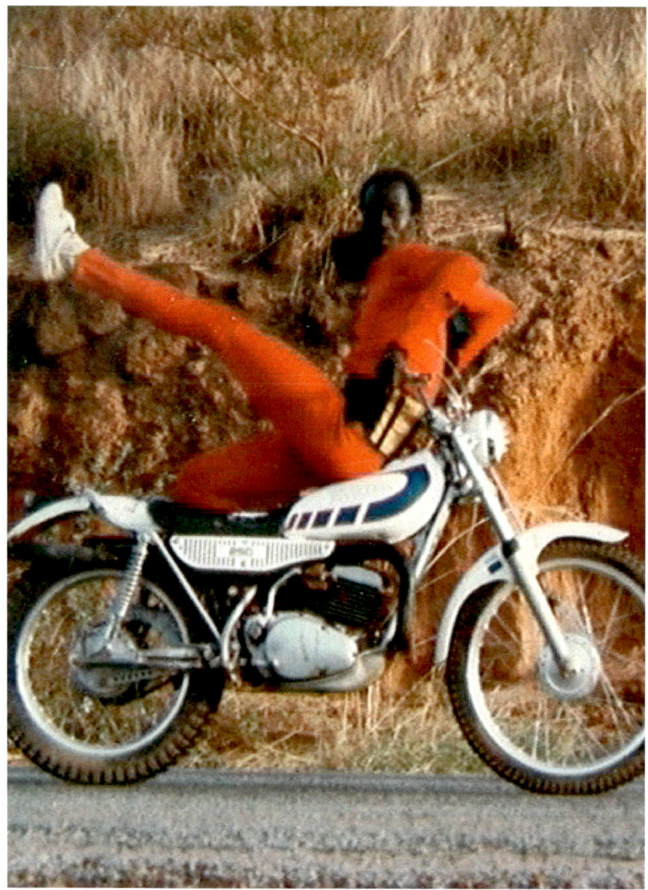
Burkina Faso, 1985 | 1999, DV-Band # 37 | 99, 01:02:57:00

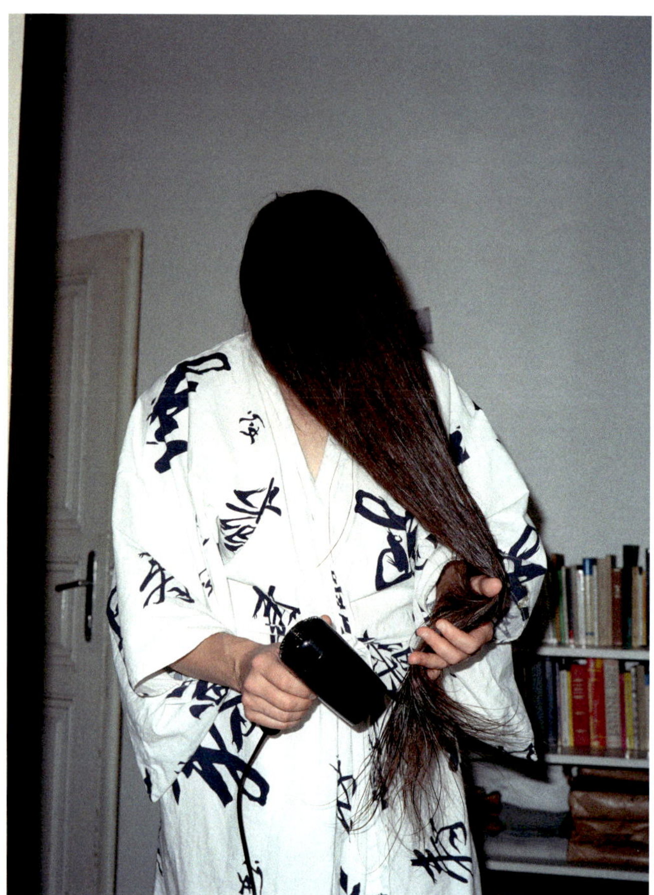
Wien, 2002

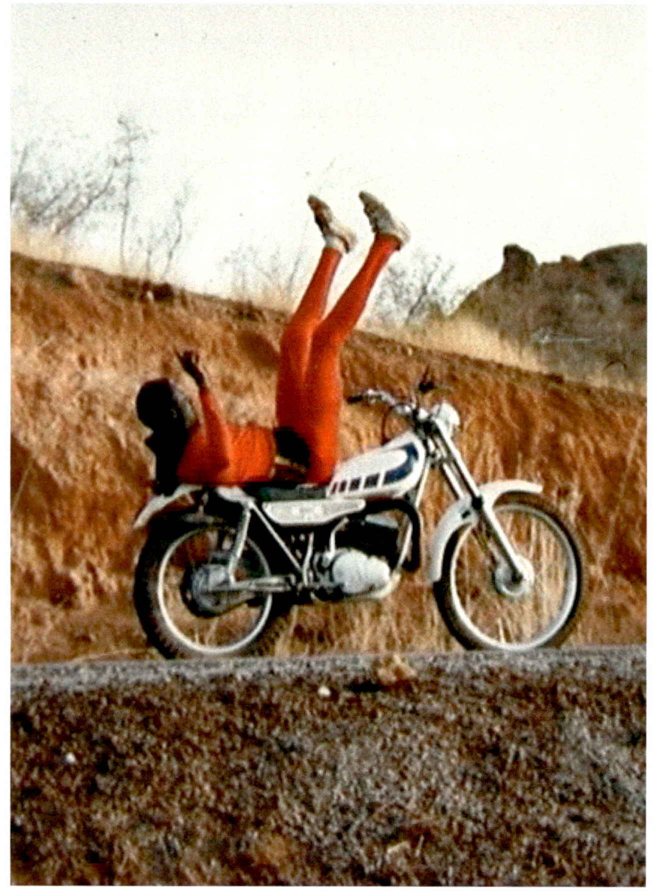
Burkina Faso, 1985 | 1999, DV-Band # 37 | 99, 01:03:04:00

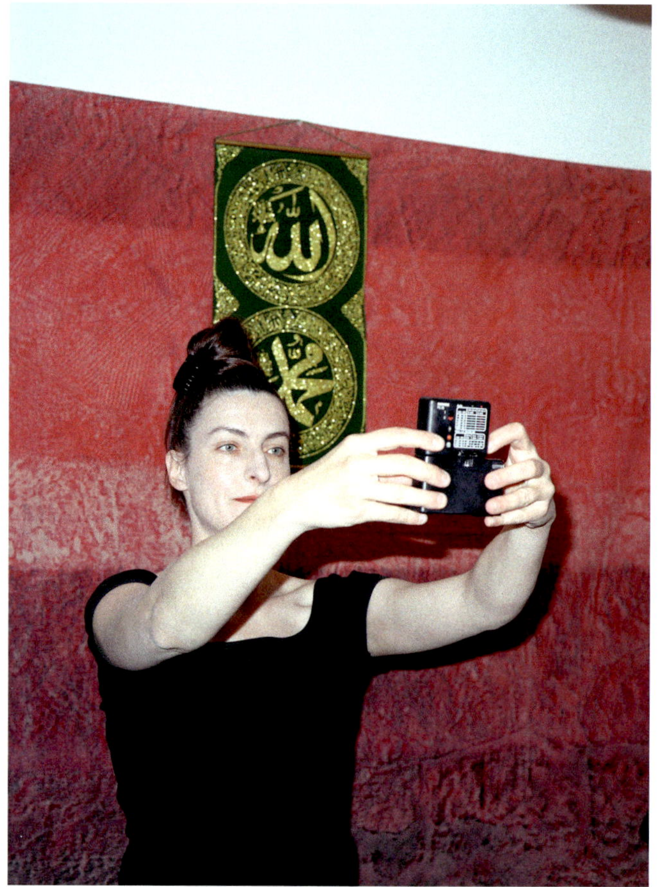
Paris, 2002

The Incomparables. From: *Impressions D'AFRIQUE,* 2006

Christian Wachter

Passage du Désir or "Is Modernity a Building Site?"

[…] When Claude is on form, he can still do a somersault with only the shortest of run-ups, almost from a stand. A couple of times he had talked about his time with the "Acrobates de Kadiogo" in the Burkina Faso of the 1980s, during the government of the revolutionary Marxist-Leninist president Thomas Sankara […] Nonetheless I was quite surprised when one afternoon in December 1999—we were back in Ouagadougou for his wedding with Tina—he handed me a package with small, yellowed, soiled photographs. I had no choice and no time. The only camera I had that allowed me to get up close enough was my video camera, and the repro work had to be completed before sundown. I like how these documents have undergone "pixelated-digital" degradation as a result, how this blends with their existing analogue, chemical-physical degradations. […]

In September 2001, after "nine eleven," with the general state of excitement also affecting our little lives, I once again felt the urge, after a long period of abstinence, to keep a "subjective" photographic chronicle. So I went out and bought a lightweight medium-format camera and, at first, I took photographs of everything and anything, and soon thereafter of Marianne too—with her tacit agreement, it seemed to me. […]

If you travel to Paris from Basel or Vienna by train, you arrive at Gare de l'Est. It's a terminus station, with the tracks ending there. But if you extend the tracks in a straight line on a map of the city and follow the line on foot through the station hall and out onto the forecourt towards the city centre, you come to Boulevard de Strasbourg. If you walk down the left-hand side of the street, you soon got past a shop with a tall, wide window. Behind it are spacious, brightly lit, immaculately clean rooms, white-tilted and whitewashed, separated by a narrow partition. One room is almost the perfect mirror-image of the other, as in a Rorschach test. In one room black women are seated in front of mirrors, having their frizzy hair washed and straightened by black stuff; in the other room, black men are having their hair cut or having a shave. It is a scene which repeats itself maybe a dozen times as you walk on (always straight ahead; don't turn into Passage du Désir!).

If it's early evening and the weather's nice, you'll see many black people standing around on the pavement in front of these windows, chatting, in groups, and not separated by gender as they are inside. And if you're with Marianne, you may well hear someone shout: "Belle coiffure, madame."

From there it's not far to the Théâtre Antoine, the venue of the outrageous performance of the dramatized adaption of Impressions d'Afrique. In 1912 the audience catcalled and booed, and only the small group around Apollinaire-Duchamp-Picabia … applauded enthusiastically (the photograph of Roussel up on stage, surrounded by the other actors, in a sailor suit, arms stoically folded across his chest.)

A little further on, at the métro station, you should finally turn off, to the right, at the Porte St. Denis, into the Boulevard de Bonne Nouvelle. At first it's slightly uphill and then slightly downhill, and then off to the right, into the little Rue de Mazagran. If the calendar now read 1934, we'd be able to call in on Michel Leiris in his room in the small hotel at No. 4, about to start work on his book on Rayxmond Roussel. He had been at the Théâtre Antoine in 1912, with his parents, at the age of eleven. […]

After his time with the "Acrobates de Kadigio" Claude was supposed to be sent to Cuba for his education and studies. Nothing came of it. There was another military coup in his homeland; his grandfather was released from prison, and rehabilitated. Instead of Havana Claude ended up in the Alsace and learnt another trade; he met Tina from Austria, and later married her, and through his diligence (and his French passport), soon found a good job in Vienna. He and Tina now have a son, and have found a nice flat in an old property in Vienna, on the ground floor, with shaded garden.

Paris/Basel/Vienna, September/October 2006

Excerpt from: Christian Wachter, "Passage du Désir or 'Is Modernity a Building Site?,'" in Impressions D'AFRIQUE, Salzburg: Fotohof edition, 2007, 161–181. Translation of the original German text by Stephen Grynwasser.

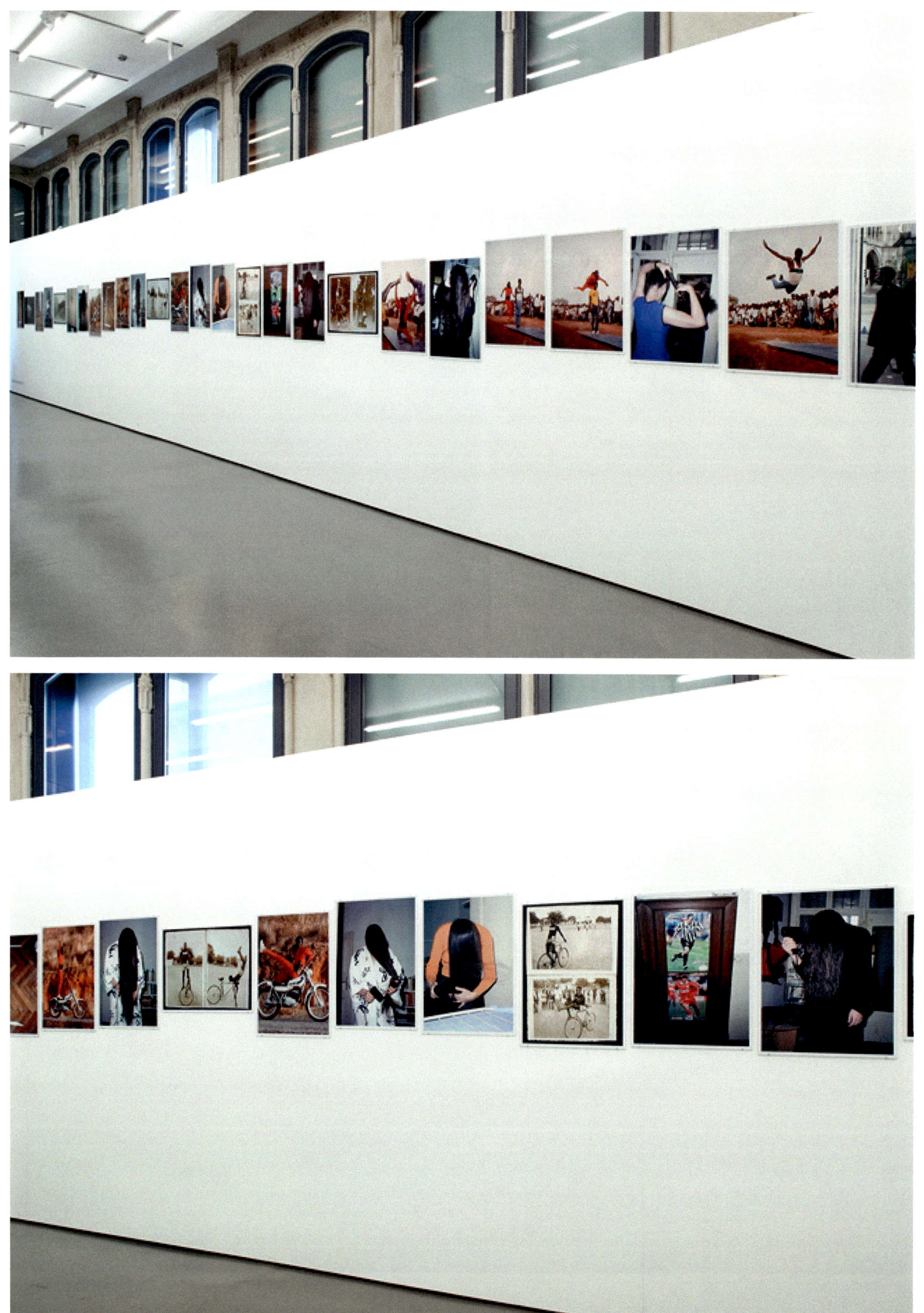

Christian Wachter, The Incomparables. From: *Impressions D'AFRIQUE* (Version 2010), Camera Austria, Graz (AT), 2010, exhibition view

Christian Wachter

Birgit Flos

LESARTEN UND SPIELFORMEN

Es gibt ein Kinderspiel, das mit einer eigenen Sprachform ritualisiert ist: Auf das Trottoir werden Rechtecke aufgezeichnet, die beispielsweise »Himmel« und »Hölle« bedeuten. In diesen Rechtecken müssen Geschicklichkeitsaufgaben bewältigt werden, Steine sind zu bewegen, erst mit beiden Beinen, dann mit nur einem Bein. Die schwierigste Aufgabe muß man mit geschlossenen Augen ausführen: Der Spieler, die Spielerin betritt die einzelnen Kreiderechtecke blind und fragt: »Bin ich?« Wenn sie oder er sicher in ein Kreiderechteck und auf keine der Linien getreten ist, kommt ein »Ja« als Antwort der Mitspielenden und es kann der nächste Schritt erfolgen. Bin ich?

Was sehe ich mit offenen und was mit geschlossenen Augen?

Christian Wachters Arbeiten sind damit befaßt, epistemologische Denkvorgänge sichtbar zu machen. Sie zeigen das Ausprobieren von Versuchsanordnungen, Skizzen des experimentellen Designs, nicht die Resultate. (Es gibt keinen abschließenden Forschungsbericht, sondern Material- und Konzeptpräsentationen, Aufforderungen zum Nachvollzug).

Wie arbeitet man mit »Fotografie nach der Fotografie«? Christian Wachters Thema sind Fragen der Wahrnehmung. Wenn er in eine Arbeit die Gleichung einbaut: *esse : percipi*, läuft im Rezipienten ein Assoziationsprogramm ab: Descartes' *cogito ergo sum*, das immer auch als: *ich zweifle, also bin ich* zu lesen ist; Ich nehme wahr, also bin ich – *esse : percipi*, beziehungsweise: Ich zeige, daß ich wahrnehme. Bin ich? Mit geschlossenen und mit offenen Augen.

Wenn Sprache und Fotografie zusammen montiert werden, vervielfältigen sich die Kombinationsmöglichkeiten der Lesarten in nicht mehr kontrollierbaren Potenzen. Das, was Wachter abbildet, auswählt, zusammenfügt, sind dazu oft bereits bearbeitete Konstrukte, zitierte Zeichen, vorgefertigte »Bilder«. Die Anzahl der Lesarten ist nicht endlich. Einige können vernachlässigt werden. Es ist schwer vorstellbar, daß er dem Realitätspotential dokumentarischer Abbildfotografie so trauen würde, daß er beispielsweise die Welt »nur« phänomenologisch darstellen würde. Die Differenz zwischen dem Abgebildeten und dem Abbild steht nicht im Vordergrund der Arbeiten, Wachter setzt diese Differenz als Arbeitskonstante voraus (das gleiche gilt für Strategien von Selbstreferenz, Dekonstruktion etc.). Er setzt sich Forschungsziele auf dem Gebiet der Kontextforschung. Einmal experimentiert er mit dem Assoziationsfeld, das den Namen »Aurora« umgibt (die Rosenfingrige? Ein Sprachbild, ein kyrillischer Schriftzug auf Matrosenmützen und anderen Marineutensilien). Er wählt historische Details aus und präsentiert sie in Rahmen, die gleichzeitig Teil an Konstruktivismuskonnotationen und an Nostalgiebedürfnissen des persönlichen Foto-Herrgottswinkels haben.

Das ist bezeichnend für die frühe Arbeitsweise Wachters: Er sammelt, collagiert, inszeniert ein Projekt über das Phänomen Erinnerung und reflektiert auch historische Präsentationsformen dieses Phänomens. Und er konstruiert mit fotografischen Methoden virtuelle Realitäten, die das Begriffsfeld zusätzlich befragen und durch ästhetische Entscheidungen deuten. Er spielt mit den Konzepten. Trotz all dieser vermeintlichen Verweigerungsstrategien (endgültige Aussagen zu machen), die ihn im extremsten Fall im *en-abyme* des Prozeßhaften und des immer weiter Hinterfragens (Schicht um Schicht) paralysieren könnten, produziert er Bilder, produziert er mit seiner ästhetischen Praxis Bild-Objekte, legt also Resultate vor. Das Abbild ist bei ihm Gedanken-/Bildkonstruktion, die in anderen Erfahrungs- und Denkvorgängen mögliche Referenten hat und nicht notwendigerweise in einer Erfahrungs- oder Objektrealität. Bei »Aurora« geht es um die Darstellung eines kognitiven Feldes, die Forschungsarbeiten bleiben noch relativ nah an den Bildvorgaben: Schiff, Russische Revolution etc. In seinem Projekt »Europe« entfernt sich

WAYS OF READING AND FORMS OF PLAYING

There is a children's game which works with its own ritualized language patterns: chalksquares are drawn on the sidewalk which may signify »Heaven« or »Hell«. Various skills have to be accomplished within these squares, one task is to move a stone, another one to do it standing on one leg only. The most difficult task is to be performed with one's eyes closed. The player enters the chalk square with his or her eyes closed and has to ask the others: »Am I?« If the player did stay within the lines and had not touched them with his/her feet, the answer of the other players is »yes« and he/she is allowed to make the next step. Am I?

What do I see with my eyes open, what do I see with my eyes closed?

Christian Wachter's works deal with the visualization of epistemological thought processes. They try out different research settings, they show sketches of experimental design but no definitive findings. (There are no final results, only the presentation of different materials and concepts and a general call for personal verification.)

How to work with »photography after photography«? Christian Wachter is concerned with questions of perception. If he includes in one of his works the equation: esse: percipi, a film of associations may be running through the head of the viewer: Descartes' dictum cogito ergo sum, which always implies I doubt therefore I am; I perceive therefore I am – esse : percipi, it follows: I am demonstrating, that I perceive. Am I? With my eyes open or closed.

If language and photography are combined in a work of art, the possibilities of variations rise to a power which defies control. In additon, the imagery Wachter selects for representation mostly consists of visual or verbal constructs that have been already worked with. He may use signs as quotations as well as quote prefabricated »images«. The quantity of different ways of reading the material is infinite. Some readings may be neglected. It is hard to imagine him just trusting in the reality potential of documentary representational photography to a point, where he would depict the world »only« on a phenomenological level. Difference between the object and its representation is not a main issue of his work. Wachter presupposes this difference as a given working factor (the same holds true for strategies of selfreference, of deconstruction etc.). The research goals he is defining for his work are to be found in the field of context research. He may for instance experiment with the associative field surrounding the name »Aurora« (the »rosefingered«? a verbal image, a cyrillic logo on sailor's caps and other naval implements). He chooses historical details and puts them in wooden frames that take part in the context of constructivist connotations and at the same time in a nostalgic notion by having an altar of sorts with personal memory items.

This seems to be a typical approach for Wachter's earlier work. He is a collector, he arranges various items in a collage, he is producing a mise-en-scène with images of memory as phenomenon and at the same time he is concerned with the representation of prefabricated presentations of the same phenomenon. And he is constructing virtual realities with photographic means, which further explore the terms in question and search for an interpretation by performing aesthetic decisions. He approaches his topics with a playful attitude. In spite of all these avoidance strategies (avoiding to make definitive statements) which, taken to their extremes, might endanger him to be paralyzed in an en-abyme process of unendingly challenging and questioning (layer for layer), he is producing pictures, his aesthetic praxis is »in fact« producing picture objects. He is presenting results after all. Representation is thus a thought and image constructing process, the referents of which are to be found in mental operations rather than in the experience of object reality. While »Aurora« is the representation of a cognitive field, research is still rather close

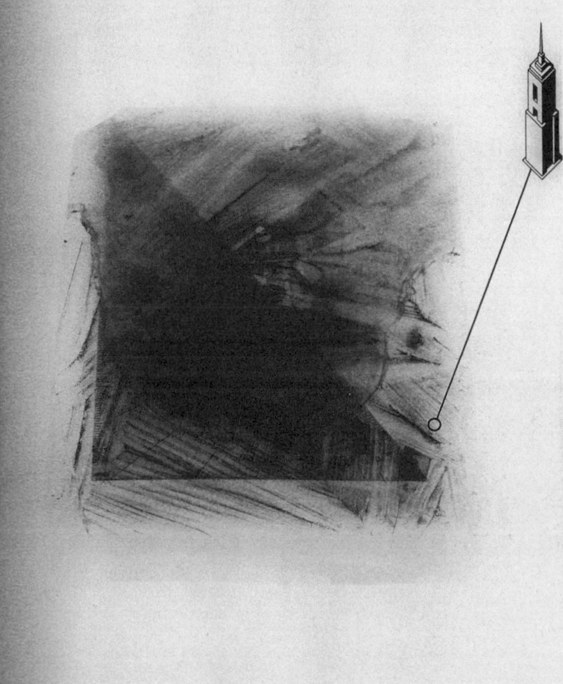

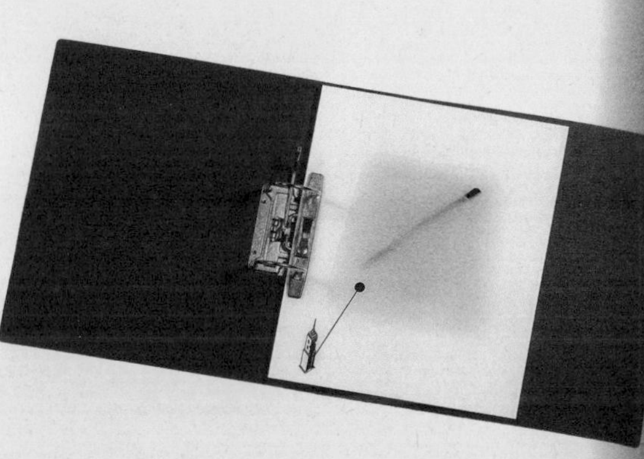

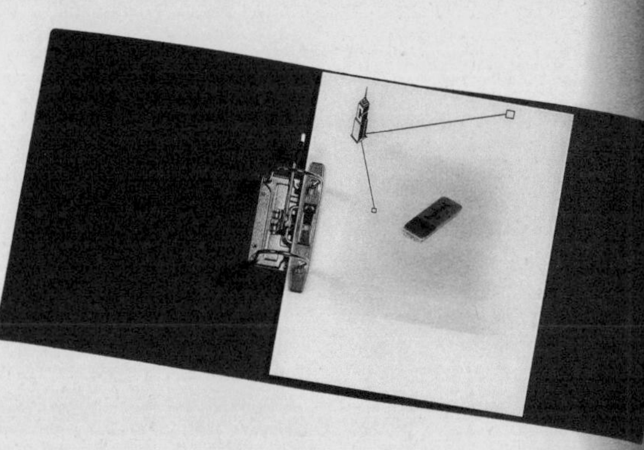

Seite/page 87 – 95:
CHRISTIAN WACHTER, Gefrorenes (aus der Werkgruppe »Netz und Knoten«)/Frozen Items (from the series »Net and Knots«), 1994/95. 16-teilig: 5 Leitzordner, jeweils 32 cm x 63 cm x 8 cm, 4 C-Prints und 1 Laserprint mit Letraset kaschiert auf Diasec, jeweils 30,5 cm x 24 cm; 11 Leitzordner, jeweils 63 cm x 32 cm x 8 cm, 11 Laserprints kaschiert auf Aluminium, jeweils 22,7 cm x 29,7 cm (19,5 cm x 29,7 cm Printgröße) und 59 Xeroxkopien, jeweils 21 cm x 29,7 cm (mit dem Text »Glasarchitektur« von Paul Scheerbart)/16 parts: 5 ring binders, each 32 cm x 63 cm x 8 cm, 4 c-prints and 1 laser print mounted on Diasec with Letraset, each 30,5 cm x 24 cm; 11 ring binders, each 63 cm x 32 cm x 8 cm, 11 laser prints mounted on aluminium, each 22,7 cm x 29,7 cm (print size: 19,5 cm x 29,7 cm) and 59 xerox copies, each 21 cm x 29,7 cm (with the text »Glass Architecture by Paul Scheerbart).

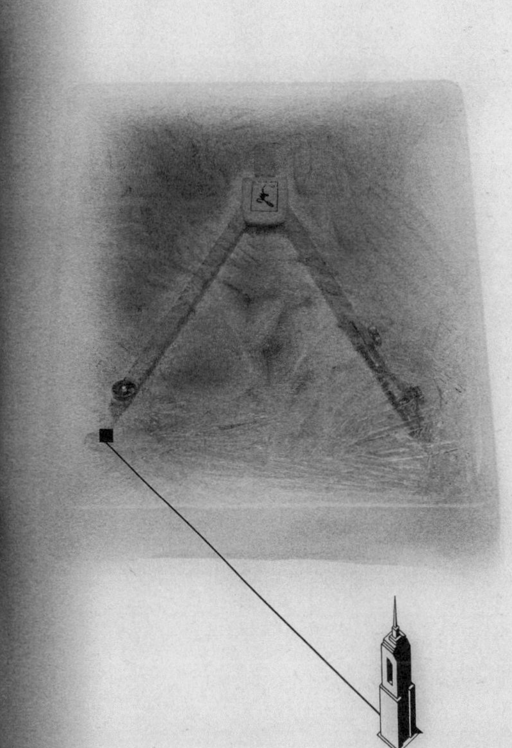

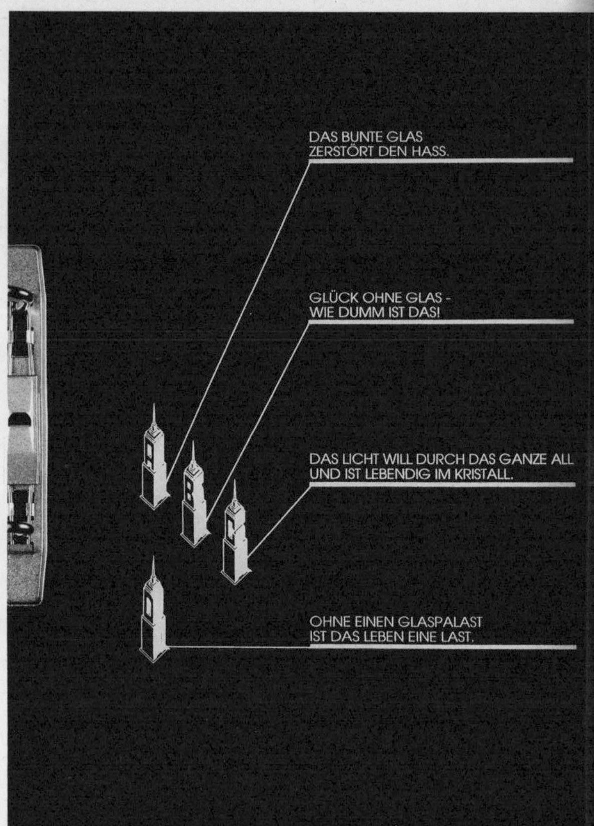

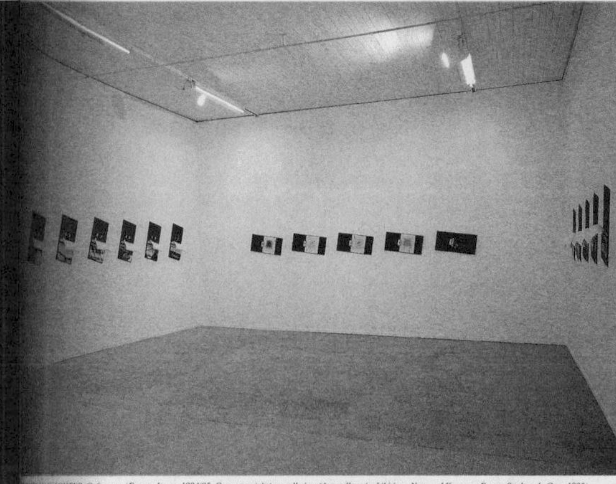

CHRISTIAN WACHTER, *Gefrorenes/Frozen Items. 1994/95. Gesamtansicht/overall view (Ausstellung/exhibition »Netz und Knoten«, Forum Stadtpark, Graz 1995).*

...Wachter weiter von solchen Vorgaben: Er formuliert selbst die Spielregeln für seine »ästhetische Rede« (Wachter): »'Europe' ist eine Konstruktion aus mehreren (formalen) Elementen: 1) Zahl/Statistik, 2) Sprache/Logos/Namen, 3) Typographie, 4) historische Formen wie jene der klassischen Vedute und jene – quasi historischen – der Dokumentarfotografie.« »Europe« ist ein Projekt, das topografischen Bezügen, imaginierten Verbindungen, einem »Netz-werk« von Gedanken verpflichtet war, bevor die Verwendung des Schlagbilds »Netz« inflationär überstrapaziert wurde.

Wachter präsentiert das vermeintlich Dokumentarische mit einem literarisch poetischen Gestus und die Unschärfen des subjektiven Ausdrucks eher dokumentarisch. Das macht den Zugang zu seinen Arbeiten »schwierig«. Erkenntnisse und Erfahrungsgewinne geschehen als Langzeit- und Prozeßeffekte, nicht punktuell als Aha-Erleb-nis, weil man etwa einen Zusammenhang plötzlich verstehen würde. Dies sind keine Rätselbilder: Es gibt keine Pointen, es werden keine Anekdoten erzählt.

Er fotografiert in seinen Versuchsanordnungen ein Ensemble, einen Vorgang, den er selbst als Autor/Künstler kontrolliert. (»Ab-tauchen ins Referenzmeer« scheint dafür ein passender Arbeitstitel, der auch die Gefahr mit anklingen läßt, die mit diesem grenzenlosen Unternehmen verbunden sein mag: das Versinken.)

Es gibt als konzeptuelle *permanents* Bezugspunkte zum narrativen Aspekt von Heisenbergs Unschärferelation (wenn Veränderung als wesentliches Element von Narration annehmbar ist), daß sich allein durch die Tatsache der Beobachtung die Forschungsobjekte vor unseren Augen wesentlich verändern. Davon ist in Wachters Arbeiten die Rede.

Die Werkgruppe »Netz und Knoten« besteht aus drei verschiede-nen Installationen: »Gefrorenes«, »Noli me tangere«, »Richard und Otto«. »Noli me tangere« ist eine Gruppe von gerahmten Bild-

given images: ship. Russian Revolution etc. In his project »Europe« Wachter is moving further away from such givens. He defines the rules for his »aesthetic speech« (Wachter) in the following way: »Europe is a construction that uses several (formal) elements: 1) figure/graphic, 2) language/logistics/names, 3) typography, 4) historical forms like those of the classical »vedutes« or those – quasi historical – of documentary photography«. With its topographic relations and its imagined links »Europe« is a project which worked with the idea of network before this term entered its inflationary phase of overuse.

Wachter is presenting the supposed documentary with a literary poetic gesture and the fuzziness of subjective expression in a rather documentary attitude. Access to his work may thus appear »difficult«. Insights and perceptive experiences develop and happen in the spectator as longterm processes and are not revealed in an »Eureka!« moment which offers the sudden intuitive understanding of the combination of various pieces. These are no visual riddles. There is no punch-line and no telling of anecdotes.

His strategy consists in photographing an ensemble, a process of which he as the author/artist is totally in control. (»Diving into the sea of references« – another Wachter project – seems to be an appropriate working title, also marking the possible dangers involved in this limitless endeavor: drowning by numbers).

There are nevertheless conceptual permanents which might be related to the narrative aspect in Heisenberg's notion of »Unschärferelation« (if one accepts the concept of change as element of the narrative process) that the very fact of observation and research changes the subject under investigation. These are the stories told in Wachter's works.

The workgroup »Netz und Knoten« (net and knots) 1995 consists of three different groups of work: »Geforenes« (frozen items), »Noli

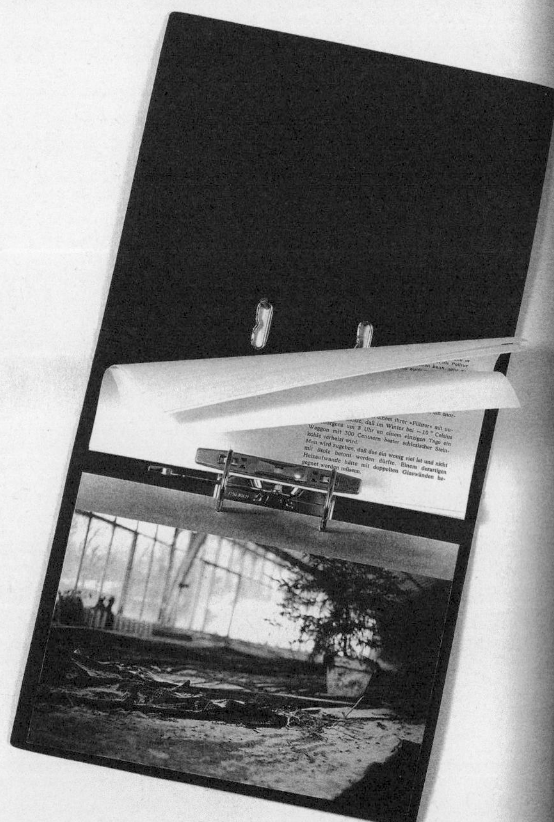

...versionen zum Verhältnis von Kognition und Sehen. Die schwarz-weißen Inszenierungen (aus Sprache, Zeichen, Fotografien) zeigen »scharfe«, überdeutliche, wohl definierte Wahrnehmungs-bedingungen. Aber Präzision und Fokussierung sagen mehr über die Methoden aus, mit denen Bedeutung konstruiert wird, als daß sie wiedererkennbare, illustrierbare Fakten darstellen. Die Klarheit scheint gemacht. Nur der Drehkopf des Stativs mit Glasplatte und eine Glühbirne sind Objekte, die affirmativ »einfach« abgebildet sind. Die Funktion eines Stativs ist beschreibbar: ein Werkzeug/Hilfsmittel der Fotografie zur Ruhigstellung des Blicks von Fotograf und Kamera während der Belichtung. Die Abbildung der Durchsichtigkeit einer Glasplatte zeigt neben einer filternden Materialverschiebung auf ein Dahinter: es ist schwarz. Aber es sind Fingerabdrücke auf dem Glas (noli me tangere), die das Medium Glas erst durch diese Störspuren sichtbar machen. Der Begriff Fotografie führt bekanntlich etymologisch auf das Malen mit Licht zurück. Die fotografische Darstellung der elektrischen Lichtquelle, der Glühbirne, mag wört-lich darauf verweisen. Von den anderen Komponenten kann man diese Anschaulichkeit nicht behaupten. Worauf bezieht sich die Fotografie eines alten Gemäldes, auf dem eine Frau ihre Augen in einer Schale vor sich her trägt und die aus dem Bild heraus den Betrachter direkt anschaut, mit zwei Augenpaaren also, von einem draußer sich selbst und von innen? Bin ich? Und immer befinden sich die Augen des Betrachters/der Betrachterin ebenfalls innerhalb der Blickkonstellation. Was geschieht zwischen dem Blick des Künstlers und dem Blick der Frau im Bild, die auf ihn zurückschaut – was nimmt man wahr, wenn man in sehende Augen sieht?

»Noli me tangere« (Berühre mich nicht) sind die Worte, die Jesus im Evangelium des Johannes an Maria Magdalena richtet, als er ihr auferstanden erscheint (Johannes, XX,17). Verschiedenste Überset-zungen in Methoden der Wahrnehmung tun sich auf (am offensicht-lichsten: Sehen ist Glauben). In diesem »Noli me tangere« ist auch die Warnung enthalten: Berühre mich nicht, sonst – verschwinde ich, ändre ich mich? Man könnte auch an diese Pflanze denken, die gedankenhaft »Kräutlein Rühr mich nicht an« heißt, deren Samen-kapseln explosionsartig zerbersten, wenn man sie nur leicht berührt. Wer spricht hier? Berühre mich nicht. Bleibt der Blick auf der Oberfläche, oder berührt der Blick, verändert, zerstört er? Es wäre verführerisch, sich den narrativen Linien, die in dieser Arbeit suggestiv angelegt sind, zu überlassen, als Projektionsfolie für eigene Gedankenkonstrukte. Ist das »Noli me tangere« eine Vorschreibung oder eine Feststellung? Hier ist eine andere mögliche Denkschiene: Die drei Wortkomponenten in dem computergenerierten Bildteil lassen sich syntaktisch am naheliegendsten so zusammen: Wahrneh-mung ist Tat. Aufmerksamkeit ist Tat. Sie konfirmieren den Betrach-ter an eine perzeptive Vorgabe. Auch die Inversion ist möglich: Ist Aufmerksamkeit Tat? Ist Wahrnehmung Tat? (Bedeutet Tat übrigens immer Aktion?) Vielleicht sollte man dem Drang der automatischen Satzbildung widerstehen, dann bleibt das Wortbild – Tat – in einem Schwebezustand als dynamisches Zeichen isoliert. Analogien führen in Sackgassen. Was ist mit der Unschärfe von Assoziationen, was ist mit Erinnerungen? In der Übersetzungsszene heißt es im Faust I zum ersten Satz der Genesis »Am Anfang war die Tat!« (und nicht »Am Anfang war das Wort«). Jede Wahrnehmung ist Übersetzung. Wenn jegliche Licht »bedeutet«, das mit Sehen konnotiert ist (ohne Licht

me tangere« and »Richard und Otto«. »Noli me tangere« is a group of framed pictorial compositions dealing with the relation of cognition and seeing. The black and white imagery (language, signs, photographs) reflects the representation of precise, »sharp«, well defined perceptive conditions. But precision and focus reveal more about methods of constructing meaning, than recognizable notions, knowable facts. The sharp edged clarity seems to be constructed. The only two objects which are represented in a rather traditional affirmative way are the mount/head of a tripod with a glass plate and a lightbulb. The function of a tripod can be defined: it is a tool used in photography to steady the photographer's/ the camera's glance during exposure. Representation of a glass plate's transparence should let us see something behind the glass, besides the shifting of materials due to the glass filter. There is nothing behind the glass, however: all is black. But one can see fingerprints on the glass (noli me tangere). It is only due to these irritating traces that the glass becomes visible. If one remembers that the term photography derives ethymologically from »painting with light« the photographic representation of the basic electric lightsource, the bulb, may be a rather literal reference to this fact. Nothing of the kind can be said about the other parts of the composition. What could be the legend of the photographic image of a painting, on which one sees a woman carrying her eyes on a plate in front of herself and who looks directly out of the picture into the spectator's eyes, – with two pairs of eyes, from outside of herself and from inside? Am I? Let us not forget that a third pair of eyes, that of the spectator, is always in the picture. What happens between the glance of the artist and the glance of the woman who looks back at him, what does one see if one is looking into seeing eyes?

»Noli me tangere« (do not touch me) are the words Jesus adressed to Mary Magdalen who sees him risen from the grave. (Ev. Johannes XX, 17) Various translations into methods of perception are possible: (the most obvious: seeing is believing). There is also a warning involved, beware, do no touch me – otherwise ... I disappear, I change? And there is also another association possible leading to an unobstrusive weed called – »Touch-me-not« – the seeds of which burst out in little explosions in case of touch. Who is talking? Don't touch me. Is the glance staying on the surface or does it touch, change, destroy? It would be a seductive thought to abandon oneself into these narrative lines, which have been suggestively laid out – freewheelingly activating a projectionscreen for subjective mental constructs. Is »Noli me tangere« merely a statement or an admonition? Another possible line of thought: Three words in the computer generated part of the composition may be syntactically linked: »Perception is (a) deed«. »Attentiveness is (a) deed«. These sentences form a perceptive program. The inversive mode is also possible: »Is perception/ attentiveness (a) deed?« (does German »Tat« necessarily translate into English-action«, by the way?) But perhaps one should resist any automatism to complete sentences. In this case there is just a wordimage – Tat/deed/action – arranged inside the graphic sign of a star, an isolated signal. Analogies tend to lead into deadend roads. What about the openess of memories and associations? In the translation scene at the beginning of Goethe's Faust I, the first sentence of Genesis is translated by Faust (every perception is a process of translation): »In the Beginning there was Action« (as

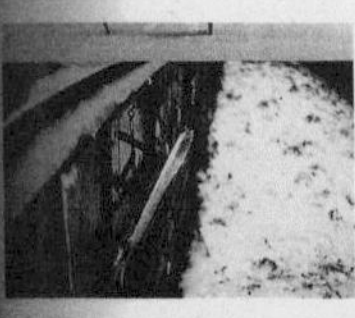
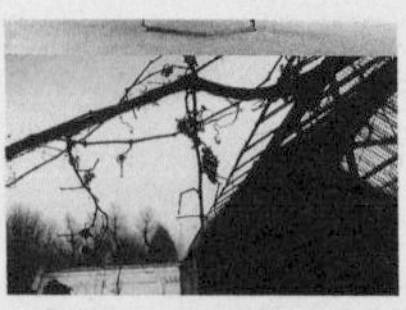
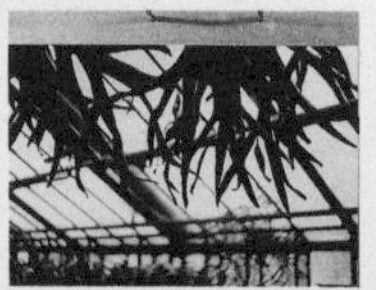

Picture &
Politics

David Goldblatt

Camera Austria Award

1995　Camera Austria Award for Contemporary Photography by the City of Graz

Participation at Symposion

1994　Symposion on Photography XV: "The Archive," lecturer

Camera Austria International

1994　David Goldblatt, "Die Struktur der Dinge hierzulande," text contribution / artist contribution and cover, *Camera Austria International* 46 / 1994

1995　David Goldblatt, "Das Archiv eines Südafrikaners," text contribution / artist contribution (journal of Symposion), *Camera Austria International* 51 – 52 / 1995

2002　Amanda Cuesta, "David Goldblatt: Fifty-one years," AXA Gallery, New York; MACBA, Barcelona; Centro Cultural de Belém, Lissabon; MoMA, Oxford, exhibition review, *Camera Austria International* 78 / 2002

2005　Sally Stein, "David Goldblatt: Fifty-one years," MACBA, Barcelona 2002; David Goldblatt: Particulars, Goodmam Gallery Editions, Johannesburg 2003, book review, *Camera Austria International* 90 / 2005

2007　David Goldblatt, "Dear Christine," text contribution, *Camera Austria International* 100 / 2007

2008　Rory Bester, "David Goldblatt: From Joburg, Goodman Gallery, Johannesburg," exhibition review, *Camera Austria International* 103 – 104 / 2008

2011　Kerstin Stremmel, "David Goldblatt: TJ 1948 – 2010, Fondation Henri Cartier-Bresson," exhibition review, *Camera Austria International* 113 / 2011

2011　"David Goldblatt: Looking at Our Structures," Reinhard Braun in conversation with David Goldblatt, text contribution, *Camera Austria International* 114 / 2011

Exhibitions

1994　*The Archive,* exhibition participation
2005　*Intersections,* solo exhibition

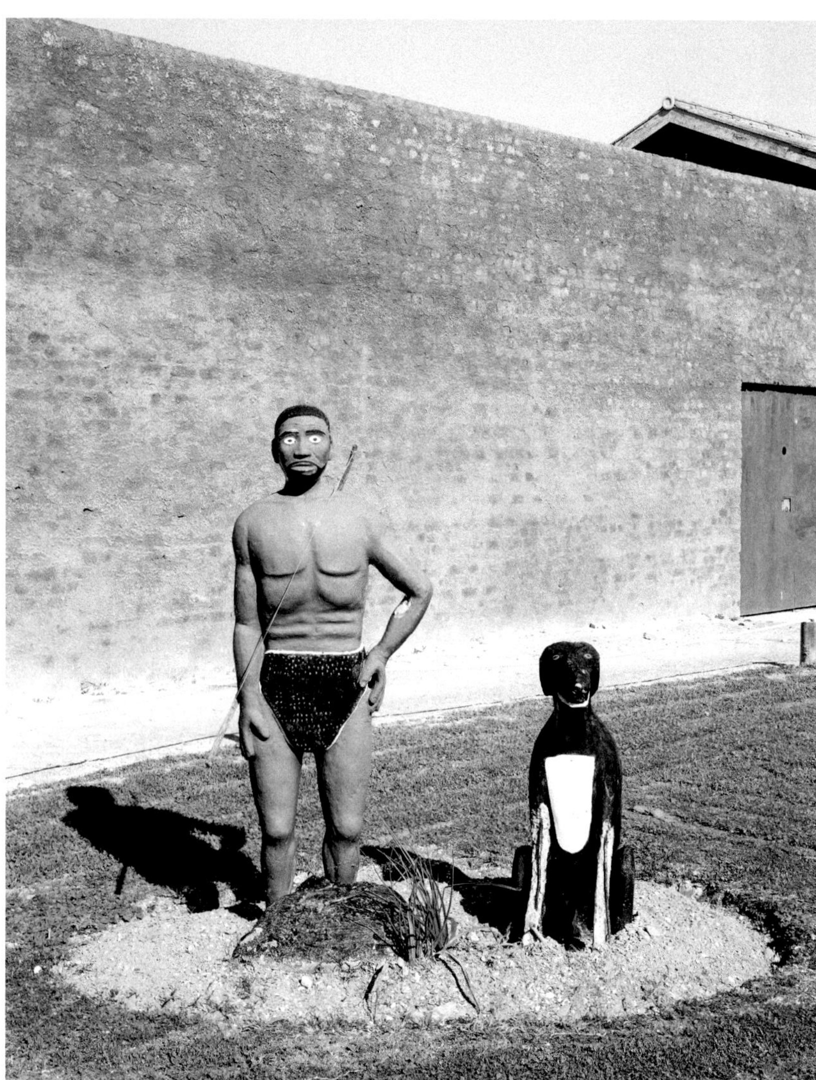

Sculpture by political prisoner Japhta Masemola, commemorating the first and the most recent political prisoners on "The Island," Robben Island, 16 July 1991, 1991

For many years political prisoners on Robben Island were subjected to conditions of punitive deprivation. Nonetheless, using every conceivable resource, they maintained a disciplined life and developed a rich culture. Japhta Masemula had a talent for making things from scraps of "nothing:" snares for hares and guinea fowl which supplemented prison diet; ingenious mousetraps; copies of a key to the prison's door, never discovered by the authorities; a life jacket for a planned escape and a model house, much admired by some warders but maliciously destroyed by others. It was partly angry reaction to this last event and partly the encouragement of an appreciative chief warder that led Masemula to sculpt this group. It commemorates the first political prisoner on the island, a Khoisan man held there in 1658 and, symbolically, through cellular underpants, the modern political prisoners. Masemula was arrested for sabotage in 1963. He died in a motor accident shortly after his release in 1989. The sculptures were destroyed by the prison authorities in 1992.

The Structures of Things Here

For the past ten years I have been photographing structures which gave expression to or were evidence of some of the forces that have shaped South African society. In particular I have been concerned with the structures of Afrikaner Christian nationalism and apartheid.

Apartheid was far more than simply a policy of enforced segregation. It was an ideological system of extraordinary complexity which deeply affected every aspect of like in South Africa. It was the tragic apotheosis of a peculiarly involuted development of Calvinism and Nationalism among Afrikaner people.

Innumerable structures—factories, houses, lavatories, government buildings, cemeteries, churches, monuments, lights, gates, roadways et al.—were erected to give effect to apartheid and to engender belief in the underlying value system of Afrikaner Christian nationalism. On the other hand, numerous and diverse structures—shacks, shops, houses, schools, mosques, churches, cemeteries, parks, monuments, signs and not a few ruins—bear witness to the profound effects of the ideology on the lives of South Africans and, in particular Black South Africans. The struggle merely to survive, as well as the struggle to resist and transcend apartheid is manifest in many of our structures.

The "zeitgeist" out of which these structures emerged and in which they had their meaning is rapidly dissipating while no distinctively post-apartheid landscape has yet taken shape. We are in the interregnum. Meanwhile, some of the structures I photographed have already disappeared or have been adapted to other uses. Many that survive are already becoming decontextualized relics, their ideological origins and meaning forgotten or mythologized. This is an appropriate time at which to look at some of the evidence of the era of White and, in particular, of Afrikaner domination and to attempt to see it in its context.

A book is planned consisting of a photographic essay with extended captions and an independent but complementary text by Marilyn Martin, architectural historian and director of the South African National Gallery in Cape Town. The text will explore structural forms and styles and the built environment in relation to our socio-political and cultural history. In particular, it will be concerned with the relationship between Afrikaner self-awareness and the development of "Afrikaner" structures from early "Cape Dutch" to the radical architecture of the extremely conservative Dutch Reformed Churches in the latter part of the 20th century. Developments in modes of building among African people, from the ancient corbelled stone hut to the sophisticated simplicity of plastic shelters in "illegal" squatter camps, to the people's parks, in the times of apartheid and revolution will be examined.

I know of no other attempt to bring together and examine these complexly interconnected matters either in photographs or in text.

In *Camera Austria International* 46/1996: 23.

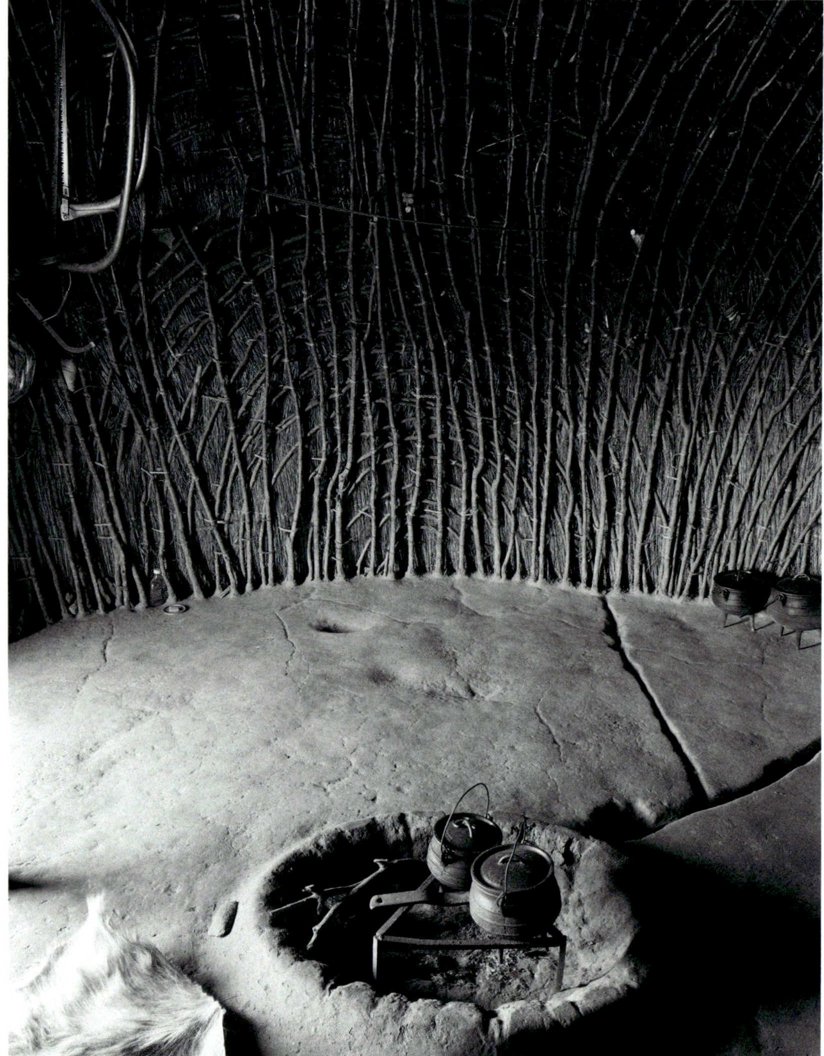

Interior of a beehive dwelling: the home of Mildred Nene, KwaCeza, KwaZulu.
31 July 1989, 1989

The home of Mildred Nene, two unmarried daughters, their three children and three other grandchildren. The hut took two months to build in 1987 from wood and grass brought on their heads by the three women. At 59 Nene did not yet qualify for a pension. Sometimes one of her seven children or the father of one of her grandchildren would send money. There was no other income. Adjacent to the hut was a rectangular room with a steel roof, the house of her son Isaac who worked in Durban and who came home for annual holidays. He sent her no money but would bring something on these visits. Near the hut was a byre for Isaac's two cows. Nene had some goats but they were stolen. She knew who took them but thought it best to keep quiet. People do not help each other, she said. The chief helps according to the size of the gift one gives him. Isaac sometimes wrote to her. What about? His chest, which gives him trouble. When asked if she ever wrote, she replied, "He knows my lift. I can't tell him anything."

NEDERDUITSE GEREFORMEERDE KERK (DUTCH REFORMED CHURCH),
Quelerina, Johannesburg, November 3, 1986.

In the face of international sanctions, rising Black resistance and the costs of enforcing apartheid, Afrikaner unity and hegemony were weakened in the seventies and eighties. The revolt of Black students in 1976 destroyed the acquiescence of Blacks in their oppression. The symbiotic relationship of the National Party, the State and the Dutch Reformed Churches, which had seemed almost monolithic, was broken. There was a great deal of self-questioning on the morality of apartheid and there were moves to soften it. As the world-wide revulsion against apartheid gathered force, the Afrikaner felt more isolated in the world and more misunderstood than ever before. He saw himself deserted, standing alone against communist ambitions in Southern Africa and defending law and order against increasingly radicalised revolutionary forces at home. Latterday Dutch Reformed Church architecture seems to reflect these changes. Churches became enclosing and inward-looking rather than outward thrusting. They have few windows in their outer walls. They suggest the fortress and the »laager«. Some, such as this one built in 1984, have become rounded rather than angular as though in quest of African shapes rather than those imposed upon Africa.

NEDERDUITSE GEREFORMEERDE KERK (NIEDERLÄNDISCHE REFORMIERTE KIRCHE),
Quelerina, Johannesburg, 3. November 1986.

Internationale Sanktionen, zunehmender Widerstand der schw[…] Bevölkerung und der hohe Preis, den die Durchsetzung der Apar[…] kostete, hat während der siebziger und achtziger Jahre Zusamm[…] und Hegemonie der Afrikaander geschwächt. Mit der 1976er Rev[…] der schwarzen Studenten war die Duldsamkeit der unterdrück[…] Schwarzen zu Ende. Das bis dahin beinahe monolithisch anmu[…] symbiotische Bündnis zwischen Nationalpartei, Staat und Niede[…] dischen Reformierten Kirchen wurde brüchig. Man begann si[…] fragen, ob Apartheid denn noch moralisch vertretbar sei, un[…] bildeten sich Bewegungen, die für eine Mäßigung der Apartheidpo[…] eintraten. In dem Maße, in dem die Welt diese Politik entschlos[…] ablehnte, fühlten sich die Afrikaander isolierter und weniger ver[…] den als je zuvor. Sie sahen sich alleingelassen gegenüber komm[…] stischen Ambitionen im Süden des Kontinents, als einsame Verte[…] ger von Gesetz und Ordnung gegenüber den zunehmend radikalisie[…] revolutionären Kräften im eigenen Land. Die jüngere Architektur[…] Niederländischen Reformkirchen erscheint wie ein Widerhall di[…] Veränderungen. Ihre Bauten vermitteln den Eindruck des […] schließens, des Nach-innen-Gekehrtseins, statt nach außen zu w[…] Die Außenwände werden nur von wenigen Fenstern durchbroch[…] Sie erinnern an Festungen oder Wagenburgen. Manche dieser an[…] sten eckigen Bauten sind rund geworden – etwa diese 1984 geb[…] Kirche –, als suchte man afrikanische Formen statt jener, die Af[…] aufgezwungen wurden.

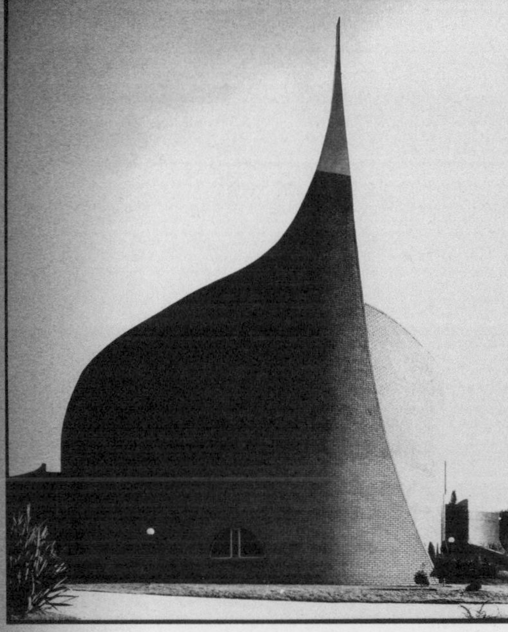

NEDERDUITSE GEREFORMEERDE KERK (DUTCH REFORMED CHURCH),
Op die Berg, Koue Bokkeveld, Cape Province, May 23, 1987.

In the nineteen forties, the extremely conservative Dutch Reformed Churches (DRC), began to build structures of increasingly radical modern design. They abandoned the Gothic which had inspired virtually all of their churches since the 17th century. It was the start of a surge of church-building that was to last for 50 years. More than thousand DR churches were built between 1940 and 1990, twice the number that existed in 1940 after 280 years of DRC activity in South Africa. This huge investment in radical architecture arose from the powerful and sustained fervour of the Christian Nationalism that gripped Afrikaners after the 1938 Voortrekker celebrations, which carried their Nationalist Party to power in the 1948 elections and which led them to create the apartheid republic. The Churches opposed atheism, communism, liberalism, humanism and racial miscegenation. They strongly propagated the ideology of Afrikaner Christian Nationalism and its radical core: apartheid. There was no paradox in conservative Calvinists building radically modern churches: they expressed precisely the spirit in which Afrikaners, with God's help, were taking control of their destiny.

NEDERDUITSE GEREFORMEERDE KERK (NIEDERLÄNDISCHE REFORMIERTE KIRCHE),
Op die Berg, Koue Bokkeveld, Kap Provinz, 23. Mai 1987.

Seit den vierziger Jahren dieses Jahrhunderts bauten di[…] konservativen Niederländischen Reformkirchen in einem S[…] zunehmend radikalerer Modernität. Die Gotik, die fast alle Ki[…] bauten seit dem 17. Jahrhundert beeinflußt hatte, wurde aufge[…] Es begann ein Kirchenbauboom, der fast 50 Jahre anhielt. V[…] bis 1990 wurden mehr als tausend Kirchen dieser Konfession[…] doppelt so viele, wie es bis dahin, nach 280-jährigem Wir[…] Niederländischen Reformkirchen in Südafrika gegeben hat[…] gewaltige Investition in radikale Architektur war Ausdru[…] machtvollen und andauernden christlichen Nationalismus[…] Afrikaander nach den 1938er Voortrekker-Gedenkfeiern erf[…] Wahlen des Jahres 1948 brachten dann die Nationalistische P[…] die Macht und führten zur Gründung der Apartheid-Repub[…] Kirchen leisteten Widerstand gegen Atheismus, Kommun[…] Liberalismus, Humanismus und Rassenvermischung. Sie tra[…] drücklich für die Ideologie des afrikaandischen chris[…] Nationalismus und deren radikale Essenz, die Apartheid, e[…] erzkonservative Calvinisten Kirchen von radikaler Modern[…] ten, war durchaus nicht paradox: Die Afrikaander nahmen, m[…] Hilfe, ihr eigenes Schicksal in die Hand, und ihre Bauten[…] Ausdruck dieses Geistes.

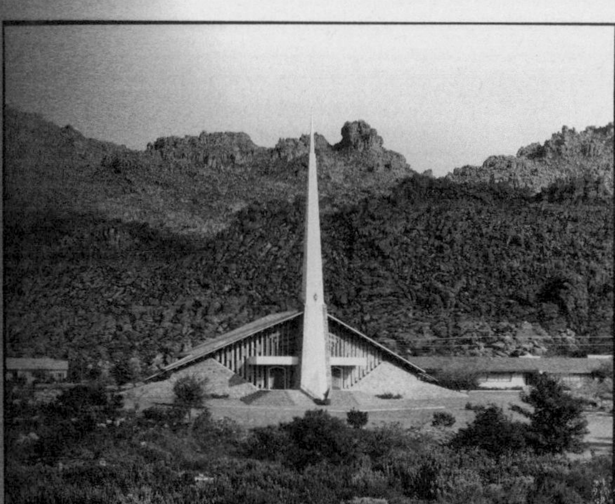

THE APOSTOLIC MULTIRACIAL CHURCH IN ZION OF SOUTH AFRICA,
Crossroads, Cape Town, October 11, 1984.

This church was part of a squatter community, which, for a time, was notable for its cohesiveness in the face of efforts by the state to destroy it. Desperately seeking escape from the destitution of the Transkei and Ciskei »homelands« and searching for work, many thousands of Africans poured into the Western Cape in open defiance of the Pass Laws. Most settled in squatter camps, the largest of which were Crossroads and KTC. Here, notwithstanding extremely harsh conditions, a community, with churches, shops, schools and civic groups emerged. But the huge sprawl, next to Cape Town's airport, was the antithesis of the apartheid planners' notions of »orderly development«. Furiously the government tried to reverse the tide. Year after year shacks were destroyed and people arrested, jailed and »endorsed out« of the region. When that failed, a new area, Khayelitsha, was demarcated for Africans. But few wanted to go there; it was much farther from the city. Meanwhile the camps were riven by power struggles between leaders. In 1986, supporters of one of these, with the apparent connivance of government security forces, attacked residents and torched their shacks. Seventy thousand people fled, many to Khayelitsha.

DIE APOSTOLISCHE MULTIRASSISCHE KIRCHE ZION VON SÜDAFRIKA,
Crossroads, Kapstadt, 11. Oktober 1984.

Diese Kirche gehörte einer Kommune von Landbesetzern, die aufgrund ihres starken Zusammenhalts angesichts staatlicher Angriffe von sich reden machte. Auf der Flucht vor der drückenden Armut den Homelands von Transkei und Ciskei und auf der Suche nach Arbeit drängten Tausende Schwarze, in offener Mißachtung staatlicher Reisebeschränkungen, in die westliche Kapregion. Die meisten ließen sich in Landbesetzerlagern nieder, deren größte Crossroads und KTC waren. Trotz härtester Lebensbedingungen entstanden in diesen Lagern Gemeinwesen mit Kirchen, Geschäften, Schulen und Bürgervertretungen. Die ausgedehnten Siedlungen rund um den Flughafen von Kapstadt waren jedoch genau das Gegenteil dessen, was sich die geistigen Väter der Apartheid unter einer »geordneten Landerschließung« vorgestellt hatten. Die Regierung versuchte mit allen Mitteln, die Einwandererflut einzudämmen. Jahr für Jahr wurden den Hütten abgerissen und ihre Bewohner festgenommen, zu Gefängnisstrafen verurteilt und ausgewiesen. Als diese Politik scheiterte, teilte man den Schwarzen als neues Siedlungsgebiet die Region Khayelitsha zu. Dort wollte allerdings kaum jemand hin – es lag wesentlich weiter von Kapstadt entfernt als vorhandene Siedlungen. Inzwischen brachen in diesen Siedlungen Machtkämpfe zwischen kommunalen Führern aus. 1986 attakierte einer von ihnen, offenbar mit Billigung der Sicherheitsbehörden, die Bewohner der Siedlung und steckte die Hütten in Brand. Siebzigtausend Menschen flohen, die meisten nach Khayelitsha.

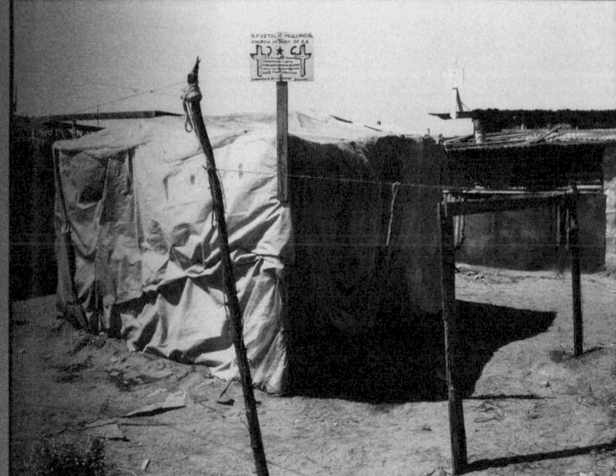

SCULPTURE OF A KHOISAN MAN IN »AERTEX« UNDERPANTS WITH DOG,
by PAC leader, Japhta Masemula in the maximum security prison for political prisoners,
Robben Island, July 16, 1991.

For many years political prisoners on Robben Island were subjected to conditions of punitive deprivation. Nonetheless, using every conceivable resource, they maintained a disciplined life and developed a rich culture. Japhta Masemula had a talent for making things from scraps of »nothing«: snares for hares and guinea fowl which supplemented prison diet; ingenious mousetraps; copies of a key to the prison's doors, never discovered by the authorities; a life jacket for a planned escape and a model house, much admired by some warders but maliciously destroyed by others. It was partly angry reaction to this last event and partly the encouragement of an appreciative chief warder that led Masemula to sculpt this group. It commemorates the first political prisoner on the island, a Khoisan man held there in 1658 and, symbolically, through cellular underpants, the modern political prisoners. Masemula was arrested for sabotage in 1963. He died in a motor accident shortly after his release in 1989. The sculptures were destroyed by the prison authorities in 1992. .

SKULPTUR VON JAPHTA MASEMULA,
PAC-Führer und politischer Häftling im Hochsicherheitsgefängnis Robben Island. Sie stellt einen Angehörigen des Khoisan-Stammes mit »Aertex«-Slip und Hund dar,
Robben Island, 16. Juli 1991.

Die politischen Häftlinge auf Robben Island wurden jahrelang schwere Entbehrungen ausgesetzt. Trotzdem führten sie, durch Ausnutzung selbst der geringsten Möglichkeiten, ein diszipliniertes Leben und entwickelten eine reichhaltige Kultur. Japhta Masemula hatte die Gabe, noch aus dem letzten Abfall etwas Brauchbares zu machen: Fangschlingen für Hasen und Vögel zur Ergänzung der Häftlingsrationen; geniale Mausefallen; einen Nachschlüssel zum Gefängnistor, den die Justizbeamten nie entdeckten; eine Schwimmweste für einen geplanten Fluchtversuch und ein Modellhaus, das manche Wärter sehr bewunderten, andere jedoch böswillig zerstörten. Die wütende Reaktion auf diesen Zwischenfall einerseits und der ermutigende Zuspruch eines leitenden Gefängnisbeamten andererseits regten Masemula an, diese Skulptur zu machen. Sie erinnert an den ersten politischen Gefangenen auf der Insel, einen Angehörigen des Khoisan-Stammes, der dort 1658 festgehalten wurde, und – durch den Slip, der Teil der heutigen Häftlingskleidung ist – an die politischen Gefangenen der Gegenwart. Masemula wurde 1963 wegen Sabotage inhaftiert. Er starb 1989 kurz nach seiner Entlassung durch einen Verkehrsunfall. Die Gefängnisbehörden zerstörten die Skulpturen 1992.

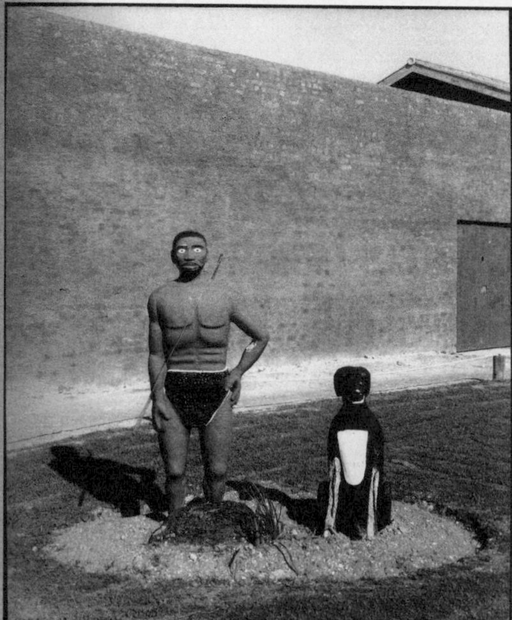

Participation at Symposion

1993   Symposion on Photography XIV, "WAR"

Camera Austria International

1994   Susan Meiselas, "Auf dem Weg nach Kurdistan," text contribution/artist contribution (journal of Symposion), *Camera Austria International* 47–48/1994

2004   Roy Exley, "Susan Meiselas – Carnival Strippers, Scout Gallery, London," exhibition review, *Camera Austria International* 86/2004

2006   Allan Sekula, "A Portable National Archive for a Stateless People: Susan Meiselas and the Kurds," text contribution, Susan Meiselas, "Kurdistan. In the Shadow of History," text contribution/artist contribution and cover, *Camera Austria International* 95/2006

2016   Verena Kuni, "Susan Meiselas: Carrying the Past, Forward, Fotografie Forum Frankfurt," exhibition review, *Camera Austria International* 134/2016

Susan Meiselas
Kurdistan

Today, "Kurdistan" does not exist on the map. Since
1918, the Kurds' homeland has remained divided
among Turkey, Iraq, Iran, Syria and what is now the
former U.S.S.R. In each country the Kurds have been
continuously threatened with either assimilation or
extermination. But as a place, Kurdistan exists in the
minds of more than twenty-five million Kurds, the
largest ethnic people in the world without a state of
its own.

From: *Kurdistan: In the Shadow of History,* 13.

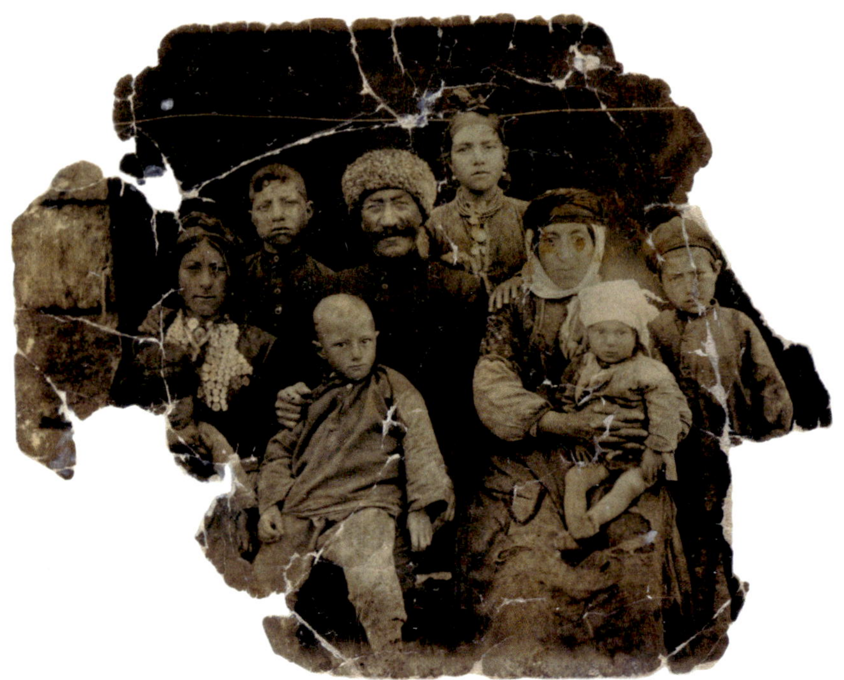

Saring Mahmoud with his family, n.d., Courtesy Akim Saringovich Farizian

From the project "Kurdistan," 1991–2008

Susan Meiselas

Allan Sekula
Atlas and Archive 2006

I recall visiting Susan Meiselas in New York while she was working on her Kurdistan book. At that moment she felt that nothing could be left out, that each and every image she had unearthed had unfathomed meaning for someone, and this demanded to be included in her archive of a stateless people. Her radical nominalism, that is, her reluctance to allow any one image to stand as a type for other images that were excluded was worthy of the utmost philosophical respect. The Kurds had been typed enough as a people. And her interest in building a provisional national archive from what were often literally buried fragments was itself the outcome of a continuing dialogic desire. She wanted to produce a book that would continue and broaden the conversations she had heard in blasted villages and refugee tents. In theory, no potential story should be thwarted by editorial selection or publisher's page counts. So we can think of this sequence: Stories–Photographs–Stories. The idea of dialogue sounds both hopeful and rather innocent. It is not always easy to convey how dangerous it has sometimes been to propose such a thing.

Later, in 1998, at the Rotterdam opening of Meiselas' "completed" Kurdistan project at what is now the Nederlands Foto Museum, an exiled Kurdish activist tells me that had he made a few more phone calls he could have had "10,000 people here for the show, in buses from Germany." Having already checked the galleries for bombs, the Dutch police are nervous about this promised opening-night blockbuster. In one vitrine we see a charred copy of Meiselas' book, retrieved from the ruins of a Kurdish cultural center in Brussels, torched by arsonists from the Turkish fascist Grey Wolves or else working with the Turkish secret police. Pragmatically Meiselas knew the project would die unborn if it aimed for the inclusivity of a telephone directory. We reached an impasse as we talked about and around this problem that afternoon in New York. Finally I suggested we take the subway uptown and walk over to see Gerhard Richter's *Atlas* at the Dia Foundation: "It won't provide any answers, but it will pose a few questions about inclusion and exclusion and the sheer mass of images in the work." And of course nothing could have been much further from Meiselas' own engagement with photojournalism, with history in the phenomenological intensity of its unpredictable unfolding.

Later, while she was still working on the book, she made an interesting comment, defending the specificity of documentary photography: "When you are working with evidence—say when you're digging up grave sites—you don't want people to think that it is conceptual art, an installation, or that it's just invented."

Richter and Meiselas: The painter's studio, on the one hand, as a philosophical ground from which to collect and view images of the world, of ones own work and ones own life in the provisionality of its remaking. And on the other hand, the photographer with a five-day visa, gazing down—not for the first time—into a mass grave and realizing that history has offered no clue for what she is seeing. Thus she begins, not with the images that already exist, that overwhelm us with familiarity and ennui, and can only be made strange by relentless categorization and repetition and judicious suspension of normative sharpness, but with the sense that where bodies are buried in secret there must also be a buried archive, limited in scope but immense nonetheless, waiting for resurrection. An archive, but not an atlas: the point here is not to take the world upon ones shoulders, but to crouch down to the earth, and dig.

This text was first published in *Camera Austria International* 95/2006, 11.

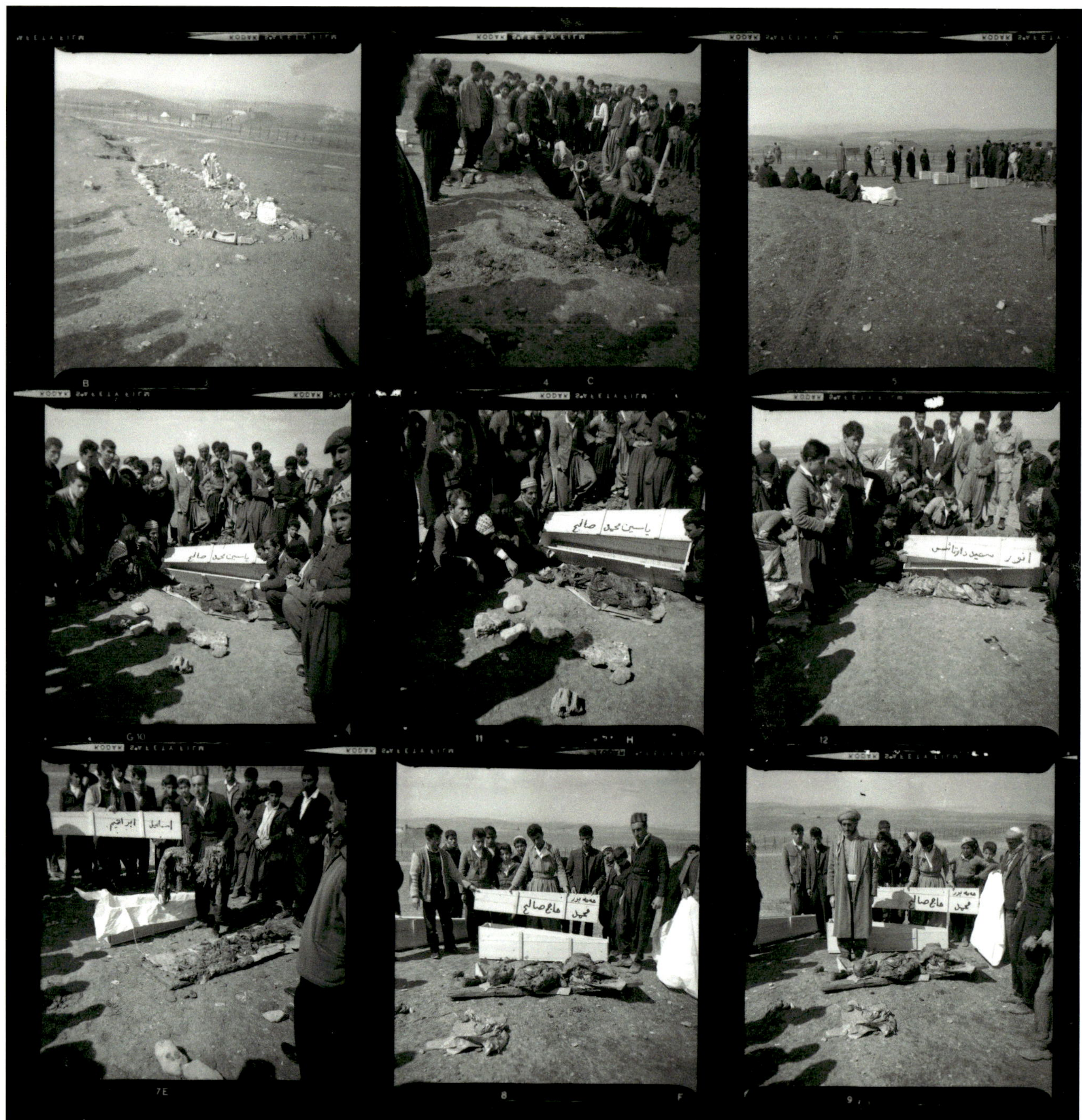

From the project "Kurdistan," 1991–2008,
exhumation, 1960s, courtesy Mamosta Ghafoor Amin Abdullah,
Sulaymaniyah, northern Iraq

LES KURDES

Ernest Chantre
French Anthropologist
Photographs by Captain Barry,
French Photographer

The Kurdish type I established after studying 332 individuals (62 women) can be summarized as follows:

The physiognomy of the Kurds breathes savagery: their characteristics are hard, their eyes, of a fierce brightness, are small and sunken under the orb. The men are most commonly dark, tall, and lean and have uncommon strength. They wear hardly anything except for a mustache and they cover their heads with a turban that is sometimes of gigantic proportions. Their step is firm, they hold their heads up with pride, and their look has a supreme arrogance. They do not laugh or talk much.

Ernest Chantre, Les Kurdes: Esquisse Historique et Ethnographique, 1897

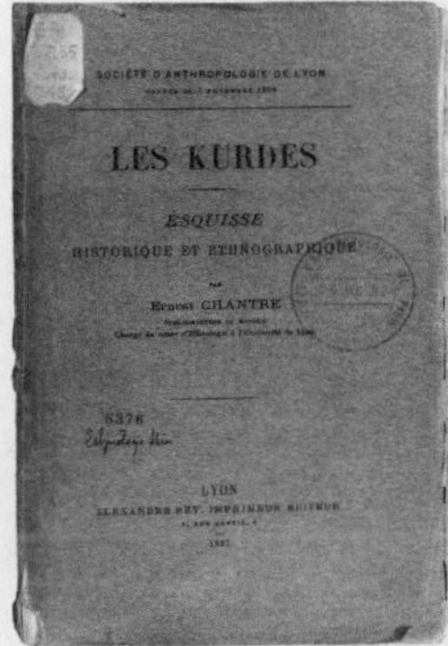

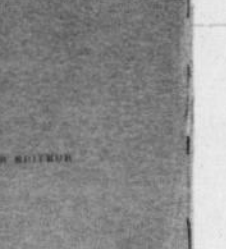

Courtesy Musée de l'Homme, Paris

"Examined from this point of view, these Aedii present a much more elongated oval than that found on the Armenians. . . . The forehead is large and slightly rounded; the frontal bumps are moderately pronounced even in male subjects."
—Ernest Chantre

Courtesy The Field Museum, Chicago

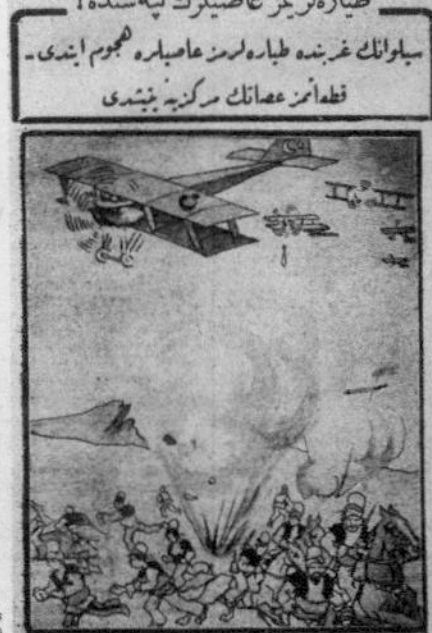

Kurdes Bourouki d'Airidja
Le Cheikh Abach et sa femme

Ernest Chantre, Missions Scientifiques en Transcaucasie, Asie Mineure et Syrie 1890–1894, Archives du Muséum d'Histoire Naturelle de Lyon, 6th Volume, 1895/Courtesy The Field Museum, Chicago

OTTOMAN EMPIRE

TURKISH KURDS

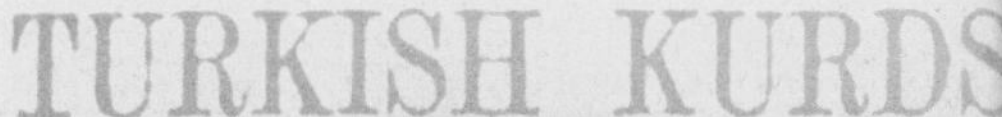

THE KURDISH REVOLT.

INSURGENT GAINS.

ABDUL HAMID'S SON AS KING.

(FROM OUR OWN CORRESPONDENT.)

CONSTANTINOPLE, Feb. 25.

The insurgent Kurds were reported yesterday to have occupied Kharput and Diarbekir el Azir and to have overrun Dersim and part of Mamuret. The insurgents have proclaimed one of Abdul Hamid's sons as King of Kurdistan. A state of siege has been proclaimed in Malatia, to the west of the Euphrates. Turkish airmen are bombing the insurgents, but pending the arrival of adequate forces no serious engagement is to be expected for a few days.

The Ghazi Pasha, Marshal Fevzi Pasha, the Chief of the General Staff, and General Kiazim Pasha, a former Minister for Defence, were present at a protracted meeting of the Cabinet, and the plan for the military campaign is said to be now completed.

At yesterday's meeting of the Popular Party no material new facts appear to have been brought to light. Fethi Bey, the Prime Minister, announced that fresh legislation would be introduced for treating as high treason the publishing of a newspaper or the making of a speech in which religion is used as a means for exciting popular sentiment, but he rejected the proposal to proclaim martial law in Constantinople. General Ismet Pasha was among those who spoke in support of the Government.

There is a general expectation that once the troops are in a position to attack the insurgents will soon be forced to surrender. But the period after the revolt has been stifled will be a very hard test for the Government. The universal tendency here is to impute the revolt to British instigation, and one newspaper this morning refuses to see the slightest trace of the existence of any Kurdish national movement either among the ignorant mountaineers or those educated Kurds who have given proofs of their attachment to Turkey, and therefore it ascribes the rebellion to ignorance and blind fanaticism, which must be annihilated at whatever sacrifice.

The Times, London, February 26, 1925

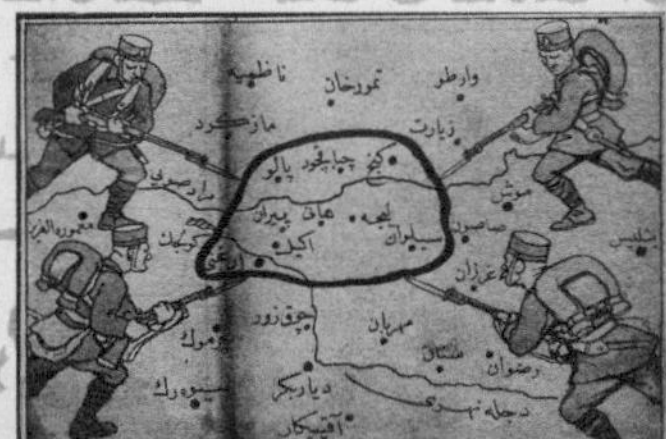

Turkish soldiers encircle Pirani, Egil, Hani, Lice, Silvan, Palu, Bingöl, and Genç, published in Cumhuriyet, a Turkish newspaper

Cumhuriyet, March 30, 1925

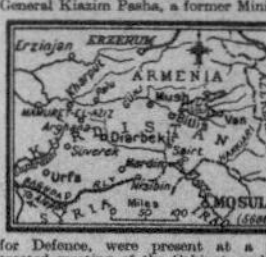

Diary of Events at Mezreh (Mamouret-el-Aziz)
(From a letter written by a European inhabitant of the town)

March 24 . . . Towards sunset sound of guns and firing of rifles and machine guns. The Vali in a car escorted by 25 mounted gendarmes fled. Soon afterwards 300 Kurds entered the town and proceeded to sack; first the Government House, and then the Department of Justice. They then opened the prison, and the prisoners showed the Kurds the houses of the officers and rich men so that the first could be made prisoners and the houses of the latter looted. In this looting the porters and wood-choppers of the town, mostly Kurds, also joined.

March 26 . . . During the day, the notables of the town tried to organise a militia amongst the population, but there was not much enthusiasm, for although most of the population was armed as it always is, they did not like to show their arms for fear of being disarmed by the rebels. However, one Hassin Bey an officer of the army managed to get some courage into the people and they eventually attacked the rebels; drove them out of the town leaving 50 dead; there were an equal number of casualties amongst the population.

March 28 . . . The Government at Angora sent its congratulations to the people and announced the early arrival of troops. Telegraphic communication which had been interrupted was reopened; but all telegrams were censored and letters had to be posted open.

British intelligence report
British Public Record Office
FO 371/10837/E2359

"Our planes are above the heads of the rebels" (top text)
"The rebels are scattered by our bombs" (bottom text)

Cumhuriyet, March 30, 1925

Since the government will not be able to admit its negligence, the explanation that the revolt was due to foreign intrigue and the forces of reaction will serve very well for dissemination through the medium of the press, of public speeches, etc. And by these means we can smother or threaten all the centers of reaction and paralyse the intrigues both of the opposition and of the foreigner.

British summary of Turkish press, March 2, 1925
British Public Record Office

"The Turk is a naked sword, Whoever crosses with him is cut apart"
Cumhuriyet, April 16, 1925

TURKEY

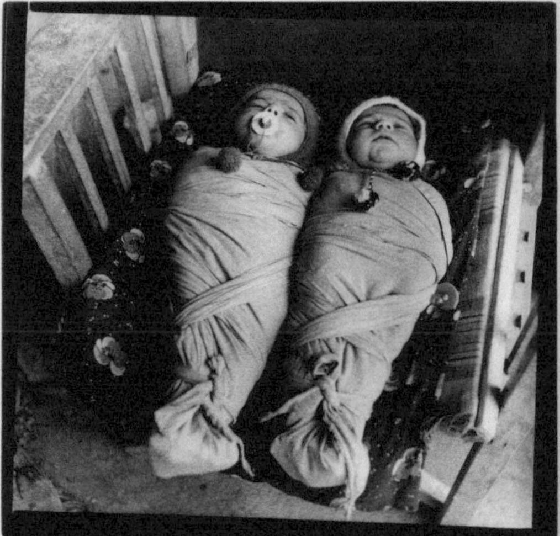

Infants swaddled in cradle, Rania

Jabar Abdulkarim Amin
Kurdish Photographer

The Iraqi police monitored shops selling three kinds of things—cassettes, photographs, and books. No one was allowed to sell a photograph or take a photograph that showed the tragedy of the Kurdish people. For example, a photographer in Sulaimania took a photograph of a poor baby with torn clothes and sold it as a postcard. The photographer was arrested for selling this photograph.

The government brought all the photographers to the secret police station of Sulaimania and ordered them to hand over all of their old negatives. We were called twice or three times a year, and they had very strict rules.

I never actually took photographs of the fighting in the mountains, but when the peshmerga took pictures they would send them to me and I would develop them. You cannot imagine how difficult life was here. We were developing the negatives for the peshmerga in the mountains at the same time that we were being watched.

In 1962, my cousin was imprisoned for ten days for carrying a photograph. In 1963, when I came to Rania, I gathered the most important photographs of the Kurdish leaders, about seventy of them, and put them in a ceramic pot and hid them outside. But when they built the road there, the photographs disappeared. I had another group inside the house, but as the Iraqi police were searching house to house, I was afraid that they would come and find the photographs with me, so I burned them.

Interview with Jabar Abdulkarim Amin, living in northern Iraq, May 1993

Sabry

Jabar Abdulkarim Amin

Most of the photographs that are left are portraits taken for official documents, such as passports, and family photographs. After the exodus I stopped taking photos. I didn't have any money, and there was no work to do. Now, I no longer have my shop. —Jabar Abdulkarim Amin

At first he did not wonder [...] why I was concerned about the Qazis since they had collaborated with the Soviets. I said that they were essentially nationalists [...] doing what they could for the betterment of their people, and the Soviets were the only ones interested in helping them [...] their execution, and in so [...] blamed by the Kurds, which [...] would be viewed with horror [...] Kurdish nationalists. He asked me what he should do about it, and I suggested that he ask the Shah to instruct Razmara to [...] bring the Qazis to Teheran for a fair and open trial.

The Ambassador asked [...] got an immediate appointment with the Shah. George [...] began by expressing a hope for the amelioration of tribal problems, including those of the Kurds; he then went on to say [...] while the Qazis had collaborated with the Soviets, they had done a lot for education—and the Shah interrupted him.

"Are you afraid I'm going to have them shot?" he asked with a smile. "If so, you can set your mind at rest. I am not."

The next day the Qazis had been hanged at dawn, "after the approval of his Imperial Majesty the Shahinshah."

One has to conclude that the Shah may have sent out the order as soon as our Ambassador had closed the door behind him.

Background illustration: William Eagleton, The Kurdish Republic of 1946

BARZANI TRIBE IN RUSSIA

Fugitives From Iraq Battled Armies of Three Countries

TEHERAN, June 19 (AP)—The Iranian War Ministry said tonight that the Barzani tribesmen who battled armies of three countries in a 200-mile trek from their homes in the Iraqi mountains had reached Russian territory.

The tribesmen had been chased out of Iraq for banditry. They crossed into Turkey, then went to Iran, where they engaged Iranian Army forces in the northwest corner of Iran within sight of the Turkish and Russian borders.

A War Ministry official said the band, estimated at 600 to 3,000 men, crossed the Araxis River five miles east of a point where the borders of the three countries meet. The tribesmen apparently swam the river and left much of their arms, equipment and pack animals behind, the official said.

The New York Times, June 20, 1947

«قاضی محمد»

Qazi Mohammad on the gallows, March 31, 1947.

In Mahabad and elsewhere hasty efforts were made by Kurdish officials to destroy all records, documents, and photographs. At the same time, individuals and families removed all traces of their involvement in the Kurdish movement by burning letters, commissions, and photographs of themselves, Qazi Mohammed and Stalin.

William Eagleton, The Kurdish Republic of 1946

These photographs were all clandestinely slipped to me by people who were trying to help me write something. But nobody talked openly about the days of Mahabad, publicly. All my investigations and interviews were done behind closed doors.

Walid Raad

Camera Austria Award

2005   Camera Austria Award for Contemporary
Photography by the City of Graz

Camera Austria International

2002   Walid Raad/Akram Zaatari, "Mapping Sitting,"
text contribution/artist contribution, *Camera
Austria International* 78/2002
The Atlas Group/Zeina Traboulsi/Walid Raad,
"Sweet Talk or Photographic Documents of
Beirut," text contribution/artist contribution,
Camera Austria International 80/2002
2006   Rainer Bellenbaum, "The Atlas Group (1989–
2004). A Project by Walid Raad, Hamburger
Bahnhof Museum für Gegenwart, Berlin,"
exhibition review, *Camera Austria
International* 96/2006
2010   Walid Raad, "Sweet Talk: Commissions
(Beirut)," text contribution/artist contribu-
tion, *Camera Austria International* 111/2010

Exhibition

2010   *Sweet Talk: Commissions (Beirut),*
solo exhibition

FAGACEAE

Trees with alternate leaves; separate ♂ and ♀ flowers on the same tree; ♂ flowers are in elongated catkins; small number of ♀ flowers; fruit is an acorn enveloped at base by scaled cupules. Economical interest.

▼ ▼ ▼ *Quercus calliprinos* Webb, **Karm-el-Mohr, > Ehden, Nahr Beirut, Aïn-Traz, Mlikh**. Common, various habitats. EMR.
Kermes oak. CHÊNE VERT. سنديان
Tree with prickly short teeth.

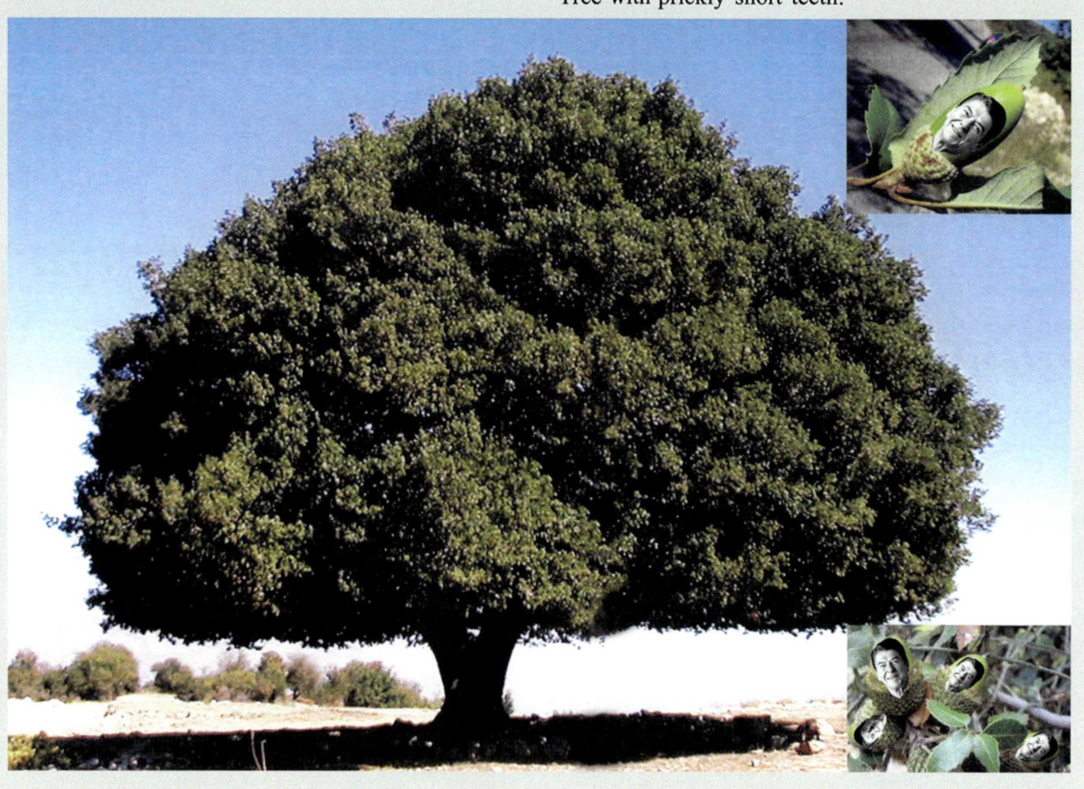

▼ *Quercus brantii look* (Ky) Mouterde, **Arz-Chouf**. Rocky ground, cedar's forest, localized. EMR.
Look's oak. CHÊNE DE LOOK. بلوط لوك

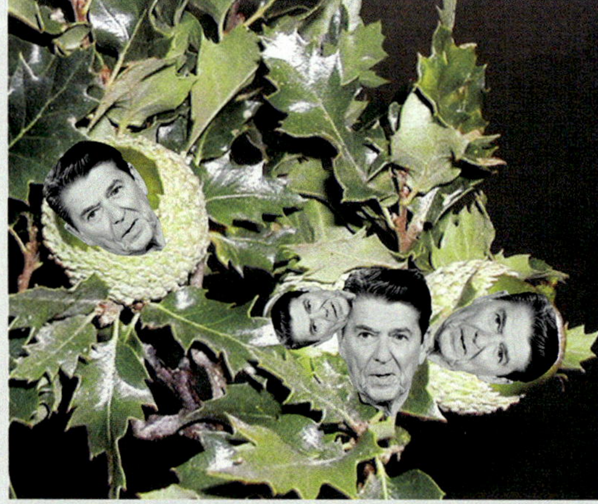

▼ *Quercus cedrorum* Ky **Horch-Ehden**. Forests. End (Leb+Tur).
Cedar oak. CHÊNE DES CÈDRES. بلوط الأرز

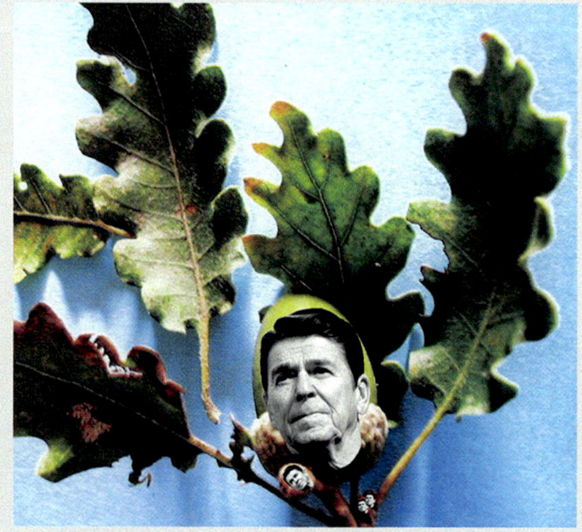

325

Walid Raad

Document title:	Better be watching the clouds
Category_File_Type_	[cat. A]_Hassoun_Logbook
Plates:	006–512
Date:	1992
Attributed to:	Fadwa Hassoun

The following plates were donated in 1992 to The Atlas Group by Fadwa Hassoun, a retired officer in the Lebanese Army. Throughout the 1970s and 1980s, Lebanon's Deuxième Bureau code-named local and international political and military leaders in the language of local flora. As a trained botanist, Hassoun's job was to assign the code names to the leaders. Hassoun kept track of all code names in a logbook where she collaged faces of the leaders onto flowers and trees. The plant's name became the politician's code name. As such, Hosni Mubarak became Dwarf Mallow; Mikhail Gorbachev, Purple Carline; Ronald Reagan, Kermes Oak; and Kamal Joumblatt, Pink Sorrell.

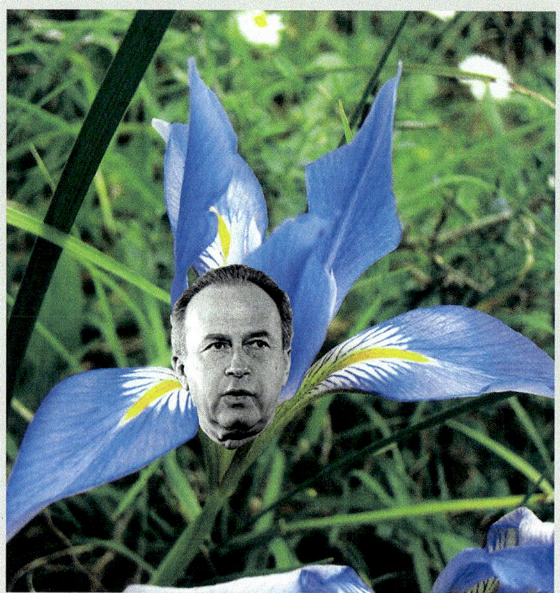

▲ *Iris unguicularis cretensis* (Janka) Mair. **Aandqet, Qoubaïyat, Akkar el-Aatiqa**. Woodland. EMR.
Cretan iris. IRIS DE CRÈTE. سوسن كريت

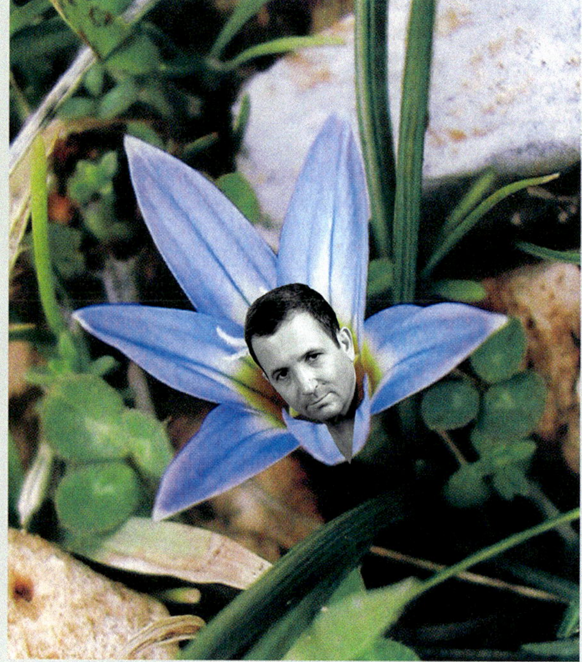

▲ *Romulea bulbocodium* (L.) Seb. & Mauri. **Sannine, Hamat, Qssaybeh, Aammiq, Kfarhouneh, Tawmat, Mlikh**. Various habitats.
Crocus-leaved romulea.
ROMULÉE BULBOCODE. حرسنة

▼ *Romulea columnae* Seb. & Mauri. **Bintael, <
Beit-Méri**. Woodland (altitude 550 m).
Sand crocus.
ROMULÉE DE COLUMNA. روملية الرمل
A rigid tunic, spitted, with 2 bracts, downy bract.

▼ *Iris westii* Dinsm. **Towmat Jezzine**. Rocky slopes.
End (Leb).
West's iris. IRIS DE WEST. سوسن وست

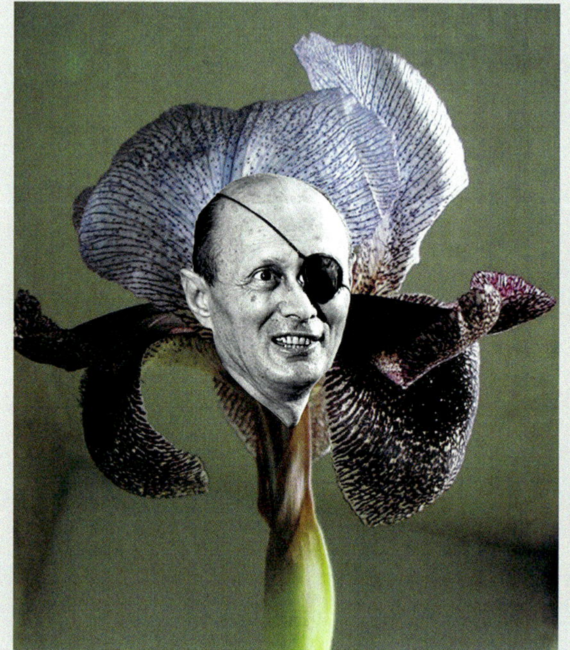

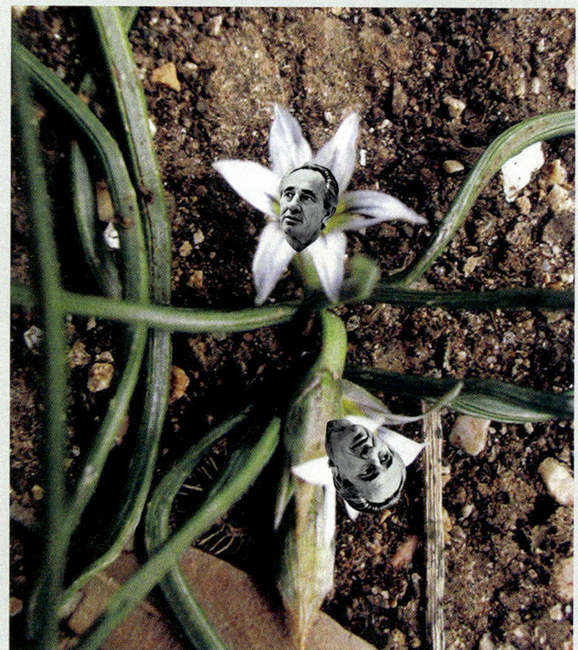

345

206

Hashem el Madani

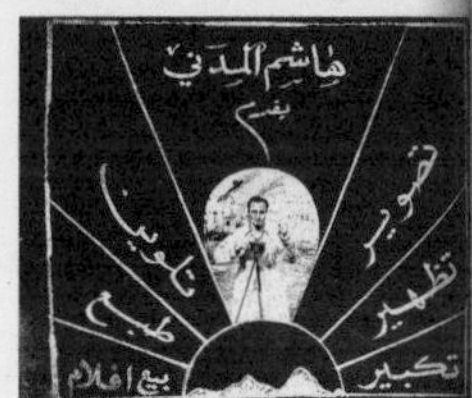

Announcement used by Hashem el Madani to promote Studio Shehrazade, with his self-portrait in the center.

PHOTOGRAPHY AS WORK

Every morning, I would take my camera and walk down the streets of the old city of Saida, where people called me to take photos of them. That was between 1948 and 1953, before I owned a studio. I walked through the souks of vegetables, shoemakers, carpenters, and textiles, then went down to the sea castle, the beach, and up until the land castle. I went as far as the orange fields outside city walls, the new bridge at Ain el-Helweh, the Bargout, Nabi Yahya, and even the Kinayat, the Eucalyptus trees by the river. Everywhere on my way, people asked me to come and take portraits of their families, since most of them did not own cameras.

I also went as far as the port area and the jetty, where people liked to be photographed. They would pose sitting or standing on the rocks, boarding on a sailboat or motorboat while it was docked. Sometimes I would go to the Zarraka pond, a natural pond with steps that continued under water. The men stood on the rocks ready to jump; they asked me to photograph them flexing, boxing, or wrestling. I would come back home around noon to have lunch and rest a little bit, before heading back to Hammam Badr (Badr beach), where the men went after work for leisure and sport.

While taking pictures, I made sure that figures filled the frame, then I adjusted the focus by measuring approximately the distance to the subject, which could not be done through the viewfinder of my Kodak Retina, manufactured in Germany. I processed the rolls in the evening at home, washed them, and went to the movies while waiting for the negatives to dry. I enlarged the prints and left them to dry until the next morning, when I would cut them and leave for another tour.

Sometimes on Sundays, I went to Damascus or the Cedars. I would cut the film stock out of 30 m bulk films, and measure each roll to equal one and a half dra'aa (arm length, which is a measuring unit used in textile retail business). I prepared 15 rolls for every out-of-city excursion, and only five for a typical city tour. I arranged my negatives in a metallic box, and labelled them according to the trips.

In the beginning, I would not ask for any money in advance when taking pictures. I was paid only after the client saw the photograph, and liked it. Ninety percent of the people used to buy their photos, while the rest of them turned them down for financial reasons. I sold 9 cm x 6 cm photographs for 25 Piasters; enlargements could be done upon special request. In the early fifties, I started making booklets with contact prints for every set of films and showing them to my clients before enlarging.

In the first year of my practice, I had no idea how to organize or classify my negatives. In the fifties I started numbering the metallic boxes, until the numbers reached 110 in the sixties (1962/63). I inscribed the number on every print as reference for future enlargements. In 1964, I was doing less outdoor photography, and started classifying my negatives every six months in one box, inscribing the dates on the cover.

Based on a series of interviews with Hashem el Madani, conducted by Akram Zaatari between 2000 – 2002.

Mapping Sitting

A project by Walid Raad and Akram Zaatari,
Fondation Arabe pour l'Image / FAI, Beirut.

In Mapping Sitting, we present geographically and culturally specific photographic works that raise questions about portraiture, performance, photography and identity in general. We proceed from the proliferation of portrait photographic practices in the Arab world in the early to mid-20th century such as passport studio photographs, institutional group portrait photographs, surprise photographs and itinerant portrait photographs by itinerant photographers to ask how the photographic portrait functioned in the Arab world as a commodity, luxury item, an adornment, as a description of individuals and groups, and as the inscription of social identities. We proceed from the thesis that the photographic practices in question are symptomatic of an evolving capitalist organization of labor and its products and established conventions of iconic representation. We also propose that these practices were not only reflective but also productive of notions of work, leisure, play, citizenship, community, and individuality.

MAPPING SITTING

Ein Projekt von Walid Raad und Akram Zaatari, Fondation Arabe pour l'Image / FAI, Beirut.

In Mapping Sitting präsentieren wir geografisch und kulturell spezifische Fotoarbeiten, die Fragen der Porträtkunst, Performance, Fotografie und Identität aufwerfen. Ausgehend von der Blüte porträtfotografischer Praktiken in der arabischen Welt von Anfang bis zur Mitte des 20. Jahrhunderts wie z. B. Atelier-Passfotos, institutionelle Gruppenporträts, Überraschungsfotos und Straßen-Porträtfotos von Wanderfotografen fragen wir, welche Rolle das fotografische Porträt in der arabischen Welt als Ware, Luxusartikel, Ziergegenstand, Beschreibung von Individuen und Gruppen sowie zur Einschreibung sozialer Identitäten gespielt hat. Unsere These lautet, dass besagte fotografische Praktiken symptomatisch für eine entstehende kapitalistische Organisation der Arbeit und ihrer Produkte sowie etablierter Konventionen ikonischer Repräsentation sind. Zudem unterstellen wir, dass diese Praktiken neue Auffassungen von Arbeit, Freizeit, Spiel, Bürgerschaft, Gemeinschaft und Individualität nicht nur widerspiegelten, sondern auch hervorbrachten.

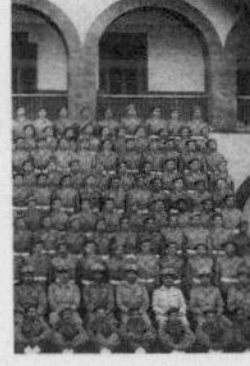 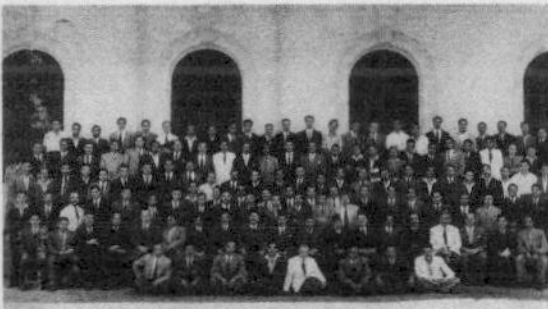 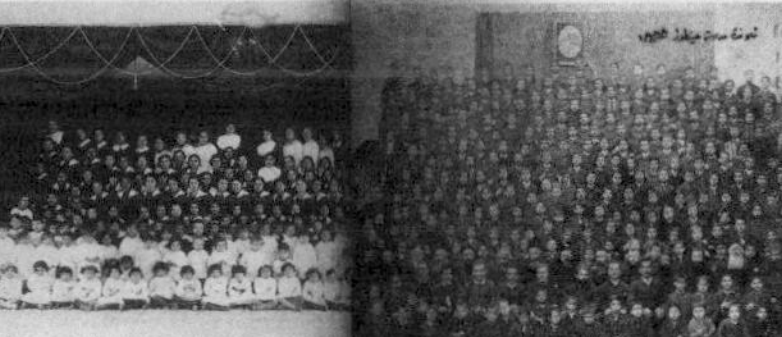 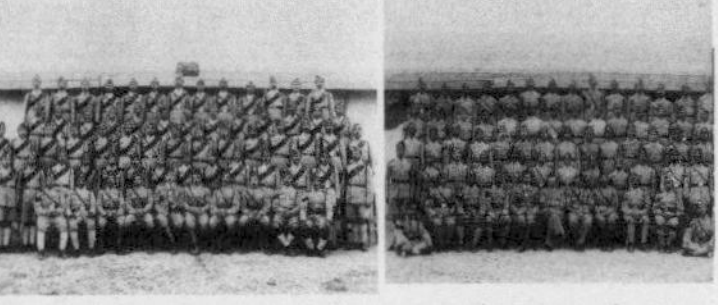

The following photographs were scaled and positioned horizontally, according to the height and baseline of standing figures in the first front row.

1. Police Academy. Cairo, Egypt 1940. Photographer: Selim Youssef. Collection FAI.
2. Unidentified group. Cairo, Egypt 1940. Photographer: Selim Youssef. Collection FAI.
3. School students. Photographer: anonymous. Collection Haifa Kokache / FAI.

4. Students of Aintoura St. Joseph school. Aintoura, Lebanon 1888. Photographer: anonymous. Collection Omar el Daouk / FAI.
5. Police Academy. Baghdad, Iraq 1934. Photographer: anonymous. Collection FAI.
6. Police Academy. Baghdad, Iraq 1930. Photographer: A. Abbosh. Collection FAI.

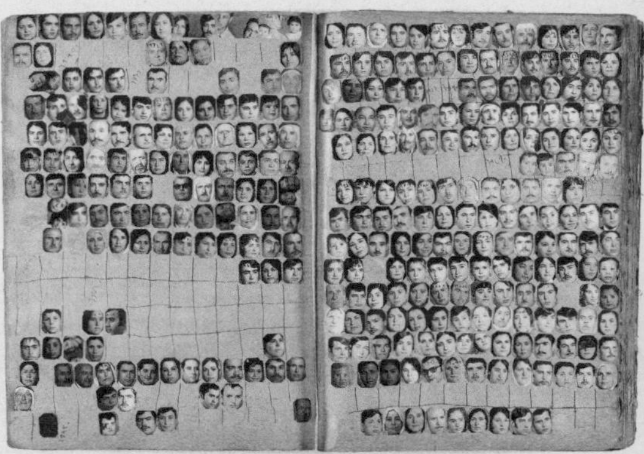

Studio Soussi portrait index. Saida, Lebanon. 100 pages, ca. 150 portraits per page, 35 cm x 50 cm x 9,5 cm. Collection FAI.
The portrait indexes simply referred to as Dafatir (notebooks) referenced most studio portraits numerically and visually.

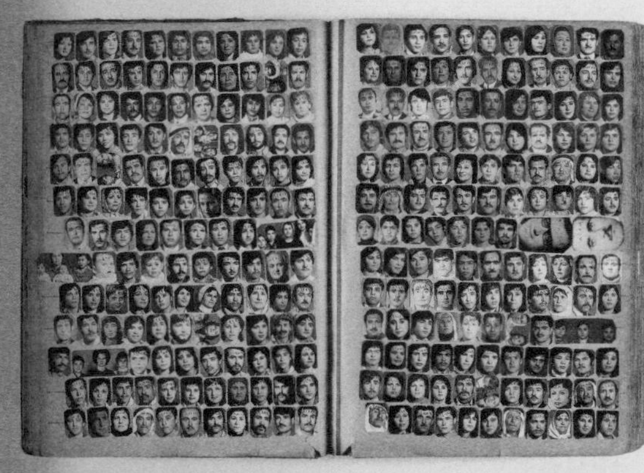

Studio Soussi portrait index. Saida, Lebanon. 100 pages, ca. 150 portraits per page, 35 cm x 50 cm x 9,5 cm. Collection FAI.
The portrait indexes simply referred to as Dafatir (notebooks) referenced most studio portraits numerically and visually.

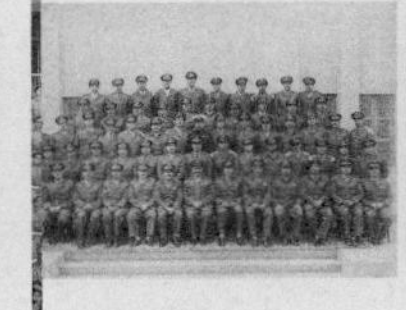 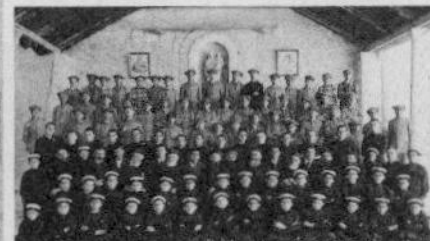 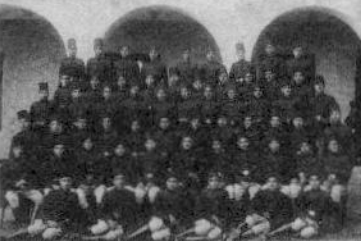 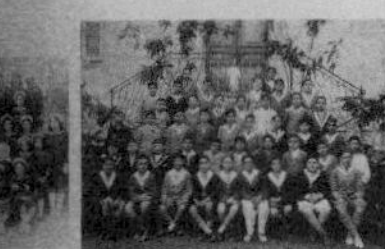 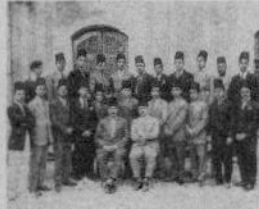 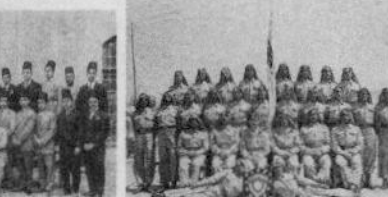 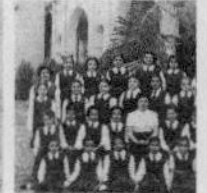

7. Police Academy. Cairo, Egypt 1940s. Photographer: Selim Youssef. Collection FAI.
8. Alsace Orphanage. Bethlehem, Palestine 1932. Photographer: anonymous. Collection FAI.
9. Police Academy. Cairo, Egypt 1927. Photographer: anonymous. Collection Amgad Negub / FAI.
10. Students of Saint Joseph de l'Apparition school. Jaffa, Palestine 1946. Photographer: anonymous. Collection Aida Shehadeh / FAI.

11. Students of Frères des Écoles Chrétiennes school. Jerusalem, Palestine 1932. Photographer: anonymous. Collection Leila Kardus / FAI.
12. Unidentified group. Syria 1940s. Photographer: Selim Youssef. Collection FAI.
13. Unidentified group. Jerusalem, Palestine 1960s. Photographer: Diana Photo Studio. Collection Ali Maher / FAI.
14. Unidentified group. Cairo, Egypt 1955. Photographer: J. Conti. Collection FAI.

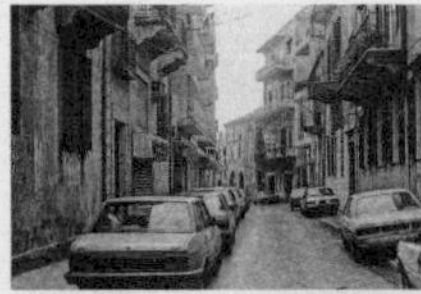
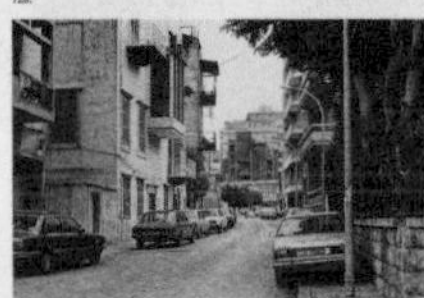
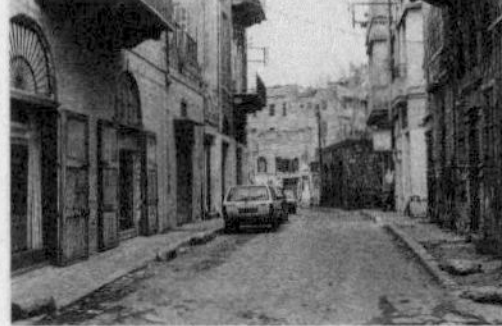
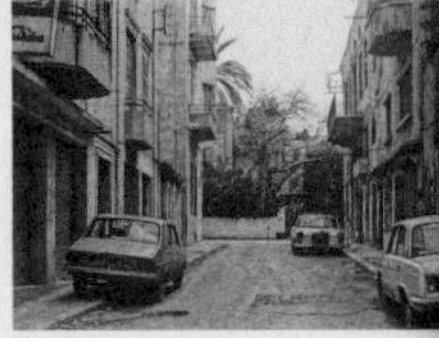
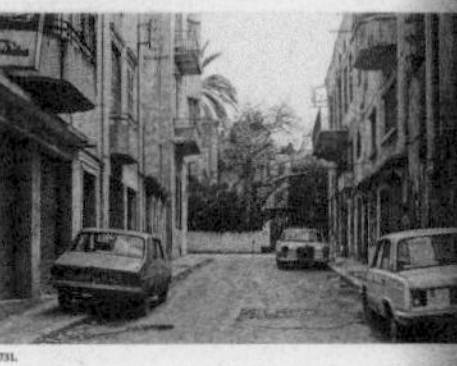
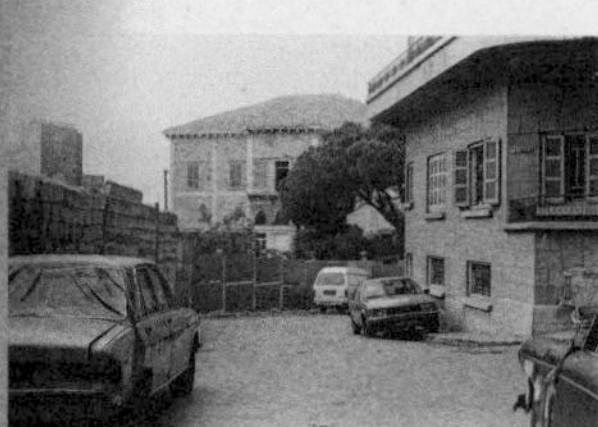
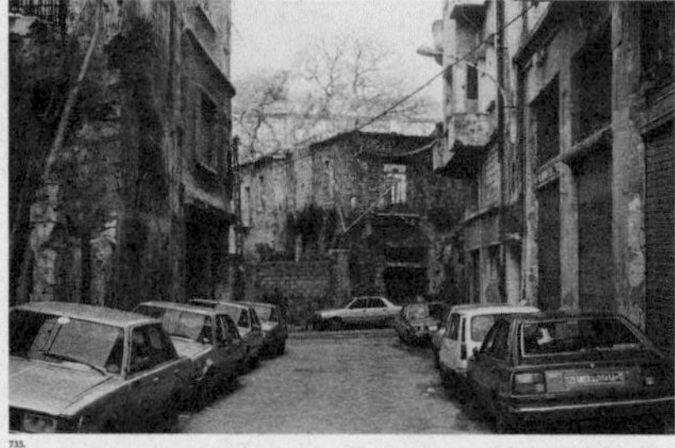

WALID RAAD, *Sweet Talk: Beirut Commissions_1991 – 1995: Plate 240*, 2010. Inkjet-print, 112 cm x 188 cm.
Courtesy: Galerie Sfeir-Semler, Hamburg; Anthony Reynolds Gallery, London; Paula Cooper Gallery, New York.

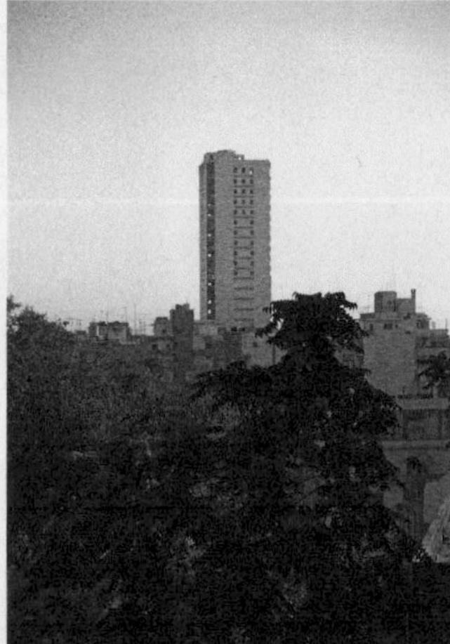
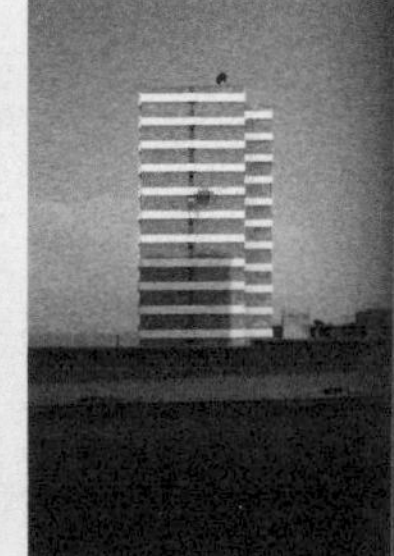
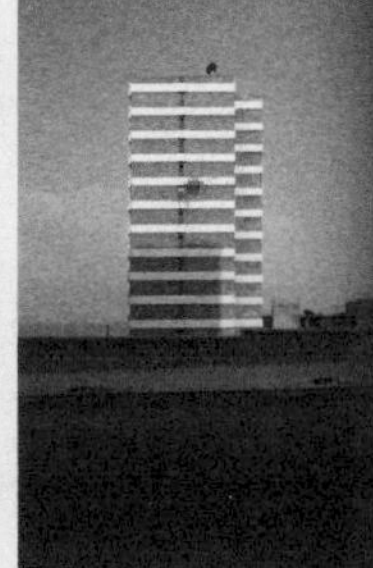
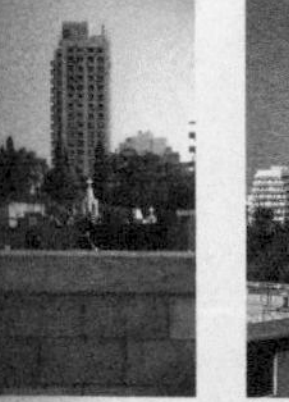
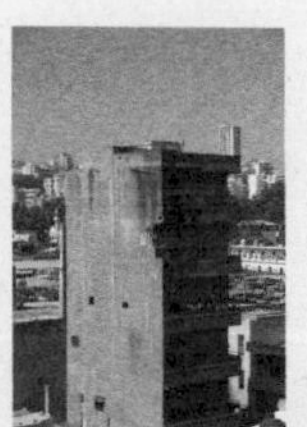

WALID RAAD, *Sweet Talk: Beirut Commissions_2005: Plate 703*, 2010. Inkjet-print, 112 cm x 188 cm.
Courtesy: Galerie Sfeir-Semler, Hamburg; Anthony Reynolds Gallery, London; Paula Cooper Gallery, New York.

Camera Austria International

2006   Ulrich Loock, "Ahlam Shibli: Resisting Oppression," text contribution, Ahlam Shibli, artist contribution, *Camera Austria International* 93 / 2006

2011   Reinhard Braun, Ahlam Shibli, "Ahlam Shibli: Einspruch gegen verordnete Unsichtbarkeit," text contribution and artist contribution, *Camera Austria International* 114 / 2011

2013   Alberto Martín, *"Ahlam Shibli: Phantom Home,* MACBA, Barcelona; Jeu de Paume, Paris; Museu de Arte Contemporânea de Serralves, Porto," exhibition review, *Camera Austria International* 122 / 2013

Exhibitions

2004   *Bleiben oder gehen / Ostati ili otići / Staying or leaving,* exhibition contribution

2015   *Disputed Landscape: Uncovering History,* exhibition contribution

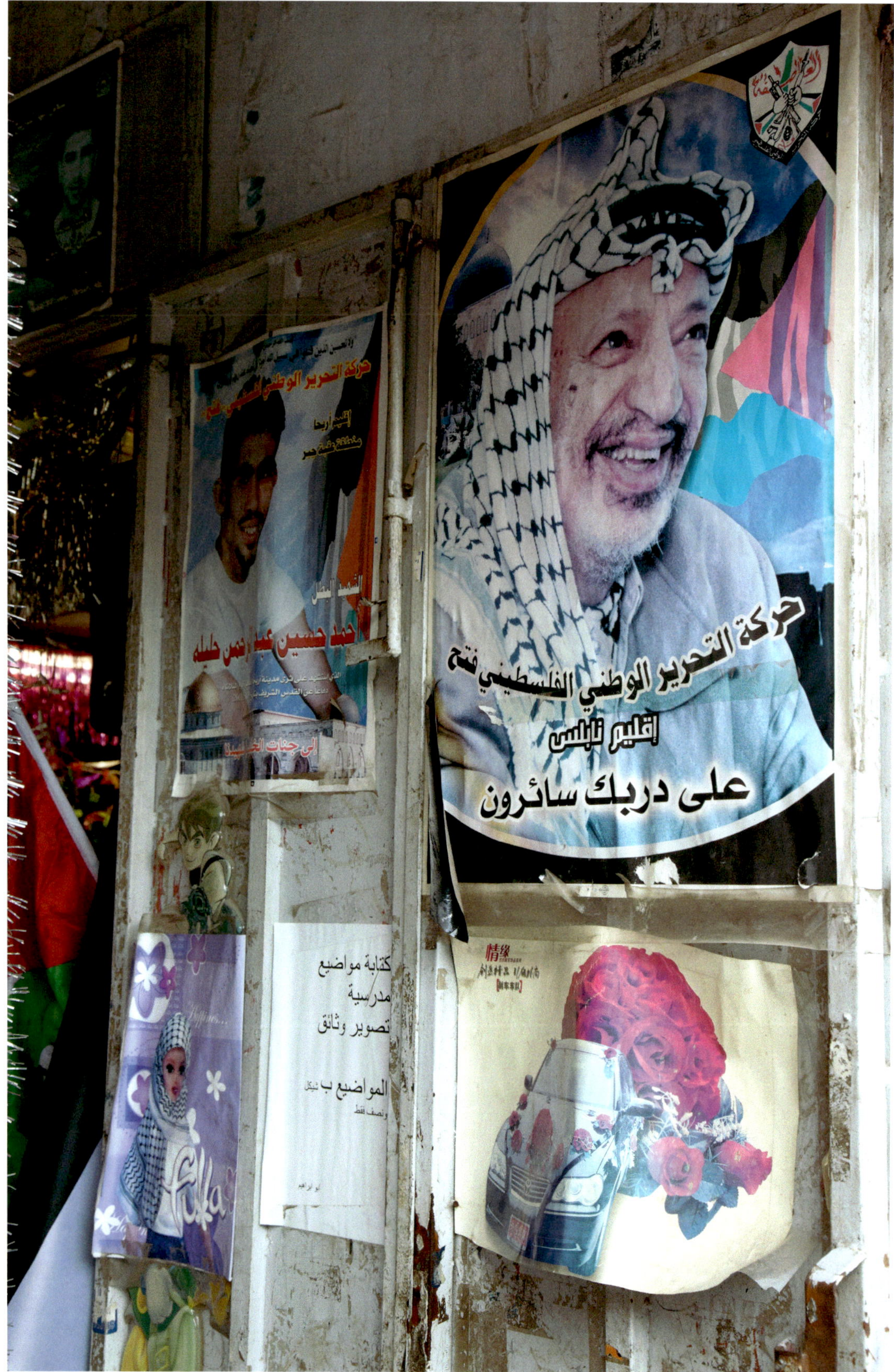

Untitled (*Death* no. 59), Palestine, 2011–2012

Balata Refugee Camp, March 6, 2012.
Posters covering the iron gate of a shop, among them a poster exhibiting the picture of Yasser Arafat and the writing, "Palestinian National Liberation Movement / Nablus region / We are following your way." A second poster is devoted to the martyr Ahmad Hleylah from Fateh, in the Jericho region, who fell in defense of Jerusalem on May 29, 2001, in 'Aqbat Jaber. The walls of the adjacent shop are covered with pictures and posters of Arafat, and different posters of martyrs.

Ahlam Shibli

Death
Palestine, 2011–2012, from a series of
68 photographs

*I shall not return until I plant my paradise on earth or else
reap a paradise from the sky or die or we all die together.*
Ghassan Kanafani

This work is based on the demand for recognition that became apparent with the Second Intifada, the Palestinian uprising against the colonial power in the territories occupied by Israel since 1967. The Second Intifada lasted from 2000 to 2005 and claimed several thousand deaths on the Palestinian side.

Death exhibits some of the ways in which the ones who are absent become present again—"represented": Palestinian fighters, who fell in the course of their armed resistance against the Israeli incursions, and victims of the Israeli military killed under different circumstances (*Shaheed* and *Shaheeda*); militants who carried out attacks which they knew would lead to their death, among them the men and women who detonated explosives on their own bodies to assassinate Israelis (*Istishhadi* and *Istishhadiya*), and the prisoners. The former are dead, the latter are alive, jailed for a large part if not the rest of their lives.

Death focuses on a limited range of means representing the martyrs and the prisoners in the closed environment of Nablus, its region, and its refugee camps: posters and occasionally graffiti in the streets; paintings, photos, posters, and other memorabilia in the homes of the martyrs' families; the graves that bear inscriptions and are sometimes ornate with pictures and items of the deceased. One supplementary element representing the prisoners are their letters and diaries—personal if one ignores the prison authority's censorship. All of these are forms of representation originated by the families, friends, and the fighters' associations.

*The question of death does not belong to the dead, but
to those who remain alive.*
Ghassan Kanafani

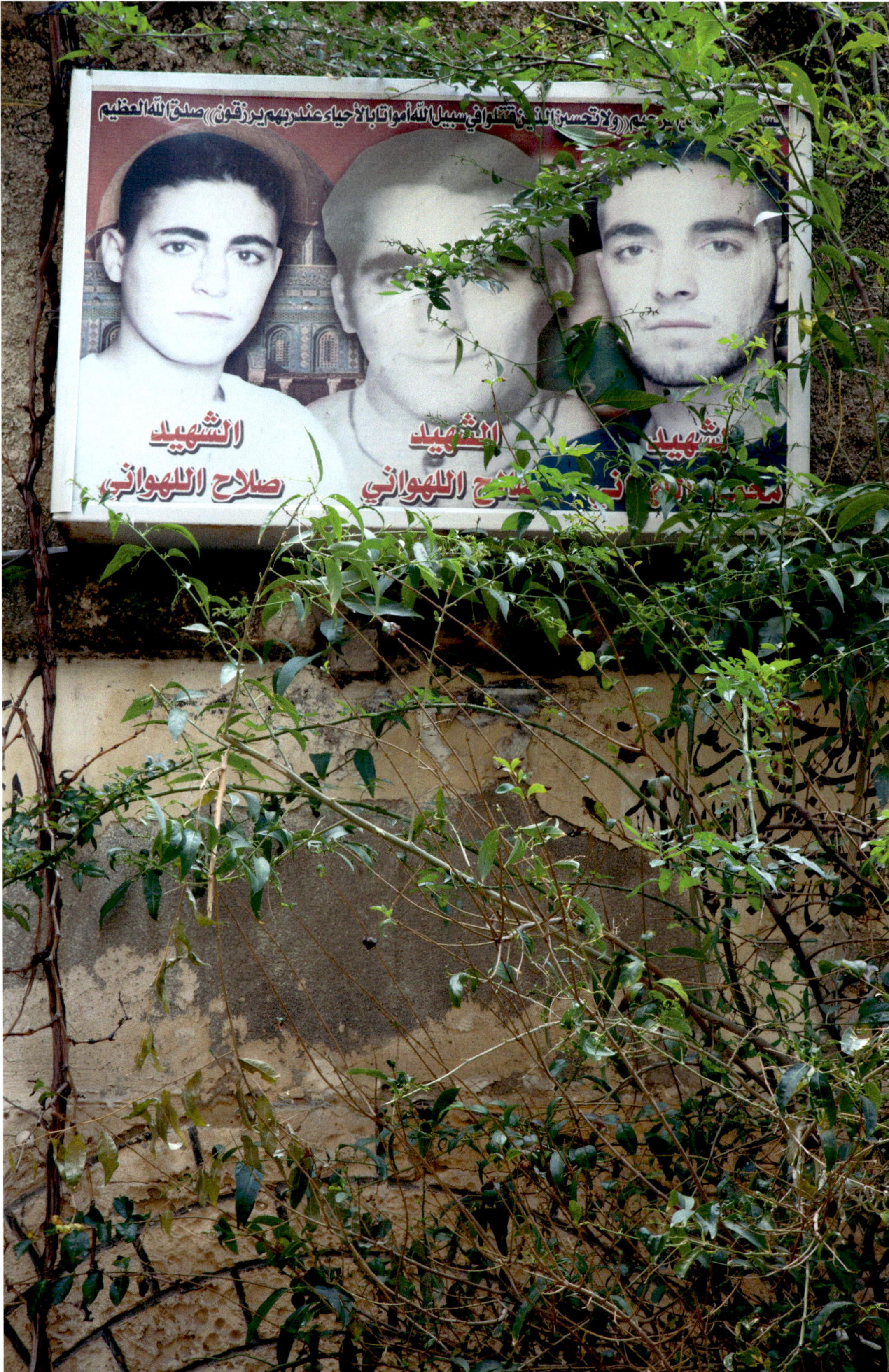

Untitled (*Death* no. 67), Palestine, 2011–2012

Balata Refugee Camp, January 28, 2012.
Next to the house of the al-Lahwaani family, a memorial for their three martyrs: the two sons, Mahmoud and Salah, and, in the middle, their father Saleh. Salah was killed on June 15, 2004 on the occasion of the funeral of the martyrs Khalil Marshoud and 'Awad Abu Zeid, by the Israeli army that also attacked Salah's own funeral, increasing the number of people from Balata who were injured that day, in addition to dozens of other citizens who suffered suffocation from tear gas, which was flooded out by the army during the martyr's funeral. On July 3, 2004, eighteen days after the death of his brother Salah, Mahmoud was shot by the Israeli army during one of their successive incursions at the same place where Salah died, the southern entrance of the camp. Years earlier a mysterious accident claimed the life of their father in Israel.

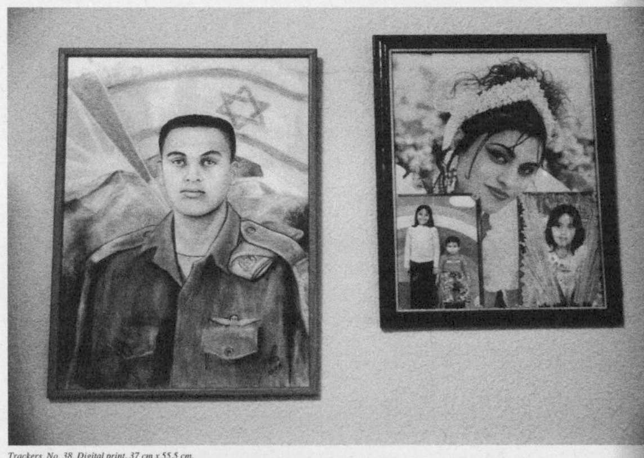

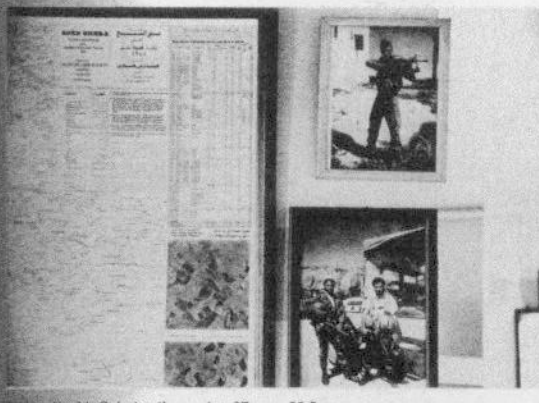
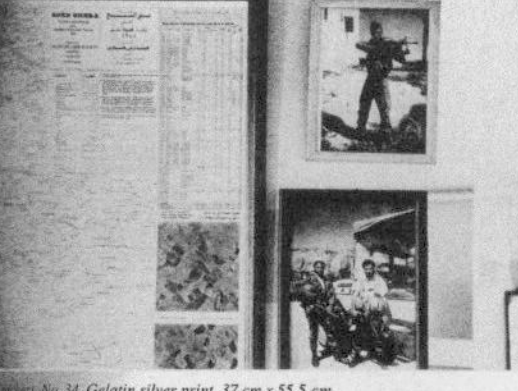
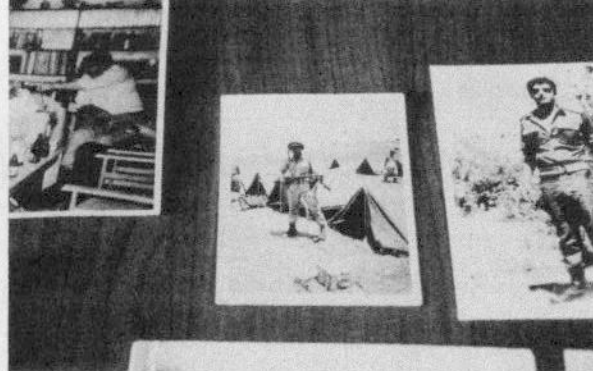

Trackers, No. 34. Gelatin silver print, 37 cm x 55,5 cm.

Trackers, No. 35. Digital print, 37 cm x 55,5 cm.

Trackers, No. 38. Digital print, 37 cm x 55,5 cm.

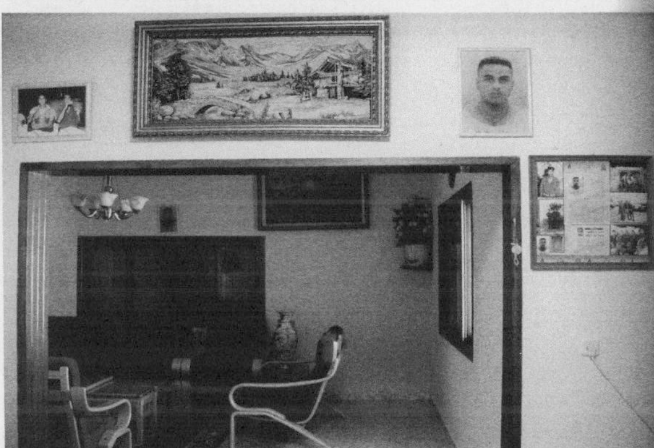

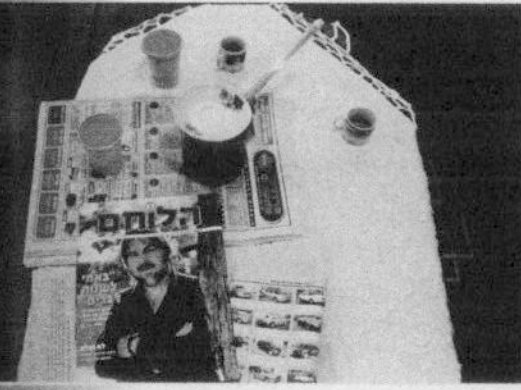
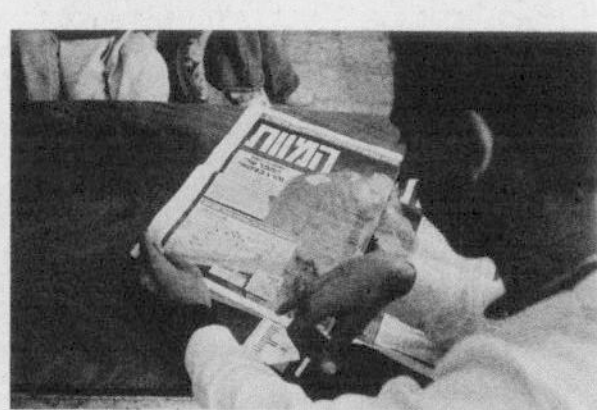

Trackers, No. 39. Gelatin silver print, 37 cm x 55,5 cm.

Trackers, No. 40. Gelatin silver print, 37 cm x 55,5 cm.

Trackers, No. 37. Digital print, 37 cm x 55,5 cm.

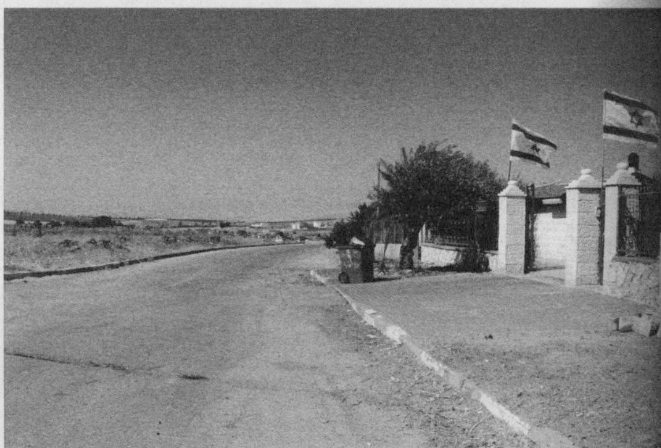

Trackers, No. 14. Digital print, 37 cm x 55,5 cm.

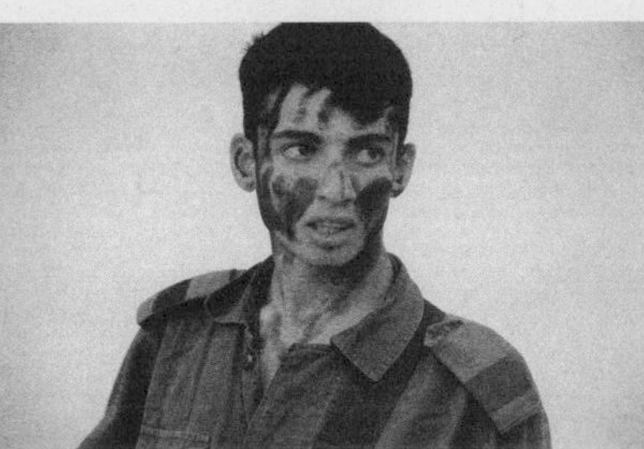

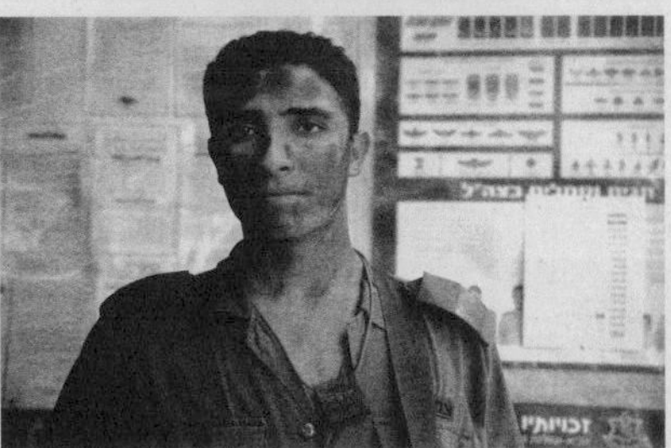

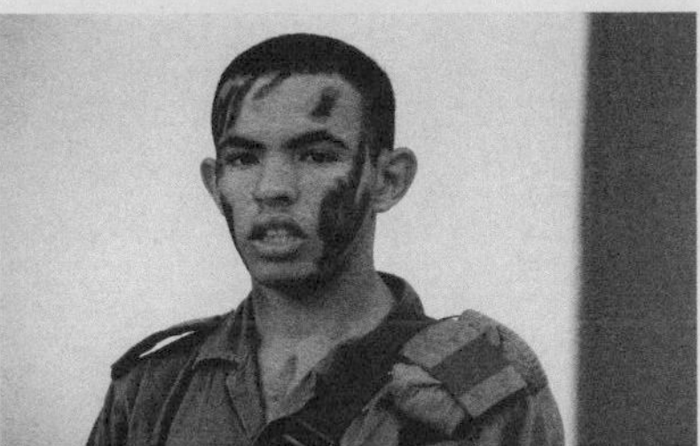

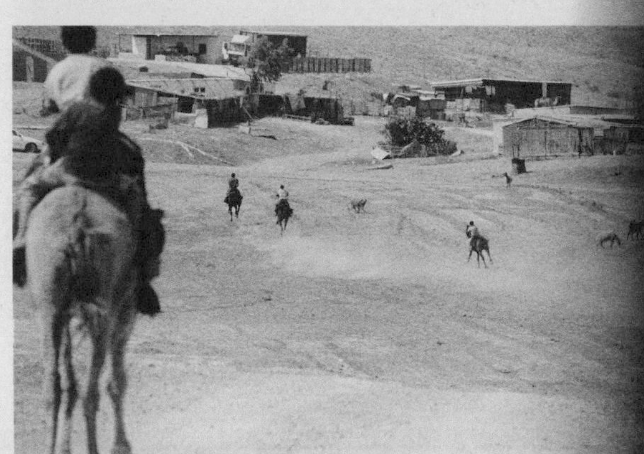
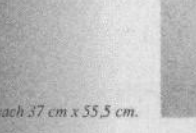

Trackers, No. 20. Gelatin silver print, 37 cm x 55,5 cm.

Trackers, No. 54
Trackers, No. 55
Trackers, No. 56
Digital print, je/each 37 cm x 55,5 cm.

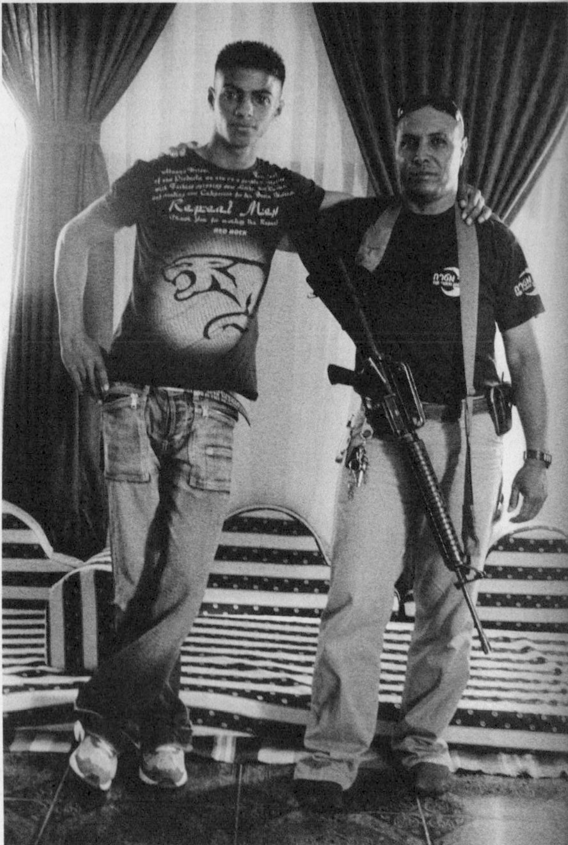

häuser in den besetzten Gebieten in einem Zustand der direkten Konfrontation. Manchmal werden die Freiwilligen als Verräter betrachtet. Auf der anderen Seite ist zu hören, es gehöre zum Charakter der Beduinen, sich auf die Seite des jeweiligen Staates zu stellen, in dem sie leben. Auf der Website der IDF (Israeli Defense Forces) schließlich wird von einem Spurenleser berichtet, der bereits in der zweiten Generation dient. Er sei in die Armee eingegangen, da er als Jugendlicher so viel von den Soldaten gehört habe, dass er nicht habe abseits stehen wollen. Ahlam Shibli beansprucht bei ihrer Auseinandersetzung mit dem Militärdienst von Palästinensern in der IDF, auf keines von diesen Erklärungsmodellen zurückzugreifen, sondern einen Beitrag zu leisten zur Soziopsychologie von Minderheiten, genauer: zur Soziopsychologie eines eingeborenen Volkes unter Kolonialherrschaft.

Die Installation von »Trackers« ist in sieben Kapiteln organisiert, die sich, obgleich nicht scharf voneinander abgegrenzt, folgendermaßen beschreiben lassen: Ausbildung an der Waffe, Häuser/Dorf, Freizeit/Familie, Dekoration der Wohnung, Friedhof, Trainingslager, Vereidigungs- und Diplomzeremonie. Ahlam Shibli fotografiert die Soldaten bei der militärischen Ausbildung, ihr Zuhause und ihre Gräber. Vollkommen fehlen Bilder, welche die Spurenleser beim Einsatz zeigen, und überhaupt gibt es kaum Fotos von Soldaten in Aktion.

Durch die Bilder von Friedhöfen gibt Ahlam Shibli ihrer Arbeit eine geschichtliche Dimension. Eine Grabplatte – der offizielle Stein der Armee – dient dem Gedenken eines 1991 im Libanon mit 35 Jahren gefallenen Soldaten. In einem anderen Foto ist auf einer mit grüner Farbe beschriebenen Tafel im Anschluss an einen Vers aus dem Koran (»Und betrachte nicht diejenigen, die auf Allahs Weg gefallen sind, als tot. Nein! Sie leben bei ihrem Herrn, und sie werden dort versorgt.«) folgende Widmung zu lesen: »Die Gräber der 14 von Gott gerechtfertigten Märtyrer, die sich für die Heimat geopfert haben und deren Identität unbekannt ist. Im Jahr 1969.« Von einem Ortsansässigen, den Ahlam Shibli auf dem Friedhof getroffen hat, weiß sie, dass Angehörige der israelischen Armee im Jahr 1969 eines Nachts die nackten Leichen von 14 Kämpfern mit unkenntlich gemachten Gesichtern gebracht und den Dorfvorsteher aufgefordert haben, sie zu begraben. Es habe sich um palästinensische Kämpfer gehandelt, die aus dem Libanon nach Israel eingedrungen seien. Die Gräber – und darin ähneln sie dem Foto – bedürfen der Beschriftung. Die Beschriftung gibt zu erkennen, wer der Tote war und was sein Schicksal war. Ohne sie sind die Gräber unterschiedslos nichts als die letzte Ruhestätte von Verstorbenen. Nebeneinander gezeigt, legen die Fotos dem Betrachter nahe, den gewaltsamen Tod eines palästinensischen Angehörigen der israelischen Armee im Jahr 1991 in Verbindung zu bringen mit dem Tod von Kämpfern gegen den jüdischen Staat, die entweder im Jahr 1948 im Zusammenhang mit der Gründung des Staates Israel aus ihrer Heimat hatten flüchten müssen oder sich als Einwohner noch später dem bewaffneten Kampf angeschlossen hatten. Unausgesprochen, durch die Auswahl der Bilder evoziert, bringt Ahlam Shibli ins Spiel, was keines der 85 Fotos von »Trackers« zeigt: die tödliche Konfrontation von Palästinensern mit Palästinensern, bewirkt durch den Staat Israel.

Mit den Fotos der Gräber von 1969 und 1991 wird eine Verbindung hergestellt zwischen dem Militärdienst der jungen Freiwilligen, deren mögliche Zukunft es ist, mit einem ähnlichen Stein wie der von 1991 begraben zu werden, und der arabischen Niederlage von 1948 und 1967 mit ihren bekannten Folgen – Annexion von palästinensischem Land, Vertreibung eines großen Teils der einheimischen Bevölkerung, Unterdrückung, kulturelle Desintegration und Diskriminierung der Zurückgebliebenen. Indem Ahlam Shibli aber die Gräber von Kämpfern für und gegen den Staat Israel fotografiert, deren Todesdaten so weit auseinander liegen, dass sie nie einander gegenüberstehen können, wahrt sie gleichzeitig eine Distanz zwischen ihnen, die jede eindeutige Aussage über ihre gegenseitige Beziehung vermeidet. Weder legen die Fotos fest, welcher Art die

Trackers, No. 41. Digital print, 90 cm x 60 cm.

Defense Forces) website, finally, features a tracker who is already serving in the second generation. He joined the army because he had heard so much about the soldiers as a young man that he did not want to be the odd one out. In her account of Palestinians doing military service in the IDF, Ahlam Shibli claims not to fall back on any of these explanatory models, but rather to contribute to the socio-psychology of minorities, and more specifically to the socio-psychology of native people under colonial rule.

The »Trackers« installation is arranged in seven chapters that, although not strictly delimited from each other, can be described as follows: training under arms, houses/village, leisure/family, interior decoration, cemetery, training camp, swearing-in and diploma ceremony. Ahlam Shibli takes photographs of the soldiers during military training, their home and their graves. There are no pictures of the trackers in a combat situation, and indeed very few photos of any soldiers in action.

With the pictures of cemeteries, Ahlam Shibli adds a historical dimension to her work. A memorial slab – the official stone of the army – serves to commemorate a soldier who fell in Lebanon in 1991 at the age of 35. In another photo, following a verse from the Qur'an (»Think not of those who are slain in Allah's way as dead. Nay, they live, finding their sustenance in the presence of their Lord«) we read the following dedication written in green on a plaque: »The graves of the 14 martyrs justified by God, who sacrificed their lives for the homeland and whose identity is unknown. In the year 1969.« From a local man whom Ahlam Shibli met at the cemetery, she knows that one night in 1969 members of the Israeli army brought the naked bodies of fourteen fighters with mutilated faces, asking the head of the village to bury them. They were Palestinian fighters who had penetrated Israel from Lebanon. The graves require inscriptions as a photograph needs a caption. The inscription indicates who the dead person was and what his fate was. Without them the graves are without exception nothing but the final resting place of dead men. Presented next to each other, the two photos lead the observer to make a connection between the violent death of a Palestinian member of the Israeli army in 1991 and the death of fighters against Israel, who either had had to flee their homeland in 1948 in connection with the foundation of the Jewish state or who had joined the armed struggle after further Palestinian defeats. Implicitly, but evoked by the choice of pictures, Ahlam Shibli brings into play what none of the 85 photos of »Trackers« shows: the deadly confrontation of Palestinians with Palestinians, brought about by the state of Israel.

With the photos of the graves from 1969 and 1991, the photographer creates a link between the military service of the young volunteers, whose possible future is to be buried with a stone similar to that of the dead man from 1991, and the Arab defeat of 1948 and 1967 with its well-known consequences – the annexation of Palestinian territory, the eviction of a large part of the native people, and the oppression, disintegration and discrimination of those who remained. However, by taking photos of the graves of men fighting for and against the state of Israel, the dates of whose deaths are so far apart that it was never possible for them to actually face each other, Ahlam Shibli preserves a distance between them that avoids any unequivocal statement regarding their mutual relationship. The photos neither specify the kind of connection between one death and the other, nor do they express an opinion on the question of right or wrong of the actions that ultimately led to the graves depicted in the photos. They do not make the Palestinian adversaries responsible for each other's death, but the state for and against whom they fought, and raise the inescapable question of how come Palestinians face each other, the ones in the service of the Jewish state and the others as its enemies.

Therefore, the photos are at the same time, and perhaps first and foremost, pictures of commemoration of the dead that is dedicated to these young Palestinians, irrespective of what side they fought on. One picture is of plastic chairs between the graves, a sign of the frequent presence of the living in this place.

The pictures show what is, the graves of the dead from 1969 and of the dead man from 1991. It is up to the observer to realise what

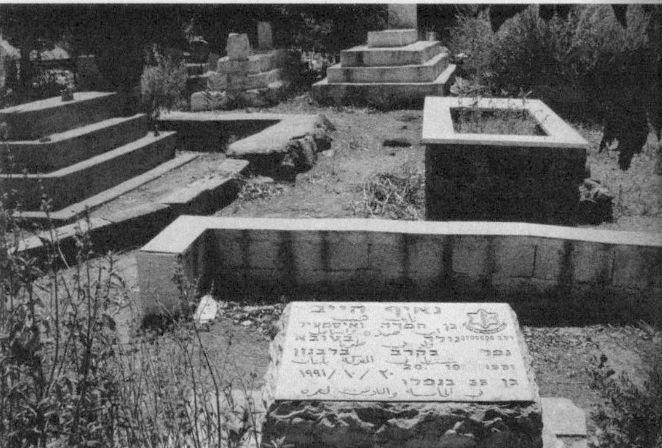

Trackers, No. 49. Digital print, 37 cm x 55,5 cm.

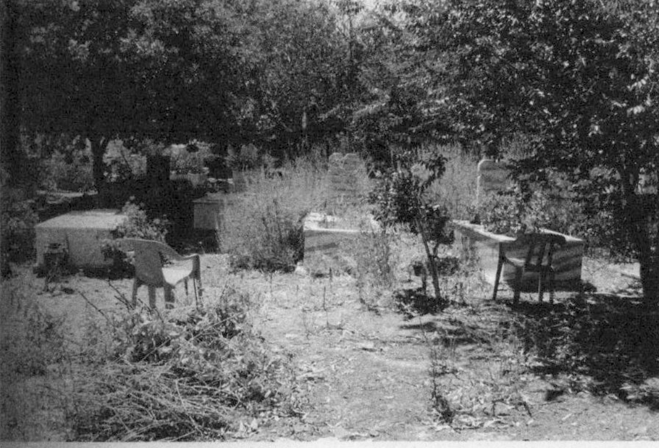

Trackers, No. 45. Digital print, 37 cm x 55,5 cm.

Verbindung zwischen dem einen und dem anderen Tod ist, noch nehmen sie Stellung zu der Frage nach Recht oder Unrecht der Handlungen, an deren Ende die abgebildeten Gräber stehen. Für den Tod der palästinensischen Kämpfer machen sie nicht die unmittelbaren Gegner verantwortlich, sondern den Staat, für oder gegen den sie kämpfen. Daher sind die Fotos zugleich und vielleicht vor allem Erinnerungs-Bilder des Totengedenkens, das diesen jungen Palästinensern unabhängig davon gewidmet ist, auf welcher Seite sie gekämpft haben. Auf einem Bild stehen Plastikstühle zwischen den Gräbern, ein Zeichen der häufigen Anwesenheit von Lebenden an diesem Ort.

Die Bilder zeigen, was ist, die Gräber der Toten von 1969 und des Toten von 1991. Zu realisieren, was sie implizieren, bleibt dem Betrachter überlassen. Alle Bilder von Ahlam Shibli charakterisiert ein ruhiges, lang dauerndes Verharren der Fotografin beim Wirklichen. Das wird deutlich im Vergleich zwischen ihren eigenen Fotos der Soldaten und den Fotos, die sie in den Häusern von deren Familien gesehen und fotografiert hat, wo sie neben anderen Bildern die Wände zieren. Die Erinnerungs-Fotos zeigen Soldaten in kämpferischer Haltung oder in der Pose von Kameraden, die sie für die Fotografen einnehmen: Ihre Körper werden zu Trägern von vereinfachten und normierten Signifikanten der soldatischen Funktion und damit ihrer Besonderheit entkleidet. Ahlam Shibli hingegen fotografiert die Soldaten nicht als solche Soldaten, sondern sie als Individuen in einer bestimmten Situation ab: Rekruten beim Militärdienst, die tun, was man als Angehöriger der Armee zu tun hat. Wie alle anderen Bilder von »Trackers« zeigen auch diese Fotos nicht die »menschliche« Seite der Armee, sondern ihre gesellschaftliche. In dieser Hinsicht erweisen sich Ahlam Shiblis Bilder viel stärker von etwas Allgemeinem geprägt als die konventionellen Bilder von Militär, die bei den Familien der Soldaten an den Wänden hängen.

Abgesehen vom dokumentarischen Wert der Innenaufnahmen mit dem Bilderschmuck (es gibt keine Bilder von der sonstigen Ein-

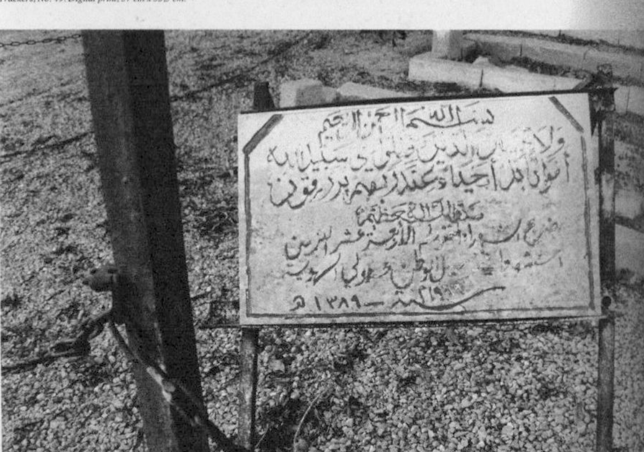

Trackers, No. 48. Digital print, 37 cm x 55,5 cm.

they may imply. All of Ahlam Shibli's pictures are characterised by the photographer's calm, patient persistence with these situations of reality. This becomes clear if you compare her own photos of the soldiers and the photos she saw and took photos of in their families' houses, where they decorate the walls alongside other pictures. The souvenir photos are of soldiers in combative or comradely poses that they take up for the photographer: their bodies become vehicles of standardised signifiers of the soldier's function and are thereby divested of their particularity. Ahlam Shibli, on the other hand, does not take photos of the soldiers as such soldiers but rather portrays individuals in a certain situation: recruits on military service doing what you have to do as a member of the army. This is particularly impressive in the three portraits of soldiers whose faces are painted for outdoor training. Like all the other »Trackers« pictures, these photos do not show the »human« side of the army but rather its social component. In this respect, Ahlam Shibli's pictures turn out to be much more strongly characterised by something universal than the conventional pictures of the military hanging on the walls of the soldiers' families' homes.

Apart from the documentary value of the interior photos with the decorative pictures (there are no pictures of the other furnishings of the houses – Ahlam Shibli does not pursue an ethnographic programme), they also serve to reflect on the aesthetic and ideological modalities of the photographic project itself.

It is characteristic of the »Trackers« pictures that they hardly ever depict the soldiers in action – quite unlike what the media they are reading suggest: in one photo, a magazine entitled The Fighter is lying on the table, and in another photo a soldier in civilian clothes is reading a newspaper in which the headline reads »Death« and a second line »My friend was killed instead of me«. But in Ahlam Shibli's photos, all that remains of night-time training are the delicate pictures of grasses and trees in the searchlight; hand grenade training is shown in a picture of a soldier fearfully and extremely cautiously holding a grenade that has just been handed out to him; and all that we see of recruits learning the

Dialog 6

Research & Archive

Anna and Bernhard Blume

Participation at Symposion

1984   Symposion on Photography VI: "The
        Power (and the Glory) of Photography,"
        26–28 October 1984, lecturer
        (Bernhard Johannes Blume)

Camera Austria International

1985   Bernhard Johannes Blume, "Natürlich,"
        text contribution/artist contribution (journal
        of Symposion),
        Camera Austria International 19–20/1985
1991   Thomas Trummer "Die Gegenstände
        sind wir selbst. Bernhard Johannes Blume.
        Fotoarbeiten 1970–1984; Anna und Bernhard
        Blume. Gegenseitig," book review, *Camera
        Austria International* 36/1991
1993   Jutta Steininger, "Anna und Bernhard Blume,"
        exhibition review, *Camera Austria
        International* 42/1993

Exhibitions

1984   *Fotografie 84,* exhibition contribution
1996   *Radical Images,* II. Austrian Triennial for
        Photography, exhibition contribution

Publication

1996   Werner Fenz and Reinhard Braun, eds,
        Radical Images 1/2, publication in two
        volumes for exhibition at II. Austrian
        Triennial for Photography, Graz: Edition
        Camera Austria, 1996.

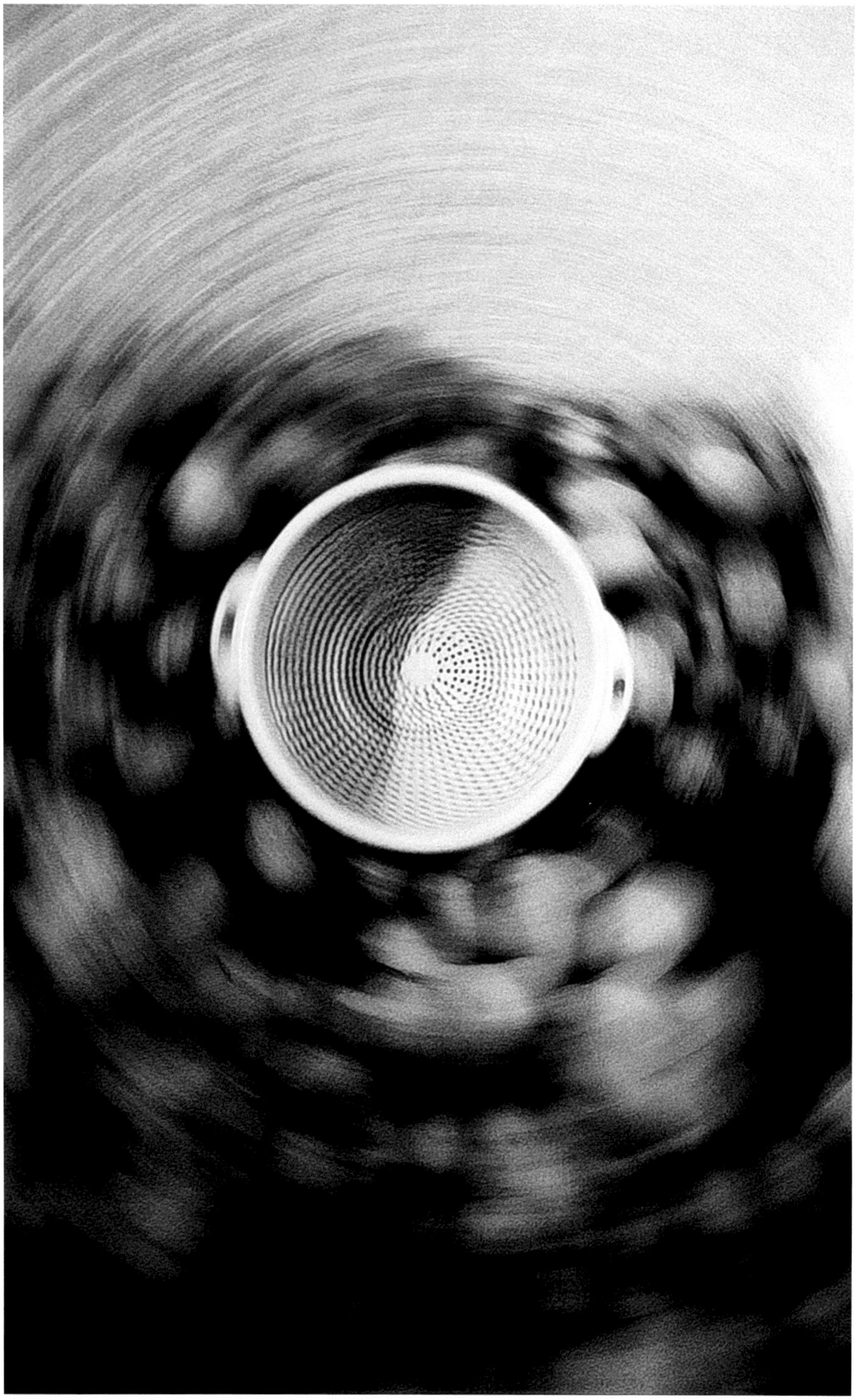

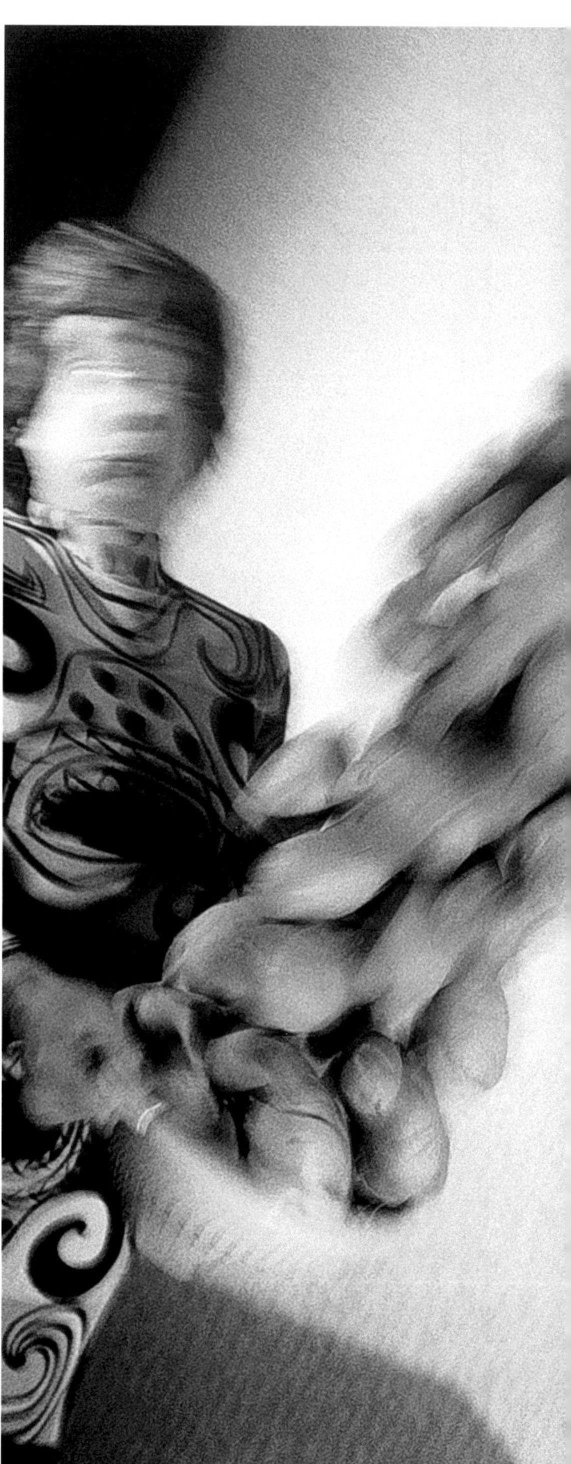

Kitchen Frenzy, 1985

Anna and Bernhard Blume

Kitchen Frenzy

Are potatoes simply potatoes, or could they be pointers to the soul? Should we not perhaps see them as lending tangible expression to desires and drives that, not indulged or divulged, have been suppressed? So could not potatoes sometimes constitute all-too-solid instinct formations, photogenic manifestations of a soul long frustrated and otherwise condemned to be mute? This potato conduct, behavior far removed from the everyday and here captured on film, would suggest that this is indeed so: they are menacing, or uncommon to say the least! What was earmarked for ingestion no longer complies with the laws of nature but rather obeys acausal forces, here, for example, housewifely spiritual powers.

Psychoanalysis here naturally dredges up for us wishes that, having been repressed into the so-called unconscious, can only become objective phenomena in potato form. Their true meaning at first remains a mystery for the housewife herself. Yet for the decerning beholder of the pictures the murky instincts at the bottom of these goings-on are as clear as day, in a manner of speaking.

So it comes as no surprise that there are photos of this flush of exuberance emanating from the unconscious. Their mission is to allow those affected to see themselves objectively for once. So they were taken as part of a photo therapy. Yet those afflicted have so far declined to perceive themselves in the aforementioned state, a refusal that naturally blocks the way to any successful therapy.

As long as the protagonists of this drama still balk at confronting the hidden truth, and cannot or will not acknowledge as their own the needs and desires that have found expression here—i.e., they continue to repress them—then there will be no shortage of such or similar occurrences and incidents. And the photographers will have a nice lot of work in store; unless our picture producers should actually turn out to be none other than the persons portrayed on the photos. If that is the case, there can be no cure!

The English version of the German statement from the US exh. cat. *Anna and Bernhard Blume. Photo-Works.* exh. cat., Milwaukee: Milwaukee Art Museum, 1996.

Bernh. Joh. Blume

natürlich

Polaroidsequenzen von 1984

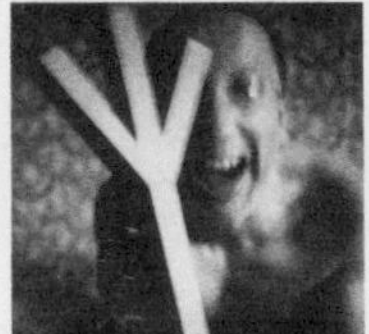 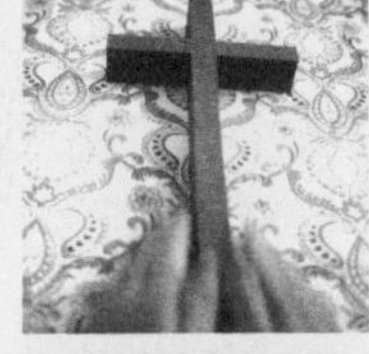
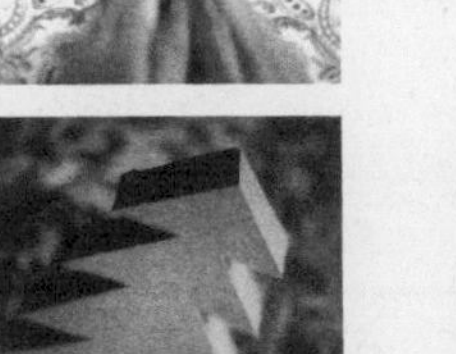
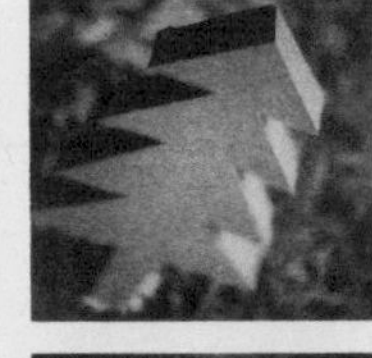
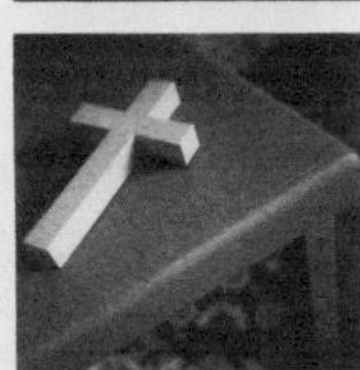
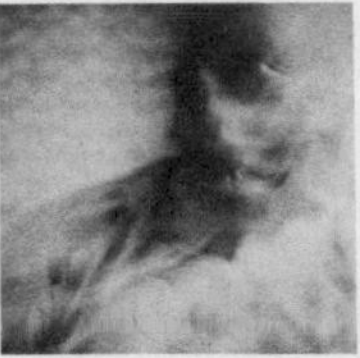

"Heilsgebilde", 1984 /
'Objects of Salvation', 1984

Vernunft, Sachzwang etc. An diesem Unsterblichkeitsprogramm unserer Zivilisation muß sich der Einzelmensch orientieren und zwecks Überlebens daran sich anpassen. Das System ist absolut und souverän. Es braucht keine Verkörperungen mehr wie Häuptling, Priester, König, Gott in einem Einzelmenschen. Unser Individuelles ist selbst schon Allgemeines, und individuelle Repräsentanten, wie Künstler es zu sein beanspruchen, sind so gesehen überflüssig. Der Künstler ist nur noch ein gutes negatives Fallbeispiel für die Neurose der Individuation, für das individuelle Leiden an der anonymen Souveränität des Systems, das in uns allen waltet. Als Romantiker des Ich wehrt er sich noch und will das Allgemeine nur im Besonderen, d.h. in *sich* verkörpern und leibhaftig souverän repräsentieren. Ein letzter Ich-Darsteller! In der Massengesellschaft will er authentisch sein, und weil das alle möchten, kann er sich noch Identifikation erhoffen.

Auch ich führe mich hier als exemplarischen Fall vor. Sagen wir mal: als Fotokünstler. Fotos werden akzeptiert, nicht unbedingt als Kunst, aber als einigermaßen wahrscheinliche Mitteilungen. Das durch Fotos vermittelte wird im objektiven Sinne immer noch für wahrer gehalten als Geschriebenes oder Gemaltes oder

immortality program of our civilisation! The individual must ori... tate itself by it and adapt to it. The system is absolute and sover... It can do without personal incarnations like chiefs, priests, kings... god. Our very individuality has become general, and individual repre... sentatives that artists claim to be, are, if one looks at it this wa... superfluous. The artist is reduced to a negative case study of the neu...

"Verwackelter Selbstvergewisserungsversuch", 1984 /
"... Attempt of Self-assurance", 1984

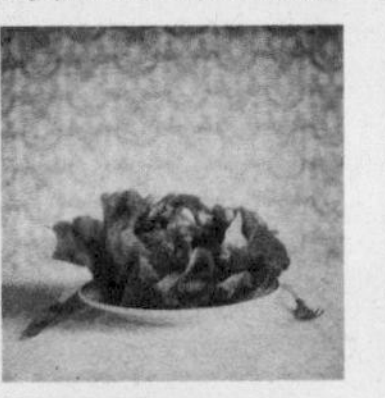 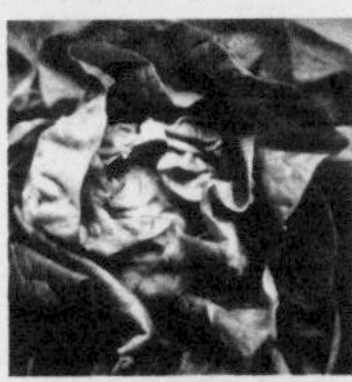
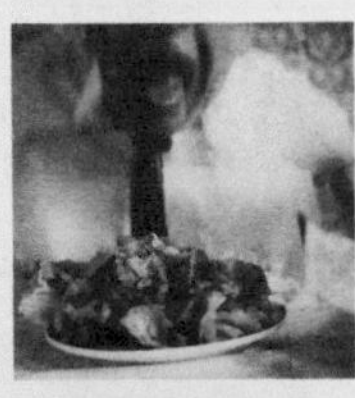 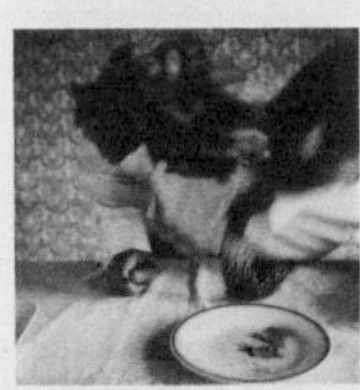
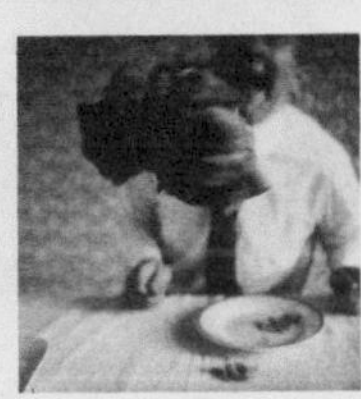 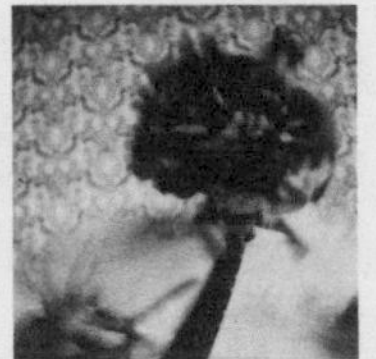

roses of individuation, of the individual suffering under the anonymous sovereignty of the system controlling us all. As a romantic of the ego he is still struggling against it and wants to embody and personally and sovereignly represent the general only in the particular, that is, in himself. One last self-representation! In a mass society he seeks to be authentic, and since this is what everyone wants, he still may hope for an identity.

als das Konkrete, Selbsterlebte, "es war im Fernsehen" ... Die Kamera, besonders die Fernsehkamera, muß ja dabei gewesen sein, die Bildherstellung geschieht ja nach Naturgesetzen, Willkür hat seine Grenzen. Die Spuren auf den Fotos sind Lichtreflexe wirklicher Gegenstände. So auch in diesen Polaroids.

Ich zeige Ihnen aber nicht bloße Gegenstandsspuren, sondern Selbstvergegenständlichungsspuren eines Subjekts, das entsprechend seinem Künstlerwahn die Fotospuren seines Objektleibes durch Gestaltung ins Exemplarisch-Subjektive zurückverwandeln will.

Das Ich will nicht nur Weltengrund, Subjekt seiner Objekte sein, sondern darüberhinaus auch Grund seiner selbst. An diesen Polaroid-sofort-Selbstbildnissen zeigt sich der Wahnsinn der Gesellschaft im Versuch des Künstlers: Er will auch noch als Objekt Subjekt bleiben. Vor und zugleich hinter der Kamera, als Erblickter dennoch Blick! Er will, wie seinerzeit so mancher bürgerliche Philosoph durch sein Begriffssystem, wie Hegel z.B, seine sterbliche Natur durch Philosophie oder wie hier durch Kunst erlösen, d.h durch Formung, Stil, also durch etwas Höheres, weil Allgemeineres, – folglich Unsterbliches, – aufheben oder überhöhen.

"Parapsychose (vegetarisch)", 1978/84 /
'Parapsychosis (vegetarian)', 1978/84

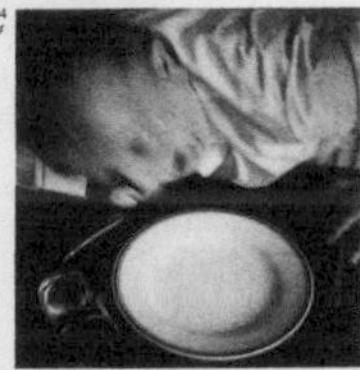

Er will den individuellen Zufall, der er selbst ist, in wenigstens ästhetische Notwendigkeit erheben.

Das ist natürlich nicht ohne Tragik, bzw. Komik. Denn auch den Selbstauslöser fertigte die Industrie. Das "Ich bin Ich" ist längst ein Sonderangebot von Polaroid, von Neckermann und Photo Porst. Das Selbst ist also schon erlöst, in eine anonyme Ware nämlich! Und wer sich durch solche Vergewisserungsangebote nicht erlösen lassen will und trotzdem fotografiert, der muß die Identifizierungsraster unterlaufen, ignorieren, parodieren und, wenn es nur ginge, transzendieren. Das sieht ganz lustig aus und ist dann doch nicht nur mit Lust verbunden. Das Ich soll ja durch Nichtung seines "bloß" körperlichen Nicht-Ich zum Zuge kommen, und das bedeutet Frust und Qual. Weil es nie richtig klappt. Deshalb nenne ich meine Fotospiele auch gerne "Masovisuelle Ipsation".

Aber durch solchen Fototod im Fotocomic hält der Fotokünstler als ein letzter Individualheroe für sich und andere noch eine negative Hoffnung zynisch wach: auf Authentizität! Sie kann

I present myself as an exemplary case. Let us say: as a photo art... Photographs are accepted, not necessarily as art but as more or le... plausible communications. The information transported by a photo... graph is thought to be, in the objective sense, more true than any... written or painted or even as anything real, experienced by self... was on TV" ... After all, the camera, especially the TV camera, m... have been there; the pictures are produced according to laws of na... re, arbitrariness has its limits. The traces on the photograph are... reflections of real things. Which is also true of these polaroids.

I will not only show you mere traces of objects, but also intro... self-materialisation of a subject tending, according to its artistic ma... nia, to change back the photographic traces of its object shape... exemplarily subjectivity through creativity.

The ego not only wants to be world purpose, subject of its objec... but, in addition, also its own purpose. The polaroid-pictures demon... strate the insanity of society in the artist's attempt: Being objec... he wants to remain subject; in front of and simultaneously behind... camera, seeing, yet seen. Like many a burgeois philosopher be...

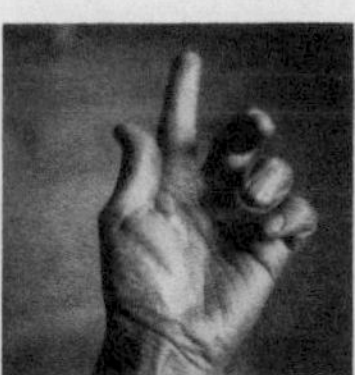
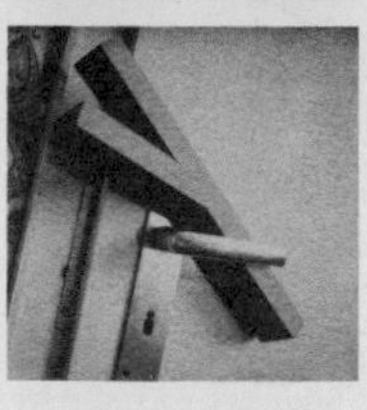
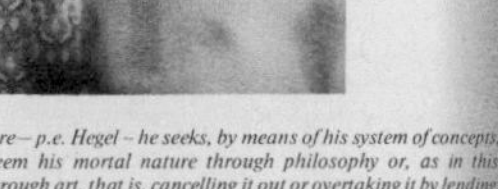

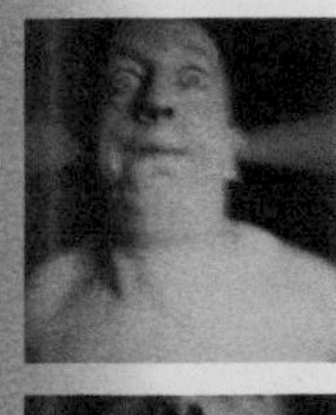
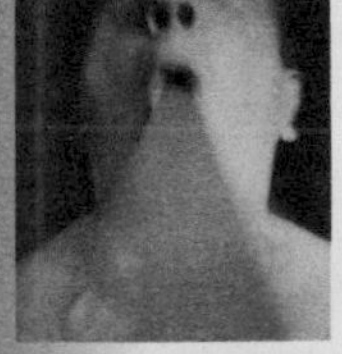

"Sakrale Kunst", aus der Serie "Zurück zur Natur, aber wie?", 1984

Tragisch perpetuiert er wie alle Fotografen, Filmer, Fernsehleute Krieg und Tod und Selbstabschaffung im Medium "interesselosen Wohlgefallens". In meinem Fall: In schönen grünen Bildern will er sein Verschwinden – und am eigenen Gemüse die Ertötung der Natur als paradoxe Lebenspraxis zeigen: Als Rasterung von Leib und Seele, Überformung, Züchtung, Ausrottung der Vielfalt, Zerstörung des Zusammenhangs, als ein Verschwinden der komplexen Mutter durch die Dominanz des männlich-eckigen Prinzips. So winkt der Künstlerpriester hier ganz deutlich dem Publikum mit grünen Heilsgebilden zu. Sehnsuchtsgebärden mit Naturkonstrukten. Aber nicht von einem imaginären Paradiese her, sondern aus seinem Wohn- und zugleich Wahnzimmer als dem gerasterten Gefängnis der Kultur.

Er gestikuliert mit immergrünen Zweigen, Plastikblumen, sogenanntem Frischgemüse aus der Tiefkühlbox. Giftgrüne Pflanzenkreuze stehen oder schweben für das Schicksal des Natürlichen und sind entsprechend stereometrisch eckig und aus dauerhaftem Material und dennoch ideoplastisch ein Verweis aufs Werden und Vergehen. Es wird also kein Fortschrittskultur zelebriert als Hoffnungsritus. Die Kreuze sollen in Erinnerung halten, daß die Kultur nicht nur ein ignorantes Wuchern, Wachsen, Sich Verzweigen sein kann, sondern auch ein Erleiden und Ersterben ist.

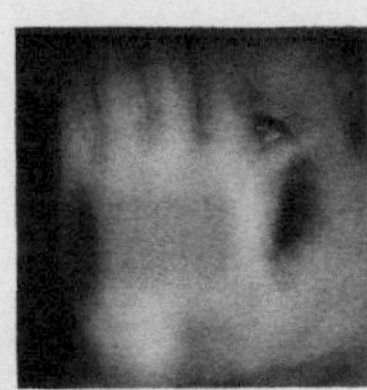 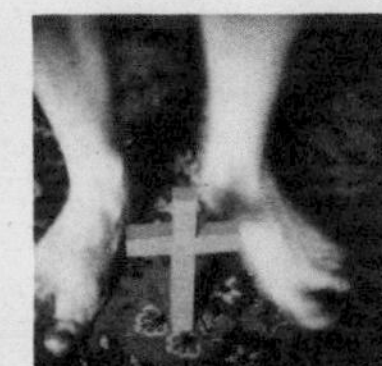

"Ecclewsiastic art", from the series "Back to Nature, but How?", 1984

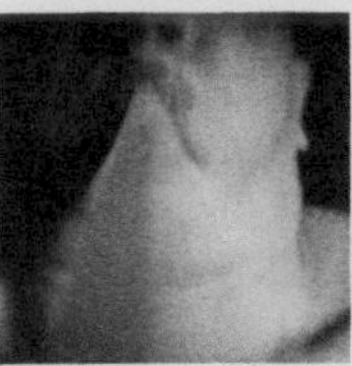
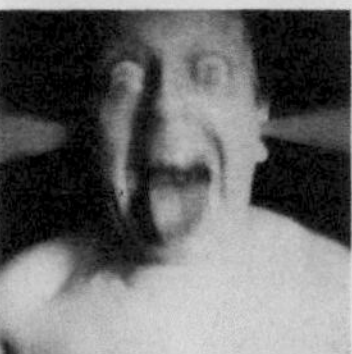
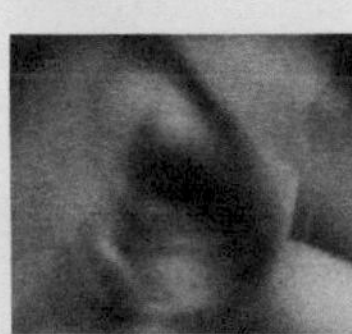

But by such photo death in a photo comic the photo artis... individual hero cynically keeps alive for himself and for the o... last negative hope: for authenticity! It can, however, only be... this side of the picture – as demonstrated by these pictures. A... from the photos of hobby and ad photographers who not o... doubt the aetheticism of the poses and patterns of social i... tion but confuse it with reality itself or pretend it to be such,... res demonstrate: The artist suffers exemplarily from the co... from himself! Here, things that normally are private, beco... and only bearable by deforming form. Here is presented th...

aber nur diesseits aller Bilder liegen, wie diese Bilder zeigen. Aber anders als die Fotos von Hobbyknipsern oder Werbefotografen, welche das Ästhetische der Posen und Muster gesellschaftlicher Identifikation ja nicht nur nicht bezweifeln, sondern mit der Realität selbst verwechseln oder sie dafür ausgeben, zeigen seine Bilder: Es krankt der Künstler exemplarisch am Kollektiv als an sich selbst! Das, was ansonsten nur privat geschieht, das ist hier öffentlich, und nur durch Deformierungen der "Form" erträglich. Hier wird die Angstlust vorgeführt, als Ich im Leib als seinem Triebgrund zu verschwinden, und der Künstler verfährt dabei mit sich wie das System mit der Natur: Er geht wie dieses über Leichen, – in seinem Falle aber ists die eigene, das macht ihn so sympathisch und exotisch! Der Selbstdarsteller zeigt in lachender Verwesung – fotoekstatisch, fototödlich – die allgemeine Selbstabschaffung. Das Heil erscheint in solcher Kunst nur negativ. Es läßt sich nicht bebildern. Sakrale Kunst ist repressiv. Der Künstler kann das ehemals Schöne, das Ästhetische nur noch als Vorschein eines Schrecklichen entlarven wollen und muß doch weiter schöne Bilder machen. Muß er?

fore – p.e. Hegel – he seeks, by means of his system of concepts, to re... deem his mortal nature through philosophy or, as in this cas... through art, that is, cancelling it out or overtaking it by lending sha... and style which is more exalted (since general) and conseque... immortal. He seeks to lift the individual coincidence that he is at lea... to the level of aesthetic necessity.

This, of course, does not lack a certain degree of tragedy or comed... for even the self-timer has been produced by industry. "Me is me" ha... long since become a special offer by Polaroid, Neckermann and Pho... Porst. The ego, thus, has already been redeemed, namely, into a... anonymous commodity! And those who refuse to be redeemed ... such offers of assurance and continue to make photography mu... evade and ignore and must, if it were possible, transcend the patter... of identification. Though this may have a funny look, there is more i... volved than fun and pleasure. The ego, after all, should, by negati... of its "merely" physical non-ego, get its chance – and that means fru... stration and pain; because it never really works. This is why I also ca... my photo games "maso-visual ipsation".

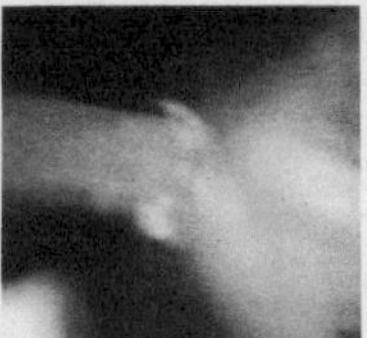 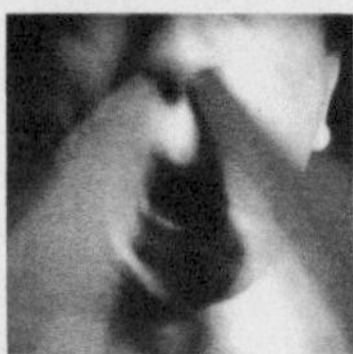 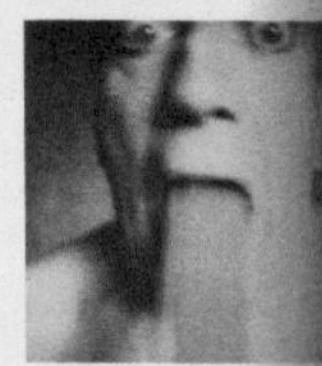

"Grünes Fluidum", aus der Serie "natürlich", 1984 / "Green Fluid", from the series "natural", 1984

Die Äpfel, Paprika und Blumenkohl sind die Metaphern für ein rundes heiles Ganzes und werden dennoch angstekstatisch oder zynisch lachend vorgewiesen. Als Wunsch und zugleich Angstsymbole. Denn das GANZE ist Geburt und Tod, nicht seine bloße Trennung und Verdrängung, Rationalisierung. Die Reine, d.h. von Trieb und Tod gereinigte Vernunft ist nämlich ungenießbar. Sie ist bloß tautologisch, und nicht ökologisch. Aber dennoch hängt dem ganzheitlich gestimmten Künstlermedium als Müsliman, Salatbeschwörer das Natürliche zuweilen idiosynkratisch aus dem Halse.

Seine Wiedervernatürlichungsekstasen geschehen unter Schmerzen, denn die weibliche Natur als grünes, fluidales Ganzes raubt dem Künstler öfter seinen männlichen Verstand. Der mütterliche Odem braust ihm dann durch Hals, Nase und Ohren. Und die Mutter Erde schickt ihm grüne Strahlen durchs Gehirn. Salat verweigert seine Zubereitung und erscheint in einer Drohgebärde. Als Wiederkehr eines Verdrängten, – narzißtisch-ideoplastisch. Doch nur gebündelt – strahlenförmig wird das mütterliche Chaos zugelassen, – d.h. ästhetisch-phallokratisch! – Denn Gott will MANN bleiben, Schöpfer aus dem Nichts und Selbsterzeu-

...get, auch als Müsliman. Die Gottesmutter wird auch weiterhin zur Jungfrau entsexualisiert. Der Hl. Geist erzeugt sich immer noch durchs Ohr der Frau, – als Wort, als Machtwort! Aber "vielleicht ist die Wahrheit ein Weib" – ahnte Nietzsche und konzipierte den Übermenschen.

Das ist zum Weinen, aber auch zum Lachen natürlich. In diesem Foto lacht für Sie der Künstler deshalb maskulin-auratisch und feminin-ekstatisch. An ihm und durch ihn als ein Medium der Wiederkehr des Weiblichen (im Manne) taucht das Verdrängte über seinem Kopfe wieder auf als Blumenkohl, als Heilsgebilde. Ein runder Apfel oder Apfelkranz erinnern uns an den Verlust der

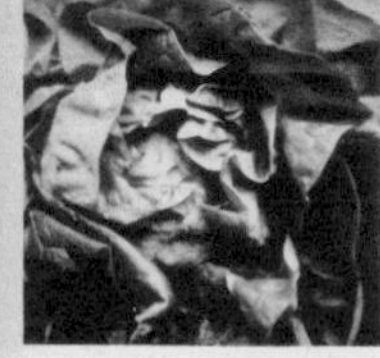

"Back to Nature, but How?", 1984

fear of the ego of disappearing in the body, in the slough of driven urges, and the artist does to himself what the system does to nature. Just like it, he walks over dead bodies – over his own dead body, as it were, and that's what makes him so amiable and exotic! In lovely decay, the artist representing himself depicts – photoecstatically and photodeadly – the general self-cancellation. Salvation in such a ... only appears negative. It refuses to be depicted. Sacred art is repressive. All that's left to the artist is to expose former beauty, former aestheticism as the mere foreshadowing of the terrible – and he ... must continue to make beautiful pictures. Or must he?

Tragically, he perpetuates, like all photographers, film-makers and TV-producers, war and death and self-cancellation within the medium of "disinterested pleasure". In my case: In beautiful green pictures he wants to show his disappearance and, using his vegetables as an example, the deadening of nature as a paradoxical practice of life, as a screening of body and soul, as overshaping, ... eradicating plurality, destroying contexts, as a vanishing of the complex mother by the domination of the masculine-right-angle principle. The artist priest clearly beckons to the audience with green symbols of salvation. Gestures of an inner longing with constructive...

...ture. But not from an imaginary paradise, no; rather from the very room and the delusion wherein he lives, from the screened jail of culture.

He is gesticulating with evergreen branches, plastic flowers, so-called fresh vegetables (from the freezer). Poison-green plant crosses stand for or hover for the destiny of all that is natural, appropriately angular, of durable material, yet an ideoplastic hint to growing and dying. No celebration of a progress cult, a rite of hope. The crosses are to be a reminder that culture is not only ignorant growth and branching out but also suffering and dying. Apples, peppers and cauliflower are metaphors of a rounded, wholesome completeness – yet

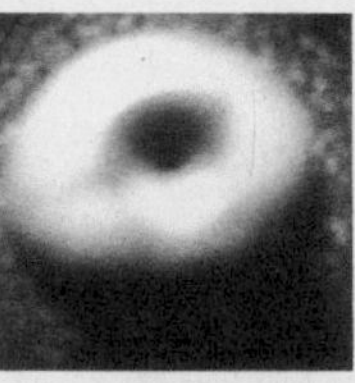 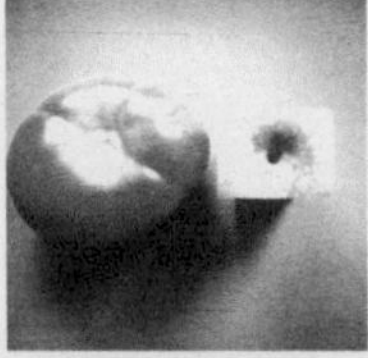 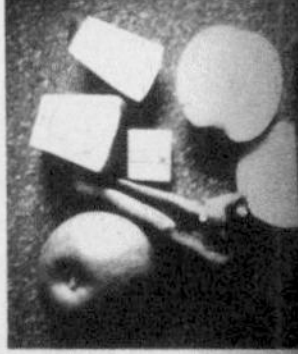 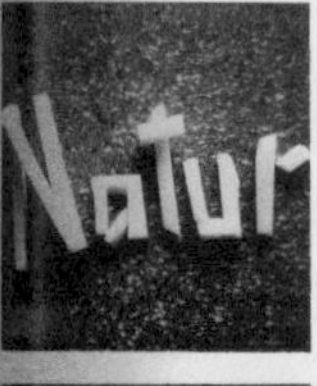 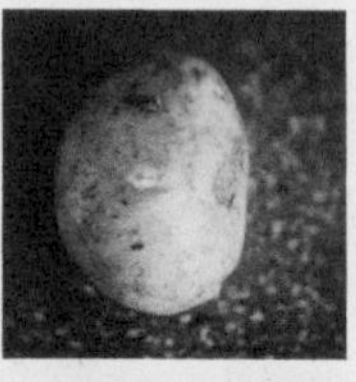

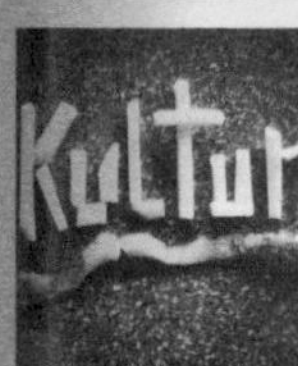 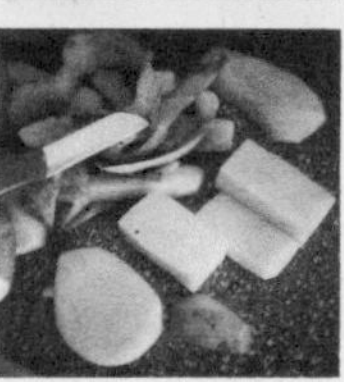

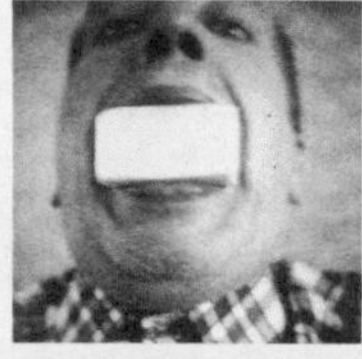

"Natur – Kultur", 1984 / "Nature – Culture", 1984

"Die runde und die eckige Vernunft", aus der Serie "Zurück zur Natur, aber wie?", 1984 / "Round and Square Reason", from the series "Back to Nature, but How?", 1984

mütterlichen Mitte. Es wird dem in ein intra-uterines Glück sich selbst Zurückverweisenden komplementär die linke Herzhand grün, wie Sie hier sehen können. Sie weist jedoch zugleich vom allzu Nahen in ein räumlich-bläulich-fernes Ungefähres. Also nur manchmal deucht ihn, – er wäre bereits angekommen. Die unvollkommen-runde Frühkartoffel wurde allerdings sogleich, nebst einigen Äpfeln, ein Opfer analytisch-geometrisch-männlicher Zerteilung. Hiernach ist sie zu einer Heilssymbolik nur bedingt geeignet. Außerdem war gerade Mittagszeit: Himmel und Erde, Pommes Frites anstatt Pellkartoffeln. Und überhaupt Gekochtes

they are held out in an ecstasis of fear or with a cynical grin, double symbols of wishes and fear. For it is the whole which is constituted of birth and death, not merely separation, displacement and rationalization. Purity, that is: reason cleansed of urges and death, is inedible, a tautology, not ecological. Nevertheless, the holistically inclined artist medium – the muesli man and salad charmer – idiosyncratically has the natural up to here.

His renaturalization ecstases are painful since female nature, the green fluid whole, often makes the artist loose his masculine reason. Motherly breath will sweep through his throat, nose and ears. And

28

und Gesottenes statt Rohkost. Und manchmal, im Schnellimbiß an der Ecke, gehen ihm die geometrisierten Happen nicht recht hinein und hinunter. Deshalb zum Nachtisch McDonalds Softeis, oral-amerikanisch-traumatisch. Weiße Muttermilch ist deshalb für alle Sehnsuchtssymbiotiker, oral-fixierte Vaginalneurotiker, ödipale Phallokraten usw. nur in der eckig-rationellen Tiefkühlpackung zugelassen.

Ansonsten aber herrscht in diesen Fotos, wie gesagt, Grün vor. Polaroidgrün mit dem leichten Blauknick in die Ferne. – Um zu verhindern, daß das mütterliche Gute mir allzu nahe kommt. Als grünes Fluidum ist es dem hier agierenden Sauerstoffekstatiker

Mother Earth sends green rays through his brain. Salad refuses ... fixed and appears menacing, as a come-back of something repressed – narcistic-ideoplastic. But the motherly chaos must only ... bundled rays, i.e. aesthetically phallocratic! For god wants to remain male, creator from the void, self-creator, even a muesli man. ... mother of god continues to be desexed as a virgin, as a word, a word of authority. But perhaps "the truth is a woman", Nietzsche suspected and conceived the superman.

That gives rise to tears, but, of course, also to laughing. And in this photo, the artist laughs for you a masculin-auratic, feminin-ecstatic laugh. About him and through him as a medium of the return ...

ohnehin allgegenwärtig. Aus- und einatmend, essend, trinkend, kotzend, pissend, scheißend, onanierend – fluktuiert das grüne Sehnsuchtsideoplasma durch alle Körperöffnungen im Rhythmus der Natur.

Ankoppeln will er sich so, in neuer Triebromantik, als eine Wunschmaschine an materiale/mütterliche und astrale Nahrungsketten. Dazu ist, wie Sie hier sehen konnten, besonnene Besinnungslosigkeit, ekstatische Kontrolle, hungrige Enthaltsamkeit, bunte Illusionslosigkeit, lachende Verzweiflung, desinteressiertes Wohlgefallen und das heißt Ästhetik, – also KUNST vonnöten.

of the female (in the male), the repressed reappears over his head, as a cauliflour, as an object of salvation. A round apple, an apple ring, brings to mind the loss of the motherly center. As you can see here, the left hand of the man directing himself back to intra-uterine contentness, coming from the heart, complimentarily turns green. At the same time, it points from that which is all too near into spacial bluish vagueness, so that only at times he feels he has arrived. The imperfectly rotund early potato immediately fell, as it were, together with several apples, victim to analytical-geometrical-masculine division. After this, they were only partially useful as objects of salvation. Moreover, it just was noon time: heaven and earth, French fries, not boiled potatoes. And generally cooked and fried instead of uncooked food. And sometimes, at the fast food on the corner, he has trouble getting the geometrically cut pieces in and down. So: McDonald's ice cream, oral-American-traumatic, for dessert. White mother's milk for symbiotics of longing, for orally fixed vagina neurotics, oedipal phallocrats etc. is only allowed in angular-rational deep-freeze packages.

But otherwise green is the dominant color in these pictures, as mentioned. Polaroid green with that slight blue kink into the distance. So as to keep the motherly good at arm's length. As a green fluid it is omnipresent anyway to the oxygen ecstatic in action here. In- and exhaling, eating, drinking, puking, pissing, shitting and masturbating – the green ideoplasma of longing fluctuates in the rhythm of nature through all the body openings.

This is how he wants to hitch up in his new romanticism of urges and drives – a wish machine linked to material-motherly and astral feeding chains. And that requires, as you can see here, thoughtful thoughtlessness, ecstatic control, hungry abstinence, a motley lack of illusion, laughing desperation, disinterested pleasure, that is: aestheticism, – so ART.

Übersetzung: Klaus Feichtenberger
Translation: Klaus Feichtenberger

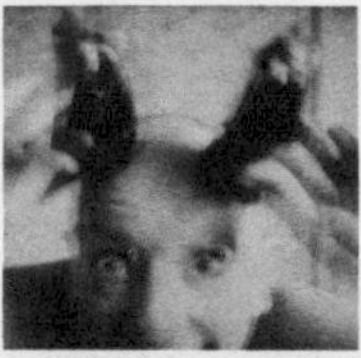 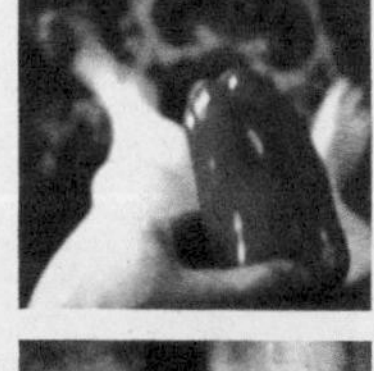
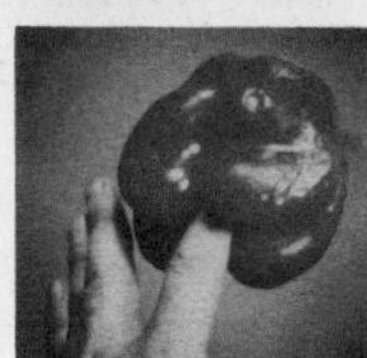 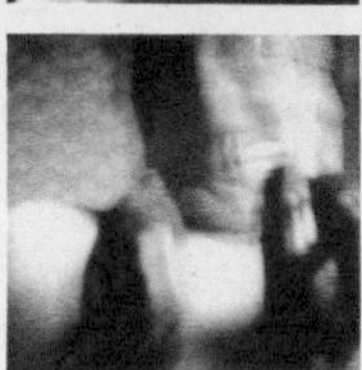

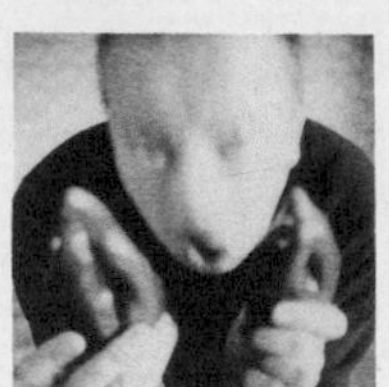 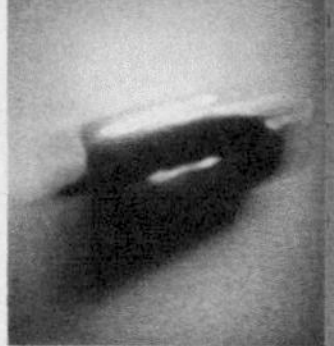

"Orgie", aus der Serie "natürlich", 1984 / "Orgy", from the series "natural", 1984

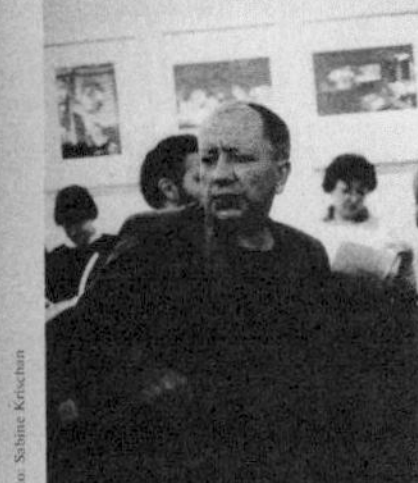

Foto: Sabine Krischan

BERNHARD JOHANNES BLUME
geboren 1937 in Dortmund, Lehre als Dekorationsmaler, Studium in Düsseldorf und Köln, lebt in Köln und München. Monographie: "Natürlich", München 1985.

BERNHARD JOHANNES BLUME
Born in 1937 in Dortmund; training as an interior decorator, studied in Düsseldorf and Köln, lives in Köln and Munich; monograph: "Natürlich", Munich 1985.

30

31

222

Camera Austria Award

2015   Camera Austria Award for Contemporary
Photography by the City of Graz

Camera Austria International

2002   Forum contribution, *Camera Austria
International* 79/2002
2008   Jens Asthoff, "Annette Kelm,"
text contribution, Annette Kelm,
artist contribution and cover,
Camera Austria International 102/2008
2014   Holger Otten, "Annette Kelm: Staub,
Kölnischer Kunstverein, Köln," exhibition
review, *Camera Austria International*
128/2014
2015   Guest editor, artist contribution and
cover, Maren Lübbke-Tidow, "Annette
Kelm: Wir wissen eigentlich nicht,
was wir sehen: Fotografieren fotografieren," text contribution, *Camera
Austria International* 131/2015

Exhibitions

2009   *Annette Kelm,* solo exhibition
2010   *Milk Drop Coronet. 30 Exhibitions on
the Virtuosity of Thingness,* exhibition
contribution

Publication

2017   Annette Kelm and Hendrik Schwantes
eds, *Hans Hansen, Atelier,* Graz: Edition
Camera Austria, 2017

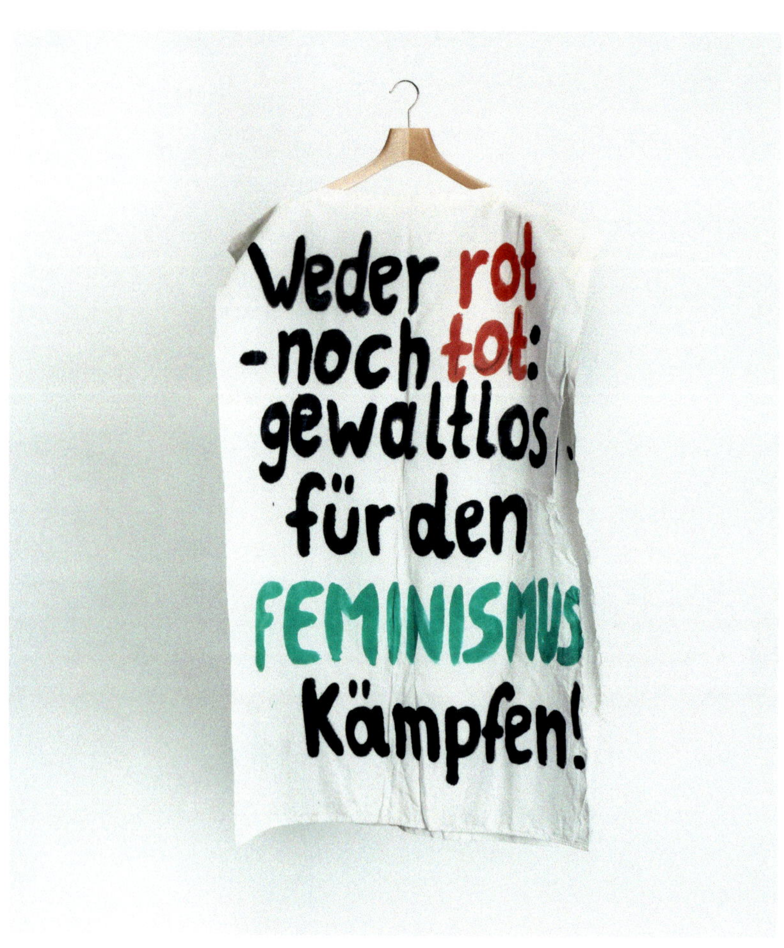

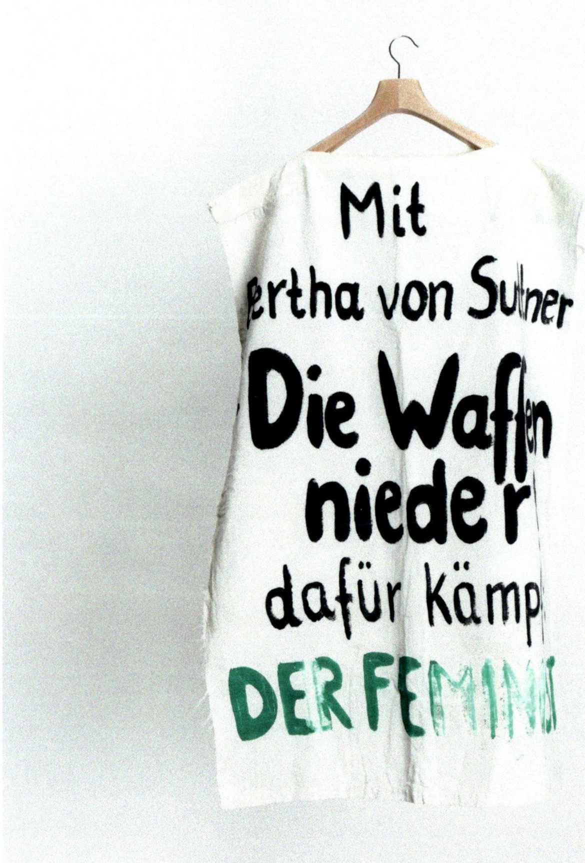

Institut für Zeitgeschichte-Archiv, Munich, file Hannelore Mabry / Bayerisches Archiv der Frauenbewegung.
From the series "Körperüberhänge" (Body Cloaks), 2014; signature ED 900, box 403, no. 2.

Annette Kelm

Body Cloaks

The body cloaks were worn by the Munich-based "Förderkreis zum Aufbau der Feministischen Partei" (Sponsor Group to Build the Feminist Party). From the beginning the group was clear about the fact that men can be feminists, and for that reason explicitly called on men to become feminists. This often led to criticism from groups that excluded men. From 1976 the group published the magazine *DER FEMINIST* (The Male Feminist). The central figure was the women's rights activist Hannelore Mabry (1930–2013). She also managed the group's archive and bequeathed it on her death to the Institut für Zeitgeschichte in Munich.

The cloaks are stored in boxes in the institute, alongside a wide variety of documents such as flyers, documentary photographs and minutes of meetings. They were tailored from old bed sheets and the group wore them for various actions. I photographed the protest cloaks in an improvised studio situation in the rooms of the archive. I find the cloaks interesting because, among other reasons, they represent an attempt to create a parallel aesthetic to the "purple dungarees" that have become a strong (and often clichéd) symbol for second wave feminism in German-speaking countries.

The Förderkreis group, which emerged from another group also founded by Maby, the Frauenforum München e.V., has been largely forgotten, although back then it is one of the first and biggest groups in the women's movement. Popular perception of second wave feminism in Germany is centered around Alice Schwarzer and purple dungarees. This central focus also emerges in the museumization of the feminist movement, for example in the Deutsches Historisches Museum in Berlin, where there is a two square meter glass showcase containing a pair of dungarees, a copy of *Emma* and *Courage*, and a flyer.

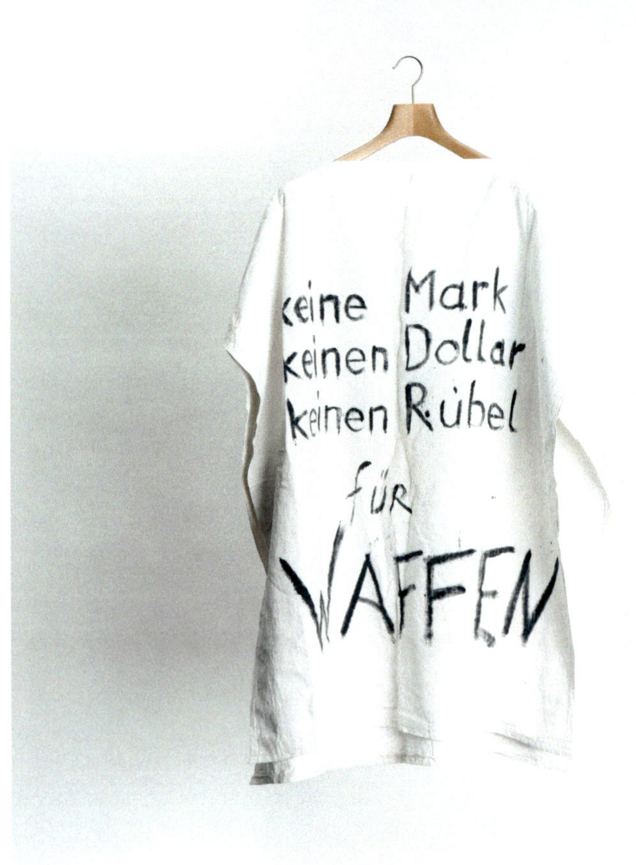

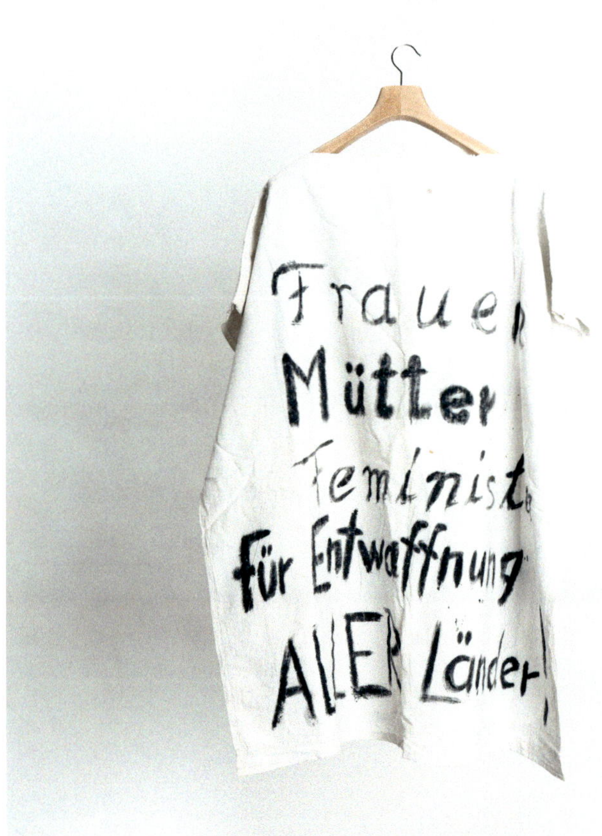

Institut für Zeitgeschichte-Archiv, Munich, file Hannelore Mabry/Bayerisches Archiv der Frauenbewegung.
From the series "Körperüberhänge" (Body Cloaks), 2014; signature ED 900, box 532

131
2015

Camera Austria
INTERNATIONAL

A/D/LUX
16,– €
CH
20,– sFr

Gastredakteurin / Guest editor

Annette Kelm

Shannon Ebner, Morgan Fisher,
Jan Groover, Hans Hansen, Louis Ducos
du Hauron, Judith Hopf, Horst P. Horst,
Barbara Kasten, David Lieske,
Dirk von Lowtzow, Maren Lübbke-Tidow,
Henrik Olesen, Arthur Ou, Josephine Pryde,
Sabine Reitmaier, Michael Schmidt,
Hendrik Schwantes, Sylvia Sleigh,
Lucie Stahl, Herbert Tobias,
Christopher Williams

Kolumne / Column
Cinenova Feminist Film and
Video Distributor

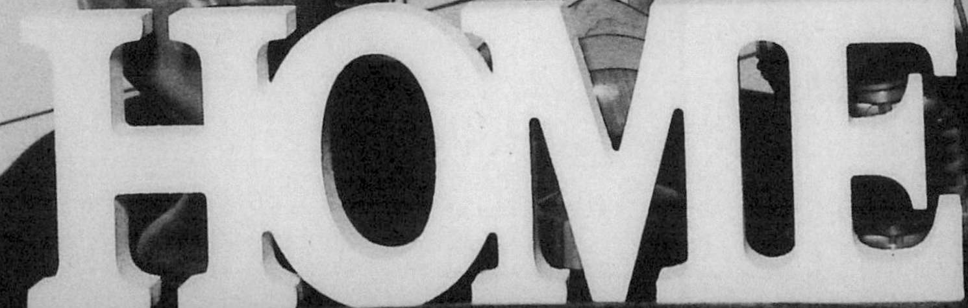

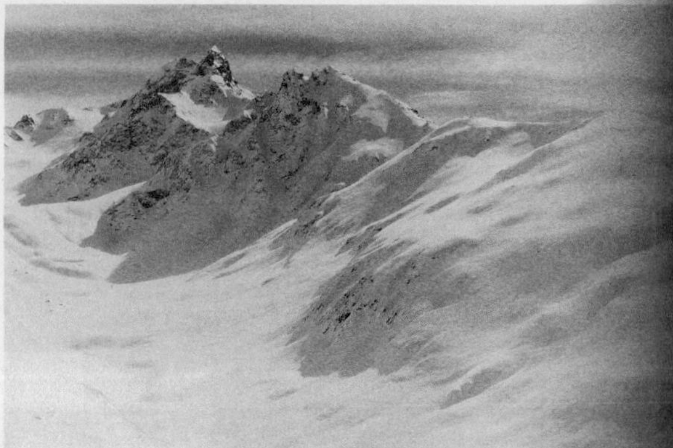

ANNETTE KELM, Berg, 2001. C-Print, 50,8 cm x 61 cm.

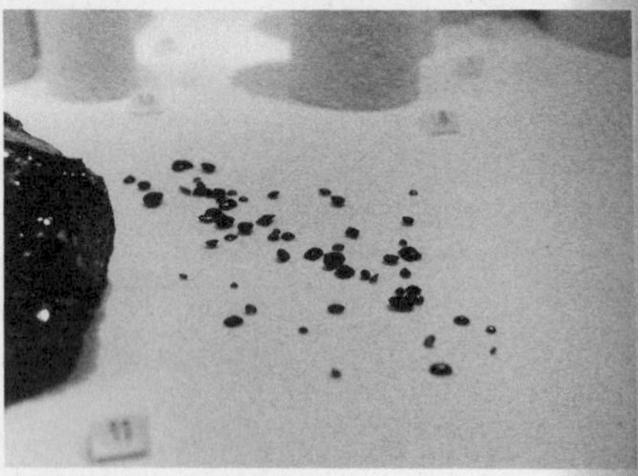

ANNETTE KELM, Rubine, 2001. C-Print, 50,8 cm x 61 cm.

Annette Kelm

geboren 1975 in Stuttgart (D); lebt in Hamburg (D); zahlreiche Ausstellungen, zuletzt: 1998 Galerie Nomadenoase, Hamburg; »Wunderwelt«, Art Agents Gallery, Hamburg; 2001 »Wir, Comawoche«, Hamburg; 2002 »andere Räume«, Kunstverein Hamburg

Rolf Sachsse

NETZ – BILD – HAUT
Bilder vom Krieg

Wer eine Bildsuchmaschine des Internets auf »Krieg« und die passenden Übersetzungen des Begriffs in die fünf Weltsprachen einstellt, erlebt das klassische Wunder eines unorganisierten Wissenszugriffs: Viele Bilder zeigen Vieles (pro Sprache rund 200.000 Zugriffe, im englischen einige mehr), aber eigentlich nur ganz selten das, was fotografischer oder televisionärer Journalismus mit dem Wort Krieg verbinden. Ruinöse Bauten als Teil abenteuerlicher Radtouren[1] oder lächelnde Uniformierte in der Sonne als Teil einer privatistischen Erinnerungsgeschichte[2] sind ebenso häufig wie symbolschwere Arbeiten einer immerhin als naiv beschriebenen Volkskunst[3], hinzu kommen sekundäre Beschreibungen von Schutzmaßnahmen oder Kriegsfolgen[4]. Assoziativ mögen die Bilder mit dem Krieg zu verbinden sein, Darstellungen sind es nicht. Selbst eine ungebührlich kurze Recherche im Internet lässt also den Schluss zu, dass trotz aller Thematisierung das Zeigen des Krieges nicht gern gesehen ist. Mit dem Finger deutet man nicht auf (tote) Menschen, so scheint es.

Ein Blick in professionelle Suchkataloge[5] ändert den Eindruck selbstverständlich. Hier dominieren nicht nur die Arbeiten der harten BildjournalistInnen, sondern auch die Motive einer entsprechenden Erwartungshaltung. Leichen im Blut, Straßen mit Löchern, herumstehende und nichts begreifende Passanten, Panzer, Soldaten, Hubschrauber, Einschusslöcher, Ruinen mit menschlichen Überresten, dazu Luftbilder mit Aufzeichnungen von Aktionen und Dokumenten der Ergebnisse – halt das ganze Montagematerial, aus dem sich für einen durchschnittlichen Mediennutzer das Bild vom Krieg zusammensetzt. Ist man jung genug, wird dieses unendlich wiederholte und damit abgenutzte Spiel der Realitäten durch die virtuelle Räumlichkeit der Computerspiele überwuchert und damit endgültig von der eigenen Lebenswirklichkeit abgetrennt. Resultat eins: Jedes Kind, das in der Vorpubertät täglich zwei Stunden vorm Ego-Shooter saß, überholt locker die bestausgebildeten Scharfschützen aller Sondereinheiten. Resultat zwei: Einem solchen Kind kann man im Fall einer persönlichen Kränkung nicht mehr mit so lächerlichen Argumenten wie der Differenz von Leben und Tod kommen. Die Vorhersage, dass sich Littleton und Erfurt wiederholen werden, haben die gleiche Ursache und Treffsicherheit wie die meteorologische Tendenz zu gigantischen Naturkatastrophen: Menschengemacht und nicht (für) wahrgenommen.

Professionelle Bilder vom Krieg ummanteln sich mit einer ethischen Perspektive, wollen selbst Moral sein: Das Zeigen des Grauens müsse doch einen jeden Menschen wachrütteln und ihn alles daran setzen lassen, Wiederholungen zu verhindern. Manchmal mag das funktionieren, meistens jedoch nicht. Im Gegenteil: Schaudern fördert die Schaulust, immer weiter, immer heftiger, immer schauriger. Jedes Bild, das lehrt schon die Erotik, ist in erster Linie ein Versprechen für ein neues Bild – um den Frust am Alten

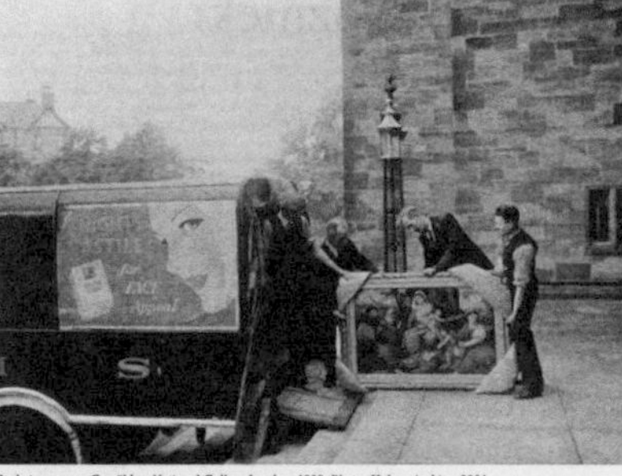

Evakuierung von Gemälden, National Gallery London, 1939. Photo: Hulton Archive, 2001.

nicht zu groß werden zu lassen, denn das kann sein Versprechen niemals halten. Itinerare (Reiseverzeichnisse) des hohen Mittelalters listeten genau auf, in welchen Städten viele und grausame Hinrichtungen ausgeführt wurden; und die Berichte von Dabeigewesenen verzeichnen genau, welche Volksbelustigung in derlei Darbietungen lag. Trotzdem mag das Märchen vom abschreckenden Wirken grausamer Bilder seine Wirkung nicht verlieren.

Bilder vom Krieg haben Konjunktur in der Medienwelt. Seit Christian Freis semi-dokumentarischen Film »War Photographer« über und mit James Nachtwey, bei dem der Protagonist näher an einem Oscar war als Nick Nolte in einer ähnlichen Rolle aus Nicaragua, türmen sich die Anfragen nach passenden Drehbüchern bei den Filmagenturen, und alle müssen nach Experten suchen, die ihnen das Funktionieren des Bildgeschäfts zu Zeiten des Internets erklären. Umgekehrt wird aus jedem klitzekleinen Fernseh-Feature über einen Lokalblatt-Bildjournalisten sofort ein Actionkrimi mit quietschenden Reifen, Kamera im Anschlag und ruckartiger Annäherung an – nun ja, meist den kleinen Verkehrsunfall zwei Straßen weiter. Aus dem Alltag wird Krieg, das haben die Computerspiele als Trend nur noch verstärkt und mit höherer Treffsicherheit ausgestattet. Die Metaphorik des Krieges hat sich zudem noch vollkommen verbraucht und ist zur Kennzeichnung eitler Auseinandersetzungen von Prominenten und denen, die sich dafür halten, verkommen.

Wie aus dem Krieg Alltag wird, ist mit stehenden und bewegten Bildern eindrucksvoller zu belegen als mit jeder anderen Darstellungsform. Didi Danquarts Film »Wundbrand« aus Sarajevo (1994) zeigt mehr Krieg in den Köpfen als auf der Straße; de facto passiert nichts, das irgendwie auf eine direkte Lebensbedrohung hinweist.[6] Doch eine Spannung liegt im Bild, und in einer späteren Diskussion erwähnt der Filmemacher eher beiläufig, dass einige der Gefilmten längst tot seien, meist an direkten Folgen der Auseinandersetzungen gestorben, also an dem, was unsere militärischen Beschützer Kollateralschäden zu nennen sich angewöhnt haben. Bilder abseits des Gesche-

hens, die doch die Last des alltäglichen Krieges zeigen, sind prinzipiell eine Domäne der Fotografinnen gewesen, von Margaret Bourke-White über die Dokumentaristinnen der Nachkriegszeit in Deutschland[7] bis etwa zur Arbeit von Sabine Sauer in Südafrika und auf dem Balkan. Weder Danquarts Film noch Sauers Bilder sind bislang publiziert – auch ein Statement zum Krieg in den Medien.

Medientechnisch liegen derlei Bilder und Filme oft weit hinter den großen Ausarbeitungen des heroischen Umgangs zurück – es gibt kaum große Scheckbücher bei der Erstellung, und es gibt wenig Farbe in der Postproduction. Im Film dominiert die Handkamera, in der Fotografie das Kleinbild, aber auch da nur mit kurzer und Normalbrennweite. Mit armen Mitteln kommt man näher an die Menschen heran, darin lag auch Goyas Wahl der Grafik für seine Kriegsbilder: Das heroische Gemälde mit seinem hohen Preis ist um 1850 ins historische Bild gewechselt, aus dem sich die Geschichte der neuen Düsseldorfer Fotografenschule direkt speist. Aber das ist eine andere Linie, und sie es hier nicht direkt geht (zumindest kenne ich kein Kriegsbild aus diesem Umfeld). Oder doch? Die Mobilmachung der Pop-Ikone Madonna, von Andreas Gursky um montierte Elemente ordnend erweitert, ähnelt verdächtig den Aufmärschen in Belgrad, die Milošević-hörige Rock-SängerInnen allnächtlich zusammenkommen ließen.

Krieg im Alltag, Alltag im Krieg, Krieg im Bild, Bilderkrieg, Bild im Krieg: die Metaphorik hat als Rotation schon einigen Leerlauf. Doch bei kurzem Anhalten der Räder wird ihr Werk sichtbar – fürchterlich.

1 http://www.adventurecycling.net/vietnamimages/krieg.jpg
2 http://www.leisurefeat.com/images/meinkrieg.jpg
3 http://adjones.net/FolkArt/summer99/krieg.jpg
4 http://www.nationalgallery.org.uk/about/default.htm
5 http://www.fotomarktplatz.de, o.ä.
6 http://ns1.zkm.de/zkm/stories/storyReader$2716
7 http://www.lkwpd.org/w/bahio/bour-mar.htm /frauenobjektiv. Fotografinnen 1940 – 1950, Ausstell.-Kat. Bonn: Haus der Geschichte, 2001.

Camera Austria International

2000 Presentation to the Forum,
Camera Austria International 72 / 2000
2002 Maren Lübbke, "Tatiana Lecomte,"
text contribution / artist contribution,
Camera Austria International 78 / 2002
2009 Rebekka Reuter, "Tatiana Lecomte:
Scriptures Without Words,"
exhibition review, *Camera Austria
International* 106 / 2009

Exhibitions

2003 *Orte,* solo exhibition
2010 *Milk Drop Coronet. 30 Exhibitions on
the Virtuosity of Thingness,* exhibition
contribution
2011 *Tatiana Lecomte,* solo exhibition
(with Šejla Kamerić)
2012 *DLF 1874. Die Biografie der Bilder,*
exhibition contribution
2015 *Archives, Re–Assemblances, and Surveys,*
Galerija Klovićevi dvori, Zagreb (HR),
exhibition contribution
Disputed Landscape: Uncovering History,
exhibition contribution
*What Was Documentary Is Now Something
Else,* Austrian Culture Institute Prague,
Fotograf Gallery and Galerie Školská 28,
Prague (CZ), exhibition contribution

Publications

2011 Reinhard Braun, ed., *Tatiana Lecomte,
Dissolution,* Graz, Edition Camera Austria,
2011.
2017 Reinhard Braun, ed., *Tatiana Lecomte,*
"Meine erste Löwin" (My First Lioness),
Graz, Edition Camera Austria, 2017

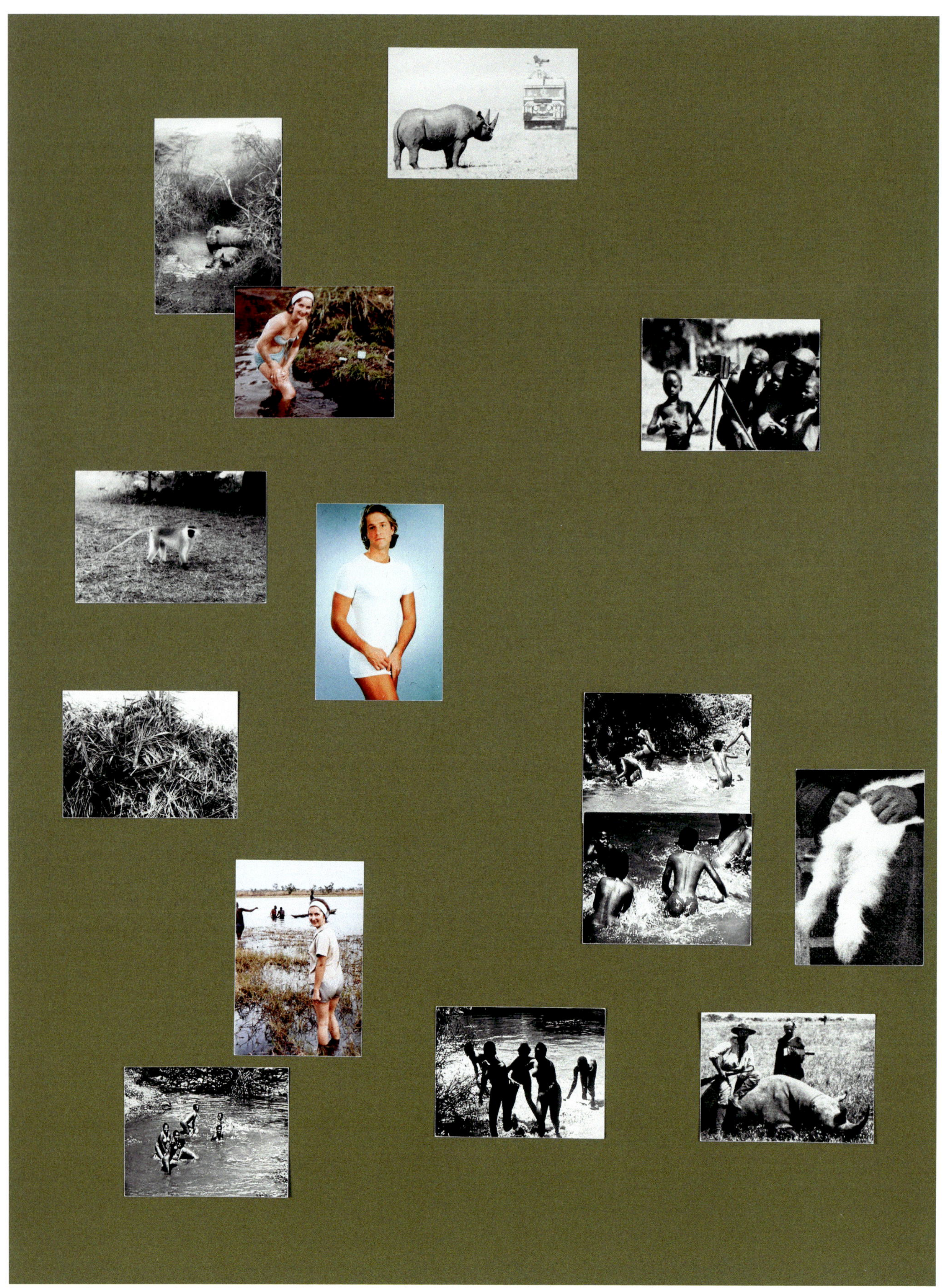

From the series "Meine erste Löwin" (My First Lioness), 2018

Tatiana Lecomte

Meine erste Löwin (My First Lioness)

The photographic source material, which Tatiana Lecomte liberally appropriates, which she "borrows," to use the artist's own words for her approach, is to be seen not only in a general historical context but most especially as being anchored in the history of photography. Images that document African safaris and stylize the slaying of animals as heroic feats, photos of animal husbandry showing a romantically glorified view, medical imagery, illustrations for cooking recipes, underwear advertising. In her work, Lecomte repeatedly references history as a laboratory for power and violence, a laboratory that is also dominated by gazes and imagery. She assumes the role of the one who shows what could already been seen and this remained hidden and secret during the act of making visible. "Meine erste Löwin" (My First Lioness) is a montage, but it also signifies reflection on the principle of montage—and ultimately on the possibilities and conditions of photography itself.

Franz Thalmair, from: *Tatiana Lecomte,* "Meine erste Löwin,"
Graz: Edition Camera Austria, 2017.

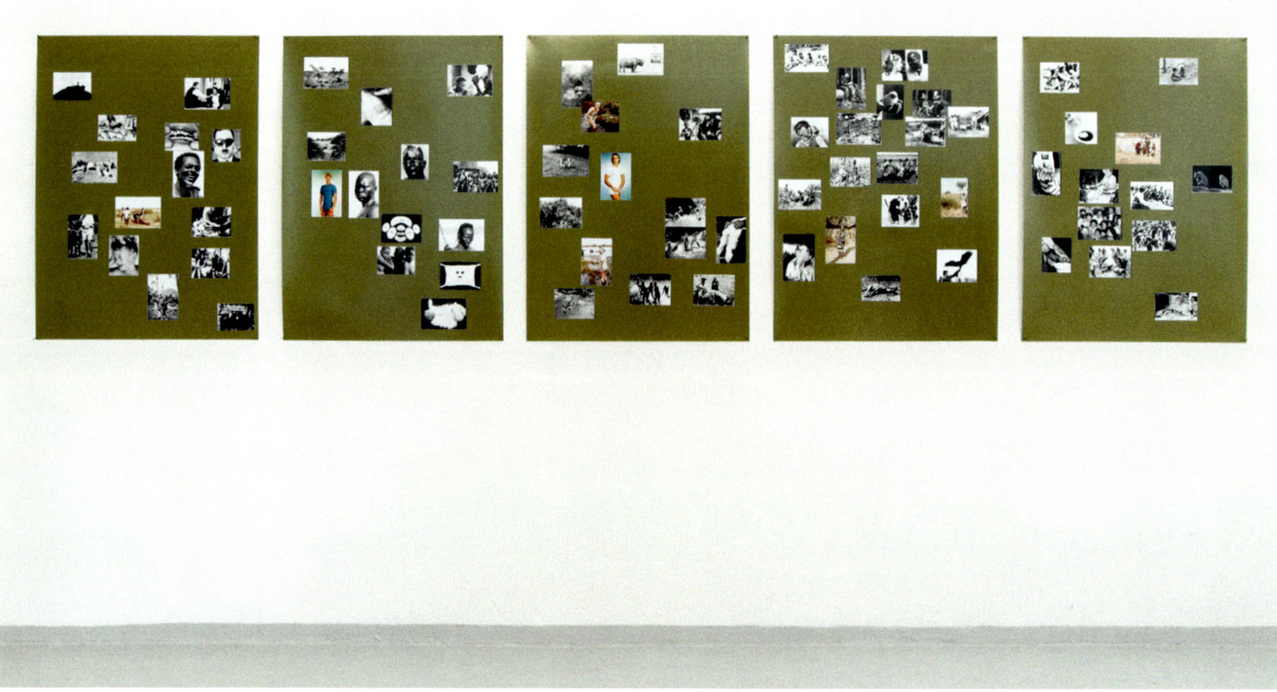

Tatiana Lecomte, *Chiasmata 17 – 18 mit Anna Artaker,* Josephinum, Vienna (AT), 2018, exhibition view

Tatiana Lecomte

geboren 1971 in Bordeaux; lebt in Wien; 1991 – 92 Académie des Beaux-arts de Lyon; 1993 – 95 Höhere technische Lehr- und Ver
anstalt, Graz; 1995 – 98 Hochschule für angewandte Kunst, Wien; 1998 – 00 G. Rietveld Academie, Amsterdam; 2000 – 01 Ateli
dium Tokio, Japan.

Ausstellungen:
1998 »nach vier kommt fünf«, Raum aktueller Kunst, Martin Janda, Wien; »come together«, Portfolio Kunst AG, Wien; 1999 »Jur
ne«, Secession Wien; 2000 »New Austrian Spotlight«, Istanbul.

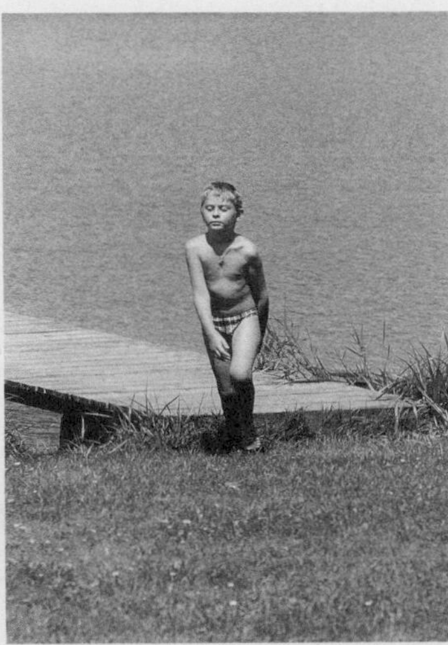

TATIANA LECOMTE, Junge, 1999. C-print, 110 cm x 76 cm.

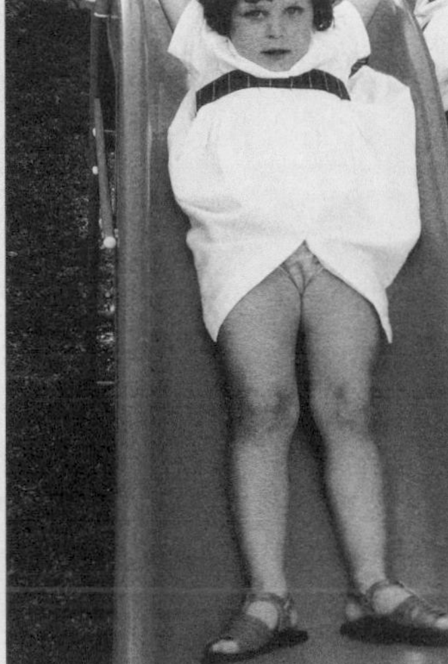

TATIANA LECOMTE, Mädchen, 1997. C-print, 124 cm x 80 cm.

Tatiana Lecomte

Maren Lüb[bke]

Seit einigen Jahren nun beobachte ich die fotografische Arbeit von Tatiana Lecomte. Was mich an ihr zunächst am meisten beeindruckte, war ihr klarer und offener Blick auf die von ihr festgehaltenen Situationen – ohne dass sich beim ersten Hinsehen auf das Dargestellte auch gleich ein spezifischer Inhalt mitteilte. Die Arbeit kam höchst unprätentiös, fast beiläufig daher, setzte sich aber gleichzeitig auf merkwürdige Weise im Gedächtnis fest. Es schien, als gäbe Lecomte mit ihren Arbeiten Rätsel auf, ohne aber selbst die Lösungen zu kennen bzw. zu ihrer Ergründung selbst in die Tiefen des Bildes einsteigen zu wollen, geschweige denn vom Betrachter diese Transferleistungen zu erwarten. Ich erinnere mich an Gespräche, in denen von Rückzug oder Zurückgezogenheit in eine private Sphäre gesprochen wurde, und von der (Un-)Zulässigkeit, den Betrachter mit diesen Arbeiten allein zu lassen. Es schien ein Mysterium auf ihnen zu lasten, ohne dass jemand auch nur eine Ahnung davon entwickeln konnte, worin dieses eigentlich hätte bestehen sollen. All das trifft insbesondere vor dem Hintergrund ihres kontinuierlichen und intensiven Arbeitens an Bildern nicht zu. Vielmehr entwickelt sich in ihrer Arbeit zunehmend – das heißt in der Zusammenschau ihrer verschiedenen Werkkomplexe – ein narrativer Faden, der zwar die ganze Arbeit zu durchlaufen scheint, der aber vom Betrachter selbst an beliebiger Stelle aufgenommen und im Gedankenspiel weiter durch die Arbeiten gelegt werden muss.

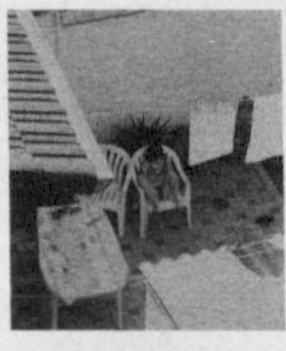

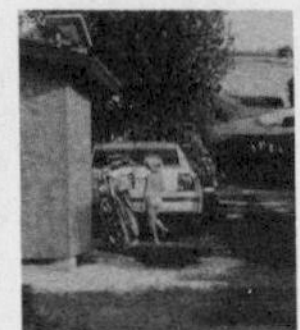

Darüber hinaus nimmt sie mit ihrer Arbeit eine ausgewiesen fotografische Position ein, ein Umstand, der mir erwähnenswert erscheint, trifft man doch in Österreich heute kaum KünstlerInnen einer jüngeren Generation, die kontinuierlich mit der Kamera arbeiten und die Möglichkeiten des Mediums systematisch erforschen, durchspielen und sich bewusst aneignen. Es gibt in Österreich keine Schule für speziell fotografisches Arbeiten wie zum Beispiel die Klasse von Bernd und Hilla Becher in Düsseldorf, die eine ganze Generation von KünstlerInnen hervorgebracht hat, und mit ihr den Diskurs um das Fotografische im zeitgenössischen Kunstdiskurs wesentlich und nachhaltig geprägt hat. Die Ausbildungssituation in Österreich ist denkbar schlecht und mittlerweile stellt sich angesichts der Tatsache, dass es kaum mehr KünstlerInnen gibt, die sich *nicht* ganz selbstverständlich der Fotografie bedienen und diese als integrativen Bestandteil ihrer Arbeit begreifen, die Frage, ob es überhaupt noch sinnvoll ist, dem Fotografischen an sich Bedeutung beizumessen und eine kritisch-diskursive, aber auch praxisorientierte Auseinandersetzung mit der Fotografie auf der Ebene der Ausbildung oder Vermittlung zu forcieren. Gerade im künstlerischen Produktionszusammenhang lösen sich die Genregrenzen immer mehr auf und eine Auseinandersetzung mit zeitgenössischer Kunst bedeutet heute immer auch, die Begriffe, mit denen wir operieren und die kategorialen Zuschreibungen, die wir RezipientInnen vornehmen, weit

TATIANA LECOMTE, aus der Serie / from the series: Mädchen und Jungen, 1999. C-prints, je / each 33 cm x 26 cm.

I have been observing Tatiana Lecomte's photographic w[ork] some years now. The thing that impressed me most first o[f] her clear, open view of the situations she captured on fi[lm] though the subject of the photos does not immediately conve[y] cific content at first glance. The work had a totally unpre[tentious] almost casual feel, but, at the same time, implanted itself i[n] in my mind. It seemed that Lecomte was posing riddles [in her] works, albeit without knowing the solutions herself or ev[en to] plumb the depths of the picture in order to get to the bo[ttom of] them, let alone expecting the viewer to perform this tra[nsfer]... remember talking about... to or seclusion in a private... and about the (in)admi[ssibility]... leaving the viewer alone wi[th the]... works. They seemed... down by a mystery, althou[gh]... one could even have gu[essed]... what this might have bee[n]... of this is true, part[icularly]... against the background... continuous, intensive... pictures. Rather, what... her work – i.e. when vie[wed]... various complexes of... as a whole – is a narrati[ve]... which, although seemin[g]... through the entire w[ork]... viewer himself must p[ick up at] any point and, in his... tinue to lay down in the... In addition, she... distinctly photographic... in her work, a fact worth... I feel, when you consider... re are hardly any young... Austria today who wo[rk]...

by Bernd and Hilla Becher in Düsseldorf, that has produc[ed a who]le generation of artists, thereby impacting profoundly an[d ...] phy in the contemporary art discourse. The training... Austria is extremely poor, and in view of the fact that... hardly any artists any more who do not use photographs... ter of course, seeing it as an integral component of th[eir]... question now is whether it makes any sense at all to... tance to photography per se and to promote a critical... but also practical analysis of photography at the level... and education. Particularly in the context of art prod[uction]... boundaries of genre are increasingly ceasing to apply,... an analysis of contemporary art always implies a broa[d]... independent conception of the terms with which we opera[te]... categorical allocations that we make as recipients. Lec[omte]... often artistic methods are being negotiated at the level o[f]... handling of the medium – the genre itself is really only o[f]... importance – to be ousted by questions of the greater con[text]...

*Seite / page 59
TATIANA LECOMTE, Ohne Titel / Untitled...
SW-Fotografien / b/w-photographs, je / each...*

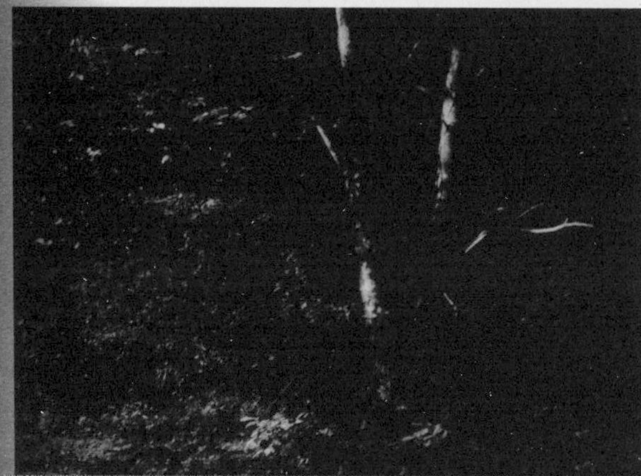

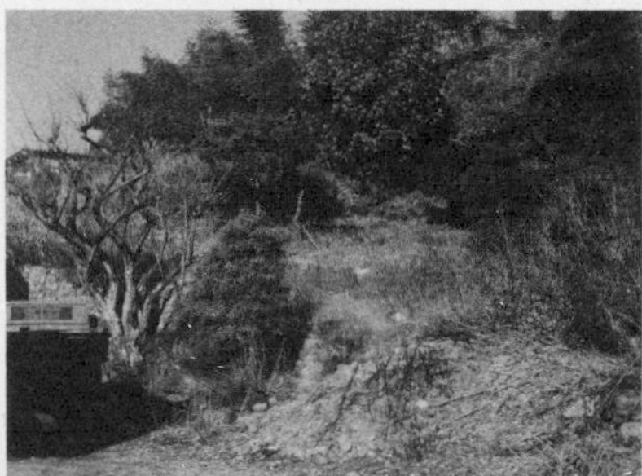

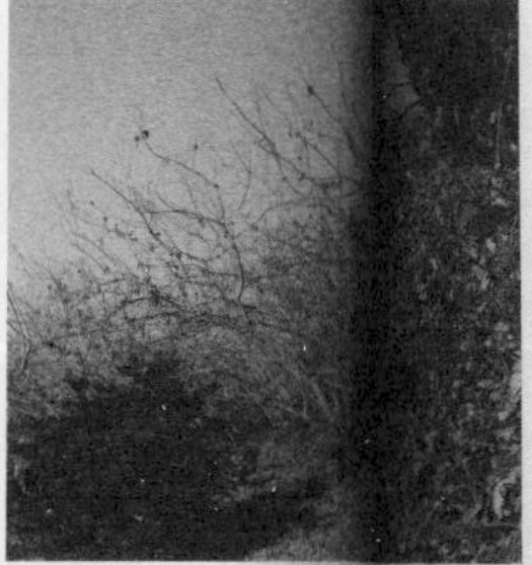

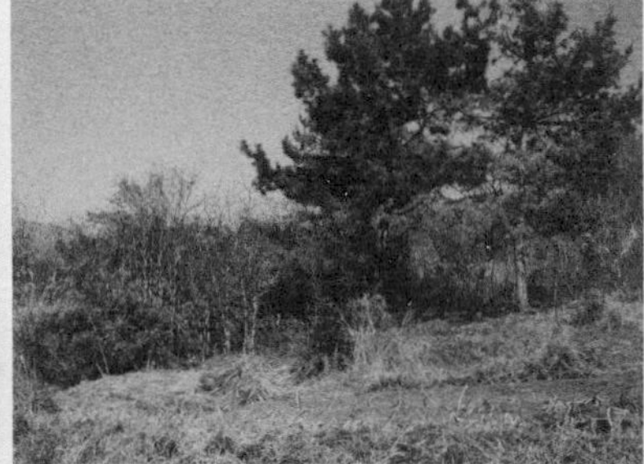

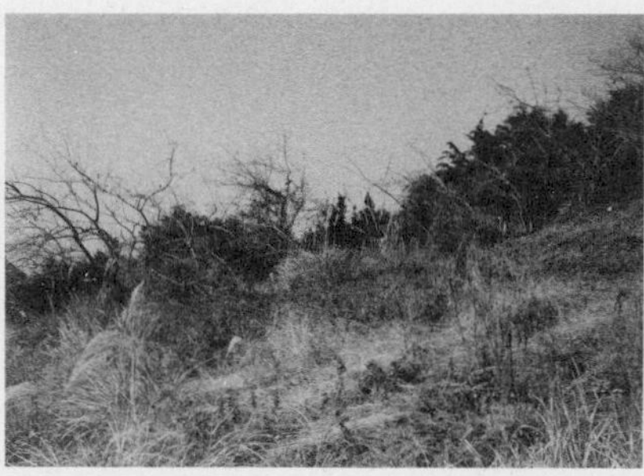

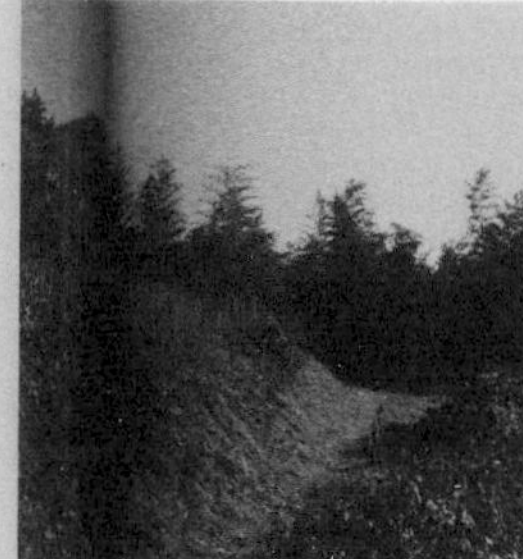

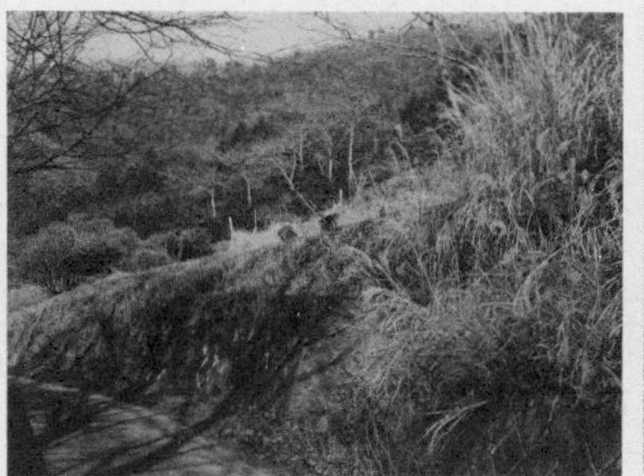

TATIANA LECOMTE, she was covered with autumn leaves, 2000. C-prints, je / each 68 cm x 95 cm.

Peter Piller

Camera Austria International

2005   Manisha Jothady, "Peter Piller: Ein Tennisball,
der beim Hecke-Schneiden zum
Vorschein kommt, erinnert an Gewölle,"
text contribution / artist contribution,
Camera Austria International 89 / 2005
2011   Forum, presented by Peter Piller,
Camera Austria International 113 / 2011
2015   Anke Hoffmann, "Peter Piller: Belegkontrolle,"
Fotomuseum Winterthur, Centre de la
photographie Genève, Städtische
Galerie Nordhorn, Kunsthalle Nürnberg,
exhibition review, *Camera Austria
International* 129 / 2015
2018   Radek Krolczyk, "Jochen Lempert /
Peter Piller: Fotografie neu ordnen: Vögel,"
MKG Museum für Kunst und Gewerbe
Hamburg, exhibition review,
Camera Austria International 141 / 2018

Exhibitions

2006   *First the artist defines meaning. On the
Paradigm of the Conceptual,* exhibition
contribution
2009   *Then the work takes place. On the Paradigm
of the Conceptual in Contemporary
Photography,* exhibition contribution

Publication

2010   Archiv Peter Piller: *Materialien (D).
Peripheriewanderung Graz,* Graz,
Edition Camera Austria, 2010

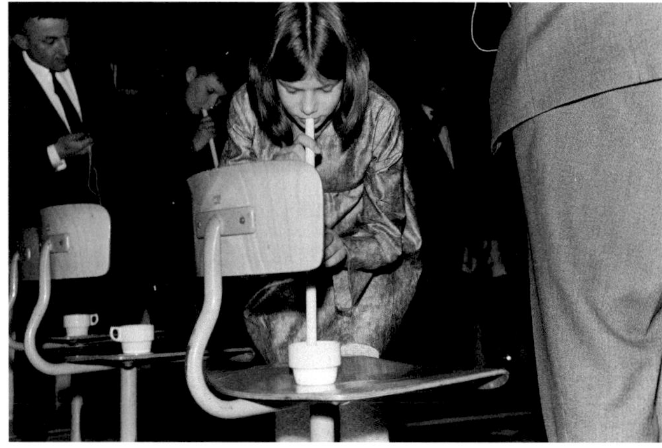

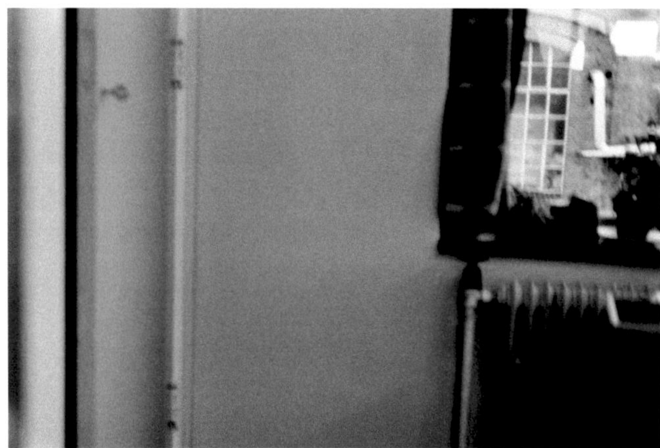

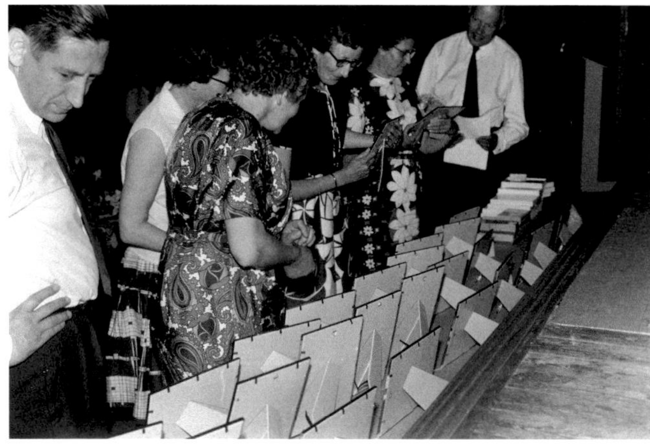

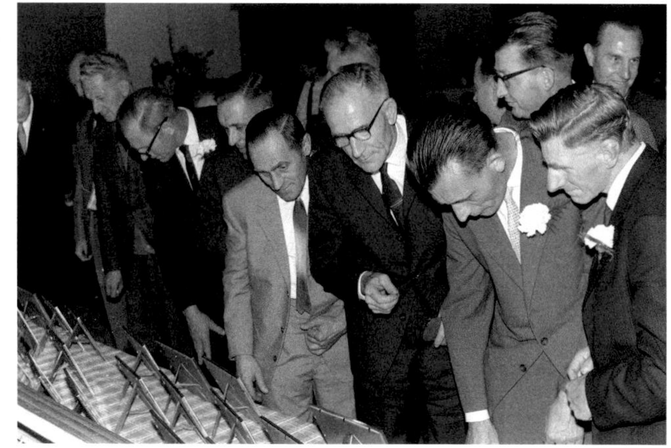

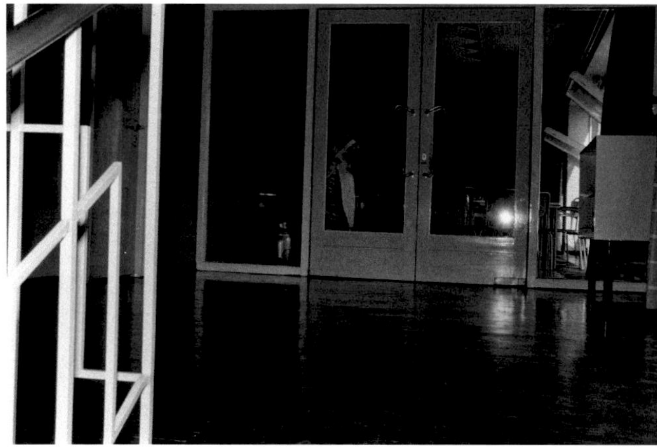

From the series "Dauerhaftigkeit" (1) (Permanence 1), 2005

Peter Piller

Permanence

All photographs are from the archive of a company newspaper from Nijverdal, in the municipality of Hellendoorn, in the Netherlands. It comprises some 15,000 negatives that were kept in eleven folders. Up until now, almost no enlarged prints have been made of any of the negatives. The company photographers documented the everyday workings of the firm from the 1950s to the 1970s.

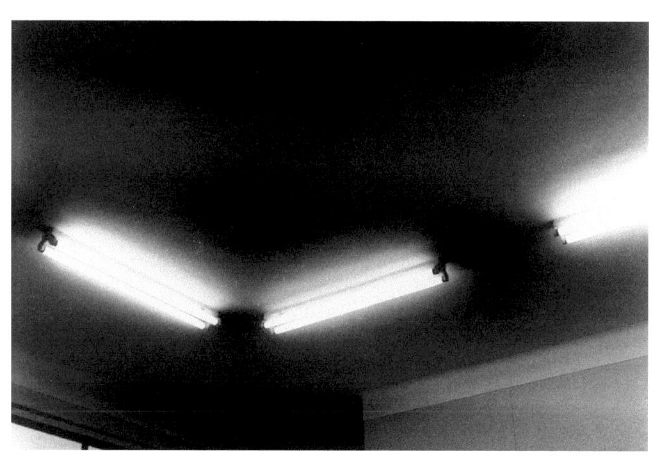

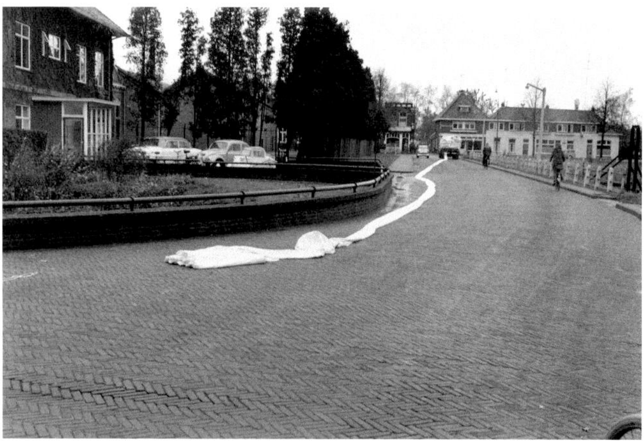

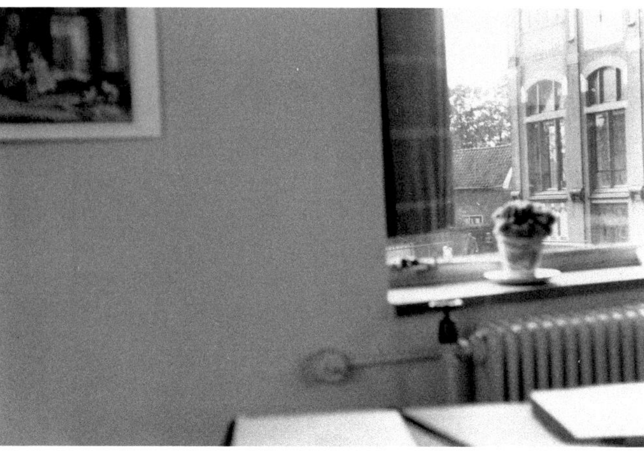

From the series "Dauerhaftigkeit" (1) (Permanence 1), 2005

Peter Piller

Manisha Jothady

EIN TENNISBALL, DER BEIM HECKE-SCHNEIDEN ZUM VORSCHEIN KOMMT, ERINNERT AN GEWÖLLE[1]

Vom 20. Juli bis 26. September 1996 umwanderte Peter Piller in 31 Streckenabschnitten das Ruhrgebiet. Insgesamt 337 Kilometer legte er dabei zurück, die letzten fünf mit dem Schiff. Das Ergebnis dieser »Peripheriewanderung« sind neben 31 Tuschezeichnungen, die den jeweils zurückgelegten Wegstrecken zugeordnet sind, und Textprotokollen, aufgenommen auf Tonband direkt vor Ort, auch Fotografien.[2] Letztere bilden den Auftakt zu einer Beschäftigung, die Pillers künstlerische Verfahrensweise im Wesentlichen heute bestimmt. Es sind Aufnahmen, auf denen nichts Maßgebliches im *eigentlichen* Sinne zu sehen ist, kein Bedeutung tragendes Detail findet sich darin ins Zentrum gerückt: Sollen wir unsere Aufmerksamkeit auf den Kanaldeckel vor dem Innenhof lenken oder auf die Betonmauer, die diesen umgibt? Ist der gelbe Gartenschlauch oder die Kinderschaukel dahinter das anvisierte Motiv? Unmöglich lässt sich sagen, was hier nun eigentlich »Sache« ist, geschweige denn, zu welchem Zweck diese Fotos gemacht wurden – ja sie scheinen sogar derart *absichtslos* aufgenommen worden zu sein, dass sich nicht einmal auf eine Einzelperson als Urheber rückschließen lässt.

Nicht nur die bundesdeutschen Regionalzeitungen zeichnen sich durch eine Überfülle von Bildmaterial aus, das durch solcherart visuelle Beiläufigkeit bestimmt ist: Aufnahmen, gemacht für einen Tag, zur Illustration von Artikeln von nicht allzu hohem überregionalem Interesse – doch immerhin Bilder, die Peter Piller, wie er einmal sagte, genau so »schon immer machen wollte«. Er findet sie in Provinzblättern, die Namen haben wie *Delmenhorster Kreisblatt*, *Trostberger Tageblatt*, *Zollern-Alb Kurier*, *Backnanger Kreiszeitung* usw. Zu etwa 80 verschiedenen Lokalzeitungen hat der in Hamburg lebende Künstler durch seinen Job bei der Medienagentur Carat Zugang, und seine Aufgabe dort besteht darin, falsch platzierte Anzeigen zu orten – eine monotone Tätigkeit sicherlich, ganz offensichtlich aber schärft sie den Blick auf für gewöhnlich unbeachtete Details. Piller beginnt 1998, die nicht für das Firmenarchiv benötigten Zeitungsfotos auszuschneiden, zu sammeln, nach bestimmten Kriterien in Motivgruppen zu kategorisieren, zu systematisieren, zu archivieren. Das »Archiv Peter Piller« umfasst derzeit zwischen 6000 und 7000 Abbildungen. Der Großteil davon stammt aus Tageszeitungen und ist in rund 100 Sammelgebiete geordnet. Eine andere Rubrik versammelt Bilder aus dem Internet. Auch einige eigene fotografische Aufnahmen sowie eine Reihe von Postkarten, die Blindgänger-Bomben aus dem Ersten Weltkrieg zeigt, gehören dazu. Die Homepage *www.peterpiller.de* gibt Einblick in all dies.

Für die meisten Rubriken waren die begleitenden Bildunterschriften titelgebend. Einige Kategorien ergeben sich »intuitiv aus dem unvoreingenommenen Einlassen auf das Material, im Dialog mit den Photos, ihren Motiven und den kleinen Details am Rande, ihren Fehlern, ihren unbewussten Aufnahmekonventionen«.[3] Der Revolver-Verlag hat bislang acht Sammelgebiete in der Reihe *Archiv Peter Piller* publiziert. Sie heißen *Durchsucht und versiegelt (Tatorthäuser)*, *Diese Unbekannten (Täter)*, *Noch ist nichts zu sehen (Bauerwartungsflächen)*, *Die Verantwortlichen sind einstimmig (Ortsbesichtigungen)*, *Schmuckstück/Schandfleck*, *Stein des Anstoßes*, *Regionales Leuchten* und *Auto berühren*.

Keiner dieser Bände zeigt Konfektionsbilder von der Art, wie sie uns die Bildverwertungsindustrie liefert. Es handelt sich vielmehr um eine Anhäufung heimatlos gewordener Illustrationen, die nicht nur vollkommen unrepräsentativ sind, sondern sich zudem durch das Herausgelöstsein aus dem ursprünglichen Textumfeld einer unmittelbaren Entschlüsselung entziehen. Entscheidend für die

Logik eines Bildes ist ja nicht nur der visuelle Befund »Was darauf abgebildet ist«. Denn was könnten uns Bilder über Menschen, die »in Löcher blicken«, Einweihungsbänder durchschneiden, oder Aufnahmen von irgendwelchen »Bauerwartungsflächen« schon Bedeutsames vermitteln? Vor allem auf bestimmte kategoriale Implikate einer Abbildung kommt es ja gewöhnlich an – sie sind der Verweis darauf, dass jedes Bild seine Bestimmungskraft aus einem konkreten Zusammenhang bezieht. Und wir können auch gar nicht anders, als das Dargestellte auf seinen vorstrukturierten Kontext hin zu betrachten. Genau hier setzt Piller an, wirkt dieser wahrnehmungspsychologischen Vorgefasstheit entgegen, wenn er die jeweiligen Abbildungen aus dem Textzusammenhang löst, durch die multiplizierende und serielle Anordnung Werte- und Bedeutungsverschiebungen erzeugt und auf diese Weise zu neuen Formen von Erzählstrukturen findet.

Pillers Entscheidung zu dieser Art Aneignungskunst gründet dabei nicht auf einer Antihaltung, man müsse der Unzahl an Bildern, die es täglich zu verarbeiten gilt, nicht noch weitere hinzufügen.[4] Vielmehr geht es ihm darum, dieses so kunstlos wirkende Material so lange zu durchforsten, bis eine unter der Oberfläche liegende Bedeutung, ein zusätzliches Potenzial offen liegt.

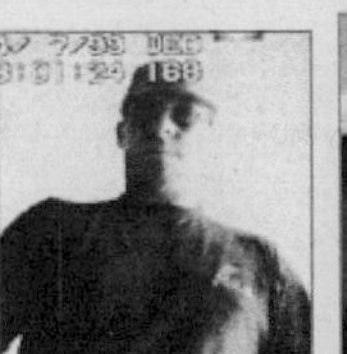
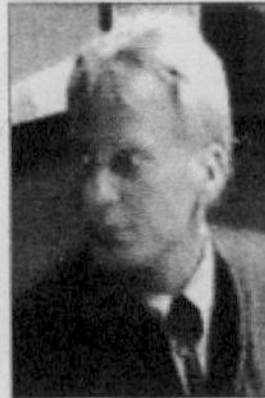
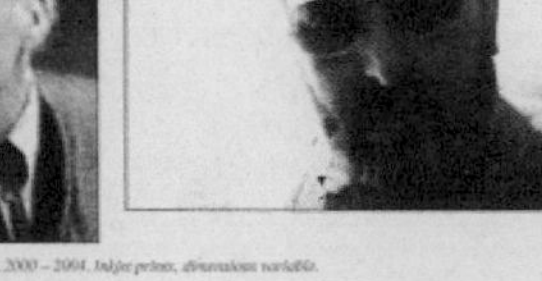
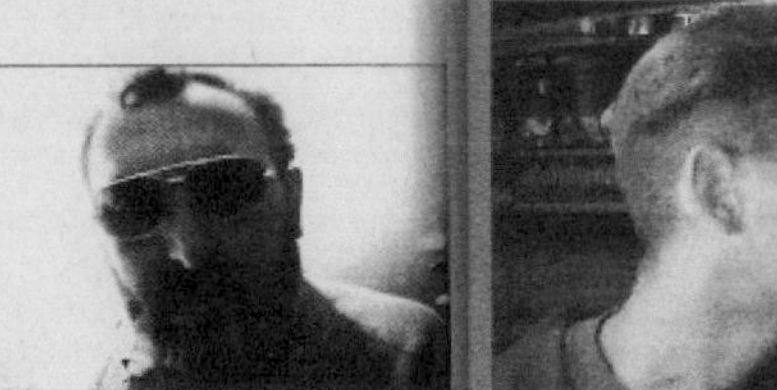

PETER PILLER, aus der Serie / from the series: Diese Unbekannten (Täter), 2000 – 2004. Inkjet prints, dimensions variable.

Die unendlich vielen Ordnungs- und Einteilungsmöglichkeiten lassen Pillers künstlerisches Tun als Projekt einer enzyklopädischen Kompetenz erscheinen, in dem das Ideal des absoluten Bildes außer Kraft gesetzt wird. Obschon einzelne Serien in ihrer Anhäufung groteske Züge annehmen, der Künstler uns hier als schelmischer Chronist des mittelständischen Alltags erscheint (»Auto berühren«, »Rätselgewinner präsentieren Geldscheine«) und man glaubt, seine Selektion lediglich an Kriterien wie Witz und Kuriosität festmachen zu können, an Bildern, die weit jenseits des persönlichen Erinnerungshaushaltes angesiedelt sind (denn wer denkt schon an die eigene Kindheit zurück und sieht dabei Menschen, die »in Löcher blicken«, vor dem inneren Auge auftauchen), so tragen manche dieser Bilder doch auch – vielleicht weil sie oftmals derart amateurhaft, ungelenk und in ihrer Bildsprache mitunter stereotyp sind – ein gewisses Identifikationspotenzial für die Betrachterinnen in sich. Eine ganze Reihe der Tatorthäuser sieht deshalb aus wie eines in der Nachbarschaft, von Freunden oder Verwandten. Hier in Österreich könnte man einen Mann aus der Serie »Diese Unbekannten (Täter)« ohne zweimal hinsehen zu müssen mit dem Austropopsänger Rainhard Fendrich verwechseln. Weitere der hier versammelten Scheckkartenbetrüger, die Baseballkappen tragen, sehen Bruce Willis verdächtig ähnlich. Und auch unter den Lokalhonoratioren (»Die Verantwortlichen sind einstimmig (Ortsbesichtigungen)«) hat der/die eine oder andere etwas gemein mit jener Person, die an der Kassa des Supermarktes sitzt oder mit uns dort in der Schlange wartet.

Pillers Arbeitsweise lässt sich als Recycling begreifen, denn nutzlos gewordene Bilder werden hier dem Bilderkreislauf unserer

Gesellschaft wieder zugeführt. Und fast möchte man an eine ikonische Prägung glauben, sind es doch gerade die Tageszeitungen, in denen sich sein Schaffen großen Zuspruchs erfreut. Spontan denkt man bei Piller an den *Mnemosyne Atlas* von Aby Warburg, obschon sich dieser Vergleich in der komparativen Analyse nach übereinstimmenden Merkmalen erschöpft. Und ungeachtet der Tatsache, dass auch Warburg das eine oder andere Zeitungsfoto gesammelt hat, hat sich er doch insgesamt dem klassischen Gegenstandsbereich seines Faches verpflichtet. Pillers Strategie des Sammelns und Kategorisierens, die Präsentation und Distribution seiner Serien in Form von Büchern sowie die individuelle Deutungs- und Erinnerungsarbeit, die sie ermöglichen, lassen auch an Hans-Peter Feldmann denken. Doch Pillers Recherche nach »visuellen Clustern« folgt nicht nur der Ordnung nach gleichen Erkennungszeichen, sondern (und hier ergeben sich hier wieder Anknüpfungspunkte zu Warburg) durch verwandtschaftliche Beziehungen, durch das Prinzip einer Nachbarschaft. Etwa dann, wenn er Aufnahmen, die ein Bombentrichter zeigen (Piller stieß übrigens durch einen Zeitungsartikel auf das) zur Dokumentation entsprechender Gefahrenzonen anlegen, mit dem Bild von einer Autoexplosion kombiniert. Ein institutionsreiches Gefüge stellen vor allem Pillers Ausstellungsprojekte dar, die er meist einzelne Vorlagen vergrößert, davon Industrie-Drucke anfertigen lässt oder sie etwa als Polaroid-Reproduktion, Graffititen und Diat... aneinander und dabei gleichsam scheinbar wirklich ... in einem reinen Sammelgebiet ... präsentieren. Dass hier die abstrahieren, Formen zu finden für eine Art Bildanekdote, klingt

---

A TENNIS BALL DISCOVERED WHILE CUTTING THE HEDGE IS LIKE A BIRD OF PREY'S PELLET[1]

Peter Piller roamed around the Ruhr district in thirty-one stages from July 20 to September 26, 1996. He covered a total of 337 kilometres, the last five by ship. In addition to thirty-one ink drawings each assigned to a particular stage of the journey, and notes recorded on tape on location, this »periphery journey« also produced a number of photographs.[2] The latter mark the start of a preoccupation that is fundamentally characteristic of Piller's artistic methodology today. These are photos of nothing substantial in any real sense, and they do not focus on any significant detail: should we pay our attention to the manhole cover outside the courtyard or to the concrete wall surrounding it? Is the yellow garden hose or the children's swing beyond the intended subject? It is impossible to say what they are all about, let alone for what purpose these photos were taken – indeed, they seem to be so unintentionally that we cannot even infer a particular individual as their author.

Not only local German newspapers display a profusion of photos of such visual triviality: pictures, taken for one day, to illustrate articles of no great national interest – and yet pictures, all the same, that Peter Piller has, as he once stated, »always wanted to take«. He finds them in backwoods newspapers with such names as Delmenhorster Kreisblatt, Trostberger Tageblatt, Zollern-Alb Kurier, Backnanger Kreiszeitung, etc. The Hamburg-based artist has access to some eighty different local papers thanks to his job at the Carat media agency, where his task is to locate any wrongly placed advertisement – a monotonous job, to be sure, but one which quite obviously keens the eye for details that we generally disregard. In 1998, Piller began cutting out the newspaper photos not required for the company's archives, collecting them, categorising them in subject groups according to certain criteria, systematising and archiving them. The »Peter Piller Archive« currently comprises between 6000 and 7000 pictures. The majority have been culled from daily newspapers and are arranged in some 100 collecting areas. Another section contains pictures from the Internet. Several of his own photos along with a number of postcards of unexploded shells from World War I are also included. The web site www.peterpiller.de provides access to all of this.

The accompanying captions lent the titles to most of the sections. Some categories result »intuitively from the unprejudiced study of the material, in a dialogue with the photos, their subjects and the little, incidental details, their flaws, their unintentional photographic conventions«.[3] Revolver-Verlag has so far published eight collecting areas in the Archiv Peter Piller series. Translated the titles are Searched and sealed (crime scene houses)[I], These unknown (offenders)[II], Nothing to see yet (sites shortly to be made available for building)[III], The authorities are unanimous (site surveys)[IV], Gem/eyesore[V], Bone of contention[VI], Regional shining[VII] and Touching car[VIII].

None of these books features off-the-peg pictures of the kind supplied to us by the image-processing industry. Rather, they are an accumulation of now homeless illustrations that are not only completely unrepresentative, but which also elude straightforward decoding as a result of their being removed from their original setting. The decisive factor for the logic of a particular picture is not only the visual fact of »what it depicts«. For what can pictures of people staring into holes, cutting inaugural ribbons, or pictures of any sites shortly to be made available for building convey to us of significance? Above all, what is usually important are certain categorial implications – these are relevant to the fact that every picture derives its determinative force from a specific context.

Indeed, we cannot help but view the content of the picture in terms of its pre-structured context. This is precisely the starting point for Piller, counteracting this psychological, conceptual preconception when he detaches the various pictures from their textual context, creating shifts in values and meanings by the multiplication and serial arrangement, and thus finding new forms of narrative structures.

Piller's decision to engage in this kind of appropriation art is not based on an anti-attitude, not wanting to add to the already huge number of pictures that we have to process every day.[4] His aim, rather, is to sift through this seemingly plain material until he discovers a meaning, an additional potential below the surface.

The infinite possible arrangements and categorisations make Piller's artistic activity appear to be a project of encyclopaedic competence, in which the ideal – the absolute image – is annulled. Although some series, in their accumulation, take on grotesque features, with the artist appearing to be an impish chronicler of everyday middle-class life (»Touching cars«, »Puzzle winners present bank notes«), whose selection would seem to be based solely on criteria of wittiness and curiosity, on pictures that go beyond the repertory of personal memories (who can think back to their childhood and see people »looking into holes« in their mind's eye), some of these pictures – perhaps because they are often so amateurish, awkward and hackneyed in their pictorial language – hold a certain potential for identification for the viewer. Many of the houses that were scenes of crimes look just like one in the neighbourhood, of friends or relatives. Here in Austria, you might mistake one man from the series »These unknown (offenders)« for the Austrian pop singer Rainhard Fendrich at cursory glance. Other cheque card fraudsters collected here wearing baseball caps bear a suspicious resemblance to Bruce Willis. And one or two of the local notabilities (»The authorities are unanimous (site surveys)«) have something in common with the person sitting at the supermarket checkout or waiting in the queue with us.

Piller's working method can be seen as recycling, as he puts pictures that have become useless back into our society's image-cycle. And it is almost an ironical coincidence considering that it is daily newspapers in which his work enjoys such great popularity. Synchronously, Piller's work reminds us of Aby Warburg's Mnemosyne Atlas although this comparison does not go any further than the comparative analysis of matching features. And regardless of the fact that Warburg also collected a few newspaper photos, on the whole he remained committed to the classical ambit of his discipline. Piller's strategy of collecting and categorising, preserving and distributing his series in the form of books, and the individual interpretation and memory work that they permit, are also reminiscent of Hans-Peter Feldmann. But Piller's research for his clusters – not only follows the order based on similar features, but also (and here again we can observe similarities to Warburg's

---

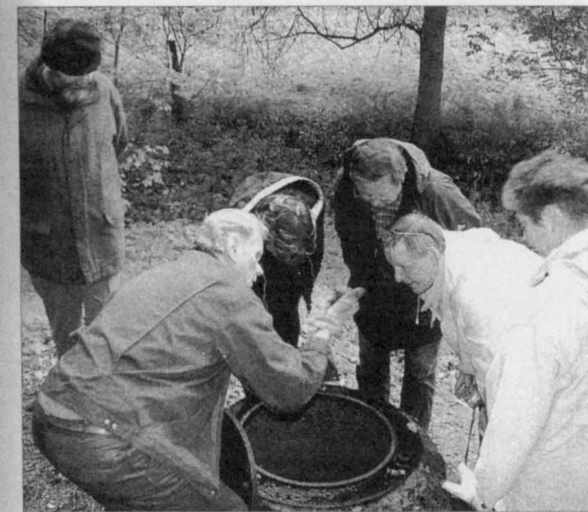

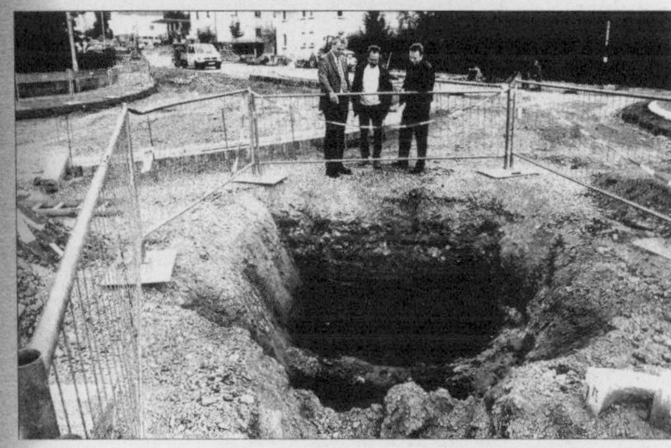

PETER PILLER, aus der Serie / from the series: In Löcher blicken / Looking into holes, 2001 – 2004. Inkjet prints, dimensions variable.

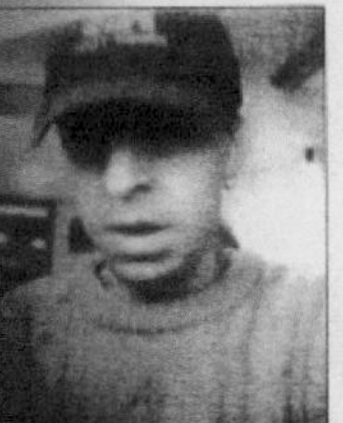
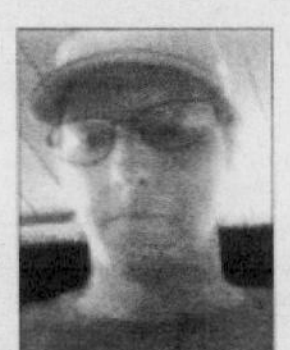
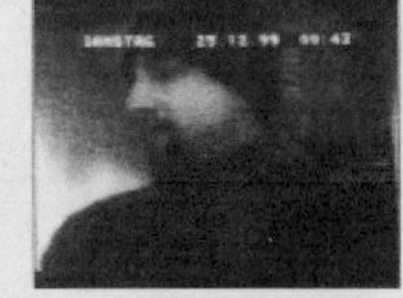
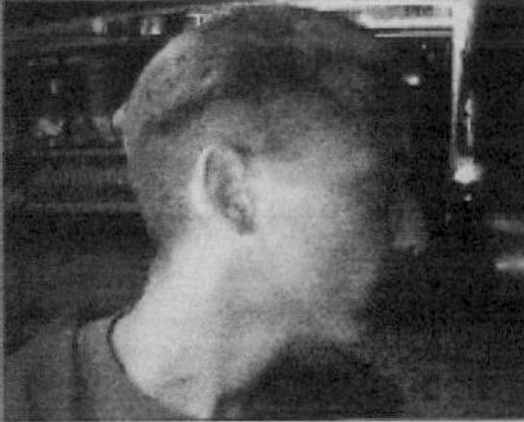
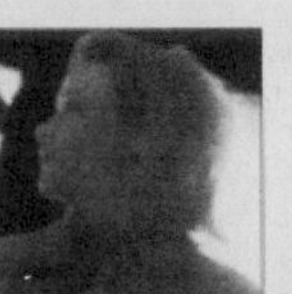
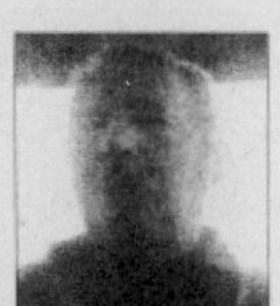
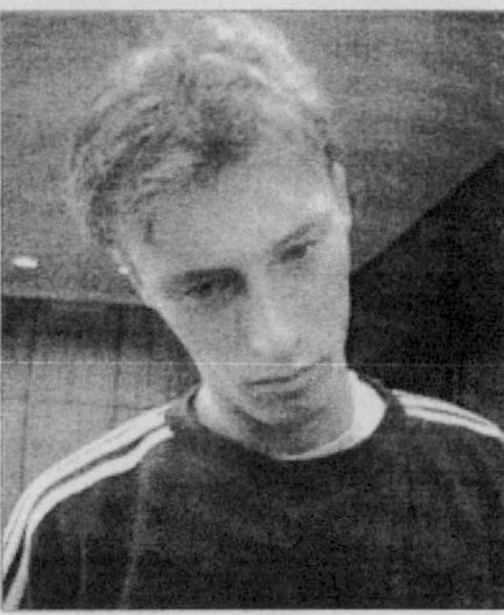

PETER PILLER, aus der Serie / from the series: Diese Unbekannten (Täter), 2000 – 2004. Inkjet prints, dimensions variable.

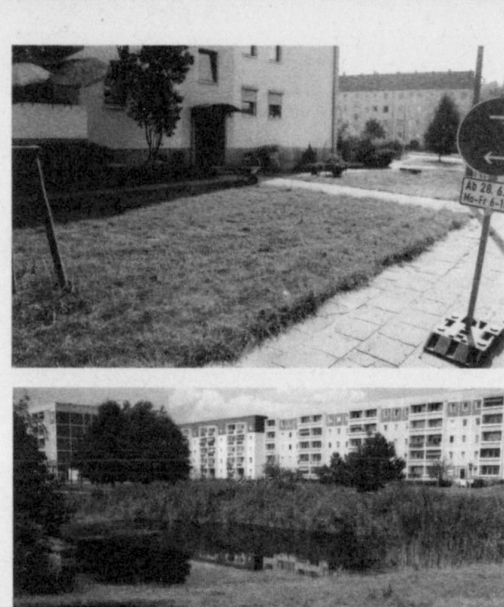

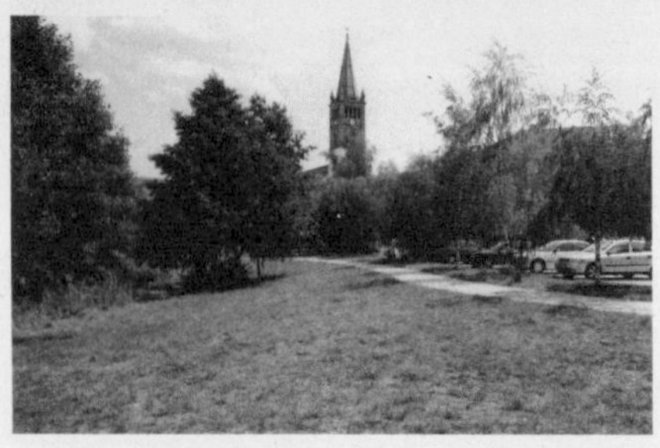

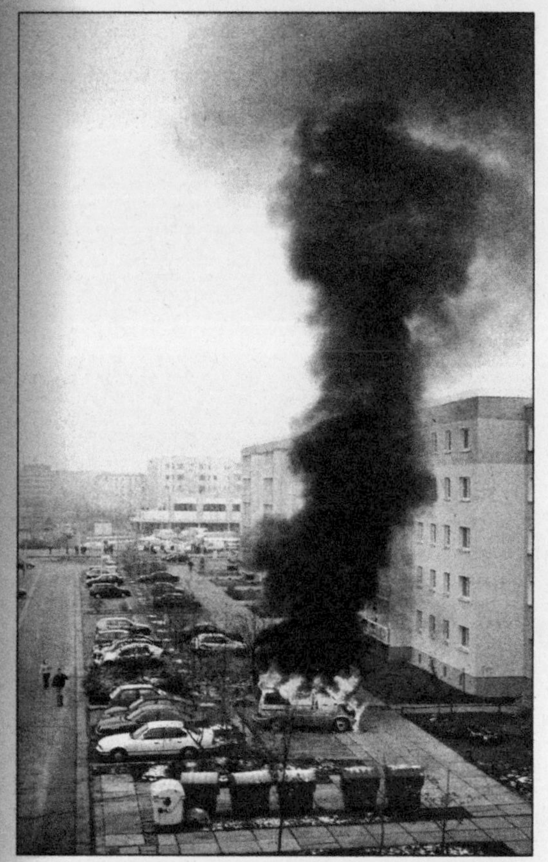

26

27

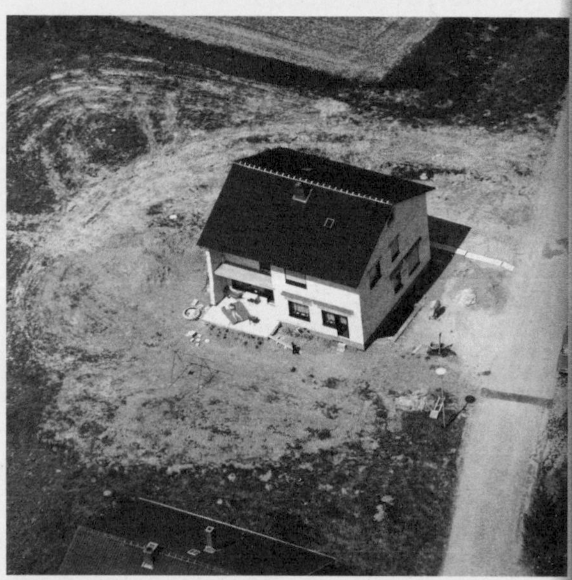

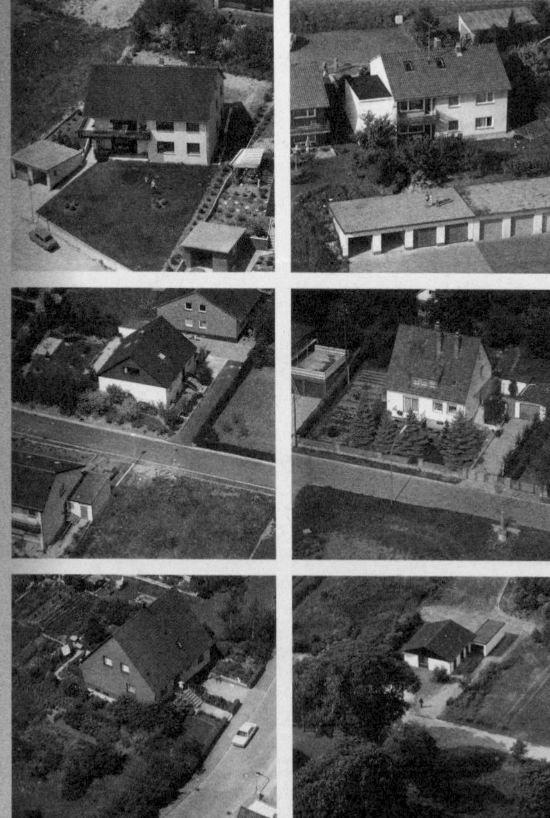

28

29

Visual Politics & Science

Sabine Bitter/ Helmut Weber

Participation at Symposion

1993   Symposion on Photography XIV, "WAR"

Camera Austria International

1996   "Sabine Bitter/Helmut Weber," artist
        contribution and cover,
        Georg Schöllhammer, "Was kann denn
        eine 'Stadtübung' sein?," text contribution,
        Camera Austria International 55/1996
2009   Maren Richter, "Sabine Bitter/Helmut Weber,
        Landesgalerie Linz," exhibition review,
        Camera Austria International 107/2009
2011   "Global Prayers," artist contribution, *Camera
        Austria International* 116/2011
2017   "Sabine Bitter/Helmut Weber," artist contri-
        bution, *Camera Austria International* 139/2017

Exhibitions

1995   *Urban Exercises,* solo exhibition
1996   *Radical Images,* exhibition at II. Austrian
        Triennial for Photography, exhibition
        contribution
2005   *Live Like This!,* solo exhibition
2011   *Communitas. The Unrepresentable
        Community,* exhibition contribution
2012   *The Urban Cultures of Global Prayers,*
        exhibition contribution
2014   *Archives, Re-Assemblances, and Surveys,*
        Galerija Klovićevi dvori, Zagreb (HR),
        exhibition contribution
        *The Militant Image. Picturing What Is Already
        Going on, Or The Poetics of the Militant Image,*
        a project by Urban Subjects
        (Sabine Bitter, Jeff Derksen, Helmut Weber)

Publications

1996   Werner Fenz and Reinhard Braun, eds,
        Radical Images 1/2, publication in two
        volumes for exhibition at II. Austrian
        Triennial for Photography, Graz, Edition
        Camera Austria, 1996.
2005   Reinhard Braun, ed., *BitterWeber,
        Live Like This!,* Graz, Edition Camera
        Austria, 2005.
2015   "Urban Subjects," in *The Militant Image
        Reader,* Sabine Bitter, Jeff Derksen,
        Helmut Weber, eds, Graz,
        Edition Camera Austria, 2015.

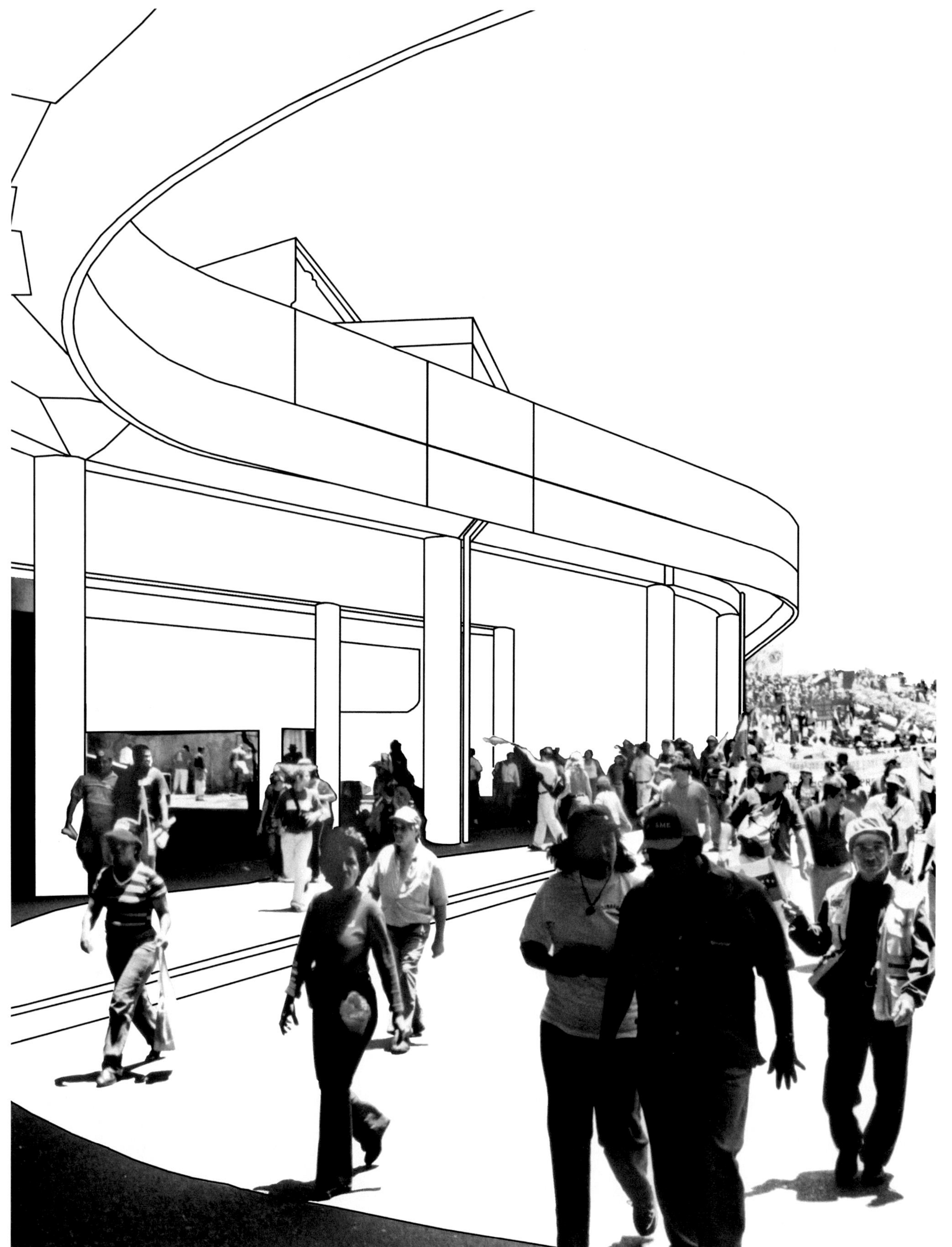

The workers are the builders of the country, Caracas, 2003

Sabine Bitter/ Helmut Weber

Super Citizens

The city is a platform for great mobilizations, new claims, and concentrations of the political. With Porto Alegre, Bombay-Mumbai, Seattle and Genoa cities are not just nodes of global commerce, but are central to a new geography of global politics. This geography breaks the center-periphery model of colonialism, negotiates the urban-rural divide, and creates a new scale for the political. In this geography, Caracas, Venezuela is a vital example of an urban platform that is simultaneously national and global.

This series of photographs of pro-Chávez demonstrations and marches in Caracas have been digitally altered—the architecture and the city-scape have been sketched out, rendering it more as an ideal or even utopian architectural drawing which recalls the optimistic aesthetics of the collage works from late-1960s architectural groups such as Archigram and Superstudio. The language of this moment of utopian architecture with terms such as "total urbanization" and "absolute egalitarianism" is replaced in our sketches with the forceful language of protest and change: "The Workers are the Builders of the Country," "International Solidarity for the Bolivarian Process!" or "The Land Belongs to the People."

By abstracting the architecture, it is reduced from the main texture and structure of the urban territory, and the citizens—with their signs and banners—are made more vital and central. Representing a transformative urbanism that is both spatial and social, their collective mobilization moves through the urban space, producing the city. The series is expanded by photographs of demonstrations and marches in Vancouver ("Say No to Sharia Court in Canada"), Los Angeles ("Students for the right to DREAM") and Vienna ("we walk till they walk out"), to articulate emerging claims of citizens, who transform cities to a new geography of global politics.

BitterWeber: Live Like This!, Edition Camera Austria, Graz: 2005, 163.

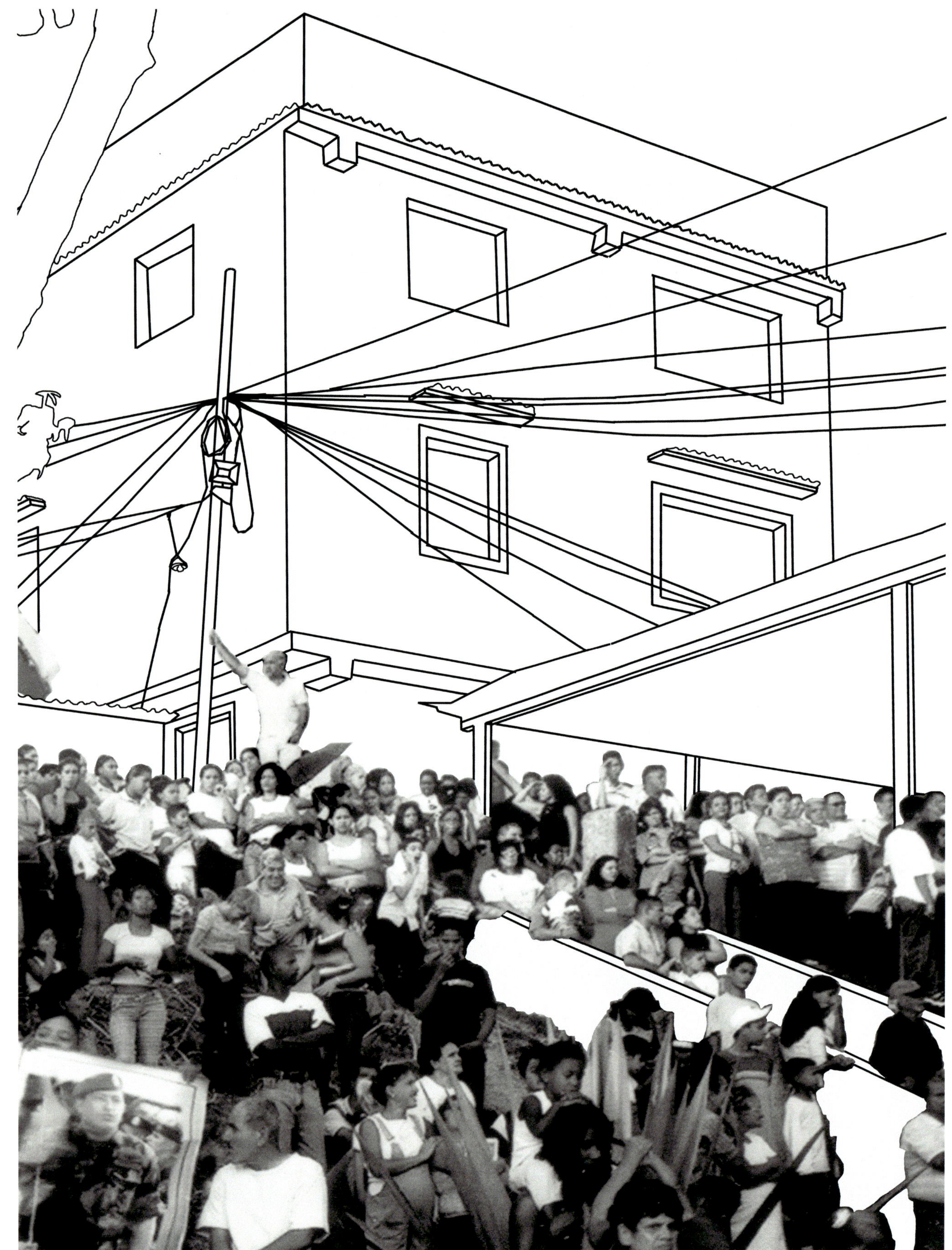

The land belongs to the people, Caracas, 2003

From the series "Super Citizens," 2003–2005

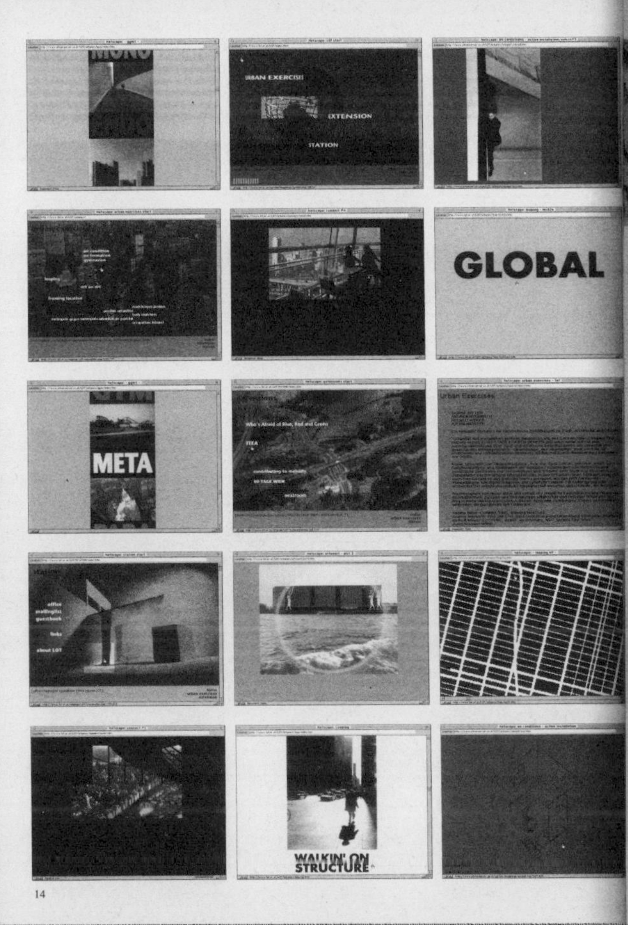

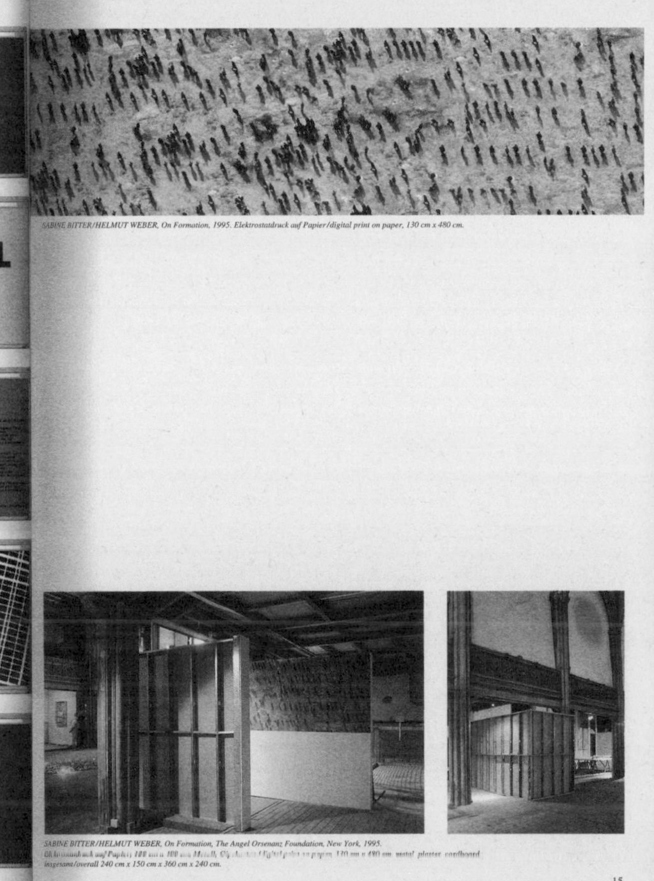

SABINE BITTER/HELMUT WEBER, On Formation, 1995. Elektrostatdruck auf Papier/digital print on paper, 130 cm x 480 cm.

SABINE BITTER/HELMUT WEBER, On Formation, The Angel Orsenanz Foundation, New York, 1995.
Glühlampdruck auf Papier, 180 cm x 100 cm, Metall, Öl (Antron)/digital print on paper, 130 cm x 480 cm, metal, plaster, cardboard, insgesamt/overall 240 cm x 150 cm x 360 cm x 240 cm.

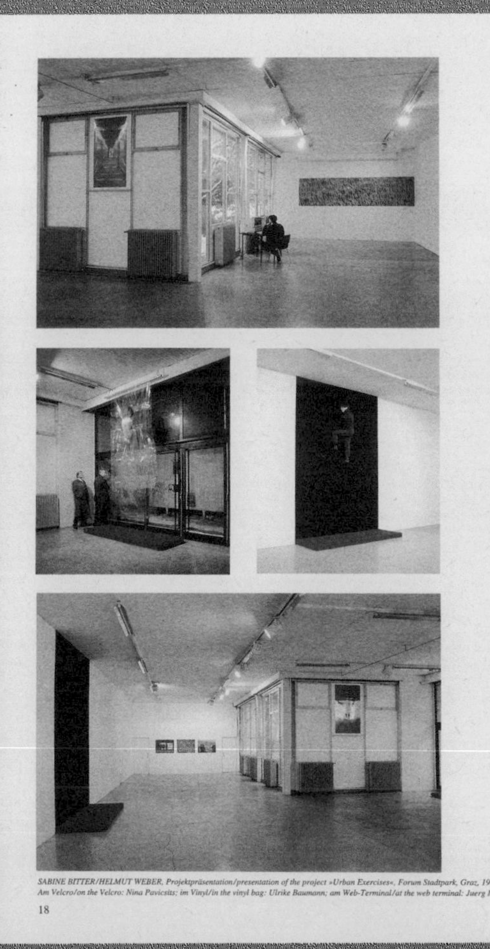

SABINE BITTER/HELMUT WEBER, Projektpräsentation/presentation of the project »Urban Exercises«, Forum Stadtpark, Graz, 1995.
Am Velcro/on the Velcro: Nina Pavicsits; im Vinyl/in the vinyl bag: Ulrike Baumann; am Web-Terminal/at the web terminal: Juerg Meister.

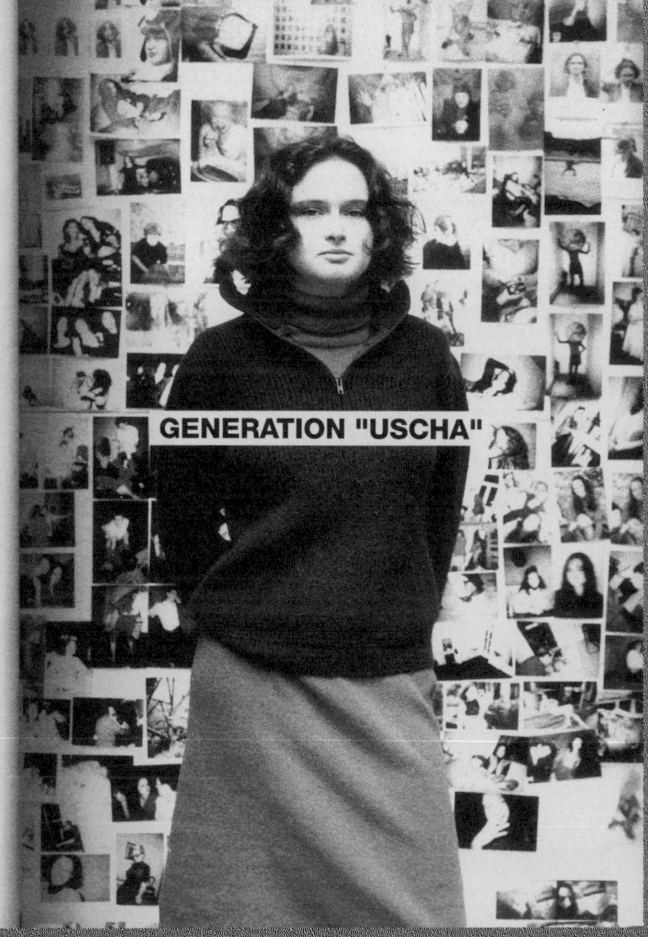

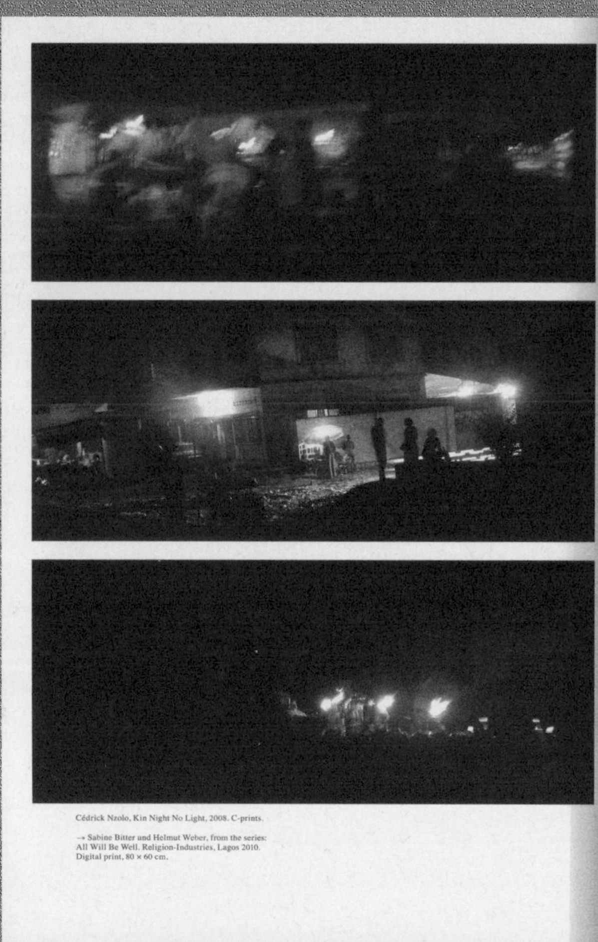

Cédrick Nzolo, Kin Night No Light, 2008. C-prints.

→ Sabine Bitter und Helmut Weber, from the series:
All Will Be Well. Religion-Industries, Lagos 2010.
Digital print, 80 × 60 cm.

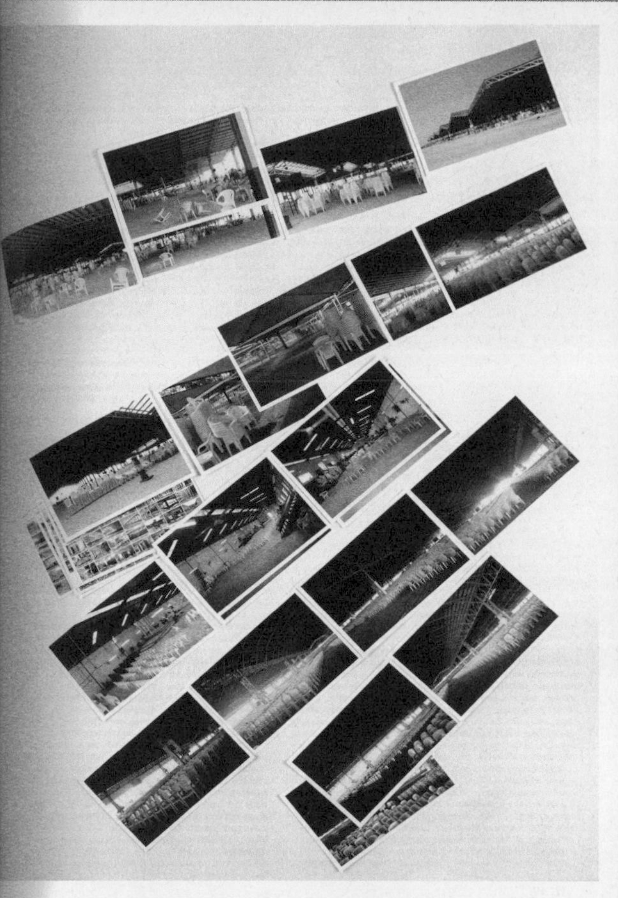

Sven Johne

Camera Austria International

2010   Naoko Kaltschmidt, "Deutsche Börse Photography Prize 2010. Sven Johne: Berichte
zwischen Morgen und Grauen, Frankfurter
Kunstverein," exhibition review, *Camera
Austria International* 111/2010

2012   Susanne Holschbach, "Sven Johne: Die
Illusion des ewigen Sommers," text
contribution, Sven Johne, artist contribution
and journal supplement Lampedusa Hotels,
Camera Austria International 118/2012

2015   Christian Egger, "Sven Johne: Anomalies of
the Early 21st Century/Some Case Studies,"
Arbeiterkammer Wien, exhibition review,
Camera Austria International 131/2015

Exhibition

2013   *Sven Johne, Where the sky is darkest,
the stars are brightest,* solo exhibition

Publication

2013   *Sven Johne, Where the sky is darkest,
the stars are brightest,* Graz, Edition
Camera Austria, 2013

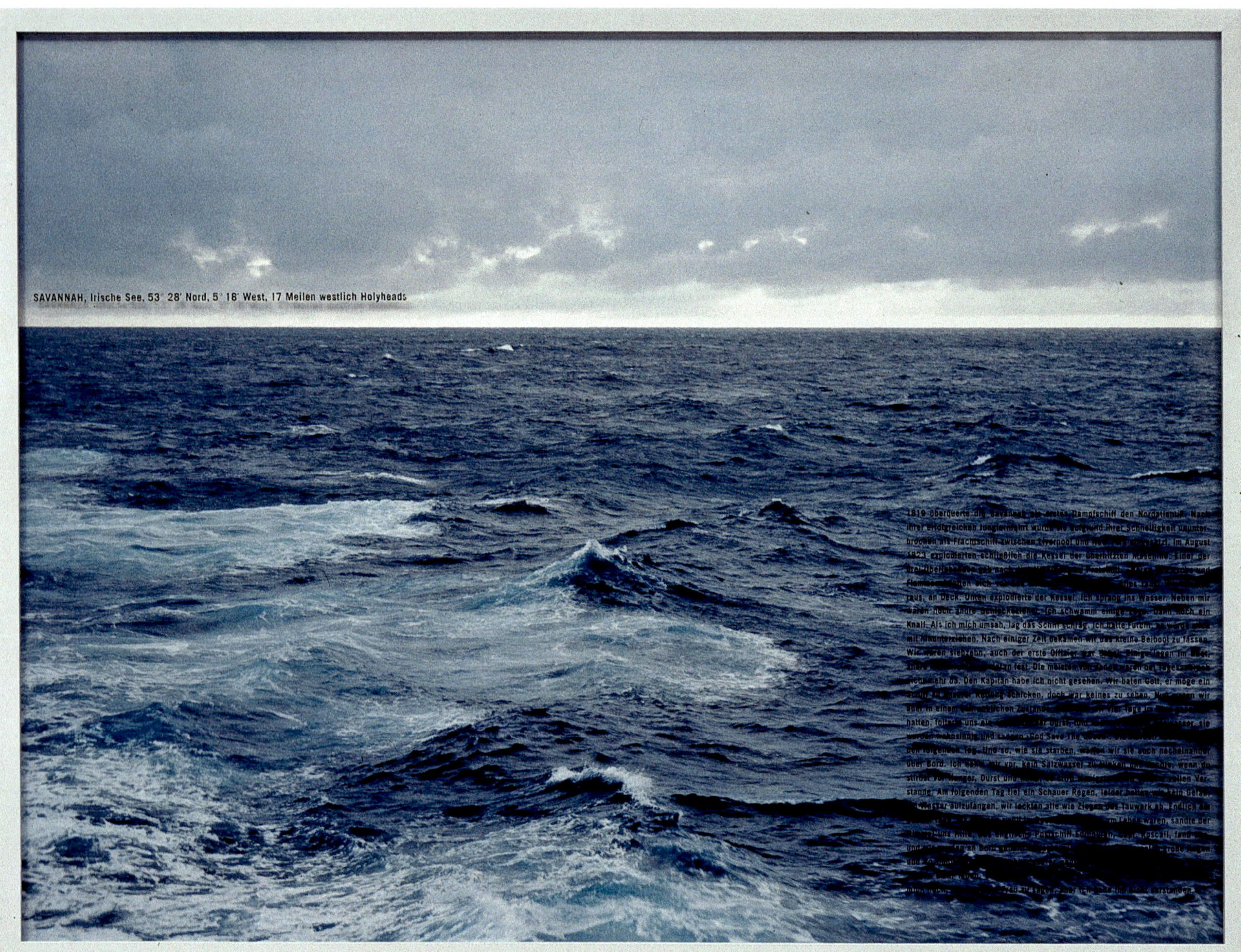

Savannah, Irish Sea, 53°28' West, 5° 18' North, 17 miles West of Holyhead

In 1819 the Savannah was the first steamship to ever cross the North Atlantic. Because of her speed, after her successful maiden voyage she sailed continuously between Liverpool and New York. In August 1823 the overheated boilers finally exploded. One of the three survivors testified about the sinking, "Heaps of ashes and flames built up in front of the boilers. Someone shouted 'Everybody out!' We ran out onto the deck. Downstairs the boilers exploded. I jumped into the water. Next to me there were other stokers. I swam a few strokes. Then there was another explosion. When I turned around the ship was tilting. I was afraid it would pull me down along with it.

After some time we were able to locate the ship's dinghy. There were seventeen of us. The first mate was there too. Some were lying in the boat, others were just holding on. Most of them were no longer there come dawn. I didn't see the captain. We prayed to God that He might send a ship to rescue us, but there was none in sight. We were in a frightful situation. After four days in the boat we were tormented by extreme thirst. Five of us drank sea water. All five went crazy and sang 'God Save The Queen.' They died, one after the other, the next day. And so we threw them overboard, one after the other, once they had died. I decided not to drink sea water and thought, if you die of hunger, thirst, and cold, at least you die with your wits about you. The next day there was a rain shower. Unfortunately we had nothing in which to collect the water, so like goats we licked the rigging. Finally, on the eighth day, when of the original twelve there were only four of us alive in the boat, heaven sent us help. The English postal ship Edinburgh under Captain Roscall found us, and we were brought on board. He later told me that I had had such enormous eyes and sunken cheeks, he thought I wouldn't last another half hour. The first mate died after three hours on board. He still managed to ask me to tell his wife something, but I couldn't understand what he said."

From the series "Ship Cancellation," 2004

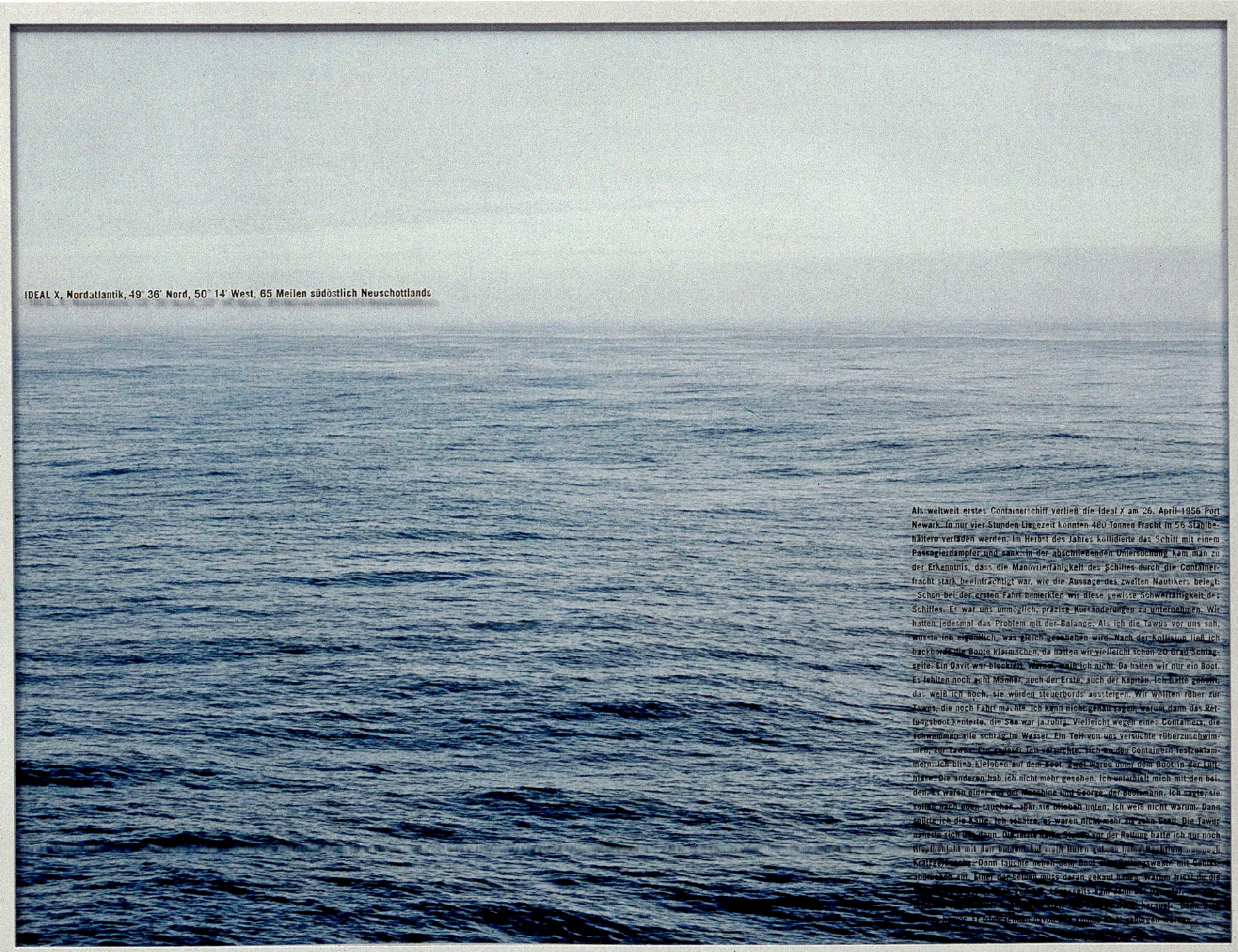

Ideal X, North Atlantic, 49° 36' North, 50° 14' West, 65 miles Southeast of Nova Scotia

The first container ship in the world, the Ideal X, left Port Newark on April 26, 1956. It took just four hours to load 480 tons of cargo in 56 steel containers. In the fall of that year the ship collided with a passenger liner and sank. During the ensuing investigation it became clear that the maneuverability of the ship was greatly impeded by the weight of the cargo, as documented in the testimony of the second navigator: "During the maiden voyage, we already noticed a certain clumsiness to the ship. It was impossible to execute precise course changes. We always had problems with balance. When I saw the Tawus ahead of us, I knew, actually, what was about to happen.

After the collision I had the portside lifeboats readied—we were already listing about 20 degrees. One davit was jammed. Why, I don't know. So we only had one lifeboat. Eight men were still missing, including the first mate and the captain. I was hoping, I remember, that they would deboard on the starboard side. We wanted to get to the Tawus, which was still sailing. I can't say exactly why the lifeboat capsized; the sea was calm, after all. Maybe because of the containers, which were bobbing sideways in the water. Some of the men tried to swim over to the Tawus. Some tried to grab onto the containers. I stayed on top of the upside-down lifeboat. Two men were under the lifeboat in the trapped air bubble. I didn't see the others anymore. I spoke with the two—one was from the engine room, the other was George, the boatswain. I told them to swim to the surface, but they stayed put. I don't know why. Then I noticed the cold. I estimated it wasn't more than ten degrees. The Tawus drew nearer to us then. During the last half hour before we were rescued I could only communicate with the two under the lifeboat by knocking on the hull. There was no reaction to my shouts, just scratching sounds. Then a life vest with bite marks floated to the surface next to the lifeboat. One of the men must have chewed on it. 'Why would you eat a life vest?' I was thinking. The passenger liner then pulled up alongside and as I climbed up the rope ladder someone yelled, There are some legs hanging out over there! Then George floated up. He quickly drifted away and couldn't be secured."

From the series "Ship Cancellation," 2004

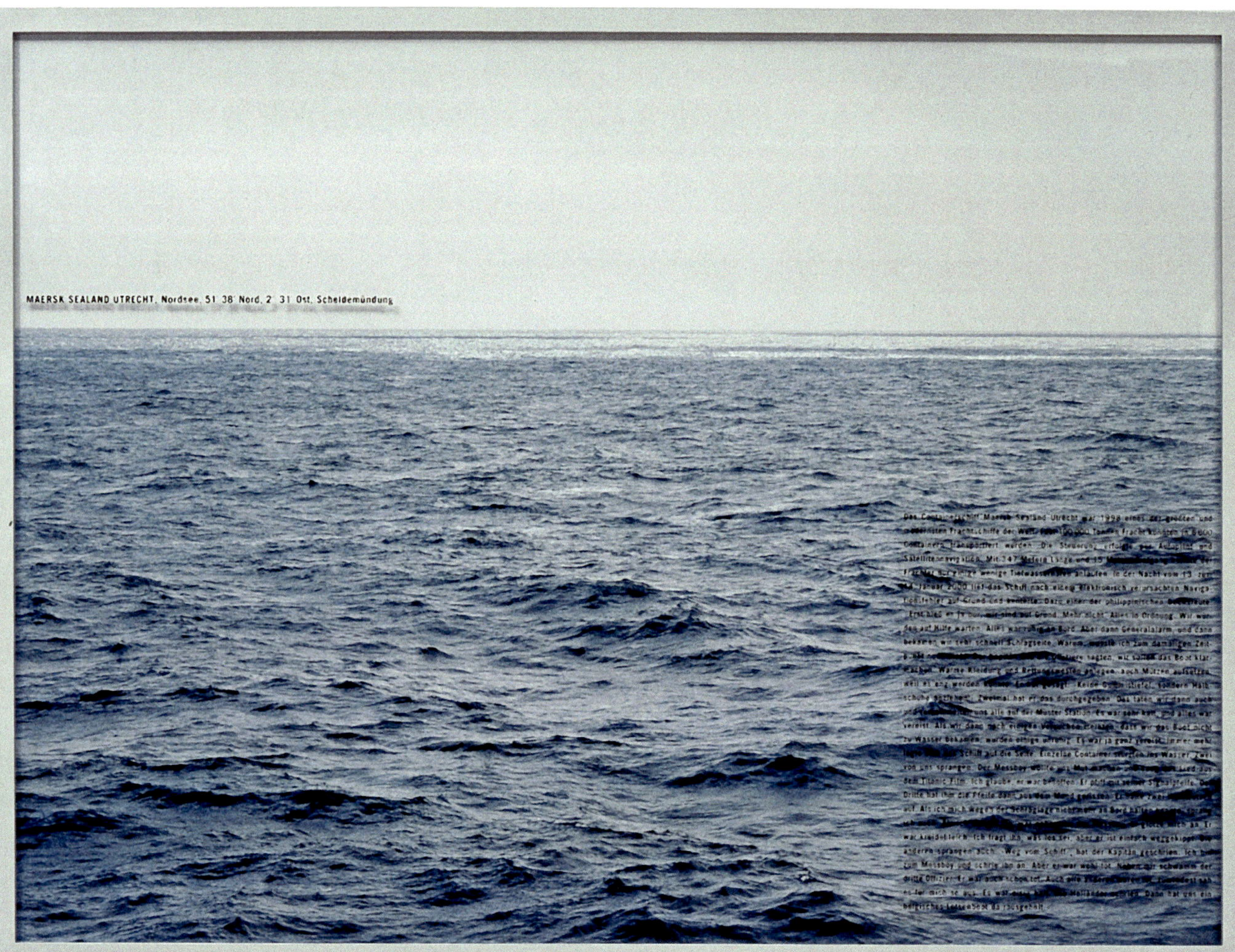

Maersk Sealand Utrecht, North Sea, 51° 38' North, 2° 31' East, Schelde Estuary

In 1998, the container ship Maersk Sealand Utrecht was one of the largest and most modern cargo ships in the world. Almost 100,000 tons of freight could be transported in 6,600 containers. The ship was controlled by auto-pilot and satellite navigation. Because of its length of 347 meters and its draft of 15 meters, the freighter could only dock at a few deep-water ports. In the night from January 13 to 14, 2000, the ship ran aground and capsized as a result of an electronically caused navigational error. One of the Philippine deck hands reported: "First they said we had run aground. Nothing else. Everything was OK. We would wait for help to arrive. All was quiet on board. But then they sounded the alarm, and then we listed very quickly. Why, at the time, I didn't know yet. The captain and the officers said we should ready the lifeboat. We should put on warm clothes and life vests, even woolen caps, because it could get dicey. He said, 'No rubber boots, just put on shoes!'

He said this twice. So we all did as he said and met again at the muster station. It was very cold, and everything was iced up. As we realized, after a few tries, that we wouldn't be able to launch the lifeboat, some people got anxious. The thing was totally iced up. The ship listed more and more. Single containers started falling into the water. Two of us jumped. The mess boy wanted to boost our morale and sang the song from Titanic. I think he was drunk. He blew his signal whistle. The third mate ripped the whistle out of his mouth. He was wearing two woolen caps. When I could no longer hold myself on board because of the listing, I jumped as well. As I surfaced, the mess boy was next to me. He was staring wide-eyed at me. He was white as a sheet. I asked him what was wrong, but he just tipped over. The others jumped too. The captain shouted 'Get away from the ship!' I went over to the mess boy and yelled at him, but he must have been dead. All the others were dead too, at least it looked that way to me. It was freezing cold. The Dutchmen were screaming. Then a Belgian pilot cutter got us out of there."

From the series "Ship Cancellation," 2004

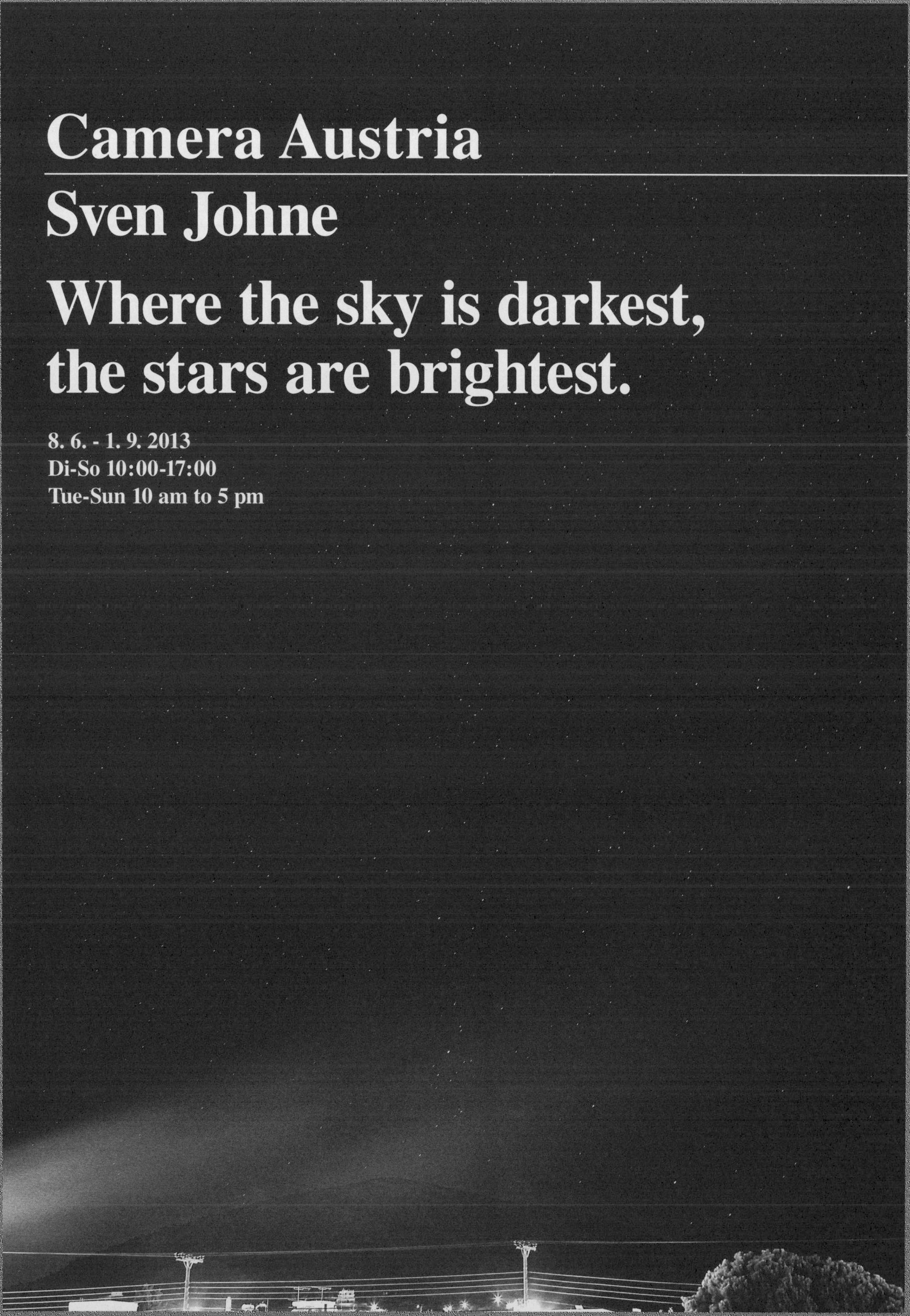

Camera Austria

Sven Johne

Where the sky is darkest, the stars are brightest.

8. 6. - 1. 9. 2013
Di-So 10:00-17:00
Tue-Sun 10 am to 5 pm

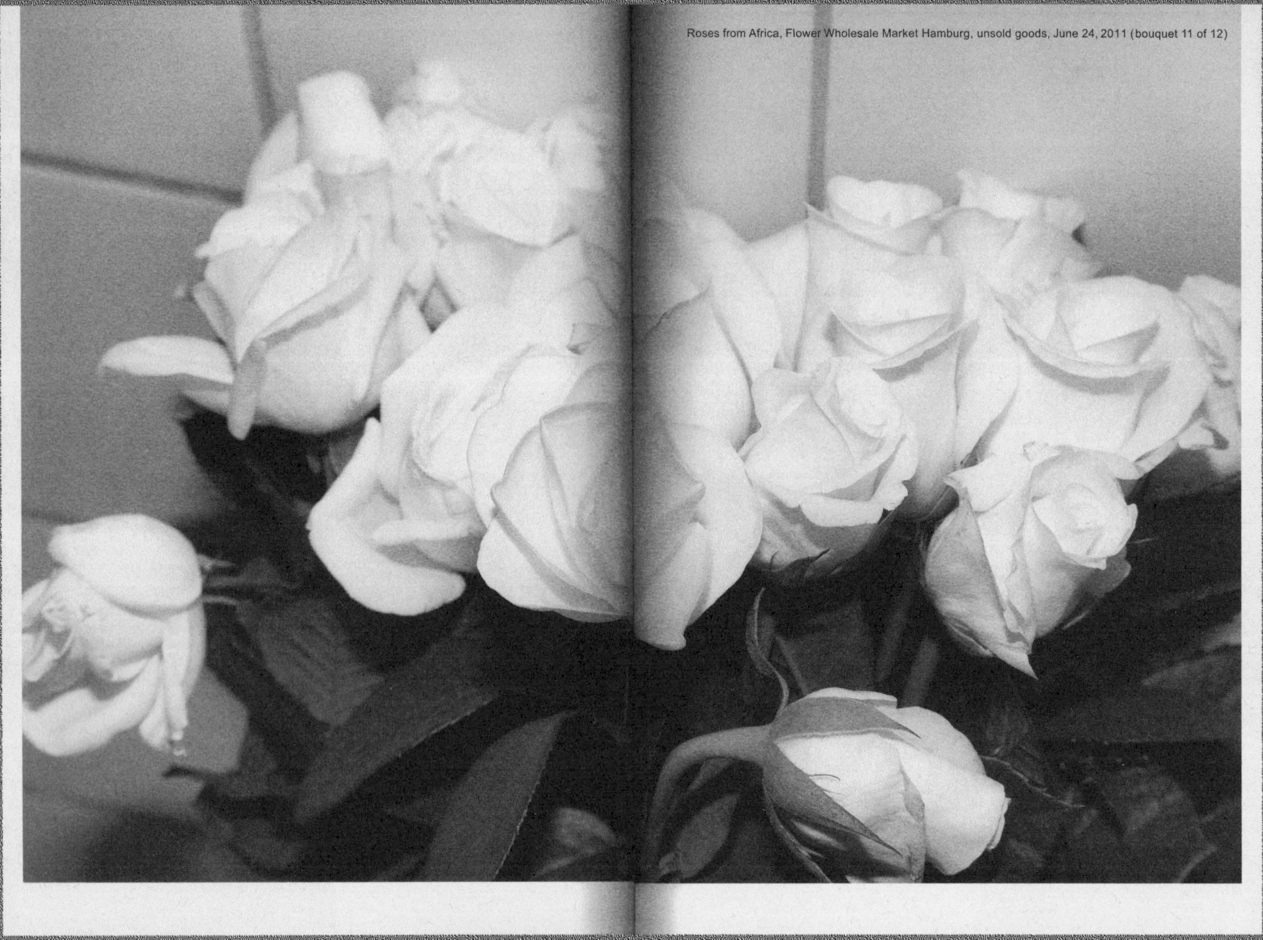

Roses from Africa, Flower Wholesale Market Hamburg, unsold goods, June 24, 2011 (bouquet 11 of 12)

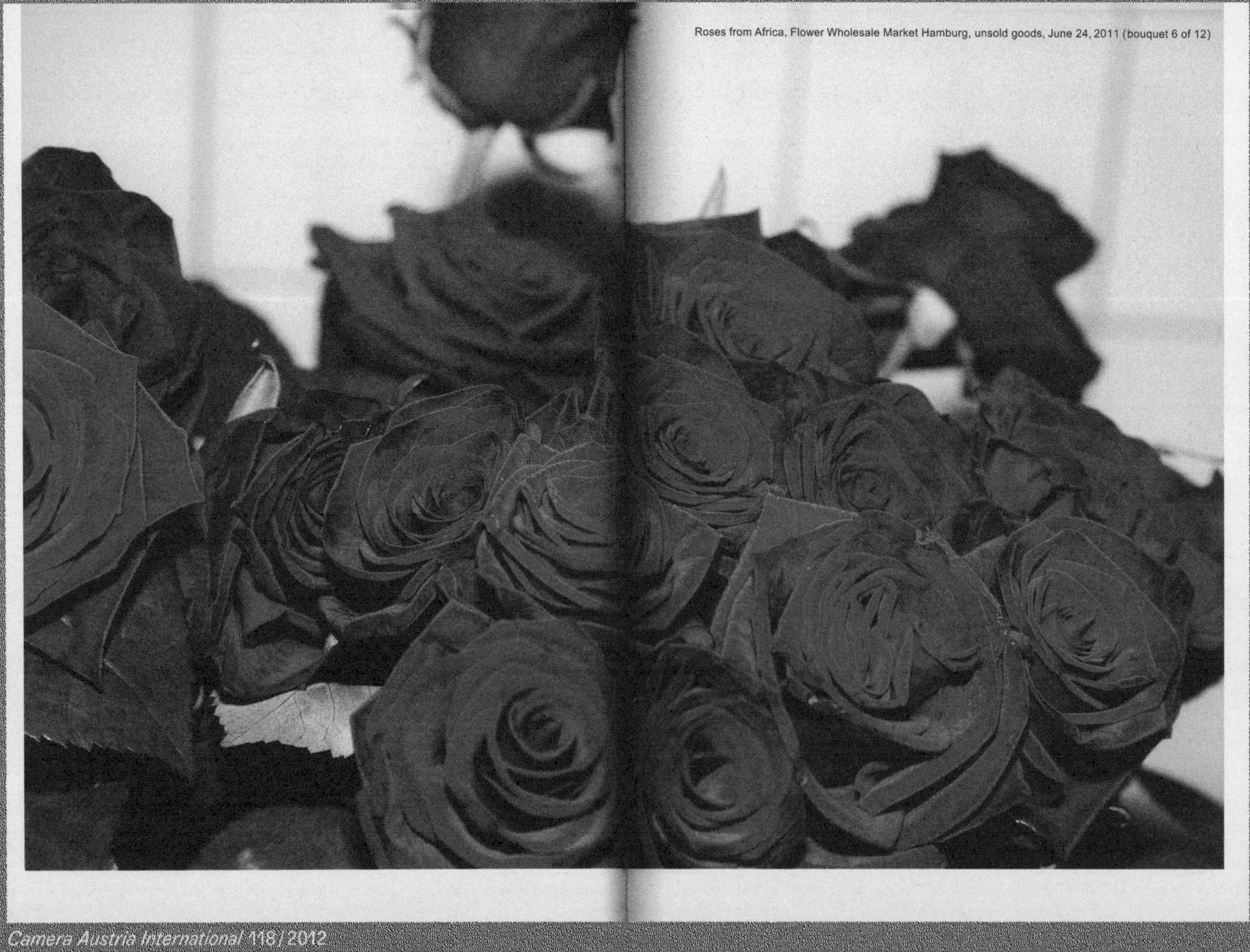

Roses from Africa, Flower Wholesale Market Hamburg, unsold goods, June 24, 2011 (bouquet 6 of 12)

Darcy Lange

Camera Austria International

2009 Mercedes Vicente, "Darcy Lange,"
text contribution,
Helen Legg, "Darcy Lange: Work
Studies in Schools," text contribution,
Darcy Lange artist contribution,
Camera Austria International 108 / 2009

Exhibition

2010 *Darcy Lange*, solo exhibition

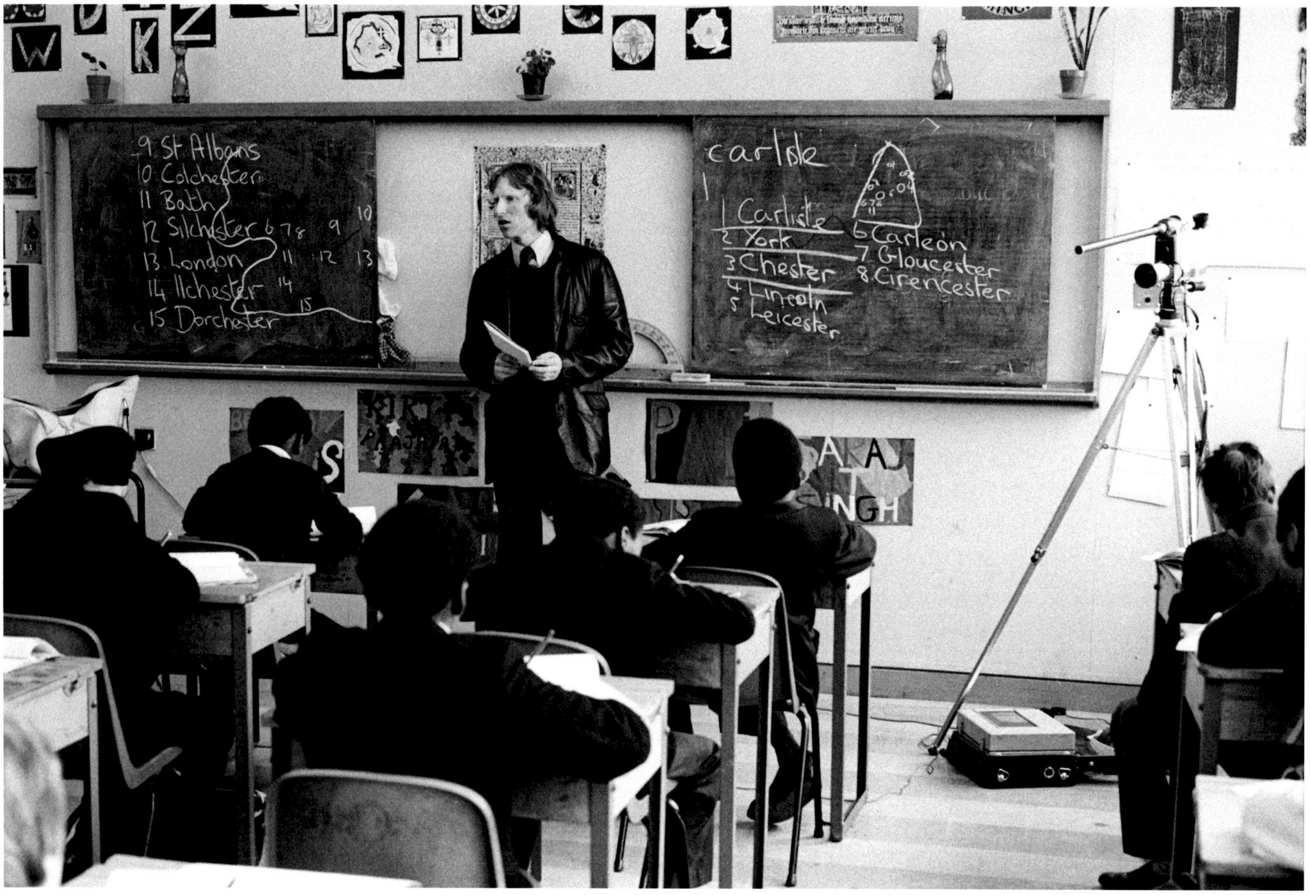

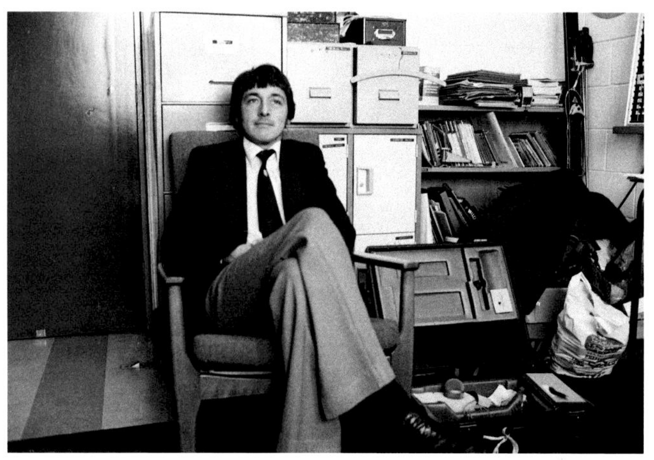
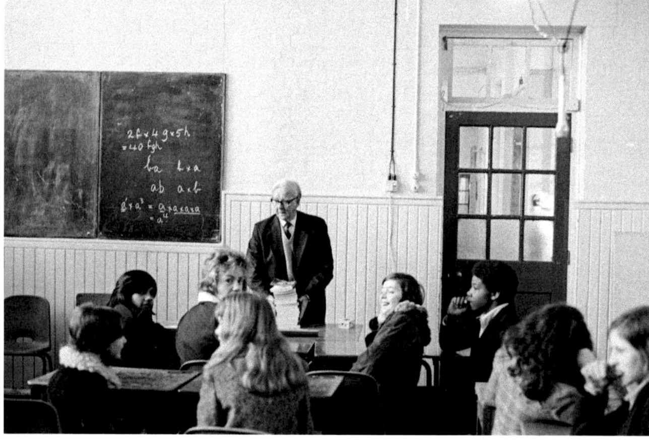
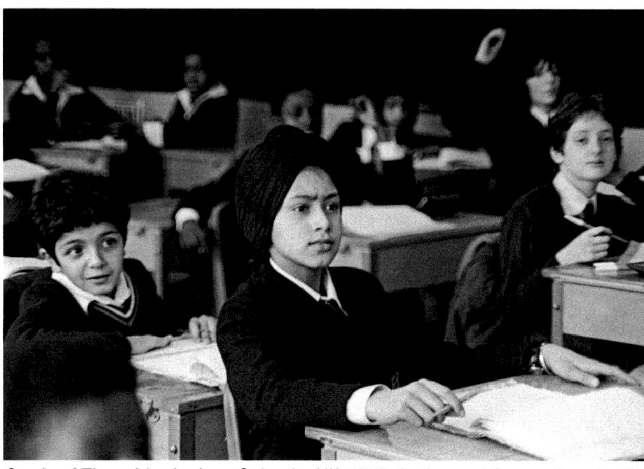
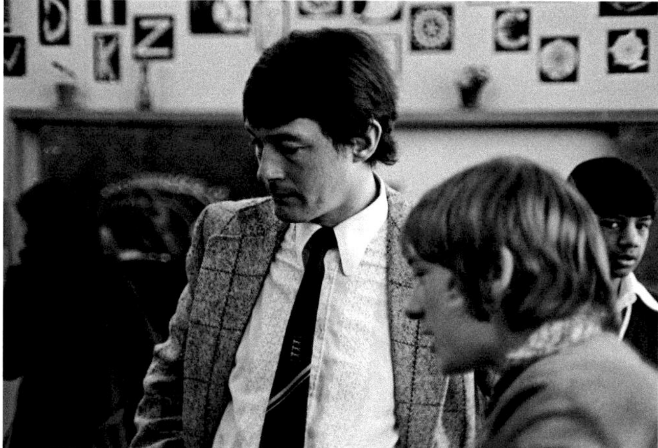

Study of Three Birmingham Schools, UK, 1976, Ladywood Comprehensive School

From the series "Work Studies in Schools," 1976–1977

Darcy Lange

Work Studies in Schools

Study of Three Birmingham Schools, UK, 1976
Studies of Teaching in Four Oxfordshire Schools, UK,
1977

Lange's "Work Studies in Schools" focus on the process of teaching and learning in the classroom. The first of these studies took place in three Birmingham schools in 1976, followed by studies in four Oxfordshire schools in 1977. In his Birmingham studies, Lange carefully chose institutions that would represent different social classes, recording in both public and private schools. He also videotaped a wide range of classes, later developing in the Oxfordshire studies a more restricted and systematic structure focused solely on the teaching of art, history, and science (see wall diagram for the structure of the Oxfordshire study). The capacity of early portable video to provide live and taped feedback made the medium a viable tool for criticism and analysis. Feedback (Lange's understanding of which was conceptually influenced by his conversations with Dan Graham at the time) became the central focus in the Oxfordshire series, where the studies of teachers' performances were extended by videotaping the teachers' and students' reactions to the recordings of the classes. The subjects' reactions thus became incorporated into the work and guided its development, while the self-reflexive process added another dimension to the studies—Lange's videotaping was itself also examined as work. Seen as "researches" and "an educational process" the videos recorded insightful discussions about the nature and motivations of Lange's project.

Lange considered the process of education as "subtly but totally political" and "concerned with the establishment of values and parameters of behaviour; its criteria of success are mostly orientated towards middle-class academic aspirations." The tapes cast teaching as a socially constructive process without assigning a value to these practices. Subscribing to the Marxist ideology common among video practitioners of the time, Lange saw "Work Studies in Schools" as "our collective truth," as a means of breaking down or making transparent such social hierarchies. Moreover, by inviting his subjects to become critical viewers, the artist introduces a radical potential for social transformation. For Lange, the power of video had to do with this immediate communicative relation with his subjects and its ability to effect change in them, which he saw as a reciprocal process.

To his disappointment, Lange never found an outside "function" for his videos, which were shown largely in the context of art galleries. This troubled him, and this frustration was presaged in a 1975 conversation with Willoughby Sharp: "This is where I need to get a lot more serious about getting the work shown to a wider audience, and making a real effort to get back to the people it was recorded from."

Mercedes Vicente, text for exhibition *Darcy Lange,* Camera Austria, Graz: 2010.

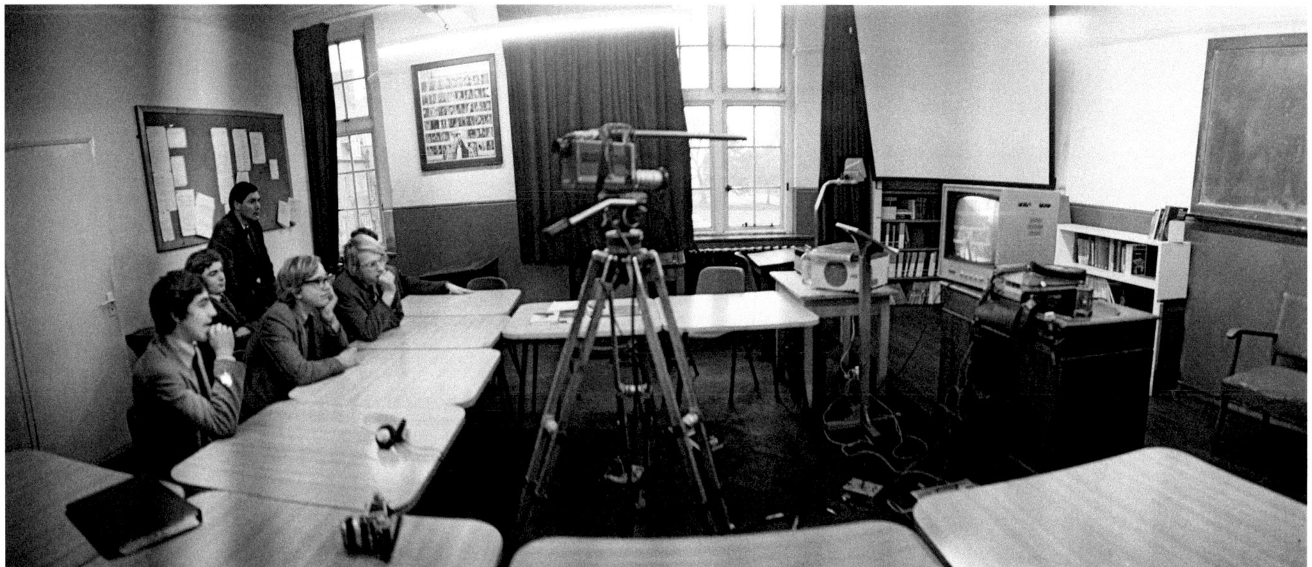

Studies of Teaching in Four Oxfordshire Schools, UK, 1977, Cheney Upper School

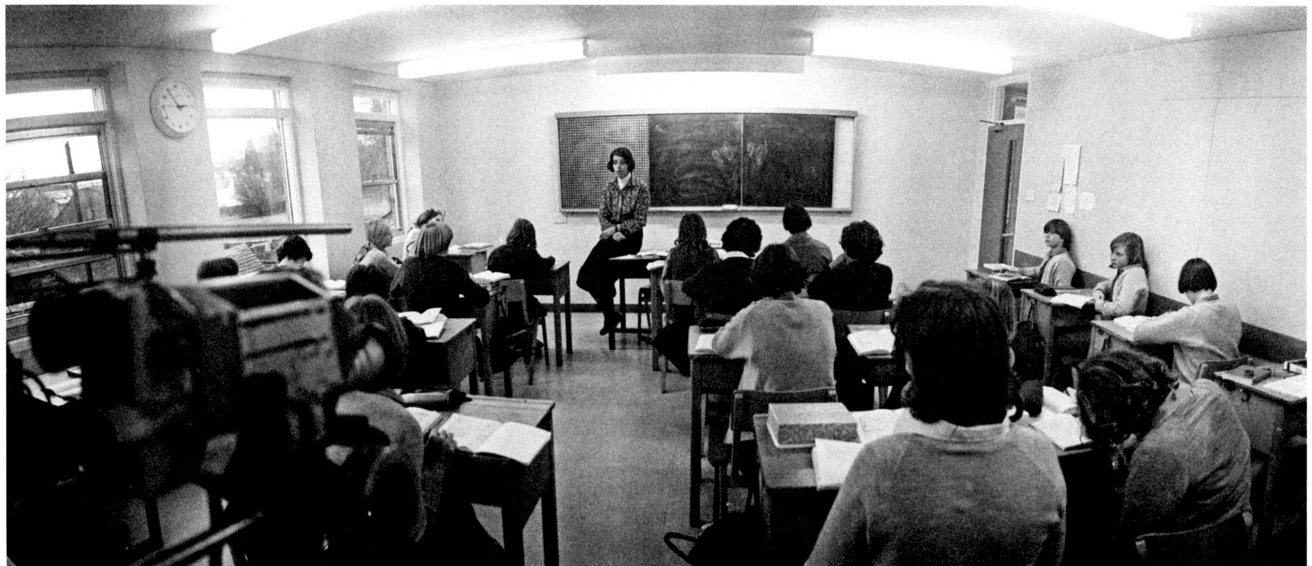

Studies of Teaching in Four Oxfordshire Schools, UK, 1977, St Mary's School

From the series "Work Studies in Schools," 1976–1977

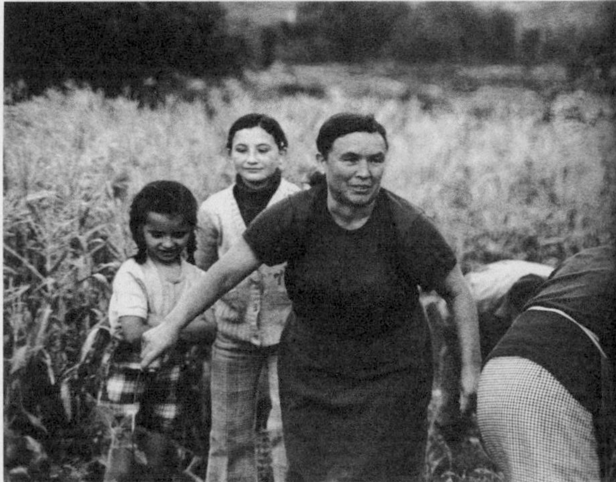

DARCY LANGE, Cantavieja, Study of Work in a Spanish Village, Spain / Spanien, 1975. B/w still photograph / SW-Fotografie.

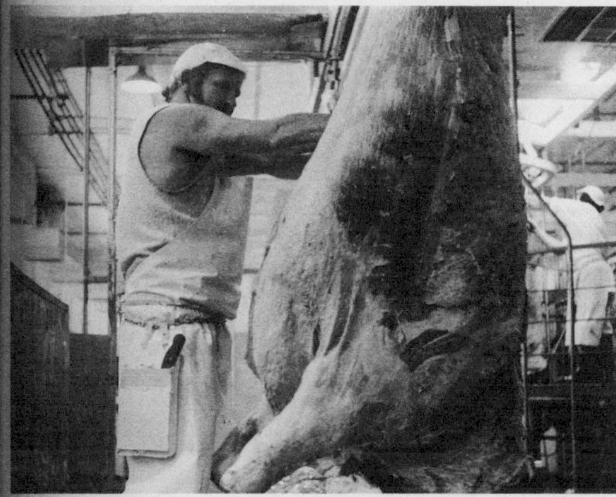

DARCY LANGE, Waitara Freezing Works / Schlachthaus Waitara, 1974. B/w still photograph / SW-Fotografie.

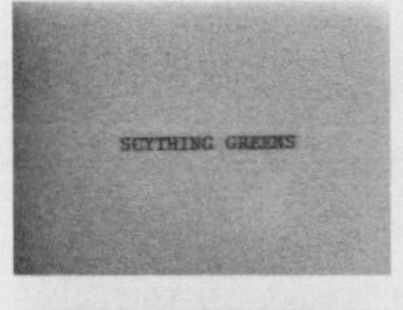

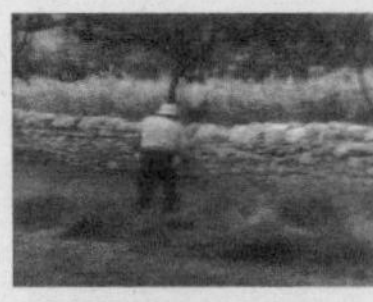
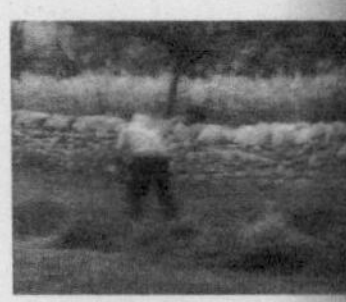

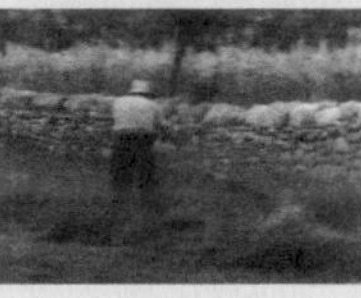
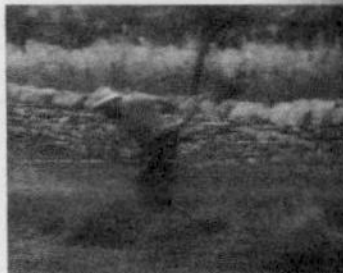
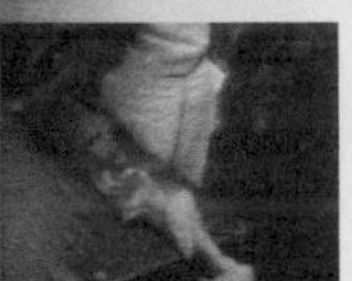

Scything Greens / Gras mähen. Video stills.

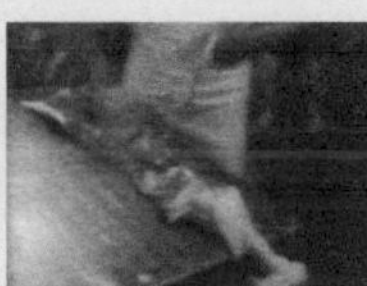
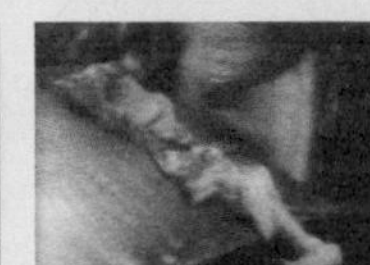
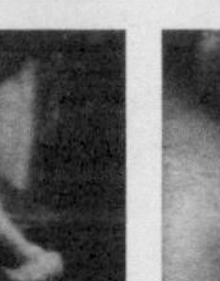
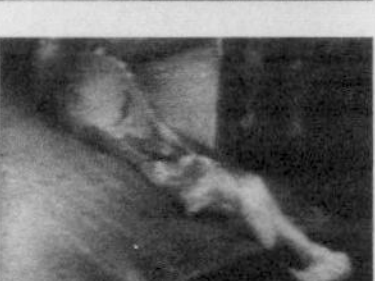

Boning Calves / Kälber auslösen. Video stills.

DARCY LANGE: WORK STUDIES IN SCHOOLS

Helen Le[gg]

Filmed exploratively in three Birmingham schools in 1976, and more systematically in four Oxfordshire schools the following year, »Work Studies in Schools« contrasts state and private schools across a range of subjects. Ostensibly a continuation of his ongoing documentation of manual labour, the project sees Lange shift his attention to the professional practice of teaching, though the issue of class remains the central axis around which the work turns. His ethnographic-style studies cast educational establishments as complex societal mechanisms engaged in the production and reproduction of class identity.

The development of this work, which can be tracked across the two years Lange spent on it, suggests someone dissatisfied with the condition of art, probing at boundaries not only of his own work, but that of the documentary genre and the orthodoxies of art in 1970's Britain. Lange felt that art had become isolated, divorced from the world around it, and so sought to develop a practice with social conscience. That he pre-empted some of the key critical issues of documentary practice is indicative of this. His videos were produced less for any external eye than for the participants themselves, to the extent that much of his footage, until quite recently, had been seen only by the subjects themselves. By playing his unedited classroom recordings back to the teachers and pupils he worked with and then asking them to respond, again on videotape, he gave a voice to those individuals he chose to represent that was crucially incorporated as a fundamental part of the work. The process of looking, thinking and questioning, that is gradually formalised as Lange grasps the functional possibility of his material, was intended above all to empower those he filmed.

In Birmingham Lange filmed classes in a secondary state comprehensive, a boy's grammar and a primary school, capturing a range of teaching styles and techniques. It was here that he would tentatively develop the three-part video format of »classroom study«, »teacher response« and »student response« that would form the basis of a clearer, more rigorous framework for the Oxfordshire studies. In Oxford Lange also made a sharper and more deliberate contrast between two state and two public schools, with comparisons drawn between the teaching of history, science and art in each. A further layer of reflection was added by the filmed discussion that took place between Lange, the art critic Guy Brett, Ron Jones, a lecturer at the School of Art Education in Birmingham and many of the teachers and pupils from the featured schools. This was filmed at the Museum of Modern Art in Oxford in 1977, during an exhibition of the Oxfordshire studies held there and was subsequently included as part of the show.

Much of Lange's methodology was, perhaps unsurprisingly, influenced by the work of other artists. Lange openly credited Dan Graham's use of video feedback as having informed his fine-tuning of the schools studies structure between Birmingham in 1976 and Oxford in 1977. The feedback process is sporadic in the Birmingham tapes; by the time of the Oxfordshire studies, Lange records teacher and pupil interviews after every classroom recording. He believed this process would produce a study that was as objective as possible, because it embodied different points of view.

Stephen Willats, with who Lange also exchanged ideas, had developed a pioneering body of work by the mid-seventies, detailed in a number of texts written by the artist including, The Artist as an Instigator of Changes in Social Cognition and Behaviour (London: Gallery House Press 1973) and the influential Art and Social Function (London: Latimer New Dimensions 1976). Willats' concern with ways in which the social structure organised and determined its own continuance through ideology, in particular through models of communication networks, and his proposal that artists might develop works as »social models«, using data from an audiences' own environment in order to trigger a shift in their self-image, clearly resonate with Lange's own thinking.

Yet Lange's strategies were also powerfully affected by practices evolving beyond the art world. Between 1971 and 1977, though based in London, he made frequent extended visits to Birmingham:

»Work Studies in Schools«, zunächst 1976 als eine explorative Untersuchung in drei Schulen in Birmingham gefilmt und ein Jahr darauf systematischer in vier Schulen in Oxfordshire, vergleicht den Unterricht an staatlichen und privaten Schulen anhand einer Reihe von Fächern. Scheinbar eine Fortführung von Langes Dokumentationsserie über manuelle Arbeit, bringt das Projekt doch eine Verschiebung seines Interesses hin zum Beruf des Unterrichtens mit sich, wiewohl auch hier die Klassenfrage im Zentrum steht. Seine ethnografisch anmutenden Studien stellen Bildungseinrichtungen als komplexe, mit der Produktion und Reproduktion von Klassenidentität befasste Gesellschaftsmechanismen dar.

In der Entwicklung dieser Arbeit, die über die gesamten zwei Jahre ihrer Entstehung nachvollziehbar ist, wird jemand sichtbar, der mit der Kunst unzufrieden war und hier nicht nur die Grenzen des eigenen Werks, sondern auch die des Dokumentargenres und britischer Kunstorthodoxien der 1970er Jahre auslotete. Lange glaubte, dass sich die Kunst abgesondert, von der sie umgebenden Welt entfernt hatte, und strebte eine künstlerische Praxis mit sozialem Gewissen an. Ein Hinweis darauf ist auch, dass er dabei einige Kernprobleme des Dokumentarismus vorwegnahm. Seine Videos wurden weniger für die Augen Außenstehender produziert als für die Beteiligten selbst, und zwar so sehr, dass die meisten seiner Aufnahmen bis vor kurzem keiner außer ihnen gesehen hat. Er spielte seine ungeschnittenen Aufnahmen aus den Klassenzimmern Lehrern und Schülern, mit denen er arbeitete, erneut vor und bat sie, der vor der Videokamera, dazu Stellung zu nehmen; so gab er denen, stellten eine Stimme, die als wesentliches Moment in die Arbeit integriert wurde. Der Betrachtungs-, Reflexions- und Befragungsprozess, der mit Langes Einsicht in die funktionalen Möglichkeiten des Materials zunehmend formalisiert wurde, sollte vor allem zur Ermächtigung der Gefilmten beitragen.

In Birmingham nahm Lange Klassen in einer staatlichen Gesamtschule, einem Knabengymnasium und einer Grundschule auf, wobei er eine Reihe unterschiedlicher Unterrichtsstile und -techniken erfasste. Dabei entwickelte er allmählich jenes dreiteilige Videoformat aus »Klassenstudie«, »Lehrerreaktion« und »Schülerreaktion«, das schließlich die Grundlage des klareren, strengeren Ansatzes der Oxfordshire-Studien bilden sollte. In Oxford traf Lange auch eine deutlichere und gezieltere Unterscheidung zwischen je zwei staatlichen und zwei privaten Schulen, in denen er das gleiche zwischen dem jeweiligen Geschichts-, Naturwissenschafts- und Kunstunterricht anstellte. Eine weitere Reflexionsebene kam mit dem Mitschnitt einer Diskussion zwischen Lange, dem Kunstkritiker Guy Brett, Ron Jones, einem Dozenten an der School of Art Education in Birmingham, und einer ganzen Reihe von Lehrern und Schülern aus den betreffenden Schulen hinzu. Diese Diskussion fand 1977 am Museum of Modern Art in Oxford im Rahmen einer Ausstellung der Oxfordshire-Studien statt und ihr Mitschnitt wurde in der Folge in die Ausstellung integriert.

Langes Methode war selbstverständlich auch durch die Arbeiten anderer Künstler beeinflusst. So führte er die Feinjustierung der Schulstudienstruktur zwischen Birmingham 1976 und Oxford 1977 explizit auf Dan Grahams Arbeit mit Videofeedback zurück. Wurde das Feedback in den Birmingham-Videos nur sporadisch eingesetzt, so nimmt Lange in den Oxfordshire-Studien nach jedem Unterrichtsmitschnitt Interviews mit Lehrern und Schülern auf. Seiner Überzeugung nach gab dies der Studie größtmögliche Objektivität durch die Verkörperung unterschiedlicher Standpunkte.

Stephen Willats, mit dem sich Lange ebenfalls austauschte, hatte bis Mitte der 1970er Jahre ein richtungsweisendes Werk geschaffen, das er in einer Reihe eigener Texte wie The Artist as an Instigator of Changes in Social Cognition and Behaviour (London: Gallery House Press 1973) und dem einflussreichen Buch Art and Social Function (London: Latimer New Dimensions 1976) ausführte. Willats' Beschäftigung mit der Art und Weise, wie die Gesellschaftsstruktur mittels Ideologie, insbesondere durch namhafte Kommunikationsnetzwerke, ihre eigene Perpetuierung bereitstellte, sein Vorschlag, Künstler sollten »Gesellschaftsmodelle« entwickeln und dabei auf Daten aus der Umgebung des Publikums zurückgreifen, um eine Veränderung in dessen Selbstbildern hervorzurufen, sind auch in Langes Denken spürbar.

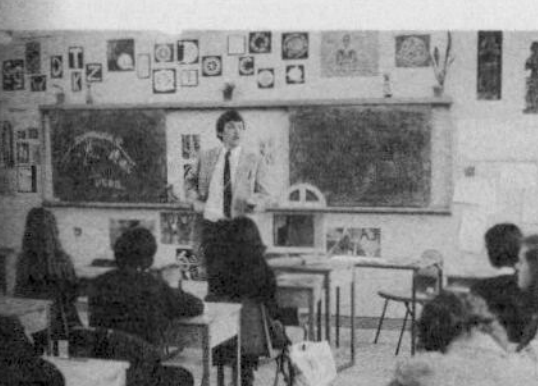

DARCY LANGE, Study of Three Birmingham Schools, UK, 1976. Mr Perks, »Animal Farm«, English Class / Englischklasse, Ladywood Comprehensive School. B/w still photograph / SW-Fotografie.

DARCY LANGE, Studies of Teaching in Four Oxfordshire Schools, UK, 1977. Chris Wright, History class / Geschichteklasse, Cheney Upper School. B/w still photograph / SW-Fotografie.

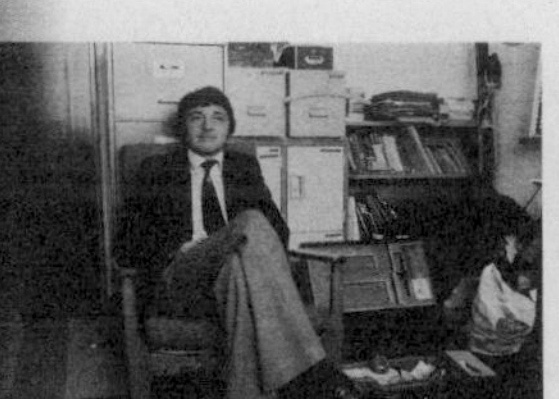
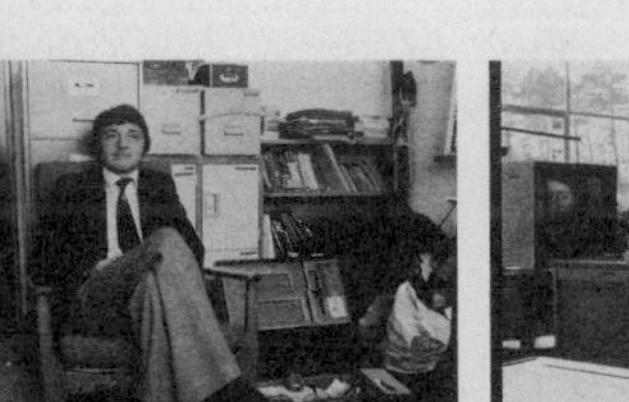

DARCY LANGE, Study of Three Birmingham Schools, UK, 1976. Mr Perks, Teacher Response / Lehrerfeedback, Ladywood Comprehensive School. B/w still photograph / SW-Fotografie.

DARCY LANGE, Studies of Teaching in Four Oxfordshire Schools, UK, 1977. Chris Wright viewing the recording of his class study / bei der Betrachtung der Aufnahmen von seinem Unterricht. B/w still photograph / SW-Fotografie.

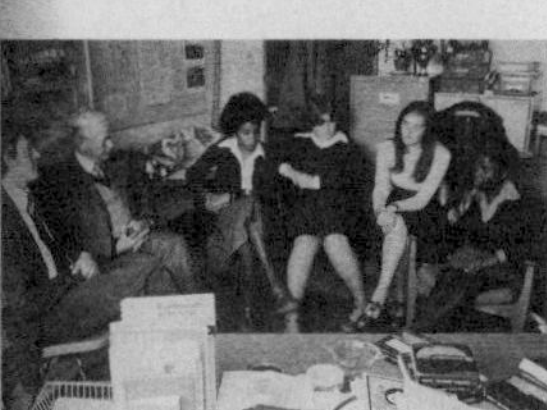
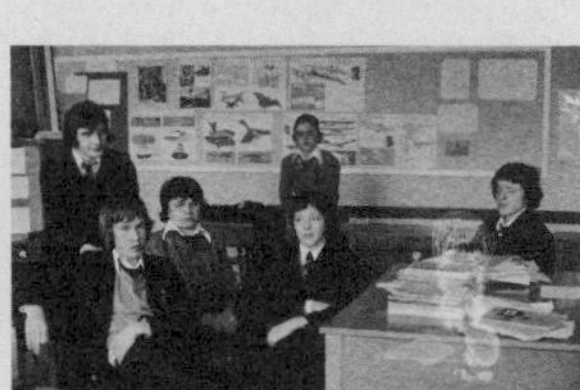

DARCY LANGE, Study of Three Birmingham Schools, UK, 1976. Mr Perks, Mr. Brendon and students discussing the recording / und Schülerinnen bei die Diskussion der Aufnahmen, Ladywood Comprehensive School. B/w still photograph / SW-Fotografie.

DARCY LANGE, Studies of Teaching in Four Oxfordshire Schools, UK, 1977. Chris Wright's students' response to his history class / Feedback von Chris Wrights Schülern auf seinen Geschichtsunterricht, Cheney Upper School. B/w still photograph / SW-Fotografie.

the city proved to be a place in which he found it possible to work, not least because the Birmingham School of Fine Art offered him a teaching position. More pertinent though, was the peculiar fact that under its auspices sat the only centre for the study of education in the country housed within an art school, an institution Lange became part of, albeit informally, sitting in on lectures and discussions and making use of its resources. The centre's liaison officer arranged access to the three schools Lange filmed and the camera used also belonged to the institution. »I went up to Phil Slight's place, a friend who taught in an educational college in Birmingham, and he showed me his video machine, and it just seemed obvious that it was what I wanted to use. And I used it. The first tape I did was in Birmingham.«[1] The camera had been purchased to record both expert and student teachers at work, after which footage was played to tutorial groups in order to dissect, analyse and appraise the skills of teaching and processes of learning – a system identical to the one developed by Lange. Pupils would discuss techniques used by teachers, their responses to and handling of the classes' behaviour, the clarity of their communication and use of teaching aids. That these considerations found their way into Lange's videos is clear; he frequently frames and focuses the camera on hand gestures and facial expression, zooms in on text books or writing and diagrams on blackboards, drawing attention to the specifics of communication in an analytical way. Books in the artist's library included volumes designed for student teachers, offering methods for the documentation of classroom situations, reinforcing the possibility that Lange was studying techniques used by educationalists.

Lange had already played film footage back to his subjects prior to 1976, but this was never conceptualised as integral to the work until the schools studies. Here, it comes to determine the entire structure, suggesting he was becoming gradually more aware of its implications for his work. The feedback process allowed Lange's subjects to view themselves within their own environment, with a degree of distance that might foster critical reflection. By recording the feedback as well, intending it to be seen by a third party audience, he created a functional portrait of thought in action. Important too was the inclusion of Lange himself as protagonist in many of the tapes; his questions and physical presence are never edited and rarely hidden except by the practical necessity of his being seated behind the camera.

Lange's positioning of himself within an institution might be seen as akin to the work of the Artist's Placement Group (APG), which, through the late 1960s and early 1970s organised placements for artists within industry and government. However, while the APG's philosophy proposed the artist as an inherently creative being, whose insight might impact in a socially progressive way upon the processes of production, Lange was sceptical about the very notions of art and the artist, preferring the idea that creativity was not »located« within certain privileged beings or forms, but rather something to be practiced, by everyone, across all fields. »Creativity in schools is not necessarily confined just to the art class … art is important because of its observation of material life. Creativity when applied through music, poetry, art, to life and work could become a protection against object worship, beyond functionalism. It might help to re-create involvement and creativity within manual work or build non-object recreational expression«[2]. Indeed in all of the »Work Studies«, Lange shows an absolute respect for the labour of individuals, seeking out creativity inherent within peoples' daily activity and aligning himself alongside others, rather than in a hierarchical relationship. It is in this radical scepticism and his subsequent positioning of himself – which was to lead him further away and ultimately beyond art's institutions – that demands Lange's serious reconsideration.

1 Darcy Lange in an interview with Willoughby Sharp, Avalanche (New York), Summer 1975.
2 Darcy Lange, from an unpublished note in the artist's archive headed »Some Conclusions«.

Langes Strategien waren allerdings auch stark durch Verfahren geprägt, die nicht aus der Kunstwelt stammten. Zwischen 1971 und 1977 hielt er sich, obwohl in London lebend, oft für längere Zeit in Birmingham auf: Die Stadt erwies sich als ein Ort, an dem er arbeiten konnte – nicht zuletzt, weil ihm die Birmingham School of Fine Art eine Lehrerstelle bot. Wichtiger aber war, dass sich dort das landesweit einzige Zentrum für Pädagogik an einer Kunstakademie befand, eine Institution, der sich Lange, zumindest informell, anschloss: er nahm an Vorlesungen und Diskussionen teil und benutzte ihre Ressourcen. Die für Außenkontakte zuständige Person des Centre vermittelte den Zugang zu den drei Schulen, an denen Lange filmte, und auch die verwendete Kamera kam vom Centre. »Ich suchte meinen Freund Phil Slight auf, der an einem pädagogischen Institut in Birmingham unterrichtete, und er zeigte mir sein Videogerät, und ich wusste sofort, dass ich damit arbeiten wollte. Und das tat ich dann auch. Mein erstes Video nahm ich in Birmingham auf.«[1] Die Kamera war angeschafft worden, um erfahrene und angehende Lehrer bei der Arbeit zu filmen mit dem Ziel, die Videos dann in Übungen zu analysieren und zu einer Bewertung der Lehrkompetenz und des Lernfortschritts zu gelangen – ein System also, ganz ähnlich dem, das Lange entwickelte. Schüler diskutierten die von den Lehrern angewandten Techniken, ihre Reaktionen auf das Verhalten der Klasse, die Klarheit ihrer Kommunikation und ihren Lehrmitteleinsatz. Dass derlei Überlegungen auch Eingang in Langes Videos fanden, ist offensichtlich; er richtet die Kamera häufig auf Handbewegungen und Gesichtsausdruck, zoomt auf Lehrbücher oder auf Texte und Diagramme an der Tafel, richtet sein Augenmerk analytisch auf Details des Kommunikationsprozesses. In der Bibliothek des Künstlers befanden sich Bücher für angehende Lehrer, in denen es um Methoden zur Dokumentation von Klassensituationen ging, was die Vermutung stützt, dass sich Lange mit in der Pädagogik gebräuchlichen Techniken beschäftigte.

Zwar hatte Lange den gefilmten Personen seine Aufnahmen auch schon vor 1976 vorgeführt, aber erst in den »School Studies« wurde dies zu einem integralen Bestandteil des Werks. In ihnen wird es strukturbestimmend, was darauf schließen lässt, dass er sich der Implikationen für seine Arbeit stärker bewusst wird. Aufgrund des Feedbackprozesses konnten sich die Dargestellten in ihrer eigenen Umgebung sehen, aus einer Distanz, die förderlich für die kritische Reflexion sein konnte. Indem er das Feedback ebenfalls aufnahm, um es einem außenstehenden Publikum zu zeigen, schuf er ein funktionales Porträt eines Denkens in Aktion. Wichtig war auch Langes eigene Einbeziehung als Protagonist in vielen Videos; seine Fragen und seine physische Präsenz wurden nie herausgeschnitten und kaum einmal verborgen – oder nur durch die praktische Notwendigkeit, dass er hinter der Kamera stand.

In Langes eigener Positionierung innerhalb einer Institution könnte man Ähnlichkeiten mit der Arbeit der Artist's Placement Group (APG) sehen, die in den späten 1960 und 1970er Jahren Künstler in Wirtschaft und Staatsführung einschleuste. Allerdings galten Künstler in der Philosophie der APG als grundlegend kreative Menschen, deren Einsichten Produktionsprozesse gesellschaftlich progressiv zu beeinflussen vermochten, wogegen Lange schon den Begriff der Kunst und des Künstlers skeptisch gegenüberstand und Kreativität eher als etwas betrachtete, das nicht irgendwelchen privilegierten Menschen oder Formen »innewohnt«, sondern von allen und auf allen Gebieten praktiziert werden kann. »Kreativität in Schulen ist nicht unbedingt auf den Kunstunterricht beschränkt … Kunst ist wichtig wegen ihrer Beachtung materiellen Lebens. Durch Musik, Poesie, Kunst zum Leben und Arbeit angewandt, könnte Kreativität Schutz vor einer Verherrlichung von Gegenständen bieten, abseits des Funktionalismus. Sie könnte zur Wiederbelebung schöpferischer Mitbeteiligung an manueller Arbeit oder zur Förderung nicht objektgebundener Ausdrucksformen in der Freizeit beitragen«[2]. In all seinen »Work Studies« zeigt Lange größten Respekt für die Arbeit derer, die er filmt, versucht stets die in der jeweiligen Tätigkeit steckende Kreativität aufzuspüren und sieht sich immer Seite an Seite mit den anderen und nicht in einem hierarchischen Verhältnis. Aufgrund eben dieser radikalen Skepsis und der aus ihr folgenden Selbstpositionierung – die ihn immer weiter und schließlich ganz von Kunstinstitutionen wegführt – ist es notwendig, sich ernsthaft mit Lange zu beschäftigen.

1 Darcy Lange in einem Interview mit Willoughby Sharp, in: Avalanche (New York), Summer 1975.
2 Darcy Lange, in einer unveröffentlichten Notiz mit der Überschrift »Some Conclusions« aus dem Archiv des Künstlers.

(Übersetzung aus dem Englischen: Wilfried Prantner)

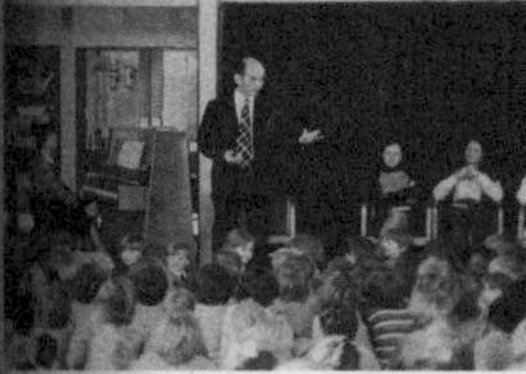

DARCY LANGE, Study of Three Birmingham Schools, UK, 1976.
Assembly / Vorschulgruppe, Leabank Junior School.
B/w still photograph / SW-Fotografie.

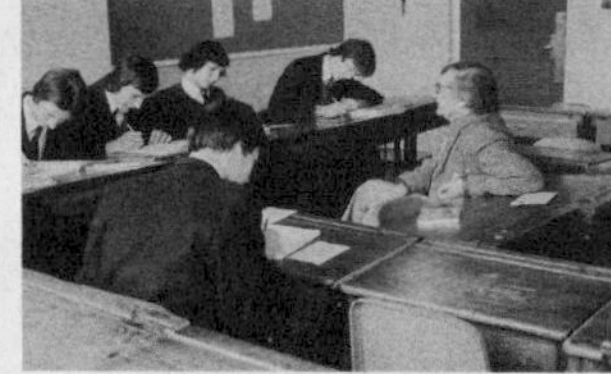

DARCY LANGE, Study of Three Birmingham Schools, UK, 1976.
Mr. Trott, English Literature and Language class / Klasse für englische Literatur und Sprache, Webster, King Edward's School. B/w still photograph / SW-Fotografie.

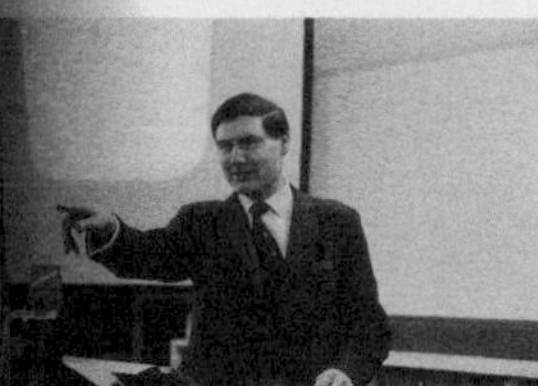

DARCY LANGE, Studies of Teaching in Four Oxfordshire Schools, UK, 1977.
Howat, History class / Geschichteklasse, Radley College.
B/w still photograph / SW-Fotografie.

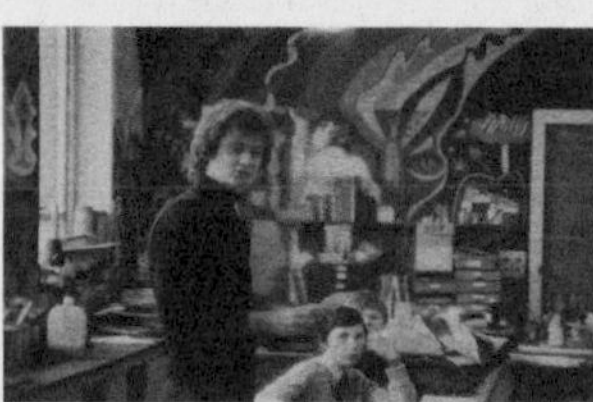

DARCY LANGE, Studies of Teaching in Four Oxfordshire Schools, UK, 1977.
Tony Morgan, Art class / Kunstklasse, Banbury School.
B/w still photograph / SW-Fotografie.

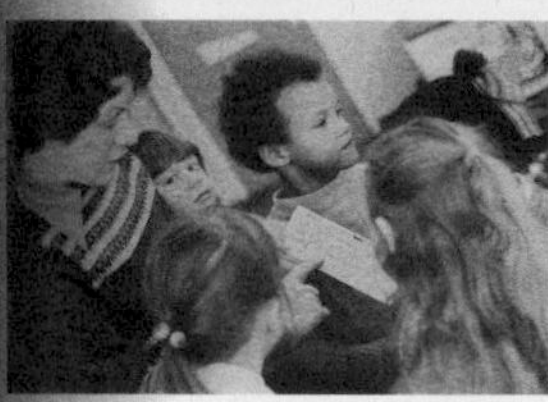

DARCY LANGE, Study of Three Birmingham Schools, UK, 1976.
Mrs. Harris, Teaching the Infants / Vorschulunterricht, Leabank Junior School.
B/w still photograph / SW-Fotografie.

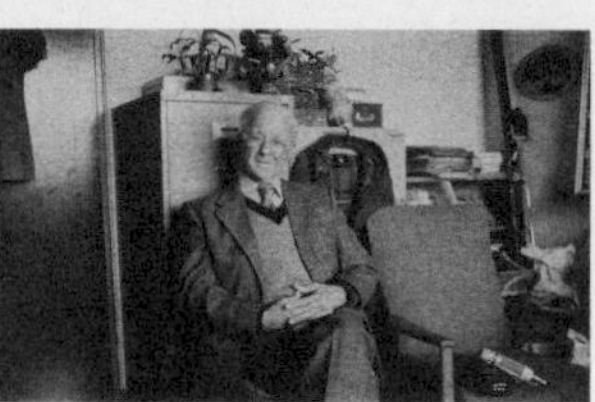

DARCY LANGE, Study of Three Birmingham Schools, UK, 1976.
Mr. Brendon, Teacher Response / Lehrerfeedback, Ladywood Comprehensive School.
B/w still photograph / SW-Fotografie.

Alle Arbeiten von / all images by Darcy Lange: Courtesy: Darcy Lange Estate.
Video und / and Film: New Zealand Film Archive Wellington;
still photographs: Govett-Brewster Art Gallery, New Plymouth.

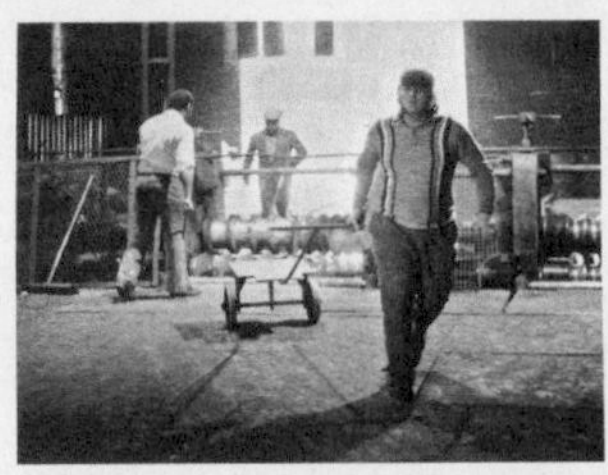

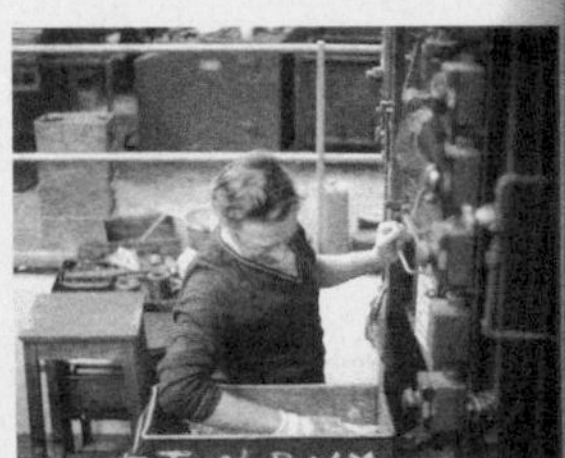

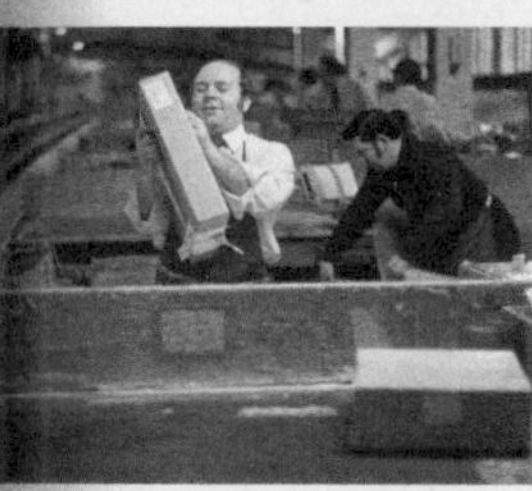

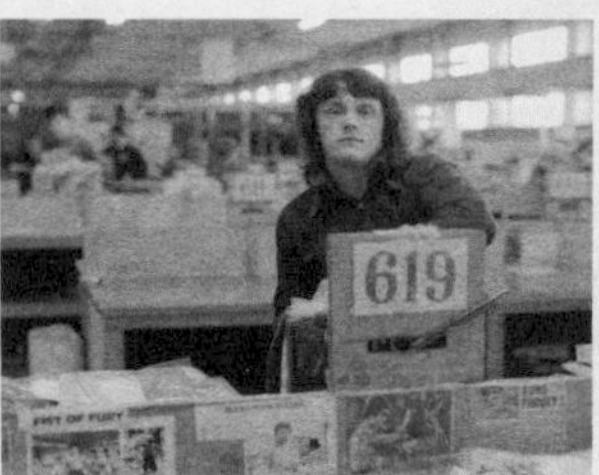

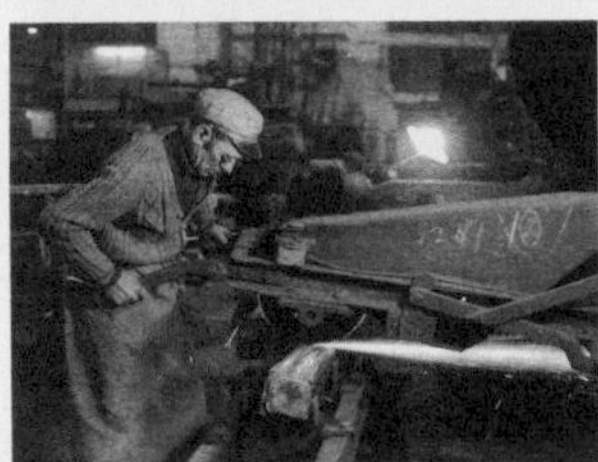

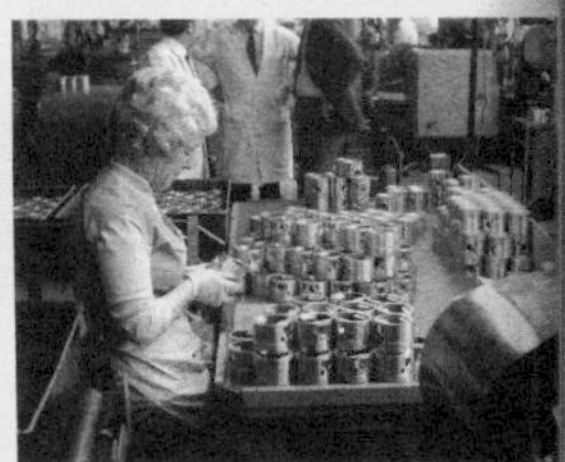

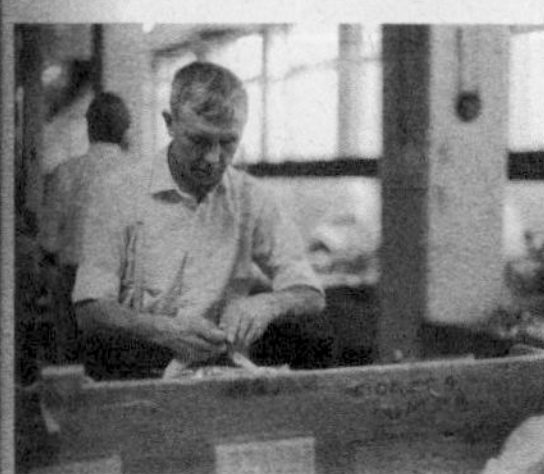

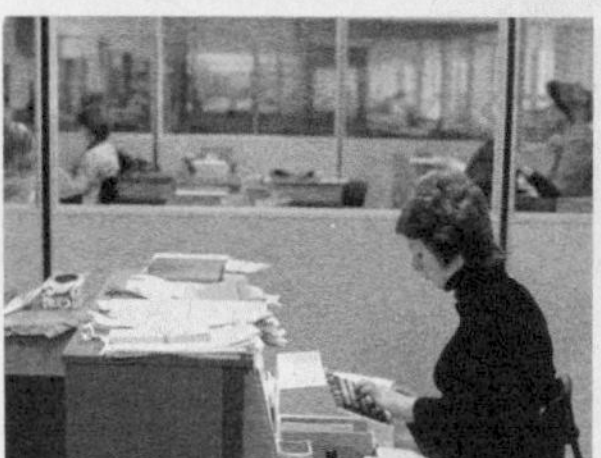

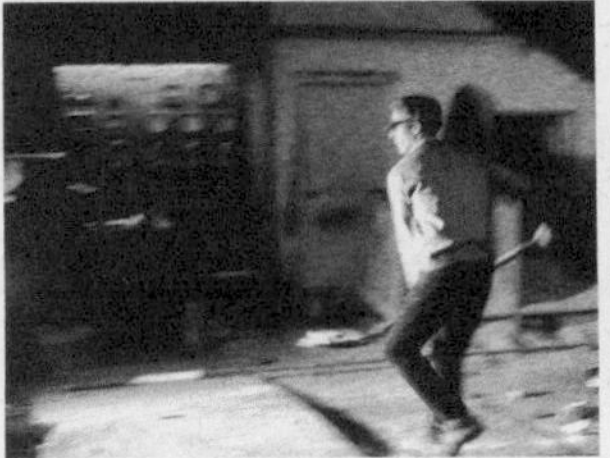

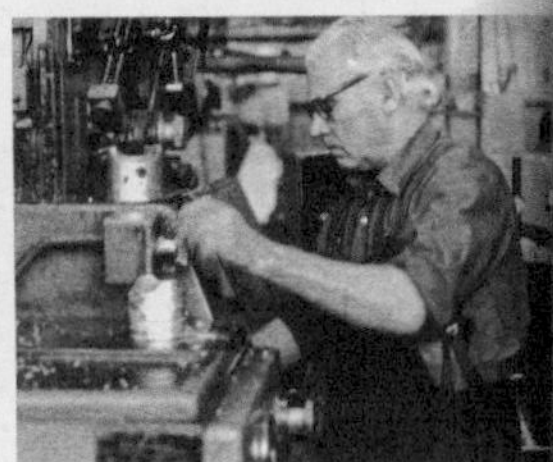

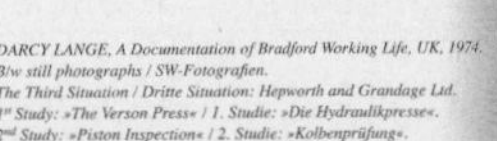

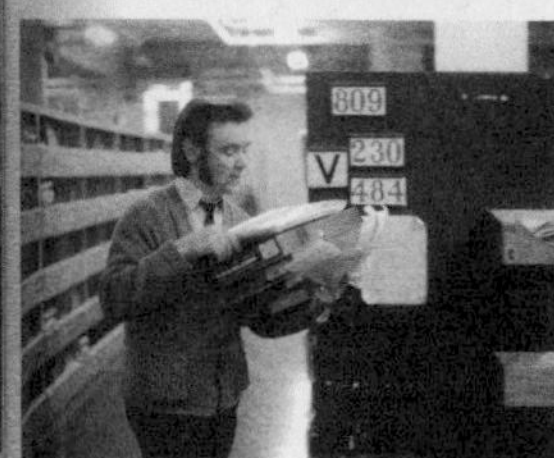

DARCY LANGE, A Documentation of Bradford Working Life, UK, 1974.
B/w still photographs / SW-Fotografien.
The First Situation / Erste Situation: Osborne Steels Ltd.
1st Study: »Rolling Mill« / 1. Studie: »Walzwerk«.
2nd Study: »The Grinding« / 2. Studie: »Schleifen«.
3rd Study: »Furnaces« / 3. Studie: »Hochöfen«.

DARCY LANGE, A Documentation of Bradford Working Life, UK, 1974.
B/w still photographs / SW-Fotografien.
The Third Situation / Dritte Situation: Hepworth and Grandage Ltd.
1st Study: »The Verson Press« / 1. Studie: »Die Hydraulikpresse«.
2nd Study: »Piston Inspection« / 2. Studie: »Kolbenprüfung«.
3rd Study: »Dual Lathes« / 3. Studie: »Doppeldrehbank«.

DARCY LANGE, A Documentation of Bradford Working Life, UK, 1974.
B/w still photographs / SW-Fotografien.
The Fourth Situation / Vierte Situation: Grattan Ltd.
1st Study: »Study of a Packer« / 1. Studie: »Packerstudie«.
2nd Study: »Study of a Packer« / 2. Studie: »Packerstudie«.
3rd Study: »Order Assembly« / »Zusammenstellen der Bestellung«.
4th Study: »Order Assembly« / »Zusammenstellen der Bestellung«.
5th Study: »Punch Card Operator« / »Lochkartenverarbeitung«.

Allan Sekula

Camera Austria Award

2001   Camera Austria Award for Contemporary Photography by the City of Graz

Participation at Symposion

1996   Symposion on Photography XVI: "Fish Story: Photography between Discourse and Document," 18–20 October 1996, concept, lecturer

Camera Austria International

1988   Allan Sekula, "Sketch for a Geography Lesson," text contribution/artist contribution, *Camera Austria International* 25/1988

1995   Allan Sekula, "Walking on Water," text contribution/artist contribution, Frits Gierstberg, "Allan Sekula: Fish Story," exhibition review, *Camera Austria International* 53/1995

1997   Allan Sekula, "Über Fish Story: Der Sarg lernt tanzen," text contribution and cover, Allan Sekula, "Dead Letter Office (Work in Progress)," artist contribution, *Camera Austria International* 59–60/1997

1998   Pia Lanzinger, "Allan Sekula: Dismal Science. Photo Works 1972–1997," Münchner Kunstverein, exhibition review, *Camera Austria International* 62–63/1997

2001   Allan Sekula, "TITANIC's Wake," text contribution/ artist contribution, *Camera Austria International* 79/2001

2003   Ruth Noack, "Allan Sekula: Performance under Working Conditions," Generali Foundation, Vienna, exhibition review, *Camera Austria International* 83/2003

2006   Allan Sekula, "A Portable National Archive for a Stateless People: Susan Meiselas and the Kurds," text contribution, *Camera Austria International* 95/2006

2008   Susanne Holschbach, "Critical Realism in Contemporary Art. Around Allan Sekula's photography, Leuven University Press, Leuven 2006," book review, *Camera Austria International* 102/2008

2010   Allan Sekula, "Condé and Beveridge: … The Red Guards Come and Go, Talking of Michelangelo," text contribution, *Camera Austria International* 109/2010

2013   Cover, *Camera Austria International* 123/2013

2014   Kaucyila Brooke, "Allan Sekula (January 15, 1951 – August 10, 2013)," text contribution, Allan Sekula, artist contribution, *Camera Austria International* 125/2014

2015   Wilfried Prantner, "Hilde van Gelder ed.: Allan Sekula. Ship of Fools/The Dockers' Museum, Leuven University Press, Leuven 2015," book review, *Camera Austria International* 131/2015

2017   Eiko Grimberg, "Allan Sekula: Photography Against the Grain, MACK, London 2016," book review, *Camera Austria International* 137/2017

Exhibitions

1988   *Sketch for a Geography Lesson,* solo exhibition

2002   *Waiting for Tear Gas*, solo exhibition

2005   *TITANIC's Wake*, solo exhibition

Publication

2003   David Barriet, David Benassayag, Beatrice Didier, Christine Frisinghelli et al., eds, *Allan Sekula, TITANIC's Wake,* Graz, Edition Camera Austria, 2003

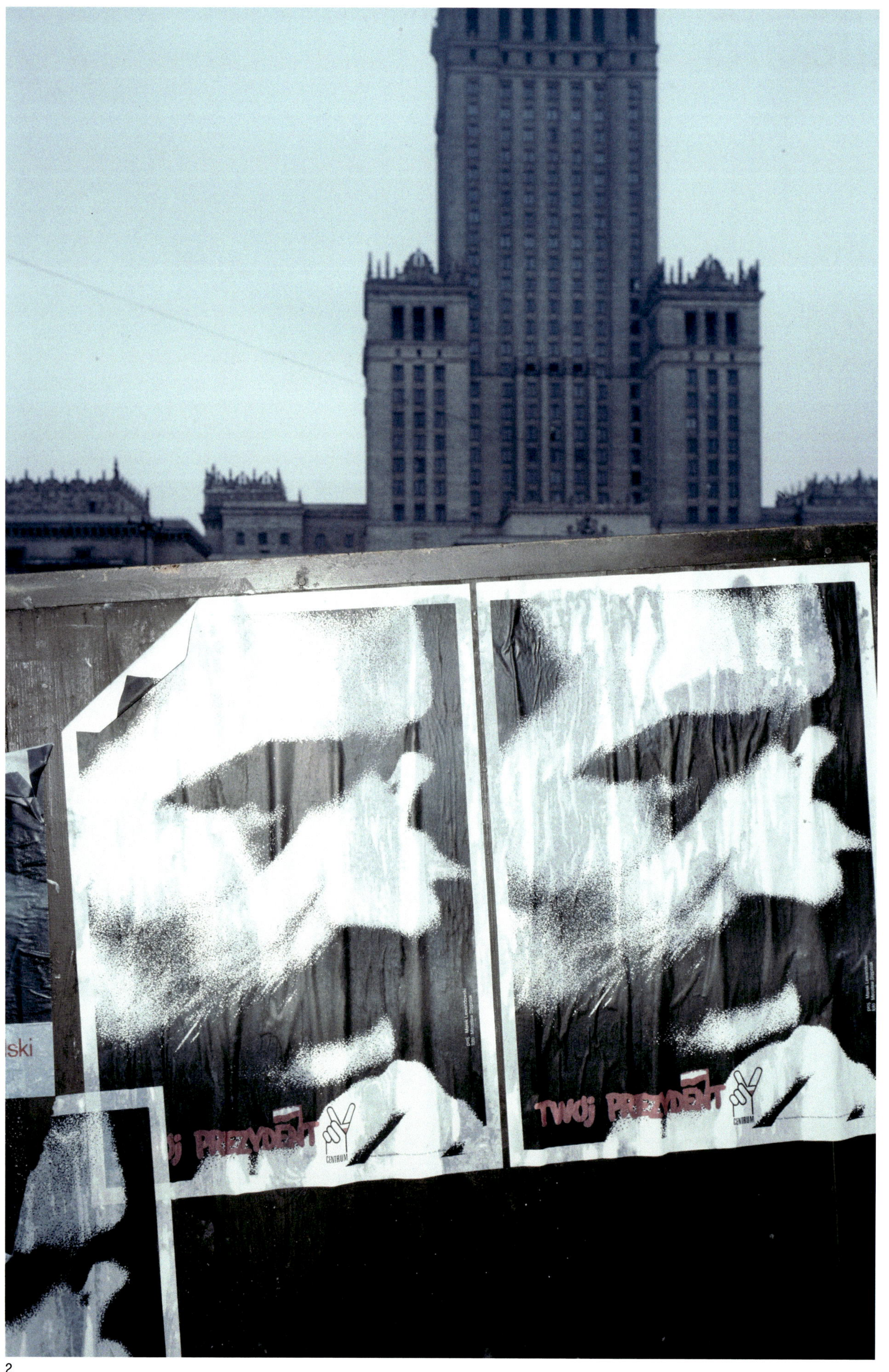
TWÓJ PREZYDENT
CENTRUM
...j PREZYDENT
CENTRUM
...ski

Allan Sekula

Walking on Water

Prologue

They build churches so that people can pray for houses.
Joke circulating in Poland, 1990

American conservatives like to believe the self-congratulatory myth that communism began to collapse at its weakest point, in Poland, because of a carefully nurtured secret alliance between Ronald Reagan and Pope John Paul II, the former Cardinal Karol Wojtyla. In the United States, it is often noted that there is a more than political explanation for the affinity between the two leaders, the former actor and the former mime. But beyond this shared theatricality, we should also consider Reagan's demonstrated love of the sea and the Pope's inheritance of a fisherman's throne. This is especially important with respect to Poland, a nation that takes the anchor for its national symbol. Poles also may believe this version of history, and may love the United States with more avidity and awe than many Americans, but they also were able to observe and endure and finally resist the blunders and abuses of the Polish communist nomenklatura at first hand. Thus Poles can understand internal and perhaps less magical explanations for the transformation of this, the "Jesus Christ of nations."
Conceding defeat, President Jaruzelski is interviewed on Polish television, late on election night. Already he is elder-statesmanlike, Nixonesque. He quotes Pope John Paul II on the triumph of good over evil, and speaks of the need to build democracy. Watching the speech, Malgosia Paradzinska, an English literature graduate student at the University of Warsaw, repeats over and over: "This is a sick country. You are visiting a sick country."

Walking on Water, 1990/1995,
Chapter 9 from *Fish Story*, 1989–1995

Selection from a series of 80 slides

2   Two double election posters for Lech Walesa. In front of the Palace of Culture and Science. Warsaw.
3   A French television correspondent reporting on the Polish elections from Zamkowy Square. Warsaw. (After the death of the artist, Dr. Hilde Van Gelder was able to identify the correspondent as the Belgian-Flemish radio and television journalist Johan Blommaert and correct this inscription.)
7   Models of Soviet ships built in the yard. Museum of the Gdansk shipyard.
9   Gdansk shipyard.
12 Work on a Soviet merchant ship. Gdansk Shipyard.
26 Shipyard apprentices living three to a room. Shipyard Workers' Home Number 1, Gdansk. "The work is too much for what I am paid."
61 A woman selling bras. Marszalkowska Street, Warsaw.
78 Crucified feet Saint Anna's Church, Warsaw.

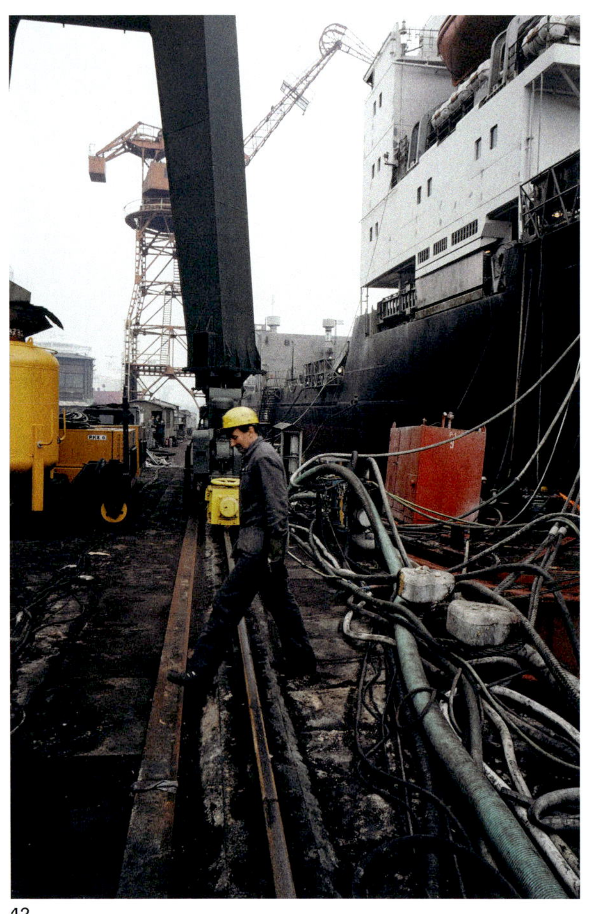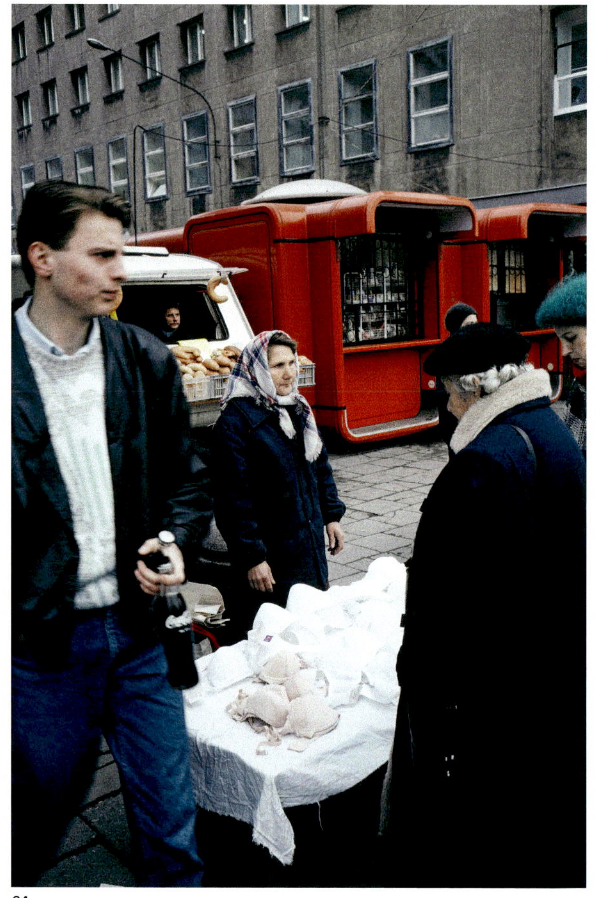

12

61

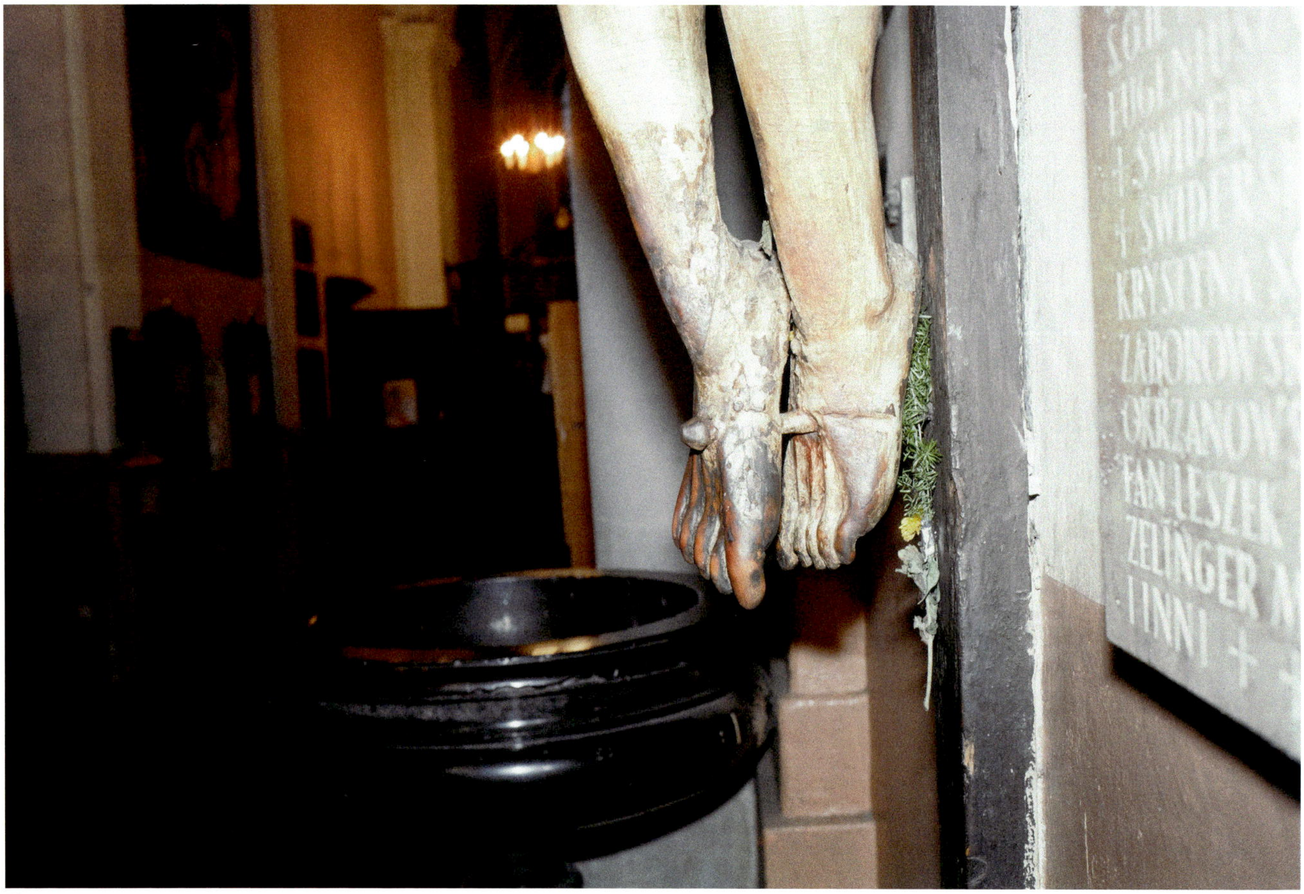

78

Allan Sekula

WALKING ON WATER

PROLOGUE

They build churches so that people can pray for houses.
Joke circulating in Poland, 1990.

American conservatives like to believe the self-congratulatory myth that communism began to collapse at its weakest point, in Poland, because of a carefully nurtured secret alliance between Ronald Reagan and Pope John Paul II, the former Cardinal Karol Wojtyla. In the United States, it is often noted that there is a more than political explanation for the affinity between the two leaders, the former actor and the former mime. But beyond this shared theatricality, we should also consider Reagan's demonstrated love of the sea and the Pope's inheritance of a fisherman's throne. This is especially important with respect to Poland, a nation which takes the anchor for its national symbol. Poles also may believe this version of history, and may love the United States with more avidity and awe than many Americans, but they also were able to observe and endure and finally resist the blunders of the Polish communist nomenklatura at first hand. Thus Poles can understand internal and perhaps less magical explanations for the transformation of this, the »Jesus Christ of nations«.

Conceding defeat, President Jaruselski is interviewed on Polish television, late on election night. Already he is elder-statesmanlike, Nixonesque. He quotes Pope John Paul II on the triumph of good over evil, and speaks of the need to build democracy. Watching the speech, Malgosia Paradzinska, an English literature graduate student at the University of Warsaw, repeats over and over: »This is a sick country. You are visiting a sick country.«

AUF DEM WASSER WANDELN

PROLOG

Sie bauen Kirchen, damit die Leute um Häuser beten können.
Polnischer Witz, 1990.

Amerikanische Konservative glauben gern den selbstherrlichen Mythos, daß der Kommunismus deshalb an seinem schwächsten Punkt, in Polen, zu bröckeln begann, weil es eine geheime Allianz gab zwischen Ronald Reagan und Papst Johannes Paul II, dem einstigen Kardinal Karol Wojtyla. In den USA ist oft die Rede davon, daß die Affinität zwischen dem ehemaligen Schauspieler Reagan und dem ehemaligen Mimen Johannes Paul nicht nur eine politische ist. Abgesehen von der gemeinsamen theatralischen Vergangenheit sollte man auch Reagans erwiesene Liebe zur See und den von einem Fischer ererbten Heiligen Stuhl in Betracht ziehen. Das ist nicht unbedeutend – gerade im Hinblick auf Polen, das im Staatswappen einen Anker trägt. Mag sein, daß auch die Polen an diese Version ihrer Geschichte glauben, und mag sein, daß sie die USA inniger und ehrfürchtiger lieben als so mancher Amerikaner, aber sie haben es auch geschafft, die »Glanzleistungen« der polnisch-kommunistischen Nomenklatura mit eigenen Augen mitanzusehen, sie zu ertragen und schließlich dagegen Widerstand zu leisten. Vielleicht verstehen sie deshalb auch die eher internen und weniger magischen Erklärungen für den Wandel Polens, dieses »Jesus Christus unter den Nationen«.

Spätabends am Wahltag wird Präsident Jaruselski im polnischen Fernsehen interviewt und gesteht seine Niederlage ein. Er wirkt bereits wie ein abgedankter Staatsmann, ein wenig wie Nixon. Er zitiert Papst Johannes Paul II im Zusammenhang mit dem Triumph des Guten über das Böse und spricht von der Notwendigkeit, eine Demokratie aufzubauen. Malgosia Paradzinska, Studentin der englischen Literatur an der Universität Warschau, verfolgt die Rede im Fernsehen und sagt immer wieder: »Dieses Land ist krank. Sie sind zu Besuch in einem kranken Land.«

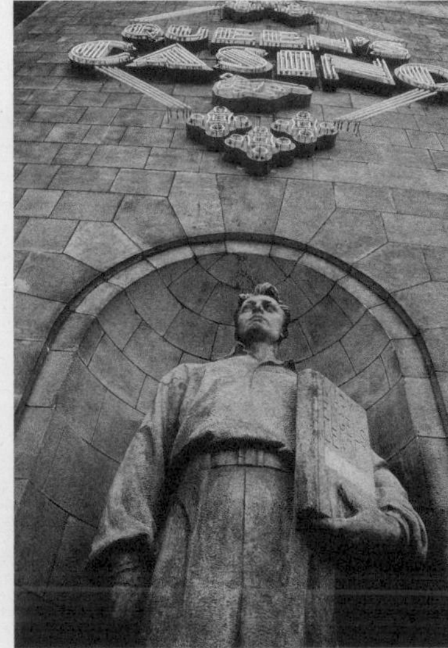

77

Warsaw – Gdansk – Warsaw, November 22 – December 3, 1990.

Warschau – Danzig – Warschau. 22. November – 3. Dezember 1990.

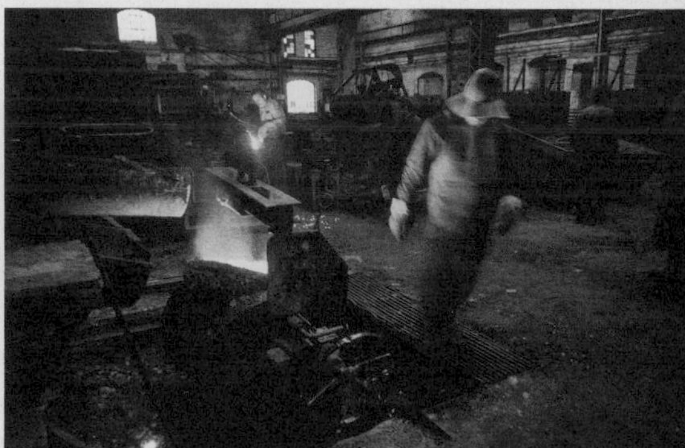

31

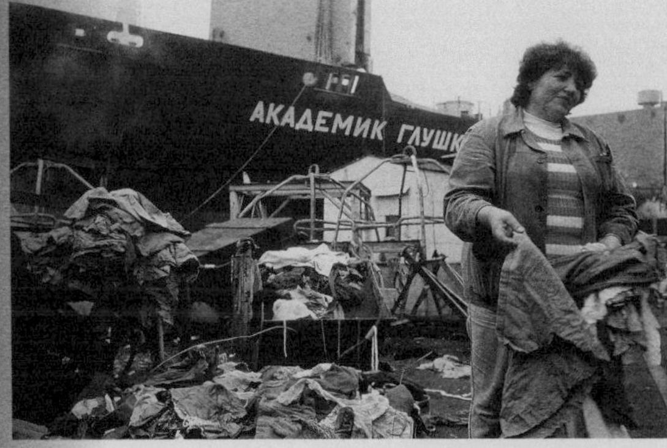

16

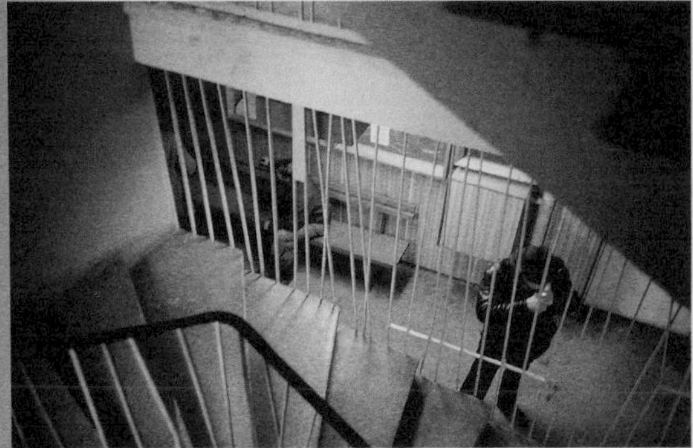

32

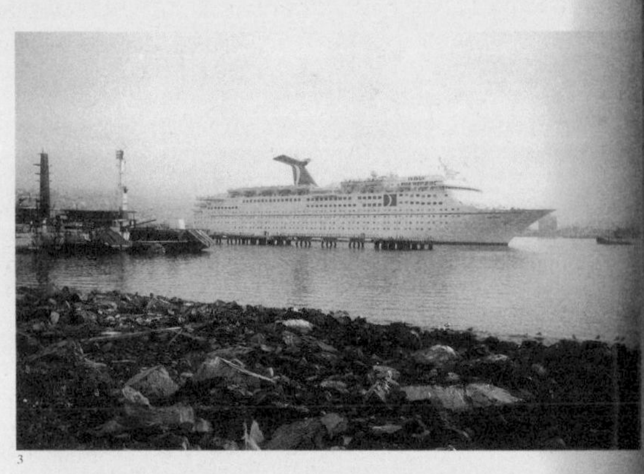

3

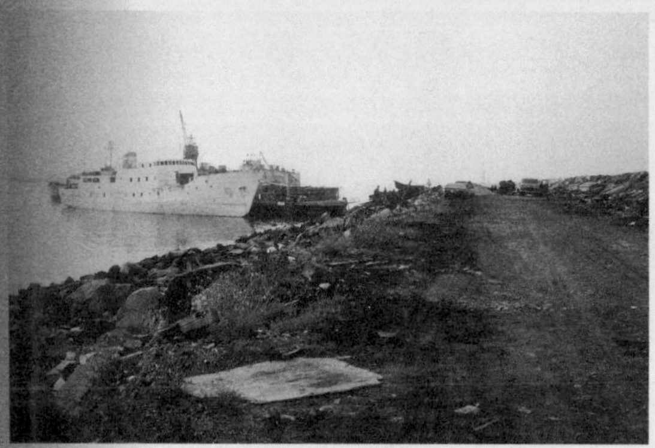

4

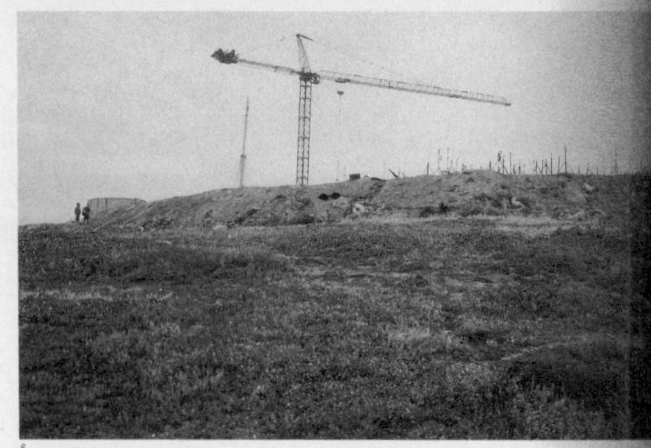

5

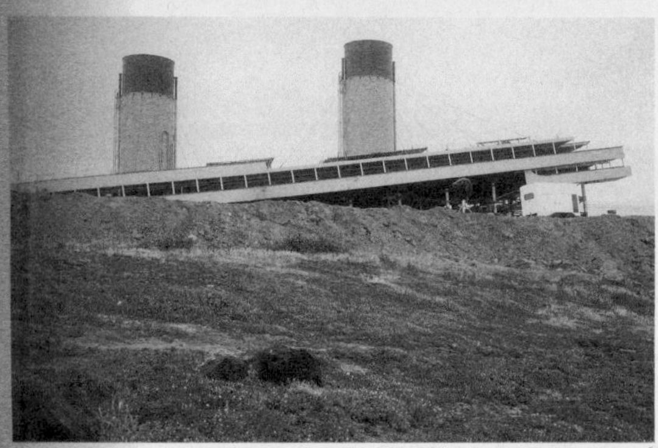

6

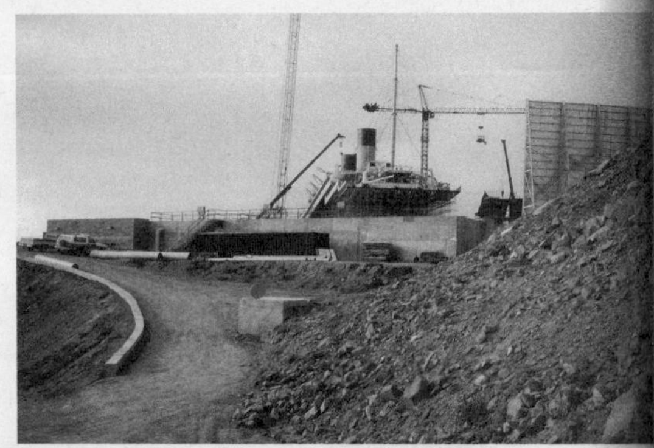

7

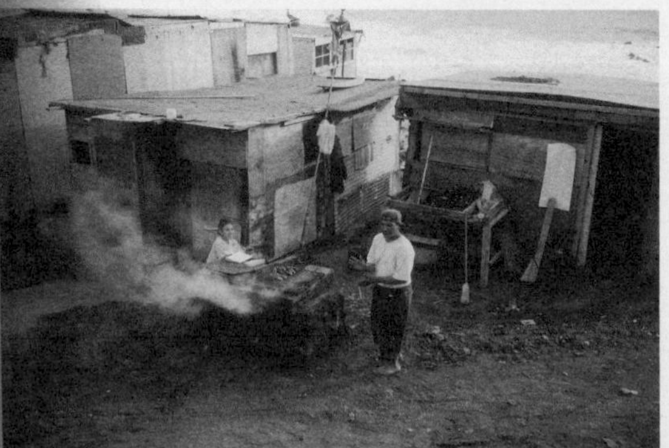

8

Dialog

Privacy &
Public Image

Nobuyoshi Araki

Camera Austria International

1993　Roland Hagenberg / Walter Vogl,
　　　　"Fotografieren ist Mord. Interview mit
　　　　Nobuyoshi Araki," text contribution,
　　　　Nobuyoshi Araki, artist contribution and
　　　　cover, *Camera Austria International* 45 / 1993
1997　"(H)ARAKI(RI) – Zu Nobuyoshi Araki:
　　　　Sexual Desire und Irina Ionesco: Nudes,
　　　　Edition Stemmle, Zürich, 1996," book review,
　　　　Camera Austria International 57 – 58 / 1997
1998　Michael Wetzel, "Jenseits des Lustprinzips.
　　　　Neues von Araki," Cantz, Ostfildern-Ruit,
　　　　Oktagon, Köln and Edition Stemmle, Zürich,
　　　　book review, *Camera Austria International*
　　　　62 – 63 / 1997
2005　Minoru Shimizu, "Zwei Realismen –
　　　　Diesseits und Jenseits der modernistischen
　　　　Fotografie. Moriyama : Shinjuku : Araki,"
　　　　exhibition review, *Camera Austria
　　　　International* 89 / 2005

Exhibitions

1992　*Akt – Tokyo. 1971 – 1991,* solo exhibition
1995　*Erotos,* solo exhibition
2001　*Akt – Tokyo. 1971 – 1991,* solo exhibition

Publication

1992　Seiichi Furuya and Manfred Willmann, eds,
　　　　Nobuyoshi Araki, Akt – Tokyo. 1971 – 1991,
　　　　Graz, Edition Camera Austria, 1992

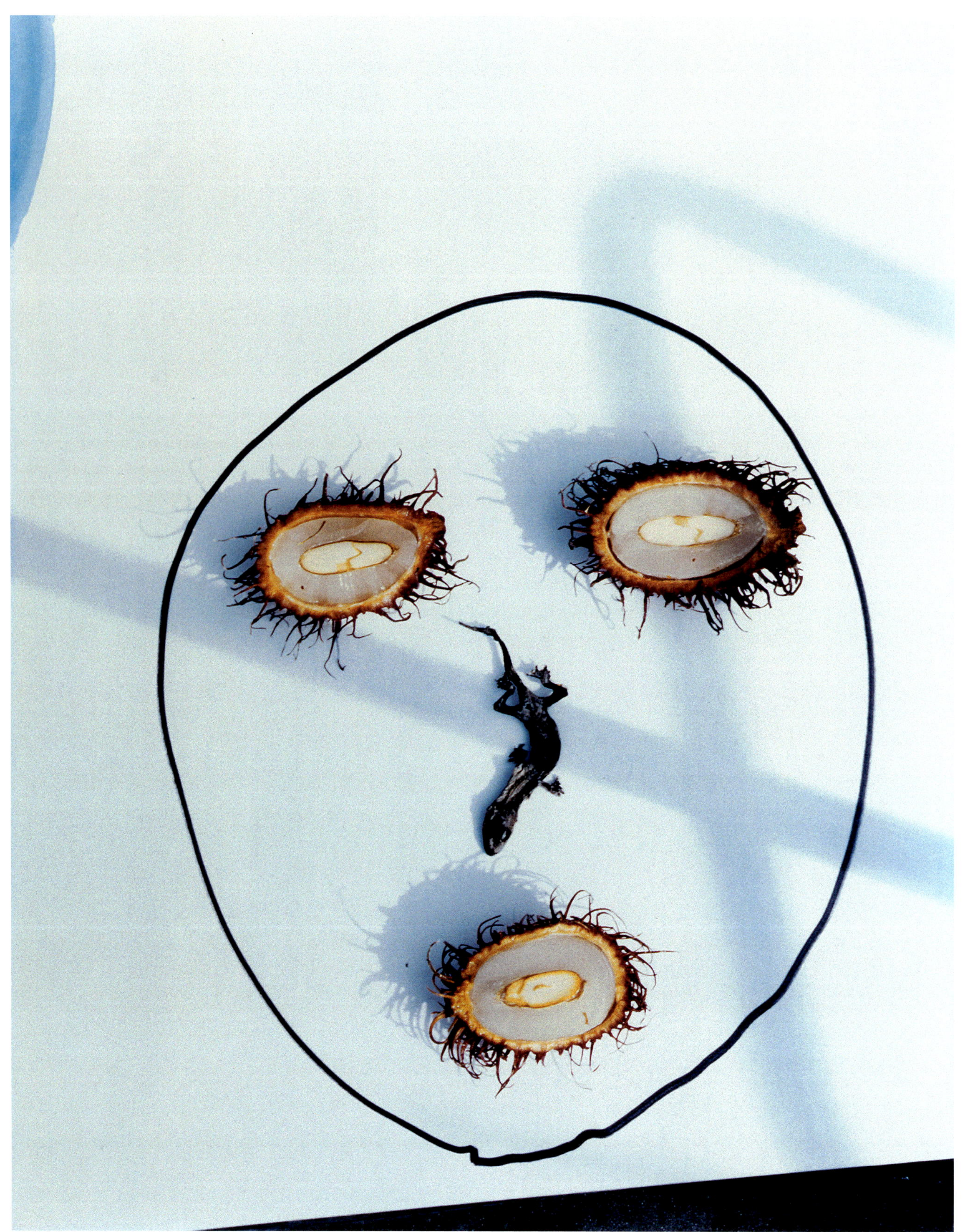

From the series "Shikikei"

Nobuyoshi Araki

Taeko Tomioka
Photographs to be read

Manfred Willmann and Seiichi Furuya have selected more than hundred of Nobyoshi Araki's photographs —out of so many! I believe this is the first time that someone other than Araki himself has made the selection of photos to be exhibited. In more than twenty years, Araki has published more than eighty books of photographs, that have been edited so as to create cleverly and carefully prepared narratives that could be "read". This show is unique then in that someone else has "read" Araki. And how will viewers read this reading?

Araki's narratives have not been mere stories. They may not be novels—I would avoid that term, but would honestly call them literature. The sequence in this show begins with a wedding photo, and ends with one of Araki wearing his deceased wife's coat and holding her portrait. (His wife died at age 42 in 1990). The sequence apparently, emulates his own style.

Part of Araki's strategy in getting his viewer to read is to present a space—a "landscape"—that lies between the quotidian and the non-quotidian, a space that belongs simultaneously to both times—and to neither. The quotidian was his wife Yoko, the non-quotidian naked (not nude) women. The bizarre appearance of these naked women is an Araki-created fiction, and the landscape consists of both the quotidian and non-quotidian equally suspended within it. If either becomes heavier than the other then the landscape fluctuates drastically. For some time after his wife's death, Araki took photographs of nothing but the sky—a landscape of its own—and later compiled them into a volume called *Skyscapes*. Her death had taken away the quotidian time / space equation from him, and so the quotidian / non-quotidian relation became unbalanced. Araki's literary orientations do not take each photo as being equivalent to, say, a word, quite the contrary. His is non-verbal literature, and he discovers it beyond—no, inside—photography. It is within photography that the quotidian and the non-quotidian are inverted and exchanged as having equal value. Photography does not effect the inversion from outside the relation.

Beings possessing substance exist by chance; they exist only temporarily in time, and have no beginning or end. Hence all things are of equal value, but time creates differences among them, Araki's work is nothing more than manifestation of his obsessive desire to confirm that things substantial or non-substanial things with or without form, are equal. From the beginning of his career he knew that this obsession would be intruded upon by that small number of photos labelled "Masterpieces" or "Decisive Moments of the Century," by photographs that would expose the obscenity of society in the cause of justice, or even with malicious intent. Araki's own shameless presence in so many of his photographs might also be due to his compelling desire to prove things equal.

Excerpt from: *Nobuyoshi Araki. AKT–TOKYO. 1971–1991*, Graz: Edition Camera Austria, 1992, 84.

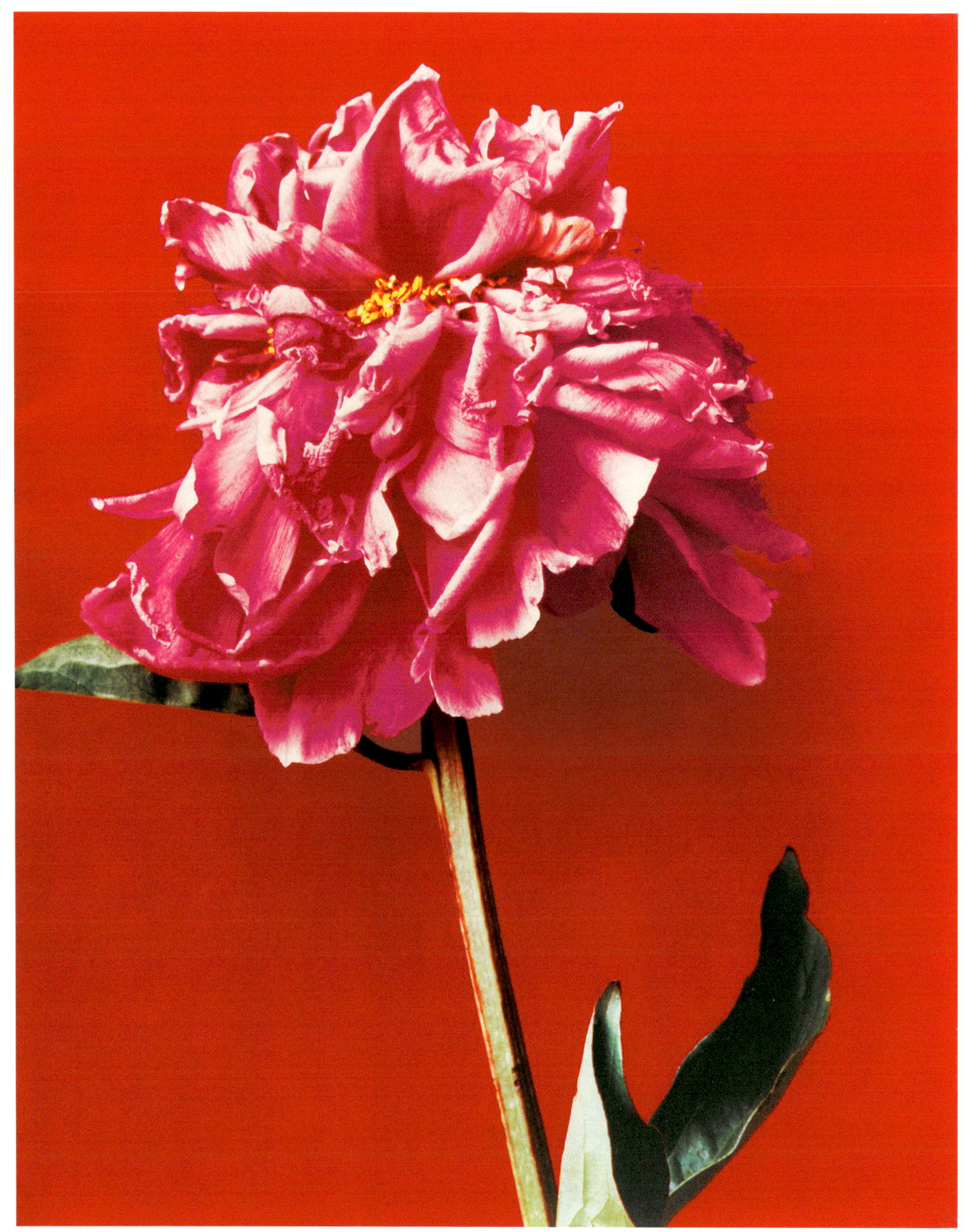

From the series "Shikikei"

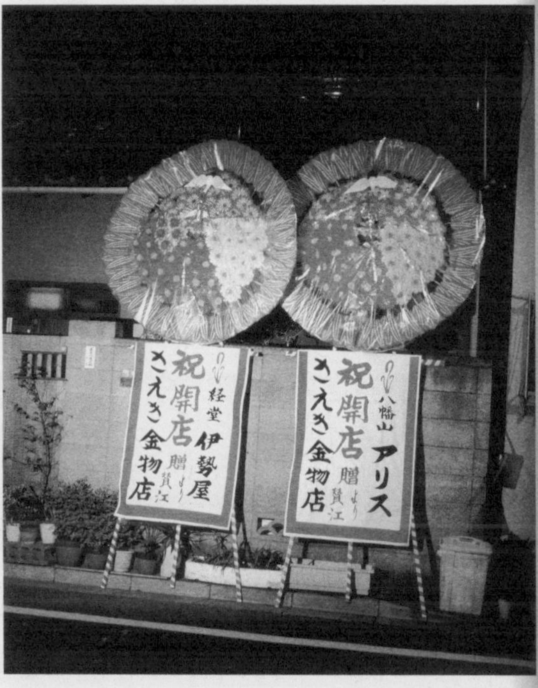

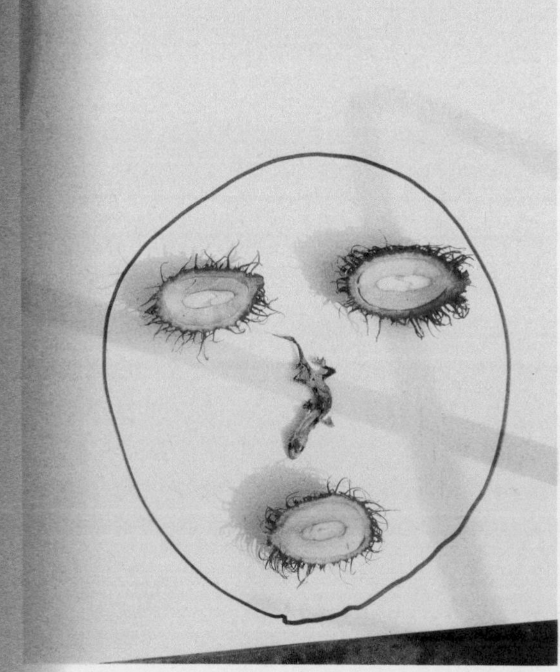

18

19

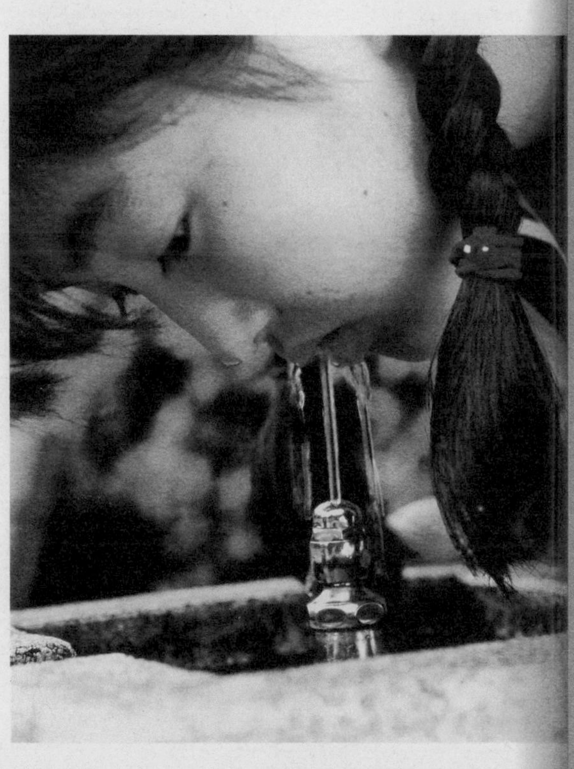

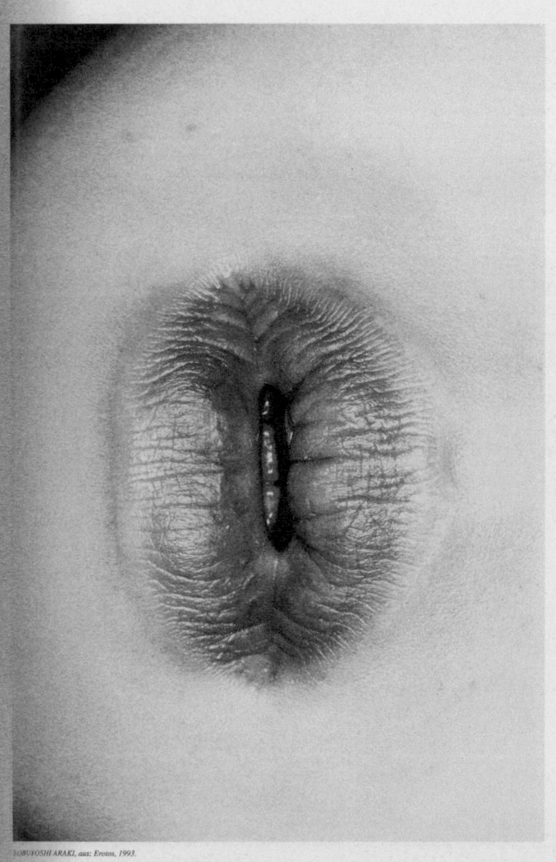

NOBUYOSHI ARAKI, aus: Erotos, 1993.

24

25

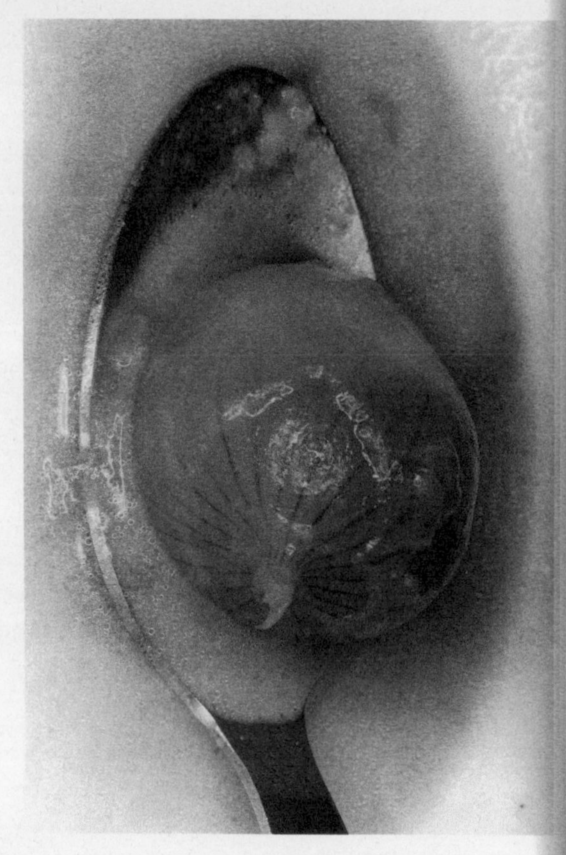

26

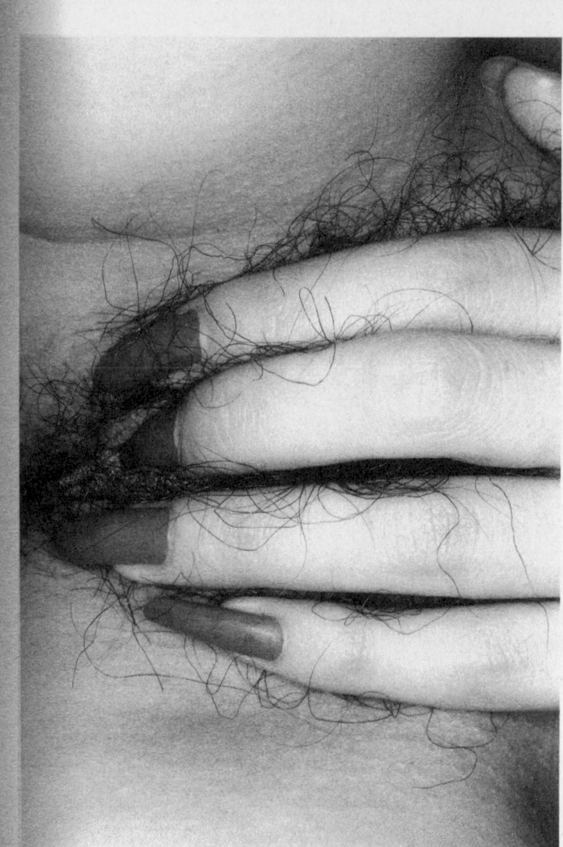

27

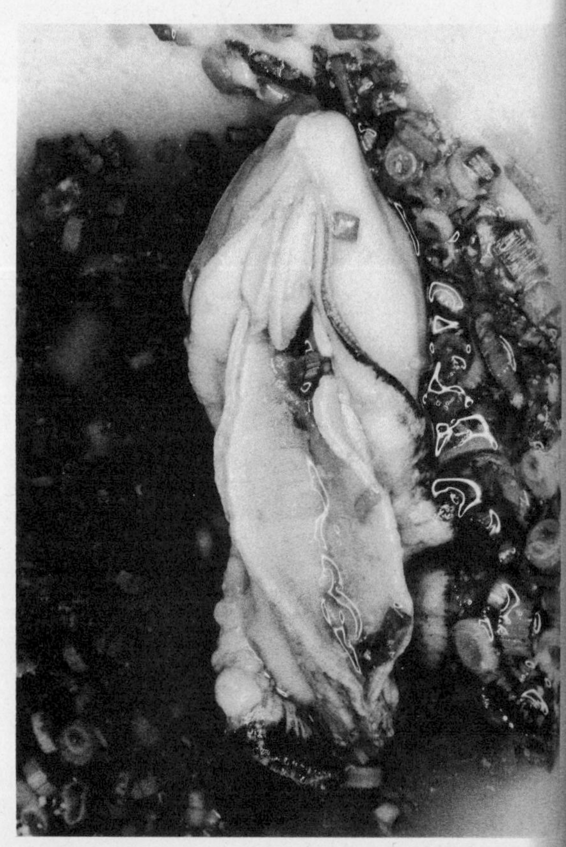

30

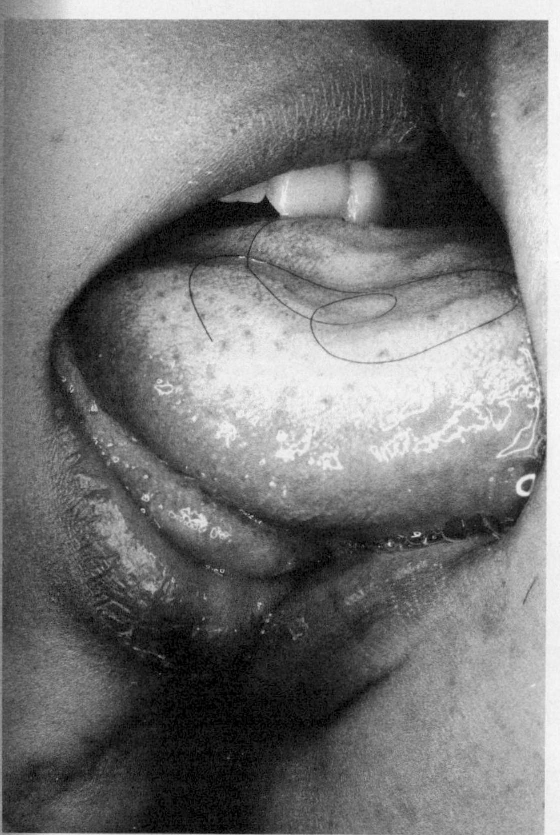

31

Petar Dabac

Camera Austria International

1984   Annie Le Brun, "Das Naturempfinden am
Ende des 20. Jahrhunderts zu den Arbeiten
von Petar Dabac," text contribution,
"Petar Dabac," artist contribution,
Camera Austria International 14/1984

1996   Želimir Koščević, "Petar Dabac," text
contribution, Petar Dabac, "Lieber Pero,"
artist contribution, *Camera Austria
International* 56/1996

2007   Manisha Jothady, "Fotografie aus Kroatien:
Petar Dabac, Mare Milin, Fotohof, Salzburg,"
exhibition review, *Camera Austria
International* 98/2007

2011   Sandra Križić Roban, "Petar Dabac: Not
Guilty, Galerija Klovicevi dvori, Zagreb,
2011," book review, *Camera Austria
International* 115/2011

Exhibitions

1975   *Fotografik in Farbe,* solo exhibition

1979   *5 Jahre Fotogalerie im Forum Stadtpark,*
exhibition contribution

1981   *Le sentiment de la nature à la fin du 20e siècle,*
solo exhibition

1983   *Aspekte der zeitgenössischen jugoslawischen
Fotografie,* exhibition contribution

1993   *Forum Stadtpark Graz, Austria,* Museum
des Zentrums für Volkskunst, Kharkiv (UA),
exhibition contribution

1994   *Siebzehn,* exhibition contribution

1996   *Stadtpark Zwei,* Art Pavilion, Zagreb (HR),
exhibition contribution

2003   *Freundschaftsspiel,* exhibition contribution

2013   *Zero Point of Meaning. Non-functional,
Non-representational, Elementary,
Experimental and Conceptual Photography
in Croatia,* exhibition contribution

Publication

1997   Manfred Willmann, ed., *Stadtpark Zwei,*
Graz, Edition Camera Austria, 1997

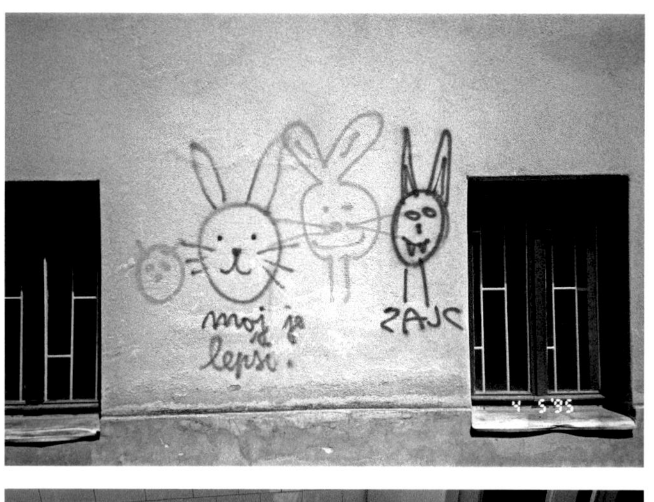
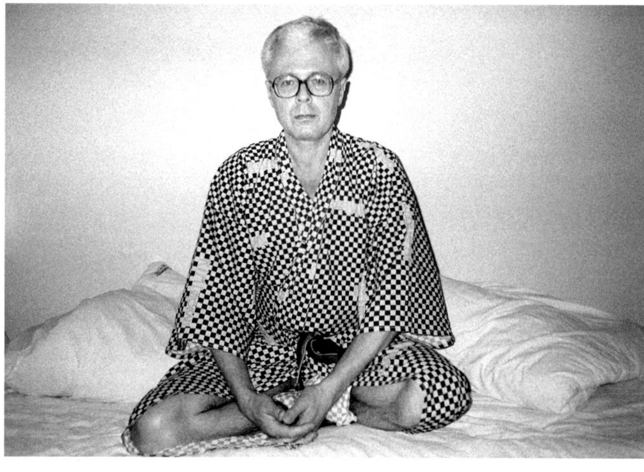
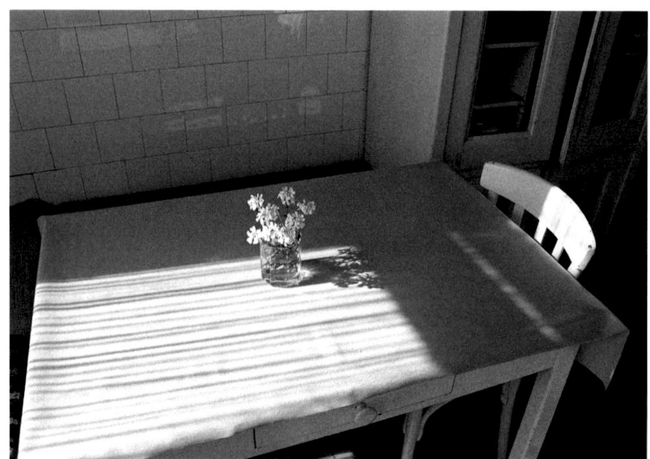
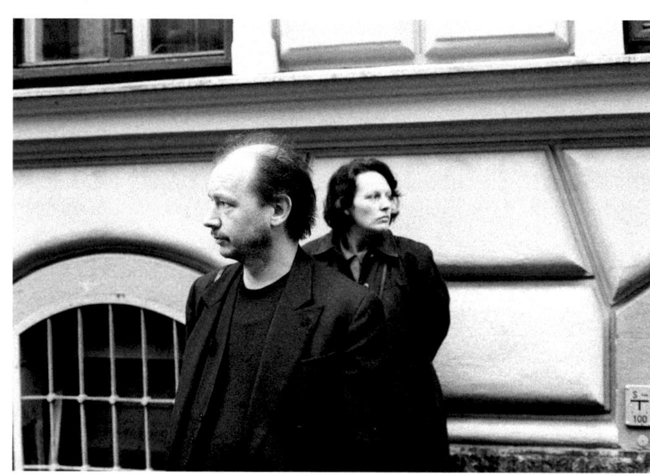
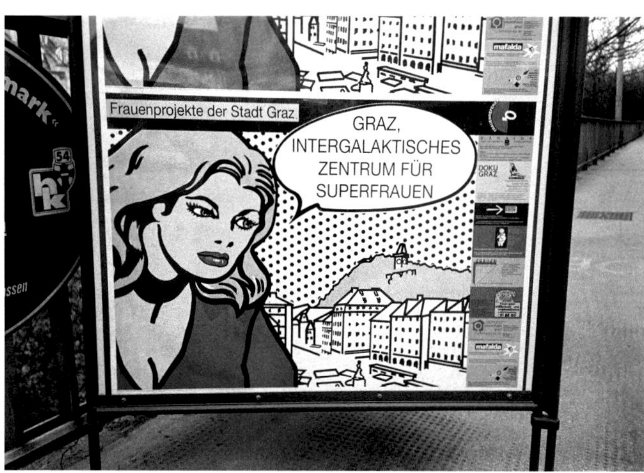
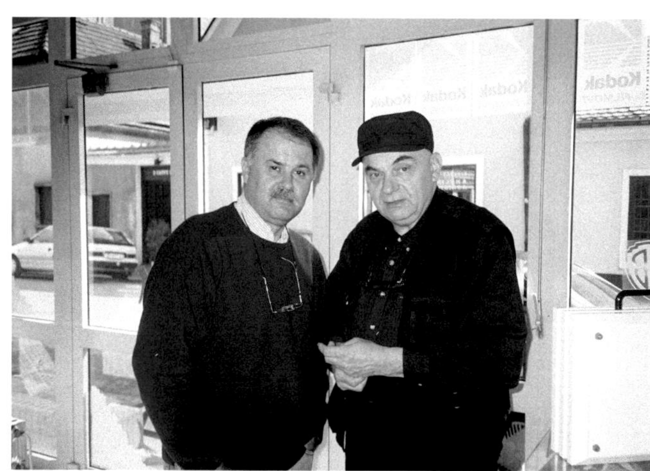
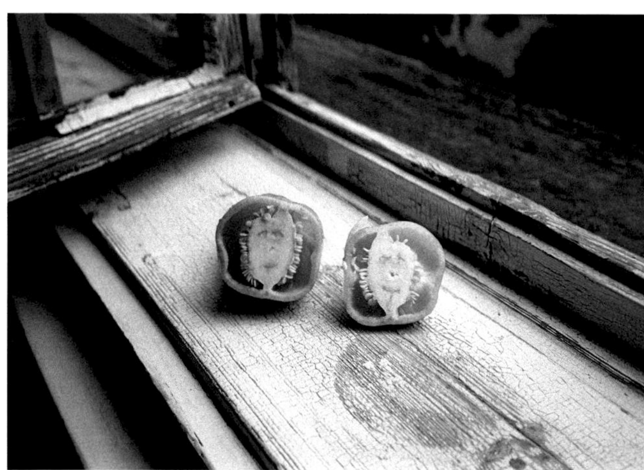
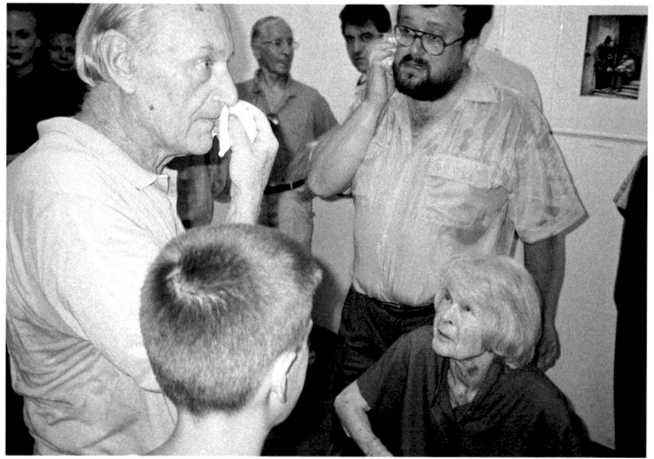

From the series "Lieber Pero" (Dear Pero), 1990

Petar Dabac

Želimir Koščević
Petar Dabac, "Lieber Pero," work in progress since 1990

In numerous discussions on the language of art, photography often eluded the theoretical discourse. Some theoreticians have justifiably disputed the adequacy of linguistic theories for an analytical approach to photography, using as an argument the panorama of surprising photographic examples from the time of the invention of photography over the period of Surrealism to present times. Indeed, as the photographic fund, worth thinking about, becomes ampler, photography is more frequently understood as an aspect of intuitive consiousness, able to select from the observed and momentary what this observed object or scene hides and what disappears in time. It is hard to say who is right here, but without any doubt I would offer the cycle "Lieber Pero" (Dear Pero) as an argument to that side which regards the photograph in its abstract dimension, "reading" from it poetic metaphors and intuitive cognition. Of course, this cycle also has its physical coordinates and its spiritual and social context. The photographs from that cycle, however, contain not only an excess of reality, but also an excess of time. They are spread over a much wider span of time, leaving us to wonder where their beginning or end is. In the nightmarish chaos of the sensuous touch with reality, Dabac has started to select the pictures of what he has experienced and observed, creating from them, little by little, one integral whole, wherein one photograph evokes the other, regardless of space or time that might be separating them. Following their diachronic series, from its conditional beginning to its conditional end, somewhere in the background we shall discern the being that, with a camera in his hands, discretely builds into the memory this world in which he is living.

From: Želimir Koščević, "Petar Dabac," *Camera Austria International* 56/1996: 23. Translation of the original Croatian text by Maja Zaninovic.

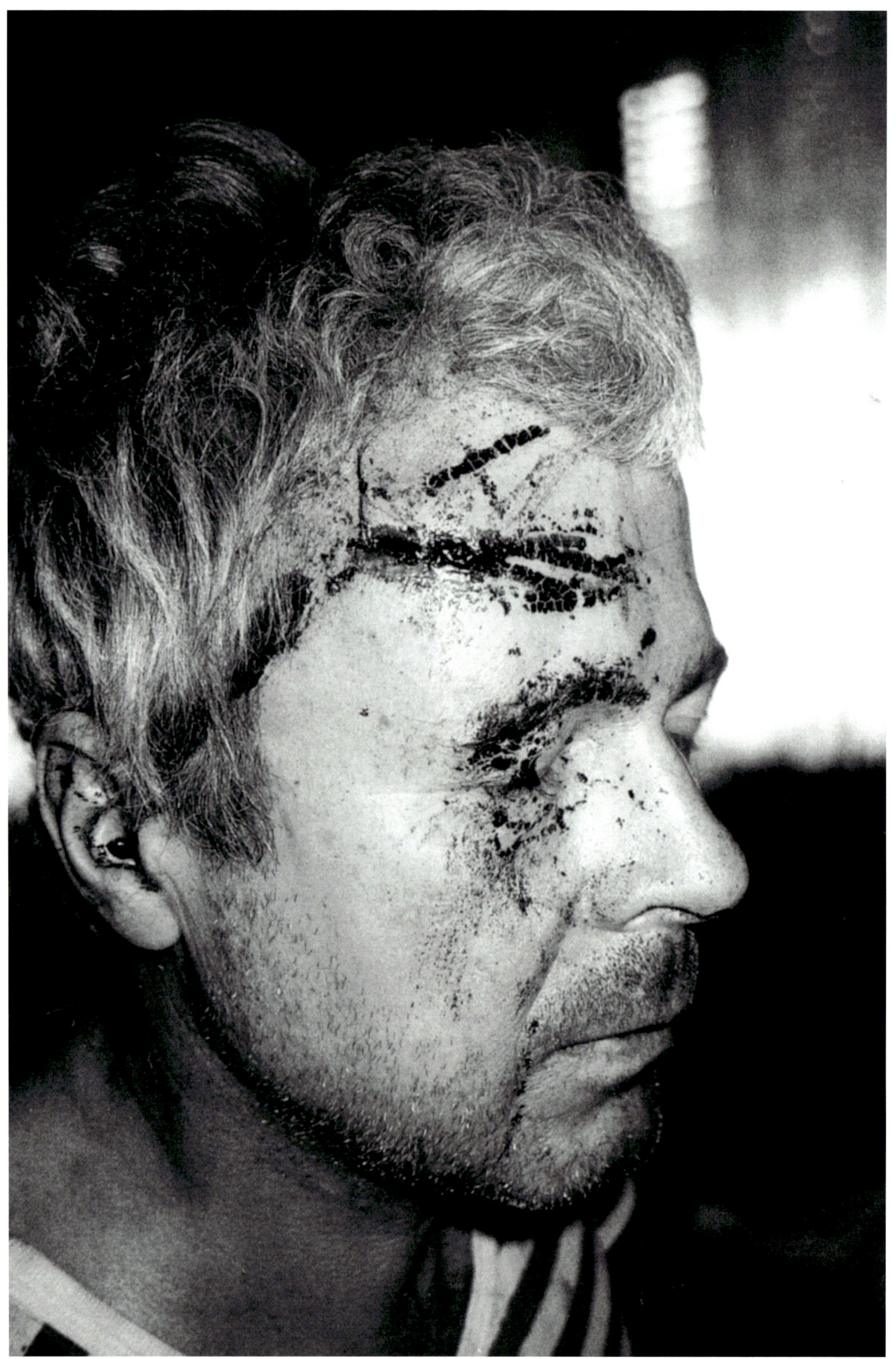

From the series "Lieber Pero" (Dear Pero), 1990

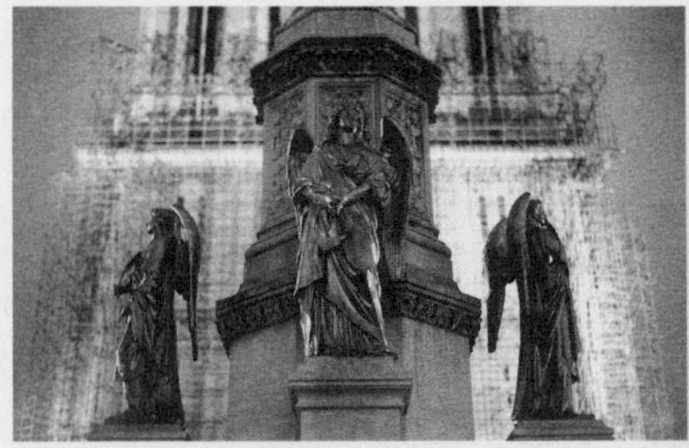
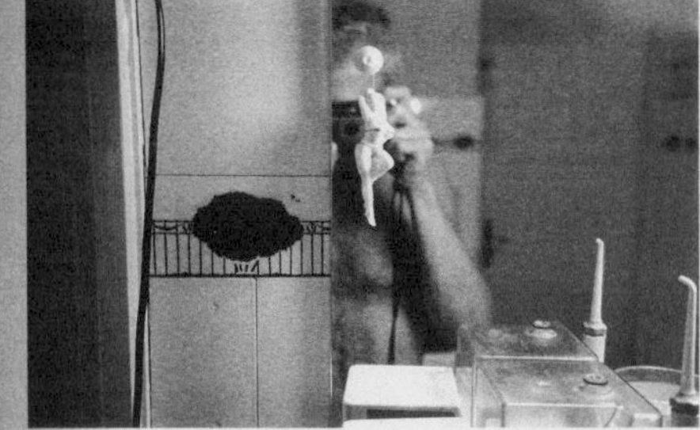
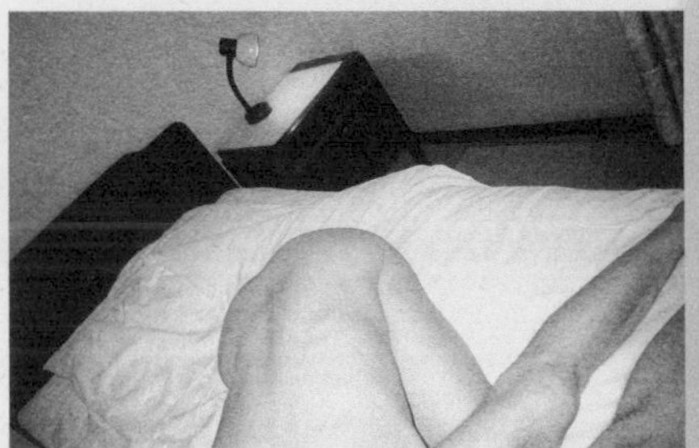
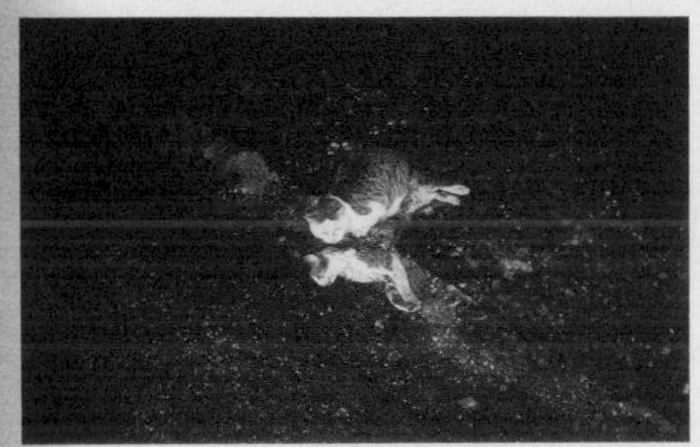

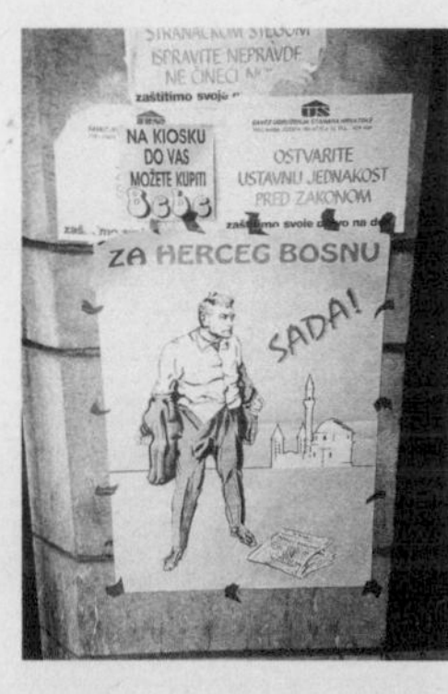
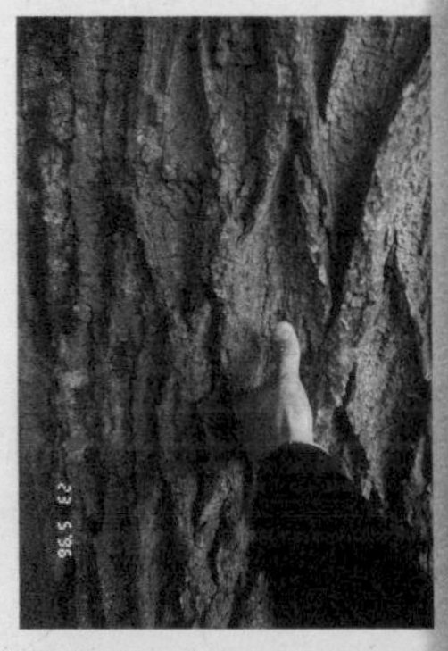
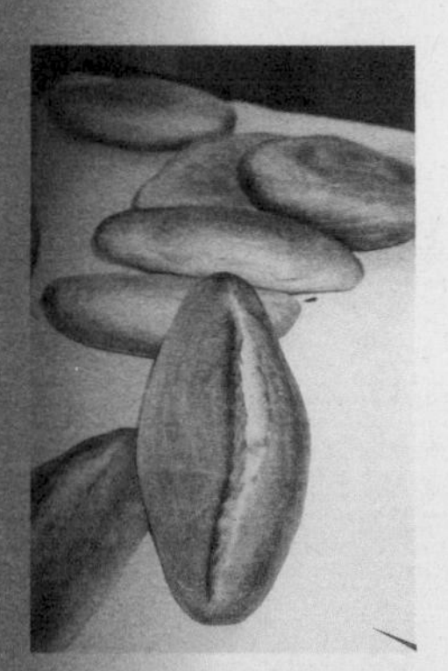
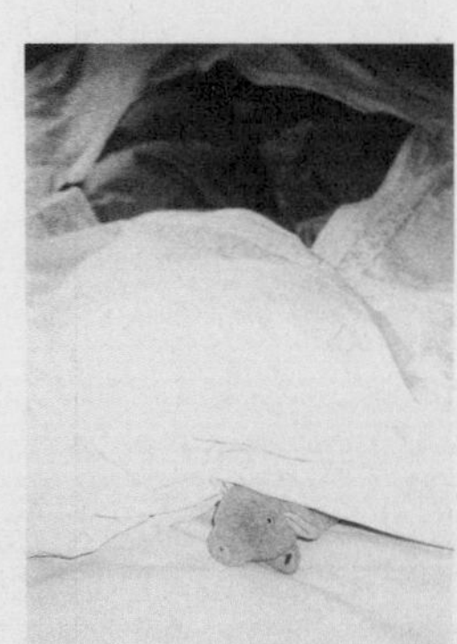
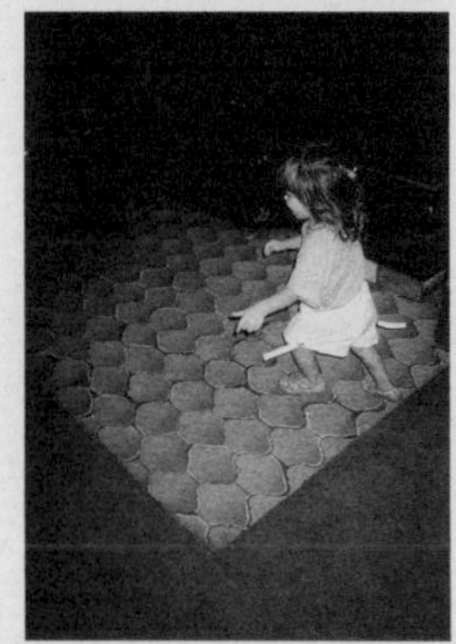
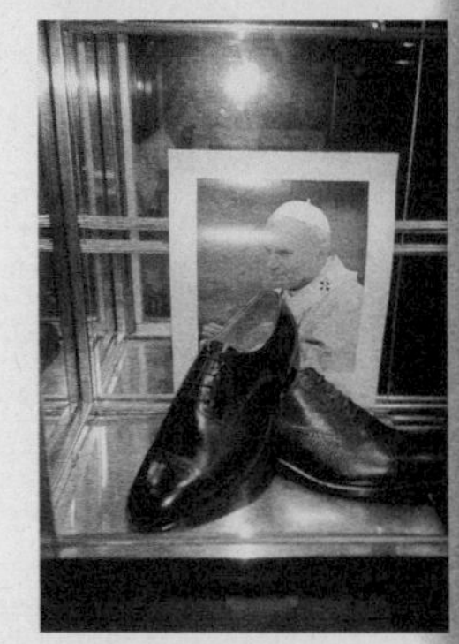
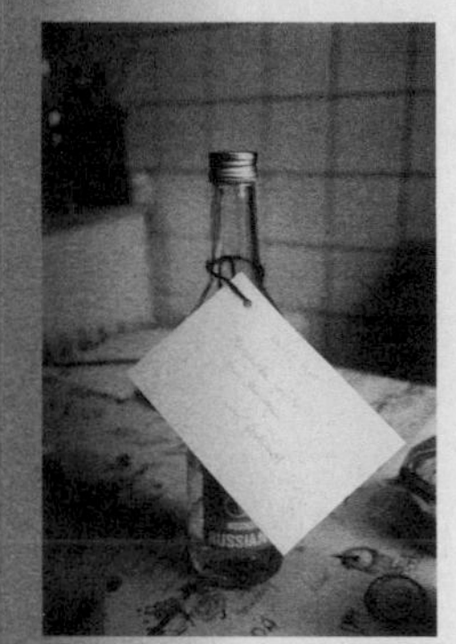
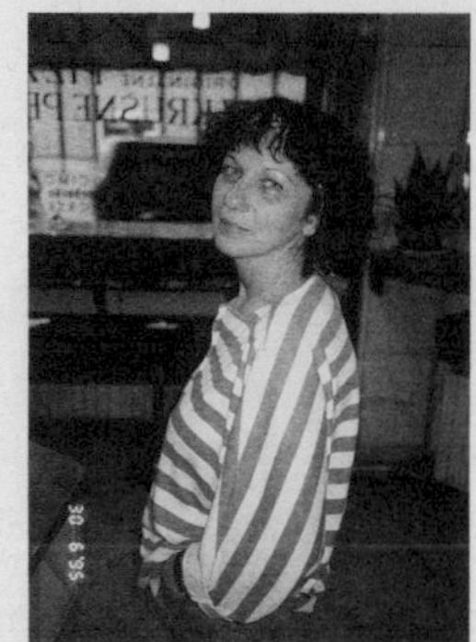

279

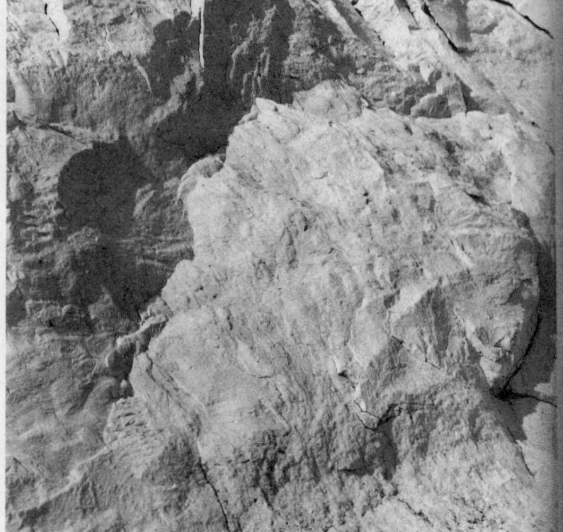

Hvar, Juli 1979

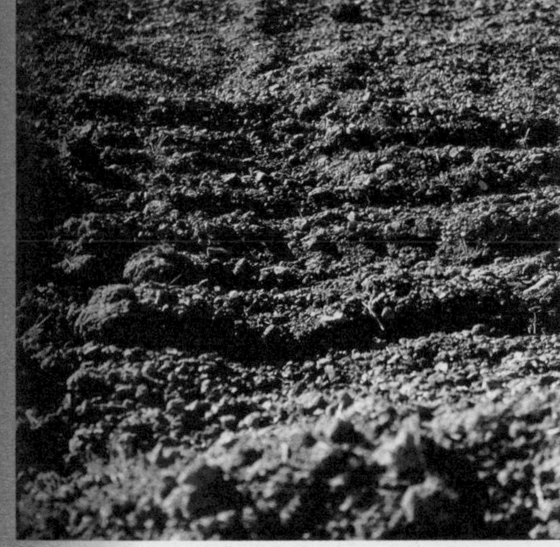

Kumrovec, Oktober 1979

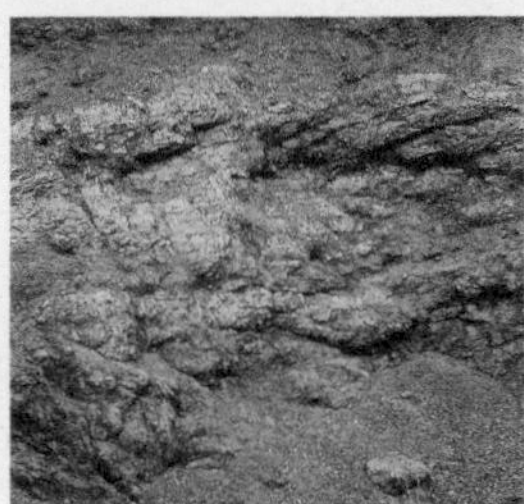

Stubičke Toplice, 1979

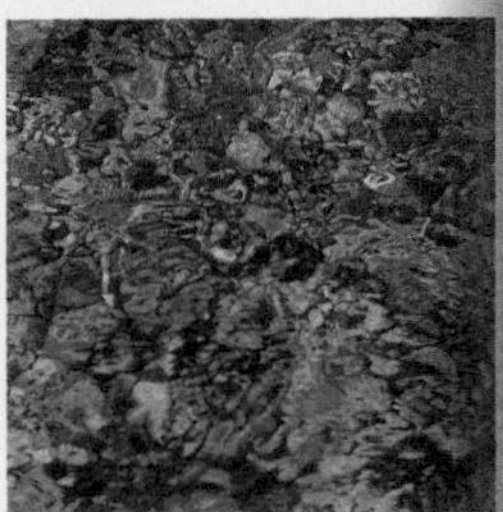

Senj, August 1979

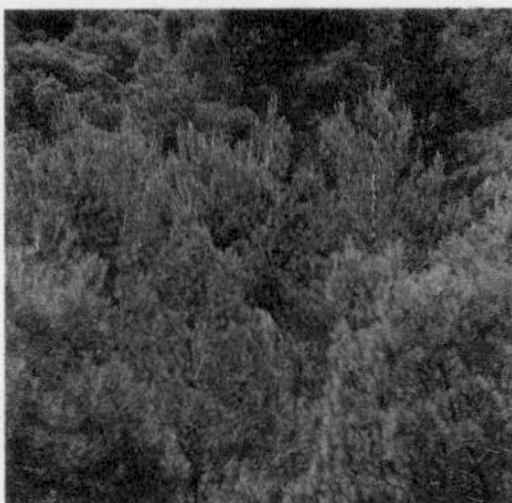

Hvar, Juli 1979

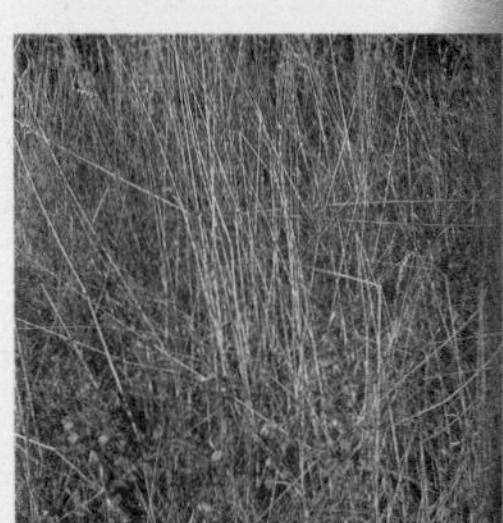

Novigrad, August 1979

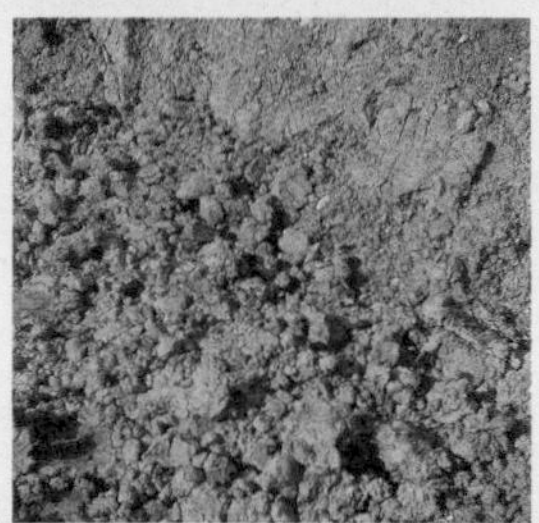

Zabok, Oktober 1979

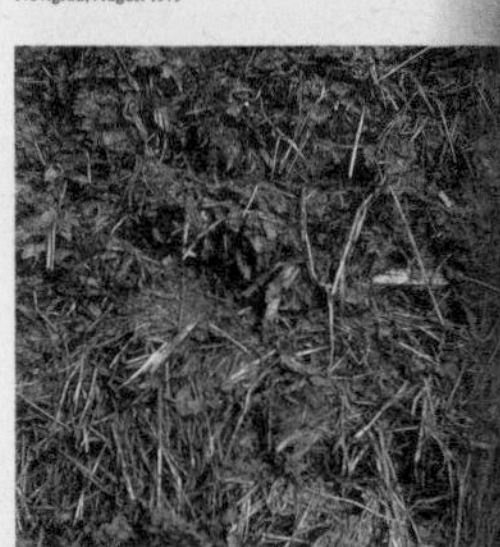

Žeinci, September 1979

eines Realismus, der nur eine Form der Konsumtion der Realität ist, und welcher uns deshalb auf eben jene totale idealistische Praxis zurückverweist. Darin liegt der äußerliche Schwindel der realistischen Darstellung: das Abbild des Objekts erweckt den Anschein von Realität, wo keine Realität ist und wo auch keine sein kann: es erweckt nämlich den Anschein einer normativen Vorstellung des Objekts.

Ich würde sogar sagen, daß im Realismus sogar die gewaltsamste Konsumtion von Zeichen vorliegt. Wird die Beziehung zum Gegenstand zu sehr geleugnet, so verschwindet dieser hinter seiner konventionellen Darstellung. Denn darin besteht sicher die Lehre aus einem Jahrhundert Fotografie: Die Darstellung des Gegenstandes dient immer mehr dazu, uns von einem Gegenstand zu entfernen, der von Bild zu Bild wie eine Fata Morgana verschwindet und wieder auftaucht. Um uns von Bild zu Bild dorthin zu bringen, wo wir niemals hinwollten. Federgewicht, Bleigewicht der Ideologie. Nehmt Euch gut in acht, das Gewicht des Wirklichen, unter dem man unsere Träume erdrücken will, hat immer die Leichtigkeit von Zeichen, und unter diesen Bedingungen erweist sich der Realismus als das falscheste Zeugnis über die Realität. Es ist unmöglich, den Anteil zu leugnen, welchen die Fotografie an dieser Ummauerung des Wirklichen durch ihre Bilder hat. Und doch läßt es sich nicht leugnen, daß die Fotografie in sich selbst die Kraft trägt, die Mauern der Wiedergabe niederzureißen. Aber wo? Wann und wie? Durch welche begnadete Revolution des Blickes könnte die Fotografie den Horizont öffnen, nachdem sie mehr als ein Jahrhundert lang systematisch dazu beigetragen hat, ihn zu verschließen, wenn man von einigen packenden Ausnahmen absieht?

„Hat nicht der Fotograf – Nachfahr der Augurn und der Haruspexe – die Schuld auf seinen Bildern aufzudecken und den Schuldigen zu bezeichnen?" fragt Walter Benjamin. Mir gefällt diese kriminalistische Metapher nicht besonders, aber immerhin kommt ihr das Verdienst zu, mit dem Zweifel ein Element der Verunsicherung einzubringen. Wenn die Fotografie nicht mehr Zeugin der Anklage gegen das Unwirkliche wäre; wenn die Fotografie nicht mehr Gewißheit wäre, sondern Frage; wenn die Fotografie aufhören würde, einen Zweck zu erfüllen. Genügt es nicht, daß dieser große realistische Betrug ein Ende hat, damit die Fotografie wieder das wird, was sie ist: ein endloses Infragestellen der Welt? Man könnte sogar von „Fotomanze" sprechen, denn die Fotografie wird weniger mit der Realität als mit dem Zufall konfrontiert. Mit dem Zufall, welcher in einem Aufblitzen das Bild, auf das wir gefaßt waren, zerreißt, um den Blick auf das gähnende Rätsel unserer Existenz freizugeben. Gerade dann wird die Fotografie gefährlich, wenn sie nicht mehr das erzählt, was man durch sie mitteilen will.

Gefährlich wie ein unerbittlicher Wettlauf zwischen der Zeit und dem Augenblick, so daß das Auge mit voller Wucht auf die Wirklichkeit prallt, ist die Fotografie zunächst ein Unfall, ein schrecklicher Zusammenstoß zweier Universen: dem der Welt und dem des Blickes, den wir auf sie werfen. Und der fotografische Raum ist eben jener ihrer Ungleichzeitigkeit, der sich im Aufflackern ihrer zufälligen Begegnung erhellt oder auch nicht. Deshalb sind wohl auch die großen Fotografien außerordentlich selten. Sie hängen ebensosehr vom Bewußtsein wie von der Technik ab, denn auch hier wird niemals ein Blick den Zufall zuschalten können. Jedes Mal ist der fotografische Raum das Ergebnis eines Einbruchs in das geschlossene Feld unserer Sicherheiten und ein Bruch mit der Ordnung der Dinge. Dieser Raum ist vor allem ein Zwischenbereich, der jede repräsentative Norm verleugnet, auch die realistische, und vor allem die realistische. Denn dieser Zwischenbereich entwickelt sich ja nur in jenen Aufblitzen des Zufalls, das das Bild erhellt, um Lebewesen und Dinge als obsessive Gestalten der Leere dahintreiben zu lassen. Zwischenbereich, überflüssiger Bereich, Bereich, den es nicht gibt, außer als Zeitpunkt des katastrophalen Zusammenpralls eines Blickes mit alledem, was er nicht ist. Ein in hohem Maße unwahrscheinlicher Bereich, der kaum noch erforscht ist; hinter unseren Augen, die schon alles gesehen haben, dehnen sich unendliche Urwälder von Perspektiven.

Sehen Sie sich die Fotos dieses Beitrages genauer an. Das sind keine Strukturen, das sind keine Landschaften. Es sind nur Abdrücke des Zufalls, hier, dort, am Morgen, am späten Nachmittag, im Winter, bei Einbruch der Nacht, sehr nahe, mitten im Hochsommer, beim Morgengrauen, sehr weit weg ... Der Asphalt lastet auf uns wie der bedrohlichste Gewitterhimmel, der Stein prägt sich als weißer Sonnenschatten ein, die Linie des Horizonts grenzt den Tag und die Nacht über dem Abgrund der Farbe aus. In welch strähniger Fülle von Wasser und Stein

have none: to a normative idea of the object to which people blithely assent.

I would go so far as to say that realism is nothing other than a frenzy of sign-consumption. For in this frantic rush to deny the relationship with the object, the object itself is eclipsed by its conventional representation. This is surely the lesson of the last hundred years in the history of photography: the representation of the object only serves to alienate us more and more from the object proper, which, shifting from image to image, vanishes and reappears in the form of an empty mirage. We are being shunted from image to image in a direction we had no wish to take. Ideology: a pound of lead, a pound of feathers. Make no mistake, the deadweight of the real with which they try to crush our dreams, cannot be dissociated from the immaterial nature of signs: and under such conditions, realism turns out to be the least faithful way of recording reality. It is impossible to deny the part which photography has played in the walling-off of the real behind its images. Yet it is equally impossible to deny that photography also carries within itself the energy necessary to lay low the barriers of representation. But where? How? Which revolution in our ways of seeing will prompt photography to open up the horizon it has spent over a century (with a few brilliant exceptions) systematically shutting off?

"As a descendant of the soothsayers and the prophets, ought not photography, through its images, to reveal the transgression and point to the guilty party?" asked Walter Benjamin. I am not too fond of this police metaphor, but it has the merit of introducing alongside doubt an element of creative disturbance: what if photography were no longer the prosecution witness called to testify against all that which is not real? What if photography were not smug certainty, but enquiry, curiosity? What if photography were to refuse to serve? Is it not true that we need only call the bluff of realism for photography to revert to its true function, and become an infinite question ing of the world? We might even speak here of „photomancy", given that photography is less a confrontation with reality than with chance. With chance, which can in a sudden flash lacerate the image we expected to see and lay open the gaping enigmas of our existence. This is where photography becomes truly subversive-at the very moment it ceases to express the thing it was supposed to express.

As dangerous as a relentless long-distance race between time and that instant when the eye crashes headlong against the real, photography is first and foremost an accident, the terrible collision of two universes, the world outside and the look we apply to it. And the space of photography is, quite precisely, the space where they fail to coincide, illuminated, or darkened, in the flash of their fortuitous encounter. Hence no doubt the extreme rarity of truly great photos: they cannot be guaranteed any more by a cast of mind than by a clever technique. Here too, the wink of an eye can never abolish chance. Time and again, the space of photography is defined by a sudden break-in that interrupts the closed circle of our certainties, along with a violation of the order of things. This space is essentially an intermediate one, and is bound by no representational norms, not even that of realism. Indeed, it specifically rejects the realist norm, since this intermediate space can only unfold along the track of that lightning-streak of chance which sets fire to the image and causes people and objects to float as irrepressible metaphors of emptiness. An intermediate space, a superfluous space, a space which does not exist, save in the moment of that cataclysmic encounter of our eyes with all that lies before us. An essentially improbable space which has still scarcely been prospected. At the back of our eyes, which we thought had seen it all, virgin perspectives stretch away to infinity.

Look closely at the photos on these pages. They are not patterns; they are not landscapes. They are simply imprints left by chance, -here, there, in the morning, in the late afternoon, in winter, at dusk, close to, at the height of summer, at daybreak, far off... Asphalt weighs upon us like threatening stormclouds; stone leaves a mark like the white shadow of the sun; the skyline scissors day from night along the precipice of colour. Into which hairy tangle of water or stone merge the golden threads of fairytale? Whatever can have happened? Nothing seems to look like itself any more.

It is however by approaching the real scrupulously and with undivided attention that Petar Dabac is able to lead us to the strange realization of a new feeling of nature. Too remote to fall prey to the technical seductions of micro-photography, too close to his material to be trapped in the social orthodoxy of landscape, he has succeeded in photographing something which had never been

Camera Austria Award

1989   Camera Austria Award for Contemporary Photography by the City of Graz

Participation at Symposion

1987   Symposion on Photography IX: "The Contemporary," 16–18 October 1987, lecturer

Camera Austria International

1988   Gisela Bartens, "Nan Goldin: The Ballad of Sexual Dependency," book review, *Camera Austria International* 25/1988
Nan Goldin, "The Ballad of Sexual Dependency," artist contribution and cover (journal of Symposion), "Liebe Nan," Christine Frisinghelli and Nan Goldin, *Camera Austria International* 26/1988

1992   Nan Goldin, "Cookie Mueller," text contribution/artist contribution, *Camera Austria International* 39/1992

1995   Nan Goldin, "Portraits 1991–1994," artist contribution, Peter Schjeldahl, "Nan Goldin: The Goldin Age," text contribution, *Camera Austria International* 50/1995

2011   Julia Gwendolyn Schneider, "Nan Goldin: Berlin Work," Berlinische Galerie, Berlin, exhibition review, *Camera Austria International* 113/2011

2014   Tobias Zielony, "Nan Goldin: A Conversation," text contribution, Nan Goldin, "The Ukraine Project," artist contribution, *Camera Austria International* 125/2014

Exhibitions

1987   *The Contemporary*, exhibition contribution
1991   *Life, Loss, Obsession*, solo exhibition

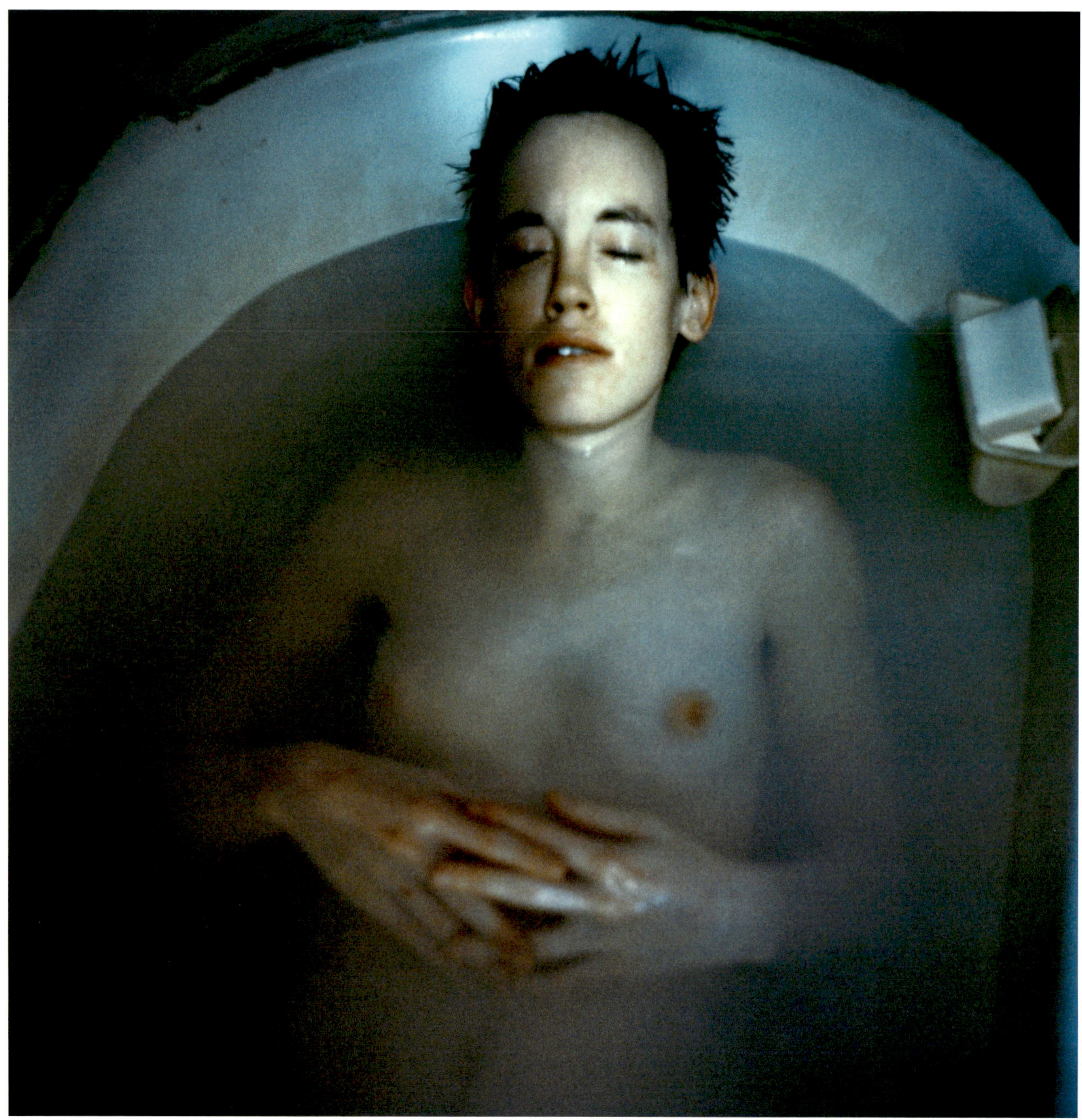

Ryan in the tub, Provincetown, Mass, 1976

From the series "The Ballad of Sexual Dependency," 1978–1986

Nan Goldin

Nan Goldin, Tobias Zielony
A Conversation

Tobias Zielony: When you were working on "The Ballad of Sexual Dependency," your pictures were shocking for a lot of people.

Nan Goldin: It changed photography. That sounds really grandiose. But I really suffered a lot of shit for it. I don't want to be famous; I just want to have done something in my life. I feel like I opened some doors that had been closed, by showing what was private. So I have always said that this was "personal documentary". This is the name that was given to this kind of photography. But, looking back on it, I consider it bullshit. "The Ballad of Sexual Dependency" (1986) was the first book like this, except the only thing that I knew before was Larry Clark's book *Tulsa* (1971). Thanks to Zweitausendeins, who published 75,000 copies of *The Ballad*, the book got to be known in the world. First it was hardcover; then they put it out as a paperback. Then the people could afford it and started to buy it. The people it was made for. The book was made for the people in it—like all my work.

Zielony: "The Ballad of Sexual Dependency" was a slide show long before the book was published. You were changing the images in the slide show all the time in the beginning, but after you made the book, did you keep on changing it?

Goldin: I continued to change it. The book came out in 1986. I changed the music that went along with the show in 1987. I never changed the music again, but even in 2008, when it was sold to the Museum of Modern Art, I changed the slides. That is what I like about slide shows versus films; it is the ability to re-edit, and re-edit.

Zielony: In an old issue of Camera Austria[1] there is a letter from Christine Frisinghelli to you. She says that she went to Houston with you for a presentation of your slide show. She said people were attacking you …

Goldin: The men were screaming at me.

Zielony: Really, why?

Goldin: Because they hated it. I wasn't popular with male photographers. There weren't that many female photographers around. I went through ten years of being screamed at. In my memory, things were being thrown at me … physical attacks. I got punched in the nose by a guy at a society for photo education. This work was so threatening to men. Still, even in the 1980s, all the dealers in New York, most of them, were saying that there is not such a thing as a good woman artist. I had forgotten what a struggle I had as a woman.

Zielony: Christine Frisinghelli said in the letter that when she came with you to Houston, she understood that people could hurt you, because they are afraid of getting hurt.

Goldin: Oh, that is beautiful. Christine had a huge influence on my life at the time—the letters she wrote, getting the grant.

Zielony: In the letter she describes how she herself was hurt by your pictures in the beginning. Maybe people sense that there is something scary in your pictures.

Goldin: Well, I guess if you provoke people to that point, it is also powerful. I didn't want power over people, but I guess that an intensity equal to moving people is also making people furious. So I kind of stayed away from that, because I was too fragile basically to deal with it. I was afraid after the book; I went into a kind of hibernation for two years. […]

1 *Camera Austria International* 26/1988
Excerpt from: *Camera Austria International* 125/2014: 11–21

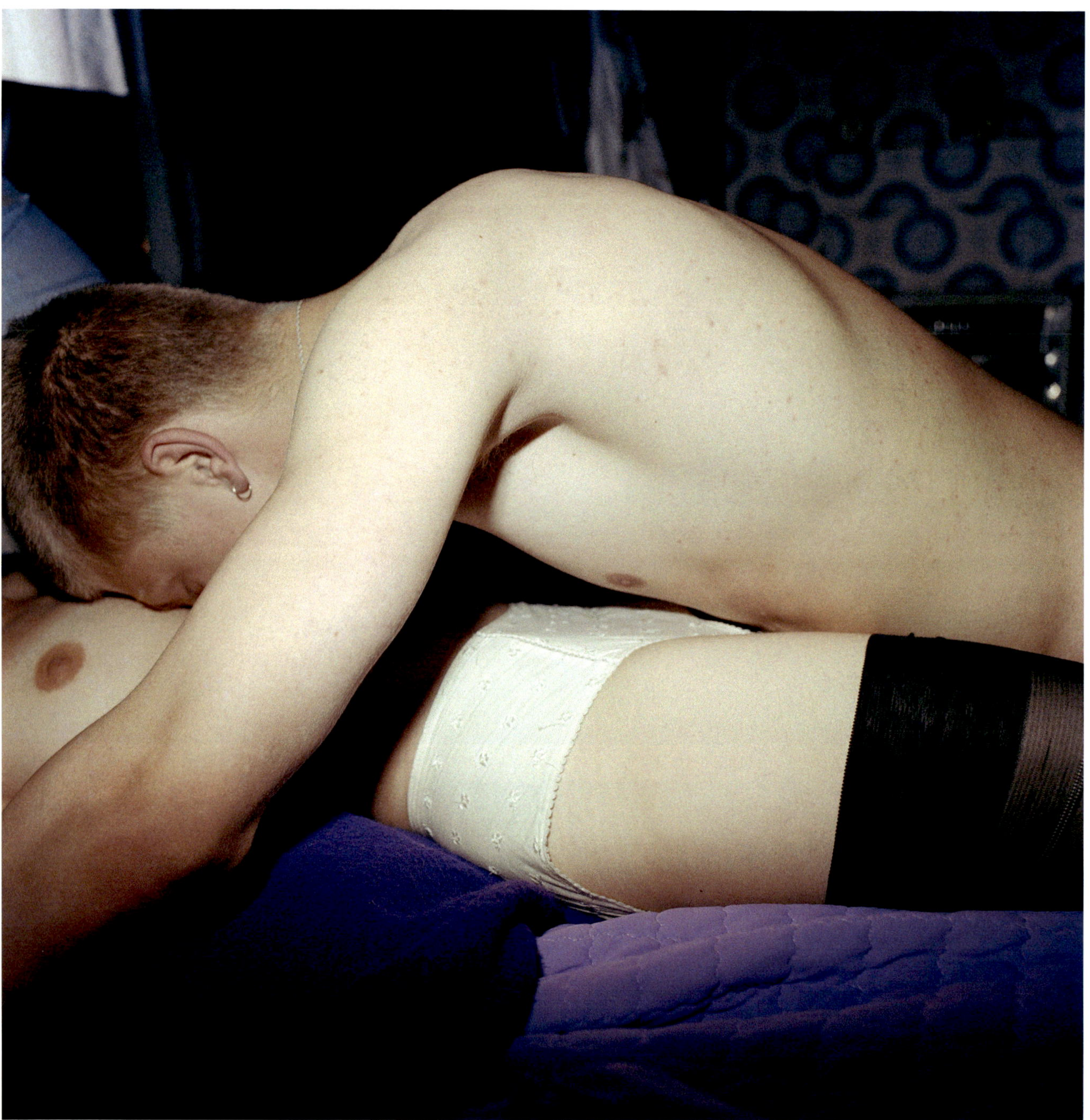

Skinhead having sex, London, 1978

From the series "The Ballad of Sexual Dependency," 1978–1986

Camera Austria

ZEITGENOSSENSCHAFT / *The Contemporary*　　26

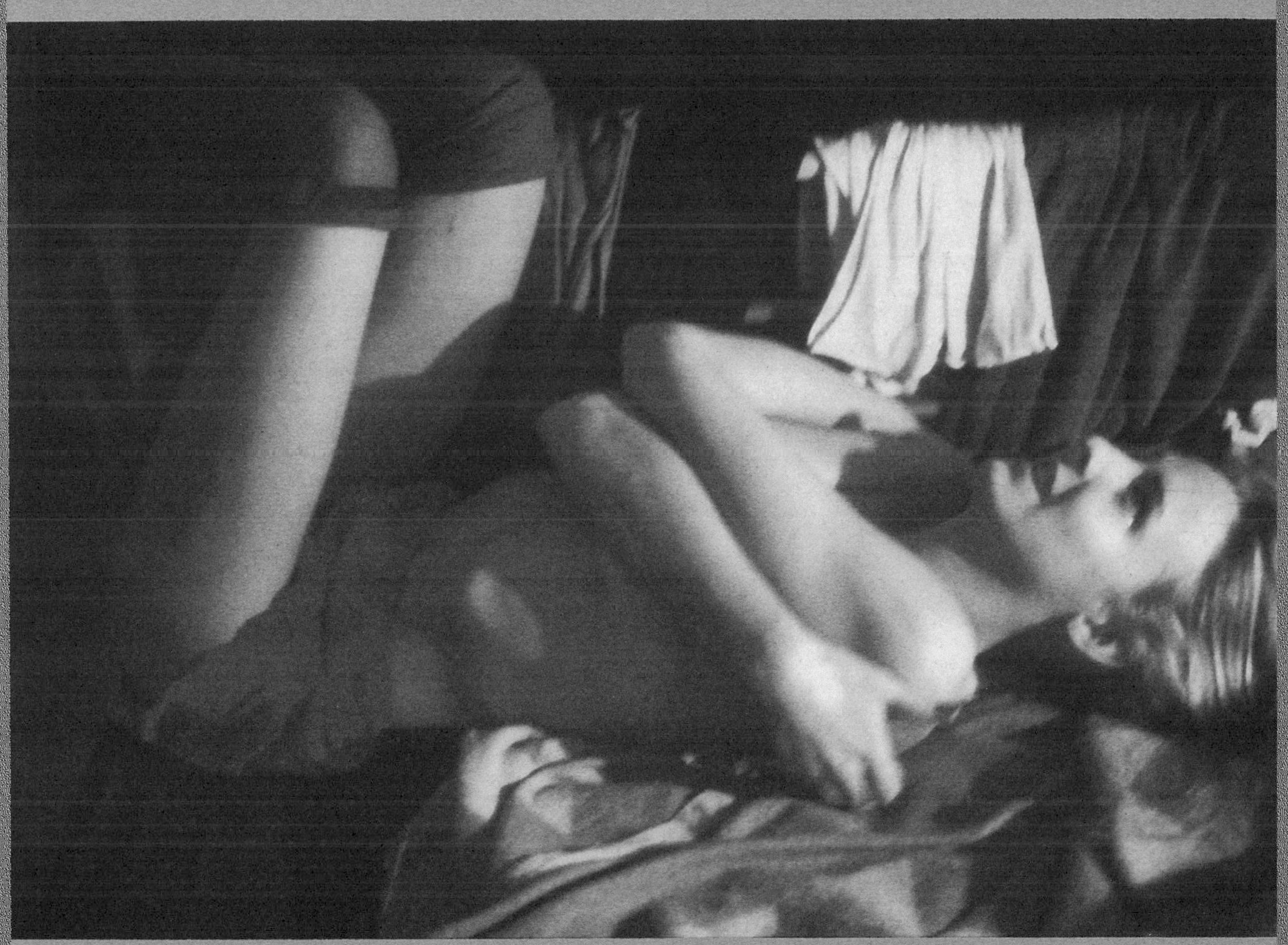

SYMPOSION ÜBER FOTOGRAFIE IX I. TEIL PIDDER AUBERGER NAN GOLDIN CLEGG & GUTT-
MANN MICHAELA MOSCOUW ROB POWELL AUSSTELLUNGEN BÜCHER NACHRICHTEN TERMINKALENDER

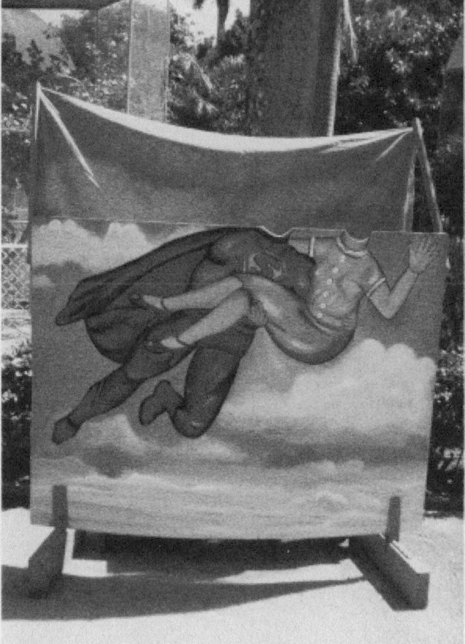

Superman with Lois Lane / Superman mit Lois Lane, The Zoo, Merida, Mexico, 1982

Liebe Nan,

»Warum schreibst nicht Du einen Text?«, hast Du mich gefragt, am 10. März in New York, als wir ziemlich spät in der Nacht (früh am Morgen) in Deiner Wohnung die Fotos für Deinen Beitrag zu diesem Heft zusammensuchten. Es stimmt, Du hast in Deinem Buch schon alles gezeigt, in Deiner Show schon alles gezeigt, und die Fotos sind da. Wir haben Bilder ausgesucht, von denen einige in Deinem Buch nicht enthalten konnten, und neuere haben wir gewählt um zu zeigen, wie Deine Arbeit weitergeht: Deine Arbeit, die darin besteht, nichts vergessen zu wollen, nichts loszulassen von dem was einmal da und bedeutend war.

Ich kann keinen »Text« schreiben, das nicht. Ich wollte Dir einen Brief schreiben: jetzt, im Haus auf dem Lande (das Du gesehen hast, in das Du einmal zurückkommen willst) scheint Deine Welt weit weg. Und obwohl ich weiß, daß mir vieles (die äußeren Umstände, die Lebensform vielleicht) fremd ist von dem, was Du beschreibst, kann ich diese Bilder aus Deiner Welt nicht so anschauen, als führten sie mir das Fremde vor Augen: ich bin berührt worden von Dir, und so nicht mehr nur Betrachter. Als Du Deine Bilder in Graz gezeigt hast, habe ich mich fast gewehrt gegen dieses Berührtsein. Ich wollte mich schützen vor der direkten Betroffenheit, vor den Gefühlen, (vor der Sentimentalität, den Clichés, wie ich das nannte für mich. Du erinnerst Dich vielleicht nicht mehr an meine Frage an Dich damals, die gerade das betraf: warum diese Abfolge, warum diese »Geschichte« so zusammenstellen, warum diese Musik dazu? warum so viel von dem zeigen, was weh tut?). In Houston dann, als ich zum zweiten Mal die Show sah, ist mir manches klarer geworden: Du hattest die Arbeit verändert (Dich verändert?). Vieles erschien mir offener (»War da mehr Hoffnung?« hast Du mich gefragt, als ich Dir das sagte); ja, manches war nicht ganz so schmerzvoll, schien mir (habe ich es nur anders gesehen?). Aber vor allem: ich sah Dich in Deinem Land, in Deiner Sprache konfrontiert mit einem Publikum, das Dich verletzte um nicht seine Verletzungen zeigen zu müssen. Ich habe erst da verstanden, daß man Deine Arbeit auch vom Standpunkt des Genießers (des Voyeurs) aus betrachten könnte; ich verstand erst da richtig, was es bedeutet für Dich, so offen zu sein, wie Du es sein willst. Ich kam mir schwach vor, weil ich zu spät verstanden habe (zu spät, um Dich zu unterstützen, Dich zu beschützen, wenn ich gekonnt hätte).

Jetzt, als ich daran gegangen bin, Dir zu schreiben, hatte ich immer nur diesen einen Satz im Kopf: wie Dir helfen, Dich zu schützen, und zugleich zu hoffen, daß Du weiterarbeiten kannst? Was (noch) können wir von Dir verlangen? Wie anders können wir Dich unterstützen als dadurch, daß wir zugeben von dem, was Du tust (wie Du bist) berührt zu sein? Als zu sagen, daß es möglich sein muß, aus dem Inneren der Vorgänge heraus zu beschreiben; in der Betrachtung (im Erleben) selbst das Sehen (Verstehen) zu beschreiben. Wie anders als durch die Arbeit des Nachdenkens über Deine Arbeit; zugeben, daß der Konflikt zwischen dem Bewahren, dem Nicht-Loslassen, und dem Weitergeben, dem Freigeben, ein wesentlicher ist, für uns alle.

Christine

NAN GOLDIN
geboren 1953 in Washington D.C., USA; lebt seit 1978 in New York City; »Die Ballade der sexuellen Abhängigkeit« wurde zuerst als Live-Präsentation in den Clubs von New York gezeigt, danach u.a. 1986 bei der »Whitney Biennial«, The Whitney Museum of American Art, New York; Berliner Filmfestspiele, 1986; Rencontres Internationales de la Photographie, Arles, 1987. Buchveröffentlichung: »The Ballad of Sexual Dependency«, New York 1986. Deutsche Ausgabe: »Die Ballade der sexuellen Abhängigkeit«, Frankfurt am Main, 1987. Letzte Einzelausstellung bei Pace/McGill, New York City, 1988.

NAN GOLDIN
born 1953 in Washington D.C., USA; lives in New York City since 1978; »The Ballad of Sexual Dependency« was first shown in New York clubs, but also at the »Whitney Biennial«, The Whitney Museum of American Art, 1986; at the Berlin Film-Festival, 1986; at the »Rencontres Internationales de la Photographie«, Arles, France 1987. The publication »The Ballad of Sexual Dependency« appeared as an Aperture monograph in New York City in 1986 (German Edition 1987). Latest one-woman-show at Pace/McGill, New York City, 1988.

Dear Nan,

"Why don't you write a text?" you asked me on March 10th in New York when, in the small hours of the morning in your appartment, we were choosing the photographs for your contribution to this issue. True, you've said it all in your book and shown it all in your show, and the photographs are there. Some of the pictures we chose could not be included in your book; we selected a few of the more recent ones in order to show how your work goes on; your work which consists in refusing to forget, refusing to let go off anything that once was and had meaning.

I can't write a text — not that. What I wanted to do is write you a letter: Now, in the country cottage (which you have seen and want to come back to one of these days), your world seems so far away. And even though I know that much of what you describe is foreign to me, I cannot look at the pictures of your world as a mere description of foreign things. I've been touched, so now I'm not just a viewer — something I almost tried to fend off when you showed your pictures in Graz. I wanted to shield myself against the way your work affected me, against the feelings (the sentimentality, the clichés, as I secretly called it; you may not remember the question I put to you which precisely aimed at this: Why this sequence? Why arranging the story as you did? Why these songs? Why showing so much that hurts?) Then, in Houston, when I saw the show for the second time, a few things became clearer. The show had changed (or was it you who had changed?). There seemed to be more openness. (When I said so, you asked: "Was there more hope?") Yes, much of your work was not as painful, it seemed (or was it my way of seeing it?). But more importantly: I saw you in your country, confronted in your language with a public that hurt you in order to hide its own hurts. This is when I understood that your work might also be seen, enjoyed even, from the voyeur's view; only then I began to understand what it means to you to be as open as you are trying to be. I felt weak because this understanding came to late (too late to support you, to protect you if I could have).

Now that I am writing to you, there is this one constantly recurring sentence in my head: How to help you, to protect yourself, so you can go on with your work? What more can we demand from you? How can we support you if not by admitting that we are touched by what you do and what you are; if not by saying that it must be possible to describe from inside the things that are happening: to describe our seeing (understanding) in the very act of viewing (experiencing)? How can we support you if not by exerting our minds to ponder your work, admitting that the conflict between preserving, not letting go, and going on, releasing, is an important one — for us all.

Christine

(translation: Klaus Feichtenberger)

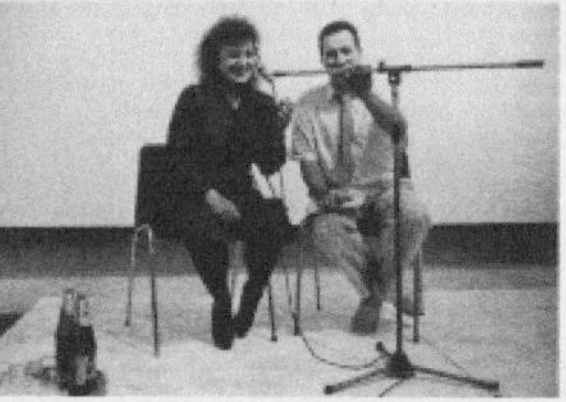

Foto: Elisabeth Kraus

Lamia Joreige

Camera Austria
International

2002　Lamia Joreige, "Replay," artist contribution,
Camera Austria International 78 / 2002

LA GUERRE DU LIBAN

IMAGES ET CHRONOLOGIE

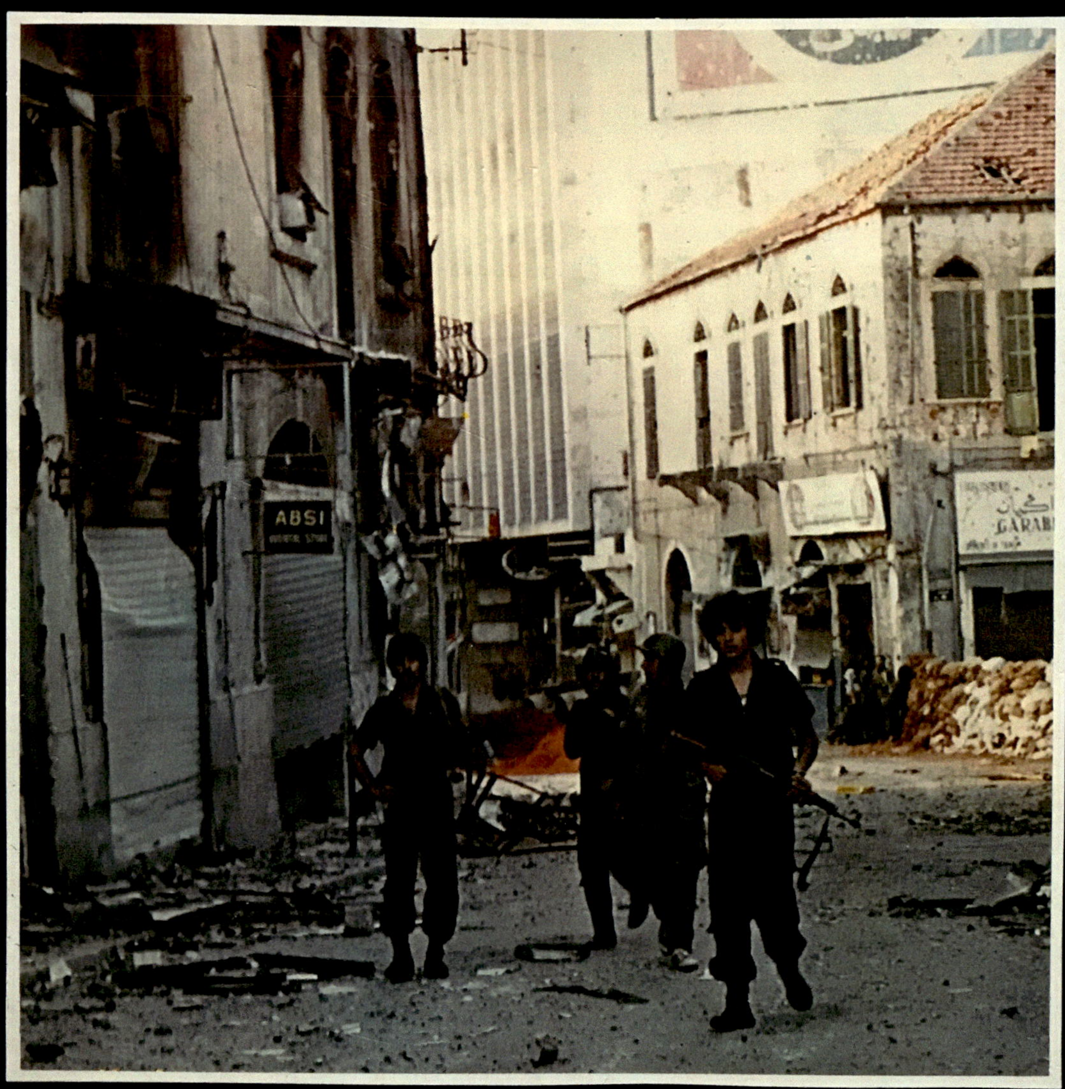

DAR AL-MASSIRA

Lamia Joreige

Replay

A street, for long an inaccessible "territory," a stage that I find essential to appropriate. As I revisit this place, I encounter nothing but rupture: A rupture of time, a rupture within time.

I think of things that did happen, things that might have happened in this place during the war—For, I only knew it during the war. I imagine that He, who was photographed while dying, might have died here; that She, who was running, escaping something terrible, might have run in the parking lot around the corner.

Perhaps it wasn't them, perhaps it wasn't here; still, I find their images inextricably linked to this place.

A fragment is captured, enlarged, repeated, thus turned into another version of itself. It carries its own memory: stories enacted (or to be enacted) in other geographies. Bodies sacrificed, murdered, executed repeatedly: a staging of violence in the absence of blood. Violence as rupture with the ever present possibility of loss. Violence projected onto any act, at that singular instant when the real and the non-real are indiscernible. Violence endlessly reenacted, always recognized.

Is there a trace that is not already withdrawn in relation to itself?

The site of irreversible rupture: the sea, that of departures, immutable, always at a close distance, a familiar yet extraordinary imagery, demands uninterrupted contemplation. Here it separates two bodies—a man and a woman—each perpetuating a vain act, revealing the impossibility for them to be.

He falls many times and does not die, though he also never stops falling, never stops dying. She runs, coming towards us again and again; she doesn't stop running, doesn't stop escaping. Icons of our present, reconstruction of a past, of an origin we can no longer recall.

LA GUERRE DU LIBAN

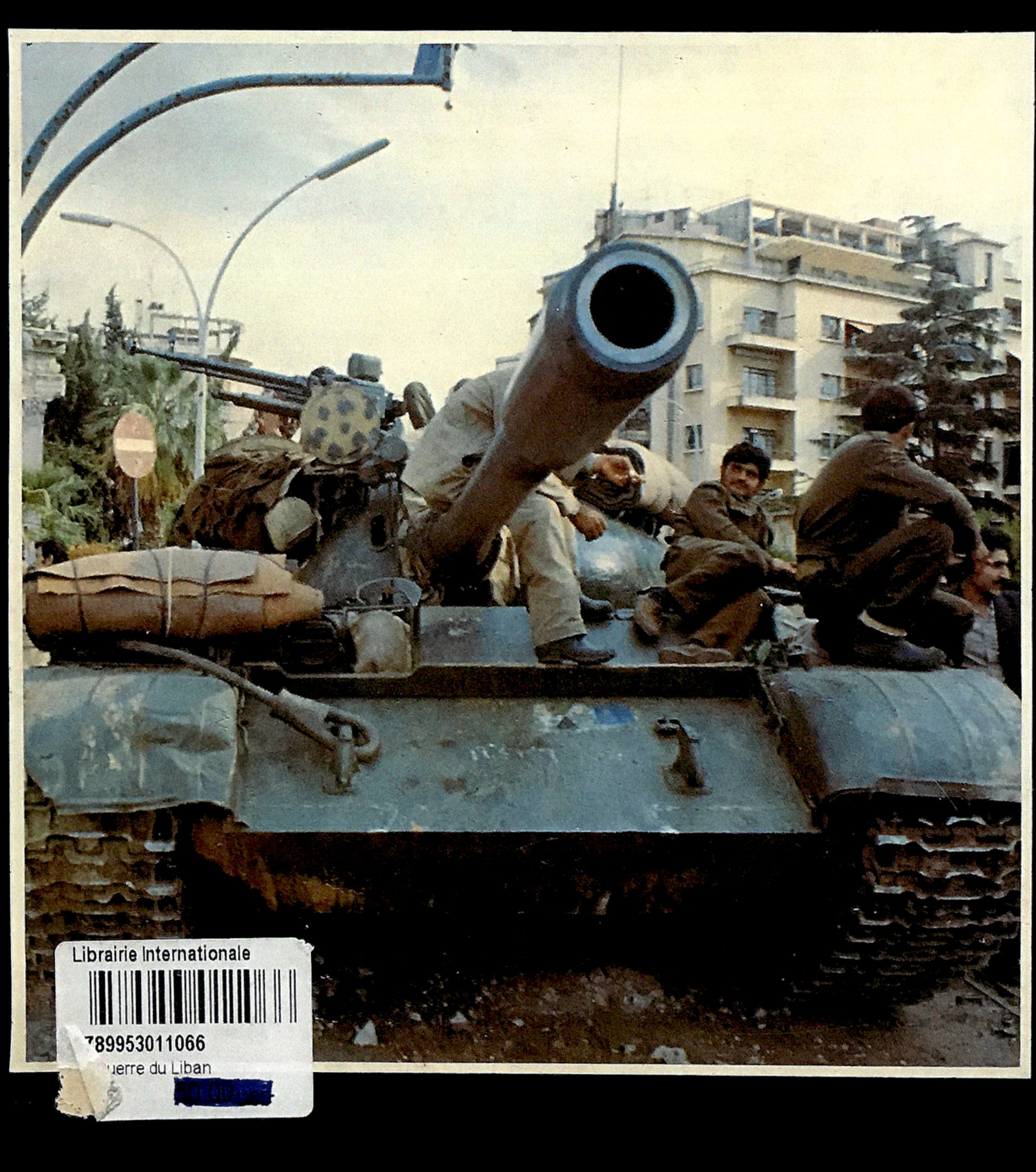

290

Camera Austria

International € 14,– 78/2002

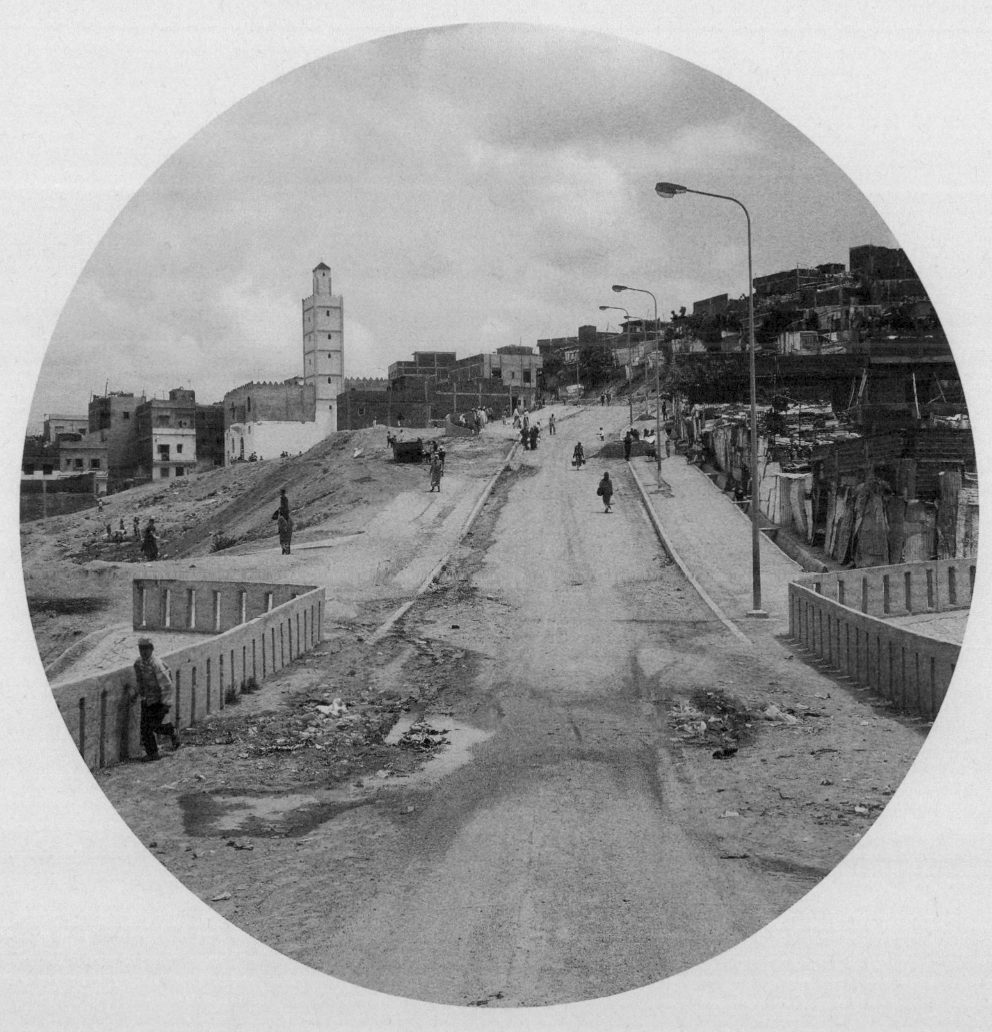

CATHERINE DAVID: DOSSIER – IMAGES DU MONDE ARABE / IMAGES FROM THE ARAB WORLD
LAMIA JOREIGE / AKRAM ZAATARI / VAN LEO / HASHEM EL MADANI / WALID RAAD /
JALAL TOUFIC / FOUAD HELMI / RANDA SHAATH / YTO BARRADA

INGRID SIMON   MONIKA SCHWÄRZLER   LOTTE LYON   ANDREAS SPIEGL

TATIANA LECOMTE   MAREN LÜBBKE

FORUM   AUSSTELLUNGEN / EXHIBITIONS   BÜCHER / BOOKS

Lamia Joreige

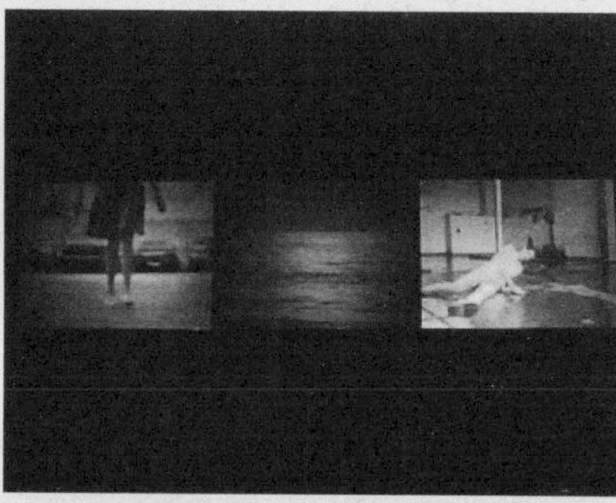

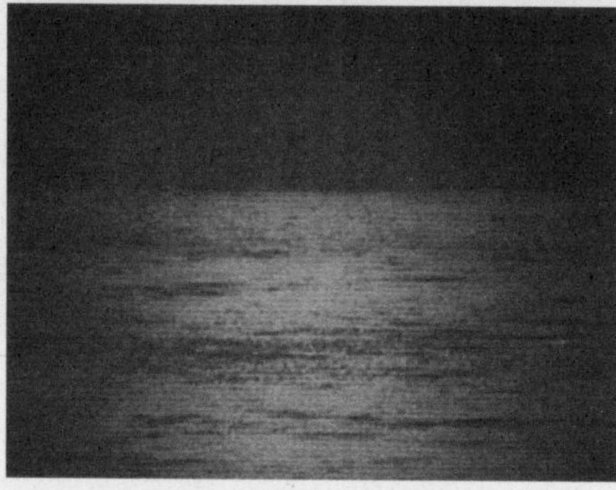

LAMIA JOREIGE, Replay, Video and photographs. Installation for: »Hamra street project«, Beirut 2000.
Images taken from: La guerre du Liban. Images et chronologie, Beirut: Dar al-Massira 1978.

REPLAY

A street, for long an inaccessible »territory«, a stage that I find essential to appropriate. As I revisit this place, I encounter nothing but rupture: A rupture of time, a rupture within time.

I think of things that did happen, things that might have happened in this place during the war – for I only knew it during the war. I imagine that He, who was photographed while dying, might have died here; that She, who was running, escaping something terrible, might have run in the parking lot around the corner.

Perhaps it wasn't them, perhaps it wasn't here; still, I find their images inextricably linked to this place.

A fragment is captured, enlarged, repeated, thus turned into another version of itself. It carries its own memory: stories enacted (or to be enacted) in other geographies. Bodies sacrificed, murdered, executed repeatedly: a staging of violence in the absence of blood. Violence as rupture with the ever present possibility of loss. Violence projected unto any act, at that singular instant when the real and the non-real are indiscernible. Violence endlessly re-enacted, always recognized.

Is there a trace that is not already withdrawn in relation to itself?

The site of irreversible rupture: the sea, that of departures, immutable, always at a close distance, a familiar yet extraordinary imagery, demands uninterrupted contemplation. Here it separates two bodies – a man and a woman – each perpetuating a vain act, revealing the impossibility for them to be.

He falls many times and does not die, though he also never stops falling, never stops dying. She runs, coming towards us again and again; she doesn't stop running, doesn't stop escaping.

Icons of our present, reconstruction of a past, of an origin we can no longer recall.

Eine Straße, lange Zeit unzugängliches »Territorium«, eine Bühne, deren Aneignung mir überaus wichtig ist. Während ich diesen Ort wieder aufsuche, sehe ich nichts als Brüche: einen Bruch der Zeit, einen Bruch in der Zeit.

Ich denke an das, was geschehen ist, was an diesem Ort geschehen sein könnte – während des Krieges, denn ich kannte ihn nur während des Krieges. Ich stelle mir vor, dass der, der beim Sterben fotografiert wurde, hier gestorben ist; dass sie, die rannte, vor etwas Schrecklichem floh, auf dem Parkplatz hier um die Ecke gerannt ist.

Vielleicht waren sie es nicht; vielleicht war es nicht hier; dennoch sind für mich die Bilder von ihnen untrennbar mit diesem Ort verbunden.

Ein Bruchstück wird eingefangen, vergrößert, wiederholt und damit in eine andere Version seiner selbst transformiert. Es besitzt sein eigenes Gedächtnis: Geschichten, die in anderen Geografien durchlebt wurden (oder noch durchlebt werden müssen). Körper, die geopfert, ermordet, mehrfach exekutiert wurden: Eine Inszenierung von Gewalt, bei der kein Blut fließt. Gewalt als Bruch mit der stets gegenwärtigen Möglichkeit des Verlustes. Gewalt, die in dem singulären Augenblick, da das Reale und das Nichtreale ununterscheidbar sind, auf jede Handlung projiziert wird. Gewalt, die immer aufs Neue durchlebt, unablässig wiedererkannt wird.

Gibt es eine Spur, die sich in ihrem Selbstbezug nicht immer schon entzogen hat?

Der Schauplatz des irreversiblen Bruchs: das Meer, das Meer der Abschiede, unveränderlich, stets in einer nahen Ferne, in vertrauten und doch außergewöhnlichen Bildern, verlangt ununterbrochene Kontemplation. Hier trennt es zwei Körper – einen Mann und eine Frau – die beide mit einem vergeblichen Akt fortfahren, der enthüllt, dass es ihnen unmöglich ist zu sein.

Er fällt viele Male, ohne zu sterben, und hört doch nie auf zu fallen und zu sterben. Sie rennt, auf uns zu, immer wieder, und hört nicht auf zu rennen, hört nicht auf zu fliehen.

Ikonen unserer Gegenwart, Rekonstruktion einer Vergangenheit, eines Ursprungs, an den wir uns nicht mehr erinnern.

(Übersetzung: Wilfried Prantner)

This text is taken from the publication Missing links. Art practices from Lebanon, 2001.
Dieser Text ist der Publikation *Missing Links. Art Practices from Lebanon*, 2001, entnommen.

6

REPLAY

A street, for long an inaccessible »territory«, a stage that I find essential to appropriate. As I revisit this place, I encounter nothing but rupture: A rupture of time, a rupture within time.

I think of things that did happen, things that might have happened in this place during the war – for I only knew it during the war. I imagine that He, who was photographed while dying, might have died here; that She, who was running, escaping something terrible, might have run in the parking lot around the corner.

Perhaps it wasn't them, perhaps it wasn't here; still, I find their images inextricably linked to this place.

A fragment is captured, enlarged, repeated, thus turned into another version of itself. It carries its own memory: stories enacted (or to be enacted) in other geographies. Bodies sacrificed, murdered, executed repeatedly: a staging of violence in the absence of blood. Violence as rupture with the ever present possibility of loss. Violence projected unto any act, at that singular instant when the real and the non-real are indiscernible. Violence endlessly re-enacted, always recognized.

Is there a trace that is not already withdrawn in relation to itself?

The site of irreversible rupture: the sea, that of departures, immutable, always at a close distance, a familiar yet extraordinary imagery, demands uninterrupted contemplation. Here it separates two bodies – a man and a woman – each perpetuating a vain act, revealing the impossibility for them to be.

He falls many times and does not die, though he also never stops falling, never stops dying. She runs, coming towards us again and again; she doesn't stop running, doesn't stop escaping.

Icons of our present, reconstruction of a past, of an origin we can no longer recall.

Eine Straße, lange Zeit unzugängliches »Territorium«, eine Bühne, deren Aneignung mir überaus wichtig ist. Während ich diesen Ort wieder aufsuche, sehe ich nichts als Brüche: einen Bruch der Zeit, einen Bruch in der Zeit.

Ich denke an das, was geschehen ist, was an diesem Ort geschehen sein könnte – während des Krieges, denn ich kannte ihn nur während des Krieges. Ich stelle mir vor, dass der, der beim Sterben fotografiert wurde, hier gestorben ist; dass sie, die rannte, vor etwas Schrecklichem floh, auf dem Parkplatz hier um die Ecke gerannt ist.

Vielleicht waren sie es nicht; vielleicht war es nicht hier; dennoch sind für mich die Bilder von ihnen untrennbar mit diesem Ort verbunden.

Ein Bruchstück wird eingefangen, vergrößert, wiederholt und damit in eine andere Version seiner selbst transformiert. Es besitzt sein eigenes Gedächtnis: Geschichten, die in anderen Geografien durchlebt wurden (oder noch durchlebt werden müssen). Körper, die geopfert, ermordet, mehrfach exekutiert wurden: Eine Inszenierung von Gewalt, bei der kein Blut fließt. Gewalt als Bruch mit der stets gegenwärtigen Möglichkeit des Verlustes. Gewalt, die in dem singulären Augenblick, da das Reale und das Nichtreale ununterscheidbar sind, auf jede Handlung projiziert wird. Gewalt, die immer aufs Neue durchlebt, unablässig wiedererkannt wird.

Gibt es eine Spur, die sich in ihrem Selbstbezug nicht immer schon entzogen hat?

Der Schauplatz des irreversiblen Bruchs: das Meer, das Meer der Abschiede, unveränderlich, stets in einer nahen Ferne, in vertrauten und doch außergewöhnlichen Bildern, verlangt ununterbrochene Kontemplation. Hier trennt es zwei Körper – einen Mann und eine Frau – die beide mit einem vergeblichen Akt fortfahren, der enthüllt, dass es ihnen unmöglich ist zu sein.

Er fällt viele Male, ohne zu sterben, und hört doch nie auf zu fallen und zu sterben. Sie rennt, auf uns zu, immer wieder, und hört nicht auf zu rennen, hört nicht auf zu fliehen.

Ikonen unserer Gegenwart, Rekonstruktion einer Vergangenheit, eines Ursprungs, an den wir uns nicht mehr erinnern.

(Übersetzung: Wilfried Prantner)

This text is taken from the publication Missing links. Art practices from Lebanon, 2001.
Dieser Text ist der Publikation *Missing Links. Art Practices from Lebanon*, 2001, entnommen.

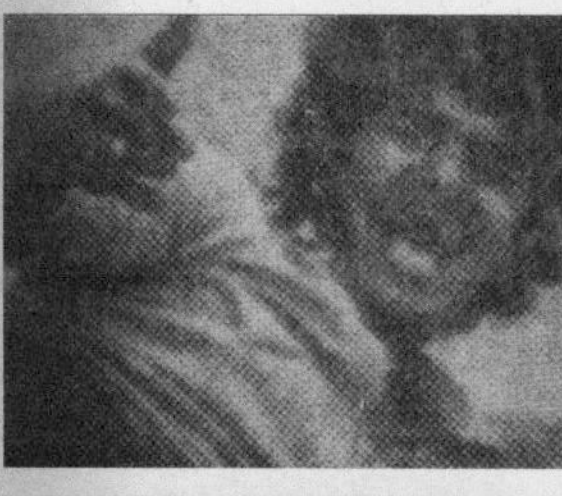

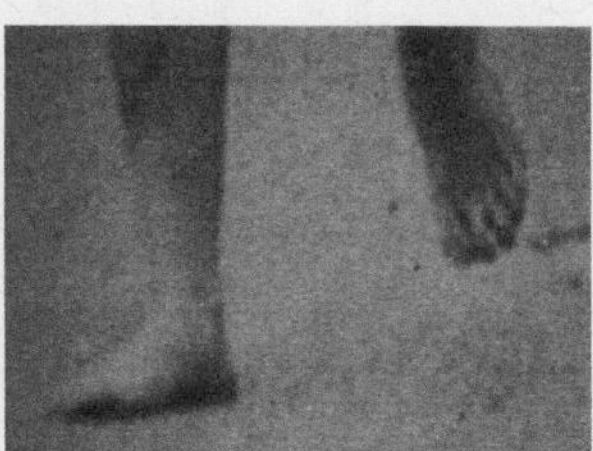

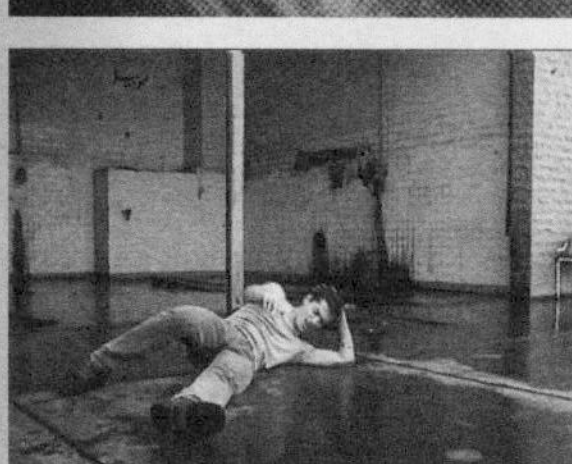

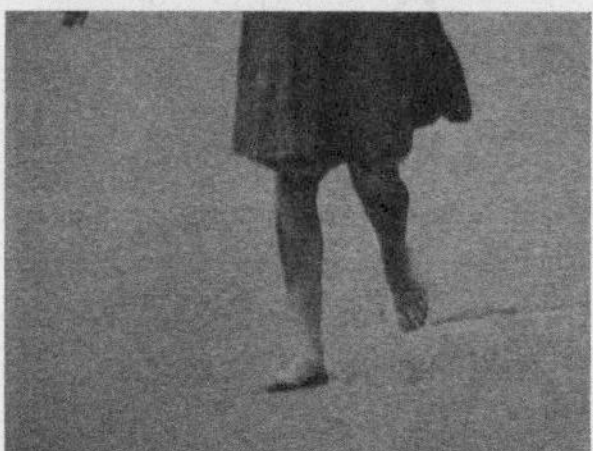

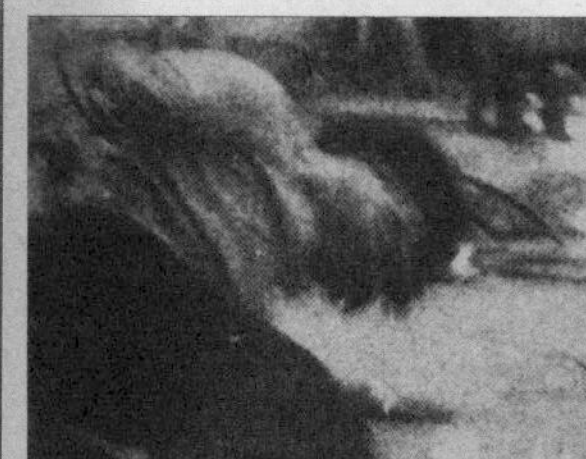

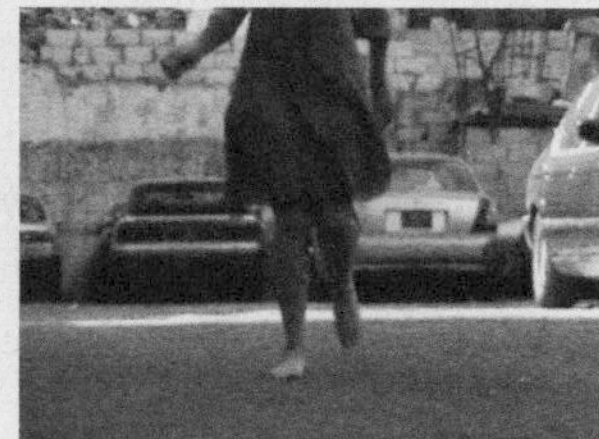

"""

Chronology

In the following, Camera Austria's activities between 1974 and 2018 are listed and divided into exhibitions, workshops and publications. Unless otherwise stated, the exhibitions took place in 1974 and 1975 in the Fotogalerie im Schillerhof, from 1976 to 1996 in the Forum Stadtpark, from 1996 to 2003 in the Galerie am Sparkassenplatz 2 and from 2003 in the Eisernes Haus.

1974

EXHIBITIONS
Helmut Trummer (AT), 10/2–11/5 1974
Christian Vogt (CH), 11/6–12/3 1974
Nikolaus Walter (AT), 12/4 1974–1/7 1975

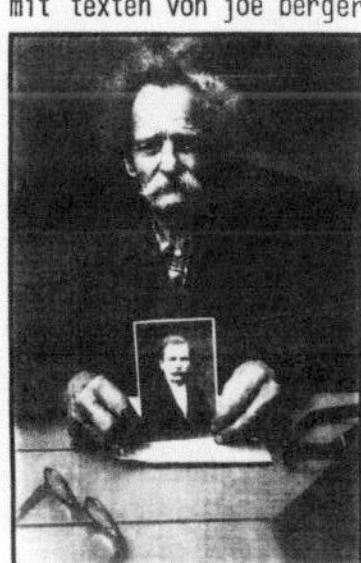

1975

EXHIBITIONS
Petar Dabac (HR), *Fotografik in Farbe,*
1/5–2/4 1975
Tina Schadler (AT), *Sequenzen,* 2/5–3/4 1975
Friedl Bondy (AT), *Autoportraits 1971–1974,*
3/12–4/2 1975
Dieter Eikelpoth (DE), 4/9–5/6 1975
Masaaki Nakagawa (JP), 5/14–6/3 1975
Gert Winkler (AT), *Experimentelle Architektur,*
6/4–6/24 1975
Seiichi Furuya (JP), *199 Fotos,* 6/25–7 1975
Branko Lenart (AT), *mirrorgraphs und andere
fotografien,* 10/8–11/3 1975
Franco Fontana (IT), *Landschaften,* steirischer
herbst '75, 11/6 1975

1976

EXHIBITIONS
Walter Hirsch (SE), 1/22–2/19 1976
Niggi Messerli (CH), 2/28–3/30 1976
Luigi Ghirri (IT), 3/31–4/27 1976
Burkhard Junghanss (DE), 4/24–5/22 1976
Französische Fotografen, with works by
Henri Cartier-Bresson, Brassaï, Izis,
Jean-Philippe Charbonnier, Édouard Boubat,
Robert Doisneau, in collaboration with
Institut Français de Graz (AT), 4/3–4/15 1976
Elisabeth Kraus (AT), *Fotos,* 6/17–7/9 1976
Rudolf Lichtsteiner (CH), *Fotografische Bilder,*
9/22–10/19 1976
Peter Pakesch (AT), *Anonyme Fotos,*
10/21–11/9 1976
Mary Ellen Mark (US), *Passport,* steirischer
herbst '76, 11/2–11/9 1976
Erich Kees (AT), *Wasser,* 11/11–11/26 1976
Christian Vogt (CH), *Rahmenbilder,*
12/14 1976–1/10 1977

1977

EXHIBITIONS
Simon Marsden (GB), 1/14–2/11 1977
Renato Gozzano (IT), 4/27–5/13 1977
American Photographers, with works by
Lewis Baltz, Lee Friedlander, Ralph Gibson,
Les Krims, Mary Ellen Mark, Duane Michals,
Stephen Shore, Neal Slavin, steirischer
herbst '77, 10/24–11/11 1977; Galerie im
Taxispalais, Innsbruck (AT), 11/22–12/4 1977;
Museum des 20. Jahrhunderts, Vienna (AT),
12/7 1977–1/8 1978

WORKSHOP
Ralph Gibson (US), 11/24–11/28 1977

PUBLICATION
Manfred Willmann, ed., *American
Photographers,* in a conversation with
Manfred Willmann and Allan Porter,
Graz: Fotogalerie im Forum Stadtpark, 1977

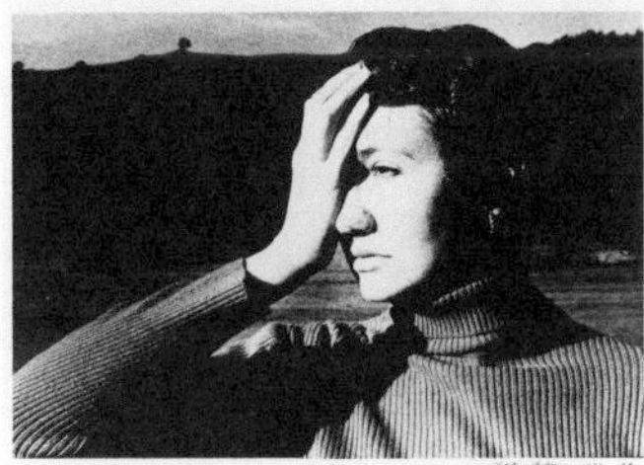

1978

EXHIBITIONS
Toshimi Kamiya (JP), *Sankai-zu,* 1/12–2/3 1978
Gwenn Thomas (US), *Color Photographs,*
2/15–3/10 1978
Fotografie im 20. Jahrhundert, 3/10–4/14 1978
Antoine (AT), *Fotochemische Arbeiten,*
3/31–4/14 1978
Max Aufischer (AT), *Fotos 1977/78,*
6/14–7/5 1978
Reportage – Fotografen, with works by
Diane Arbus (US), Manuel Alvarez Bravo (MX),
Robert Frank (US), Joseph Koudelka (CZ),
Homer Sykes (GB), Shomei Tomatsu (JP),
Nikolaus Walter (AT), steirischer herbst '78,
10/25–11/21 1978; Museum des 20. Jahr-
hunderts, Vienna (AT), 2/21–3/25 1979

WORKSHOP
Mary Ellen Mark (US), 10/25–10/30 1978

PUBLICATION
Manfred Willmann, ed., *Reportage Fotografen,*
with texts and works by Diane Arbus,
Manuel Alvarez Bravo, Robert Frank,
Josef Koudelka, Homer Sykes, Shomei
Tomatsu, Nikolaus Walter, Graz, Fotogalerie
im Forum Stadtpark, 1978

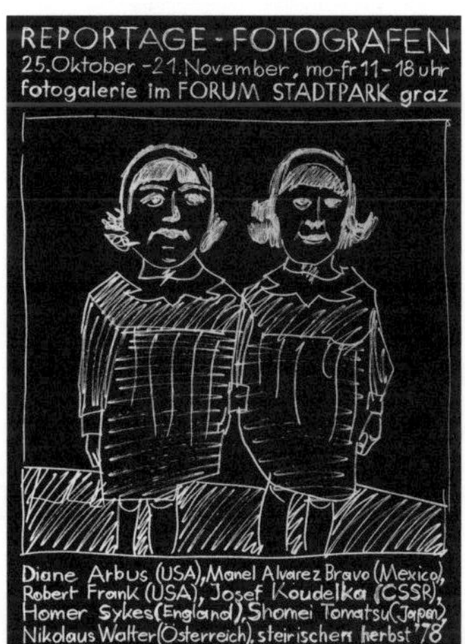

1979

EXHIBITIONS
Erich Tschinkel (AT), *Oszillographik,*
3/4–3/23 1979
Wilhelm Schürmann (DE), *Stadtlandschaften
und Stilleben,* 3/28–4/13 1979
Lotte Hendrich-Hassmann (AT),
4/18–5/11 1979
Pino Settanni (IT), 4/18–5/11 1979
New York, with works by Weegee (US),
Tsuneo Enari (JP), Manfred Willmann (AT),
5/18–6/15 1979
Helmut Tezak (AT), *Photograph's – who's,*
5/22–6/13 1979
5 Jahre Fotogalerie im Forum Stadtpark, with
works by Antoine, Max Aufischer, Lewis Baltz,
Petar Dabac, Tsuneo Enari, Franco Fontana,
Lee Friedlander, Seiichi Furuya,
Luigi Ghirri, Ralph Gibson, Renato Gozzano,
Lotte Hendrich-Hassmann, Walter Hirsch,
Toshimi Kamiya, Erich Kees, Elisabeth Kraus,
Les Krims, Friedl Kubelka-Bondy, Branko
Lenart, Rudolf Lichtsteiner, Mary Ellen Mark,
Niggi Messerli, Masaaki Nakagawa, Wilhelm
Schürmann, Stephen Shore, Neal Slavin,

Homer Sykes, Helmut Tezak, Gwenn Thomas, Shomei Tomatsu, Helmut Trummer, Christian Vogt, Nikolaus Walter, Manfred Willmann, 9/28–10/2 1979
Verkaufsausstellung '79, 12/14–12/16 1979

WORKSHOP
Wilhelm Schürmann (DE), 3/27 1979

SYMPOSION ON PHOTOGRAPHY I
steirischer herbst '79, 9/29–10/2 1979
Lecturers: Lee Friedlander (US),
Robert Heinecken (US), Klaus Honnef (DE),
Joseph Kosuth (US), Ingeborg Lüscher (CH),
Pedro Meyer (MX), Manfred Mixner (AT),
Allan Porter (CH/US), Peter Schlessinger (US),
Georg F. Schwarzbauer (DE),
John Szarkowski (US), Peter Turner (GB),
Manfred Willmann (AT)

PUBLICATION
Christine Frisinghelli and Manfred Willmann, eds, *Symposion on Photography,* with a preface by the editors, texts and works by Lee Friedlander, Robert Heinecken, Klaus Honnef, Joseph Kosuth, Ingeborg Lüscher, Pedro Meyer, Manfred Mixner, Allan Porter, Peter M. Schlessinger, Georg F. Schwarzbauer, John Szarkowski, Peter Turner, Manfred Willmann, Graz: Fotogalerie im Forum Stadtpark, 1980

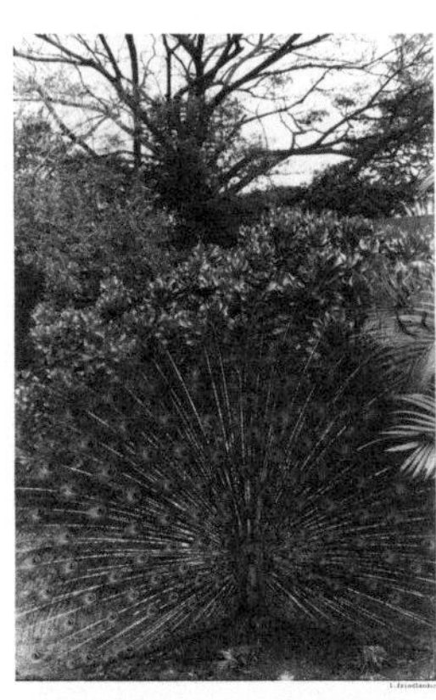

1980

EXHIBITIONS
Seiichi Furuya (JP), *Porträts von Christine,* 1/16–2/8 1980
Triptych, with works by Linda Connor, Robert Heinecken, Tony Ray-Jones, Burk Uzzle, Charles Harbutt, Ralph Gibson, Mark Goodman, in collaboration with Apeiron Workshops Inc., Millerton, New York (US), 2/12–2/29 1980
Joe Maloney (US), 3/12–3/21 1980
John Pfahl (US), 3/12–3/21 1980
Daidoh Moriyama (JP), *Das ist Japan,* 4/15–5/10 1980
Richard Kratochwill (AT), *Wirklichkeiten,* 4/17–5/11 1980
Europäische Fotografen, Teil 1: Steiermark, with works by Stefan Amsüss, Max Aufischer, Adolf Michael Begsteiger, Heinrich Charusa, Karl Darnhofer, J. K. Feichtinger, Friedrich Fischer, Gerd Frisch, Ernst Matthäus Fürböck, Seiichi Furuya, Franz Grüll, Hans Gsellmann, Antoine Haller, Richard Heintz, Othmar Herbst, Peter Gerwin Hoffmann, Hasso Hohmann, Peter Horak, Eilfried Huth, Rosina Ircher, Hans-Georg Jost, Klaus Kada, Erich Kees, Hermann Kiehsl, Michael Kirchengast,

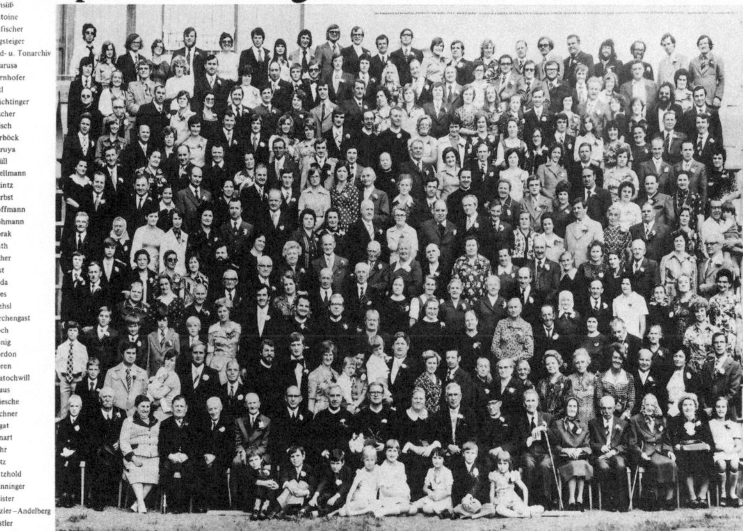

Werner Koch, Regina König, Renate Kordon, Harald Koren, Richard Kratochwill, Elisabeth Kraus, Richard Kriesche, Josef Lechner, A. Legat, Branko Lenart, Egon Lohr, Helmar Lotz, Peter Manninger, Peter Matzhold, Norbert Meister, Rainer Mezler-Andelberg, Norbert Nestler, Friederike J. Nestler-Rebeau, Ferdinand Neumüller, Holger Neuwirth, Wolfram Orthacker, Franz Pacher, Gudrun Panzenbeck, Gerhard Pelko, Peter Philipp, Karl Pierer, Max Puntigam, Karl Pürer, Gerhard Roth, Albin Schrey, Eckart Schuster, Friedrich A. Schuster, Michael Schuster und Hartmut Skerbisch, Johann Schuster, Erwin Schwab, Alfred Seiland, Gerhard Skrapits, Aktion Spielbus, Heinz Stammberger, Peter Starchel, Gerhard Steffen, Harald Strobl, Walter Supper, Wolfgang Temmel, Helmut Tezak, Sepp Tezak, Hans Georg Tropper, Helmut Trummer, Wolfgang Veit, Hanns Waltinger, Felix Weber, Leo Weiss, Hans Wiesenhofer, Horst Wiesner, Manfred Willmann, Alfons Wimmers, Irmfried Windbichler, Rüdiger Wischenbart, Gery Wolf, Raimund Wrana, Alois Zechner, steirischer herbst '80, 10/20–10/31 1980

WORKSHOPS
Peter M. Schlessinger (US), 5/23–5/26 1980
Lewis Baltz (US), 9/26–9/28 and 10/3–10/5 1980

SYMPOSION ON PHOTOGRAPHY II
steirischer herbst '80, 10/20–10/22 1980
Lecturers: Alain Desvergnes (FR),
Ute Eskildsen (DE), Jochen Gerz (DE),
Peter MacGill (US), Albert Goldstein (HR),
Dieter Hacker/Andreas Seltzer (DE),
Richard Kriesche (AT), Rudolf Lichtsteiner (CH),
Nathan Lyons (US), Herbert Molderings (DE),
John Taylor (GB), Peter Weibel (AT)
Contributions published in:
Camera Austria International 4/1980

EDITIONS CAMERA AUSTRIA INTERNATIONAL
1/1980, 2/1980, 3/1980, 4/1980

1981

EXHIBITIONS
Petar Dabac (AT), *le sentiment de la nature à la fin du 20e siècle,* 2/6–2/20 1981
Alfred Seiland (AT), 2/27–3/27 1981
Dokumentation eines Workshops mit Peter Schlessinger, with works by Seiichi Furuya,
Michael Heimerl, Branko Lenart, Johannes Singer, Peter Starchel, Helmut Tezak, Manfred Willmann, 3/31–4/24 1981
Siete Portafolios Mexicanos, with works by Aníbal Angula Cosio, Lázaro Blanco, Victoria Blasco, Graciela Iturbide, Pedro Meyer, Pablo Ortiz Monasterio, José Luis Neyra, 6/3–6/30 1981, in collaboration with Pedro Meyer und dem Consejo Mexicano de Fotografía, Ciudad de México (MX)
Andreas Müller-Pohle (DE), *Konstellationen–Extractions,* 6/9–6/30 1981
Robert Mapplethorpe (US), 9/11–9/29 1981
Issei Suda (JP), 9/11–9/29 1981
Neue Fotografie aus Österreich, with works by Heinz Cibulka, Seiichi Furuya, Leo Kandl, Elisabeth Kraus, Branko Lenart, Elfriede Mejchar, Josef Pausch, Helmut Tezak, Nikolaus Walter, Manfred Willmann, 10/15.–10/31 1981
Seiichi Furuya (JP), *AMS,* 12/4–22 1981
Branko Lenart (AT), *Millerton Project,* 12/4–12/22 1981
Österreichische Fotografen, with works by Heinz Cibulka, Seiichi Furuya, Erich Kees, Elisabeth Kraus, Richard Kratochwill, Branko Lenart, Elfriede Mejchar, Josef Pausch, Alfred Seiland, Walter Supper, Manfred Willmann, in collaboration with the Consejo Mexicano de Fotografía, Ciudad de México (MX), 6/30 1981 (Opening)

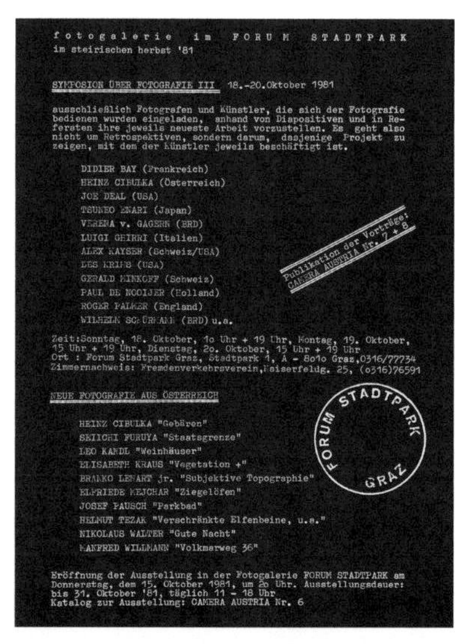

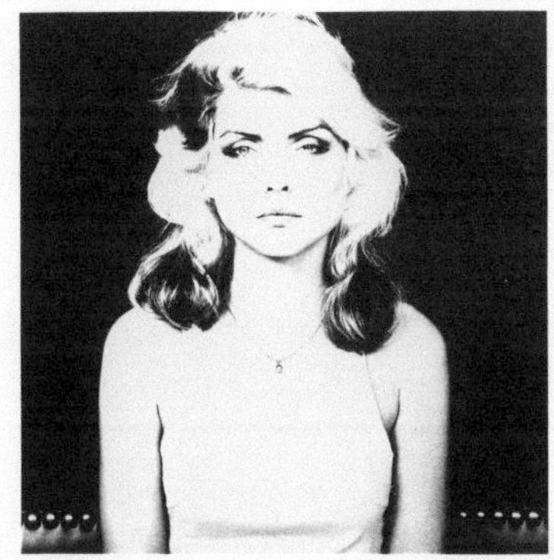

ROBERT MAPPLETHORPE

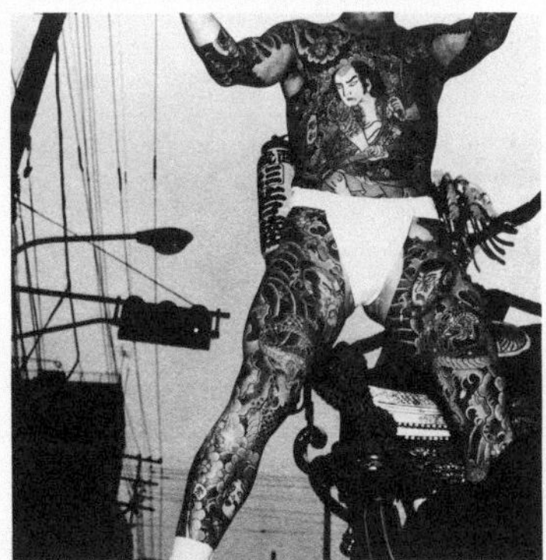

ISSEI SUDA

Fotogalerie im FORUM STADTPARK, Graz
11.–29. September '81. Montag–Freitag 11–18 Uhr

WORKSHOP
Verena von Gagern (DE), 6/6–6/8 and
6/12–6/14 1981

LECTURE
Al Souza (US), 6/22 1981

SYMPOSION ON PHOTOGRAPHY III
steirischer herbst '81, 10/18–10/22 1981
Lecturers: Didier Bay (FR), Heinz Cibulka (AT),
Joe Deal (US), Tsuneo Enari (JP),
Verena von Gagern (DE), Luigi Ghirri (IT),
Alex Kayser (CH), Paul de Nooijer (NL),
Roger Palmer (GB), Wilhelm Schürmann (DE)
Contributions published in: *Camera Austria
International* 7/1981 and 8/1982

PUBLICATIONS
Seiichi Furuya, AMS, with a text by
Klaus Honnef, Graz, Edition Camera
Austria, 1981
Manfred Willmann, "Schwarz und Gold,"
with a text contribution by Albert Goldstein,
Graz, Edition Camera Austria, 1981

EDITIONS CAMERA AUSTRIA
INTERNATIONAL
5/1981, 6/1981, 7/1981–1982

1982

EXHIBITIONS
Franco Fontana (IT), *Presenze,* 1/14–2/3 1982
André Gelpke (DE), *Sex-Theater,* 2/5–3/5 1982
Kurt Matt (AT), *Bilder aus der Luft und Der Tod
des Hirsches,* 3/9–4/2 1982
Gerhard Skrapits (AT), *Eingriffe,*
3/18–4/16 1982
Michael Schmidt (DE), 4/16–5/2 1982
Christoph Scharff (AT), 4/17–5/10 1982
Spiel ohne Grenzen, master class for photog-
raphy of the Kunstgewerbeschule Zürich
(Head Rudolf Lichtsteiner), 5/7–5/28 1982
Peter Dressler (AT), 5/13–6/7 1982
Joan Fontcuberta (ES), 5/21–6/30 1982
John Gossage (US), 6/5–7/2 1982
Fotografie 1982, with works by Lewis Baltz
(US), Nick Hedges (US), Duane Michals (US),
Gabriele and Helmut Nothhelfer (DE),
Gerhard Roth (AT), Michael Schuster/Hartmut
Skerbisch (AT), steirischer herbst '82,
10/1–10/31 1982
Dagmar Hartig (DE), 10/15–11/5 1982

Hitoshi Fugo (JP), *Floating Around,*
11/8–11/25 1982
Bill Brandt (GB), *Retrospektive,*
in collaboration with British Council,
11/22–12/7 1982
Helmut Tezak (AT), *Zürich/Ein Essay,*
11/26–12/23 1982
Graz 1982, with works by Antoine Haller,
Max Aufischer, Hermann Candussi,
Seiichi Furuya, Gerhard Jurkovic, Erich Kees,
Richard Kratochwill, Elisabeth Kraus,
Erich Lázár, Branko Lenart, Michael Markart,
Max Puntigam, Alfred Seiland, Gerhard
Skrapits, Peter Starchel, Harald Strobl, Helmut
Tezak, Manfred Willmann, Alfons Wimmers,
Ursula Wüst, 10/1–10/19 1982; Galerija
Sinagoga, Maribor (SI), 12/9–12/26 1982

WORKSHOPS
Franco Fontana (IT), 1/22–1/24 1982
André Gelpke (DE), 2/6–2/7 1982
Michael Schmidt (DE), 4/17–4/18 1982
Joan Fontcuberta (ES), 5/22–5/23 1982
John Gossage (US), 6/4–6/6 1982

LECTURE
Harald Rumpf (DE), "52 junge deutsche
Fotografen," 3/27 1982

SYMPOSION ON PHOTOGRAPHY IV
steirischer herbst '82, 10/17–10/19 1982

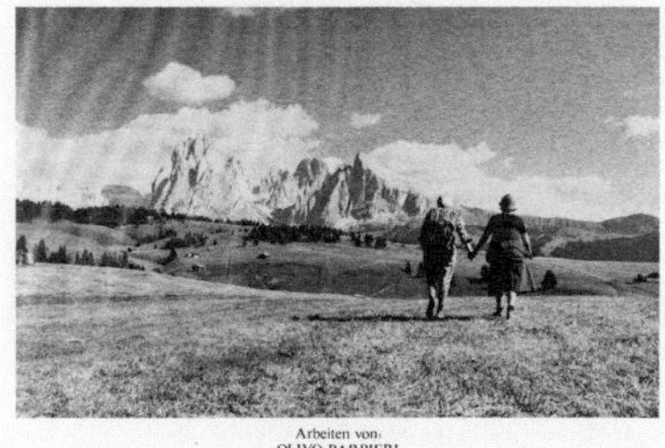

Lecturers: Lewis Baltz (US), Gus Blaisdell (US),
Antje von Graevenitz (DE/NL), Mark Haworth-
Booth (GB), Duane Michals (US), Gabriele
and Helmut Nothhelfer (DE), Gerhard Roth
(AT), Burghart Schmidt (DE), Michael
Schuster/Hartmut Skerbisch (AT)
Contributions published in: *Camera Austria
International* 11–12/1983

PUBLICATION
Manfred Willmann ed., *Graz 1982,* with text
contribution by Antoine Haller, Max Aufischer,
Hermann Candussi, Seiichi Furuya, Gerhard
Jurkovic, Erich Kees, Richard Kratochwill,
Elisabeth Kraus, Erich Lázár, Branko Lenart,
Michael Markart, Max Puntigam, Alfred
Seiland, Gerhard Skrapits, Peter Starchel,
Harald Strobl, Helmut Tezak, Manfred
Willmann, Alfons Wimmers, Ursula Wüst,
Graz: Fotogalerie im Forum Stadtpark, 1982

EDITIONS CAMERA AUSTRIA
INTERNATIONAL
8/1982, 9/1982, 10/1982

1983

EXHIBITIONS
Ursula Wüst (AT), *Arbeiten 1982,*
1/11–2/2 1983
Hermann Candussi (AT), *Mit freundlicher
Mitarbeit von …,* 1/14–2/2 1983
Elisabeth Kraus (AT), *Vegetation +,*
2/2–2/25 1983
Rupert Larl (AT), *L'arl pour L'arl,* 2/3–2/25 1983
*Aspekte der zeitgenössischen jugoslawischen
Fotografie,* with works by Milan Aleksić,
Dragan Arrigler, Željko Borčić, Petar Dabac,
Božidar Dolenc, Ivan Dvoršak, Marko Gosar,
Lado Jakša, Vladimir Jovanović, Stojan
Kerbler, Boyana Komadina, Sloba Konjović,
Milan Pajk, Dragan Papić, Neša Paripović,
Dragan Pešić, Marko Pešić, Ivan Posavec,
Janez Pukšič, Bojan Radovič, Ljubomir
Šimunić, Tone Stojko, Alenka Vidrgar,
Jugoslav Vlahović, Zoran Vogrinčič,
in collaboration with Ffotogallery Cardiff,
Kurator William Messer, 2/7–3/4 1983
Humberto Rivas (AR/ES), *Porträts,*
3/1–4/8 1983
Harald Strobl (AT), 3/3–3/25 1983
Gerhard Jurkovic (AT), *Für meine Freunde,*
4/6–5/4 1983
Andreas Horlitz (DE), *Arbeiten 1980–1983,*
4/11–4/29 1983
Peter Starchel (AT), *In München,* 5/2–5/27 1983
*PENISOLA – Una Linea della Fotografia Italiana
a Colori,* with works by Olivo Barbieri, Antonio
Battistella, Vincenzo Castella, Giovanni
Chiaramonte, Mario Cresci, Vittore Fossati,
Luigi Ghirri, Guido Guidi, Mimmo Jodice,
Ernesto Tuliozi, Fulvio Ventura, Kurator Luigi
Ghirri, 6/3–7/7 1983
William Eggleston (US), *Kenia,* in collaboration
with Wilmar Koenig, Werkstatt für
Photographie, Berlin (DE), 6/8–7/7 1983
Dino Pedriali (IT), *Pier Paolo Pasolini,*
10/3–10/30 1983
Fotografie 1983, with works by John Baldessari
(US), Christian Boltanski (FR), Friedl Kubelka-
Bondy (AT), Michael Schmidt (DE), Cindy
Sherman (US), Hermann Stamm (DE),
Hiromi Tsuchida (JP), 10/6–10/30 1983
Branko Lenart (AT), *Heimatbilder,*
10/24–11/11 1983
Einar Schleef (DE), *Zuhause,* 11/24–12/22 1983

WORKSHOPS
William Messer (US), 2/12–2/13 1983
Huberto Rivas (AR/ES), 3/2–3/4 1983
William Eggleston (US), 5/7–5/8 1983
Luigi Ghirri (IT), 6/4–6/5 1983

Michael Schmidt (DE), 12/9 1983
Helmut Tezak (AT), Presentation of Portfolio
ZirkaNeunIntroVersionen, 4/27 1983

SYMPOSION ON PHOTOGRAPHY V
steirischer herbst '83, 10/7–10/9 1983
Lecturers: John Baldessari (US), Christian
Boltanski (FR), Friedl Kubelka-Bondy (AT),
Michael Schmidt (DE), Cindy Sherman (US),
Hermann Stamm (DE), Hiromi Tsuchida (JP),
Franco Vaccari (IT)
Contributions published in: *Camera Austria
International* 15–16/1984

EDITIONS CAMERA AUSTRIA
INTERNATIONAL
11–12/1983, 13/1983

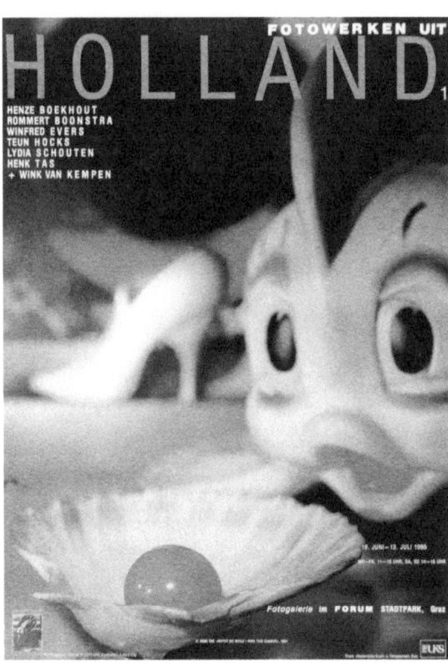

1984

EXHIBITIONS
Max Aufischer (AT), *Wer MA sagt, muss auch
× sagen*, 1/24–2/24 1984
Claus Schöner (AT), *Retrospektivisch*,
3/12–4/6 1984
Gerhard Jurkovic (AT), *– ich – ist ein anderes*,
3/14–4/3 1984
Christian Wachter (AT), *Wiener Porträts*,
3/14–4/3 1984
Johanna Kandl (AT), *Skulptur*, 3/14–4/3 1984
Wilmar Koenig (DE), *Porträts 1981–1983*,
4/4–4/25 1984
Wolfgang Volz (DE), *Christo: Surrounded
Islands*, 4/9–5/11 1984
Liesl Ujvary (AT), *Menschen – Pflanzen –
Porträts*, 4/11–5/4 1984
Bodo Hell (AT), *Stadtschrift*, 4/11–5/4 1984
Hugo Jaeggi (CH), *Widerschatten – Die andere
Seite des Spiegels*, 6/8–6/29 1984
Fotografie '84, with works by Gottfried
Bechtold (AT), Bernhard Johannes Blume (DE),
Giovanni Chiaramonte (IT), Bernard Faucon
(FR), John Gossage (US), Inge Morath-Miller
(AT), Helmut Newton (DE), steirischer
herbst '84, 10/3–10/31 1984
Shomei Tomatsu (JP), *Japan 1952–1981*,
12/14 1984–1/18 1985; Exhibition of Salzburger
Landessammlungen Rupertinum (AT),
2/8–3/10 1985; Austrian Picture Archive at
Museum moderner Kunst, Vienna (AT),
Eröffnung 3/13 1985; Galerie im Körnerpark,
Berlin (DE), 2/8–3/9 1986; Fotoforum Bremen,
Galerie in der Böttcherstraße, Bremen (DE),
4/25–6/18 1986; Städtische Galerie, Erlangen
(DE), 10/25–11/23 1986; Museet for Fotokunst,
Brandts Klaedefabrik, Odense (DK),
7/17–8/30 1987

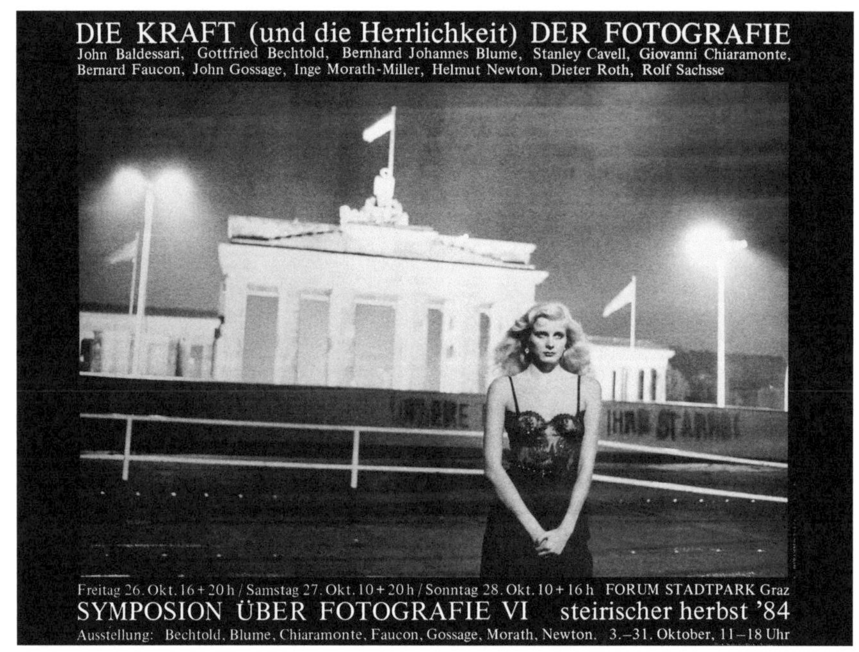

WORKSHOP
Hugo Jaeggi, 6/9–6/10 1984

SYMPOSION ON PHOTOGRAPHY VI
"The Power (and the Glory) of Photography"
steirischer herbst '84, 10/26–10/28 1984
Lecturers: John Baldessari (US), Gottfried
Bechtold (AT), Bernhard Johannes Blume (DE),
Stanley Cavell (US), Giovanni Chiaramonte
(IT), Bernard Faucon (FR), John Gossage (US),
Inge Morath-Miller (AT), Helmut Newton (DE),
Rolf Sachsse (DE)
Contributions published in: *Camera Austria
International* 19–20/1985

PUBLICATIONS
Seiichi Furuya and Manfred Willmann, eds,
Shomei Tomatsu, Japan 1952–1981, with an
introduction from the editors, texts by
Shomei Tomatsu and text contributions by
Otto Breicha, Kazuo Nishii and Toshiharu
(Shunji) Ito,
Graz, Edition Camera Austria, 1984
Helmut Tezak, DAKAR, Graz, Edition Camera
Austria, 1984

EDITIONS CAMERA AUSTRIA
INTERNATIONAL
14/1984, 15–16/1984

1985

EXHIBITIONS
*Meisterwerke der Fotokunst – Sammlung
Tillmann & Vollmer*, 2/5–3/11 1985
Erich Lázár (AT), *Blaue Augen – Aus Graz*,
3/5–3/27 1985
Toto Frima (NL), 4/12–5/5 1985
Henze Boekhout (NL), 4/12–5/5 1985
Fotografie aus der DDR, with works by Sibylle
Bergemann, Arno Fischer, Christina Glanz,
Wolfgang Gregor, Thomas Kläber,
Hans Wulf Kunze, Sieghard Liebe, Ute Mahler,
Roger Melis, Helga Paris, Thomas Sandberg,
Rudolf Schäfer, Gundula Schulze,
Uwe Steinberg, Helfried Strauss, Ulrich Wüst,
Kurator Michael Schmidt, 6/12–7/7 1985,
Museum moderner Kunst Palais Liechtenstein,
Vienna (AT), 9/8 1985
Larry Fink (US), *Social Graces*, 6/14 –7/7 1985
*EUROPA – AMERIKA: Hello – Good Bye, Good
Bye – Hello*, with works by Gosbert Adler (DE),
Lewis Baltz (US), Bernd und Hilla Becher (DE),
William Eggleston (US), Robert Frank (US),

André Gelpke (DE), Luigi Ghirri (IT), Wilmar
Koenig (DE), Christoph Scharff (AT),
Michael Schmidt (DE), steirischer herbst '85,
9/17–10/7 1985
Six Austrian Photographers, with works by
Heinz Cibulka, Seiichi Furuya, Friedl Kubelka-
Bondy, Branko Lenart, Helmut Tezak, Manfred
Willmann; Arbitrage Gallery, New York City
(US), 5/16–6/11 1985; Municipal Art Gallery,
Los Angeles (US), steirischer herbst '85 in the
USA, 7/9–8/18 1985
Rudolf Lichtsteiner (CH), *Tischgeschichten*,
9/19–10/7 1985

WORKSHOP
Larry Fink, 6/15–6/16 1985

SYMPOSION ON PHOTOGRAPHY VII
"Europa – Amerika: Hello – Good Bye,
Good Bye – Hello"
steirischer herbst '85, 10/4–10/6 1985
Lecturers: Gosbert Adler (DE),
Lewis Baltz (US), William Eggleston (US),
Robert Frank (US), André Gelpke (DE),
Luigi Ghirri (IT), Marc Holborn (US),
Wilmar Koenig (DE), Herbert Molderings (DE),
Weston Naef (US), Christoph Scharff (AT),
Michael Schmidt (DE), Roberta Valtorta (IT)
Contributions published in: *Camera Austria
International* 21/1986 and 22/1987

EDITIONS CAMERA AUSTRIA
INTERNATIONAL
17/1985, 18/1985, 19–20/1985

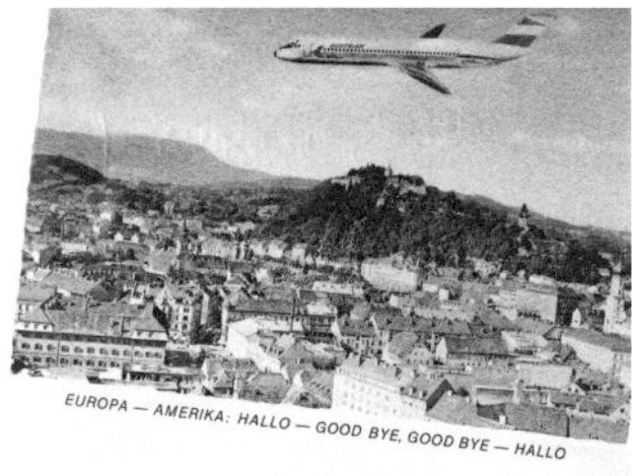

1986

EXHIBITIONS
Self-Images / World-Images, with works by
Peter Dressler, Elisabeth Kraus, Erich Lázár,
Paul Albert Leitner, Sylvia Mascher, Michaela
Moscouw, Claus Schöner, Peter Starchel,
Helmut Tezak, Christian Wachter, Manfred
Willmann, Ursula Wüst, 5/14–6/4 1986
Fotowerken uit Holland, with works by
Henze Boekhout, Rommert Boonstra,
Winfred Evers, Teun Hocks, Lydia Schouten,
Henk Tas, Wink Van Kempen, 6/18–7/13 1986
Gosbert Adler (DE), *Nadja 1986,*
6/18–7/13 1986
Image : Text, with works by Rolf Dieter
Brinkmann (DE), Peter Dressler (AT),
Allen Ginsberg (US), John Hilliard (GB),
Martin Kippenberger (DE), Einar Schleef (DE),
Peter Weibel (AT), steirischer herbst '86,
10/14–11/7 1986
Hubert Schmalix (AT), *F (Fotos),*
11/15.–11/27 1986

LECTURE
Hripsimé Visser and Bas Vroege, "Fotowerken
uit Holland," 6/18 1986

SYMPOSION ON PHOTOGRAPHY VIII
"Image : Text"
steirischer herbst '86, 10/18–10/19 1986
Lecturers: Hubertus von Amelunxen (DE),
Victor Burgin (GB), Regina Carstensen (DE),
Peter Dressler (AT), Frieda Grafe (DE),
Bodo Hell (AT), John Hilliard (GB),
Martin Kippenberger / Albert Oehlen (DE),
Timm Starl (AT), Peter Weiermair (AT)
Contributions published in: *Camera Austria
International* 24 / 1987 and 25 / 1988

EDITIONS CAMERA AUSTRIA
INTERNATIONAL
21 / 1986

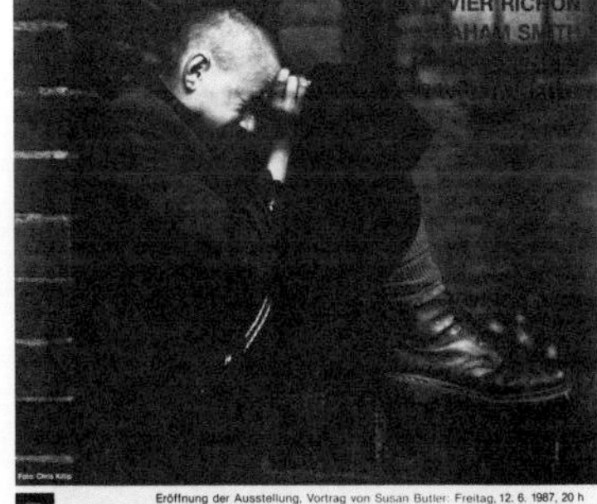

1987

EXHIBITIONS
Max Aufischer (AT), *Schwarzbunte Bilder,*
1/19–2/7 1987
André Kertész (HU / US), *70 Fotografien
1912–1966,* 2/27–3/22 1987
John Baldessari (US), *Neue Arbeiten,* 1986,
2/27–3/22 1987
Fotografie in Österreich, with works by
Peter Dressler, Herwig Kempinger, Paul Albert
Leitner, Michaela Moscouw, Christian
Wachter, Ursula Wüst, Manfred Willmann,
Museum Folkwang, Essen (DE), 3/8–4/18 1987
Königreich. Fotoarbeiten aus Großbritannien,
with works by Paul Graham, John Hilliard,
Chris Killip, Karen Knorr, Martin Parr,
Olivier Richon, Graham Smith, Jo Spence /
David Roberts, in collaboration with the
British Council, 6/12–7/12 1987
The Contemporary, with works by Pidder
Auberger (DE), phoenix production
(Walter Berger / Ona B., (AT)), Barbara Ess
(US), Peter Fischli / David Weiss (CH),
Nan Goldin (US), Axel Hütte (DE),
Karen Knorr (GB), Michaela Moscouw (AT),
Henk Tas / Wink van Kempen (NL),
steirischer herbst '87, 10/15–11/7 1987

SYMPOSION ON PHOTOGRAPHY IX
"The Contemporary"
steirischer herbst '87, 10/16–10/18 1987
Lecturers: Pidder Auberger (DE),
Walter Berger / phoenix production (AT),
Michael Clegg (US), Barbara Ess (US),
Nan Goldin (US), Axel Hütte (DE), Karen Knorr
(GB), Michaela Moscouw (AT), Rob Powell
(GB), Henk Tas / Wink van Kempen (NL)
Contributions published in: *Camera Austria
International* 26 / 1988 and 27 / 1988

PUBLICATION
Manfred Willmann, ed., *Hans Frank,
Hinter den Kulissen,* with a conversation
between Michael Mauracher and Hans Frank,
Graz, Edition Camera Austria, 1987

EDITIONS CAMERA AUSTRIA
INTERNATIONAL
22 / 1987, 23 / 1987, 24 / 1987

1988

EXHIBITIONS
Allan Sekula (US), *Sketch for a Geography
Lesson,* in collaboration with Ute Eskildsen,
Museum Folkwang, Essen (DE),
2/18–3/11 1988
Arc Lémanique, with works by Gabriele
Basilico (IT), Jacques Berthet (CH),
Luc Chessex (CH), Nicolas Faure (CH),
Luigi Ghirri (IT), Anne-Marie Grobet (CH),
Claude Nori (FR), Olivier Richon (CH/GB),
Christian Vogt (CH), Manfred Willmann (AT),
in collaboration with Musée de l'Elysée,
Lausanne (CH), 5/25–6/17 1988
Die Rache der Erinnerung, with works by
Christian Boltanski (FR), Hannah Collins (GB),
Günther Förg (DE), Masahisa Fukase (JP),

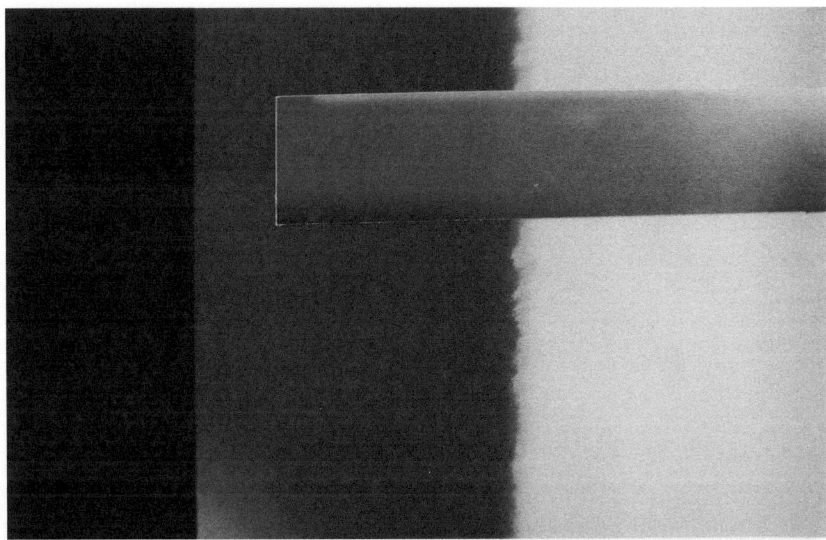

Seiichi Furuya (JP), Christiane Richter (DE),
Henk Tas (NL), Manfred Willmann (AT),
steirischer herbst '88, 9/25–10/7 1988
Walter Dahn (DE), *Fotoarbeiten,* in
collaboration with the Austrian Picture
Archive at Museum moderner Kunst,
Vienna (AT), 11/16–12/8 1988
Questioning Europe, with works by
Seiichi Furuya, Horáková & Maurer,
Manfred Willmann, Austrian contribution to
the Photo Biennale Rotterdam (NL)
Über–Lebens–Energie, Workshops and
exhibition with Gosbert Adler in Kindberg;
Herrmann Candussi in Weiz; Heinz Cibulka
in Köflach; Seiichi Furuya in Kapfenberg;
Wilmar Koenig in Judenburg; Michael Schmidt
in Eisenerz; Christian Wachter in
Mürzzuschlag; Manfred Willmann in Leoben,
exhibitions of all contributions in conjunction
with steirischer herbst '88, Ostbahnhof Graz
(AT), in cooperation with the Steirische
Kulturinitiative

EDITIONS CAMERA AUSTRIA
INTERNATIONAL
25 / 1988, 26 / 1988, 27 / 1988, 28 / 1988

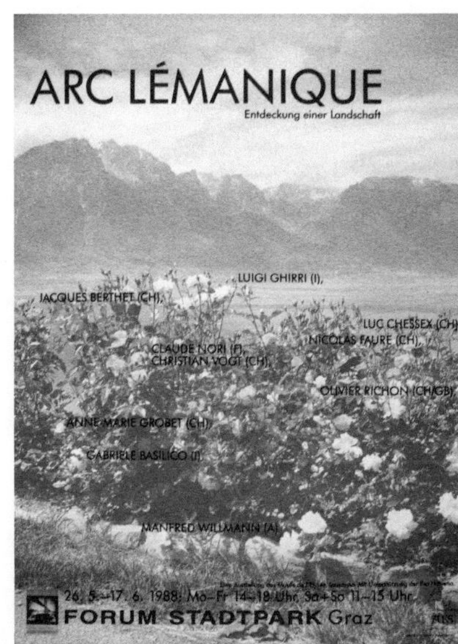

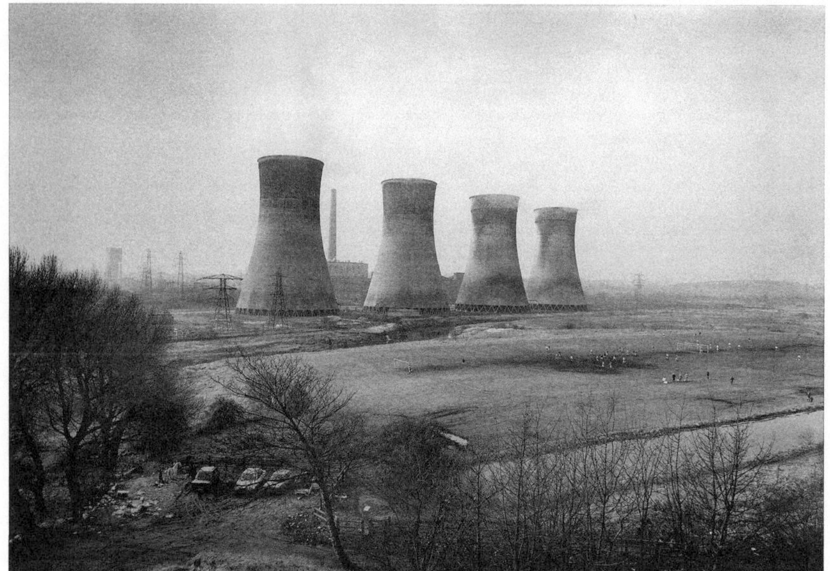

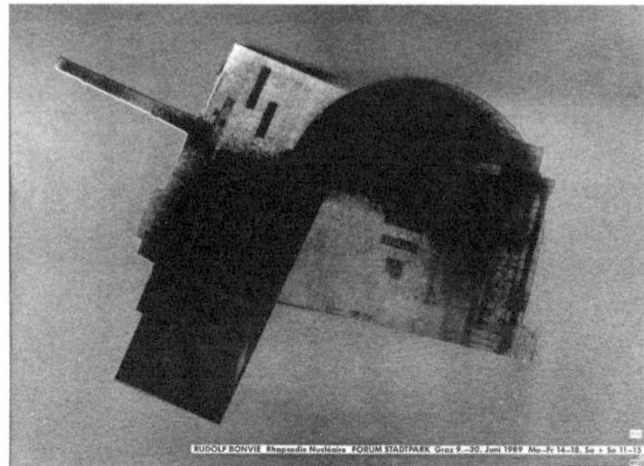

1989

EXHIBITIONS
Eva Maria Ocherbauer (AT / DE), *Katatingi*,
3/2–4/8 1989
Erich Lázár (AT), *Tierra del Fuego*, 3/2–4/8 1989
Manfred Willmann (AT), *Die Sieger*,
5/10–5/31 1989
Christian Eigner (AT), *Die Möglichkeit*,
5/10–5/31 1989
Stadtpark Eins, with works by Max Aufischer,
Seiichi Furuya, Tamara Horáková & Ewald
Maurer, Erich Lázár, Branko Lenart, Eva Maria
Ocherbauer, Michael Schuster, Helmut Tezak,
Christian Wachter, Manfred Willmann;
Kunsthaus Zug, Zug (CH), 1989; Muzej
Suvremene Umjetnosti, Zagreb (HR), 1990;
Austrian Cultural Institute, Paris (FR),
in conjunction with Mois de la Photo '92,
11/2–12/1 1992; 1600 Smith in Cullen Center,
Houston, TX (US), 5/18–8/7 1993
Rudolf Bonvie (DE), *Rhapsodie Nucléaire*,
6/9–7/2 1989
John Davies (GB), *A Green and Pleasant Land*,
6/8–6/30 1989
*Zwischen Himmel und Erde. 22 Grazer
Fotoarbeiten*, Stadtmuseum, Graz,
8/18–9/10 1989
Astrid Klein (DE), *Fotoarbeiten 1984–1989*,
in collaboration with Carsten Ahrens
and Hildegund Amanshauser, in cooperation
with the ICA, London (GB), the Wiener
Secession (AT) and the Kestnergesellschaft,
Hannover (DE), 9/19–10/7 1989
The New Concept, with works by
John Baldessari (US), Volker Heinze (DE),
Alfredo Jaar (CL), Gerald Van Der Kaap (NL),
Herwig Kempinger (AT), David Levinthal (US),
David Robbins (US), Michael Schuster/
Hartmut Skerbisch (AT),

steirischer herbst '89, 11/9–11/30 1989
Clegg & Guttmann (US), *Landscapes,*
12/14 1989–1/20 1990

SYMPOSION ON PHOTOGRAPHY X
"The New Concept"
steirischer herbst '89, 11/10–11/12 1989
Lecturers: John Baldessari (US), Volker Heinze
(DE), Alfredo Jaar (CL), Ronald Jones (US),
Gerald Van Der Kaap (NL), Herwig Kempinger
(AT), David Levinthal (US), Gerhard Johann
Lischka (CH), Michael Schuster / Hartmut
Skerbisch (AT), Herta Wolf (AT)
Contributions published in: *Camera Austria
International* 33–34 / 1990

PUBLICATIONS
Manfred Willmann, ed., *Stadtpark Eins,* with
an introduction by Helmut Strobl and a
text contribution by Gisela Bartens, Graz,
Edition Camera Austria, 1989
Carsten Ahrens, Hildegund Amanshauser
and Christine Frisinghelli, eds, *Astrid Klein,
Fotoarbeiten 1984–1989,* with a preface
from the editors and text contributions by
Noemi Smolik and Carsten Ahrens,
Graz, Edition Camera Austria, 1989

CAMERA AUSTRIA AWARD
for Contemporary Photography by the
City of Graz: Nan Goldin (US)

EDITIONS CAMERA AUSTRIA
INTERNATIONAL
29 / 1989, 30 / 1989

1990

EXHIBITIONS
Paul Albert Leitner (AT), *Weltverwirrung,*
1/12–2/4 1990
Brian Griffin (GB), *Work,* 2/10–3/4 1990
David Levinthal (US), *Hitler Moves East,*
4/26–5/20 1990
Christian Wachter (AT), *ABPOPA / AURORA,*
4/26–5/20 1990
Hans Danuser (CH), *In Vivo,* 5/23–6/22 1990
*Withdrawal Symptoms of Existence. Objects /
Signs / Commodities,* with works by Helen
Chadwick (GB), Willie Doherty (IE), Horáková
& Maurer (AT), Thomas Locher (DE), Olivier
Richon (CH / GB), Rolf Walz (DE), Allan
McCollum (US), steirischer herbst '90,
10/18–11/11 1990

SYMPOSION ON PHOTOGRAPHY XI
"Withdrawal Symptoms of Existence. Objects/
Signs/Commodities", steirischer herbst '90,
9/29–10/2 1990
Lecturers: Helen Chadwick (GB),
Willie Doherty (IE), Paul Groot (NL),
Horáková & Maurer (AT), Thomas Locher (DE),
Olivier Richon (CH/GB), Peter Weibel (AT),
Michael Wetzel (DE), Slavoj Žižek (SI)
Contributions published in: *Camera Austria
International* 37 / 1991 and 38 / 1991

PUBLICATION
Christian Wachter, *ABPOPA / AURORA,*
with text contributions by Timm Starl,
Elisabeth Schlebrügge, Susanne Neuburger,
Graz, Edition Camera Austria, 1990

EDITIONS CAMERA AUSTRIA
INTERNATIONAL
31–32 / 1990, 33–34 / 1990, 35 / 1990

1991

EXHIBITIONS
Gosbert Adler (DE), *Sog,* 2/12–3/3 1991
Wladimir Kuprijanow (RU), *Mittelrussische
Landschaft,* 4/9–4/30 1991
Andrea van der Straeten (AT), *Accidental
Artists,* 5/7–5/29 1991
Nan Goldin (US), *Life, Loss, Obsession,*
in collaboration with Museum Folkwang,
Essen (DE), 9/9–9/29 1991
The Public Image, with works by Rudolf Bonvie
(DE), Vince Leo (US), Mark Lewis (CA), David
Robbins (US), Annie Sprinkle (US), Mitra
Tabrizian (GB), steirischer herbst '91,
10/4–11/3 1991

SYMPOSION ON PHOTOGRAPHY XII
"The Public Image"
steirischer herbst '91, 10/4–10/7 1991
Lecturers: László Beke (HU),
Rudolf Bonvie (DE), Antonín Dufek (CZ),
Werner Fenz (AT), Vince Leo (US),
Mark Lewis (CA), David Robbins (US),
Sally Stein (US), Mitra Tabrizian (GB)
Michael Klier (DE), *Der Riese,* film projection
Contributions published in: *Camera Austria
International* 40 / 1992 and 41 / 1992

CAMERA AUSTRIA AWARD
for Contemporary Photography by the
City of Graz: Olivier Richon (CH/GB)

EDITIONS CAMERA AUSTRIA
INTERNATIONAL
36 / 1991, 37 / 1991, 38 / 1991

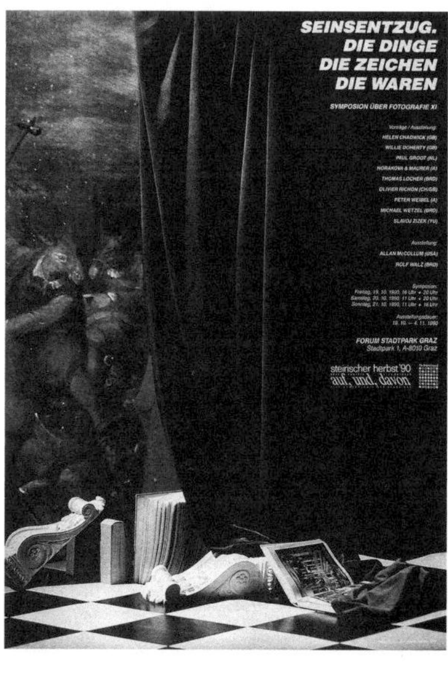

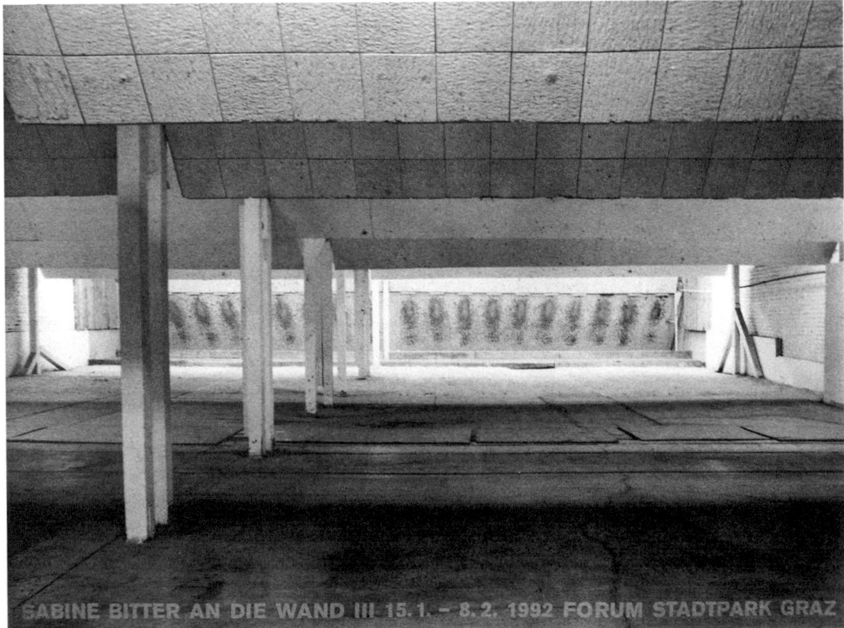

1992

EXHIBITIONS
Sabine Bitter (AT), *An die Wand III*,
1/14–2/16 1992
Boris Mikhailov (UA), *Fotoarbeiten*,
3/17–4/10 1992
Nobuyoshi Araki (JP), *Akt – Tokyo. 1971–1991*,
6/17–7/12 1992; Galorie Fotohof, Salzburg (AT),
7/28–8/30 1992; Galerie Museum, Bozen (IT),
1/21–2/27 1993; Kunsthal, Rotterdam (NL),
4/20–5/16 1993; Museum Folkwang,
Essen (DE), 6/10–7/25 1993; Vorarlberger
Kunstverein, Bregenz (AT), 8/6–8/29 1993;
Fotomuseum im Münchner Stadtmuseum,
Munich (DE), 9/9–10/24 1993;
Torch Gallery, Amsterdam (NL), 2/4–3/5 1994;
Nordliga Fotocentret, Oulu (FI), 5/6–6/7 1994;
Zone Gallery, Newcastle (GB), 3/22–4/30 1995;
Galerie Bob van Orsouw, Zürich (CH),
8/19–9/30 1995
Matta Wagnest/Nicolas Eder (AT), *1 000 1*,
9/9–9/27 1992
So oder so nicht sein/Identities, with works by
Miyako Ishiuchi (JP), Mary Kelly (US),
Jeff Koons (US), Wladimir Kuprijanow (RU),
Boris Mikhailov (UA), Jack Pierson (US),
Jo Spence (GB), steirischer herbst '92,
10/15–11/4 1992
Leo Kandl (AT), *Kollektion,* 12/1–12/20 1992

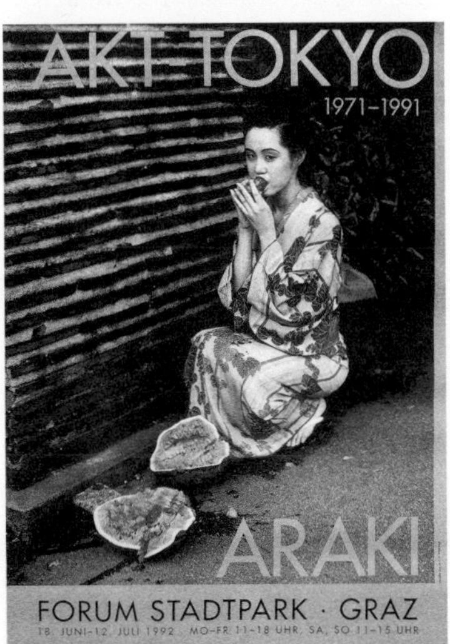

SYMPOSION ON PHOTOGRAPHY XIII
"Identities"
steirischer herbst '92, 9/16–9/18 1992
Lecturers: Boris Groys (DE),
Miyako Ishiuchi (JP), Mary Kelly (US),
Jeff Koons (US), Wladimir Kuprijanow (RU),
Rosy Martin (GB), Eva Meyer (DE),
Boris Mikhailov (UA), Irit Rogoff (IL/GB)
Contributions published in *Camera Austria
International* 43–44/1993

PUBLICATIONS
Sabine Bitter, *An die Wand,* with text
contributions by Dietmar Steiner
and Georg Schöllhammer,
Graz, Edition Camera Austria, 1992.
Seiichi Furuya and Manfred Willmann eds.,
Nobuyoshi Araki, AKT–TOKYO. 1971–1991,
with text contributions by Hiromi Ito,
Toshiharu Ito, Taeko Tomioka and Nobuyoshi
Araki aswell as an epilog from the editors,
Graz, Edition Camera Austria, 1992.

EDITIONS CAMERA AUSTRIA
INTERNATIONAL
39/1992, 40/1992, 41/1992

1993

EXHIBITIONS
Thomas Florschuetz (DE), *Fotoarbeiten,*
3/4–4/2 1993
Forum Stadtpark Graz, Austria, with works
by Max Aufischer, Hermann Candussi, Petar
Dabac, Seiichi Furuya, Horáková & Maurer,
Erich Kees, Elisabeth Kees-Kraus, Richard
Kratochwill, Erich Lázár, Branko Lenart,
Eva Maria Ocherbauer, Michael Schuster,
Gerhard Skrapits, Helmut Tezak, Christian
Wachter, Nicolas Eder/Matta Wagnest,
Manfred Willmann, Museum des Zentrums
für Volkskunst, in collaboration with Boris
Mikhailov, Kharkiv (UA), 4/15–5/15 1993
Mistaken Identities, with works by Jimmie
Durham (US), Guillermo Gómez-Peña
(MX/US), Theresa Hak Kyung Cha (KR/US),
Connie Hatch (US), Mary Kelly (US), Glenn
Ligon (US), Yong Soon Min (KR/US), Adrian
Piper (US), Armando Rascón (MX/US),
Marlon Riggs (US), Martha Rosler (US), Lorna
Simpson (US), Mitra Tabrizian/Andy Golding
(GB), Carrie Mae Weems (US), Pat Ward
Williams (US). Curators Abigail Solomon-
Godeau and Constance Lewallen,

in collaboration with the University Art
Museum Santa Barbara (US), Museum
Folkwang, Essen (DE), und Louisiana Museum,
Humlebaek (DK), 4/30–5/30 1993
KRIEG., I. Austrian Triennial for Photography,
with works by Dennis Adams (US), Iris
Andraschek (AT), Art in Ruins (GB), Bader &
Tanterl (DE), John Baldessari (US), Sabine
Bitter (AT), Christopher Bledowski (CH),
Krzysztof Cichosz (PL), Michel Dector/
Michel Dupuy (FR), Willie Doherty (IE), Seiichi
Furuya (JP/AT), Georg Herold (DE), Horáková
& Maurer (AT), Gerald van der Kaap (NL),
Herwig Kempinger (AT), Astrid Klein (DE),
Verena Kraft/Kurt Petz (DE), Elke Krystufek (AT),
Zofia Kulik (PL), Wladimir Kuprijanow (RU),
Paper Tiger Television (US), Philippe Perrin (FR),
Pierre et Gilles (FR), Martha Rosler (US),
Michael Schuster (AT), Andrea Sodomka (AT),
Andrea van der Straeten (AT), Matta Wagnest
(AT), Nick Waplington (GB), Manfred
Willmann (AT), in collaboration with Werner
Fenz, in cooperation with the Neue Galerie
am Landesmuseum Joanneum, Graz,
9/16–10/31 1993
Eva Maria Ocherbauer (AT), *Still Alive,*
12/6–12/22 1993

LECTURES
Mistaken Identities, in cooperation with the
Kunstverein Graz
Diedrich Diederichsen, "PC zwischen PoMo
und MuCu. Ein Erfahrungsbericht," 5/21 1993
Rada Iveković, "Mistaken Identities:
Jugoslawien," 6/22 1993
Silvia Eiblmayr, "Die Frau als Medium – Eine
symptomatische Verschiebung," 6/25 1993

SYMPOSION ON PHOTOGRAPHY XIV
"WAR."
steirischer herbst '93, 10/2–10/4 1993
Lecturers: Art in Ruins (GB), Sabine Bitter (AT),
Heinz Emigholz (DE), Paul Lowe (GB),
Zofia Kulik (PL), Susan Meiselas (US),
Sophie Ristelhueber (FR), Martha Rosler (US),
Burghart Schmidt (DE), John Taylor (GB)
Contributions published in: *Camera Austria
International* 47–48/1994

PUBLICATIONS
Werner Fenz and Christine Frisinghelli eds.,
KRIEG, publication in two volumes for
exhibition at I. Austrian Triennial for
Photography, with text contributions by
the editors, Art in Ruins, Bogdan Bogdanović,
Harun Farocki, Dževad Karahasan, Martha
Rosler, Dubravka Ugrešić, Herta Wolf,
Graz, Edition Camera Austria, 1993
Horáková & Maurer, *BUFET Tugendhat,*
with text contributions by Petr Nedoma,
Monika Faber and Werner Fenz,
Graz, Edition Camera Austria, 1993
Eva Maria Ocherbauer, *Still alive,*
Graz, Edition Camera Austria, 1993

CAMERA AUSTRIA AWARD
for Contemporary Photography by the
City of Graz: Seiichi Furuya (JP/AT)

EDITIONS CAMERA AUSTRIA
INTERNATIONAL
42/1993, 43–44/1993, 45/1993

1994

EXHIBITIONS
Another Continent, with works by Gosbert Adler (DE), Rudolf Bonvie (DE), Peter Fischli/David Weiss, (CH) Aglaia Konrad (AT), Zofia Kulik (PL), Annelies Štrba (CH), Jindřich Štreit (CZ), Manfred Willmann (AT), Tokyo Metropolitan Museum of Photography (JP), 1/28–3/22 1994
Wout Berger (NL), *Poisoned Landscape,* 3/3–3/27 1994
Walter Niedermayr (IT), *Die bleichen Berge,* 3/3–3/27 1994
Erich Lázár (AT), *Private Eye,* 4/22–5/15 1994
Jindřich Štreit (CZ), *Vesnice je svet/The Village Is the Globe,* 4/22–5/15 1994
Nick Waplington (GB), *Living Room II,* 4/22–5/15 1994
Sylvia Mascher (AT), *M.Y.S.D.Y.S,* 6/10–7/8 1994
Seiichi Furuya (JP/AT), *Zuhause in Berlin-Ost, 1985–1987,* 9/8–9/27 1994
Olivier Richon (CH/GB), *After DL,* 9/8–9/27 1994
The Archive, with works by Henry Bond/Liam Gillick (GB), Cor Dera (NL), Hans-Peter Feldmann (DE), David Goldblatt (ZA), Leo Kandl (AT), Inez van Lamsweerde (NL), Ken Lum (CA), Peter Roehr (DE), Andrea van der Straeten (AT), Jindřich Štreit (CZ), Christopher Williams (US), steirischer herbst '94, 10/13–11/2 1994
Alle haben Alles gesehen, with works by Herwig Kempinger, Hartmut Skerbisch, Michael Schuster, Manfred Willmann, Austrian contribution to *Il ruolo della critica,* Modena per la Fotografia 1994, Palazzo Comunale, Modena (IT), 10/28–11/27 1994
Three Photographers: Seiichi Furuya, Erich Lázár, Manfred Willmann, Stadtgalerie Bratislava (SK), European Month of Photography Bratislava, October/November 1994
siebzehn, with works by Max Aufischer, Hermann Candussi, Katrin Cebul, Petar Dabac, Beba Fink, Seiichi Furuya, Klaus Dieter Hartl, Horáková & Maurer, Erich Kees, Elisabeth Kees-Kraus, Richard Kratochwill, Branko Lenart, Inge Morath, Eva Maria Ocherbauer, Heinz Pöschko, Michael Schuster, Manfred Willmann, 12/1–12/22 1994

SYMPOSION ON PHOTOGRAPHY XV
"The Archive"
steirischer herbst '94, 10/14–10/16 1994
Lecturers: Monique Behr (DE), Henry Bond/Liam Gillick (GB), Cor Dera (NL), Hans-Peter Feldmann (DE), David Goldblatt (ZA), Leo Kandl (AT), Ken Lum (CA), Roberta McGrath (GB), Andrea van der Straeten (AT), Jindřich Štreit (CZ), Christopher Williams (US), Herta Wolf (AT)
Contributions published in: *Camera Austria International* 51–52/1995

Horáková & Maurer (AT), *BUFET Tugendhat,* book presentation and conversation, 3/1 1994

EDITIONS CAMERA AUSTRIA INTERNATIONAL
46/1994, 47–48/1994, 49/1994

1995

EXHIBITIONS
Yve Lomax (GB), *Sometime(s),* 2/27–3/31 1995
Christian Wachter (AT), *Netz und Knoten,* 2/27–3/31 1995
Robert Adams (US), *Listening to the River,* 5/17–6/11 1995
Nobuyoshi Araki (JP), *Erotos,* steirischer herbst '95, 9/27–10/22 1995; Galleri Index, Stockholm (SE), 1/28–3/5 1995; Galerie Wang, Oslo (NO), 3/30–5/7 1995

Sabine Bitter/Helmut Weber (AT), *Urban Exercises,* 12/12–12/22 1995
Johanna Kandl (AT), *Der Kreis ist noch lange nicht geschlossen,* 12/12–12/22 1995

PUBLICATION
Olivier Richon, *After D.L.,* with a text from the artist and a conversation between Olivier Richon and Parveen Adams, Graz, Edition Camera Austria, 1995

CAMERA AUSTRIA AWARD
for Contemporary Photography by the City of Graz: David Goldblatt (ZA)

EDITIONS CAMERA AUSTRIA INTERNATIONAL
50/1995, 51–52/1995, 53/1995

1996

EXHIBITIONS
Stadtpark Zwei, with works by Max Aufischer, Petar Dabac, Seiichi Furuya, Klaus Dieter Hartl, Horáková & Maurer, Erich Kees, Elisabeth Kees-Kraus, Erich Lázár, Branko Lenart, Inge Morath, Eva Maria Ocherbauer, Michael Schuster, Christian Wachter, Manfred Willmann, Art Pavilion, Zagreb (HR), 10/22–11/12 1996; Photography Museum of Thessaloniki (GR), 6/26–7/25 1996
hybrid, with works by Katharina Copony, Thomas Feuerstein, Mathias Fuchs, Christina Göstl, Kurt Hengstschläger/Ulf Langheinrich, Helmut Mark, Christine Meierhofer, Norbert Pfaffenbichler, Herwig Turk, 6/12–7/7 1996
Radikale Bilder, exhibition for the II. Austrian Triennial for Photography, with works by Faisal Abdu'Allah/Clive Allen (GB), Art in Ruins (GB), Gilles Barbier (FR), Richard Billingham (GB), Sabine Bitter/Helmut Weber (AT), Anna and Bernhard Blume (DE), Henry Bond (GB), Alain Bublex (FR), Daniele Buetti (CH), Manuela Burkart (DE), Helen Chadwick (GB), Critical Art Ensemble (US), Petér Csikvári (HU), Thomas Demand (DE), Darko Fritz (HR), Rainer Ganahl (AT), G.R.A.M. (AT), Michael Hofstetter (DE), Gerald van der Kaap (NL), Ali Kepenek (DE), Ivana Keser (HR), Jürgen Klauke (DE), Allan McCollum/Laurie Simmons (US), John Miller (US), Christoph Nebel (AT), Shirin Neshat (IR/US), Tony Oursler (GB/US), Beate Passow (DE), Jack Pierson (US), Richard Prince (US), Sophie Ristelhueber (FR), Ugo Rondinone (CH), Klaus Scherübel (AT), Bruno Serralongue (FR), Andres Serrano (US), Cindy Sherman (US), Martin Sjoberg (SE), Stephen Willats (GB), in collaboration with Werner Fenz, Neue Galerie am Landesmuseum Joanneum, Graz, 6/15–7/28 1996

LECTURE
Granular – Synthesis, 6/14 1996

SYMPOSION ON PHOTOGRAPHY XVI
"Allan Sekula: Fish Story. Photography between Discourse and Document"
steirischer herbst '96, 10/18–10/20 1996
Lecturers: Michael Asher (US), Hartmut Bitomsky (DE/US), BüroBert (DE/CH), Chan-Kyong Park (KR), Kristin Ross (US), Allan Sekula (US), James Welling (US), Brigitte Werneburg (DE), Herta Wolf (AT/DE)
Billy Woodbury (US), *Bless Their Little Hearts,* film projection
Contributions published in: *Camera Austria International* 59–60/1997

PUBLICATION
Werner Fenz and Reinhard Braun, eds, *Radikale Bilder 1/2,* publication in two volumes for exhibition at II. Austrian Triennial for Photography, with text contributions from the editors and Art in Ruins, Paolo Bianchi, Francesco Bonami, Andreas Broeckmann, Critical Art Ensemble, Frits Gierstberg, Yve Lomax, Beate Passow, Andreas Spiegl, Michael Wetzel, Graz, Edition Camera Austria, 1996

EDITIONS CAMERA AUSTRIA INTERNATIONAL
54/1996, 55/1996, 56/1996

1997

EXHIBITIONS
Christian Wachter (AT), *Im Referenzmeer tauchen …,* 5/26–6/27 1997
Herwig Kempinger (AT), *The World Is Half Night,* 5/26–6/27 1997
Mitra Tabrizian (GB), *Minimal Utopia,* steirischer herbst '97, 10/18–11/14 1997

SYMPOSION ON PHOTOGRAPHY XVII
"Agents and Agencies: Photography between Discourse and Document II"

steirischer herbst '97, 10/17–10/19 1997
Lecturers: Geoffrey Batchen (US/AU),
Timothy Druckrey (US), Douglas Fogle (US),
Christian Höller (AT), Yve Lomax (GB),
Susanne Lummerding (AT), Sam Samore (US),
Beat Streuli (CH), Mitra Tabrizian (GB),
Ricardo Zulueta (US)
Contributions published in: *Camera Austria
International* 65–66/1998

PUBLICATION
Manfred Willmann, ed., *Stadtpark Zwei,*
with a text contribution by Reinhard Braun,
Graz, Edition Camera Austria, 1997

EDITIONS CAMERA AUSTRIA
INTERNATIONAL
57–58/1997, 59–60/1997

1998

EXHIBITIONS
Fotoarbeiten, with works by Maria
Hahnenkamp (AT), Matthias Herrmann (DE),
Elke Krystufek (AT), Friedl Kubelka (AT),
Cora Pongracz (AT), 4/18–5/29 1998
Branko Lenart (AT), *Kaddisch: 23 Nekro-
gramme,* 11/10–12/4 1998

PUBLICATIONS
*Friedl Kubelka, Schaulust. Ein Photobuch
der Schule für Künstlerische Photographie,*
Graz, Edition Camera Austria, 1998
Branko Lenart, Kaddisch, with a text
contribution by Johannes Schmidt,
Graz, Edition Camera Austria, 1998

EDITIONS CAMERA AUSTRIA
INTERNATIONAL
61/1998, 62–63/1998, 64/1998

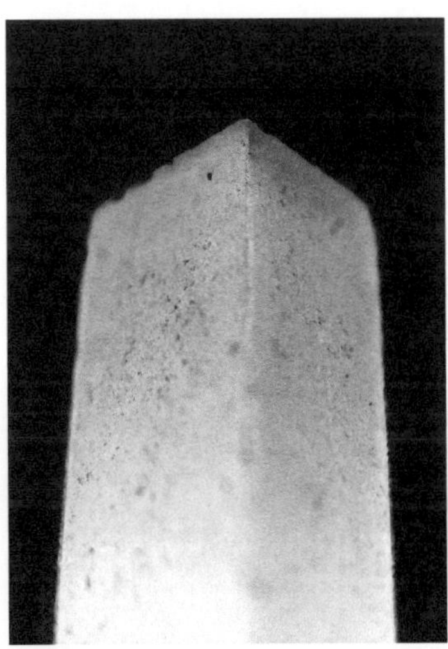

1999

EXHIBITIONS
Martin Parr (GB), *Common Sense,*
3/19–4/23 1999
Camera Austria 64–65, with works by Vlasta
Delimar (HR), Teresa Hubbard/Alexander
Birchler (GB/CH), Lois Renner (AT),
Joke Robaard (NL), Ed Ruscha (US),
Wolfgang Tillmans (DE), Lois Weinberger (AT),
Franz West (AT), 4/17–5/12 1999
Gottfried Bechtold (AT)/Hans Schabus (AT),
Fotoprofile, 9/3–9/17 1999
Dub Housing, with works by Dan Holdsworth
(GB), Tedros Haile (GB), Mark Hall (GB),
Nick Knight (GB), Cathie Pilkington (GB), in
collaboration with Jason Evans, in conjunction
with the project RE-MAKE/RE-MODEL,
steirischer herbst '99, 9/25–10/24 1999

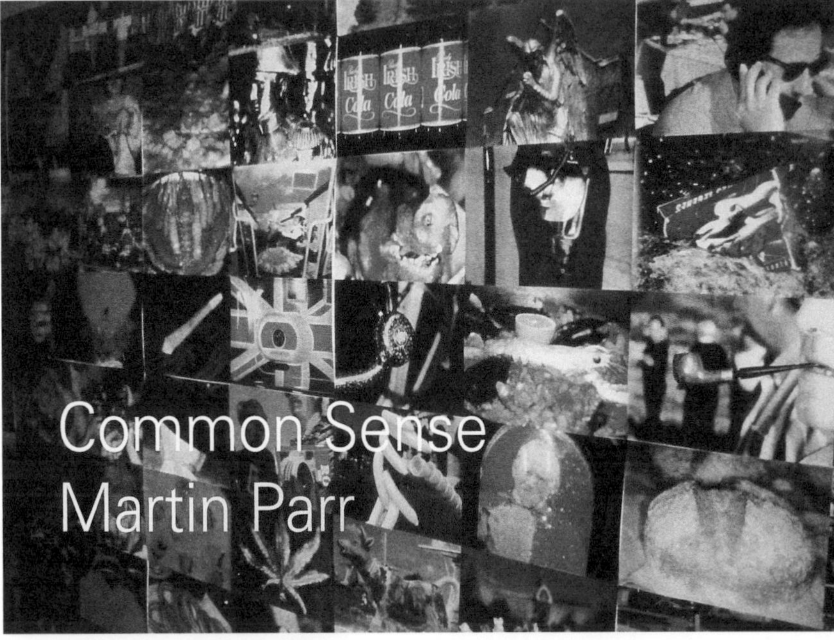

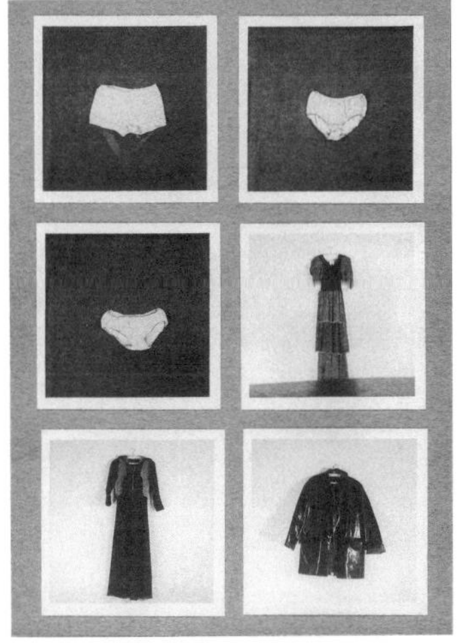

Hans-Peter Feldmann (DE), *Künstlerbücher,*
12/3–12/23 1999

PUBLICATION
Rosa Brueckl and Gregor Schmoll, *Das
Frühwerk,* Graz, Edition Camera Austria, 1999

CAMERA AUSTRIA AWARD
for Contemporary Photography by the
City of Graz: Hans-Peter Feldmann

EDITIONS CAMERA AUSTRIA
INTERNATIONAL
65/1999, 66/1999, 67/1999, 68/1999

2000

EXHIBITIONS
Michael Janiszewski (DE), *Fotoarbeiten
1990–1999,* 4/9–5/19 2000
Milica Tomić (YU), *I am Milica Tomić,*
5/25–5/31 2000
Milica Tomić (RS) and Róza El-Hassan (HU),
Thinking about Overpopulation, Performance/
stroll through Graz, documented by Seiichi
Furuya, 5/26 2000
Camilo José Vergara (US), *The New American
Ghetto,* an event by HdA – Haus der Architektur
in collaboration with Camera Austria,
7/11–9/1 2000
Art in Ruins (GB), *Party Time,*
steirischer herbst 2000, 10/8–11/5 2000

PUBLICATION
Manfred Willmann ed., *Michael Janiszewski,
Fotoarbeiten 1990–1999,* with a text
contribution by Heinz Schütz,
Graz, Edition Camera Austria, 2000

EDITIONS CAMERA AUSTRIA
INTERNATIONAL
69/2000, 70/2000, 71/2000, 72/2000

2001

EXHIBITIONS
Seiichi Furuya (JP/AT), *Portrait,* 3/28–5/4 2001
Nobuyoshi Araki (JP), *Akt–Tokyo. 1971–1991,*
6/29–8/10 2001
Jörg Schlick (AT), *Poésie Noire. Für Elisabeth
Printschitz,* steirischer herbst '01,
10/7–10/28 2001
Ulrike Lienbacher (AT), *Pin up Übungen,* 2001
and *10+10 Fotografien,* 2000,
12/7 2001–1/31 2002

CAMERA AUSTRIA AWARD
for Contemporary Photography by the
City of Graz: Allan Sekula (US)

EDITIONS CAMERA AUSTRIA
INTERNATIONAL
73/2001, 74/2001, 75/2001, 76/2001

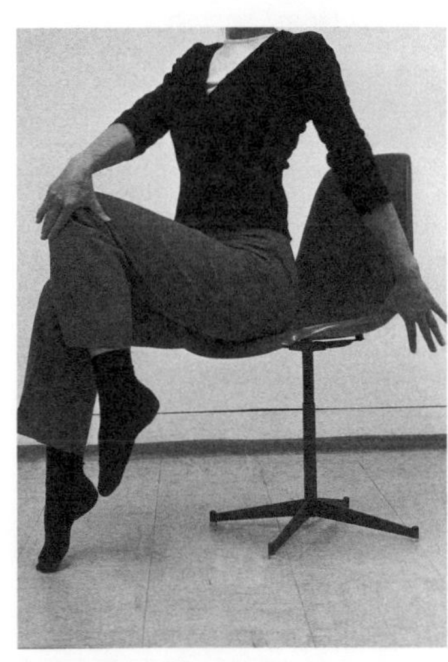

2002

EXHIBITIONS
Alexandra Vogt (DE), *Stay With Me,*
4/21–5/17 2002
Allan Sekula (US), *Waiting for Tear Gas,*
10/4–10/18 2002
Michael Schuster (AT), *DROMBEG,*
10/27–11/24 2002

PUBLICATION
Hans-Peter Feldmann, *Graz,*
Graz, Edition Camera Austria;
Düsseldorf, 3 Möven Verlag, 2002

EDITIONS CAMERA AUSTRIA
INTERNATIONAL
77/2002, 78/2002, 79/2002, 80/2002

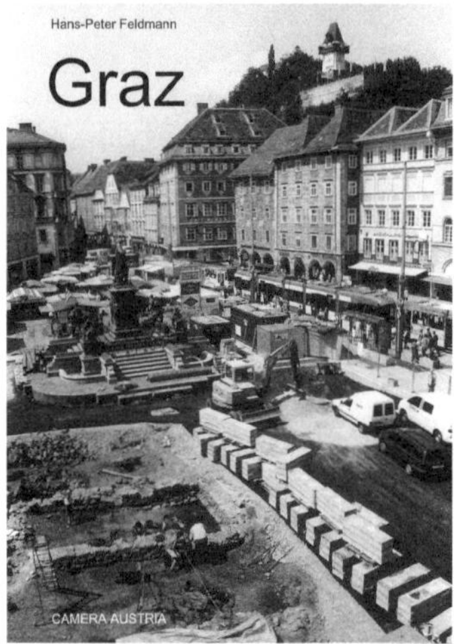

2003

EXHIBITIONS
Hans-Peter Feldmann (DE), *Graz,*
1/10–2/28 2003
Tatiana Lecomte (FR/AT), *Orte,*
3/10–4/11 2003
Freundschaftsspiel, with works by Rudolf
Bonvie, Petar Dabac, Seiichi Furuya, Matthias
Herrmann, Rainer Iglar, Wilmar Koenig,
Timm Rautert, Anja Rösch, Hans Schabus,
Jörg Schlick, Michael Schuster, Wolfgang
Vollmer, Christian Wachter, Manfred Willmann,
4/27–5/30 2003
European Eyes on Japan, with works by
Michael Danner (DE), Margherita Spiluttini
(AT), Agnieszka Wolodzko (PL), Palais Thienfeld,
Graz, 7/26–8/24 2003, a project from Graz
2003 – Capital of Culture Europe, realized with
support from EU Japan Fest, Tokyo
Positions in Japanese Photography, with works
by Mao Ishikawa, Keizo Kitajima, Kisei
Kobayashi, Mika Ninagawa, Sakiko Nomura,
Masafumi Sanai, Tomoko Sawada, Risaku
Suzuki, Kyoichi Tsuzuki, 10/4–11/2 2003,
a project from Graz 2003 Capital of Culture
Europe, realised with support by EU Japan
Fest, Tokyo
*Pierre Bourdieu, In Algerien. Zeugnisse der
Entwurzelung,* 11/15 2003–2/6 2004, in
collaboration with Franz Schultheis,
Fondation Bourdieu, St. Gallen, a project by
Camera Austria in collaboration with Graz
2003 – Capital of Culture Europe; the
exhibition in Graz was preceded by the
presentation of the project in Paris,
*Pierre Bourdieu. Images d'Algérie. Une affinité
élective,* 1/23–3/2 2003, Institut du Monde
Arabe, Paris, further exhibition stops:
Institut Franco-Japonais de Tokyo, Tokyo (JP),
4/20–5/22 2004;

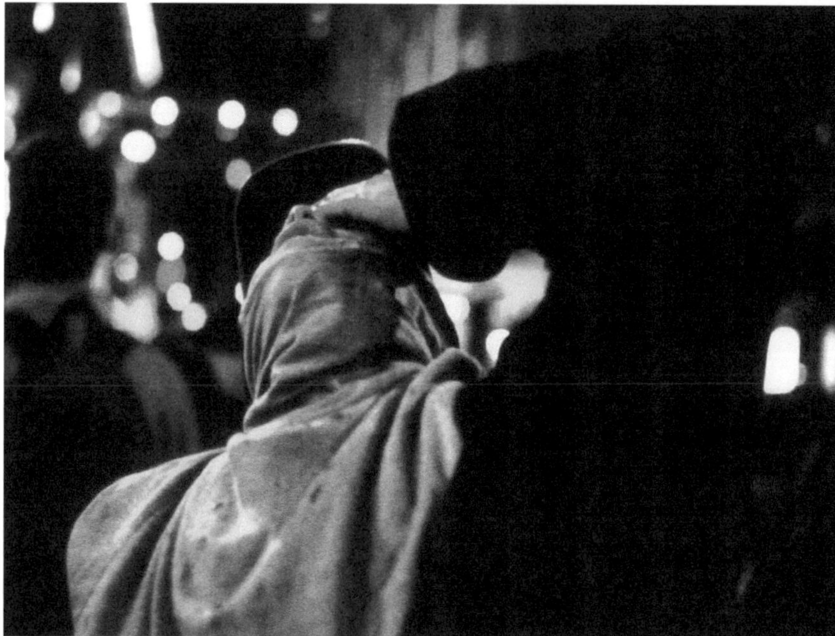

Daelim Contemporary Art Museum, Seoul (KR),
6/11–7/18 2004; The Photographers' Gallery,
London (GB), 10/15–11/28 2004;
BildMuseet, Umeå universitet, Umeå (SE),
10/31 2004–1/23 2005; Gallery of Contempo-
rary Art, Celje (SI), 1/25–2/24 2005; Aspekte
Galerie der MVHS im Gasteig, Munich (DE),
3/8–5/8 2005; Centre de la Photographie,
Genève (CH), 3/15–4/9 2005; Centre Culturel
Français, Freiburg i.Br. (DE), 4/15–5/28 2005;
Galerie im Taxispalais, Innsbruck (AT),
9/9–10/16 2005; Shedhalle, Rote Fabrik,
Zürich (CH), 2/28–5/7 2006;
Bibliothèque Nationale d'Algérie, Algier (DZ),
3/1–3/31 2006, Centre Culturel Français,
Constantine (DZ), 4/7–5/11 2006;
Centre Culturel Français, Tlemcen (DZ),
5/20–6/10 2006; Deichtorhallen, Hamburg
(DE), 6/22–9/3 2006; Goldsmiths College,
University of London, London (GB),
October 2006 – June 2007; Kahn Liberal Arts
Institute, Smith College, Northampton (US),
1/15–3/21 2007; Karşı Sanat Çalışmaları,
Istanbul (TR), 5/3–6/1 2007;
ENS/Ecole normale supérieure Lettres et
sciences humaines, Lyon (FR), 5/5–6/15 2008;
Universität Konstanz, Konstanz (DE),
1/17–3/2 2009; MUCEM/Musée des
Civilisations de l'Europe et de la Méditerranée,
Marseille (FR), 11/5–12/6 2009;
Círculo de Bellas Artes, Madrid (ES),
10/13 2011–1/15 2012; Université de
Strasbourg (FR), 11/26 2011–2/12 2012;
Centre du Patrimoine Arménien, Valence (FR),
3/15–5/27 2012; Università di Modena e
Reggio Emilia, Modena (IT), 5/11–6/30 2012;
Jeu de Paume/Château de Tours, Tours (FR),
6/16–11/4 2012

SYMPOSION ON PHOTOGRAPHY XVIII
"Positions in Japanese Photography"
10/31–11/1 2003
Lecturers: Masafumi Fukagawa, Toshiharu Ito,
Mao Ishikawa, Michiko Kasahara,
Kazue Kobata, Shino Kuraishi, Minoru Shimizu,
Kyoichi Tsuzuki, Toshiya Ueno
Contributions published in: *Camera Austria
International* 84/2003

PUBLICATIONS
David Barriet, David Benassayag, Beatrice
Didier, Christine Frisinghelli et al., eds,
Allan Sekula, TITANIC's wake,
Graz, Edition Camera Austria, 2003
Christine Frisinghelli and Franz Schultheis, eds,

*Pierre Bourdieu: In Algerien. Zeugnisse der
Entwurzelung,* Graz, Edition Camera Austria,
2003

CAMERA AUSTRIA AWARD
for Contemporary Photography by the
City of Graz: Aglaia Konrad (AT)

EDITIONS CAMERA AUSTRIA
INTERNATIONAL
81/2003, 82/2003, 83/2003, 84/2003

2004

EXHIBITIONS
Der Widerstand der Fotografie, with works by
Lisa Holzer (AT), Sabina Hörtner (AT),
Werner Kaligofsky (AT), Ulrike Lienbacher (AT),
Barbara Probst (DE), Klaus Schuster (AT),
2/14–3/28 2004
Sol LeWitt, Photography, 4/3–5/30 2004,
in collaboration with George Stolz,
in cooperation with Kunsthaus Graz
Aglaia Konrad (AT), *KOPIE/CITY-Graz 2004,*
5/12–8/1 2004
Gerald van der Kaap (NL), *Jump Cut,*
8/14–9/26 2004
*Bleiben oder Gehen/Ostati ili otići/Staying or
Leaving,* with works by Ana Hušman (HR),
Oliver Musovik (MK), Dan Panaitescu (RO),
Maria Papadimitriou (GR), Randa Shaath (ET),
Ahlam Shibli (PS), Efrat Shvily (IL), Mladen

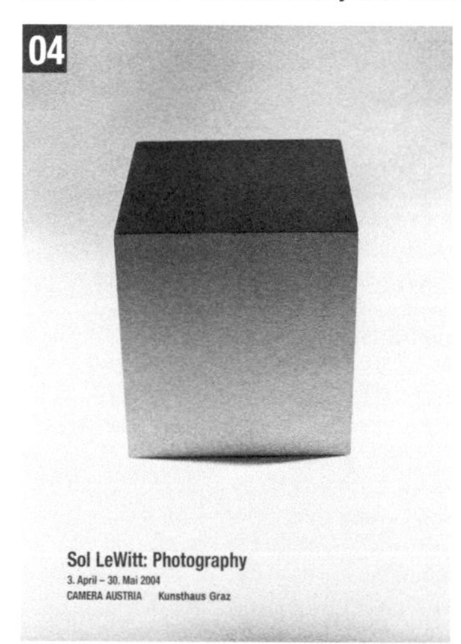

"

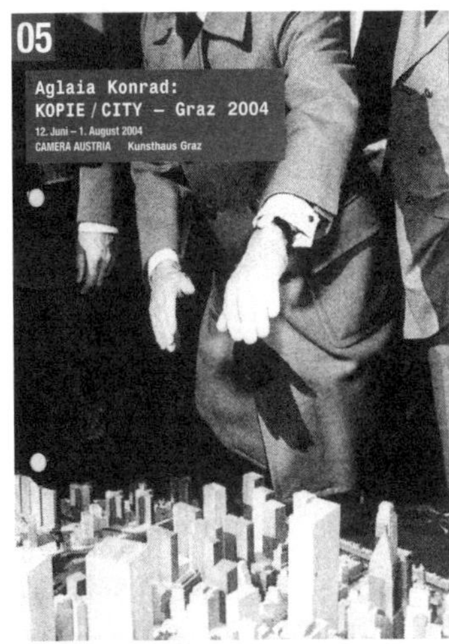

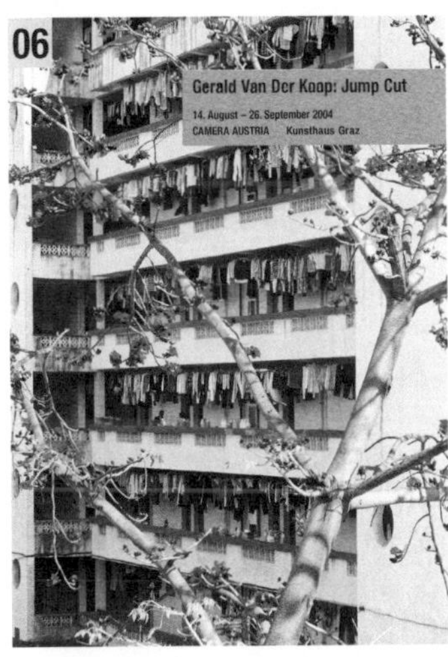

Stilinović (HR), 10/9–11/28 2004; 9/8–9/27 2004, Umjetnički Paviljon, Zagreb (HR), in collaboration with Sandra Križić Roban and Hrvatski fotosavez, Zagreb, and in cooperation with steirischer herbst '04
Seiichi Furuya (JP/AT), *alive,* 12/11 2004–1/23 2005, curator Monika Faber

SYMPOSION ON PHOTOGRAPHY XIX
"Pierre Bourdieus View on the Social World,"
1/23–1/24 2004
Lecturers: Christian Fleck (AT), Elisabeth Katschnig-Fasch (AT), Franz Schultheis (CH), Jochen Becker (DE), Cathren Müller (AT), Ulf Wuggenig (DE)

PUBLICATION
Künstlerhaus Wien, Sandro Droschl, and Norbert Pfaffenbichler, eds, *Abstraction Now,* with texts by Miguel Carvalhais, Sandro Droschl, Christian Höller, Lev Manovich, Norbert Pfaffenbichler, Marc Ries, Marie Röbl, Graz, Edition Camera Austria, 2004

EDITIONS CAMERA AUSTRIA INTERNATIONAL
85/2004, 86/2004, 87/2004, 88/2004

2005

EXHIBITIONS
Double Check. Die Re-Definition von Raum in der Fotografie: Gegen-Räume, synchrone Geschichte(n), 2/5–3/20 2005, with works by Carlos Aires (ES), Barbara Caspar (AT), Eclipse (SLO), Petra Gerschner (DE), Frances Goodman (SA), Emma Hedditch (GB), IRWIN (SI), Dorit Margreiter (AT), Aydan Mürtezaoglu

(TR), Tanja Ostojić (YU), Jack Pierson (US), Oliver Ressler (AT), Erzen Shkololli (Kosovo), Kamera Skura (CZ), Weekend Art (HR), Anita Witek (AT), in collaboration with Marina Gržinić and Walter Seidl, in cooperation with the Gallery of Contemporary Art, Celje (SI) Allan Sekula (US), *TITANIC's wake,* 4/2–5/22 2005
Chikaku. Zeit und Erinnerung in Japan, with works by Masaki Fujihata, Rieko Hidaka, Takashi Ito, Emiko Kasahara, Tadashi Kawamata, Yayoi Kusama, Trinh T. Minh-ha, Hiroyuki Moriwaki, Daido Moriyama, Takuma Nakahira, Tetsuya Nakamura, Motohiko Odani, Taro Okamoto, Yoko Ono, Yutaka Sone, Yoshihiro Suda, Hiroshi Sugimoto, Masaaki Yamada, Makoto Sei Watanabe, Miwa Yanagi, 6/5–9/11 2005, Kurator Toshiharu Ito, Tokyo National University of Fine Arts and Music, Tokio, in collaboration with Adam Budak, Kunsthaus Graz, Seiichi Furuya, Camera Austria and Miki Okabe, The Japan Foundation BitterWeber (AT), *Live Like This!,* 10/1–11/18 2005; Plattform, Berlin, 4/21–5/28 2006, in cooperation with steirischer herbst 2005
David Goldblatt (ZA), *Intersections,* 11/26 2005–2/26 2006

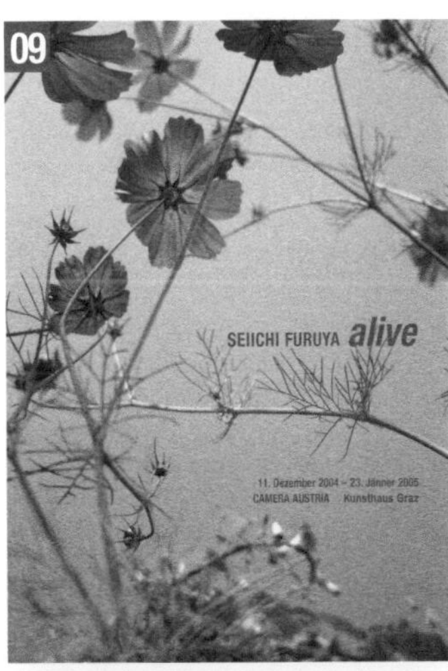

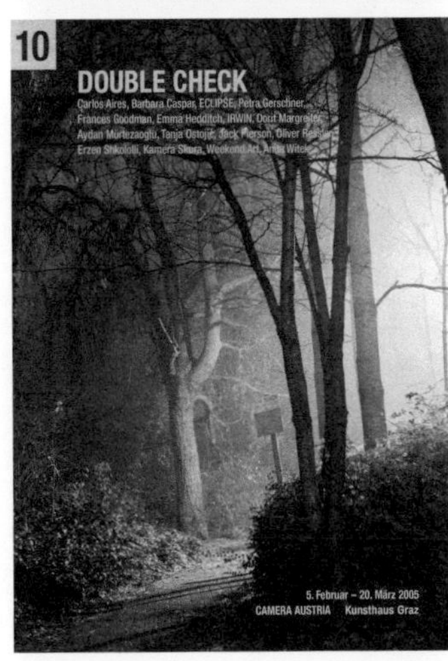

PUBLICATION
Reinhard Braun, ed., *BitterWeber, Live Like This!,* with texts by Catherine David, Reinhard Braun, Jeff Derksen, and Neil Smith, as well as a conversation of the artists with Bik Van der Pol [Liesbeth Bik, Jos van der Pol], Ken Lum, Andrea Geyer, Jayce Salloum, Marina Gržinić, David Thorne and Julia Meltzer (The Speculative Archive), Graz, Edition Camera Austria, 2005

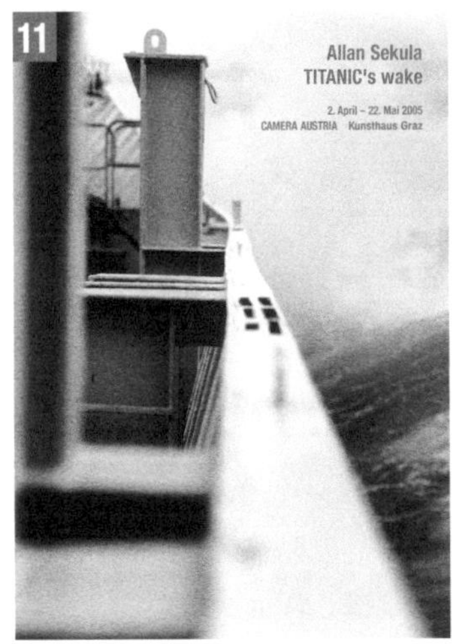

CAMERA AUSTRIA AWARD
for Contemporary Photography by the City of Graz: Walid Raad (LB)

EDITIONS CAMERA AUSTRIA INTERNATIONAL
89/2005, 90/2005, 91/2005, 92/2005

2006

EXHIBITIONS
Jo Spence, Beyond the Perfect Image, 4/1–6/25 2006, in collaboration with Jorge Ribalta and Terry Dennett, in cooperation with the Museu d'Art Contemporani de Barcelona (ES)
First the artist defines meaning. Zum Paradigma des Konzeptuellen, with works by Miles Coolidge (CA), Ralf Hoedt (DE), Joachim Koester (DK), Peter Piller (DE), Nicole Six & Paul Petritsch (AT), Christine Würmell (DE), 7/8–9/10 2006
knowing you, knowing me. Zur Komplizenschaft mit Bildern, 9/24–11/26 2006, with works by Thomas Feuerstein (AT), Andrea Geyer/Sharon Hayes (DE/US), G.R.A.M. (AT), Rainer Oldendorf (DE), Marco Poloni (CH), Mark Raidpere (EE), in cooperation with steirischer herbst 2006
Peter Dressler (AT), *Greifbare Schönheit,* 12/8 2006–2/25 2007

PUBLICATIONS
Max Aufischer, Werner Fenz, and Manfred Willmann, eds, *Erich Kees, in mir,* with texts by Jasmin Haselsteiner-Scharner and Monika Faber, Graz, Edition Camera Austria, 2006
Diedrich Diederichsen, Christine Frisinghelli, Christoph Gurk, Juliane Rebentisch et al., eds, *Golden Years. Materialien und Positionen zu queerer Subkultur und Avantgarde zwischen 1959 und 1974,* with texts by the editors and by Mike Kelley, Terre Thaemlitz, Jim Hoberman, Jerry Tartaglia, Douglas Crimp, AA Bronson, et al., in cooperation with steirischer herbst 2006, Graz, Edition Camera Austria, 2006

EDITIONS CAMERA AUSTRIA INTERNATIONAL
93/2006, 94/2006, 95/2006, 96/2007

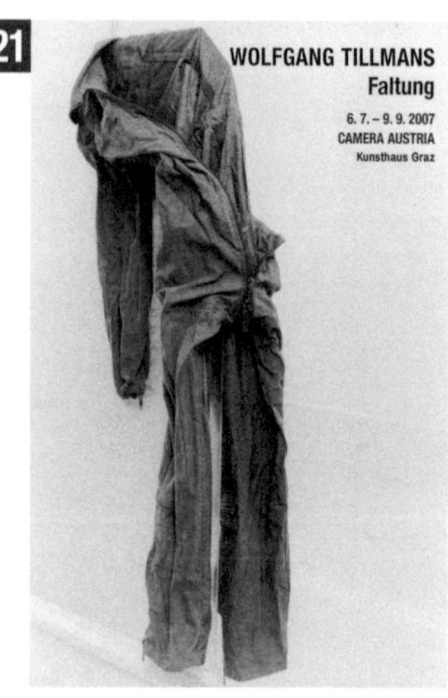

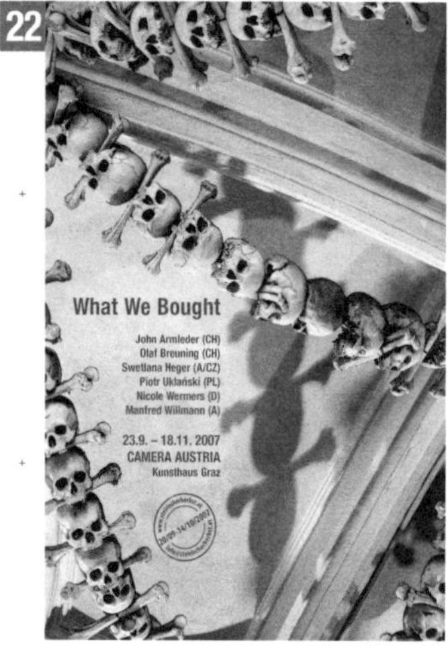

2007

EXHIBITIONS
Sie befinden sich hier, with works by Marika Asatiani (GE), Christoph Grill (AT), Sylvia Henrich (DE), Karina Nimmerfall (AT), SofijaSilvia (HR), Verena Winkelmann (NO), Andrea Witzmann (AT), 3/10–5/1 2007
Einar Schleef, Kontaktbögen, 5/12–6/24 2007, in collaboration with Regine Herrmann and the Akademie der Künste, Berlin (DE)
Wolfgang Tillmans (DE), *Faltung,* 7/6–9/9 2007
What We Bought, 9/23–11/18 2007, with works by John Armleder (CH), Olaf Breuning (CH), Swetlana Heger (AT/CZ), Piotr Uklański (PL), Nicole Wermers (DE), Manfred Willmann (AT), in cooperation with

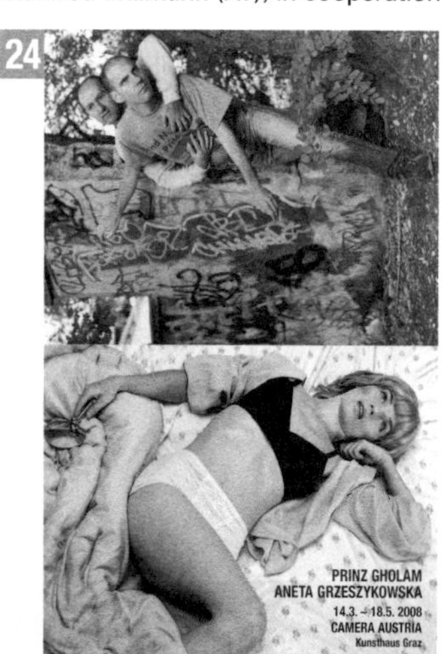

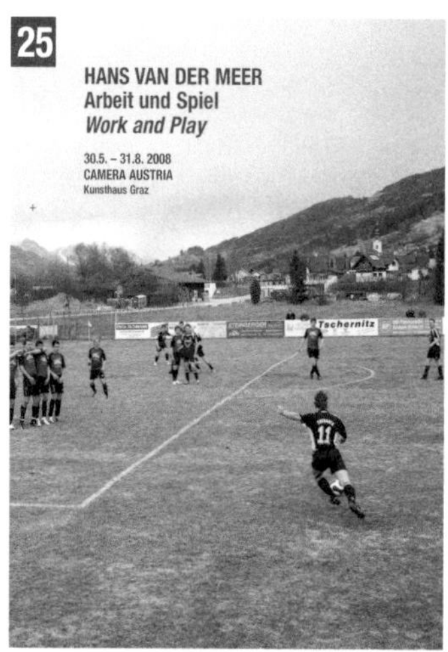

steirischer herbst 2007
I am not afraid. The Market Photo Workshop, Johannesburg, with works by Bonile Bam, Jodi Bieber, Lerato Maduna, Sabelo Mlangeni, Zanele Muholi, Nontsikelelo Veleko, 12/1 2007–3/2 2008, further exhibition stops: Aspekte Galerie, Volkshochschule Munich (DE); Langhans Galerie Prag (CZ); Johannesburg Art Gallery, Johannesburg (ZA)

SYMPOSION ON PHOTOGRAPHY XX
"The Market Photo Workshop, Johannesburg/Camera Austria Nr. 100"
12/1 2007
Lecturers: John Fleetwood (ZA), Nontsikelelo Veleko (ZA), Zanele Muholi (ZA), Marika Asatiani (GE), Herta Wolf (AT)
Contributions published in: *Camera Austria International* 100/2007

PUBLICATIONS
Maren Lübbke-Tidow, ed., *Karina Nimmerfall, cinematic maps,* with an introduction by Raimar Stange and an essay by Norman M. Klein, Graz, Edition Camera Austria, 2007
Manfred Willmann, ed., *Camera Austria International: Index Nr. 1/1980–100/2007,* edited by Heidi Oswald and Anja Rösch, Graz, Edition Camera Austria, 2007

CAMERA AUSTRIA AWARD
for Contemporary Photography by the City of Graz: Marika Asatiani (GE)

EDITIONS CAMERA AUSTRIA INTERNATIONAL
97/2007, 98/2007, 99/2007, 100/2007

2008

EXHIBITIONS
Prinz Gholam (DE/LB), Aneta Grzeszykowska (PL), 3/14–5/18 2008
Hans van der Meer (NL), *Arbeit und Spiel,* 5/30–8/31 2008, in collaboration with Frits Gierstberg and the Nederlands Fotomuseum, Rotterdam (NL)
Elke Krystufek (AT), *Für das Glück zuständig,* 10/5 2008–1/18 2009, in cooperation with steirischer herbst 2008

PUBLICATIONS
Christine Frisinghelli, ed., *Elke Krystufek, Nein,* with a text by the artist, Graz, Edition Camera Austria, 2008
Reinhard Braun, ed., *Common Affairs,* with texts by Ursula Biermann, Reinhard Braun, Mladen Bizumic, Petra Gördüren, a conversation between Josephine Meckseper and Simone Schimpl aswell as a conversation between Lily van der Stocker and Amy Kellner,

steirischer herbst 2008, Graz, Edition Camera Austria, 2008.

EDITIONS CAMERA AUSTRIA INTERNATIONAL
101/2008, 102/2008, 103–104/2008

2009

EXHIBITIONS
Bahman Jalali (IR), 1/30–4/13 2009, in collaboration with Catherine David and the Fundació Antoni Tàpies, Barcelona (ES)
Then the work takes place. Zum Paradigma des Konzeptuellen in der zeitgenössischen Fotografie, with works by Marine Hugonnier (FR), Joachim Koester (DK), Sharon Lockhart (US), Jean-Luc Mylayne (FR), Peter Piller (DE), Hans Schabus (AT), Christopher Williams (US), 4/25–6/28 2009
Annette Kelm (DE), 7/10–9/13 2009
Artur Żmijewski (PL), *Democracies und andere Arbeiten,* 9/27 2009–1/17 2010, in cooperation with steirischer herbst 2009

LECTURES
Peter Piller (DE), "Vorzüge der Absichtslosigkeit," 4/23 2009
Yilmaz Dziewior (DE), "Referenz und Abstraktion im Werk von Annette Kelm," 7/8 2009

CAMERA AUSTRIA AWARD
for Contemporary Photography by the City of Graz: Sanja Iveković (HR)

EDITIONS CAMERA AUSTRIA INTERNATIONAL
105/2009, 106/2009, 107/2009, 108/2009

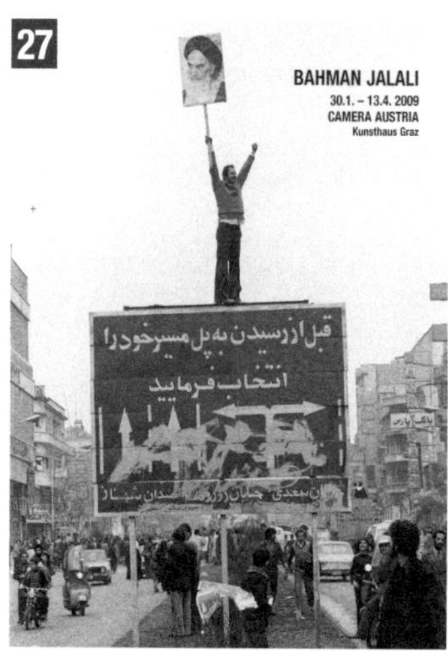

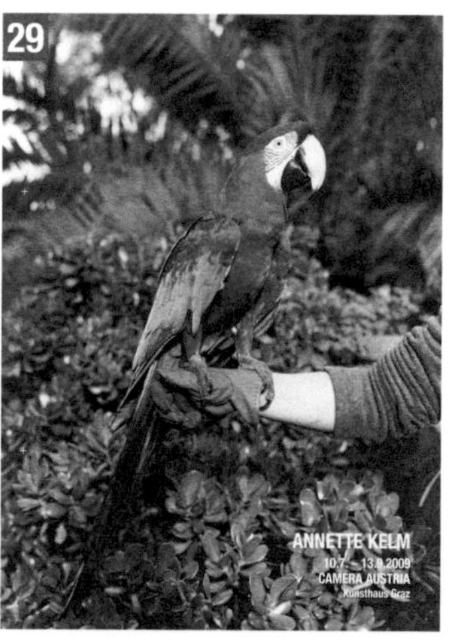

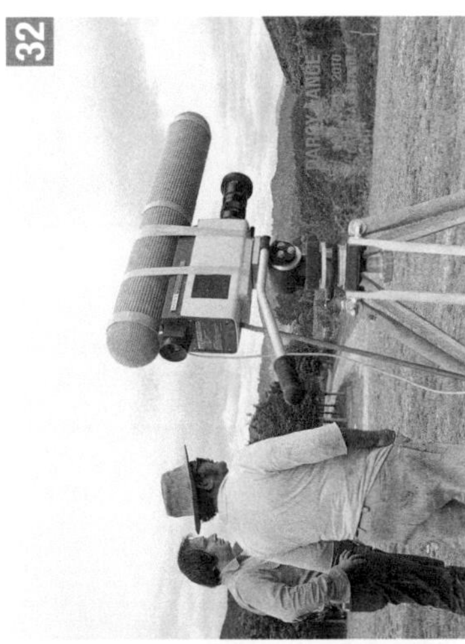

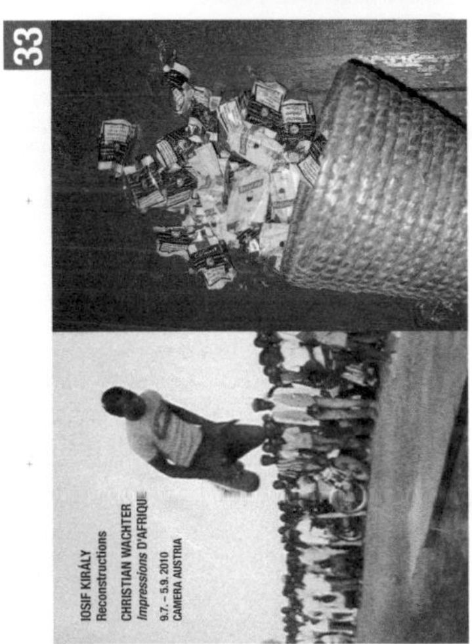

2010

EXHIBITIONS

Walid Raad (LB), *Sweet Talk: Commissions (Beirut),* 1/29–4/5 2010
Darcy Lange (NZ), 4/17–6/27 2010, in collaboration with Mercedes Vicente and the Govett-Brewster Art Gallery, New Plymouth (NZ), with support by the Darcy Lange Estate and the New Zealand Film Archive
Iosif Király (RO), *Reconstructions*
Christian Wachter (AT), *Impressions D'AFRIQUE,* 7/9–9/5 2010
Milk Drop Coronet. 30 Ausstellungen zur Virtuosität des Dinglichen, with works by Thomas Bayrle (DE), Walead Beshty (GB), Björn Braun (DE), Agnieszka Brzeżańska (PL), Natalie Czech (DE), Jeanne Faust (DE), Hans-Peter Feldmann (DE), Aurélien Froment (FR), Sylvia Henrich (DE), Horáková + Maurer (CZ/AT), Susan Howe/James Welling (US), Margarete Jakschik (PL), Annette Kelm (DE), Herwig Kempinger (AT), Heinz Peter Knes (DE), Ernst Koslitsch (AT), Tatiana Lecomte (FR/AT), Jochen Lempert (DE), Ulrike Lienbacher (AT), Lotte Lyon (AT), Eva Maria Ocherbauer (AT), Markéta Othová (CZ), Michael Schmidt (DE), Gregor Schmoll (AT), Roman Schramm (DE), Stefanie Seufert (DE), Dirk Stewen (DE), Josef Strau (AT), Barbara Trautmann (DE), Susanne Winterling (DE), 9/26 2010–1/9 2011, in cooperation with steirischer herbst 2010

LECTURE

Mercedes Vicente, "Darcy Lange: Beyond Observation," 4/15 2010

305

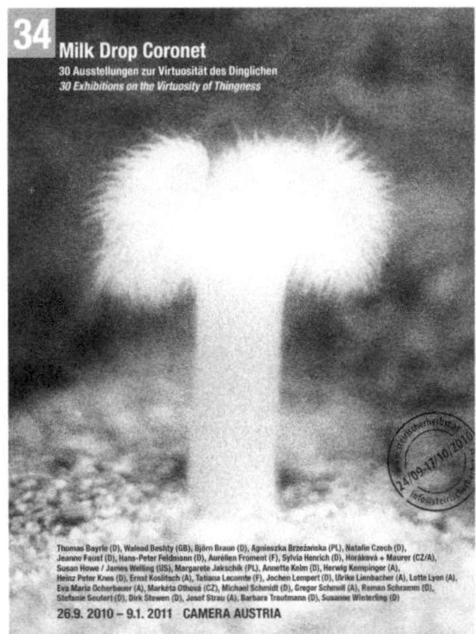

PUBLICATIONS

Archiv Peter Piller: Materialien (D). Peripheriewanderung Graz, Graz: Edition Camera Austria, 2010.
Koko Okano and Christine Frisinghelli, eds, *Seiichi Furuya: Mémoires. 1984–1987,* with a text by Einar Schleef, Graz, Edition Camera Austria, 2010

EDITIONS CAMERA AUSTRIA INTERNATIONAL

109/2010, 110/2010, 111/2010, 112/2010

2011

EXHIBITIONS

Šejla Kamerić (BA), Tatiana Lecomte (FR/AT), 1/21–3/27 2011
Communitas. Die unrepräsentierbare Gemeinschaft, with works by Martin Beck (AT/US), Sabine Bitter/Helmut Weber (AT/CA), Sharon Hayes (US), Heidrun Holzfeind (AT/US), Maryam Jafri (PK/US), Sanja Iveković (HR), Clemens von Wedemeyer (DE), 4/9–6/19 2011
Tobias Zielony (DE), *Manitoba,* 7/8–9/4 2011
Communitas. Unter anderen, with works by Yael Bartana (IL), Laurence Bonvin (CH), Peggy Buth (DE), Rabih Mroué (LB), Artur Żmijewski (PL), ArtTerritories: Ursula Biemann (CH)/Shuruq Harb (PS) with contributions by: Rheim Alkadhi (IQ/US), Youmna Chlala (LB), Ganzeer (EG), Ahmad Hosni (EG), Michael Kennedy (US), Yazan Khalili (SY/PS), Karem Said (EG), VJ Um Amel (EG), 9/25 2011–1/1 2012, in cooperation with steirischer herbst 2011

PUBLICATION

Reinhard Braun ed., *Tatiana Lecomte, Dissolution,* with texts by Reinhard Braun and Manuela Ammer, Graz, Edition Camera Austria, 2011

CAMERA AUSTRIA AWARD

for Contemporary Photography by the City of Graz: Heidrun Holzfeind (AT)

EDITIONS CAMERA AUSTRIA INTERNATIONAL

113/2011, 114/2011, 115/2011, 116/2011

2012

EXHIBITIONS

The Urban Cultures of Global Prayers, with works by Gilles Aubry (CH), Sabine Bitter/Helmut Weber (AT/CA), Lía Dansker (AR), Aryo Danusiri (ID), Katja Eydel (DE), Frida Hartz (MX), Magdalena Kallenberger/
Dorothea Nold (DE), Verónica Mastrosimone (AR), Rika Collective (KE), Sandra Schäfer (DE), Surabhi Sharma (IN), Sevgi Ortaç (TR), Jens Wenkel/Lagos Film Workshop (NG), Paola Yacoub (LB), 1/28–4/1 2012, an exhibition by NGBK in conjunction with "Erlösung und Befreiung in der Stadt," by global prayers, in cooperation with Camera Austria
Margherita Spiluttini (AT), *und dann (reframing architecture),* 4/21–6/10 2012
DLF 1874. Die Biografie der Bilder, with works by Annegang, Werner Feiersinger, Michael Höpfner, Rainer Iglar, Krüger & Pardeller, Tatiana Lecomte, Mahony, Dorit Margreiter, Christian Mayer, Susanne Miggitsch, Gregor Neuerer, Tina Ribarits, Constanze Ruhm, Günther Selichar, Michael Strasser, Anita Witek, 6/30–9/2 2012, an exhibition by the austrian Photocollection of the Federation, in collaboration with Ruth Horak
Art Is Concrete. And So Is Truth?, with works by Anna Jermolaewa (RU), subREAL (RO), Helmut and Johanna Kandl (AT), Stefan Panhans (DE), G.R.A.M. (AT), Stefanie Seibold (DE), Christodoulos Panayiotou (CY), 9/30 2012–2/17 2013, in cooperation with steirischer herbst 2012

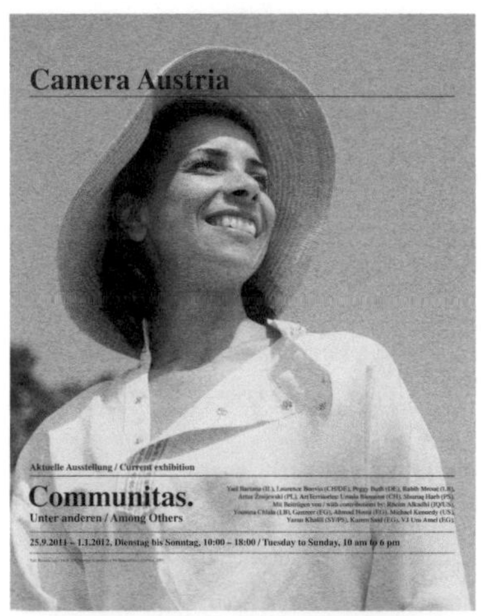

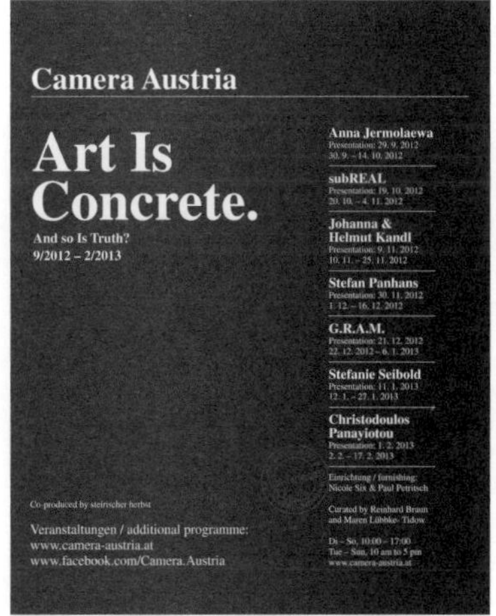

PUBLICATIONS

Bundesministerium für Unterricht, Kunst und Kultur ed., *DLF 1874. Die Biografie der Bilder,* Graz, Camera Austria, Vienna, Edition Fotohof, 2012
Stefanie Seufert, with texts by Florian Ebner and Christine Heidemann, Graz, Edition Camera Austria, 2012

EDITIONS CAMERA AUSTRIA INTERNATIONAL

117/2012, 118/2012, 119/2012, 120/2012

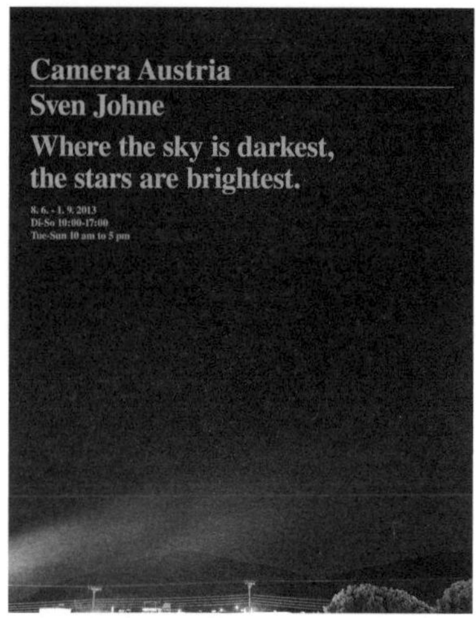

2013

EXHIBITIONS

Zero Point of Meaning. Non-functional, Non-representational, Elementary, Experimental and Conceptual Photography in Croatia, with works by Boris Cvjetanović, Petar Dabac, Sandro Đukić, Igor Eškinja, Ivan Faktor, Tomislav Gotovac, Boris Greiner, Miljenko Horvat, Vlatka Horvat, Željko Jerman, David Maljković, Antun Maračić, Enes Midžić, Marijan Molnar, Ivan Posavec, Davor Sanvincenti, Edita Schubert, Mladen Stilinović, Slaven Tolj, Goran Trbuljak, Josip Vaništa, Mirjana Vodopija, Fedor Vučemilović, 3/9–5/26 2013, in collaboration with Sandra Križić Roban and Ivana Hanaček, in cooperation with Institute of Art History, Zagreb (HR), and Croatian Photographic Union, Zagreb (HR)
Sven Johne (DE), *Where the sky is darkest, the stars are brightest,* 6/8–9/1 2013
Unexpected Encounters, with 0gms [(Sofia) Kamen Stoyanov, Ivan Moudov in collaboration with Nemanja Cvijanović, Anetta Mona Chisa/Lucia Tkáčová, Pravdoliub Ivanov]; Beirut [(Kairo) Jens Maier-Rothe, Sarah Rifky, Antonia Alampi, Habiba Effat in collaboration with Malak Helmy, Hassan Khan, Mada Masr, Jasmina Metwaly]; Kontekst collective [(Belgrad) in collaboration with Nina Höchtl, KURS, Bojana Piškur/Đorđe Balmazović (REC/Škart)], 9/22–11/17 2013, in cooperation with steirischer herbst 2013
Skulptur, with works by Laurie Kang (CA), Kasia Klimpel (PL/NL), Lotte Lyon (AT), Christian Mayer (AT), Peter Puklus (HU), Carly Steward (US), Michael Strasser (AT), Anita Witek (AT), 12/7 2013–2/16 2014

PUBLICATIONS

Stefanie Seibold, *images = images. Re-Reading the Performance Works of Gina Pane,* Graz, Edition Camera Austria, 2013
Sven Johne, *Where the sky is darkest, the stars are brightest,* Graz, Edition Camera Austria, 2013
Reinhard Braun ed., *Martin Behr, Martin Osterider, Triester,* Edition 1–8, Graz, Edition Camera Austria, 2013

CAMERA AUSTRIA AWARD

for Contemporary Photography by the City of Graz: Joachim Koester (DK)

EDITIONS CAMERA AUSTRIA INTERNATIONAL

121/2013, 122/2013, 123/2013, 124/2013

2014

EXHIBITIONS

Joachim Koester (DK), *The Ghost Shop,* 3/15–5/25 2014
once documentary, with works by Sven Augustijnen (BE), Eric Baudelaire (FR), Peggy Buth (DE), Maryam Jafri (US), 6/6–9/7 2014
The Militant Image. Picturing What Is Already Going on, Or The Poetics of the Militant Image, with works by Raymond Boisjoly (CA), Harun Farocki (DE), Peter Friedl (AT), Sharon Hayes (US), Marine Hugonnier (BE), Alfredo Jaar (US), Emily Jacir (PS), Walid Sadek (LB), Jayce Salloum (CA), Ines Schaber (DE), Paola Yacoub (LB), 9/28–11/16 2014, a project by Urban Subjects (Sabine Bitter, Jeff Derksen, Helmut Weber) in collaboration with Camera Austria, in cooperation with steirischer herbst 2014
Archives, Re-Assemblances, and Surveys, with works by Sabine Bitter/Helmut Weber, Heidrun Holzfeind, Michael Höpfner, Krüger & Pardeller, Tatiana Lecomte, Christian Mayer, Karina Nimmerfall, Nicole Six & Paul Petritsch, Michael Strasser, Anita Witek, Galerija Klovićevi dvori, Zagreb (HR), 9/10–11/2 2014; Muzej likovnih umjetnosti, Osijek (HR), 11/7–11/30 2014, in collaboration with Sandra Križić Roban, in cooperation with Croatian Photographic Union, Galerija Klovićevi dvori and Austrian Cultural Forum, Zagreb (HR)
Erik van der Weijde (NL), *Gebilde,* 12/6 2014–2/15 2015

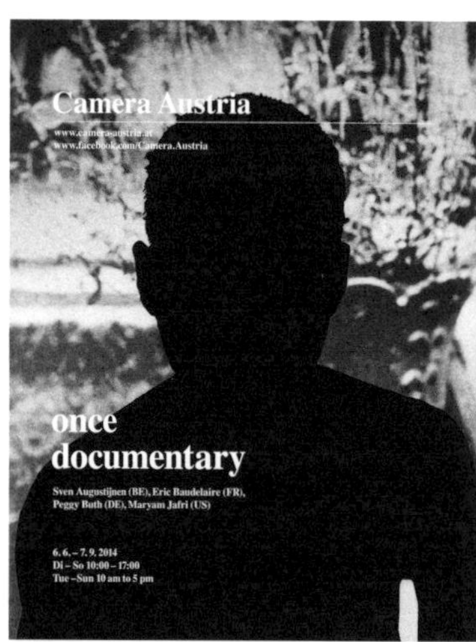

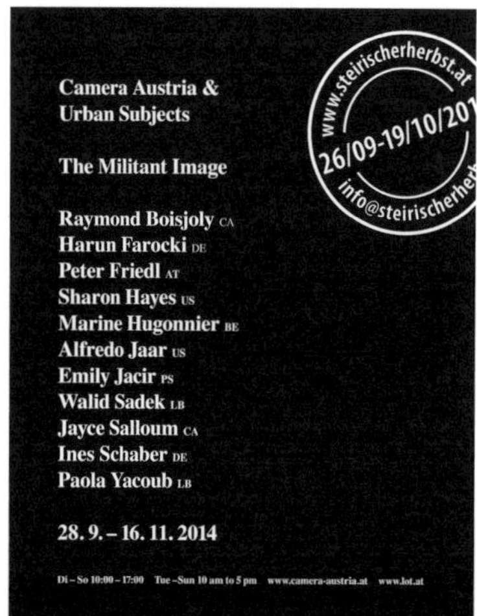

WORKSHOP

Militant Image – Workshop in conjunction with steirischer herbst, Urban Subjects (CA/AT), Marina Gržinić (SI), Jaleh Mansoor (CA), Stefan Römer (DE), Sandra Schäfer (DE), 10/9–10/10 2014

PUBLICATIONS

Archives, Re – Assemblances, and Surveys, with a preface by Reinhard Braun and texts by Maren Lübbke-Tidow and Sandra Križić-Roban, Graz, Edition Camera Austria, 2014
Maren Lübbke-Tidow ed., *Erik van der Weijde, Gebilde,* with text contributions by Pierre Dourthe, Frits Gierstberg, Maren Lübbke-Tidow, Dan Rule, Erik van der Weijde, Jan Wenzel, Graz, Edition Camera Austria, 2014
Reinhard Braun ed., *Martin Behr, Martin Osterider, Triester,* edition 9, Graz, Edition Camera Austria, 2014

EDITIONS CAMERA AUSTRIA INTERNATIONAL

125/2014, 126/2014, 127/2014, 128/2014

2015

EXHIBITIONS

Disputed Landscape, an exhibition project in three parts in cooperation with Kunsthaus Graz; further exhibition stops in Graz: Kunsthaus Graz, Universalmuseum Joanneum, Kunst im öffentlichen Raum Steiermark
Disputed Landscape: The Visual Paradigm, with works by Stephanie Kiwitt (DE/BE), Christian Mayer (AT), Ricarda Roggan (DE), Nicole Six & Paul Petritsch (AT), 3/13–5/10 2015
Disputed Landscape: Uncovering History, with works by Anthony Haughey (IE), Tatiana Lecomte (FR/AT), Jo Ractliffe (ZA), Ahlam Shibli (PS), Efrat Shvili (IL), 5/16–7/5 2015
Disputed Landscape: Enacting Landscape, with works by Philip Gaißer (DE), Michael Höpfner (AT), Sharon Ya'ari (IL), 7/11–9/6 2015
What Was Documentary Is Now Something Else, with works by Philip Gaißer, Michael Höpfner, Helmut and Johanna Kandl, Stephanie Kiwitt, Markus Krottendorfer, Tatiana Lecomte, Austrian Culture Institute Prague, Fotograf Gallery and Galerie Školská 28, Prag (CZ), 10/1–10/31 2015, a coproduction with Fotograf Festival 2015 Documentary Strategies and Austrian Culture Institute Prague (CZ)
To What End?, with works by Heba Y. Amin (EG), Takashi Arai (JP), Mohamed Bourouissa (DZ/FR), Hrair Sarkissian (SY), Vangelis Vlahos (GR), 9/27–11/22 2015, in collaboration with Gülsen Bal, in cooperation with steirischer herbst 2015
Efrat Shvili (IL), *The Jerusalem Experience,* 12/12 2015–2/21 2016, a project by

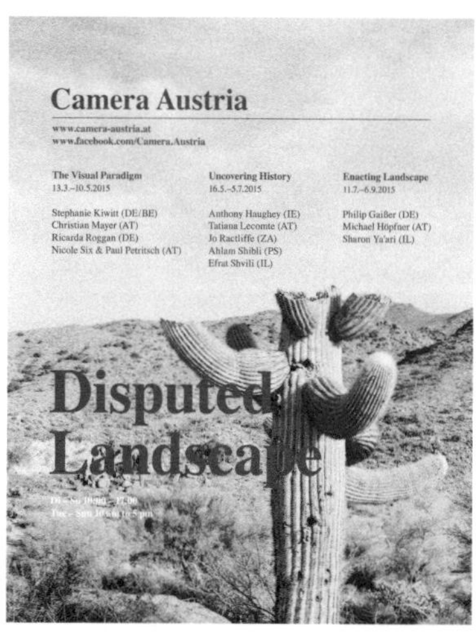

Efrat Shvili in cooperation with Oren Myers,
Centre de la Photographie Genève (CH),
6/2–8/20 2017

PUBLICATIONS
Katrin Bucher Trantow and Peter Pakesch, eds,
Landschaft. Konstruktion einer Realität, with
a preface by Peter Pakesch and text
contributions by Estelle Blaschke and
Reinhard Braun, Katia Huemer, Alanna
Lockward, Dirck Möllmann, Robert Smithson,
Thomas Weski et. al., Cologne, Verlag der
Buchhandlung Walther König, 2015.
Reinhard Braun ed., *Karina Nimmerfall,
1953. Possible Scenarios of a Discontinued
Future,* Graz, Edition Camera Austria, 2015
Philip Gaißer, *Ants 1,* with a text by
Philip Gaißer and A.K. Lenz,
Graz, Edition Camera Austria, 2015
Urban Subjects ed., *The Militant Image Reader,*
with text contributions by Reinhard Braun,
Urban Subjects, Jeff Derksen, Marina Gržinić,
Jayce Salloum, T.J. Demos, Sandra Schäfer,
Stefan Römer, Paola Yacoub, Michel Lasserre,
Jaleh Mansoor,
Graz, Edition Camera Austria, 2015
Reinhard Braun ed., *Martin Behr, Martin
Osterider, Triester,* edition 10,
Graz, Edition Camera Austria, 2015

CAMERA AUSTRIA AWARD
for Contemporary Photography by
the City of Graz: Annette Kelm (DE)

EDITIONS CAMERA AUSTRIA
INTERNATIONAL
129/2015, 130/2015, 131/2015, 132/2015

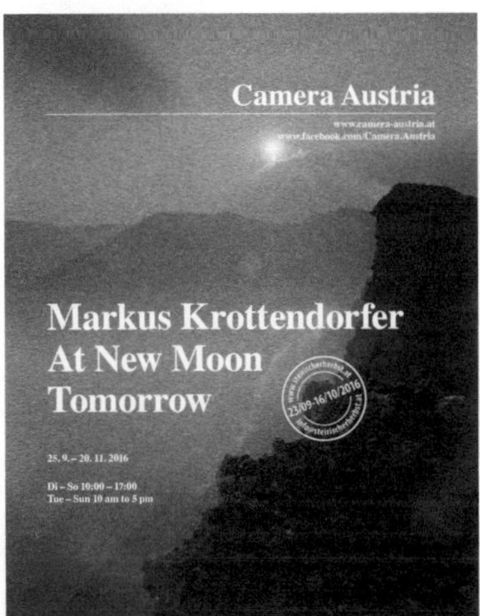

2016

EXHIBITIONS
Shirana Shahbazi (IR/CH), *Group Show,*
3/12–5/22 2016
Friedl Kubelka (AT), *Atelier d'Expression
(Dakar),* 6/11–8/14 2016
Markus Krottendorfer (AT), *At New Moon
Tomorrow,* 9/25–11/20 2016,
in cooperation with steirischer herbst 2016
Stephanie Kiwitt (DE), *Dialogues,*
12/8 2016–2/19 2017

PUBLICATIONS
Reinhard Braun ed., *Martin Behr, Martin
Osterider, Triester,* edition 11,
Graz, Edition Camera Austria, 2016
Maren Lübbke-Tidow ed., *Friedl Kubelka,
Atelier d'Expression (Dakar),* with text
contributions by Adama Diouf, Georg Gröller,
Maren Lübbke-Tidow, Graz, Edition Camera
Austria, 2016
Reinhard Braun ed., *Stefanie Seufert,
Wood Survives in the Form of Postholes,* with

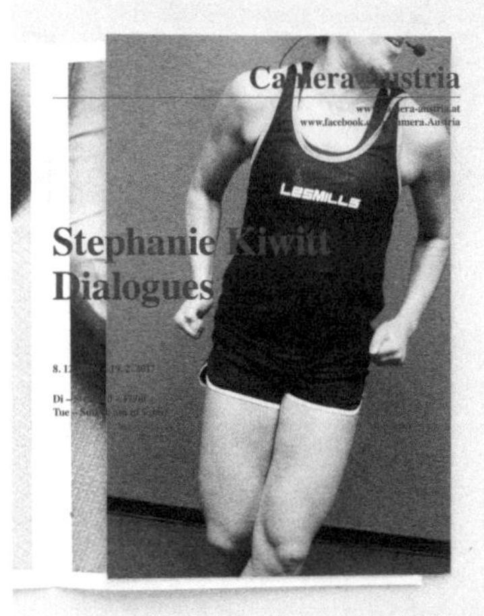

text contributions by Reinhard Braun,
Maren Lübbke-Tidow, Stefan Panhans,
Graz, Edition Camera Austria, 2016
Reinhard Braun ed., *Markus Krottendorfer,
At New Moon Tomorrow,* with text
contributions by Reinhard Braun,
Anette Freudenberger, Bernhard Kellner,
Thomas Wisser,
Graz, Edition Camera Austria, 2016
Reinhard Braun ed., *Stephanie Kiwitt,
Dialogues,* with contributions by Reinhard
Braun, Steven Humblet, Stephanie Kiwitt,
Tina Schulz, Carsten Tabel,
Eveline Vanfraussen, Bart Verschaffel,
Graz, Edition Camera Austria, 2016

EDITIONS CAMERA AUSTRIA
INTERNATIONAL
133/2016, 134/2016, 135/2016, 136/2016

2017

EXHIBITIONS
Hans Hansen: Atelier, 3/18–6/4 2017,
in collaboration with Annette Kelm and
Hendrik Schwantes
*Un-Curating the Archive.
Basierend auf einem Handapparat von
Nicole Six und Paul Petritsch,
Teil I: 1974–1989,* 6/24–8/13 2017
Özlem Altin (DE), *Processing,* 9/24–11/19 2017,
in cooperation with steirischer herbst 2017
*Un-Curating the Archive II.
Basierend auf einem Handapparat von
Nicole Six und Paul Petritsch,
Teil II: 1990–2002,* 12/8 2017–2/18 2018

PUBLICATIONS
Reinhard Braun, ed., *Martin Behr, Martin
Osterider, Triester,* edition 12, Graz, Edition
Camera Austria, 2017
Reinhard Braun, ed., *Tatiana Lecomte,* "Meine
erste Löwin," with a text contribution by Franz
Thalmair, Graz, Edition Camera Austria, 2017
Annette Kelm and Hendrik Schwantes, eds,
Hans Hansen, Atelier, with a preface by
Annette Kelm and Hendrik Schwantes,
and text contributions by Reinhard Braun
and Anna Voswinckel,
Graz, Edition Camera Austria, 2017
Reinhard Braun ed., *Özlem Altin, Dance,*
Graz, Edition Camera Austria, 2017

CAMERA AUSTRIA AWARD
for Contemporary Photography by the City
of Graz: Jochen Lempert (DE)

EDITIONS CAMERA AUSTRIA
INTERNATIONAL
137/2017, 138/2017, 139/2017, 140/2017

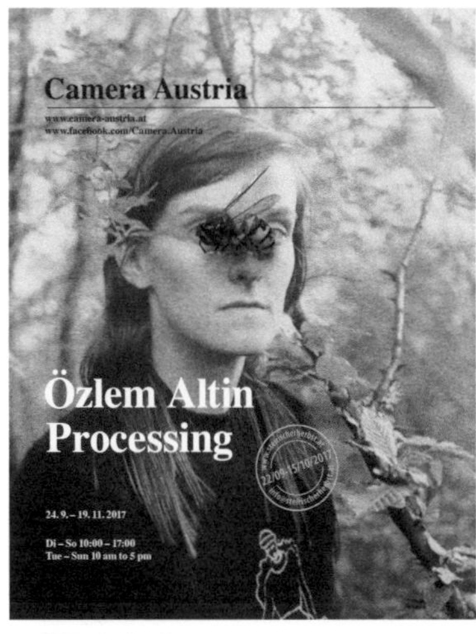

2018

EXHIBITIONS
Horáková + Maurer (AT), *TPX – Index,*
3/10–4/29 2018
Karina Nimmerfall (DE), *Indirect Interviews
with Women,* 5/19–7/1 2018
Heidi Specker (DE), *Fotografie,* 7/13–8/26 2018
Ines Schaber (DE), *Notes on Archives,*
9/23–11/18 2018
Tetsugo Hyakutake (JP), *Postwar Conditions,*
12/8 2018–2/17 2019

SYMPOSION ON PHOTOGRAPHY XXI
"The Violence of Images" 10/5–10/6 2018
Lecturers: Christine Frisinghelli (AT),
Marina Gržinić (HR), Ana Hoffner (RS/(AT)),
Tom Holert (DE), Jakub Majmurek (PL),
Guy Mannes-Abbott (GB), Ines Schaber (DE),
Ana Teixeira Pinto (PT/DE), Ala Younis (KW)
In cooperation with steirischer herbst 2018

PUBLICATIONS
Reinhard Braun ed., *Martin Behr,
Martin Osterider, Triester,* edition 13,
Graz, Edition Camera Austria, 2018
Reinhard Braun ed., *Karina Nimmerfall. Indirect
Interviews with Women,*
Graz, Edition Camera Austria 2018
Reinhard Braun ed., *Heidi Specker, Fotografie,*
with a text contribution by Reinhard Braun
and Heidi Specker,
Graz, Edition Camera Austria, 2018
Ines Schaber ed., *Ines Schaber: Notes on
Archives 1. Obtuse, Flitting By, and in Spite of
All – Image Archives in Practice,* with texts by
Ines Schaber and a conversation with
Madhusree Dutta (eng.), Berlin: Archive
Books; Graz, Edition Camera Austria, 2018
Ines Schaber ed., *Ines Schaber: Notes on
Archives 2. Culture Is Our Business,*
with texts by Reinhard Braun and Ines
Schaber and a conversation with
Diethart Kerbs (eng.), Berlin: Archive Books;
Graz, Edition Camera Austria, 2018
Ines Schaber ed., *Ines Schaber: Notes on
Archives 4. Dear Jadwa,* with texts by
Ines Schaber and a conversation with
Mustafa Kabha (eng.), Berlin: Archive Books;
Graz, Edition Camera Austria, 2018

EDITIONS CAMERA AUSTRIA
INTERNATIONAL
141/2018, 142/2018, 143/2018, 144/2018

Camera Austria Association: Laboratory for Photography and Theory

Locations

Location Café Schillerhof, Graz
1974 – Fotogalerie im Schillerhof, privately organized

1975 – 1996 Forum Stadtpark Artists' Association, Stadtpark 1, Graz
1975 – 1976 Fotogalerie im Schillerhof, hosted by the artists' association
1976 creation of the Photo Department from the Film & Photo Department; incorporation of the photo gallery in the Artists' Association
1990 founding of the branch association Camera Austria – Forum Stadtpark

1996 – 2003 Sparkassenplatz 2, Graz
1997 founding of the Camera Austria Association: Laboratory for Photography and Theory

2010 – 2015 editorial team Berlin Kunst-quartier Bethanien, Mariannenplatz 2, Berlin

since 2003 Eisernes Haus, Lendkai 1, Graz

Organization

Directors, board, curators, and editors

MANFRED WILLMANN
1974 – 2010 artist and curator, artistic director
1980 – 2010 founder and editor of *Camera Austria International*
1997 – 2009 founder and chairman of the Association

CHRISTINE FRISINGHELLI
since 1976 curator, author
1980 – 2010 co-founder and editorial director of *Camera Austria International*
1997 – 2009 co-founder and deputy chairwoman
2009 – 2011 chairwoman of the Association
since 2001 curator of the Pierre Bourdieu photo archive

SEIICHI FURUYA
since 1978 artist, curator; organization of projects on Japanese photography
1980 co-founder of *Camera Austria International*
1997 co-founder of the Association

REINHARD BRAUN
since 1992 author, editor, and curator
1993 – 1997 and since 2010 member of the board
since 2011 artistic director and editor of *Camera Austria International*
since 2012 chairman of the Association

MAREN LÜBBKE-TIDOW
since 1997 author, curator, and editor
since 2002 member of the board
2010 – 2017 vice-chairwoman of the Association
2010 development of the editorial location in Berlin
2010 – 2014 editorial director, *Camera Austria International*

HEIDI OSWALD
2000 – 2002 assistant to the directors
2008 – 2017 member of the board

WILFRIED PRANTNER
since 1980 translator and copy edtior
since 2013 member of the board

WALTER SEIDL
since 2005 author and curator
since 2013 member of the board

CHRISTINA TÖPFER
since 2013 author and editor
since 2017 member of the board of the Association
since 2018 editorial director, *Camera Austria International*

Artists, Works in the exhibition

The works are arranged alphabetically by artist and chronologically within their works. Original titles are in italics. Unless otherwise stated, these are vintage prints, later prints are indicated in brackets. The measurements are given in height before width and refer to the picture size.

Robert Adams

1937 Orange, NJ, US – Astoria, OR, US

Robert Adams began his career as a linguist. He studied English at the University of Southern California from 1956 to 1960 and was an assistant professor at Colorado College from 1962 to 1970 before devoting himself entirely to photography. Today he is referred to as "the" photographer of the American West. While Ansel Adams reproduced the landscapes of the same region in sublime and almost heroic photographs, Adams dissected the relationship between nature and man. His works are concerned primarily with the evolving landscape and moments of transition: the suburbanization of Denver, a changing Los Angeles of the 1970s and 1980s, and the deforestation of Oregon in the 1990s. He examines the role played by human intervention and advancing industrialization, and the effects the exploitation of the landscape is having on its inhabitants. His motifs can appear desolate, but in the way he presents them they are by no means a swan song, but rather a representation of his attitude: to criticize the assault on the environment, but also to seek the opportunity to reconcile oneself with this world through a photographic examination of its destruction. In addition to large landscapes, it is the small, unspectacular moments, such as those in the series *Around the House* (2016) that he captures in frontally constructed images. In 2010, Yale University Art Gallery organized a retrospective that explored four decades of his work and was subsequently shown at the Los Angeles Museum of Art, the Museo Nacional Centro de Arte Reina Sofia in Madrid, and the Jeu de Paume in Paris. Although Adams has been publicly exhibited since the 1970s, his actual medium is the photo book. To date, he has published more than 60 picture essays in book form. His works can be found in large museum collections all over the world.

- *Farmyard. South of Arriba, Colorado*, 1969 (1977), gelatin silver print, 6 ¼ × 8 in (15.9 × 20.3 cm)
- *A farm pond about to be destroyed by earthmoving Machinery, Northglenn, Colorado*, 1973 (1996), gelatin silver print, 7 × 8 ¾ in (17.8 × 22.2 cm)
- *North of Briggsdale, Colorado*, 1973 (1977), gelatin silver print, 7 ¼ × 9 ½ in (18.4 × 24.1 cm)
- *Clear-cut and burned, east of Arch Cape, Oregon (Clatsop County, Oregon)*, 1976 (1980), gelatin silver print, 9 × 11 ⅛ in (22.9 × 28.6 cm)
- *South of the Rocky Flats Nuclear Weapons Plant, Jefferson County, Colorado*, 1976 (1979), gelatin silver print, 8 ½ × 11 ⅛ in (21.6 × 28.3 cm)
- *Grand Junction, Mesa County, Colorado*, 1978 (1979), gelatin silver print, 9 × 11 ⅛ in (22.9 × 28.3 cm)

Courtesy Fraenkel Gallery, San Francisco and Galerie Thomas Zander, Cologne

Nobuyoshi Araki

1040 Tokyo, JP – Tokyo, JP

Nobuyoshi Araki studied photography and film science at the University of Chiba from 1959 to 1963. In that same year, he began working as an advertising photographer for Dentsu, one of the largest agencies in the world. In addition to commercial photography, he began to develop his own photographic ideas. The artist declared 1970 the "first year of Araki." He began with various artistic experiments because he was increasingly dissatisfied with the status quo of mainstream photography. He perceived deception and dishonesty in style of photography that was popular and predominant in Japan at the time and set himself the goal of showing the true face of a rapidly changing society through his kind of photography. In 1971 he married his wife Yoko. He published the documentation of his honeymoon in the small photo book *Sentimental Journey,* the first of more than 600 books to date. He is not only one of the most productive, but also one of the most provocative photographers of our time in Japan. His work spans a diverse spectrum from erotic depictions of women to still lifes, plant photographs, reportages, and diary-like self-portraits. For this genre, he developed the term I-photo, which refers to the Japanese literary genre of the I-novel. In it, the authors' experience and the most realistic representation possible serve as the starting material for a fictional story. In 1992 Seiichi Furuya and Manfred Willmann organized the first solo exhibition of Araki outside Japan. In 2018 the Museum der Moderne Salzburg showed an excerpt of his 125 works from the Araki Collection under the title *I-Photo.*

From the series "Shikikei," 15 chromogenic prints, 19 ⅝ × 24 ⅝ in (49.8 cm × 62.5 cm) Exhibition prints 1992 Camera Austria

Archive Nobuyoshi Araki

Lewis Baltz

1945 Newport Beach, CA, US – 2014 Paris, FR Lewis Baltz studied at the Art Institute in San Francisco and at the Claremont Graduate School from 1969 to 1971. In 1970 he was already a lecturer in photography at the California Institute of Arts' Pomona College. Until 2003 he taught as Visiting Professor at various American and European universities and art schools. Baltz is one of the most important representatives of the so-called "New Topographics." The name is derived from the 1975 exhibition *New Topographics: Photographs of a Man-altered Landscape* at the George Eastman House in Rochester, New York, which featured works by Baltz, Robert Adams, Bernd and Hilla Becher, Joe Deal, Stephen Shore, and Henry Wessel. Baltz's projects are documentations of industrial areas, urbanization, wasteland or new housing estates, which meticulously reproduce in large series how the everyday environment presents itself. It's not a critique, as he says himself, but an inventory that gets by without an author and art. With this reduction and coolness, he transformed the documentary approach into a conceptual process that took its cue from contemporary art. Between 1974 and 2012 he also published numerous articles in magazines such as *Art in America, The Times Literary Supplement or L'Architecture d'Aujourd'hui.* They provide insights into his understanding of art and politics and analyze the development of American photography. Baltz studied the work of his contemporaries, including Robert Adams, Michael Schmidt, William Eggleston, Chauncey Hare, Anthony Hernandez, and Allan Sekula. His works are represented in over 50 museum collections worldwide, in Austria in the Albertina, Vienna.

- "Park City," 1978–1980, 102 gelatin silver prints, each 8 × 10 in (20.3 × 25.4 cm)

Deichtorhallen Hamburg / Falckenberg Collection

Sabine Bitter / Helmut Weber

1960 Aigen, AT – Vienna, AT; Vancouver, CA 1975 Dorf/Pram, AT – Vienna, AT

Sabine Bitter and Helmut Weber completed their studies in Visual Design at the University of Art and Design Linz under Laurids Ortner in 1987. Since 1994, they have been working on joint projects that investigate the interplay between people and the urban space with its public, institutional and private spheres. Among other things, they examine the question of how the promise of social housing relates to the actual experience of its inhabitants, and critically question official interpretations of the construction history of high-prestige buildings, which often conceal the eradication of existing cultural spaces that was necessary for their realization. The works are structured in series and preceded by intensive research, as in the residential project Pedregulho in Rio de Janeiro, which was planned and realized between 1946 and 1954 as a political and social showcase project (in *Live Like This!,* 2000). Another work was created on the campus architecture of the IIT (Illinois Institute of Technology) in Chicago, which was created between 1942 and 1958 under the direction of Mies van der Rohe and is regarded as an icon of modern architecture (*Bronzeville,* 2007). In a further step, Bitter and Weber manipulate the images of these spaces and architectures through montage and new combinations. With these interventions, they disrupt political and ideological notions of places whose function includes the representation of systems and ideologies. Through their artistic approach to urban studies, often carried out in collaboration with the author and critic Jeff Derksen, they initiate discussions on the political and ideological instrumentalization of images of urban living space, which they see as a "platform for the mobilization [...] and condensation of the political."

From the series "Super Citizens," 2003–2006
8 digital prints on photo paper,
Each 19 ⅝ × 24 ⅝ in (49.8 × 62.5 cm)

Sabine Bitter / Helmut Weber

Anna and Bernhard Blume

1937 Bork, DE – Cologne, DE
1937 Dortmund, DE – 2011 Cologne, DE

Anna Helming and Bernhard Johannes Blume met as students at the Staatliche Kunstakademie Düsseldorf, where they both studied from 1960 to 1965. Bernhard Blume also studied philosophy at the University of Cologne from 1967 to 1970. From 1987 Anna Blume was a guest lecturer at various art academies, Bernhard Blume worked as a professor at the Hochschule für bildende Künste in Hamburg. Initially, their work was predominantly in graphics. In the 1960s and 1970s, Bernhard Blume combined abstract concepts with everyday objects in striking drawings. His photographic works already refer stylistically to the later photo sequences. The works are often accompanied by "quasi-philosophical" texts, as in the Symposion on Photography VI in 1984. Since 1980, the Blumes have been working intensively on the joint project of a "lifelong photo novel." For their large-format black-and-white photo sequences, the Blumes stage themselves in performances intended solely for the camera. As leading actors, they are part of a tableau of quotidian middle-class life that threatens to descend into chaos at any time. The photographs have the character of blurred snapshots. Yet photography does not serve to document a visible reality but to construct a new reality. Their works can be found in the Hamburger Bahnhof - Museum für Gegenwart, the

Stiftung Preußischer Kulturbesitz in Berlin, the Museum für Moderne Kunst Frankfurt am Main or the Museum of Modern Art, New York.

– *Küchenkoller* (Kitchen Frenzy), 1985/2016
  5 inkjetprints, each 50 × 32 in (127 × 81.5 cm)

Anna and Bernhard Blume,
Courtesy Buchmann Galerie, Berlin

Petar Dabac

1942 Zagreb, HR – Zagreb, HR

Petar Dabac is a key figure of the contemporary Croatian photo scene. He studied mechanical engineering and shipbuilding at the University of Zagreb before turning to photography in 1960 when he began working in the photo studio of his uncle, the renowned photographer Tošo Dabac (1907–1970). After his uncle's death he took over the studio and managed the extensive estate; he is the organizer of numerous international exhibitions and editor of publications on his uncle's work. Since 2007, the Tošo Dabac Archive has been managed by the Muzej Suvremene Umjetnosti at the archive site. Already during Tošo Dabac's lifetime, his studio was an important meeting place for the Zagreb art scene. In 1978 Petar Dabac opened the Arhiv TD gallery in the studio and until 1998 he organized more than 40 exhibitions with national and international artists. From 1990 he taught photography at the Academy of Visual Arts in Ljubljana.
Since 1966 Petar Dabac has worked as a freelance artist, and in 1972 he co-founded the photo magazine *spot*. He explores the possibilities of deconstructing and reconstructing the photographic image, working playfully and experimentally with the photographic material, with photograms, simple enlargement techniques, and photocopies. Since 1990 the diary-like series "Lieber Pero" has been created as work in progress. The title repeats the opening lines of personal letters, the series gathers photographic records of everyday events, urban environments, and portraits, and resembles an extended family album. As part of the comprehensive retrospective *Petar Dabac. Nisam krivi | Not Guilty* 2011 of the Galerija Klovićevi dvori Zagreb was published a Catalogue raisonné. Works are located in the Museum of Contemporary Art Zagreb.

From the series "Lieber Pero" (Dear Pero), 1990
110 xerox copies, each 16 ⁹⁄₁₆ × 11 ¹¹⁄₁₆ in
(42 × 29,7 cm)

Petar Dabac

William Eggleston

1939 Memphis, TN, US – Memphis, TN, US

William Eggleston comes from a wealthy Southern family and grew up on a cotton plantation in Mississippi. In addition to his love of music, he became interested in photography at an early age and studied at Vanderbilt University in Nashville and Delta State College, Cleveland, Mississippi. From the end of the 1950s, he worked as a freelance photographer and from 1965 onwards

he experimented with color photography. In 1976, John Szarkowski curated a solo exhibition of his works at the Museum of Modern Art, New York, which instantly made his pictures known to the public. The prints were made by Eggleston as dye-transfer, a color image process used mainly for advertising and creating a kind of hyper-reality. Despite massive criticism, this presentation marks a milestone in the history of photography, and it is mostly because of it that Eggleston is regarded as the founder of artistic color photography.
With trivial themes, Eggleston draws a very personal picture of the American South. In the epilogue to his book *The Democratic Forest,* he describes his artistic method as "democratic," since he regards all phenomena as equal. With his works, he invites the viewer to risk a second glance at things that would normally be overlooked. He also transferred this call for a new way of looking to the long-term project *The Democratic Forest,* which he presented without comment at the Symposion on Photography VII in 1984. He photographs each motif only once, thus reinforcing the singularity of the moment. But unlike Cartier-Bresson, it's not the events depicted that make his pictures feel familiar and mysterious, but rather the ordinary. His works can be found in large museum collections all over the world.

– *Huntsville, Alabama,* 1969/1970, Dye-Transfer,
  18 ⅜ × 12 ¾ in (46.6 × 32.3 cm)
– *Memphis / Brazier (BBQ pit),* 1969–1971
  (1981), Dye-Transfer, 12 ⅝ × 19 ⅛ in
  (32 × 48.6 cm)
– *Memphis,* 1970 (1986), Dye-Transfer,
  13 ³⁄₁₆ × 20 ¼ in (33,5 × 51,5 cm)
– *Near Minter City and Glendora, Mississippi,*
  1970 (1999), Dye-Transfer, 14 ⅜ × 21 ¾ in
  (36.5 × 55.3 cm)
– *Memphis, Tennessee,* 1971 (1999),
  Dye-Transfer, 21 ¹³⁄₁₆ × 14 ⅞ in (55.4 × 36.7 cm)
– *Sumner, Mississippi, Cassidy Bayou in
  background,* 1971 (1999), Dye-Transfer,
  14 ⁷⁄₁₆ × 21 ¹³⁄₁₆ in (36.7 × 55.4 cm)
– *En route to New Orleans,* around 1978,
  Chromogenic print, 15 ¹⁄₁₆ × 10 ¼ in
  (38.2 × 26 cm)
– *Memphis, Tennessee,* 1978 (1999),
  Dye-Transfer, 17 ¹⁵⁄₁₆ × 11 ⅞ in
  (45.5 × 30.1 cm)
– *Memphis, Tennessee,* 1989 (1999),
  Dye-Transfer, 17 ¹⁵⁄₁₆ × 11 ⅞ in
  (45.5 × 30.1 cm)

Museum Folkwang, Essen

Hans-Peter Feldmann

1941 Düsseldorf, DE – Düsseldorf, DE

In the 1960s, the German photographer and conceptual artist Hans-Peter Feldmann first studied painting at the Kunstschule Linz, now the Academy for Art and Design. From 1968 onwards he began his photographic work and compiled his own as well as found photographs into series, which he self-published until 1975 in a total of 35 artist's books under the title *Bilderhefte.*
Feldmann's photographic work would often take a cue from so-called "found footage" material from all areas of photography. He is interested in press and magazine photos as well as anonymous private photos or postcard

motifs that would be dismissed as kitschy, which he then combines with his own photos. Feldmann's focus lies above all on the inconspicuous everyday motifs that he collects and arranges with a careful eye and a definite love of photography. Through a subsequent serial production and presentation, the original context of the images is dissolved. With this approach, Feldmann positions himself against an elevation of the artist's individual work. He deconstructs common categorizations of art.
In 1972 and 1977, Feldmann participated in documenta 5 and 6 in Kassel where he presented his *Sonntagsbilder* (Sunday Pictures) as wall-sized installations of black-and-white copies. In 2003 he was represented at the 50th Biennale di Venezia. In 2011, the Salomon R. Guggenheim Museum in New York dedicated a solo exhibition to Feldman on the occasion of being awarded the Hugo Boss Prize the previous year, followed in 2013 by a solo exhibition in Hamburg's Deichtorhallen under the title *Kunstausstellung.*

– *Alle Kleider einer Frau* (All of a Woman's Clothes), 1974, 70 gelatin silver prints, each 3 9/16 × 3 9/16 in (9 × 9 cm)

Hans-Peter Feldmann

Seiichi Furuya

1950 Izu, JP – Graz, AT

Seiichi Furuya studied architecture at Tokyo Polytechnic University. In 1973 he left Japan and traveled to Europe on the Trans-Siberian Railway. He initially lived in Vienna before moving to Graz in 1975, where Manfred Willmann organized the first exhibition of his work. It was here that he met his future wife Christine Gössler in 1978. In 1982 he moved to Vienna, where he co-founded the Austrian Photo Archive in the Museum of Modern Art the following year, Acting as its first chairman. In 1984 Furuya accepted a position as an interpreter and moved with his family first to Dresden, then one year later to East Berlin. Since 1987, Furuya has been living in Graz again. A central motif of his work is his examination of the life and death of his wife Christine, whom he portrayed from her first meeting until her suicide in 1985. With the exhibition *Mémoires* 1989 at the Neue Galerie in Graz he started again to work with this collection of portraits and continues and continues to present them in ever-changing combinations to this day. Another important theme of Furuya's work is that of the border, which he presents in his series *Staatsgrenze* (Border) (1981–1983), a journey along the Austrian border to the countries of the former Eastern Bloc; in *Limes* (1986-1988), he draws attention to the Berlin Wall from the perspective of East Berlin. In 2016 he focused on the debate surrounding migration in Europe in his work *Spielfeld* (2016). Furuya's works can be found in numerous international and Austrian collections, including the Metropolitan Museum and the Museum of Modern Art in New York, the Tokyo Metropolitan Museum of Photography, the Albertina and the Museum Moderner Kunst in Vienna, and the Österreichische Fotogalerie at the Museum der Moderne Salzburg.

From the series "AMSterdam," 1980 24 gelatin silver prints, Each 12 × 15 15/16 in (30.4 × 40.4 cm)

Seiichi Furuya

Luigi Ghirri

1943 Scandiano, IT – 1992 Roncocesi, IT

Luigi Ghirri trained as a surveyor, as a photographer he was self-taught. His first photos were taken at the end of the 1960s in Modena and the surrounding area. Ghirri was part of the city's lively intellectual art scene, which also included the conceptual artist and theorist Franco Vaccari, who wrote the text for his first small catalogue in 1972. In 1978 Ghirri was a co-founder of the publishing house Punto e Virgola. In the same year, he published his first important monograph *Kodachrome,* in which he summarized his thinking about photography in texts and image series. "Fotografare è relazionarsi con il mondo" (Photography means to connect with the world), he says, photography is for him a means of analysis to examine the selectivity between representation and interpretation, to question the world around us but also the world of images surrounding us. *Kodachrome* concludes with an image of a discarded daily newspaper with the headline: "Come pensare per immagini" (How Can One Think in Images?). As an artist, author and thinker, Luigi Ghirri has raised this question again and again. A project of far-reaching impact was *Viaggio in Italia* in 1984, an exhibition and a book with a text by Arturo Carlo Quintavalle of the University of Parma, where Ghirri's first retrospective publication was published in 1990. The confrontation with the Italian landscape became the central theme of Italian photography of this decade. In 1992, the year of his early death, the Fotomuseum Winterthur curated the first retrospective outside Italy in collaboration with his widow Paola Borgonzoni. Luigi Ghirri's ideas and works are currently being made accessible again in the international retrospective *Karte und Gebiet* (Map and Area) (Museum Folkwang Essen, Jeu de Paume Paris, and Centro de Arte Reina Sofia Madrid). His works can be found in many international collections.

– *Atlante* (Atlas), 1973 (2008), chromogenic print, 5 ½ × 8 ¼ in (14 × 21 cm)
– *Modena*, 1973, chromogenic print, 5 ½ × 8 ¼ in (14 × 21 cm)
– *Reggio Emilia*, 1973, chromogenic print, 5 ½ × 8 ¼ in (14 × 21 cm)
– *Lido di Spina*, 1974, chromogenic print, 5 ½ × 8 ¼ in (14 × 21 cm)
– *Orbetello*, 1974, chromogenic print, 5 ½ × 8 ¼ in (14 × 21 cm)
– *Rimini*, 1977, chromogenic print, 8 ¼ × 5 ½ in (14 × 21 cm)
– *Roma* (Rome), 1977, chromogenic print, 4 ⅛ × 7 ⅞ in (10.5 × 20 cm)
– *Lido di Spina*, 1978 (2008), chromogenic print, 5 ½ × 8 ¼ in (14 × 21 cm)
– *Roma* (Rome), 1978, chromogenic print, 8 ¼ × 5 ⅛ in (21 × 13 cm)
– *Alpe di Siusi* (Seiser Alm), 1979 (2008), chromogenic print, 5 ½ × 8 ¼ in (14 × 21 cm)
– *Ferrara*, 1980 (2008), chromogenic print, 4 15/16 × 8 ¼ in (12,5 × 21 cm)
– *Parma*, 1983, chromogenic print, 5 5/16 × 8 ¼ in (13,5 × 21 cm)
– *Bologna*, 1985, chromogenic print, 5 ¾ × 8 ¼ in (14,6 × 21 cm)
– *Marina di Ravenna*, 1986, chromogenic print, 5 ½ × 8 ¼ in (14 × 21 cm)
– *Roncocesi*, 1992, chromogenic print, 5 15/16 × 8 ¼ in (15 × 21 cm)

Estate of Luigi Ghirri

– *Salisburgo* (Salzburg), 1977, chromogenic print, 4 ¾ × 7 1/16 in (12 × 18 cm)

Collection Michael Mauracher

David Goldblatt

1930 Randfontein, ZA – 2018 Johannesburg, ZA

The South African photographer David Goldblatt was born near Johannesburg as the son of Jewish emigrants. Although he began taking photographs in his youth, he initially worked in his father's business for twelve years. After his father's death, Goldblatt devoted himself exclusively to photography and worked for international magazines such as *Life* and *Picture Post Magazine.* Goldblatt documented life in South Africa under apartheid. Through his own experiences with racism and anti-Semitism, he was increasingly affected by the ideology of apartheid, which from 1948 began to control all areas of daily life in South Africa for whites and blacks alike. As a photographer, he focused primarily on everyday scenes in which racism and power structures are expressed in a subtle way. His opus magnum is *The Structures of Things Then,* a collection of images and texts developed over more than a decade, in which the social and political experiences of the apartheid era are made visible in architecture, the built structures of his country. He is regarded as one of the most important chroniclers of the apartheid era in South Africa.
Goldblatt's photographic series are essay-like, accompanied by short texts that reflect his views on the society he was a part of. In 1987, for fear of the secret police and to safeguard his work, he donated a collection of 115 prints to the Victoria and Albert Museum in London. In 1989 he founded the Market Photo Workshop in Johannesburg, a school for photography open to people of all ethnicities. In 1998, he was the first South African to have a solo exhibition at the Museum of Modern Art in New York. 2001 the Witte de With in Rotterdam followed suit with a retrospective. In 2002, Goldblatt was represented at documenta 11. Shortly before his death, the Centre Pompidou Paris presented another major retrospective. Goldblatt won the prestigious Hasselblad Prize (2006) and the Henri Cartier-Bresson Prize (2009).

– *The Apostolic Multiracial Church in Zion of South Africa. Crossroads, Cape Town, 11 October 1984 (4_3603)*, 1984, inkjet print, 13 × 16 ½ in (33 × 42 cm)
– *Mother and child in their home after the destruction of its shelter by officials of the Western Cape Development Board Crossroads, Cape Town, 11 October 1984 (4_3614)*, 1984, inkjet print, 13 × 16 ½ in (33 × 42 cm)
– *Dutch Reformed Church, completed in 1984, Quellerina, Johannesburg, 3 November 1986 (4_4627)*, 1986, inkjet print, 16 ½ × 13 in (42 × 33 cm)
– *Dutch Reformed Church, inaugurated on 31 July 1966, Op-die-Berg, Koue Bokkeveld, Cape, 23 May 1987 (4_5076)*, 1987, inkjet print, 13 × 16 ½ in (33 × 42 cm)
– *House near Phuthaditjhaba, QwaQwa, 1 May 1989 (4_5971)*, 1989, gelatin silver print, 15 × 19 ¾ in (38 × 50 cm)

— *Sculpture by political prisoner Japhta Masemola, Robben Island (4_7130)*, 1991, (Skulptur von Japhta Masemola, politischer Häftling, Robben Island), Inkjet print, 16 ½ × 13 in (42 × 33 cm)

Courtesy David Goldblatt and Goodman Gallery

Nan Goldin

1953 Washington, D.C., US – New York, NY, US; Berlin, DE; Paris, FR

Nan Goldin is one of the most important photographers of her generation. She started her career as an amateur photographer before attending the School of the Museum of Fine Arts in Boston. Her camera serves as a kind of tool for capturing personal memories and experiences. Goldin is known as a chronicler of the New York underground of the 1980s. She develops a true as well as sentimental image of the community, of her circle of friends, which she also calls her family and portrays unfiltered, omitting neither sex, violence or drugs. Her early work always revolved around her own drug use. In the 1970s to 1990s, she concentrated on life in the big cities, which was dramatically marked by HIV and AIDS. Her work is based on the direct aesthetics of snapshot photography and presents her personal painful experiences intimately, formally beautiful and with intense use of color. Her artistic breakthrough came with "The Ballad of Sexual Dependency," a slide show created between 1980 and 1986. In 1989, she published the 15-part portfolio Cookie Mueller, a portrait of her friend who died of AIDS. In parallel, she worked with Araki and David Wojnarowicz and organized the exhibition *Witnesses: Against Our Vanishing* in New York. It was the first big show in which works by people with AIDS or people who had died of AIDS were shown. Currently, Nan Goldin is a pioneer in the protest movement against the misuse of the painkiller Oxycontin, which has led her into a new dependency. She uses art platforms like *Artforum* to take on the manufacturers who are courted as generous patrons of the arts. Her works are represented in over 40 public collections worldwide, including the Sammlung Verbund in Vienna.

From the series "The Ballad of Sexual Dependency," 1978 – 1986

— *Ryan in the tub, Provincetown, Mass*, 1976, cibachrome, 19 ⅞ × 19 ½ in (image) [50,5 × 49.5 cm], 24 × 20 ¹⁄₁₆ in (sheet) [61 × 51.0 cm]
— *Mark tattooing Mark, Boston*, 1978, chromogenic print, 13 ³⁄₁₆ × 19 ⁵⁄₁₆ in (image) [33.5 × 49 cm], 15 ¹⁵⁄₁₆ × 20 ¹⁄₁₆ in (sheet) [40.5 × 51 cm]
— *Skinhead having sex, London*, 1978, cibachrome, 19 ⁵⁄₁₆ × 19 ⁵⁄₁₆ in (49 × 49 cm)
— *Brian with the Flintstones, New York City*, 1981, chromogenic print, 13 ³⁄₁₆ × 19 ¹¹⁄₁₆ in (image) [33.5 × 50.0 cm], 15 ¹⁵⁄₁₆ × 20 ¹⁄₁₆ in (sheet) [40.5 × 51 cm]
— *Nan and Brian in bed, New York City*, 1983, cibachrome, 12 × 19 ¹¹⁄₁₆ in (30.5 × 50 cm)
— *Nan after being battered*, 1984, cibachrome, 12 ¹³⁄₁₆ × 19 ¹¹⁄₁₆ in (32.5 × 50 cm)

Collection Manfred Willmann

Sanja Iveković

1949 Zagreb, HR – Zagreb, HR

Sanja Iveković became known as a member of Nove umjetničke prakse / New Art Practice, a group of artists in the Socialist Republic of Yugoslavia which was formed in the wake of the student protests of 1968. The group rejected the official modernist art paradigm and initiated a far-reaching critical analysis of social, cultural and institutional issues, drawing on performances and video art. From these beginnings, Iveković went on to critically examine the construction of gender roles, the relationship between private and public space, and the institutional frameworks of the cultural sector. Iveković's convinced feminist attitude remains a constant in her long artistic career, from pioneering works such as *Double Life* (1975), *Triangle* (1979) and *Personal Cuts* (1982) to large-scale public art projects of recent years realised in collaboration with activist groups, including *Women's House* (1998 – 2003) and *Mohnfeld* (2007) for documenta 12. For documenta 14, she reconstructed the plinth of the memorial to Karl Liebknecht and Rosa Luxemburg, which was commissioned by the Communist Party of Germany in 1926, designed by Ludwig Mies van der Rohe and destroyed by the Nazis in 1935. The reconstruction questions the relationship between revolution and remembrance and triggers a debate on the construction and deconstruction of public memory. Her works can be found mainly in European collections, but also in the Vancouver Art Gallery and the Museum of Modern Art New York.

From the series "Dvostruki Život," 1974 – 75 (Double Life), 12 photomontages 2 parts each, 1 full-page color or black-and-white advertisement from a magazine, 1 black-and-white photograph, mounted on paper, each framed 23 ⁵⁄₈ × 31 ½ in (60 × 80 cm)

— *(Untitled), Proljece 1961. 5. razred baletne Škole.* (Spring 1961 / 5th Class of the Ballet School)

— *BRIGITTE, oktobar 1975, decembar 1963. Sa Romanom Capek i njenim rodakom pred odlazak na docek Nove Godine* (December 1963. With Romana Capek and Her Relative before Going Out to Celebrate New Year's Eve)
— *ELLE, decembar 1974, 1966. U Krajiskoj* (1966. In Krajiska Apartment)
— *ELLE, novembar 1974, 1967. Prag* (1967. Prague), 1975
— *GRAZIA, novembar 1975, 1969. Na Silbi. Na Staru Godinu.* (1969. On Silba. New Year's Eve), 1975
— *BRIGITTE, may 1975, Septembar 1969. Na terasi vikendice na Silbi.* (September 1969. On the Terrace of the Summer House on Silba), 1975
  —*MARIE CLAIRE, oktobar 1975, Proljece 1970. Tuskanac, u parku kuce R. Supeka sa Mladenom Marticem* (Spring 1970. Tuskanac, in the Garden of R. Supek's House with Mladen Martic), 1975
— *GRAZIA, novembar 1974*, 1972
— *MARIE CLAIRE, decembar 1975, Proljece 1972* (Spring 1972), 1975
— *ANNA BELLA, oktobar 1975, Novembar 1974* (November, 1974), 1975
— *BRIGITTE, novembar 1975, decembar*

1975. Jutro pri stavljanju sminke. (December 1975. Morning Make-Up), 1975
— *MARIE CLAIRE, novembar 1975, august 1975. Supetar. Kod tate u vikendici,* (August 1975. Supetar. At my Father's Summer House), 1975

Generali Foundation Collection — Permanent Loan to the Museum der Moderne Salzburg WG0030300.00.0-2001

Sven Johne

1976 Bergen, DE – Berlin, DE

The German conceptual artist Sven Johne studied German language and literature as well as journalism before moving to Timm Rautert's photography class at the Hochschule für Grafik und Buchkunst Leipzig. In 2006 he graduated as a master student.
In his photographic and video works, Johne develops combinations consisting of image and text. He expands sober photographs of landscapes, places, and objects with captions and texts that are an integral part of the artwork. His series refer to collective and individual human destinies, which he researches carefully. Johne operates like an investigative journalist. The stories told about the picture-text constellations often seem to refer to the complex system of economy, politics, working and living conditions. Ultimately, however, it remains open whether Johne's composed photo reportages are documentary or fiction. Johne has been a visiting professor for photography at the Hochschule für Grafik und Buchkunst Leipzig since 2010. In 2016 he was awarded the Berlin Art Prize of the Akademie der Künste. Eight monographic books on his work have been published since 2007. His works are represented in the collections of the Pinakothek der Moderne, Munich and the Centre Pompidou, Paris.

— "Ship Cancellation," 2004, 5 lambda prints, silkscreen print on glass each 43 ⁵⁄₁₆ × 59 ¹⁄₁₆ in (110 × 150 cm)

Collection Ivo Wessel, Berlin

Lamia Joreige

1972 Beirut, LB – Beirut, LB

Lamia Joreige is a visual artist and filmmaker who uses archive documents and fictional elements to reflect on the relationship between individual stories and the collective history of Lebanon and the Middle East. Her work examines the trauma of the Lebanese wars, with a focus on her hometown of Beirut. Joreige's work *Objects of War*, an ongoing series of documentary video works, was started in 2000. In the first part, the artist conducted interviews about the things that were important to respondents during the civil war. The selected objects included a guitar, a wallet, a deck of cards and a bag with the Muppet figure Miss Piggy on the front. Seemingly banal, these things hold very personal memories and associations about its owner. In 2011, this video installation was the first work of Lebanese art to be purchased for the collection by London's Tate Modern. Joreige studied painting and film at the École Supérieure d'Arts Graphiques in Paris in 1990 and at the Rhode Island School of Design in

Providence in the United States. Together with Sandra Dagher, Joreige founded the Beirut Art Center, which she also managed from 2009 to 2014. In 2016/17 she was a scholarship holder at the Radcliffe Institute for Advanced Studies at Harvard University. Since the late 1990s, her works have been exhibited internationally. In 2018 she is represented at the Liverpool Biennale.

Replay, 2000, Three-channel video installation (color, silent), book, text, 4 min.

Lamia Joreige

Annette Kelm

1975 Stuttgart, DE – Berlin, DE

The German conceptual artist and photographer Annette Kelm studied at the Hochschule für bildende Künste Hamburg from 1997. She cites the German non-fiction photographer Hans Hansen as an important inspiration behind her artistic development. Hansen is known above all for his advertising campaigns for Volkswagen and Kodak, among others. Kelm is interested in objects and the way they are represented in the medium of photography. Her colour photographs of objects are staged still lifes she creates in her studio. She hides the context and shows things for what they are. Kelm thus participates in the theoretical considerations on the border between representation and dissolution of the representational in photography.
Kelm's works are shown at international solo and group exhibitions, most recently in 2017 at the Kestnergesellschaft in Hanover, in 2016 at the Museum of Contemporary Art in Detroit and in 2013 at the Museum of Modern Art, New York. In 2011 she participated in the 54th Biennale di Venezia. Kelm's works are represented in the collections of the Tate Modern in London, the Museum of Modern Art in New York, the Solomon R. Guggenheim Museum in New York, and the Centre Pompidou in Paris.

From the series "Körperüberhänge" (Body Capes), 2014, 2 chromogenic prints each each 34 × 31 in (86.3 × 78.5 cm); each framed 34 ½ × 31 ½ × 1 ½ in (87.8 × 80 × 4 cm)

Archive of the Institute of Contemporary History, Munich, Inventory Hannelore Mabry / Bavarian Archive of Feminist Movement

– Signature ED 900, box 526 body cape: "Frau Carrar und die Gewehre – Nicht Brecht Frau Carrar hatte Recht – Gewehre gehören vergraben! Das letzte Wort der Mutter dem Patriarchen nicht !" / "Frau Carrar und die Gewehre – Nicht Brecht Frau Carrar hatte Recht – Gewehre gehören vergraben! Das letzte Wort der Mutter dem Patriarchen nicht !"
– Signature ED 900, box 403 no. 2. body cape: "weder rot noch tot: gewaltlos für den Feminismus kämpfen!" / "Mit Bertha von Suttner – Die Waffen nieder! Dafür kämpft DER FEMINIST"
– Signature ED 900, box 403 no. 8. body cape: "Die Waffen NIEDER!" / "keine Mark keinen Dollar keinen Rubel für WAFFEN"
– Signature ED 900, box 403 no. 7. body cape: "Frauen Mütter Feministen kämpfen für Abrüstung und Entwaffnung aller Länder" / "Wir fordern Abrüstung bis zum Küchenmesser"
– Signature ED 900, box 531 body cape: "Keine Mark, kein Dollar, kein Rubel für Waffen! Der Feminist" / "Menschenrecht statt Männerrecht"
– Signature ED 900, box 403 no. 1. body cape: "Kinder brauchen Liebe, Vertrauen und Geborgenheit keine Pershing II und SS 20" / "Mütter und Väter erzieht eure Kinder zu Kriegsdienstverweigerern"
– Signature ED 900, box 532 body cape: "Keine Mark, kein Dollar, kein Rubel für Waffen!" / "Frauen, Mütter, Feministen für Entwaffnung aller Länder!"
– Signature ED 900, Box 403, no. 3 body cape: "Wir brauchen keine Vaterländer. Wir brauchen Muttererde" / "Menschenrecht statt Männerrecht"
– Signature ED 900, Box 403, no. 3 body cape: "Mit Margarethe Lenore Selenka kämpfen wir!," "Für die Gewalt des Rechts – gegen das Recht der Gewalt" / "Für die Gewalt des Rechts – gegen das Recht der Gewalt" Margarethe Lenore Selenka

Annette Kelm and König Galerie, Berlin / London

Iosif Király

1957 Resita, RO – Bucharest, RO

The Romanian photographer and architect Iosif Király co-founded the Institute of Photography and Media Art at the National University of the Arts (UNArt) in Bucharest in 1995 and continues teaching there until today. Since 2013 he has also been teaching Visual Studies in the Master's Programme of the Şcoala Naţională de Studii Politice şi Administrative in Bucharest. In his artistic and architectural-historical work, Király examines the relationships between perception, time and memory in post-communist Romania, as documented in his major photographic oeuvre, the image montages *Reconstructions, a work in progress* since 2000. A further focus of his work is the artistic performative project *Art History Archive,* which he developed in collaboration with Călin Dan under the label *subREAL.* Here the artists work on and with the image archive of the Romanian art magazine *Arta,* which appeared from 1953 to 1990. In addition, Király initiates research projects with architects, artists, and scientists, such as a long-term study of Romanian architecture that has been ongoing since 2007: the *RO_Archive, An Archive of Romania in Times of Transition* (Bucharest 2017, UNArte, www.roarchive.ro). In addition to his extensive journalistic activities, Király has exhibited in numerous solo and group exhibitions. Most recently, in 2018, the Muzeul Naţional de Artă Contemporană (MNAC - National Museum of Contemporary Art) in Bucharest presented a retrospective of his work, especially is early performative pieces influenced by Fluxus. Király's works are represented in the collections of the Stedelijk Museum, Amsterdam, and the Hamburger Bahnhof – Museum für Gegenwart in Berlin.

From the series "Sinapses" (Mogoşoaia, Găina Mountain, Piatra Neamţ, Roman, Huneodoara, Văratec, Berlin), 2006 – 2017

– *Idols were human beings too,* 12 chromogenic prints, 9 × 14 ⅛ in (23 × 36 cm), 9 × 24 ¾ in (23 × 63 cm), 9 × 7 ⅞ in (23 × 20 cm), 9 × 13 ¾ in (23 × 35 cm), 42 ⅛ × 102 ⅜ in (107 × 260 cm), 9 × 12 ¼ in (23 × 31 cm), 9 × 7 ½ in (23 × 19 cm),
42 ⅛ × 57 ⅛ in (107 × 145 cm), 8 ¼ × 14 ⅛ in (21 × 36 cm), 7 ⅞ × 15 ¾ in (20 × 40 cm), 7 ⅞ × 16 ⅞ in (20 × 43 cm), 7 ⅞ × 5 ⅞ in (20 × 15 cm)

Iosif Király

Joachim Koester

1962 Copenhagen, DK – New York, NY, US

The artist studied at the Royal Danish Academy of Fine Arts in Copenhagen from 1987 to 1993. He combines film, photography, and text in extensive multimedia installations. The starting point for his work is wide-ranging research, often beginning with a story linked to a particular place. His visual inquiry revolves around researchers of the late 19th century, occultists of the early 20th century or radicals of the 1968 scene. In *Morning of the Magicians* (2005), the artist follows the buried traces of the British occultist Aleister Crowley (1875–1947) to Sicily, where he founded the Abbey Thelema between 1920 and 1923. For Koester, the history of the occult is also a history of obscurantism. A mysterious story of ideas that seeps through the darkness of the centuries before suddenly reappearing in the "mystical" 1960s and establishing itself as a small but constant presence in mainstream consumer culture, as he explains in the accompanying text to the work. Since the early 1990s, Koester has participated in exhibitions, in 1997 he was represented at documenta 10 in Kassel, two years later he had a solo exhibition at PS 1 New York. In 2018, Bergen Kunsthall is staging a major solo exhibition entitled *Bringing Something Back,* in which the artist merges all of the museum's gallery spaces into a single large-scale installation. Koester's works can be found in the collections of the Centre Pompidou, Paris, the Moderna Museet, Stockholm, the Museum of Modern Art, New York, and the Museo Nacional Centro de Arte Reina Sofia, Madrid.

– *Morning of the Magicians,* 2005 – 2006, Film, 16mm (black-and-white, silent) 4:50 min, 6 gelatin silver prints, 4 chromogenic prints, each 18 ¹¹⁄₁₆ × 23 ¾ in (47.5 × 60.3 cm)

Courtesy Joachim Koester and Jan Mot, Brussels

Zofia Kulik

1947 Wrocław, PL – Warsaw, PL

The Polish artist Zofia Kulik studied sculpture between 1965 and 1971 at the Akademia Sztuk Pięknych (Academy of Fine Arts) in Warsaw and subsequently set up the artist collective KwieKulik with Przemysław Kwiek, working in the fields of performance, object art, film, and photography. In 1974 the duo founded the independent gallery Studio of Activities, Documentation and Propagation (PDDiU) in their private apartment with an affiliated archive of Polish art from the 1970s and 1980s. Since 1987, Kulik has been working alone and under his own name. Her photographic works are large-scale series consisting of individual black-and-white photographs created by a process of multiple exposures, which she assembles into mosaic-like, geometrically ordered tableaux. In terms of content, Kulik deals with the staging of war and the use of propaganda to stabilize political systems in power. The starting point is her personal experience as the daughter of a Polish soldier during the Warsaw Pact. Symbols of military power, the pathos of socialist ideology and religious signs mix with fragmentary shots of protest marches, executions, and revolts.

She repeatedly uses representations of her model and fellow artist Zbigniew Libera, whose poses reference the representation of masculinity throughout the history of art. Kulik constructs strictly structured pictorial spaces whose aestheticization stands in contrast to the brutality of the subject matter. Kulik's works were exhibited at the 47th Biennale di Venezia in 1997 and at documenta 12 in 2007. Works can be found in the collections of the Centre Pompidou, Paris, the Museum of Modern Art, New York, the Stedelijk Museum, Amsterdam, the Moderna Museet, Stockholm, and the London Tate Modern.

– *The Human Motif I,* 1989, 32 gelatin silver prints, total 94 ½ × 189 in (240 × 480 cm)

Zofia Kulik, Courtesy Gallery Żak | Branicka, Berlin

Darcy Lange

1946 – 2005 Auckland, NZ

New Zealand artist, filmmaker and political activist Darcy Lange studied sculpture at the Elam School of Fine Arts in Auckland from 1964 before graduating from the Royal College of Art in London. From 1972, he began working with photography, film, and video, focusing on people and work. Between 1972 and 1977 he produced *Work Studies* and *A Documentation of Bradford Working Life,* in which he captured the everyday working lives of people in British factories and mines in long uncut and uncommented shots using what he himself called an "encyclopaedic" method. Lange also taught at the Birmingham School of Fine Arts and began to explore the British school system. Over a period of two years, he produced "Work Studies in Schools" (1976/77), a survey of a total of seven British schools that compares different school types and teaching methods and is influenced by Dan Graham's critical-analytical method of video feedback. In the late 1970s, Lange returned to New Zealand, where he joined the struggle of Māori activists fighting for their rights to their lands. He documented this struggle in *Māori Land Project* (1977–1981). From the 1980s he began to focus more on music and developed audiovisual projects, including the multimedia operas *People of the World* (1983) and *Aire del Mar* (1988). Darcy Lange, who is considered a pioneer in the field of politically and socially engaged conceptual documentary films of the 1970s and was involved in the 1976 Venice Biennale and early reviews of video art at the Museum of Modern Art in New York, among others, was internationally forgotten after his return to New Zealand and his early death. Ikon Gallery Birmingham organised a comprehensive retrospective in 2010, in collaboration with the Govett-Brewster Gallery in New Plymouth, New Zealand,

which is in charge of the estate. In 2016, the Tate Modern in London organized a two-day program of Lange's films and videos.

From the series "Work Studies"
– Cantavieja, *Study of Work in a Spanish Village,* 1975, video (black-and-white, sound), 120 min.
– *Ruatoria, Study of Sheep Gathering and a Māori Shearing Gang, East Coast,* 1974, video (black-and-white, sound), 161 min.
– *Waitara Freezing Works, Taranaki,* 1974, video (black-and-white, sound), 73 min.
– *Vern Hume Aerial Top Dressing, Taranaki,* 1974, video (black-and-white, sound), 50 min.

From the series "Work Studies in Schools," 1976–1977
– *Study of Three Birmingham Schools, UK,* 1976, *Ladywood Comprehensive School,* 6 inkjet prints, 1 video (black-and-white, sound), 30 min.
– *Studies of Teaching in Four Oxfordshire Schools, UK,* 1977, *Cheney Upper School,* 6 inkjet prints, 1 video (black-and-white, sound), 70 min.
– *Studies of Teaching in Four Oxfordshire Schools, UK,* 1977, *St Mary's School,* 6 inkjet prints, 1 video (black-and-white, sound), 70 min.

Courtesy of Govett-Brewster Art Gallery and Darcy Lange Estate

Tatiana Lecomte

1971 Bordeaux, FR – Vienna, AT

Tatiana Lecomte studied at the Académie des Beaux-Arts in Lyon from 1991 to 1992 and attended the master class for painting in Graz between 1993 and 1995. In 2002 she graduated from the University of Applied Arts in Vienna. Between 1998 and 2000 she studied at the Gerrit Rietveld Academie in Amsterdam. In her photographic works, Lecomte often uses found pictorial material, which she manipulates using analogue photographic procedures (changing detail, sharpness, size, exposure) and rearranges as a reproduction. The originals, historical photographs or illustrations from antiquarian books, mostly stem from the period of National Socialism, a period in which the production of images was assigned a specific representational function. The examination of representation strategies in these photographs, the appropriation and manipulation of the material, characterises Lecome's conceptual approach, through which she participates in the ongoing discourse on the politics of images. Lecomte's works have been shown in group and solo exhibitions, including in 2004 at the Fotohof, Salzburg, in 2013 at the Jewish Museum, Vienna, and most recently in 2018 at the Josephinum, Vienna. In 2015 Lecomte was awarded the "European Month of Photography Arendt Award". Her works can be found in the Federal Photographic Collection at the Museum der Moderne Salzburg. The Lentos Kunstmuseum Linz will dedicate a solo exhibition to Lecomte in autumn 2018.

From the series "Meine erste Löwin" (My first Lioness), 2018
5 inkjet prints, each 39 ⅜ × 2 ¹⁵/₁₆ in (100 × 75 cm)

Tatiana Lecomte

Susan Meiselas

1948, Baltimore, MD, US – New York, NY, US

The American documentary photographer Susan Meiselas studied visual communication at Harvard University before teaching film and photography at public schools in New York from 1972 to 1974. At the same time, she worked on her first photographic project, which she published in 1976 in the book *Carnival Strippers.* It chronicles the lives of striptease dancers at small fairs in New England. In the same year, she joined the Magnum photo agency, of which she has been a full member since 1980.

Meiselas' photographs of the Sandinista uprising in Nicaragua in 1978/79 gained worldwide attention and iconic status through her book Nicaragua and publications in international magazines such as *The New York Times, GEO* and *Paris Match.* Her documentation of the 1981 El Salvador El Mozote massacre also attracted attention. Deeply shaken by a trip to northern Iraq, where she helped document the exhumations of Kurdish mass graves in 1991, Meiselas set herself the task of creating a collective image archive for the stateless Kurdish people. After six years of research and collecting, Meiselas finally published her project in 1997 in the publication *Kurdistan: In the Shadow of History,* in which she documents the history of Kurdistan with photographs taken over the past 100 years. Meiselas was awarded the Hasselblad Prize in 1994 and the Robert Capa Gold Medal in 1997.

From the project *Kurdistan,* 1991–2008
1 map, 72 ¹/₁₆ × 96 ¹/₁₆ in (183 × 244 cm), booklets, 17 reproductions from historic photographs, sizes variable

Susan Meiselas

Zanele Muholi

1972 Umlazi, ZA – Johannesburg, ZA

Zanele Muholi studied photography at the Market Photo Workshop, the photography school in Johannesburg founded by David Goldblatt in 1989. Her first exhibition *Urban Life Sexuality* was shown at the school's affiliated gallery in 2004 and made her intimate portraits of black lesbian couples known throughout the country. In 2006, she began her portrait series "Faces & Phases," which was conceived as a *work in progress* and today numbers more than 300 works. Muholi photographs her models, as well as herself, in calm poses against clear backgrounds and assembles these images into large tableaux. Her work is an important contribution to giving a face to queers, lesbians, and the transgender community, from an insider perspective. Collectively, the portraits are a visual statement and archive that aims to mark, map, and preserve the often invisible communities for posterity. As a photographer, Muholi sees herself as an activist. 2014 saw the publication of the book of the same name on "Faces & Phases," where the images are accompanied by texts and interviews that tell of the dangerous reality in a homophobic society. In 2017 the Stedelijk Museum,

Amsterdam, dedicated a large solo exhibition to her and also purchased works for the collection.
From the series "Faces & Phases," 2006–ongoing, digital prints of 30 portraits, each 30 1/8 × 19 7/8 in (76.5 × 50.5 cm)

Zanele Muholi, Courtesy of Stevenson, Cape Town / Johannesburg and Yancey Richardson, New York

Peter Piller

1968 Fritzlar, DE–Hamburg, DE

The German conceptual artist Peter Piller studied fine arts at the Hochschule für bildende Künste in Hamburg from 1993 to 2000. At the end of the 1990s, he began to study the aesthetics of images in regional daily newspapers and to collect them as newspaper clippings. He sorted the found pictorial material thematically into groups and provided them with succinct titles such as *In Löcher blicken* (Looking Into Holes) or *Autos berühren* (Touching Cars), or like his first series *Noch ist nichts zu sehen (Bauerwartungsflächen)* (Nothing Can Be Seen Yet [Development Sites]), which emerged from sales advertisements for building land and which Piller published in his first artist's book. The resulting "Archive Peter Piller" now also includes pictorial material from company archives and private collections. With the serial reorganization of images and their titling in his installations and artist books, Piller visualizes an aesthetic of the unintentional and casual that leaves room for new and free chains of associations. Since 2006, Piller has held a professorship for photography in the field of contemporary art at the Hochschule für Grafik und Buchkunst in Leipzig.

— "Dauerhaftigkeit" (1) (Permanence), 2005
  21 gelatin silver prints,
  each 8 9/16 × 11 13/16 in (21.7 × 30 cm)
— "Dauerhaftigkeit" (3) (Permanence), 2005
  24 gelatin silver prints,
  each 8 9/16 × 11 13/16 in (21,7 × 30 cm)

Courtesy Capitain Petzel, Berlin

Walid Raad

1967 Chbanieh, LB–New York, NY, US

Walid Raad examines Lebanon's recent past and the construction of history in general through photographs, videos, installations, and texts. Posing as a fictitious collective, The Atlas Group, Raad set up a fictional archive in 1989 to allegedly document Lebanon's contemporary history on the basis of documentary sources. The thematic focus is on descriptions of the Lebanon wars from 1975 to 1991.
The archive is also available online and claims to be authentic. It contains numerous photographs, videos, and notebooks that were either donated by (supposedly) contemporary witnesses who left their documents to the Atlas Group or have been unearthed by the collective's own research. The retrievable documents are ultimately Raad's own artistic works, some of which are based on actual archive material. By presenting these documents, which are not immediately recognizable as a mixture of facts and fiction, as authentic, Raad demonstrates that the concept of truth and authorship in historiography can be deceptive and manipulative. In 2004 Raad declared the project completed after 15 years. In 2011 he was awarded the prestigious Hasselblad Prize and in 2016 the Infinity Award, which has been presented by the International Center of Photography New York since 1985. His works were presented at documenta 11 in Kassel, among other venues. The New York Museum of Modern Art dedicated a solo exhibition to him in 2015. Raad teaches at the Cooper Union in New York.

— "Better be watching the clouds," 1992 / 2017
  12 pigmented inkjet prints, each 30 × 20 in
  (76.2 × 50.8 cm)

Courtesy Walid Raad and Sfeir-Semler Gallery, Hamburg / Beirut

Einar Schleef

1944 Sangerhausen, DE–2001 Berlin, DE

Einar Schleef was a German theater director, writer, stage designer, painter, graphic artist, actor, and photographer. Since the 1970s, his theater work, in particular, has set standards, but also met with strong criticism. Schleef began his studies in photography in 1964 at the Kunsthochschule Berlin-Weißensee. He attended the class of Arno Fischer, who taught his students that they should make their personal experiences their subject: observed pictures not staged ones. During this time Schleef lived in a backyard apartment in Weißensee together with four older ladies, whose social life he documented. Under the title *Nachbarn* (Neighbours), he presented part of the series in his diploma examination. Fischer described it as one of the best works he had ever seen. Starting in 1970, he painted a portrait of Sangerhausen, his birthplace in the Harz Mountains, which he published in 1981 in the photo book *Zuhause* (At Home), which was published between the first and second volumes of his novel *Gertrud* and focuses on an inner monologue of his mother. Schleef had left the GDR in 1976, and his mother continued to live in Sangerhausen. With this book, he also takes action against his obsessive homesickness and opens it with the sentence: "Never to go back, to get over it, to flee until you have your own home, which suffocates and eats you up". Schleef's photographs depict a very direct, unembellished view of reality, the prints seem raw. He worked with the West Berlin photographer Michael Schmidt on his photo book *Waffenruhe* (Ceasefire), for which he provided staccato texts; today it is regarded as one of the most important photo books from post-war Germany. Schleef wrote the text "Schwarz-Rot-Gold" for Seiichi Furuya's GDR photographs; it was published in the 2010 photo book *Mémoires* 1984-1987. Schleef's estate is housed at the Akademie der Künste Berlin, which has honored his photographic work in a retrospective and a comprehensive 2010 catalogue.

— *Frau V. hat Besuch,* (Mrs V. has visitors), 1965,
  fanfold, 12 gelatin silver prints,
  each 7 1/16 × 9 7/16 in (18 × 24 cm)

Akademie der Künste, Berlin,
Einar-Schleef-Archive no. 480_1–12

— *Zuhause* (At Home), 1970, 10 gelatin silver
  prints, each 11 13/16 × 15 3/4 in (30 × 40 cm)

Akademie der Künste, Berlin, Einar-Schleef-Archive no. 569_4, 569_5, 569_7, 569_9, 570_12, 570_18, 571_23, 572_32, 72_44, 573_53

— 5 contact sheets, each 16 9/16 × 11 11/16 in
  (42 × 29.7 cm)

Akademie der Künste, Berlin, Einar-Schleef-Archive no. 960, 961, 962, 963, 964, 965

Archive Akademie der Künste, Berlin

Jörg Schlick

1951–2005 Graz, AT

The Austrian concept artist Jörg Schlick studied art history under Wilfried Skreiner in Graz and saw himself as a musician, painter, curator, author, choreographer, and stage designer. Schlick espoused an extended concept of art. His object art, based on seriality and combinatorics, stood in the tradition of Fluxus and was intended to reconcile high and everyday culture. From May 1991, he was the editor of the magazine *Sonne Busen Hammer* (Sun Breasts Hammer), the central organ of the legendary Lord Jim Loge, a (pseudo-)elitist, fraternity-esque nonsense group of artists founded in 1985 by Schlick, Martin Kippenberger, Albert Oehlen, and Wolfgang Bauer, among others. In his function as head of the Department of Fine Arts at the Forum Stadtpark Graz, a position he held from 1986 to 1991, Schlick successfully advocated an international perception of the Graz art scene. From 1996 to 2001 he was a visiting professor for artistic design at the Graz University of Technology, and from 2003 he taught information design at the Joanneum University of Applied Sciences. In 1997 Schlick received the Outstanding Achievement Award in the Visual Arts of the City of Graz and in 2005 the Outstanding Achievement Award of the State of Styria. In 2015, the Künstlerhaus, Halle für Kunst & Medien in Graz organized a comprehensive retrospective with an accompanying publication, which for the first time contained a complete catalogue of his work.

— *Poésie Noire* (Black poetry), 2001,
  24 chromogenic prints, each 23 5/8 × 23 5/8 in
  (60 × 60 cm)

Estate of Jörg Schlick

Michael Schmidt

1945–2014 Berlin, DE

Today, Michael Schmidt is regarded as one of the most important photographers and mediators of post-war Germany. In a programmatic text, he states that his images should remain as neutral as possible. Things should represent only themselves in the picture. In this manner, he dealt with the reality of life in West Berlin, from the 1970s onwards. After the fall of communism, he expanded his interests to the whole of Germany, leading to series such as *EIN-HEIT* (Unity) (1996) and *Irgendwo* (Somewhere) (2005) and thematic blocks such as *Women* (2000), *Food* (2012) and *NATURE* (2014). From 1969 Schmidt taught photography at the Volkshochschule Berlin-Kreuzberg. From this activity arose the idea for the Werkstatt für Photographie, which he founded in 1976 and ran until 1981. It is thanks to him that the Berlin photo scene was able to make contact with international photographers through the Kreuzberg workshops and presentations. In 1979/80 Schmidt held a teaching position at the University/GHS Essen, the successor to the Steinert Chair at the Folkwang Hochschule. Schmidt's versatile commitment to photography is comparable to that of Manfred Willmann.

Schmidt and his wife Karin were friends with Willmann and Christine Frisinghelli. During a workshop in Graz in 1984 Schmidt first became acquainted with the work of Einar Schleef, which was exhibited there at the same time. Schmidt came into personal contact with Schleef in Berlin following an introduction by the Frisinghellis. The book *Waffenruhe* (Ceasefire), published in 1987, is a cooperative project of the two. His works can be found in the Berlinische Galerie, the Museum of Modern Art, New York, the Sprengel Museum Hannover, and the Museum Folkwang, Essen.

From the series *Waffenruhe* (Ceasefire)
1985–1987, 20 gelatin silver prints,
each 19 ^{11}/$_{16}$ × 15 ¾ in (50 × 40 cm)

Galerie Claes Nordenhake/Stiftung für Fotografie und Medienkunst with Archive Michael Schmidt

8 gelatin silver prints, each 19 ^{11}/$_{16}$ × 15 ¾ in (50 × 40 cm)

Collection Hoppenstedt—Burgwedel/Berlin

Michael Schuster/ Hartmut Skerbisch

1956 Graz, AT–Graz, AT 1945 Ramsau am Dachstein, AT–2009 Gleisdorf near Graz, AT

While studying architecture at the Graz University of Technology, Hartmut Skerbisch began to engage with new media technologies in the context of an expanded concept of space. In 1969 he made his first artistic appearance with the spatial arrangement *Putting Allspace in a Notshall* developed together with Manfred Wolff-Plottegg. With this installation of cameras and monitors, he is regarded as one of the early representatives of Austrian media art. He studied the construction of reality using new technologies. Michael Schuster graduated from the Kunstgewerbeschule in Graz. His conceptual photography, sculpture and media work explores the apparatus technologies we employ to form an image of the world. In many works, the camera itself becomes the image content, as in *Autofocusfalle* (Autofocus Trap) / (1989) and // (1991). In his *Amerika-Arbeit* (America Work) (1993), the Kodak colour wedge becomes the central image object, which also serves to challenge an objective representation of the American landscape. Schuster expands the spectrum of reflection on the perception of reality to include perceptible deceptions— an often irritating dimension.

A 20-year collaboration linked both artists. Between 1980 and 1990, they joint created their main piece, *Szene aus dem gleichnamigen Stück* (Scene from the Play by the Same Name), in which they "evoke a state in which we could already live: the state of everyone has seen everything." The title, Szene, refers to a situation that creates a context for individual, very different stages and stagings of the work: an edition of postcards; the staging of the exhibition as a scene in which the postcards are again exhibited as objects; the Hasselblad camera object with four original lenses, supplemented by the statement *Alle haben Alles gesehen* (All Have Been Seen by All), replicated and reproduced in volume as a silkscreen edition.

The functionalities of photography become the object of the investigation and are at the same time the tool with which the investigation is carried out.

In 2015 the Kunsthaus Graz dedicated the exhibition *Das Paradies der Untergang—Medienarbeiten* (Paradise, Demise—Media Works) posthumously to Hartmut Skerbisch, accompanied by a comprehensive catalogue of his works.

– *Alle haben Alles gesehen* (All Have Been Seen by All), 1989 serigraph on alucobond, 32 ¼ × 66 ^{9}/$_{16}$ in (82 × 169 cm)

Private collection Graz

Allan Sekula

1951 Erie, PA, US—2013 Los Angeles, CA, US

The American artist, filmmaker and photography theorist Allan Sekula studied fine arts at the University of California in San Diego from 1968 to 1974. After starting with performative works and installations, which he himself called "critical realism" and which were influenced by Marxism, he turned to photography in 1972. However, his works cannot be classified either in the tradition of American social documentaries or in that of artistic-conceptual photography. Sekula's multidisciplinary artistic work, which encompasses photography, film, and text as extended documentary practice, as well as his groundbreaking essays, have profoundly and lastingly changed the debate on photography, on the representation of the economic, political, and social in the current discourse on art and society. Aiming at maximum realism, he developed visual recordings which he annotated in detail and which were first created in his immediate environment, for example in *Aerospace Folktales* (1973). Later, he extended his research to include complex global connections between economy and politics and their consequences in conditions of work, production, and life. Sekula uses visual research to question the connections between low wages, resource consumption and the distribution of goods. His main work is the nine-part work *Fish Story* (1995), for which he documented the ports of Barcelona, Gdansk, Hong Kong, and Rotterdam and the living conditions in these cities between 1988 and 1994. With this work, Sekula was represented at documenta 11 in Kassel in 2002. From 1985 until his death Sekula taught at the California Institute of the Arts. His monograph *Photography Against the Grain* (1984) summarises his fundamental theoretical and artistic contributions to photography and was recently reprinted. His works can be found in collections such as the Museu d'Art Contem-

porani de Barcelona, Getty Research Institute, Los Angeles, Centre Pompidou Paris and the Generali Foundation Collection at the Museum der Moderne Salzburg.

– *Walking on Water*, 1990/1995, chapter 9 from "Fish Story," 1989–1995, Slide projection, 80 slides (35mm, color), 14 min.

Thyssen-Bornemisza Art Contemporary Collection

Ahlam Shibli

1970 Arab al-Shibli, PS–Haifa, PS/IL

Palestinian photographer Ahlam Shibli first studied art and archaeology at the Hebrew University in Jerusalem and completed her master's degree in film and television at Tel Aviv University in 2004. In her documentary photographs, Shibli deals with the concept of homeland, its loss, and the struggle to regain it. At the same time, she includes the ambivalence of this concept, which can also signify restriction and its geographical and spiritual interpretations. Thematically, she orbits both the history and present day of Palestine as well as the experiences of loss and trauma in other places. In her photography, Shibli is primarily concerned with revealing that "which is obscured by politics, ideology, social forces, and tradition." Shibli's' works are shown internationally in solo and group exhibitions, most recently at documenta 12 in Kassel and Athens, with the two large-scale series *Heimat* and *Occupation* (both 2016/17).

From the series "Death. Palestine," 2011–2012
– No. 59–68, 10 out of 68 chromogenic prints, each 39 ^{3}/$_8$ × 27 ^{9}/$_{16}$ in (100 × 70 cm)

Ahlam Shibli

Lieko Shiga

1980 Aichi, JP–Miyagi, JP

Lieko Shiga studied at Chelsea University of Art and Design in London and received a BA in Fine Arts New Media in 2004. In 2008 she received the prestigious Ihee Kimura Photography Award and one year later moved to Kitakama, a coastal city in the Tohoku region of Japan. Here she documented festivals and other official events and simultaneously recorded interviews on the history of the region. These experiences had a great influence on her artistic practice. Shiga's photographs from Kitakama differ from her earlier works in that they were created as long-term projects over a period of more than four years in direct collaboration with the local residents. Shiga acts as a translator of pictorial ideas and personal, figurative memories of the residents. Her works are surreal and seem more like recordings of theatrical performances. Kitakama was badly hit by the tsunami in March 2011; these experiences permeate the staged visual worlds, but they are very different from other documentaries of the catastrophe. In 2013 Shiga summarized the series in the photo book *Rasen Kaigan,* which has acquired something of a cult status.

From the series "Rasen Kaigan," (Spiral Coast)
2008–2012 (2018), 8 chromogenic prints,
35 ⅞ × 2 ⅜ in (91.1 × 60 cm)

Lieko Shiga

Jo Spence

1934–1992 London, GB

Jo Spence has been an established figure in the photographic discourse in Great Britain since the 1970s. Through her diverse projects, she is known for her political approach to photography and her portrayal of her personal struggle against cancer. She began her career as an assistant in a commercial photo studio and specialized in family portraits. Her classical training led her to a deep understanding of photographic technology and served as a starting point for her theoretical considerations and texts. In the early 1970s, Spence's work shifted from commercial activity to a more interrogative and critical approach to documentation, although she later criticised orthodox documentary practices. For almost two decades she worked together with Terry Dennett on social, artistic and photographic projects. The aim of the collaborative project "Re-Modelling Photo History" (1982) was to question predominant models of visual representation in photography through a form of "photo theatre". They alienated typically Western genres of photography such as exotic travel photography or the erotic nude in order to rethink the traditional relationship between photographer and model and thus rewrite the history of photography through the medium itself. The series was exhibited at documenta 12 in 2007. Works by Spence can be found in the Museo Nacional Centro de Arte Reina Sofia in Madrid and the Museum Folkwang in Essen.

— "Re-Modelling Photo History," 1981–1982, collaboration with Terry Dennett, 13 gelatin silver prints, each 9 13/16 × 7 7/8 in (25 × 20 cm)

Courtesy The Estate of Jo Spence, Courtesy Richard Saltoun Gallery, London

Christian Wachter

1949 Oberwart, AT – Wien, AT

The Austrian artist Christian Wachter studied medicine in Graz from 1970 to 1977. Wachter came to photography in 1980 through the photographer and exhibition organizer Manfred Willmann. He presented his first works in 1981 in the Atelier Lang in Graz. Wachter is primarily interested in the construction and perception of history and identities. His works, often developed in lengthy research and production processes, consist of a combination of image and text. He mixes supposed facts with fiction and allows for several levels of meaning that enable the viewer to create his own references. Exemplary for this is his early work *AURORA* (1988/89), which he implemented both as an installation and as an artist's book. Here he refers both to the ancient goddess of dawn and to the name of a Russian battleship that was deployed to conquer the Winter Palace in St. Petersburg in 1917, marking the beginning of the October Revolution. The series *The Incomparables. Impressions D'AFRIQUE* (2006) is based on Raymond Roussel's novel *Impressions d'Afrique* of 1910 and deals with the question of identity and difference between Europe and Africa, a topic that is of greater political relevance today than ever before.
Wachter's works are represented in public collections, among others in the Museum Folkwang, Essen, Museum Moderner Kunst, Vienna, and in the Federal Photographic Collection at the Museum der Moderne Salzburg.

— *L'incomparable*. From: *Impressions D'AFRIQUE*, (Impressions from Africa, The Incomparables), 12 out of a series with 62 chromogenic prints, Version 2006, each 23 3/8 × 21 1/4 in (59.5 × 54 cm)

Austrian Federal Photography Collection at the Museum der Moderne Salzburg, DLF 1698_12, 13, 19, 20, 21, 25, 29, 30, 33, 34, 40, 41

Manfred Willmann

1952 Graz, AT – Graz, AT

Manfred Willmann is a freelance photographer, curator, and publicist. In addition to his training at the Graz School of Applied Arts, his photographic education received important stimuli from Erich Kees and the Graz photo group of the TVN (Tourist Association of Friends of Nature). Otto Breicha became aware of Willmann at an early age and exhibited him together with renowned Austrian photographers. In 1974 Willmann began organizing exhibitions in the Fotogalerie im Schillerhof; from 1975 he was able to continue this work as the Forum Stadtpark. From 1976 onwards, as head of the photo department of the Künstlervereinigung, he set up a continuous exhibition programme (in which Seiichi Furuya also participated) aimed at bringing Austrian photography into an exchange with international positions. Together with Christine Frisinghelli he initiated the Symposion on Photography, which took place from 1979 to 1997 as a contribution to the festival steirischer herbst in Graz. In order to make the contributions to the symposia accessible to a wider public, he founded the magazine *Camera Austria International* in 1980 and remained its editor-in-chief until 2010. After separating from the Forum Stadtpark in 1997, he co-founded the association Camera Austria, Laboratory for Photography and Theory, and served as its chairman until 2010. Willmann is interested in the photographer's engagement with the world, with documentary and conceptual approaches being of equal importance to him. The form of the artist's book accommodates his work in thematic projects with autobiographical references, such as the monographs "Schwarz und Gold" (Black and Gold) (1981), *Das Land* (The Land) (2000) and *Blitz und Enzianblau* (Lightning And Gentian Blue) (2017). In 2005 the catalogue raisonné *Werkblick* was published for the retrospective of his work in the Neue Galerie in Graz. Works can be found in the Albertina, Vienna, the Joanneum Graz, the Museum Folkwang, Essen, the Museo di Fotografia Contemporanea, Cinisello Balsamo, and the Museum of Modern Art, New York.

From "Schwarz und Gold" (Black and Gold), 1979–1981, part 3
Ich träume nie! (I Never Dream!)
16 gelatin silver prints, each 24 × 20 1/8 in (60.8 × 51 cm)
Museum der Moderne Salzburg,
F 131_1–15_5, 6, 12, 13; GF 132_1–25_1, 2, 3, 5, 7, 10, 14, 15, 18, 20, 22, 25

Tobias Zielony

1973 Wuppertal, DE – Berlin, DE

Tobias Zielony studied film and documentary photography at the University of Wales in Newport before moving to Timm Rautert's class at the Hochschule für Grafik und Buchkunst in Leipzig in 2001. He graduated here as a master student. Zielony is known for his portrayal of minority youth in the suburbs, a subject he had already addressed during his studies in Newport. For his first book project *Behind the Block* (2004), he extended his research to a total of four European cities to observe young people in public spaces, often at night. *Trona* (2008) shows young people from the desert city of the same name not far from Los Angeles. When the former industrial town fell into economic decline, many of its inhabitants began to anaesthetize themselves with the drug Crystal Meth. Trona stands for many towns in impoverished rural America. Zielony examines the consequences of disintegrating social and institutional structures and people being left to their own devices. He deals with social realities, structural change, migration, drug abuse, and sex work as in *Jenny, Jenny* (2013). In 2015 he participated with his work *The Citizen* (2015) in the presentation of the German Pavilion at the 56th Biennale di Venezia.

Haus der Jugend (House of Youth) 2017, Two-channel installation, digital slide show (color, silent), 12:13 min., 11:44 min.

Courtesy KOW, Berlin

Authors

Reinhard Braun

was born in Linz, AT, in 1964. He studied art history at the Karl Franzens-University in Graz and has been the artistic director of Camera Austria and editor of the magazine *Camera Austria International* since 2011. His most recent curatorial projects include: Özlem Altin: Processing (2017), *Un-Curating the Archive* (2017 and 2018), *Karina Nimmerfall: Indirect Interviews with Women* and Heidi Specker: *Photography* (both 2018). Publisher of Edition Camera Austria, most recently: *Horáková + Maurer: TPX Index, Karina Nimmerfall: Indirect Interviews with Women* and *Heidi Specker: Photography* (all 2018). Braun lives and works in Graz.

Christine Frisinghelli

is a curator and author focusing on contemporary photography. From 1976 she worked with Manfred Willmann on the development of Forum Stadtpark Graz's photography program with exhibitions and workshops by international photographers. From 1979 to 1997 Frisinghelli organized annual Symposion on Photography as a contribution to the contemporary art festival steirischer herbst. In 1980 she was a co-founder of the magazine *Camera Austria International* and editor-in-chief for 112 issues until 2010. From 1996 to 1999 Frisinghelli was artistic director of steirischer herbst. Since 2001 she has been the custodian of the Pierre Bourdieu photo archive, which is managed by Camera Austria. Frisinghelli was a visiting professor at the University of Applied Arts Vienna from 1992 to 1993 and a lecturer at the Hochschule für Gestaltung Zurich from 1993 to 2004. Since 2012 she teaches at the Fondazione Modena Arti Visive in Modena, IT.

Toshiharu Ito

was born in Akita, JP, in 1953. In 1983, he graduated in history from the University of Tokyo. From 1988 he was a first assistant professor and from 1994 full professor at the Tama Art University in Tokyo. Since 2002 he has taught in the Department of Intermediality at the National University of Fine Arts and Music in Tokyo. In 2005 Ito headed the Design Committee for the Expo 2005 in Aichi. He is a member of the board of the Tokyo Metropolitan Museum of Photography. Ito's focus is on the history of photography, but he also researches and publishes across disciplines on the interconnections of art, design, science, and technology. Ito lives in Tokyo.

Sandra Križić Roban

is an art critic, curator, lecturer, author and works as a scientific coordinator at the Institute of Art History at the University of Zagreb, HR. From 2000 to 2017 she was editor-in-chief of the art magazine *Život umjetnosti,* as well as director of the project *Postmedia and Non-institutional Art Practices from the 1960s.*
Her research focuses on contemporary art, the history and theory of photography, post-war architecture, discourses in public space, and contemporary war memorials. She is the author of the only two comprehensive studies on contemporary photography and painting in Croatia: *At Second Glance: The Positions of Contemporary Croatian Photography* (2010) and *Croatian Painting from 1945 to Today* (2013). She has curated a series of retrospectives and thematic exhibitions and has published several books and numerous reviews, essays and scientific papers; she works for print media, but also for radio and television. Together with others, in 2013 she founded the Büro für Fotografie, a non-profit organization dedicated to researching and promoting contemporary photography.

Christiane Kuhlmann

was born in Essen, DE, in 1967 and has been curator for photography and media art at the Museum der Moderne Salzburg, AT, since 2016. She holds a doctorate in art history with a focus on photography and media of the 20th and 21st centuries and has many years of scientific and practical experience as a curator and conservator. From 2001 to 2011 she was a research associate at the Photographic Collection at the Museum Folkwang in Essen, and worked as a freelance curator for the Rijksmuseum Amsterdam, NL, the Museo Picasso Malaga, ES, and Art Museum Bern, CH. She explores the media interfaces of photography and dance and works on forms of representation of photography. At the Berlinische Galerie she dealt with the re-evaluation of the press photographer Erich Salomon. She works as an author and was a lecturer in the theory and history of photography at the FH Dortmund, DE, from 2010 to 2015.

Maren Lübbke-Tidow

works as a freelance author and curator in Berlin. From 1997 to 2014 she was closely associated with the Camera Austria project as an author, curator, editor, and editor-in-chief. Her texts appear in numerous magazines, catalogues, and monographs. In 2018, she curated Jochen Lempert's *Some Plant Volatiles* at the Kunsthaus Wien, AT, his *Botanical Box* at the French Pavilion in Zagreb, HR, (together with Sandra Križić-Roban), and *Stillleben. Eigensinn der Dinge* at the Kunsthaus Wien, AT. For the latter, she edited the book *Eigensinn der Dinge, Bilder, Fotografie. Still Life in Photographic Concepts of the Present* which was published by Spector Books, Leipzig. In 2018/19 she was on the jury of the f/12.2 Project Scholarship at DZ Bank, Frankfurt, DE.

Roberta Valtorta

was born in Milan, IT, in 1952. She is a historian and critic of photography, Vice President of the Italian Society for the Study of Photography (SISF) and member of the scientific advisory board of the journal RSF. From 2004 to 2016, Valtorta was Scientific Director of the Museum of Contemporary Photography in Cinisello Balsamo, IT. She has taught at the Universities of Udine, Rome, and Milan. Since 1984 she has taught at the Centro Bauer in Milan.
She has curated numerous exhibitions in Italy and other European countries, including several publicly funded projects on photography and landscape, and published numerous books and essays.

Colophon

Exhibition

This catalogue has been published in conjunction with the exhibition
*Camera Austria International –
Labor für Fotografie und Theorie*
November 24, 2018 to March 3, 2019

Organized by

Museum der Moderne Salzburg

Director: Dr. Thorsten Sadowsky
Curator: Dr. Christiane Kuhlmann, Curator
Photography and Media Art,
and Curatorial Assistant Mag. Christina
Penetsdorfer
Guest curator: Christine Frisinghelli
Registrar: Susanne Greimel
Assistant to the Registrar:
Lena McFadden BSc.
Conservation: Mag. art. Maria Emberger,
Mag. art. Theresa Wagner
Exhibition Installation: hs art service austria
Technicians Museum der Moderne Salzburg:
DI (FH) Gerald Horn (Head),
Max Wittmann (Audiovisual Media),
Christian Hauer, Alija Salihovic
External technique: Sound & Image,
Rankweil, Thomas Irger, Michael Krupica
Marketing and Communication:
Mag. Susanne Susanka (Head),
Anna Feiler MA
Press and Public Relations:
Martin Moser BA
Art Education: Mag. Martina Pohn (Head),
Mag. Elisabeth Ihrenberger,
Victoria Fahrengruber
Insurance: AON

The exhibition was organized in
collaboration with

Camera Austria

Artistic direction, editor: Reinhard Braun
Editing: Christina Töpfer (editor-in-chief),
Margit Neuhold
Foto-Archive Pierre Bourdieu:
Christine Frisinghelli
Managing directors: Katrin Müller
Assistant curator,
Exhibition management: Angelika Maierhofer
Assistance of the exhibition
management: Katharina Oberegger
Distribution: Barbara Stummvoll
Advertising manager: Barbara Stöcker
Research library: Barbara Stummvoll,
Margit Neuhold
Art education: Barbara Augustinović, Clara
Frühwirth, Lena Kinast, Daniela Zehetner
Board: Sabine Bitter, Reinhard Braun, Karina
Nimmerfall, Wilfried Prantner, Walter Seidl,
Christina Töpfer, Helmut Weber

Lenders to the Exhibition

Akademie der Künste, Berlin
Sabine Bitter/Helmut Weber, Vienna
Buchmann Galerie, Berlin
Camera Austria, Graz
Capitain Petzel, Berlin
Petar Dabac, Zagreb
Deichtorhallen Hamburg/Sammlung
Falckenberg
Hans-Peter Feldmann, Düsseldorf
Museum Folkwang, Essen
Fraenkel Gallery, San Francisco
Seiichi Furuya, Graz
Goodman Gallery, Johannesburg
Nachlass Luigi Ghirri, Modena
Dietrich H. Hoppenstedt
Estate Darcy Lange and Govett-Brewster
Art Gallery, New Plymouth
Lamia Joreige, Beirut
König Galerie, Berlin
KOW, Berlin
Tatiana Lecomte, Vienna
Michael Mauracher, Salzburg
Jan Mot, Brussels
Susan Meiselas, New York
Galerie Nordenhake, Berlin
Privatsammlung, Graz
Nachlass Jörg Schlick, Graz
Galerie Sfeir-Semler, Hamburg/Beirut
Ahlam Shibli, Haifa
Nachlass Jo Spence und Richard Saltoun
Gallery, London
Stevenson, Capetown
Stiftung für Fotografie und Medienkunst mit
Archiv Michael Schmidt
Sammlung Thyssen-Bornemisza Art
Contemporary
Galerie Thomas Zander, Cologne
Ivo Wessel, Berlin
Manfred Willmann, Graz
Gallery Żak | Branicka, Berlin

Acknowledgments

Laura Bielau, Sabine Breitwieser,
Seiichi Furuya, Fraenkel Gallery
(San Francisco), Gabriele Gerecke,
Ilaria and Adele Ghirri, Stefan Gronert,
Toshiharu Ito, Kurt Kaindl,
Verlag der Buchhandlung Walther König,
Lana Lovrenčić, Maren Lübbke-Tidow,
Hans-Ulrich Müller-Schwefe,
Michael Neubacher, Slavica Perkovic,
Karin Schmidt, Steidl Verlag,
Estate of Jo Spence, Sally Stein,
Petra Steinhardt, Suhrkamp Verlag,
Mercedes Vicente, Thomas Weski,
Manfred Willmann, Paul Zach,
David Zwirner Gallery (New York/London/
Hong Kong)

Museum der Moderne Salzburg

Director: Dr. Thorsten Sadowsky
Assistant of the Director: Dr. Sabine Haydl,
Dipl. Kulturw. Anna Rechberger

Executive Office
Marketing and communication:
Mag. Susanne Susanka (Head),
Anna Feiler MA
Press and Public Relations:
Martin Moser BA
Library: Mag. Stefanie Grünangerl BA
(Generali Foundation Studienzentrum)
Museum guard, head:
Thomas Fenninger and team
Technique: DI (FH) Gerald Horn (Head),
Max Wittmann (Audiovisual media),
Christian Hauer, Alija Salihovic

Exhibitions and collections
Curators: Dr. Barbara Herzog (collection and
digitization/image archive),
Dr. Christiane Kuhlmann (Photography and
Media Art), Mag. Antonia Lotz MA (curator
collection Generali Foundation),
Dr. Lena Nievers (curator and head of the
collection, Modern Art),
Mag. Tina Teufel MAS (Contemporary Art)
Registrar: Susanne Greimel
Assistant to the Registrar:
Lena McFadden BSc.
Assistant of exhibition production:
Stefanie Jones BA
Technician art depot: Bernhard Bernardi
Assistant to the Registrar Landessammlung:
Annemarie Rettenbacher
Assistant curator:
Mag. Christina Penetsdorfer
Curatorial assistants:
Mag. Andrea Lehner-Hagwood
(Photography and Media art),
Marijana Schneider MA (management)
Art education: Mag. Martina Pohn (Head),
Mag. Elisabeth Ihrenberger,
Victoria Fahrengruber

Administration
Head of administration and finance:
Mag. Friedrun Schwanzer
Assistant to the head of administration
and Finance: Daniela Eibl
Head of accounting: Christina Latocha
Museum store: Brigitte Fortner (head)
and team

Supervisory board
Dr. Heinrich Schellhorn (chairman)
Dr. Brigitta Pallauf (vice chairwoman)
Dr. Gertrud Frauenberger
Heideswinth Kurz

The Museum der Moderne Salzburg is
sponsored with funds provided by the
Province of Salzburg.

Publication

Edited by the
Museum der Moderne Salzburg

Mönchsberg 32
5020 Salzburg, Austria
T + 43 662 84 22 20–0
F + 43 662 84 22 20–700
info@mdmsalzburg.at
www.mdmsalzburg.at

Texts by: Reinhard Braun,
Christine Frisinghelli, Toshiharu Ito,
Christiane Kuhlmann, Maren Lübbke-Tidow,
Sandra Križić Roban, Roberta Valtorta,
with an introduction from Thorsten Sadowksy
Editing: Christine Frisinghelli,
Christiane Kuhlmann, Christina Penetsdorfer
Head of Production: Jan Wenzel, Spector Books
Copy editing: Michael Pilewski
Translation from German into English:
Jan Caspers, Simon Cowper,
Mike Hembury, Robert Savage
Graphic design: Markus Dreßen,
Hannes Drißner, Spector Books
Typeface: Agipo, www.radimpesko.com
Lithographs: ScanColor, Leipzig
Paper: Fly extraweiß, 90 g/m^2, LuxoArt Gloss
130 g/m^2, PrimatColor grau 90 g/m^2
and kanariengelb 160 g/m^2
Printing and Binding: DZA Druckerei zu
Altenburg GmbH

© 2018 Museum der Moderne Salzburg,
the authors, and Spector Books

Bibliographic information published by the
Deutsche Nationalbibliothek
The Deutsche Nationalbibliothek lists
this publication in the Deutsche
Nationalbibliografie; detailed bibliographic
data are available in the internet at
http://dnb.dnb.de.

Published by
Spector Books OHG
Harkortstraße 10
04107 Leipzig
Germany
T + 49 (0) 341 264 510 12
F + 49 (0) 341 212 24 11
mail@spectorbooks.com
www.spectorbooks.com

Distribution:
Germany/Austria:
GVA, Gemeinsame Verlagsauslieferung
Göttingen GmbH&Co.KG,
www.gva-verlage.de
Switzerland: AVA Verlagsauslieferung AG,
www.ava.ch

ISBN 978-3-95905-233-7

Printed in Germany

Copyright

Text Credits

© Copyrights for the texts by the authors
Branka Andjelkovic, "How, 'persons and
objects' become political in Sanja Iveković's
art?," in *Sanja Iveković: Selected Works*, exh.
cat., Fundació Antoni Tàpies, Barcelona: 2008,
© Fundació Antoni Tàpies.
Lewis Baltz, "Anmerkungen zu Park City"
and "Notizen zu Waffenruhe," in Lewis Baltz,
Texte, Göttingen: Steidl Verlag, 2013,
(p. 49–58) and (p. 93–97), © Lewis Baltz Trust.
Lewis Baltz, "Konsumterror:
Die spätindustrielle Entfremdung,"
in *Camera Austria International* 18/1985,
(p. 16–27). © Lewis Baltz Trust.
Monika Faber, "'Ich suche keine Antwort,'
Seiichi Furuya im Gespräch mit Monika Faber,"
in *Seiichi Furuya: Mémoires*, exh. cat.,
Tokyo: Tokyo Metropolitan Museum of
Photography, 2010.
Christopher Isherwood, *Good-bye to Berlin*,
London: The Hogarth Press, 1939.
© The Christopher Isherwood Foundation,
All rights reserved.
Monika Pessler, "Jörg Schlick, Poésie Noire,"
in Jörg Schlick, *Gleich scheuen Hirschen
in Wäldern versteckt zu leben*,
Cologne: Verlag der Buchhandlung Walther
König, Cologne 2001, © steirischer herbst.
Einar Schleef, *Tagebuch 1977–1980*,
Winfried Menninghaus, Sandra Janßen and
Johannes Windrich eds, Wien Frankfurt Berlin:
Suhrkamp Verlag Frankfurt am Main, 2007,
(p. 234). © Suhrkamp Verlag Berlin.
All rights reserved.
Georg Schöllhammer, "Die Welt ist schön?,"
in *Manfred Willmann, Werkblick*,
Cologne: Verlag der Buchhandlung Walther
König, 2005, © Neue Galerie am
Landesmuseum Joanneum Graz.
Taeko Tomioka, "Zu lesenden Fotos,"
in *Nobuyoshi Araki. AKT–TOKYO. 1971–1991*,
Graz: Edition Camera Austria, 1992, (p. 84).
© Taeko Tomioka

Image Credits

© Copyrights for the images reserved by
artists, photographers and legal successors.
© Camera Austria for all reproductions from
Camera Austria International.
Robert Adams: © Robert Adams, Courtesy
Fraenkel Gallery, San Francisco (p. 60–62).
Ketuta Alexi-Meskhishvili: © the artist and
Galerie Frank Elbaz, Paris/Dalles (p. 18).
Lewis Baltz: © The Lewis Baltz Trust,
© Lewis Baltz. Used by permission.
Courtesy Thomas Zander, Cologne (p. 66–68).
William Eggleston: © Eggleston Artistic Trust,
Courtesy David Zwirner, New York/London/
Hong Kong (p. 72–74).
Luigi Ghirri: © Eredi di Luigi Ghirri (p. 78–80).
Annette Kelm: © Courtesy of the artist,
Institut für Zeitgeschichte, Munich and König
Galerie, Berlin (p. 224–226).
Darcy Lange: © Darcy Lange Estate and
Govett-Brewster Art Gallery (p. 256–258).
Michael Schmidt: © Stiftung für Fotografie
und Medienkunst with Archive Michael
Schmidt (p. 23, 138–140).
Allan Sekula: © Courtesy of the Allan Sekula
Studio (p. 262–264).
Jo Spence: © Estate of Jo Spence and Richard
Saltoun Gallery, London (p. 116–118).
Margherita Spiluttini: © Architekturzentrum
Wien, Sammlung (p. 25).
Wolfgang Tillmanns: © the artist and Galerie
Buchholz, Berlin/Cologne (p. 18).
© Bildrecht Wien 2018 for: Anna and Bernhard
Blume (p. 218–219), Hans-Peter Feldmann
(p. 104–106), Annette Frick (p. 28, 29, 35),
Isa Genzken (p. 34), Sven Johne (p. 250–252),
Tatiana Lecomte (p. 230–231), Peter Piller
(p. 236–238), Einar Schleef (p. 132–134),
Nicole Six & Paul Petritsch (p. 135, 150, 220).
© Badischer Kunstverein, Karlsruhe
(Marianne Wex), (p. 27).
© Walead Beshty (correspondance), (p. 34).
© documenta Archive (Akinbode Akinbiyi),
(p. 13).
© Fondation Bourdieu, St. Gallen, Courtesy
Camera Austria, Graz (p. 23).
© Fotogalerie im Forum Stadtpark Graz
(cover *American Photographers,* cover catalog
Tomatsu), (p. 25, 31).
© Nan Goldin (p. 282–284).
© Wiebke Loeper (p. 17).
© Galerie im Taxispalais Innsbruck (cover
Photographie als Kunst 1839–1979), (p. 21).
© Suhrkamp Verlag Frankfurt am Main 1981
(cover Einar Schleef), (p. 26).
© The Regents of the University of California
(cover *Mistaken Identities*), (p. 15).
© Verein zur Erarbeitung der "Geschichte der
Fotografie in Österreich" (cover *Geschichte
der Fotografie in Österreich*), (p. 22).

Photo Credits

Stephan Baumann, bild_raum
(Marianne Wex), (p. 27); Gianmarco Bresadola
(Fig. Volksbühne), (p. 23); Brian Forrest
(Walead Beshty), (p. 34); Felix Grünschloss
(Marianne Wex), (p. 27); Markus Krottendorfer
(Fig RB. Archiv, Schlick), (p. 37, 39); Stefan Lux,
(p. 232); Roman März, (p. 13); Margherita
Spiluttini (correspondance), (p. 25); Christian
Wachter (Lange, *Un-Curating*, diverse), (p. 28,
136);
photography of reproductions Museum der
Moderne Salzburg: Rainer Iglar,
(p. 15, 16, 17, 18, 22, 23, 25, 26, 29, 30, 31).

Figure frontispiece: Mark Haworth-Booth
and Manfred Willmann, Symposion on
Photography VI: "The Power (and the Glory)
of Photography," 1984, Photo Harald Strobl